Catalogue of the WORLD'S most popular COINS

By Fred Reinfeld
and Burton Hobson

Eleventh Edition
Edited by Robert Obojski

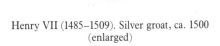

Henry VII (1485–1509). Silver groat, ca. 1500
(enlarged)

Sterling Publishing Co., Inc.   New York
Distributed in the U.K. by Blandford Press

ACKNOWLEDGMENTS

The late Robert Friedberg supplied valuable advice and information in the development of this book. Sawyer McA. Mosser and the American Numismatic Society were most helpful in supplying pictures. In the expansion of listings for this eleventh edition, Leo Dardarian gave many knowledgeable suggestions. To them, and the many others who assisted with previous editions, the authors' and editor's thanks are due.

Eleventh edition copy-edited and designed by Frederick Sard

Library of Congress Cataloging in Publication Data

Reinfeld, Fred, 1910–1964.
    Catalogue of the world's most popular coins.

    Includes index.
    1. Coins—Catalogs. I. Hobson, Burton. II. Obojski,
Robert. III. Title.
CJ63.R4 1983   737.4029'4   83-606
ISBN 0-8069-6078-7
ISBN 0-8069-6079-5 (lib. bdg.)
ISBN 0-8069-7708-6 (pbk.)

CONTENTS

HOW TO USE THIS BOOK

Bear in mind that *the prices quoted in this book are what a typical dealer will charge for coins in the condition in which the particular issue is usually encountered*. That is to say, prices are quoted for "Fine" ("F") condition for coins issued before 1880 (including ancient coins, except where otherwise stated). From 1800 to the early 1900's, "Very Fine" ("VF") is the condition. For modern foreign coins the condition is "Extra Fine" ("EF") or "Uncirculated" ("Unc."). Some ancient coins are "VG" ("Very Good").

These dates for determining condition and price are only approximate and vary with different countries. Coins in superior condition (especially those that are uncirculated) may be worth considerably more than the prices quoted here. Similarly, coins in inferior condition (especially those mutilated or damaged in any way) may be worth very much less.

When an inclusive range such as "1925–50" is used, it does not necessarily mean that the coin exists for every intervening date. But it does mean that the first and last dates are known.

When descriptions are omitted, coins may be assumed to belong to the same type as the last previously described coin of a higher denomination. Pictured coins are described directly below unless otherwise indicated by a reference number.

The term "varieties" indicates minor design changes over a period of time in respect to portrait type or inscription or both.

For silver coins the composition is not indicated, except in special situations that might be unclear—e.g., where the same denomination coin was struck in two different metals. Composition is given by means of the following abbreviations:

A or Al (aluminum)	Mg (magnesium)
Ac (acmonital)	N or Ni (nickel)
Bi (billon)	Pl (platinum)
Bra (brass)	S (silver)
Br or Bro (bronze)	St (steel)
C (copper)	T (tin)
G (gold)	Z (zinc)
I (iron)	

The indication "comp." refers to "composition metal"—20 percent low-grade "base" silver, 80 percent copper.

DATING SYSTEMS

The system of dating used on coins often reflects a nation's culture. In the Western world, the familiar A.D. (*anno Domini*—"in the year of our Lord") system refers to the birth of Christ. In the Moslem nations, the calendars are based on A.D. 622, the year of Muhammad's flight ("Hegira") from Mecca to Medina. (See chart, p. 11.)

Two important dating systems are based on the year 622. The A.H. system employs a lunar calendar with 354 days per year. To find the equivalent A.D. date, you must take 3 percent of the A.H. date (there are about 3 percent fewer days in a lunar year than a solar year), subtract the nearest whole number, then add 622. For instance, A.H. 1396 equals A.D. 1976, since 1396 − 42 + 622 = 1976. You will find examples of A.H. dating on the coins of Saudi Arabia and the early coinage of Afghanistan.

Some Moslem nations employ a solar year, making the conversion between systems simpler. To convert S.H. dates to A.D., just add 621 to the S.H. date. For instance, S.H. 1355 equals A.D. 1976, since 1355 + 621 = 1976. Examples of S.H. dating are found on the modern coinage of Afghanistan and Iran.

Several dating systems are confined to the coinage of a particular nation. The dates on Israeli coins refer to the Hebrew calendar, which is based on a lunar year and begins about 3760 B.C., the traditional time of Adam. Ethiopia has its own distinctive system, called the Ethiopian Era, which commenced at 7 years 8 months A.D. Many nations, particularly in the Orient, date their coins according to the year of the current ruler's reign.

For convenience, the catalogue listings give the A.D. equivalent for the date actually shown on the coin. For the purpose of identification, you should be aware that the A.D. date given does not necessarily appear in that form on the coin itself.

F.A.O. COIN PLAN

Although the United Nations has issued no money in its own right, a number of member governments have released special coins in cooperation with the U.N. Food and Agricultural Organization's "Freedom from Hunger" campaign launched in 1968. The coins are sold at a premium over their face value, with the extra revenue going towards agricultural development. The designs show food or include inscriptions that call attention to the F.A.O. project.

By the end of 1976, some 80 countries were participating in the F.A.O. coin plan, with total mintage of all specimens surpassing five million. By the end of 1982, nearly 100 countries were participating, with total mintage running into the tens of millions. For one special occasion alone, World Food Day, observed on October 16, 1981, approximately 40 nations issued more than 60 varieties of F.A.O. coins.

AFARS AND ISSAS

Formerly French Somaliland (q.v.), this French overseas territory in 1967 became French Territory of the Afars and the Issas. Then on June 27, 1977 it became the independent Republic of Djibouti (q.v.).

1. 100 Francs (C-N) 1970, '75. Bust of Republic.
   Rev: Camels   2.50
2. 50 Francs (C-N) 1970   1.75

3. 20 Francs (A-Br) 1968, '75. Bust of Republic.
   Rev: Arabian dhow and ocean liner   1.50
4. 10 Francs (A-Br) 1969, '70, '75   1.00

5. 5 Francs (A) 1968, '75. Bust of Republic. Rev:
   Antelope head   .65
6. 2 Francs (A) 1968, '75   .50
7. 1 Franc (A) 1969, '71, '75   .50

AFGHANISTAN

Bordered by the U.S.S.R., Pakistan and Iran, Afghanistan was a constitutional monarchy until 1973, then a republic until 1979, when it was occupied by Soviet troops.

100 Puls = 1 Afghani

1. 2½ Afghani 1926. Throne room. Rev: Toughra
   and Arabic inscription   50.00

2. 1 Afghani 1927   15.00
3. ½ Afghani 1927   7.50

5.

4. 25 Puls (C) 1930   4.00
5. 10 Puls (C) 1926   5.00

0	1	2	3	4	5

6	7	8	9	10

AFGHANISTAN (continued)

MOHAMMED ZAHIR SHAH 1933–
(A.H. 1351–)

NOTE: Solar year dating begins A.D. 1935 (S.H. 1313)

6.	5 Afghani (Al) 1958. Type of #1, modified	5.00
7.	2 Afghani (Al) 1958	3.00
8.	50 Puls (N-St or Br) 1951–55	2.00
9.	25 Puls (A, Br or C-N) 1951–55	1.00
10.	10 Puls (C-N) 1937	.75
11.	5 Puls (Bro) 1937	.50
12.	3 Puls (Bro) 1937	.50
13.	2 Puls (Bro) 1937	.40

14.	5 Afghani (N-St) 1961– . Bust of King. Rev: Value	2.00

15.	2 Afghani (N-St) 1961– . Winged sun. Rev: Value	1.50

16.	1 Afghani (N-St) 1962– . Three wheat stalks. Rev: Value	1.00
17.	5 Afghani (C-N-St) 1973. Arms. Rev: Value, grain	2.00
18.	50 Puls (C-St) 1973, '75. Rev: Value, stars	1.00
19.	25 Puls (Bra-St) 1973, '75	.75
20.	10,000 Afghani (G) 1978. Marco Polo sheep. Rev: Arms. (World Wildlife Conservation Program)	700.00
21.	500 Afghani 1978. Stork	50.00
22.	250 Afghani 1978. Leopard	35.00
23.	500 Afghani 1981. Arms. Rev: F.A.O. emblem; INCREASE FOOD PRODUCTION. (World Food Day)	30.00
24.	5 Afghani (Bra) 1981	3.00

ALBANIA

Albania is in southeastern Europe on the Adriatic Sea. It was a republic from 1925 to 1928, a kingdom under Zog I from 1928 to 1939, and under Italian domination during World War II. Since 1946 it has been the People's Socialist Republic of Albania.

100 Qindar = 1 Lek
5 Lek = 1 Franga Ar
(1 Lek = 1 Lira)

1.	20 Franga Ar (G) 1926–27. Head of Zog. Rev: Double-headed eagle	300.00
2.	10 Franga Ar (G) 1927	225.00

3.	20 Franga Ar (G) 1926–27. Bust of Skanderbeg. Rev: Winged lion	350.00

4.	5 Franga Ar 1925–27. Head of Zog. Rev: Plowing scene	300.00

5.	2 Franga Ar 1926–28. Sower. Rev: Eagle	175.00

6.	1 Franga Ar 1927–28. Helmeted head. Rev: Prow of galley	125.00

7.	1 Lek (N) 1926–27, '30–31. Classical head. Rev: Horseman	10.00

8.	½ Lek (N) 1926. Hercules and lion. Rev: Double-headed eagle	10.00
8a.	½ Lek (N) 1930–31. Type of #8. Rev: Arms on shield	7.50
9.	¼ Leku (N) 1926–27. Lion. Rev: Oak spray and value	10.00
10.	10 Qindar Leku (Bro) 1926. Eagle head. Rev: Value between sprays	30.00
11.	5 Qindar Leku (Bro) 1926. Lion head. Rev: Value over oak spray	20.00
12.	2 Qindar Ar (Bro) 1935. Double-headed eagle. Rev: Value and spray	10.00
13.	1 Qindar Ar (Bro) 1935	10.00

14.	2 Franga Ar 1935. Head of Zog. Rev: Arms	30.00
15.	1 Franga Ar 1935, '37	25.00
16.	20 Franga Ar (G) 1937. Head of Zog. Rev: Arms. (25th anniversary of independence)	400.00
17.	2 Franga Ar 1937	50.00
18.	1 Franga Ar 1937	30.00

UNDER ITALIAN DOMINATION

VICTOR EMMANUEL III as king and emperor

19.	10 Lek 1939. Head of Victor Emmanuel III. Rev: Albanian arms and fasces	55.00
20.	5 Lek 1939	25.00

21.	2 Lek (Ac) 1939–41. Helmeted bust	7.50
22.	1 Lek (Ac) 1939–41. Bust facing right	5.00
23.	0.50 Lek (Ac) 1939–41. Bust left	3.00
24.	0.20 Lek (Ac) 1939–41. Bust right	3.00

ALBANIA (continued)

25. 0.10 Lek (A-Br) 1940–41. Head of Victor Emmanuel III. Rev: Branch and value   5.00
26. 0.05 Lek (A-Br) 1940–41   3.00

37. 50 Qindarka (Al) 1969. Rev: Worker and soldier holding torch   2.00

PEOPLE'S REPUBLIC 1946–

27. 5 Lekë (Z) 1947, '57. Arms and stars. Rev: Value and stars   4.00

38. 20 Qindarka (Al) 1969. Rev: Value   1.50
39. 10 Qindarka (Al) 1969   1.00
40. 5 Qindarka (Al) 1969   .75

28. 2 Lekë (Z) 1947, '57   2.50
29. 1 Lek (Z) 1947, '57   3.50
30. ½ Leku (Z) 1947, '57   2.50

31. 1 Lek (Al) 1964. Arms. Rev: Value   4.00
32. 50 Qindarka (Al) 1964   2.00
33. 20 Qindarka (Al) 1964   1.50
34. 10 Qindarka (Al) 1964   1.25
35. 5 Qindarka (Al) 1964   1.00

36. 1 Lek (Al) 1969. Arms. Rev: Soldier subduing enemy. (25th anniversary of liberation)   2.50

ALGERIA

Formerly a semi-autonomous department of France, this North African country became an independent republic in July 1962.

100 Centimes = 1 Franc = 1 Dinar

1. 100 Francs (C-N) 1950–53. Head of the Republic. Rev: Value ... 3.50
2. 50 Francs (C-N) 1949–50 ... 3.00
3. 20 Francs (C-N) 1949–56 ... 2.00

13. 5 Dinar 1972. Wheat and oil derrick. Rev: Value. (Commemorates 10th anniversary of independence.) ... 15.00

4. 1 Dinar (C-N) 1964– . Arms. Rev: Value ... 1.50
5. 50 Centimes (Al-Br) 1964– ... .75
6. 20 Centimes (Al-Br) 1964– ... .65
7. 10 Centimes (Al-Br) 1964– ... .50
8. 5 Centimes (Al) 1964– ... .35
9. 2 Centimes (Al) 1964– ... .30
10. 1 Centime (Al) 1964– ... .20

14. 1 Dinar (C-N) 1972. Tractor and clasped hands. Rev: Value. (F.A.O. coin plan.) ... 2.00

15. 20 Centimes (Bra) 1972. Cornucopia with fruit. Rev: Value. (F.A.O. coin plan.) ... 1.00
16. 5 Dinar (N) 1974. Soldier. Rev: Value. (Commemorates 20th anniversary of revolution.) ... 3.50

11. 5 Centimes (A) 1970. Dates of four-year plan in half-cogwheel, wreath. Rev: Value. (F.A.O. coin plan.) ... .50

17. 5 Centimes (A) 1974. Dates of second four-year plan in half-cogwheel, half-wreath. Rev: Value ... .35

18. 50 Centimes (Bra) 1975. Kufic inscription. Rev: Value. (Commemorates 30th anniversary of Revolt of May 8, 1945.) ... 1.50
19. 10 Dinars (Br) 1979. Kufic inscription. Rev: Value ... 4.00

12. 50 Centimes (C-N-Z) 1971. Compass, flask and open book. Rev: Value ... .65

ANGOLA

This former Portuguese colony on the west coast of Africa became independent in 1975. After months of civil war between rival factions the People's Republic of Angola was established in 1976.

100 Centavos = 1 Escudo
5 Centavos = 1 Macuta

1. 50 Centavos (N) 1922–23. Liberty head. Rev: Arms — 7.00

2. 20 Centavos (C-N) 1921–22. Rev: Value — 7.00
3. 10 Centavos (C-N) 1921–23 — 5.00

4. 5 Centavos (Br) 1921–23. Arms. Rev: Value — 10.00
5. 2 Centavos (Br) 1921 — 17.50
6. 1 Centavo (Br) 1921 — 7.50

NEW GOVERNMENT (PORTUGAL) 1926

7. 50 Centavos (N-Bro) 1927–28. Bust of the Republic. Rev: Arms and value — 8.50

8. 20 Centavos (N-Bro) 1927–28 — 5.00
9. 10 Centavos (N-Bro) 1927–28 — 6.00
10. 5 Centavos (N-Bro) 1927 — 3.50
11. 20 Escudos 1952–55. Crowned arms and value. Rev: Arms in cross — 7.50
12. 10 Escudos 1952–55 — 5.00

15.

13. 2½ Escudos (C-N) 1953–74 — 1.00
14. 1 Escudo (Br) 1953–74. Crowned arms. Rev: Value — .75
15. 50 Centavos (N-Br) 1948–50 — 1.50

15a. 50 Centavos (Br) 1953–62. "Colonia de" dropped from legend — .40
16. 20 Centavos (Br) 1948–49 — 2.00

16a. 20 Centavos (Br) 1962 — .75
17. 10 Centavos (Br) 1948–49 — .50
18. 10 Escudos (C-N) 1969–70 — 2.50

19. 20 Escudos (N) 1971–72 — 4.00

20. 5 Escudos (C-N) 1972, '74 — 10.00

REPUBLIC 1975

21. 10 Kwanzas (C-N) 1975. Rev: Value — 4.00

22. 5 Kwanzas (C-N) 1975. Arms. Rev: Value — 3.00
23. 2 Kwanzas (C-N) 1975 — 2.00
24. 1 Kwanza (C-N) 1975 — 1.50
25. 50 Lwei (C-N) 1975. Arms. Rev: Value — 1.25
26. 20 Kwanzas (C-N) 1978. Arms. Rev: Value — 6.00

ANTIGUA

An island in the Leeward group, it was discovered by Columbus on his 1493 voyage and settled by the British in 1632. Antigua, a member of the short-lived Federation of the West Indies (1958–62), in 1967 became a member of the West Indies Associated States, with Britain controlling foreign affairs and defense.

1. 1 Farthing (C) 1836. Palm tree. Rev: Value   150.00

2. 4 Dollars (C-N) 1970. Arms with ibexes. Rev: Bananas, sugar cane and value. (F.A.O. coin plan)   15.00

ARGENTINA

Discovered 1515–16 by Spanish explorers, it remained a Spanish colony until the provinces, in a successful revolution (May 25, 1810), established an independent republic. For many years thereafter the provinces issued their own coinage.

Provinces of the Rio de la Plata

1 Real = 1 Sueldo

1.	8 Reales 1813, '15, '26–37. Arms. Rev: Sunburst	200.00
2.	4 Reales 1813, '15	100.00
3.	2 Reales 1813, '15	50.00

4.	1 Real 1813, '15, '24, '25	30.00
5.	½ Real 1813, '15	50.00
6.	8 Sueldos 1815. Type of #5, except with "S" (Sueldo) instead of "R" (Real)	125.00
7.	4 Sueldos 1815, '28, '32	65.00

8.	2 Sueldos 1815, 1824–26	25.00
9.	1 Sueldo 1815	65.00
10.	½ Sueldo 1815	65.00

La Rioja Province

11.	8 Reales 1838–40. Mount Famatina, with flags and cannon crossed. Rev: Arms	150.00
12.	4 Reales 1846, '49, '50	30.00
13.	2 Reales 1843, '44	40.00

14.	2 Reales 1842. Bust of Gen. Rosas. Rev: Arms	75.00
15.	2 Reales 1859, '60. Arms. Rev: Prov. de la Rioja	35.00
16.	½ Real 1854	25.00

ARGENTINE CONFEDERATION

100 Centavos = 1 Real

17.	4 Centavos (C) 1854. Sun. Rev: Value	15.00
18.	2 Centavos (C) 1854	20.00
19.	1 Centavo (C) 1854	20.00

ARGENTINE REPUBLIC

100 Centavos = 1 Peso

20.	1 Peso 1881–83. Liberty head. Rev: Arms	100.00
21.	50 Centavos 1881–83	15.00
22.	20 Centavos 1881–83	7.50
23.	10 Centavos 1881–83	3.00

24.	50 Centavos (N) 1941. Liberty head. Rev: Value	2.00
25.	20 Centavos (C-N) 1896–1942	.60
26.	10 Centavos (C-N) 1896–1942	.50
27.	5 Centavos (C-N) 1896–1942	.40
28.	2 Centavos (Br) 1882–96. Liberty head. Rev: Arms	2.00
29.	1 Centavo (Br) 1882–96	1.25

30.	2 Centavos (Br) 1939–50. Arms. Rev: Value	.75
31.	1 Centavo (Bro) 1939–48	.75

32.	20 Centavos (A-Br) 1942–50. Liberty head. Rev: Value	.50
33.	10 Centavos (A-Br) 1942–50	.40
34.	5 Centavos (A-Br) 1942–50	.40

35.	50 Centavos (N-St) 1952–56. Gen. San Martín. Rev: Value	.75
36.	20 Centavos (C-N) 1950. Gen. José de San Martín. Rev: Value. (100th anniversary of his death)	2.00
36a.	20 Centavos (C-N) 1951, '52; (N-St) 1952–56. "Centenario" legend dropped	.60

37.	10 Centavos (C-N) 1950	1.50
37a.	10 Centavos (C-N) 1951–52; (N-St) 1952–56	.25
38.	5 Centavos (C-N) 1950	1.25

38a.	5 Centavos (C-N) 1951–53; (N-St) 1953–56	.35

39.	1 Peso (N-St) 1957–62. Liberty Head. Rev: Value	.65
40.	50 Centavos (N-St) 1957–61	.40

41.	20 Centavos (N-St) 1957–61	.35
42.	10 Centavos (N-St) 1957–59	.25
43.	5 Centavos (N-St) 1957–59	.35

44.	1 Peso (St) 1960. Old town hall in Buenos Aires. Rev: Coat of arms	1.50

45.　10 Pesos (St) 1962–68. Gaucho. Rev: Value.
(Dodecagonal planchet)　　　　　　　　.65

46.　5 Pesos (St) 1961–68. Sailing ship. Rev: Value.
(Dodecagon)　　　　　　　　　　　　.50

47.　25 Pesos (St) 1964–68. Replica of #1. (First coin
of independent Argentina; dodecagon)　2.00

48.　10 Pesos (St) 1966. Museum. Rev: Value. (150th
anniversary of declaration of independence;
dodecagon)　　　　　　　　　　　　1.00

49.　25 Pesos (N-St) 1968. Head of Sarmiento (President, 1868–74). Rev: Value. (Dodecagon)　1.50

CURRENCY REVALUATION

1 New Peso = 100 Old Pesos

50.　50 Centavos (Bra) 1970–76. Liberty head. Rev:
Value　　　　　　　　　　　　　　.50
51.　20 Centavos (Bra) 1970–75　　　　　.35
52.　10 Centavos (Bra) 1970–75　　　　　.25
53.　5 Centavos (Al) 1970–75　　　　　　.25
54.　1 Centavo (Al) 1970–75　　　　　　.25

55.　1 Peso (A-Br) 1974–76. Sun. Rev: Value, laurel
branch　　　　　　　　　　　　　　.65
56.　5 Pesos (A-Br) 1976–77　　　　　　.60
57.　10 Pesos (A-Br) 1977. Admiral Guillermo
Brown. Rev: Value. (Bicentennial of birth of
father of Argentine army)　　　　　1.50
58.　5 Pesos 1977　　　　　　　　　　.50

59. 3000 Pesos 1977–78. Globe with map of Argentina.
Rev: Value, emblem of World Cup Soccer
Tournament. (1977 and 1978 World Cup
events in Buenos Aires)　　　　　　30.00

60.　　　　　　　　　　　　　　　　61.

60. 2000 Pesos 1977–78. Arms　　　　　15.00
60a. 1000 Pesos 1977–78. World Soccer Championships　10.00
61.　1 Peso 1977. Sun symbol　　　　　12.50

ARGENTINA (continued)

62.	100 Pesos (C-A-N) 1977–78. Arena	2.00
63.	50 Pesos (C-A-N) 1977–78. Soccer player	2.00
64.	20 Pesos (C-A-N) 1977–78. Soccer players	2.00
65.	100 Pesos (C-A-N) 1978. Bust of José de San Martín. Rev: Value	3.00
66.	100 Pesos (A-Br) 1979–	2.00
67.	100 Pesos (A-Br) 1979. Equestrian statue. Rev: Value. (Centennial of conquest of Patagonia)	2.00

ASCENSION

Ascension, covering an area of 34 square miles, is a volcanic island in the South Atlantic Ocean lying 900 miles south of Liberia. It was annexed in 1922 to the British crown colony of St. Helena.

1.	1 Crown (C-N) 1978. Bust of Elizabeth II. Rev: British lion over Ascension turtle. (Queen's Silver Jubilee)	5.00
1a.	1 Crown 1978 (S). (Silver Jubilee)	30.00
2.	1 Crown 1981. Bust of Elizabeth II. Rev: Arms over Ascension turtle. (Wedding of Prince Charles and Lady Diana)	75.00

AUSTRALIA

Settlement of Australia began January 26, 1788; six separate colonies developed: New South Wales, Tasmania, Western Australia, South Australia, Victoria and Queensland. The colonies became a federation of states in 1901 as the Commonwealth of Australia, which is today a self-governing member of the British Commonwealth of Nations.

COLONIAL ISSUES
New South Wales

The name originally applied to much of the continent; by 1840 the area had been reduced to the eastern third. During the early years of settlement, practically any coin that came to the colony was used in trade. In 1800, Governor Philip Gidley King proclaimed that certain British and foreign coins were to circulate at fixed rates. By about 1830 sufficient numbers of gold and silver coins had arrived from England to replace the foreign pieces in use. Small denomination coins were still scarce, however, and bronze penny and halfpenny tokens issued by various merchants came into circulation. These tokens relieved the shortage of small change and provided a means of advertising for the issuers as well. They passed out of use during the 1860's, replaced by regular issue British bronze coins from London.

PROCLAMATION COINS OF 1800

1.	English Guinea. (Type of #186, Great Britain)	
2.	Johanna. (Type of #1, Portugal)	
3.	Half Johanna. (Type of #2, Portugal)	
4.	Ducat (Type of #13, the Netherlands)	
5.	Gold Mohur. (Type of #5, India)	
6.	Pagoda. (Type of #36, India)	
7.	Spanish Dollar. (Type of #36, Mexico)	
8.	Rupee. (Type of #34, India)	
9.	Dutch Guilder. (Type of #3, the Netherlands)	
10.	English Shilling. (Type of #188, Great Britain)	
11.	Copper coin of 1 oz. (Type of #199, Great Britain)	

12. 5 Shillings 1813, called "ring dollar" or "holey dollar." NEW SOUTH WALES 1813 counterstamped around hole. Rev: FIVE SHILLINGS counterstamp. (Emergency issue made by cutting center out of Spanish milled dollar) 5000.00

13. 15 Pence 1813, called "dump." (Center, restamped, of #12) 800.00

Trade Coins

VICTORIA 1837–1901

14. 1 Sovereign (G) 1855, '56. Young head with ribbon hair band. Rev: Inscription 3000.00
15. ½ Sovereign (G) 1855, '56 2500.00
16. 1 Sovereign (G) 1857–70. Young head with wreath of native Australian leaves. 300.00

17. ½ Sovereign (G) 1857–66 350.00

19.

18. 1 Sovereign (G) 1871–87. Young head with ribbon hair band. Rev: St. George and dragon. (Same design as regular English issue but with Sydney mint mark "S" below head) 175.00
19. 1 Sovereign (G) 1871–87. Rev: Shield. ("S" mint mark below head or shield) 200.00
20. ½ Sovereign (G) 1871–87 150.00

23.

21. 1 Sovereign (G) 1887–93. Jubilee head. Rev: St. George and dragon ("S" mint mark below horse) 175.00
22. ½ Sovereign (G) 1887, '89, '91. Rev: Shield ("S" mint mark below) 200.00
23. 1 Sovereign (G) 1893–1901. Veiled head. Rev: St. George and dragon ("S" mint mark below horse) 175.00
24. ½ Sovereign (G) 1893, 1897, 1900 150.00

AUSTRALIA (continued)

Queensland

Originally part of New South Wales, Queensland became a separate colony in 1859.

25. 1 Penny token (C) 1852–68, also undated. Various types issued by merchants and tradesmen (mostly Sydney) ... 7.50
26. ½ Penny token (C) ... 7.50

36. 1 Penny token (C) 1863–65, also undated. Various types issued by merchants and tradesmen ... 10.00
37. ½ Penny token (C) ... 15.00

Victoria

Originally part of New South Wales, Victoria became a separate colony in 1851.

VICTORIA 1837–1901

27. 1 Sovereign (G) 1872–87. Young head. Rev: St. George and dragon. (Type of #18 with Melbourne mint mark "M" below head) ... 200.00
28. 1 Sovereign (G) 1872–87. Rev: Shield. (Type of #19 with "M" mint mark below head or shield) ... 200.00
29. ½ Sovereign (G) 1873–87 ... 150.00
30. 1 Sovereign (G) 1887–93. Jubilee head. Rev: St. George and dragon. (Type of #21 with "M" mint mark below horse) ... 200.00
31. ½ Sovereign (G) 1887, '93. Rev: Shield ("M" mint mark below) ... 150.00
32. 1 Sovereign (G) 1893–1901. Veiled head. Rev: St. George and dragon. (Type of #23 with "M" mint mark below horse) ... 185.00
33. ½ Sovereign (G) 1896–1900 ... 140.00

South Australia

Settlement of this area began about 1836; South Australia was made a separate colony in 1842.

38. 1 Pound (G) 1852. Crown. Rev: Value ... 3000.00

39. 1 Penny token (C) 1858, also undated. Various types issued by merchants and tradesmen ... 10.00
40. ½ Penny token (C) 1857 ... 15.00

34. 1 Penny token (C) 1849–63, also undated. Various types issued by merchants and tradesmen (mostly Melbourne) ... 6.50
35. ½ Penny token (C) ... 7.50

Western Australia

Declared a separate colony in 1829.

41. 1 Sovereign (G) 1899–1901. Veiled head. Rev: St. George and dragon. (Type of #23 with Perth mint mark "P" below horse) ... 175.00
42. ½ Sovereign (G) 1899, 1900 ... 150.00

43. 1 Penny token (C or Br) 1865–74, also undated.
    Various types issued by merchants and trades-
    men   15.00

48.	1 Florin (2 shillings) 1910. Crowned bust. Rev: Arms	150.00
49.	1 Shilling 1910	40.00
50.	6 Pence 1910	20.00
51.	3 Pence 1910	15.00

Tasmania

Discovered in 1642 by Abel Tasman, the island was
named Van Dieman's Land. At first a dependency of New
South Wales, Van Dieman's Land was declared a separate
colony in 1825. The name was changed to Tasmania in
1856.

GEORGE V   1910–36

52.	1 Sovereign (G) 1911–31. Bare head. Rev: Type of #46	200.00
53.	½ Sovereign (G) 1911–16	135.00
54.	1 Florin 1911–36. Crowned bust. Rev: Arms	15.00
55.	1 Shilling 1911–36	10.00
56.	6 Pence 1911–36	6.50
57.	3 Pence 1911–36	3.50

44. 1 Penny token (C) 1850–74, also undated. Vari-
    ous types issued by merchants and tradesmen   10.00
45. ½ Penny token (C) 1855, also undated   12.50

58.	1 Penny (Br) 1911–36. Rev: Value	.75
59.	½ Penny (Br) 1911–36	.75

COMMONWEALTH ISSUES

EDWARD VII   1901–10

12 Pence = 1 Shilling
2 Shillings = 1 Florin

60. 1 Florin 1927. Rev: Parliament buildings.
    (First meeting of Parliament at Canberra)   30.00

46. 1 Sovereign (G) 1902–10. Bare head. Rev: St.
    George and dragon (same design as regular
    English issue but with Australian mint
    mark—"S," "M," or "P"—below horse)   200.00
47. ½ Sovereign (G) 1902–10   140.00

61. 1 Florin 1935. Rev: Rider on horseback. (100th
    anniversary of settlement at Melbourne)   350.00

AUSTRALIA (continued)

GEORGE VI 1936–52

NOTE: Coins issued after 1948 are without IND IMP
(Emperor of India) in legend

67.	1 Penny (Br) 1938–48. Rev: Kangaroo	.75
67a.	1 Penny (Br) 1949–52	.75

68.	½ Penny (Br) 1938, '39. Rev: Value	1.50

62. 1 Crown 1937, '38. Bare head. Rev: Crown   30.00

69.	½ Penny (Br) 1939–48. Rev: Kangaroo	.60
69a.	½ penny (Br) 1949–52	.75

63.

64.

63.	1 Florin 1938–47. Rev: Modified arms	7.50
63a.	1 Florin 1951, '52	10.00
64.	1 Shilling 1938–48. Rev: Head of Merino Ram	5.00
64a.	1 Shilling 1950, '52	6.50

70.	1 Florin 1951. Rev: Sword, mace, crown and stars in form of Southern Cross constellation. (50th year jubilee of Commonwealth)	10.00

65.

66.

65.	6 Pence 1938–48. Rev: Arms. (Type of #48)	2.00
65a.	6 Pence 1950–52	1.50
66.	3 Pence 1938–48. Rev: Wheat stalks	1.00
66a.	3 Pence 1949–52	.75

NOTE: Australian silver coins were struck at the U.S. mints in Denver and San Francisco 1942–44. "D" and "S" mint marks appear on the reverse of these issues

AUSTRALIA (continued)

ELIZABETH II 1952–

NOTE: Coins issued 1955–64 have "F.D." in legend

79. 20 Cents 1966– . Rev: Platypus .50
80. 10 Cents 1966– . Rev: Lyre bird .35

71. 1 Florin 1953, '54. Laureate head. Rev: Arms.
(Type of #63) 10.00
71a. 1 Florin 1956–63 12.50
72. 1 Shilling 1953, '54. Rev: Head of merino ram.
(Type of #64) 6.00
72a. 1 Shilling 1955–63 6.50
73. 6 Pence 1953–54. Rev: Arms. (Type of #48) 3.00
73a. 6 Pence 1955–63 4.00
74. 3 Pence 1953–54. Rev: Wheat stalks. (Type of
#66) 6.50
74a. 3 Pence 1955–64 2.00
75. 1 Penny (Br) 1953. Rev: Kangaroo. (Type of
#67) 2.00
75a. 1 Penny (Br) 1955–64 2.00
76. ½ Penny (Br) 1953–55. Rev: Kangaroo. (Type
of #69) 1.50
76a. ½ Penny (Br) 1959–64 1.75

81. 5 Cents 1966– . Rev: Spiny anteater .25
82. 2 Cents (Br) 1966– . Rev: Frilled lizard .15

83. 1 Cent (Br) 1966– . Rev: Flying mouse .15

77. 1 Florin 1954. Rev: Lion and kangaroo. (Royal
visit of Queen Elizabeth and Prince Philip) 10.00

84. 50 Cents (CN) 1970. Rev: Captain Cook and
map. (200th anniversary of Cook's discovery;
dodecagonal planchet) 5.00

DECIMAL COINAGE

100 Cents = 1 Dollar

78. 50 Cents (S) 1966. Draped bust with coronet.
Rev: Arms 12.50
78a. 50 Cents (CN) 1969– . (Dodecagonal planchet) 1.75

85. 50 Cents (CN) 1977. Rev: Wattle blossom (Silver
Jubilee of Queen Elizabeth; dodecagonal
planchet) 3.00

86.   200 Dollars (G) 1980. Draped bust with coronet.
        Rev: Koala bear   350.00
86a. 200 Dollars (G) 1980. Proof   400.00

87.   200 Dollars (G) 1981. Rev: Conjoined portraits of
        Prince Charles and Lady Diana. (Marriage of
        Charles and Diana)   350.00
88.   50 Cents (C-N) 1981   3.00

89.   200 Dollars (G) 1982. Rev: Hurdler. (Twelfth
        Commonwealth Games, Brisbane)   350.00
89a. 200 Dollars (G) 1982. Proof   400.00

90.   10 Dollars 1982. Rev: Commonwealth Games
        logo superimposed on map of Australia   20.00

AUSTRIA

For centuries the Habsburgs of Austria were among the most powerful reigning families of Europe. The Austrian Habsburgs extended their rule to include the duchies of Styria and Carinthia, the kingdoms of Hungary and Bohemia, and the countries of Tyrol and Schlick. From 1438 to 1806 the head of the Holy Roman Empire was always a Habsburg.

Besides the Imperial and Austrian Archducal coinages the numerous Habsburg lands produced several local issues struck by members of the family. Coins from the various Habsburg lands are of similar designs, with some variation in mint symbols, armorial devices or legends.

In 1867 the Dual Monarchy was established under the title of Austria-Hungary. After World War I, Austria was cut down to a tiny fraction of its previous size, and became a republic.

AUSTRIAN EMPIRE
(REGIONAL ISSUES)
Tyrol
SIGISMUND 1439–96

1. ½ Guldengroschen 1484. Half-length bust. Rev: Mounted knight in armor   850.00

2. 1 Guldengroschen 1486. Duke standing   2000.00

NOTE: The two coins above are the first full-dated coins ever struck

Schlick
COUNT STEPHEN 1487–1526

3.

3. Joachimstaler 1516–26. St. Joachim. Rev: Standing lion. (Large silver pieces from Joachim's valley [*thal*] were called "thalers" at first, changing to "taler," to "daler" and finally to "dollar")   500.00

TEUTONIC ORDER
ARCHDUKE MAXIMILIAN 1588–1618

4. Double Taler 1614. Archduke as Grand Master. Rev: Knight on horseback   750.00

HOLY ROMAN EMPIRE
(Coins of the Emperors)
FERDINAND 1556–64

5. Taler undated. Bust   400.00

MAXIMILIAN II   1564–76

6.   Taler, undated. Bust   350.00

RUDOLF II   1576–1612

7.   Taler, undated. Bust   300.00

MATTHIAS II   1612–19

8.   Taler, undated. Bust   400.00

FERDINAND II   1619–37

9.   Double taler 1626. Conjoined busts of Leopold
      and Claudia de' Medici. Rev: Eagle. (Issued
      by Archduke Leopold to commemorate his
      marriage)   750.00

FERDINAND III   1637–57

10.   Taler, undated. Bust   275.00

LEOPOLD I   1658–1705

11.   Double Taler, undated. Bewigged bust in armor   750.00
12.   Taler, undated. Bust   175.00

JOSEPH I   1705–11

13.   Taler, undated. Bust   200.00

CHARLES VI   1711–40

14.   Taler, undated. Bust   175.00

MARIA THERESA 1740–80

15.   Taler 1741–80. Head. Rev: Imperial eagle   85.00

16.   Trade Taler 1780. Older bust   20.00

JOSEPH II 1765–90

From the time of his father's death in 1765, Joseph II ruled jointly with his mother Maria Theresa until her death in 1780.

17.   Taler 1765–90. Bust. Rev: Arms   85.00

LEOPOLD II 1790–92

18.   Taler 1790–92. Head. Rev: Imperial eagle   275.00

FRANCIS (II, 1792–1806; I, 1806–35)

Leopold's successor, Francis, ruled as Holy Roman Emperor Francis II from 1792 to 1806, when the Empire was abolished. Thereafter he ruled as Francis I of Austria.

19.

19.   Taler 1804–06. Head. Rev: Imperial eagle   300.00

FERDINAND I 1835–48

20.   Taler 1835–48. Laureated head. Rev: Imperial eagle   75.00
21.   ½ Taler 1839–49   50.00
22.   20 Kreuzer 1837–48   12.50
23.   10 Kreuzer 1836–42   15.00
24.   5 Kreuzer 1836–48   15.00
25.   3 Kreuzer 1839–48   10.00

FRANZ JOSEPH 1848–1916

26.   Double Taler 1854. Conjoined heads of Franz Joseph and Elizabeth. Rev: Marriage scene. (Marriage issue)   250.00

27.   Double Taler 1857. Laureated head. Rev: Lighthouse, engine, boat, and shields. (Opening of South Austrian Railways)   1250.00
28.   Double Taler 1865–68. Laureated head. Rev: Imperial eagle   650.00

29. 2 Florins 1858–92. Laureated head. Rev: Imperial eagle (varieties) 100.00

30. 2 Florins 1879. Accolated heads of Franz Joseph and Elizabeth. Rev: Seated female figure. (Silver wedding anniversary) 60.00

31. 2 Florins 1887. Laureated head. Rev: Cathedral. (Reopening of Kuttenberg silver mines) 1750.00
32. Taler 1852–56. Laureated head. Rev: Imperial eagle 135.00
32a. Taler 1857–67. (Size reduced) 50.00

33. 1 Florin 1857–92 12.50

34. ¼ Florin 1857–75 10.00
35. 20 Kreuzer 1868–72 5.00
36. 10 Kreuzer 1858–72 3.00
37. 5 Kreuzer 1858–67. Rev: Value 5.00
38. 4 Kreuzer (C) 1860–64. Double-headed eagle. Rev: Value 10.00
39. 3 Kreuzer (C) 1851 15.00
40. 1 Kreuzer (C) 1858–91 1.00
41. ⁵⁄₁₀ Kreuzer (C) 1858–91 4.00

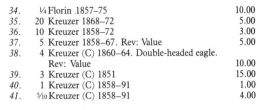

42. 5 Corona 1900, '07, '09. Laureated old head. Rev: Imperial eagle in laurel and crown wreath 30.00

43. 5 Corona 1908. Rev: Running figure of Fame. (60th year of reign) 35.00
44. 2 Corona 1912–13. Head. Rev: Imperial eagle 10.00
45. 1 Corona 1892–1907. Laureated head 6.50
46. 1 Corona 1908. Old head. Rev: Crown over monogram. (60th year of reign) 8.50
47. 1 Corona 1912–16 4.00

48. 20 Heller (N) 1892–1914. Eagle 1.50
49. 10 Heller (N) 1892–1916 1.00
50. 2 Heller (Bro) 1892–1915 .50
51. 1 Heller (Bro) 1892–1916 .50

AUSTRIA (continued)

REPUBLIC

100 Heller = 1 Corona
10,000 Kronen = 1 Schilling
100 Groschen = 1 Schilling

52. 20 Kronen (G) 1923–24. Arms. Rev: Value in
     wreath   1250.00

53. 100 Schillings (G) 1926–31, '33–34. Rev: Value in
     sprays   550.00
54. 25 Schillings (G) 1926–31, '33–34   175.00

55. 100 Schillings (G) 1935–38. Double-headed ea-
     gle. Rev: Madonna of Mariazell   1500.00
56. 25 Schillings (G) 1935–37. Rev: St. Leopold   800.00

57. 1 Schilling 1924. Parliament. Rev: Shield and
     value   8.50
58. 1 Schilling 1925–26, '32. Reduced size   6.00

59. 1000 Kronen (C-N) 1924. Tyrolese woman. Rev:
     Value in wreath   7.50

60. 200 Kronen (Bro) 1924. Teutonic cross. Rev:
     Value   5.00

61. 100 Kronen (Bro) 1923–24. Eagle's head. Rev:
     Value   4.00
62. 5 Schillings 1934–36. Type of #55   45.00

63. 1 Schilling (C-N) 1934–35. Eagle. Rev: Value   7.50

64. ½ Schilling 1925–26. Arms. Rev: Value   5.00

65. 50 Groschen (C-N) 1934–36. Eagle. Rev: Value   40.00
66. 10 Groschen (C-N) 1925, '28–29. Type of #59   2.50
67. 5 Groschen (C-N) 1931–38. Type of #60   3.00
68. 2 Groschen (Bro) 1925–30, '34–38. Cross. Rev:
     Value   1.50

69. 1 Groschen (Bro) 1925–38. Head of eagle. Rev:
     Value   1.50

AUSTRIA (continued)

COMMEMORATIVE SERIES

70. 2 Schillings 1928. Value within circle of 11 shields. Rev: Head of Schubert ... 20.00

71. 2 Schillings 1929. Rev: Head of Dr. Billroth ... 40.00
72. 2 Schillings 1930. Rev: Seated figure of Walther von der Vogelweide ... 25.00

73. 2 Schillings 1931. Rev: Bust of Mozart ... 70.00
74. 2 Schillings 1932. Rev: Bust of Haydn ... 150.00

75. 2 Schillings 1932. Rev: Bust of Dr. Seipel ... 75.00
76. 2 Schillings 1935. Rev: Bust of Dr. Lueger ... 65.00

77. 2 Schillings 1934. Arms with double-headed eagle. Rev: Head of Dr. Dollfuss ... 50.00

78. 2 Schillings 1936. Rev: Head of Prince Eugene of Savoy ... 50.00
79. 2 Schillings 1937. Rev: Karlskirche in Vienna ... 40.00

POSTWAR ISSUES

80. 5 Schillings (A) 1952, '57 ... 10.00

81. 2 Schillings (A) 1946–52 ... 6.50

82. 1 Schilling (A) 1946–57. Rev: Standing figure ... 2.00

83. 50 Groschen (A) 1946–55. Eagle. Rev: Value ... 2.00
84. 20 Groschen (A-Bro) 1950–54 ... 1.50

AUSTRIA (continued)

85. 10 Schillings 1957–73. Female head   6.00
85a. 10 Schillings (C-N) 1974–   1.50

86. 5 Schillings 1960–68. Lipizzaner stallion and rider   5.00
86a. 5 Schillings (C-N) 1968–   .75

87. 1 Schilling (A-Bro) 1959– . Edelweiss   .50

88. 50 Groschen (A-Bro) 1959– . Shield   .40

89. 10 Groschen (Z) 1947–49. Eagle. Rev: Value   3.00

89a. 10 Groschen (A) 1951–   .25
90. 5 Groschen (Z) 1948–   .25
91. 2 Groschen (A) 1950–   .25
92. 1 Groschen (Z) 1947   1.00

COMMEMORATIVE SERIES

93. 25 Schillings 1955. Muse with mask, two girls drawing curtains. Rev: Value in circle of nine shields. (Commemorating reopening of Bundestheater)   50.00
94. 25 Schillings 1956. Statue of Mozart. Rev: Value in circle of nine shields   15.00

95. 25 Schillings 1957. Mariazell Abbey. Rev: Circle of nine shields around value   15.00
96. 25 Schillings 1958. Head of von Welsbach. (100th anniversary of scientist's birth)   15.00

97. 50 Schillings 1959. Head of Andreas Hofer (leader of revolt against Napoleon's occupation of Tyrol). Rev: Eagle in circle of shields   25.00

98. 25 Schillings 1959. Head of Archduke Johann (commander in Napoleonic War). Rev: Lion of Styria in circle of shields   20.00

99. 25 Schillings 1960. Carinthian Plebiscite   25.00

103. 25 Schillings 1963. Prince Eugen. (300th anniversary of birth of field marshal)   15.00

104. 50 Schillings 1964. Olympic Winter Games   17.50
105. 25 Schillings 1964. Franz Grillparzer, poet   15.00

100. 25 Schillings 1961. Hayden church. (40th anniversary of Burgenland's incorporation into Austrian Republic)   50.00

106. 50 Schillings 1965. Rudolf of Habsburg. Rev: Circle of shields. (Founding of Vienna University in 1365)   20.00
107. 25 Schillings 1965. J.J.R. von Prechtl. Rev: Circle of shields. (150th year of Vienna Technical High School)   15.00

101. 25 Schillings 1962. Head of Anton Bruckner   15.00

108. 50 Schillings 1966. Bank building. Rev: Circle of shields. (150th anniversary of Austrian National Bank)   25.00
109. 25 Schillings 1966. Portrait of Ferdinand Raimund (1790–1836). Rev: Circle of shields. (Honors Viennese poet)   20.00

102. 50 Schillings 1963. Shields of Austria and Tyrol. (600th anniversary of union of Tyrol with Austria)   17.50

110. 50 Schillings 1967. Half-length figure of Johann Strauss. Rev: Circle of shields. (100th anniversary of Blue Danube Waltz) 17.50

114. 50 Schillings 1969. Bust of Holy Roman Emperor Maximilian I. Rev: Circle of shields. (450th anniversary of his death) 20.00

115. 25 Schillings 1969. Portrait of Peter Rosegger. Rev: Circle of shields. (125th anniversary of writer's birth) 17.50

111. 25 Schillings 1967. Portrait of Empress Maria Theresa (1717–1780). Rev: Circle of shields. (250th anniversary of birth) 15.00

116. 50 Schillings 1970. University of Innsbruck seal. Rev: Circle of shields. (300th anniversary of founding) 15.00

117. 50 Schillings 1970. Portrait of Dr. Karl Renner (1870–1950), Federal President 1945–1950. Rev: Circle of shields 17.50

112. 50 Schillings 1968. Parliament building. Rev: Circle of shields. (50th anniversary of Austrian Republic) 25.00

118. 25 Schillings 1970. Head of Franz Lehar. Rev: Circle of shields. (100th anniversary of composer's birth) 15.00

119. 50 Schillings 1971. Portrait of Julius Raab (1891–1964), Federal Chancellor 1953–1961. Rev: Circle of shields 15.00

113. 25 Schillings 1968. Belvedere Palace. Rev: Circle of shields. (300th anniversary of architect Lukas von Hildebrandt) 25.00

120. 25 Schillings 1971. Stock exchange building. Rev: Circle of shields. (200th anniversary of Vienna Bourse) 12.50

120. 121.

121. 50 Schillings 1972. University seal. Rev: Circle
of shields. (350th anniversary of Salzburg
University) 17.50

122. 124.

122. 50 Schillings 1972. School building. Rev: Circle
of shields. (100th anniversary of Agricultural
University) 17.50

123. 25 Schillings 1972. Portrait of Carl Michael
Ziehrer (1843–1922). Rev: Circle of shields.
(50th anniversary of composer's death) 15.00

124. 50 Schillings 1973. Inn. Rev: Circle of shields.
(500th anniversary of Bummerlhaus in Steyr) ... 17.50

125. 50 Schillings 1973. Bust of Theodor Körner
(1873–1957). Rev: Circle of shields. (100th
anniversary of birth of former Federal Presi-
dent) 17.50

126. 50 Schillings 1973. Portrait of Max Reinhardt
(1873–1943). Rev: Circle of shields. (100th
anniversary of theatrical director's birth) 15.00

127. 128.

127. 50 Schillings 1974. Stylized radio transmitter.
Rev: Circle of shields. (50 years of Austrian
radio) 15.00

128. 50 Schillings 1974. Bishops Rupert and Virgil
holding model of Salzburg Cathedral. Rev:
Circle of shields. (1200th anniversary of cathedral) 15.00

129. 130.

129. 50 Schillings 1974. Arms and Federal Police insignia. Rev: Circle of shields. (125th anniversary of Federal Police) 15.00

130. 50 Schillings 1974. Floral design. Rev: Circle of
shields. (International Garden Exhibition) 15.00

131. 100 Schillings 1975. Johann Strauss monument in
Vienna City Park. Rev: Circle of shields.
(150th anniversary of composer's birth) 20.00

132. 100 Schillings 1975. Modern eagle over value.
Rev: Sower in field. (50th anniversary of
schilling coinage) 20.00

133.   *135.*

133. 100 Schillings 1975. Eagle. Rev: Design symbolizing occupation. (20th anniversary of State Treaty)   12.50

134. 1000 Schillings (G) 1976. Knight on horseback. Rev: Arms. (Austrian Millennium)   300.00

135. 100 Schillings 1976. Emblem of Winter Olympics. Rev: Circle of shields. (1976 Games in Innsbruck)   10.00

136. 100 Schillings 1976. Eagle. Rev: Hasegg Mint, Olympic rings in background. (1976 Olympics)   10.00

137. 100 Schillings 1976. Rev: Modernistic skiier. (1976 Olympics)   10.00

138. 100 Schillings 1976. Rev: Bergisel ski jump. (1976 Olympics)   10.00

138a. 100 Schillings 1976. View of Burgtheater. (200th anniversary)   10.00

139. 100 Schillings 1976. (Carinthia commemorative)   10.00

140. 100 Schillings 1976. Portrait of Johann Nestory. (Austrian dramatist and actor)   10.00

141. 100 Schillings 1977. View of Hohensalzburg fortress. (900th anniversary)   10.00

142. 100 Schillings 1977. Chalice. (Founding of Kremsmunster Monastery in 777)   10.00

143. 100 Schillings 1977. Knight on horseback. (500th anniversary of mint at Hall)   10.00

144. 100 Schillings 1978. Eagle. (700th anniversary of Gmunden)   17.50

145. 100 Schillings 1978. (700th anniversary of Battle of Durnkrut and Jedenspeigen)   17.50

146. 100 Schillings 1978. Rev: City view. (1100th anniversary of the founding of Villach)   17.50

147. 100 Schillings 1978. Value over shields. Rev: Joined hands, mountains in background. (Opening of Arlberg Tunnel)   17.50

AUSTRIA (continued)

148.	50 Schillings 1978. Value within circle of shields. Rev: Bust of Franz Schubert. (150th anniversary of composer's death.)	10.00
149.	100 Schillings 1979. Arms. Rev: Cathedral facade. (Centennial of Wiener Neustadt Cathedral)	17.50
150.	100 Schillings 1979. Arms. (200th anniversary of Inn District)	17.50
151.	100 Schillings 1979. Arms. (Vienna International Center)	17.50
152.	100 Schillings 1979. Buildings. Rev: Value within circle of shields. (Festival and Congress Hall at Bregenz)	17.50
153.	500 Schillings 1980. City view. Rev: Value within circle of shields. (Millennium of city of Steyr)	50.00
154.	500 Schillings 1980. Government buildings. Rev: Value within circle of shields. (25th anniversary of Austrian State Treaty)	50.00
155.	500 Schillings 1980. Bust of Maria Theresa. Rev: Value. (200th anniversary of Queen's death)	50.00
156.	500 Schillings 1980. Bust. Rev: Value. (Centennial of Austrian Red Cross)	50.00
157.	500 Schillings 1981. Rev: Value. (800th anniversary of Verdun)	50.00
158.	500 Schillings 1981. Bust of Anton Wildgans. Rev: Value. (Centennial of birth of Austrian poet and dramatist)	50.00
159.	500 Schillings 1981. Bust of Otto Bauer. Rev: Value. (Centennial of birth of Austrian statesman and educational reformer)	50.00
160.	500 Schillings 1981. Value. (200th anniversary of religious tolerance in Austria)	50.00

AZORES

The Azores comprise three groups of islands in the Atlantic Ocean just west of Portugal, which were known as far back as the fourteenth century. For centuries the islands were Portuguese colonies; finally they were made part of Portugal for administrative purposes.

1000 Reis = 1 Crown

NOTE: Similar coins with values given in Roman numerals were issued for Portugal proper

MARY II   1828–53

1.	80 Reis (C) 1829. Crowned shield. Rev: Value in wreath	40.00
2.	20 Reis (C) 1843	15.00

3.	10 Reis (C) 1843	10.00
4.	5 Reis (C) 1843	15.00

LOUIS I   1861–89

5.	20 Reis (C) 1865, '66	10.00
6.	10 Reis (C) 1865, '66	7.50
7.	5 Reis (C) 1865–80	6.50

CHARLES I   1889–1908

8.	10 Reis (C) 1901	12.50
9.	5 Reis (C) 1901	10.00

BAHAMAS

Columbus's first landing, in 1492 in the name of Spain, was on one of the 700 islands of the Bahamas. British influence began in the 17th century; in 1729 the Bahamas became a crown colony. In 1973 it gained full independence, with membership in the Commonwealth of Nations.

1.   1 Penny (C) 1806. Bust of George III. Rev: Three-masted man-of-war   55.00

2.   5 Dollars 1966–70. Portrait of Queen Elizabeth with coronet. Rev: Coat of arms   30.00

3.   2 Dollars 1966–70. Rev: Two flamingos   20.00

4.   1 Dollar 1966–70. Rev: Conch shell   12.50

5.   50 Cents 1966–70. Rev: Blue marlin   7.50
6.   25 Cents (N) 1966–70. Rev: Native sloop   2.00

7.   15 Cents (C-N) 1966–70. Rev: Hibiscus blossom. (Square planchet)   1.00
8.   10 Cents (C-N) 1966–70. Rev: Two bonefish. (Scalloped-edge planchet)   .75

9.   5 Cents (C-N) 1966–70. Rev: Pineapple   .65
10.   1 Cent (Bra) 1966–70. Rev: Starfish   .35

11.   100 Dollars (G) 1967. Elizabeth II. Rev: Columbus with flag   1000.00

12. 50 Dollars (G) 1967, '71, '72. Rev: *Santa Maria,*
flagship of Columbus   450.00

25. 5 Dollars 1972, '73. Rev: Newly designed arms   30.00

13. 20 Dollars (G) 1967, '71, '72. Rev: Lighthouse   200.00
14. 10 Dollars (G) 1967, '71, '72. Rev: Fort   100.00
15. 100 Dollars (G) 1971, '72. Type of #2   850.00

26. 100 Dollars (G) 1973. Rev: Arms   250.00

27. 50 Dollars (G) 1973. Rev: Crawfish   125.00
28. 20 Dollars (G) 1973. Rev: Four flamingos   50.00
29. 10 Dollars (G) 1973. Rev: Tobacco dove   40.00

16. 5 Dollars 1971. Elizabeth II. Rev: Arms   30.00
17. 2 Dollars 1971–73. Rev: Type of #3   20.00
18. 1 Dollar 1971–73. Rev: Type of #4   12.50
19. 50 Cents 1971–73 (C-N) Rev: Type of #5   7.50
20. 25 Cents (N) 1971–73. Rev: Type of #6   2.00
21. 15 Cents (C-N) 1971–73. Rev: Type of #7   2.25
22. 10 Cents (C-N) 1971–73. Rev: Type of #8   1.75
23. 5 Cents (C-N) 1971–73. Rev: Type of #9   1.25
24. 1 Cent (N-Bra) 1971–73. Rev: Type of #10   .65

30. 50 Dollars (G) 1973. Rev: Two flamingos, inscription. (Independence Day)   200.00
31. 10 Dollars 1973. Rev: *Santa Maria,* inscription.
(Independence Day)   50.00

BAHAMAS (continued)

32. 200 Dollars (G) 1974–77. Elizabeth II, date of
  independence. Rev: Type of #26   300.00
33. 150 Dollars (G) 1974–77. Rev: Type of #27   215.00
34. 100 Dollars (G) 1974–77. Rev: Type of #28   150.00
35. 50 Dollars (G) 1974–77. Rev: Type of #29   75.00

36. 100 Dollars (G) 1974. Two flamingos, inscription.
  Rev: Arms. (Independence Day)   225.00

37. 10 Dollars (C-N) 1974. Head of Sir Milo B.
  Butler, governor general. Rev: Arms   35.00

38. 5 Dollars (C-N) 1974– . Arms. Rev: Flag   12.50
39. 2 Dollars (C-N) 1974– . Rev: Type of #3   8.50
40. 1 Dollar (C-N) 1974– . Rev: Type of #4   3.50
41. 50 Cents (C-N) 1974– . Rev: Type of #5   2.00
42. 25 Cents (N) 1974– . Rev: Type of #6   1.25
43. 15 Cents (N) 1974– . Rev: Type of #7.
  (Square planchet)   .75
44. 10 Cents (C-N) 1974– . Rev: Type of #8.
  (Scalloped planchet)   .75
45. 5 Cents (C-N) 1974– . Rev: Type of #9   .30
46. 1 Cent (N-Bra) 1974– . Rev: Type of #10   .20

47. 100 Dollars (G) 1975–77. Parrot. Rev: Arms.
  (Second anniversary of independence)   300.00

48. 10 Dollars 1975– . Yellow elder, national flower.
  Rev: Arms. (Independence Day)   35.00
48a. 10 Dollars (C-N) 1975–   35.00

49. 10 Dollars 1978. Head of Sir Milo B. Butler. Rev: Arms. (Fifth anniversary of independence.) Issued in proof only — 40.00

50. 10 Dollars 1978. Head of Prince Charles. Rev: Arms. (Fifth anniversary of independence.) In proof only — 40.00
51. 250 Dollars (G) 1979. Bust of Princess Anne. Rev: Arms. (250th anniversary of Bahamian Parliament) — 250.00

52. 25 Dollars 1979. Arms. Rev: Parliamentary Mace of Bahamas. (250th anniversary of Bahamian Parliament) — 50.00
53. 10 Dollars 1980. Arms. Rev: Flag, map of Caribbean. (10th anniversary of Caribbean Development Bank.) In proof only — 30.00
54. 500 Dollars (G) 1981. Elizabeth II. Rev: Conjoined portraits of Prince Charles and Lady Diana. (Marriage of royal couple.) In proof only — 500.00
55. 100 Dollars (G) 1981. (Charles and Diana.) In proof only — 100.00
56. 10 Dollars 1981. (Charles and Diana.) In proof only — 50.00

52.

43

BAHRAIN

An independent Arab state made up of the island of Bahrain and several smaller islands in the Persian Gulf near the east coast of Saudi Arabia. Bahrain was under the protection of Great Britain from 1861 until 1971, when it became an independent nation.

1.	100 Fils (C-N) 1965. Tree in circle. Rev: Value	2.00
2.	50 Fils (C-N) 1965	1.25
3.	25 Fils (C-N) 1965	.75
4.	10 Fils (Br) 1965	.60
5.	5 Fils (Br) 1965	.50
6.	1 Fil (Br) 1965	.35

7.	10 Dinars (G) 1968. Bust of Sheik Isa bin Sulman Al Khalifah. Rev: Arms. (Opening of Isa Town)	425.00
8.	500 Fils 1968	17.50

9.	250 Fils (C-N) 1969. Dhow and date palm. (F.A.O. coin plan)	4.00
10.	100 Dinars (G) 1978. Sheik Isa bin Sulman Al Khalifah. Rev: Arms. Issued in proof only	650.00
11.	50 Dinars (G) 1978. In proof only	400.00

44

BANGLADESH

Formerly East Pakistan; became independent in 1971.

1.   50 Poisha (C-N) 1973. Arms. Rev: Bird   2.00

2.   25 Poisha (St) 1973. Rev: Fish   .65

3.   10 Poisha (A) 1973, '74. Rev: Leaf   .50

4.   5 Poisha (A) 1973. Rev: Cogwheel, plow   .35

5.   25 Poisha (St) 1974–78. Rev: Carp, bananas and
     gourd. (F.A.O. coin plan)   .60

6.   10 Poisha (A) 1974–79. Rev: Tractor, seedlings
     and rice. (F.A.O.)   .50

7.   5 Poisha (A) 1974–76. Rev: Cogwheel, plow.
     (F.A.O.)   .35

8.   1 Poisha (A) 1974. Rev: Value   .25

9.   1 Taka (C-N) 1975–77. Rev: Family of four.
     (F.A.O.)   1.25
10. 50 Poisha (C-N) 1977– . Arms. Rev: Bananas
     and gourd. (F.A.O. coin plan)   1.00
11. 25 Poisha (C-N) 1977– . Arms   .60
12. 10 Poisha (A) 1977– . (F.A.O. coin plan)   .50
13. 5 Poisha (A) 1977– . (F.A.O. coin plan)   .35

BARBADOS

The most easterly of the West Indian islands, Barbados was originally explored by the Portuguese, but in 1627 it became a British colony. In 1966 it became independent, with membership in the Commonwealth of Nations.

5.   10 Dollars 1973– . Arms. Rev: Seated figures of
      Neptune   20.00
5a. 10 Dollars (C-N) 1974   12.50

1.   1 Penny (C) 1788. Negro head with crown
     and plume of three ostrich feathers. Rev:
     Pineapple   35.00

6.   5 Dollars 1973– . Rev: Shell fountain in
     Bridgetown   12.50
6a. 5 Dollars (C-N) 1974   8.50

2.   1 Penny (C) 1792. Type of #1. Rev: Neptune   20.00
3.   1 Halfpenny (C) 1792. Type of #2   30.00

7.   2 Dollars (C-N) 1973– . Rev: Two fish, coral   5.00

4.   4 Dollars (C-N) 1970. Arms. Rev: Bananas and
     sugar cane. (F.A.O. coin plan, East Carib-
     bean Territories)   5.00

8.   1 Dollar (C-N) 1973– . Rev: Flying fish.
     (Heptagonal planchet)   2.50

BARBADOS (continued)

9. 25 Cents (C-N) 1973. Rev: Morgan Lewis Sugar Mill ... 1.25
10. 10 Cents (C-N) 1973– . Rev: Tern ... .50

11. 5 Cents (Bra) 1973– . Rev: Lighthouse ... .75
12. 1 Cent (Br) 1973– . Rev: Trident ... .50

13. 100 Dollars (G) 1975. Arms. Rev: Sailing ship. (350th anniversary, English landing at Barbados) ... 65.00
14. 10 Dollars (C-N; also S) 1976. Type of #5. Obverse: 1966 INDEPENDENCE 1976 added ... 25.00
15. 5 Dollars (C-N; also S) 1976. Type of #6. 1966 INDEPENDENCE 1976 ... 25.00
16. 2 Dollars (C-N) 1976. Type of #7. 1966 INDEPENDENCE 1976 ... 7.50
17. 1 Dollar (C-N) 1976. Type of #8. 1966 INDEPENDENCE 1976 ... 5.00
18. 25 Cents (C-N) 1976. Type of #9. 1966 INDEPENDENCE 1976 ... 1.25
19. 10 Cents (C-N) 1976. Type of #10. 1966 INDEPENDENCE 1976 ... .50
20. 5 Cents (Bra) 1976. Type of #11. 1966 INDEPENDENCE 1976 ... 1.00
21. 1 Cent (Bra) 1976. Type of #12. 1966 INDEPENDENCE 1976 ... .25
22. 100 Dollars (G) 1978. Arms. Rev: Hands holding scroll. (Human Rights) ... 125.00

23.

23. 25 Dollars 1978. Elizabeth II. Rev: Supported crown. (Queen's Coronation Jubilee) ... 50.00
24. 200 Dollars (G) 1979. Arms. Rev: Stylized symbol of children. (International Year of Child) ... 200.00
25. 25 Dollars 1980. Arms. Rev: Flag, map of Caribbean. (10th anniversary of Caribbean Development Bank.) Issued in proof only ... 40.00
26. 150 Dollars (G) 1981. Arms. Rev: Poinciana. (National flower.) In proof only ... 175.00
27. 25 Dollars 1981. Arms. Rev: Stylized art symbol. (Caribbean Festival of Arts.) In proof only ... 40.00

28. 10 Dollars 1982. Arms. Rev: Seal of Central Bank of Barbados. (10th anniversary of bank.) ... 20.00

47

BELGIAN CONGO

Almost 100 times larger than Belgium, this huge territory in central Africa in 1885 became the private property of Leopold II of Belgium. In 1908 it became a Belgian colony, and in 1960 achieved independence as the Republic of the Congo (q.v.). The name was changed to Zaire (q.v.) in 1971.

100 Centimes = 1 Congo Franc

LEOPOLD II 1865–1909

1.	5 Francs 1887–96. Head. Rev: Crowned arms supported by lions	165.00
2.	2 Francs 1887–96. Rev: Crowned arms in wreath	50.00
3.	1 Franc 1887–96	25.00
4.	50 Centimes 1887–96	15.00

5.	10 Centimes (C) 1888–94. Crowned initials. Rev: Star. (Center hole)	5.00
6.	5 Centimes (C) 1887–94	3.50
7.	2 Centimes (C) 1887–88	3.00
8.	1 Centime (C) 1887–88	4.50
9.	20 Centimes (C-N) 1906–09	5.00
10.	10 Centimes (C-N) 1906–09	5.00
11.	5 Centimes (C-N) 1906–09	3.50

ALBERT I 1909–34

12.	1 Franc (C-N) 1920–30. Laureate head. Rev: Palm tree	7.50

13.	50 Centimes (C-N) 1921–29	4.00

14.	20 Centimes (C-N) 1910–11	4.00
15.	10 Centimes (C-N) 1910–28	2.00
16.	5 Centimes (C-N) 1910–28	2.00
17.	2 Centimes (C) 1910, '19	10.00
18.	1 Centime (C) 1910, '19	5.00

LEOPOLD III 1934–51
(under authority of Banque du Congo Belge)

19.	5 Francs (N-Bro) 1936–37. Head of Leopold III. Rev: Lion	75.00
20.	50 Francs 1944. Elephant. Rev: Value	125.00

21.	2 Francs (Bra) 1943. Elephant. Rev: Value. (Hexagonal)	25.00
22.	2 Francs (Bra) 1946, '47. (Round)	5.00
23.	1 Franc (Bra) 1944–49	5.00

COINAGE FOR BELGIAN CONGO AND RUANDA-URUNDI TRUST TERRITORY

24.	5 Francs (Bra) 1952. Palm tree. Rev: Star	8.00

25.	5 Francs (A) 1956–59. Crowned arms. Rev: Palm tree	2.50
26.	1 Franc (A) 1957–60	1.50
27.	50 Centimes (A) 1954, '55	1.25

48

BELGIUM

Formerly ruled by the Habsburgs, Belgium fell to the French Republic in 1794. In 1815, following Napoleon's downfall, it became part of the Netherlands. In 1830 Belgium proclaimed its independence and elected Prince Leopold of Saxe-Coburg-Gotha King.

As two languages are spoken in Belgium, coins issued from 1886 on have both French and Flemish inscriptions.

100 Centimes = 1 Franc

LEOPOLD I   1831–65

1.	5 Francs 1832–49. Laureate head. Rev: Value	75.00

2.	5 Francs 1849–65. Bare head. Rev: Arms	50.00
3.	2½ Francs 1848–50	225.00
4.	2 Francs 1834–44	550.00
5.	1 Franc 1833–44, '49, '50	150.00
6.	½ Franc 1833–44, '49, '50	125.00
7.	¼ Franc 1834–44, '49, '50	85.00

8.	20 Centimes (S) 1852–58; (C-N) 1860, '61	7.50

9.	10 Centimes (C) 1832–56; (C-N) 1861–64. Lion. Rev: Monogram	5.00
10.	5 Centimes (C) 1832–60; (C-N) 61–64	6.00
11.	2 Centimes (C) 1833–65	2.50
12.	1 Centime (C) 1832–62	5.00

LEOPOLD II   1865–1909

13.	20 Francs (G) 1867–82. Bearded head. Rev: Crowned arms	120.00

14.	5 Francs 1865–76. Rev: Crowned arms in wreath	20.00
15.	2 Francs 1866–87. Rev: Crowned arms	15.00
15a.	2 Francs 1904, '09. Rev: Value in wreath	10.00
16.	1 Franc 1866–69, '86, '87	10.00
16a.	1 Franc 1904, '09. Rev: Value in wreath	12.50
17.	50 Centimes 1866–1899	10.00
17a.	50 Centimes 1907, '09. Rev: Value in wreath	5.00

18.	25 Centimes (C-N) 1908, '09. Crowned "L"s. Rev: Value and spray. (Center hole)	2.00
19.	10 Centimes (C-N) 1894–1906	2.00
20.	5 Centimes (C-N) 1894–1907	.30
21.	2 Centimes (C) 1869–76, 1902–09. Lion and shield. Rev: Crowned script	.75
22.	1 Centime (C) 1869–1902, 1907	1.50

BELGIUM (continued)

23.   5 Francs 1880. Conjoined heads. (50th anniversary of independence)   350.00
24.   2 Francs 1880. Rev: Crowned arms   150.00
25.   1 Franc 1880   75.00

ALBERT I   1909–34

26.   20 Francs (G) 1914. Uniformed bust. Rev: Shield on crowned mantle   120.00
27.   2 Francs 1910–12. Head. Rev: Value in wreath   10.00
28.   1 Franc 1910–14   3.00
29.   50 Centimes 1910–14   7.00
30.   25 Centimes (C-N) 1910–13, 1920–29. (Center hole)   .75
31.   10 Centimes (C-N) 1920–29; (N-Bra) 1930–32   .50
32.   5 Centimes (C-N) 1910–14, 1920–32; (N-Bra) 1930–32   .50
33.   20 Francs (N) 1931, '32. Head. Rev: Shield   80.00

34.   10 Francs (N) 1930 (Centenary of independence). Heads of the two Leopolds and Albert. Rev: Value   120.00
35.   5 Francs (N) 1930–34. Head. Rev: Value   2.50

36.   2 Francs (N) 1923, '24, '30. Allegory of Belgium wounded but victorious. Rev: Caduceus   1.00

37.   1 Franc (N) 1922–35   .50
38.   50 Centimes (N) 1922–34   .50

LEOPOLD III   1934–51
(Regency 1944–51)

39.   50 Francs 1935. St. Michael and the Dragon. Rev: Exhibition hall. (Railroad Centenary)   350.00

40.   50 Francs 1939, '40. Head. Rev: Shields of nine provinces   15.00
41.   20 Francs 1934, '35. Rev: Crowned laurel, wheat and oak   7.00
42.   5 Francs (N) 1936, '37. Rev: Value   8.00

43.   5 Francs (N) 1938, '39. Lion. Rev: Shields   3.00
44.   1 Franc (N) 1939, '40   .75

45.   25 Centimes (N-Bra) 1938, '39; (Z) 1942–47. Crowned "L"s. Rev: Shields. (Center hole)   .75
46.   10 Centimes (N-Bra) 1938, '39; (Z) 1941–46   .50
47.   5 Centimes (N-Bra) 1938–40; (Z) 1941–43   .75

BELGIUM (continued)

Postwar

48. 100 Francs 1948–54. Heads of the four kings. (Dedicated to the Belgian dynasty)   25.00

56a.   56.

56. 50 Francs 1958 (Brussels Fair). Head of king. Rev: Building and value; symbol of Fair in field. French legend   20.00

56a. 50 Francs 1958. Type of #56, Flemish legend instead. (Brussels Fair)   20.00

49. 50 Francs 1948–54. Mercury head   15.00
50. 20 Francs 1949–55   8.50

57. 50 Francs 1960. Conjoined heads of Baudouin and Fabiola. Rev: Crowned arms of Belgium and Aragon. (Marriage commemorative)   20.00

51. 5 Francs (C-N) 1948– . Ceres head   .45
52. 1 Franc (C-N) 1950–   .25

BAUDOUIN I   1951–

53. 50 Centimes (Br) 1952– . Miner's head   .20
54. 20 Centimes (Br) 1953–63   .35

58. 10 Francs (N) 1969– . Head of King Baudouin. Rev: Arms   .75

59. 250 Francs 1976. Head of King. Rev: Crowned monogram   25.00

60. 500 Francs 1980. Cameo portraits of Belgium's five kings: Leopold I, Leopold II, Albert I, Leopold III and Baudouin I. Rev: Inscription and value. French legend (also issued with Flemish legend instead)   25.00

55. 25 Centimes (C-N) 1964– . Crowned monogram. Rev: Value   .20

BELIZE

Formerly known as British Honduras (q.v.).

1. 5 Cents (N-Bra) 1973–76; (A) 1976– . Queen
    Elizabeth II. Rev: Value .... .25

7. 5 Dollars (C-N) 1974– . Rev: Keelbilled toucan ... 20.00

2. 1 Cent (Br) 1973–76; (A) 1976– .... .15

8. 1 Dollar (C-N) 1974– . Rev: Scarlet macaws 15.00

3. 50 Cents (C-N) 1974– 2.50

4. 25 Cents (C-N) 1974– 1.00
5. 10 Cents (C-N) 1974– .... .50

9. 50 Cents (C-N) 1974. Rev: Birds in flight 4.00
9a. 50 Cents (C-N) 1975– . Type of #9 (value stated
    as numeral) 2.00

10. 25 Cents (C-N) 1974. Rev: Bird on branch 1.00
10a. 25 Cents (C-N) 1975– . Type of #10 (value
     stated as numeral) 2.00
11. 10 Cents (C-N) 1974. Rev: Bird on branch .... .50
11a. 10 Cents (C-N) 1975– . Type of #11 (value
     stated as numeral) 1.00

6. 10 Dollars (C-N) 1974– . Arms. Rev: Great
    curassow 20.00

BELIZE (continued)

12. 5 Cents (N-Bra) 1974. Rev: Two birds on branch .50
12a. 5 Cents (N-Bra) 1975–76; (A) 1977– . Type of #12 (value stated as numeral) .50
13. 1 Cent (Br) 1974. Rev: Birds in flight .15
13a. 1 Cent (Br) 1975–76; (A) 1977. Type of #13 (value stated as numeral; scalloped planchet) .15

18. 25 Dollars 1978. Elizabeth II. Rev: Crown supported by Tudor Greyhound and English Lion. (Coronation Jubilee) 40.00

14. 100 Dollars (G) 1975. Arms. Rev: National Assembly Building 90.00

19. 100 Dollars (G) 1979. Arms. Rev: Queen angelfish 90.00
20. 100 Dollars (G) 1979. Arms. Rev: Star of Bethlehem 90.00

15. 100 Dollars (G) 1976. Arms. Rev: Ancient Mayan symbols 90.00

21. 10 Dollars (C-N) 1979. Arms. Rev: Jabiru birds. Also issued in silver proof 20.00

16.   17.

16. 100 Dollars (G) 1977. Arms. Rev: Kinich Ahau, Mayan sun god 90.00
17. 100 Dollars (G) 1978. Arms. Rev: Itzamna, Mayan god 90.00

22. 100 Dollars (G) 1980. Arms. Rev: Moorish idol (reef fish). Issued in proof only 100.00
23. 100 Dollars (G) 1980. Arms. Rev: Orchids. In proof only 100.00

BELIZE (continued)

24. 10 Dollars (C-N) 1980. Arms. Rev: Scarlet ibis.
     Also in silver proof   20.00
25. 100 Dollars (G) 1981. Arms. Rev: Yellow swal-
     lowtail butterfly. In proof only   125.00
26. 50 Dollars (G) 1981. Arms. Rev: White-necked
     Jacobin hummingbird   80.00

27. 10 Dollars 1982. Arms. Rev: Yellow-headed par-
     rot. In proof only   30.00

BERMUDA

Six hundred miles off the Carolina coast of the United
States, Bermuda is made up of some 300 islands. It was
discovered about 1510 by Juan de Bermudez and settled by
the British a century later. In 1968 this crown colony
obtained internal autonomy.

1.   1 Penny (Bro) 1793. Bust of George III. Rev:
     Three-masted fighting ship of the line   65.00

2.   1 Crown (C-N) 1959. Crowned head of Eliz-
     abeth II. Rev: Map and ships. (350th anniver-
     sary of founding of colony)   25.00

3.   1 Crown 1964. Head of Elizabeth II. Rev: Lion
     supporting Bermuda arms   12.50

BERMUDA (continued)

DECIMAL COINAGE

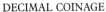

10.   1 Dollar 1972. (Elizabeth II's silver wedding anniversary)   10.00

11.   20 Dollars (G) 1970. Rev: Seagull   750.00

4.   1 Dollar 1970. New portrait of Queen with coronet. Rev: Map of Bermuda. (Issued in proof only)   80.00

12.   100 Dollars (G) 1975. Rev: Royal monograms and parliamentary mace. (Royal visit)   150.00

5.   50 Cents (C-N) 1970– . Rev: Lion supporting arms   1.50

6.   25 Cents (C-N) 1970– . Rev: Bird of spring   .70
7.   10 Cents (C-N) 1970– . Rev: Bermuda lilies   .35

8.   5 Cents (C-N) 1970- . Rev: Angelfish   .25
9.   1 Cent (Br) 1970– . Rev: Wild hog   .15

13.   25 Dollars 1975   50.00

BERMUDA (continued)

14. 100 Dollars (G) 1977. Rev: *Deliverance*, first ship constructed in Bermuda. (Queen's Silver Jubilee) 150.00
15. 50 Dollars (G) 1977. Rev: Sailboat. (Silver Jubilee) 75.00
16. 25 Dollars 1977. Rev: Three-masted fighting ship of the line. (Silver Jubilee) 60.00
17. 250 Dollars (G) 1981. Rev: Dual portraits of Prince Charles and Lady Diana. (Marriage of Charles and Diana) 400.00
18. 1 Dollar (C-N) 1981. (Charles and Diana) 5.00

BHUTAN

Located in the eastern Himalayas, Bhutan was formerly a protectorate of British India but now has complete control of both domestic and foreign affairs and is a member of the United Nations.

1. ½ Rupee 1928. Bust of Maharajah. Rev: Eight lucky Buddhist symbols with inscription in center 50.00
2. ½ Rupee (N) 1928, '50 ..... 7.50
3. 1 Paisa (Br) 1928 ..... 60.00

4. 1 Paisa (Bro) 1951. Eight Buddhist symbols. Rev: Symbols 2.50

DECIMAL COINAGE

100 Paisa (Chetrums) = 1 Rupee (Ngultrum)
100 Rupees = 1 Sertum

5. 5 Sertums (G) 1966. Bust of Maharajah. Rev: Arms. (40th anniversary of reign) 800.00
6. 2 Sertums (G) 1966 ..... 350.00
7. 1 Sertum (G) 1966 ..... 175.00
8. 3 Rupees (C-N) 1966 ..... 7.50
8a. 3 Rupees 1966. (Silver proof) 50.00
9. 1 Rupee (C-N) 1966 ..... 2.00
10. 50 Naya Paisa (C-N) 1966 ..... 1.50
11. 25 Naya Paisa (C-N) 1966 ..... 1.00

12. 1 Sertum (G) 1970 ..... 175.00

BHUTAN (continued)

13. 15 Ngultrums 1974. Farmer cultivating rice.
    Rev: Arms. (F.A.O. coin plan)   15.00

14. 1 Ngultrum (C-N) 1974, '75. Bust of Maharajah. Rev: Thunderbolt within cross, ribbons, value   1.50

15. 25 Chetrums (C-N) 1974, '75. Rev: Two fish
    with ribbons, value   .75
16. 20 Chetrums (A-Br) 1974. Type of #13. (F.A.O.
    coin plan)   .75

17. 10 Chetrums (A) 1974. Rev: Buddhist symbol
    with ribbons, value. (Scalloped-edge
    planchet)   .50
18. 5 Chetrums 1974, '75. Rev: Buddhist wheel of
    life   .25
19. 30 Ngultrums 1975. Young woman. Rev: Cross
    with thunderbolt. (International Women's
    Year)   20.00
20. 3 Ngultrums (C-N) 1979. Bust of Maharajah.
    Rev: Buddhist symbols   10.00
21. 1 Ngultrum (C-N) 1979. Arms. Rev: Buddhist
    symbols   5.00
22. 50 Chetrums (C-N) 1979   4.00
23. 25 Chetrums (C-N) 1979   2.50
24. 10 Chetrums (Bro) 1979   1.50
25. 5 Chetrums (A) 1979   .75

BIAFRA

A short-lived nation, Biafra came into being in 1967 when the Ibos of the eastern region of Nigeria (q.v.) proclaimed an independent nation. This sparked a war which lasted nearly three years, ending with the surrender of Biafran forces in 1970.

1. 2½ Shillings (A) 1969. Coconut palm. Rev: Lion   7.00

2. 1 Shilling (A) 1969. Rev: Eagle on elephant
   tusk   6.00

3. 3 Pence (A) 1969. Rev: Value   7.50

BOLIVIA

Once part of the Inca empire, Bolivia was a Spanish colony for three centuries. Gaining independence in 1825, the new nation was named for Simón Bolívar, the famed Liberator.

Early issues of the Spanish colony bear the name of the reigning Spanish monarch. The designs are similar to those of other Spanish-American mints. The Potosí mint mark appears in monogram or with the name spelled out in full. Early planchets are irregular in form and crudely engraved.

The legendary gold doubloons, issued from 1772 to 1820, bear the head of the reigning Spanish monarch and are valued at $1200.00. Many of them are from the Potosí mint.

8 Reales (Sueldos) = 1 Peso or Piece-of-Eight
100 Centavos = 1 Boliviano

Gold doubloon (8 escudos) 1791		1200.00

PHILIP IV   1621–65

1.	8 Reales 1651–61. Shield and Quartered arms. Rev: Pillars	200.00

2.	2 Reales 1652–64	35.00
3.	1 Real 1652–64	20.00

CHARLES II   1665–1700

4.	8 Reales 1676–94	75.00

5.	4 Reales 1692	75.00
6.	2 Reales 1665–94	40.00
7.	1 Real 1671–89	25.00

PHILIP V   1700–46

8.	8 Reales 1723–38	175.00
9.	2 Reales 1703–42	40.00

10.	1 Real 1733–41	25.00

FERDINAND VI   1746–59

11.	8 Reales 1746–59	125.00
12.	4 Reales 1749–54	75.00
13.	2 Reales 1750–58	35.00
14.	1 Real 1752–59	25.00

CHARLES III   1759–88

FIRST COINAGE: Same as preceding type (shield and arms)

15.	8 Reales 1760–73	100.00
16.	4 Reales 1767–69	85.00
17.	2 Reales 1763–76	30.00
18.	1 Real 1763	25.00

SECOND COINAGE: Crowned arms. Rev: Globes between pillars. Mint mark appears as monogram in legend.

19.	8 Reales 1767–70	150.00

20.	4 Reales 1767–70	135.00
21.	2 Reales 1768–70	35.00
22.	1 Real 1767–70	50.00

THIRD COINAGE: Laureate bust to right. Rev: Crowned arms between pillars.

23.	8 Reales 1774–89	65.00

24.	4 Reales 1773–89	40.00
25.	2 Reales 1773–89	15.00
26.	1 Real 1773–89	20.00
27.	½ Real 1773–89	20.00

CHARLES IV   1788–1808

28.	8 Reales 1789, '90. Bust of Charles III	80.00
29.	4 Reales 1789	125.00
30.	2 Reales 1789, '90	25.00
31.	1 Real 1789, '90	15.00
32.	½ Real 1790	17.50

33.	8 Reales 1791–1808. Bust of Charles IV	60.00
34.	4 Reales 1791–1808	50.00
35.	2 Reales 1791–1808	15.00
36.	1 Real 1791–1808	12.50
37.	½ Real 1791–1808	12.50
38.	¼ Real 1796–1808. Castle. Rev: Lion	25.00

FERDINAND VII   1808–25

39.	8 Reales 1808–25. Draped bust	60.00
40.	4 Reales 1808–25	50.00
41.	2 Reales 1808–25	20.00
42.	1 Real 1816–25	15.00

43.	½ Real 1816–25	17.50
44.	¼ Real 1809–25. Castle. Rev: Lion	35.00

REPUBLIC OF BOLIVIA 1825–

45.	8 Sueldos 1827–40. Uniformed bust of Bolívar. Rev: Tree between two llamas	50.00
46.	4 Sueldos 1827–30	30.00
47.	2 Sueldos 1827–30	15.00

48.	1 Sueldo 1827–30	12.50
49.	½ Sueldo 1827–30	12.50
50.	8 Sueldos 1848–51. Bare head of Bolívar	65.00
51.	8 Sueldos 1852–59. Laureated head of Bolívar	100.00
52.	4 Sueldos 1853–59	20.00
53.	2 Sueldos 1854–59	25.00
54.	1 Sueldo 1854–57	20.00
55.	½ Sueldo 1853–59	12.50
56.	¼ Sueldo 1852, '53. Llama. Rev: Mountain	20.00
57.	1 Peso 1859–63. Weight 400 grains	40.00
58.	½ Peso 1860. Weight 200 grains	75.00
59.	¼ Peso 1859–63. Weight 100 grains	12.50
60.	⅛ Peso 1859–63. Weight 50 grains	10.00
61.	1/16 Peso 1859–63. Weight 25 grains	8.50

DECIMAL COINAGE

100 Centavos = 1 Boliviano

62.	1 Boliviano 1864–79. Shield of arms. Rev: Value in wreath	35.00
63.	50 Centavos 1873–1909	15.00
64.	20 Centavos [⅕ Boliviano] (S) 1864–66, '70, 1904, '09	6.50
65.	10 Centavos [1/10 Boliviano] (S) 1864–67, 1870–1900; (C-N) 1883, 1892	6.50
66.	5 Centavos [1/20 Boliviano] (S) 1864, '65, 1871–1900; (C-N) 1883, 1892	4.00
67.	2 Centavos (C) 1878, '83	12.50
68.	1 Centavo (C) 1878, '83	7.50

BOLIVIA (continued)

69.	50 Centavos (C-N) 1939; (Bro) 1942. Native scene. Rev: Caduceus	3.00
70.	20 Centavos (Z) 1942	3.00
71.	10 Centavos (C-N) 1893–1919, '35, '37, '39; (Z) 1942	1.50
72.	5 Centavos (C-N) 1893–1919, '35	1.25

NEW STANDARD

73.	10 Bolivianos (Bro) 1951. Bolívar head	5.00
74.	5 Bolivianos (Bro) 1951. Arms.	2.00
75.	1 Boliviano (Bro) 1951. Native scene	1.75

CURRENCY REVALUATION

1 Peso Boliviano = 1000 Old Bolivianos

76.	1 Peso Boliviano (Ni-St) 1968– . Arms. Rev: Value	.80
77.	50 Centavos (N-St) 1965– . Arms. Rev: Value	.50
78.	20 Centavos (N-St) 1965–73	.25
79.	10 Centavos (C-St) 1965–73	.20
80.	5 Centavos (C-St) 1965–70	.15

81.	1 Peso Boliviano (Ni-St) 1968. Native scene. Rev: Value. (F.A.O. coin plan)	10.00
82.	25 Centavos (C-N) 1971, 1972. Native scene. Rev: Value. (Dodecagonal planchet)	60.00

83.	500 Pesos Boliviano 1975. Conjoined heads of Bolívar and President Banzer. Rev: Arms	40.00
84.	250 Pesos Bolivianos 1975	25.00
85.	100 Pesos Bolivianos 1975	15.00

86.	4000 Pesos Bolivianos (G) 1979. Condor over shield. Rev: Sun and seated child. (International Year of Child.) Proof	400.00

BOTSWANA

Formerly the British Protectorate of Bechuanaland, Botswana lies between South Africa, Zimbabwe and Southwest Africa (Namibia). It became an independent state on September 30, 1966, and is a member of the British Commonwealth.

1.	50 Cents 1966. Head of Seretse Khama. Rev. Arms	12.50
2.	10 Thebe (G) 1966	200.00

3.	25 Thebe (C-N) 1976. Brahma bull (F.A.O. coin plan)	1.50

4.	10 Thebe (C-N) 1976. Gemsbok	.75
5.	5 Thebe (Br) 1976. Bird	.50
6.	1 Thebe (A) 1976. Head of bird	.25
7.	5 Pula 1976. Seretse Khama. Rev: National Assembly Building. (10th anniversary of independence)	17.50

8.	1 Pula (C-N) 1976. Zebra. (Scalloped planchet)	4.00
9.	50 Thebe (C-N) 1976. Eagle with fish	2.50
10.	150 Pula (G) 1978. Rev: Brown hyena. (World Wildlife Conservation Program)	600.00
11.	10 Pula 1978. (Wildlife Conservation)	30.00
12.	5 Pula 1978. (Wildlife Conservation)	25.00

BRAZIL

The largest country in South America, with an area slightly greater than that of the U.S.A. Discovered in 1500 by Pedro Alvares Cabral, Brazil remained a Portuguese colony until 1822, when it declared its independence and became an empire. In 1889 the emperor was deposed and Brazil became a republic.

Issues of the colonial era bear the name of the reigning Portuguese monarch.

1000 Reis = 1 Milreis

COLONIAL COINAGE

1.	960 Reis 1809–18, 1818–22	25.00
2.	640 Reis 1695–1701, 1749–68, 1787–1805, 1809–22. Crowned arms of Portugal. Rev: Glove and cross	20.00

3.	320 Reis 1695–1701, 1749–68, 1783–1802, 1809–21	15.00
4.	160 Reis 1695–99, 1751–73, 1779–90, 1810–21	25.00
5.	80 Reis (S) 1696–99, 1751–71, 1787–96; (C) 1811–18	8.00
6.	40 Ries (C) 1694–99, 1715–99, 1802–18	7.00
7.	20 Reis (C) 1694–99, 1715–99, 1802–18	4.75
8.	10 Reis (C) 1695–97, 1715–99, 1802–18	4.00
9.	5 Reis (C) 1753–91	4.00

10.	Counterstamped Dollar. Portuguese arms and value counterstamped on both sides of Spanish dollars from the various New World mints	65.00

EMPIRE OF BRAZIL   1822–1889

PEDRO I   1822–1831

 *(Pedro I coin image)*

11.	80 Reis (C) 1823–31. Value in wreath. Rev: Crowned arms	6.00
12.	40 Reis (C) 1823–31	6.00
13.	20 Reis (C) 1823–30	4.50
14.	10 Reis (C) 1824–28	7.50

PEDRO II   1831–1889

15.	2000 Reis 1851–89	40.00
16.	1000 Reis 1849–89	12.50

17.	500 Reis 1849–89	4.00

BRASIL (continued)

18. 200 Reis (S) 1854–69; (N) 1871–89   3.00
19. 100 Reis (N) 1871–89   2.00
20.   50 Reis (N) 1886–88   5.00

REPUBLIC OF BRAZIL   1889–

21. 2000 Reis 1906–34. Liberty head with cap. Rev:
    Value in wreath   6.00
22. 1000 Reis (S) 1889, 1906–13; (A-Bro) 1924–31   2.50

23. 500 Reis (S) 1889, 1906–13; (A-Bro) 1924–30   2.00
24. 400 Reis (C-N) 1901, 1918–35. Liberty Head
    type   3.00

25. 200 Reis (C-N) 1889–1901, 1918–35   1.00
26. 100 Reis (C-N) 1889–1901, 1918–35   1.00
27.   50 Reis (C-N) 1918–31   1.00
28.   40 Reis (Bro) 1889–1912   1.50
29.   20 Reis (Bro) 1889–1912   1.50

FOURTH CENTENNIAL OF DISCOVERY
(an issue of outstanding interest)

30. 4000 Reis 1900. Pedro Alvares Cabral, explorer   750.00

31. 2000 Reis 1900   450.00

32. 1000 Reis 1900   250.00

33. 400 Reis 1900   150.00

BRAZIL (continued)

CENTENNIAL OF INDEPENDENCE

41. 200 Reis (C-N) 1932. Globe. Rev: Ship   5.00

34. 2 Milreis 1922. Dom Pedro and Pres. Pessoa.
Rev: Shields of the Empire and Republic   4.50
35. 1 Milreis (A-Br) 1922. Rev: Torch, crown and
liberty cap   2.50
36. 500 Reis (A-Br) 1922   1.25

42. 100 Reis (C-N) 1932. Bust of Cazique Tiberica   7.50

FOURTH CENTENNIAL OF COLONIZATION

CELEBRATED MEN SERIES

37. 2000 Reis 1932. Bust of John III   7.50

43. 5000 Reis 1936–38. Santos Dumont   7.50

38. 1000 Reis (A-Bro) 1932. Da Sousa   10.00

44. 2000 Reis 1935. Caxias facing left   7.50
44a. 2000 Reis (A-Br) 1936–38. Caxias facing right   7.00

39. 500 Reis (A-Bro) 1932. Bust of Ramalho   12.50

45. 1000 Reis (A-Bro) 1935–38. Father Anchieta   8.50

40. 400 Reis (C-N) 1932. Map of South America   10.00

46. 500 Reis (A-Bro) 1935–38. Feijo   10.00

BRASIL (continued)

47. 400 Reis (C-N) 1936–38. Cruz   4.00

48. 300 Reis (C-N) 1936–38. Gomes   5.00

49. 200 Reis (C-N) 1936–38. Maua   4.00

50. 100 Reis (C-N) 1936–38. Tamandare   4.50

51. 2000 Reis (A-Bro) 1939. Marshal Peixoto   5.00

52. 1000 Reis (A-Bro) 1939. Tobias Barreto   5.00

53. 500 Reis (A-Bro) 1939. Machado de Assis   4.00

54. 400 Reis (C-N) 1938–42. Bust of President Vargas 1.50
55. 300 Reis (C-N) 1938–42   .75
56. 200 Reis (C-N) 1938–42   1.00
57. 100 Reis (C-N) 1938–42   .85

NEW MONETARY STANDARD 1942

100 Centavos = 1 Cruzeiro

58. 5 Cruzeiros (A-Bro) 1942, '43. Map of Brazil   1.75

59. 2 Cruzeiros (A-Bro) 1942–56   1.50
60. 1 Cruzeiro (A-Bro) 1942–56   1.25

61. 50 Centavos (C-N) 1942–43; (A-Bro) 1943–47.
    Bust of President Vargas   1.00
62. 20 Centavos (C-N) 1942–43; (A-Bro) 1943–48   .75
63. 10 Centavos (C-N) 1942–43; (A-Bro) 1943–47   .40

64. 50 Centavos (A-Bro) 1948–56. President Dutra.
    Rev: Value   .60

65. 20 Centavos (A-Bro) 1948–56. Rui Barbosa   .50

66. 10 Centavos (A-Bro) 1947–55. José Bonifacio   .50

67. 2 Cruzeiros (A-Bro) 1956; (A) 1957–61 Star.
     Rev: Value   .75
68. 1 Cruzeiro (A-Bro) 1956; (A) 1957–61   .75
69. 50 Centavos (A-Bro) 1956; (A) 1957–61   .40
70. 20 Centavos (A) 1956–61   .40
71. 10 Centavos (A) 1956–61   .30

72. 50 Cruzeiros (C-N) 1965. Liberty head. Rev:
     Value   .75

73. 20 Cruzeiros (Al) 1965, Map   .50
74. 10 Cruzeiros (Al) 1965   .35

CURRENCY REVALUATION

1 New Cruzeiro = 1000 Old Cruzeiros

75. 1 Cruzeiro (N) 1970; (C-N) 1975– . Head of
     Brasilia. Rev: Floral spray   1.25

75.

76.   77.

76. 50 Centavos (N) 1967; (C-N) 1970– . Rev: Ship   1.00
77. 20 Centavos (CN) 1967, '70; (St) 1975. Rev: Oil
     derrick   .40
78. 10 Centavos (CN) 1967, '70; (St) 1974   .25
79. 5 Centavos (St) 1967, '69. Rev: Value   .25
80. 2 Centavos (St) 1967, '69   .15
81. 1 Centavo (St) 1967, '69   .15

82. 300 Cruzeiros (G) 1972. Faces of Pedro I, first
     ruler of Brazil, and General Emilio Gar-
     rastazu Medici, current president. Rev: Map.
     (150th anniversary of independence)   375.00
83. 20 Cruzeiros 1972   15.00
84. 1 Cruzeiro (N) 1972   1.50

85. 5 Centavos (St) 1975. Head of Brasilia. Rev:
     Cow (F.A.O. coin plan)   .25
86. 2 Centavos (St) 1975. Rev: Soja tree. (F.A.O.)   .20
87. 1 Centavo (St) 1975. Rev: Sugar plant. (F.A.O.)   .20
88. 10 Cruzeiros (St) 1980– . Map. Rev: Value   .50
89. 5 Cruzeiros (St) 1980– . Plant. Rev: Value   .75

BRITISH CARIBBEAN TERRITORIES

Made up of Windward and Leeward Islands, Trinidad and Tobago, Jamaica, and Barbados, this was strictly a monetary grouping, with no political significance. The unified currency ceased with the establishment of the East Caribbean Territories (q.v.) in 1965.

ELIZABETH II   1952–

1. 50 Cents (C-N) 1955. Crowned head. Rev: Britannia above arms of territories   5.00

2. 25 Cents (C-N) 1955–65. Rev: *Golden Hind*   1.50
3. 10 Cents (C-N) 1955–65   .75
4.   5 Cents (N-Bra) 1955–65   .60

5. 2 Cents (Bro) 1955–65. Rev: Value in wreath   .50
6. 1 Cent (Bro) 1955–65   .35

7. ½ Cent (Bro) 1955–58. Rev: Value   1.50

BRITISH GUIANA

Situated on the northeast coast of South America, rich in diamond and aluminum deposits, British Guiana was a crown colony starting in the 17th century. Coins bear the image of the reigning British monarch. Since 1966 it has been an independent state as Guyana (q.v.).

20 Stivers = 1 Guilder
2 Guilders = 1 Shilling
50 Pence = 1 British Guiana Dollar

GEORGE III   1760–1820

1. 3 Guilders 1809, '16. Laureate bust. Rev: Crowned value 450.00

2.	2 Guilders 1809, '16	250.00
3.	1 Guilder 1809, '16	75.00
4.	½ Guilder 1809, '16	65.00
5.	¼ Gilder 1809, '16.	25.00

6.	1 Stiver (C) 1813	20.00
7.	½ Stiver (C) 1813	15.00

WILLIAM IV   1830–37

8.	3 Guilders 1832. Bust	500.00
9.	2 Guilders 1832	350.00
10.	1 Guilder 1832, '35, '36. (1836 Coins bear inscription BRITISH GUIANA on reverse)	60.00
11.	½ Guilder 1832, '35, '36	50.00
12.	¼ Guilder 1832, '35, '36	30.00
13.	⅛ Guilder 1832, '35, '36	20.00

VICTORIA   1837–1901

14.	4 Pence 1891–1901. Head. Rev: Value	6.00

EDWARD VII   1901–10

15.	4 Pence 1903, 1908–10. Crowned bust. Rev: Value	12.50

GEORGE V   1910–36

16.	4 Pence 1911, '13, '16–31, '36. Crowned bust. Rev: Value	10.00

GEORGE VI   1936–52

17.	4 Pence 1938–45. Crowned head. Rev: Value	4.00

BRITISH HONDURAS

A British crown colony in Central America, British Honduras changed its name to Belize (q.v.) in 1973.

100 Cents = 1 British Honduras Dollar

VICTORIA   1837–1901

1.	50 Cents 1894–1901. Diademed head. Rev: Value in double circle	35.00
2.	25 Cents 1894–1901	25.00
3.	10 Cents 1894	20.00
4.	5 Cents 1894	15.00
5.	1 Cent (Br) 1885–94	12.50

EDWARD VII   1901–10

6.	50 Cents 1906–07. Crowned bust. Rev: Type of #1	50.00
7.	25 Cents 1906–07	25.00

8.	5 Cents (C-N) 1907–09	50.00
9.	1 Cent (Bro) 1904, '06, '09	35.00

GEORGE V   1910–36

10.	50 Cents 1911–19. Crowned bust. Rev: Type of #1	35.00
11.	25 Cents 1911–19	15.00
12.	10 Cents 1918–19, '36	12.50
13.	5 Cents (C-N) 1911–19, '36. Rev: Type of #8	7.50
14.	1 Cent (Bro) 1911–13	115.00
15.	1 Cent (Bro) 1914–36. Rev: Value in ornamental wreath, type of #19	8.00

GEORGE VI   1936–52

NOTE: Coins after 1947 drop EMPEROR OF INDIA legend

16.	10 Cents 1939–46. Crowned head. Rev: Type of #1	6.00
17.	25 Cents (C-N) 1952	5.00
18.	5 Cents (C-N) 1939; (N-Bra) 1942–47	6.00
18a.	5 Cents (N-Bra) 1949–52	2.50

19.	1 Cent (Bro) 1937–51	2.00

ELIZABETH II   1952–

20.	50 Cents (C-N) 1954–71. Head. Rev: Value	3.00
21.	25 Cents (C-N) 1955–73	1.50
22.	10 Cents (C-N) 1956–70	1.00
23.	5 Cents (N-Bra) 1956–73	.50

24.	1 Cent (Bro) 1954	2.00

24a.	1 Cent (Bro) 1956–73. (Scalloped edge)	.35

BRITISH VIRGIN ISLANDS

These 36 islands in the Caribbean Sea were formerly part of the Leeward Islands. In 1956 they became a separate crown colony.

1.   1 Dollar 1973. Queen Elizabeth II. Rev: Frigate birds   25.00
1a.   1 Dollar (C-N) 1974–   8.00

2.   50 Cents (C-N) 1973– . Rev: Pelicans   2.25

3.   25 Cents (C-N) 1973– . Rev: Mangrove cuckoos   1.00
4.   10 Cents (C-N) 1973– . Rev: Ringed kingfisher   .80

5.   5 Cents (C-N) 1973– . Rev: Zenaida doves   .35
6.   1 Cent (Br) 1973– . Rev: Carib and hummingbird   .15

7.   100 Dollars (G) 1975. Queen Elizabeth II. Rev: Royal tern   160.00

8.   100 Dollars (G) 1976. Elizabeth II. Rev: Crowned monogram over shield. (Queen's 50th birthday)   125.00

NOTE: Silver Jubilee sets below (1977 and 1978) issued in proof only

9.   100 Dollars (G) 1977. Elizabeth II. Rev: Crown. (Queen's Silver Jubilee)   125.00
10.   1 Dollar 1977. Frigate birds. (Silver Jubilee)   30.00
11.   50 Cents 1977. Rev: Pelicans. (Silver Jubilee)   12.50
12.   25 Cents 1977. Rev: Mangrove cuckoos. (Silver Jubilee)   7.50
13.   10 Cents 1977. Rev: Ringed kingfisher. (Silver Jubilee)   5.00
14.   5 Cents 1977. Rev: Zenaida doves. (Silver Jubilee)   3.50
15.   1 Cent 1977. Rev: Carib and hummingbird. (Silver Jubilee)   2.50

BRITISH VIRGIN ISLANDS (continued)

16. 100 Dollars (G) 1978. Elizabeth II. Rev: Crown on sceptres. (25th anniversary of coronation)   125.00
17. 25 Dollars 1978. Rev: Supported crown. (Coronation Jubilee)   40.00
18. 1 Dollar 1978. Rev: Frigate birds. (Coronation Jubilee)   30.00
19. 50 Cents 1978. Rev: Pelicans. (Coronation Jubilee)   15.00
20. 25 Cents 1978. Rev: Mangrove cuckoos. (Coronation Jubilee)   8.50
21. 10 Cents 1978. Rev: Ringed kingfisher. (Coronation Jubilee)   6.50
22. 5 Cents 1978. Rev: Zenaida doves. (Coronation Jubilee)   4.50
23. 1 Cent 1978. Rev: Carib and hummingbird. (Coronation Jubilee)   3.50

26. 100 Dollars (G) 1980. Rev: *Golden Hind* (400th anniversary of Drake's around-the-world voyage)   150.00
27. 5 Dollars 1980. Rev: Great blue heron   15.00
28. 100 Dollars (G) 1981. Rev: Knighting of Sir Francis Drake   150.00
29. 5 Dollars 1981. Rev: Royal tern. Also issued in silver proof   10.00

24. 100 Dollars (G) 1979. Elizabeth II. Rev: Bust of Sir Francis Drake in high ruffed collar   125.00

25. 5 Dollars 1979. Rev: Snowy egret   20.00

BRITISH WEST AFRICA

British West Africa comprised British Cameroons, British Togoland, Gambia, Gold Coast, Nigeria and Sierra Leone, which have all become independent states. Part of the Cameroons joined the former French Cameroun to form the Federal Republic of Cameroun; the Gold Coast and British Togoland became the Republic of Ghana. Nigeria absorbed most of Togoland. (See also Cameroon, Gambia, Ghana, Nigeria.)

12 Pence = 1 Shilling

EDWARD VII   1901–10

1.	1 Penny (C-N) 1907–10. Six-pointed star. Rev: Crowned value. (Center hole)	5.00
2.	⅒ Penny (A) 1907–08	6.00
2a.	⅒ Penny (C-N) 1908–10	2.00

GEORGE V   1910–36

3.	2 Shillings 1913–20. Crowned bust. Rev: Palm tree	12.50
3a.	2 Shillings (Bra) 1920–28, '36	8.00
4.	1 Shilling 1913–20	5.00
4a.	1 Shilling (Bra) 1920–28, '36	4.00
5.	6 Pence 1913–20. Rev: Value in wreath	5.00
5a.	6 Pence (Bra) 1920–36	5.00
6.	3 Pence 1913–20	4.50
6a.	3 Pence (Bra) 1920–36	2.50

7.	1 Penny (C-N) 1911. Type of #1	45.00
7a.	1 Penny (C-N) 1912–36	4.00
8.	½ Penny (C-N) 1911	20.00
8a.	½ Penny (C-N) 1912–36	3.00

9.	⅒ Penny (C-N) 1911	5.00
9a.	⅒ Penny (N) 1912–36	1.50

EDWARD VIII   1936

10.	1 Penny (C-N) 1936. Type of #1	3.00

11.	½ Penny (C-N) 1936	2.00
12.	⅒ Penny (C-N) 1936	1.50

GEORGE VI   1936–52

NOTE: Coins issued after 1948 drop IND. IMP. from legend

13.	2 Shillings (N-Bra) 1938–48. Crowned head. Rev: Type of #3	4.50
13a.	2 Shillings (N-Bra) 1949–52	6.00
14.	1 Shilling (N-Bra) 1938–48	2.50
14a.	1 Shilling (N-Bra) 1949–52	1.75

15.	6 Pence (Bra) 1938–47, '52	2.50
16.	3 Pence (C-N) 1938–48	1.50
17.	1 Penny (C-N) 1937–47. Type of #1	1.00
17a.	1 Penny (C-N) 1951	25.00
18.	½ Penny (C-N) 1937–47	1.00
18a.	½ Penny (C-N) 1949–51	7.50
19.	⅒ Penny (C-N) 1938–47	1.25
19a.	⅒ Penny (C-N) 1949–50	4.00
20.	1 Penny (Br) 1952. Type of #1	1.50
21.	½ Penny (Br) 1952	2.00
22.	⅒ Penny (Br) 1952	4.00

ELIZABETH II   1952–

23.	3 Pence (C-N) 1957. Head. Rev: Value	80.00
24.	1 Penny (Bro) 1956–58	7.50

25.	⅒ Penny (Bro) 1954–57. (Center hole)	5.00

BRUNEI

A self-governing sultanate situated in northwest Borneo between Sabah and Sarawak, Brunei's external affairs and defense are the responsibility of the British Government. Brunei remained outside the Federation of Malaysia when Sabah and Sarawak joined in 1963, but it used Malaysian coins.

1.	50 Sen (C-N) 1967. Head of Sultan Omar Ali Saifuddin III. Rev: Ornamental design	1.50

11.	1 Dollar (C-N) 1970, '79. Rev: Cannon	35.00
12.	10 Dollars 1977. (10th anniversary of dollar)	50.00
13.	10 Dollars 1978. Head of Sultan. Rev: Mosque. (10th anniversary of Sultan's coronation)	50.00
14.	50 Dollars 1980. (Year of Hegira, 1400)	60.00

2.	20 Sen (C-N) 1967	.85
3.	10 Sen (C-N)	.50

4.	5 Sen (C-N) 1967	.35
5.	1 Sen (Br) 1967	.25

6.	50 Sen (C-N) 1968– . Head of Sultan Hassanal Bolkiah. Rev: Native ornament	.75
7.	20 Sen (C-N) 1968–	.50
8.	10 Sen (C-N) 1968–	.30
9.	5 Sen (C-N) 1968–	.20
10.	1 Sen (Br) 1968, '79	.15

BULGARIA

Bulgaria was a Turkish province up to the Russo-Turkish War, which resulted in Bulgaria's liberation in 1877. After World War II, this Balkan kingdom became a People's Republic.

100 Stotinki = 1 Lev

ALEXANDER II 1879–86

1.	5 Leva 1884–85. Crowned arms. Rev. Value in wreath	25.00
2.	2 Leva 1882	10.00
3.	1 Lev 1882	6.00
4.	50 Stotinki 1883	5.00
5.	10 Stotinki (C) 1881	4.00
6.	5 Stotinki (C) 1881	7.50
7.	2 Stotinki (C) 1881	8.00

FERDINAND I 1887–1918

8.	20 Leva (G) 1912. Head. Rev: Arms. (25-year Jubilee)	300.00
9.	5 Leva 1892, '94. Head. Rev: Value in wreath	25.00

10.	2 Leva 1891–94, 1912–13	10.00

10a.	2 Leva 1910. Head right	8.50
11.	1 Lev 1891–94, 1912–13	10.00
11a.	1 Lev 1910. Head right	8.50

12.	50 Stotinki 1891, 1912–13	3.00
12a.	50 Stotinki 1910. Head right	4.00

13.	20 Stotinki (C-N) 1888, 1906–13. Crowned arms. Rev: Value in wreath	3.00
14.	10 Stotinki (C-N) 1888, 1906–13	2.00
15.	5 Stotinki (C-N) 1888, 1906–13	1.50
16.	2½ Stotinki (C-N) 1888	5.00
17.	2 Stotinki (Bro) 1901, '12	2.00
18.	1 Stotinki (Bro) 1901, '12	2.50

BORIS III 1918–43

19.	100 Leva 1930–37. Head. Rev: Value	15.00
20.	50 Leva (S) 1930–34; (C-N) 1940	7.50
21.	20 Leva (S) 1930; (C-N) 1940	3.00

22.	10 Leva (C-N) 1930. Cavalier of Madara. Rev: Value in wreath	2.50
23.	5 Leva (C-N) 1930	2.00

24.	2 Leva (A) 1923; (C-N) 1925. Arms on mantle. Rev: Value in wreath	.75
25.	1 Leva (A) 1923; (C-N) 1925	.60
26.	50 Stotinki (A-Bro) 1937	.50

SIMEON II 1943–46

27. 10 Leva (N-St) 1943. Arms. Rev: Value in wreath — 3.00
28. 5 Leva (N-St) 1943 — 2.00

29. 2 Leva (I) 1943– — 2.00

COMMUNIST ISSUES

37.

30. 25 Stotinki (C-N) 1951– . Type of #37 — .75
31. 10 Stotinki (C-N) 1951– — .40
32. 5 Stotinki (Bra) 1951– — .30
33. 3 Stotinki (Bra) 1951– — .25
34. 1 Stotinka (Bra) 1951 — .20
35. 20 Stotinki (C-N) 1952– — .50
36. 50 Stotinki (C-N) 1959. Arms. Rev: Value — 1.00
37. 1 Lev (C-N) 1960. Arms. Rev: Value — 1.50
38. 1 Lev (Ni-Bra) 1962. Arms. Rev: Value — 1.75
39. 50 Stotinki (N-Bra) 1962 — 1.00
40. 20 Stotinki (N-Bra) 1962 — .50
41. 10 Stotinki (N-Bra) 1962 — .40
42. 5 Stotinki (Bra) 1962 — .25
43. 2 Stotinki (Bra) 1962 — .20
44. 1 Stotinka (Bra) 1962 — .20

45. 5 Leva 1963. Saint Cyril and Saint Methodius. Rev. Value. (1100th anniversary of Cyrillic script and Slavonic alphabet) — 30.00

46.

46. 5 Leva 1964. Head of Georgi Dimitrov, former Premier. Rev: Flag above value (20th anniversary of republic) — 25.00

47. 2 Leva (C-N) 1966. Robed figure. Rev: Ancient pillars. (1050th anniversary of death of scholar Kliment Ochridsky) — 4.00

48. 2 Leva (C-N) 1969. Liberty monument. Rev: Value. (25th anniversary of Socialist Revolution) — 4.00

49. 1 Lev (C-N) 1969. Guerilla fighter's monument — 2.00

50. 2 Leva (C-N) 1969. Battle scene, defense of Shipka Pass. Rev: Value. (90th anniversary of liberation from the Turks) — 4.00

BULGARIA (continued)

51. 1 Lev (C-N) 1969. Czar Alexander II monument — 2.00

55. 2 Leva (C-N) 1972. Head of Dobri Chintulov. Rev: Value (150th anniversary of scholar's birth) — 4.00

52. 5 Leva 1970. Head of Ivan Vazov. Rev: Arms. (120th anniversary of writer's death) — 15.00

56. 5 Leva 1973. Head of Vasil Levski. Rev: Arms, value. (100th anniversary of patriot's death) — 20.00
57. 5 Leva 1973. Figures with flag. Rev: Arms. (50th anniversary of anti-fascist uprising) — 20.00

53. 5 Leva 1971. Head of Georgi Rakovski. Rev: Arms. (150th anniversary of birth of patriot, revolutionary writer) — 25.00

58. 5 Leva 1974. Head of Alexander Stambolisky. Rev: Arms. (50th anniversary of politician's death) — 20.00
59. 5 Leva 1974. Two soldiers. Rev: Arms. (30th anniversary of Socialist Revolution) — 20.00
60. 10 Leva 1975. Two wrestlers. Rev: Arms (10th Olympic Congress of 1973) — 40.00

54. 5 Leva 1972. Paissii Chilendarski holding open book. Rev: Arms, value. (250th anniversary of historian's birth) — 20.00

61. 50 Stotinki (C-N) 1977. Athlete bearing torch. Rev: Arms — 1.50

62.	5 Leva 1976. Head of Kristo Botev. Rev:.Arms. (Centennial of patriot's death in battle against Turks)	20.00
63.	5 Leva 1976. Standing knight. Rev: Arms. (Centennial of April uprising against Turks)	20.00
64.	5 Leva 1977. Head of Petko Slavekov, patriot. Rev: Arms	20.00
65.	10 Leva 1978. Lion upon monument. Rev: Arms. (Centennial of liberation from Turkey)	20.00
66.	5 Leva 1978. Head of Pelo Javoroff, painter. Rev: Arms	20.00
67.	5 Leva 1978. Facade of the National Library, Sofia. Rev: Arms. (Centennial of National Library)	20.00
68.	20 Leva 1979. Fortress atop Sofia personified. Rev: Arms. (Centennial of Sofia as national capital)	40.00
69.	10 Leva 1979. Group of children. Rev: Arms. (International Year of Child)	20.00
70.	5 Leva 1979. Stylized radio tower. Rev: Arms. (Centennial of Bulgaria's communications system)	20.00
71.	10 Leva 1980. Space ship. Rev: Arms. (Bulgarian–Soviet Union Cosmonaut Flight)	20.00
72.	5 Leva 1980. Soccer players. Rev: Arms. (World Cup Soccer Games)	20.00

BURMA

The British administered Burma as a part of India up to 1937, when they gave Burma self-government as far as internal affairs were concerned. During World War II, Burma was overrun by the Japanese, and in 1948 became a completely independent republic.

16 Annas = 1 Rupee
100 Pyas = 1 Kyat or Tical

MINDON MIN 1852–78

1.	1 Rupee 1852. Peacock. Value in wreath	25.00
2.	½ Rupee 1852	20.00
3.	¼ Rupee 1852	20.00
4.	⅛ Rupee 1852	25.00
5.	¹⁄₁₀ Rupee 1852	35.00

REPUBLIC 1948–

6.	8 Annas (N) 1949–50. Lion. Rev: Value in wreath	8.00

7.	4 Annas (N) 1949–50	5.00
8.	2 Annas (C-N) 1949–51. (Square planchet)	2.50

9.	1 Anna (C-N) 1949–51. (Scalloped edge)	2.50
10.	½ Anna (C-N) 1949. (Square)	1.00

11.	1 Kyat (C-N) 1952– . (Round)	4.00
12.	50 Pyas (C-N) 1952–66	2.00

13.	25 Pyas (C-N) 1952–65. (Scalloped)	1.00
14.	10 Pyas (C-N) 1952–65. (Square)	.50
15.	5 Pyas (C-N) 1952–66. (Scalloped)	.40
16.	1 Pya (Bro) 1952–66. (Round)	.35

17.	50 Pyas (A) 1966. Head of Gen. Aung San. Rev: Value in wreath	2.00

18.	25 Pyas (A) 1966 (Scalloped)	.75
19.	10 Pyas (A) 1966 (Square)	.60
20.	5 Pyas (A) 1966 (Scalloped)	.60
21.	1 Pya (A) 1966 (Round)	.35

22.	1 Kyat (C-N) 1975. Rice plant. Rev: Value in lotus blossom frame. (F.A.O. coin plan)	2.50
23.	25 Pyas 1980. Rice plant. Rev: Value. (F.A.O.)	1.00

BURUNDI

Formerly part of the Belgian U.N. Trusteeship of Ruanda-Urundi, it became an independent kingdom in July 1962. The republic was established in 1966.

MWAMBUTSA IV 1962–66

1. Franc (Bra) 1965   1.00

REPUBLIC 1966–

2. 10 Francs (C-N) 1968, '71. Inscription. Rev: Value within circle of grain stalks. (F.A.O. coin plan)   1.50

3. 5 Francs (Al) 1968–71, '76. Inscription. Rev: Value   1.50

4. 1 Franc (A) 1970. Sunrise. Rev: Value   .75

CAMBODIA

Cambodia became an independent constitutional monarchy in 1953 after nearly a century of French control. In 1970 the monarchy fell and the Khmer Republic was established.

100 Centimes = 1 Franc

3.

1. 1 Piastre 1860. Head of King Norodom I. Rev: Arms and value   600.00
2. 4 Francs 1860   150.00
3. 2 Francs 1860   50.00
4. 1 Franc 1860   25.00
5. 50 Centimes 1860   15.00
6. 25 Centimes 1860   12.50
7. 10 Centimes (Br) 1860   10.00
8. 5 Centimes (Br) 1860   9.00

9. 50 Centimes (A-Mg) 1953. Royal emblems. Rev: Value in wreath   2.00

10. 20 Centimes (A-Mg) 1953. Urn   1.50
11. 10 Centimes (A-Mg) 1953. Bird   1.00

DECIMAL COINAGE

100 Sen = 1 Riel

12. 50 Sen (A-Mg) 1959. Type of #9, new currency values   .75
13. 20 Sen (A-Mg) 1959. Type of #10   .60
14. 10 Sen (A-Mg) 1959. Type of #11   .50

CAMEROON

A French Associated Territory on the west coast of Africa; originally mandated to France after World War I. In 1960 it achieved independence and in 1961 became the Federal Republic of Cameroon after being joined by part of the British Cameroons (see also British West Africa). It is associated with the French Community, and is a member of the Central African States monetary union (q.v.; formerly Equatorial African States).

100 Centimes = 1 Franc

1.	2 Francs (A-Bro) 1924–25. Liberty head. Rev: Value between sprays	12.50
2.	1 Franc (A-Bro) 1924–26	5.00
3.	50 Centimes (A-Bro) 1924–26	3.00

4.	1 Franc (A-Bro) 1943. Rooster. Rev: Cross of Lorraine	8.50
5.	50 Centimes (A-Bro) 1943	3.00

6.	2 Francs (A) 1948. Bust of the Republic. Rev: Antelope head	1.50
7.	1 Franc (A) 1948	1.25

NOTE: In 1958 coinage was combined with that of French Equatorial Africa

8.	25 Francs (A-Br) 1958. Three antelope heads. Rev. Value	2.00

9.	10 Francs (A-Br) 1958	.75
10.	5 Francs (A-Br) 1958	.50

INDEPENDENT STATE 1960

11.	50 Francs (A-Br) 1960. Three antelope heads. Rev: Value. ("1er Janvier" legend commemorates independence)	15.00

12.	100 Francs (N) 1966–68	10.00

13.	100 Francs (N) 1971, '72	5.00

14.	100 Francs(N) 1975	3.00

CANADA

After settling in Canada, the French waged a struggle of continental proportions with the British for control of the fur trade. Finally in 1763 Canada became a British colony. In 1867 it was made a Dominion of the British Empire with considerable powers of self-government. In 1926 Canada became a completely self-governing Dominion within the framework of the British Commonwealth of Nations.

Prior to the general Canadian issue of coinage in 1858 a number of private tokens were struck; some of the commoner types are shown below. Several provinces—New Brunswick, Newfoundland, Nova Scotia and Prince Edward Island—had their own coinages before they were incorporated into the Dominion of Canada (see separate listings for these coins).

As for issues of the Dominion, prices are given for the commonest date of each variety. Canadian coins are popularly collected by date. Consequently, many specific dates command prices higher than those quoted here.(See *Coin Collectors' Handbook* [Reinfeld; Sterling Publishing Co. and Doubleday] for more details.)

100 Cents = 1 Dollar

EARLY TOKENS

1. Penny token (Deux Sous) (C) 1837. PROVINCE DU BAS CANADA (Quebec)   7.50

2. Penny token (C) 1850–57. BANK OF UPPER CANADA (Ontario)   3.00

3. Bouquet Sou (C) undated (issued 1835–37)   5.00

PROVINCE OF CANADA

VICTORIA 1837–1901

4.	20 Cents 1858. Head. Rev: Value	100.00
5.	10 Cents 1858	40.00
6.	5 Cents 1858	20.00
7.	1 Cent (Bro) 1858–59	3.00

DOMINION OF CANADA

VICTORIA 1837–1901

8.	50 Cents 1870–1901. Diademed head. Rev: Crowned value in wreath	80.00
9.	25 Cents 1870–1901	20.00
10.	10 Cents 1870–1901	15.00
11.	5 Cents 1870–1901	5.00

12.	1 Cent (Bro) 1876–1901. Rev: Value in dotted circle	2.50

EDWARD VII 1901–10

13.	50 Cents 1902–10. Crowned bust. Rev: Type of #8	120.00
14.	25 Cents 1902–10	50.00
15.	10 Cents 1902–10	25.00
16.	5 Cents 1902–10	7.50

17.	1 Cent (Bro) 1902–10. Rev: Type of #12	3.00

CANADA (continued)

GEORGE V 1910–36

18. 10 Dollars (G) 1912–14. Crowned bust. Rev: Arms with maple leaves   700.00
19. 5 Dollars (G) 1912–14   300.00

20. 1 Dollar 1935. Rev: Voyageurs in canoe. (Jubilee year)   60.00

21. 1 Dollar 1936. Type of #20 without commemorative inscription. (Regular issue)   55.00
22. 50 Cents 1911–36. Rev: Type of #8   75.00
23. 25 Cents 1911–36   20.00
24. 10 Cents 1911–36   12.50

25. 5 Cents 1911–21   5.00

26. 5 Cents (N) 1922–36   8.50
27. 1 Cent (Bro) 1911–20. Rev: Type of #12. (Large size)   3.00
28. 1 Cent (Bro) 1920–36. (Reduced size)   2.00

GEORGE VI 1936–52

NOTE: Coins issued 1937–47 have the title D.G. REX ET IND. IMP. Coins issued 1948–52 bear the title DEI GRATIA REX.

29. 1 Dollar 1937–38, '45–52. Head of King George. Rev: Voyageur and Indian in canoe   25.00

30. 1 Dollar 1939. Head. Rev: Parliament buildings in Ottawa, legend FIDE SVORVM REGNAT—"The King reigns on the loyalty of his subjects." (Royal visit of King George VI and Queen Elizabeth)   30.00

31. 1 Dollar 1949. Head. Rev: Sailing ship *Matthew* of discoverer John Cabot. (Newfoundland's entrance into Dominion)   35.00

32. 50 Cents 1937–52. Rev: Arms of Canada   17.50
33. 25 Cents 1937–52. Rev: Caribou head   8.50

34. 10 Cents 1937–52. Rev: Fishing schooner   5.00

35.   5 Cents (N) 1937–42. Rev: Beaver   1.50

36.   5 Cents (Tombac-Bra) 1942. Type of #35.
      (Dodecagonal planchet)   2.50
36a. 5 Cents (N) 1946–50; (St) 51–52   .85

37.   5 Cents (Bra) 1943; (St) 44–45. Rev: Large "V"
      and torch with motto in Morse Code: "We win
      when we work willingly"   1.25

38.   5 Cents (N) 1951. Rev: Refining plant over ma-
      ple leaves. (Bicentennial of nickel industry;
      dodecagonal planchet)   2.50

39.   1 Cent (Bro) 1937–52. Rev: Maple leaves   .35

ELIZABETH II 1952–

40.   1 Dollar 1953–63. Head. Rev: Voyageurs   17.50

41.   50 Cents 1953–58. Rev: Arms of Canada   10.00
41a. 50 Cents 1959–64. New reverse   8.50
42.   25 Cents 1953–64. Rev: Caribou head   3.50
43.   10 Cents 1953–64. Rev: Fishing schooner   2.00
44.   5 Cents (St) 1953–54. Rev: Beaver.
      (Dodecagon)   1.75
44a. 5 Cents (N) 1955–62. (Dodecagon)   .40
44b. 5 Cents (N) 1963–64. (Round)   .20
45.   1 Cent (Br) 1953–64. Rev: Maple leaves   .15

46.   1 Dollar 1958. Head. Rev: Raven totem pole,
      Canadian Rockies in background (100th anni-
      versary of British Columbia's entrance into
      Dominion)   20.00

47.   1 Dollar 1964. Head. Rev: Floral emblems,
      fleur-de-lis, shamrock, thistle and rose—rep-
      resenting the four main nationality groups of
      Canada: French, Irish, Scotch and English.
      (1864 conference of Fathers of the Confedera-
      tion at Charlottetown, Prince Edward Island,
      which led to Confederation Conference at
      Quebec in 1867)   20.00

CANADA (continued)

58.	10 Cents 1967. Rev: Mackerel	
59.	5 Cents (N) 1967. Rev: Rabbit	1.50
60.	1 Cent (Br) 1967. Rev: Dove	.50
		.25

48.	1 Dollar 1965, '66. New portrait of Queen with coronet. Rev: Voyageurs	20.00
48a.	1 Dollar (N) 1968– . (Smaller planchet)	1.50
49.	50 Cents 1965, '66. Rev: Arms of Canada	8.00
49a.	50 Cents (N) 1968– . (Smaller planchet)	.75
50.	25 Cents 1965–68. Rev: Caribou head	2.50
50a.	25 Cents (N) 1968–	.40
51.	10 Cents 1965, '66; (50% S) 1968. Rev: Fishing schooner	1.00
51a.	10 Cents (N) 1968	.25
51b.	10 Cents (N) 1969– . Rev: Redesigned, smaller ship	.20
52.	5 Cents (N) 1965– . Rev: Beaver	.15
53.	1 Cent (Br) 1965– . Rev: Maple leaves	.10

61.	1 Dollar (N) 1970. Rev: Crocus plant. (Manitoba centennial)	3.00

54.	20 Dollars (G) 1967. Rev: Coat of arms. (Centennial of Confederation)	400.00

62.	1 Dollar (N) 1971. Rev: Arms, dogwood blossoms above. (Bicentennial, entry of British Columbia into Confederation)	3.00
63.	1 Dollar 1971. Rev: Arms of British Columbia. (Struck in size of pre-1968 silver dollars, sold as numismatic item)	25.00

55.	1 Dollar 1967. Rev: Canada goose in flight	25.00

56.	50 Cents 1967. Rev: Howling wolf	10.00
57.	25 Cents 1967. Rev: Wildcat	4.00

64.	1 Dollar (N) 1973. Rev: Legislature building. (Prince Edward Island bicentennial)	3.00

CANADA (continued)

65. 1 Dollar 1973. Rev: Officer of Royal Canadian
Mounted Police on horseback. (100th anniversary of R.C.M.P.)   17.50

66. 25 Cents (N) 1973. Rev: R.C.M.P. officer in
parade uniform, with banner   1.50

NOTE: Nos. 67–74, 77–88, 90–98 commemorate the 1976
Olympic Games

69. 5 Dollars 1973. Rev: Yachts, city of Kingston   25.00

70. 5 Dollars 1973. Rev: Map of North America,
Canada highlighted   25.00

71. 10 Dollars 1974. Rev: Temple of Zeus   40.00

67. 10 Dollars 1973. Rev: Skyline of Montreal   40.00
68. 10 Dollars 1973. Rev: World map, Canada highlighted (Olympics)   40.00

72. 10 Dollars 1974. Rev: Head of Zeus   40.00
72a. 10 Dollars 1974. Rev: Temple of Zeus   40.00

85

| 73. | 5 Dollars 1974. Rev: Laurel wreath and five-ring Olympic symbol | 25.00 |
| 74. | 5 Dollars 1974. Rev: Athlete holding Olympic torch | 25.00 |

| 79. | 5 Dollars 1975. Rev: Oarsman | 20.00 |
| 80. | 5 Dollars 1975. Rev: Indian paddling | 20.00 |

| 75. | 1 Dollar 1974. Rev: Value, old and new city scenes. (100th anniversary of founding of Winnipeg) | 15.00 |
| 76. | 1 Dollar (N) 1974 | 3.00 |

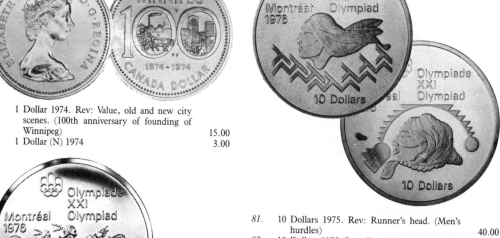

| 81. | 10 Dollars 1975. Rev: Runner's head. (Men's hurdles) | 40.00 |
| 82. | 10 Dollars 1975. Rev: Female head. (Shotput) | 40.00 |

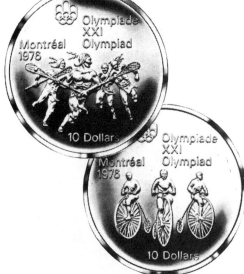

| 77. | 10 Dollars 1975. Rev: Indians playing lacrosse | 40.00 |
| 78. | 10 Dollars 1975. Rev: Cyclists | 40.00 |

| 83. | 5 Dollars 1975. Rev: Female javelin thrower | 20.00 |
| 84. | 5 Dollars 1975. Rev: Marathon runner | 20.00 |

90. 100 Dollars (G) 1976. Queen Elizabeth II. Rev:
    Athena with athlete   225.00

85. 10 Dollars 1975. Rev: Symbolic figure paddling   40.00
86. 10 Dollars 1975. Rev: Two abstract figures.
    (Sailing)   40.00

91. 10 Dollars 1976. Rev: Soccer scene   40.00
92. 10 Dollars 1976. Rev: Field hockey scene   40.00

87. 5 Dollars 1975. Rev: Abstract swimmer   20.00
88. 5 Dollars 1975. Rev: Abstract woman diver   20.00

89. 1 Dollar 1975. Rev: Cowboy on bucking horse.
    (100th anniversary of founding of Calgary)   12.50
89a. 1 Dollar (N) 1975   12.50

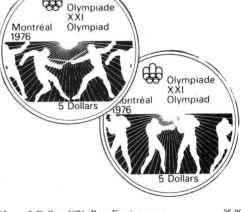

93. 5 Dollars 1976. Rev: Fencing scene   25.00
94. 5 Dollars 1976. Rev: Boxing scene   25.00

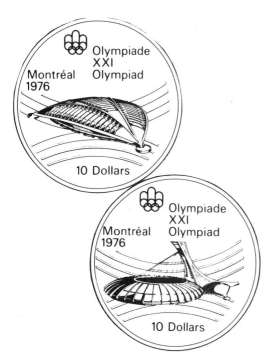

95. 10 Dollars 1976. Rev: Velodrome building   40.00
96. 10 Dollars 1976. Rev: Olympic stadium   40.00

104. 100 Dollars (G) 1979. Rev: Group of children playing. (International Year of Child.) Issued in proof only   200.00
105. 50 Dollars (G) 1979– . Rev: Maple leaf. Issued as a bullion coin (value determined by bullion market fluctuations)   . . . .
106. 1 Dollar 1979. Rev: Sailing ship *Griffon*   15.00
107. 100 Dollars (G) 1980. Rev: Canoeist. (Centennial of Arctic Territories.) In proof only   250.00
108. 1 Dollar 1980. (Arctic Territories)   15.00
109. 100 Dollars (G) 1981. Rev: Stylized musical motif. (Canada's National Anthem.) In proof only   250.00
110. 1 Dollar 1981. Rev: Railroad   15.00
111. 100 Dollars (G) 1982. Rev: Open book showing national arms, maple leaf. (New Canadian Constitution)   250.00
112. 1 Dollar 1982. Rev: Bison skull   15.00

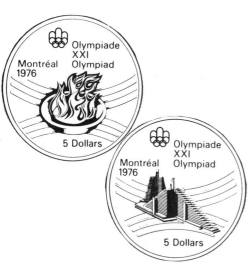

97. 5 Dollars 1976. Rev: Olympic flame   25.00
98. 5 Dollars 1976. Rev: Olympic village   25.00
99. 1 Dollar 1976. Rev: Library of Parliament at Ottawa   15.00
100. 100 Dollars (G) 1977. Rev: Flowers. (Queen's Silver Jubilee.) Issued in proof only   300.00
101. 1 Dollar 1977. (Silver Jubilee)   15.00
102. 100 Dollars (G) 1978. Rev: Birds. (Canada's Unification.) In proof only   200.00
103. 1 Dollar 1978. Rev: Stylized circle of athletes. (Eleventh Commonwealth Games, Edmonton, Alberta)   15.00

CAPE VERDE ISLANDS

This group of islands about 375 miles off the west coast of Africa became a Portuguese possession at the end of the 15th century. The Cape Verdes became an independent republic on July 5, 1975.

100 Centavos = 1 Escudo

1. 1 Escudo (N-Bro) 1930. Bust of Republic. Rev: Arms in wreath over value ... 17.50
2. 50 Centavos (N-Bro) 1930 ... 6.50

3. 20 Centavos (Bro) 1930. Head of Republic ... 3.00
4. 10 Centavos (Bro) 1930 ... 2.00
5. 5 Centavos (Bro) 1930 ... 1.50

6. 1 Escudo (N-Bro) 1949. Arms over date. Rev: Value ... 2.75
7. 50 Centavos (N-Bro) 1949 ... 1.50

8. 10 Escudos 1953. Arms over value. Rev: Shield over date ... 10.00
9. 5 Escudos (C-N) 1968 ... 3.00
10. 2½ Escudos (N-Bro) 1953–68 ... 2.00

11. 1 Escudo (Bro) 1953, '68 ... 2.00
12. 50 Centavos (Bro) 1968 ... 1.25

13. 250 Escudos 1976. Fish. Rev: Map ... 20.00

14. 2½ Escudos (Bra) 1977. Arms. Rev: Farmer planting coffee. (F.A.O. coin plan) ... 2.00

15. 1 Escudo (N-Bra) 1977. Arms and value. Rev: Schoolboy. (F.A.O. coin plan, rural education) ... 2.00

16. 50 Escudos (C-N) 1977. Rev: Amilca Lopes Cabral (1924–73), agricultural engineer ... 5.00

17.   20 Escudos (C-N) 1977. Rev: Domingos Ramos
      (1935–66), hero of liberation movement   3.50

18.   10 Escudos (C-N) 1977. Rev: Dr. Eduardo
      Mondlane (1920–69), founder of Mozam-
      bique liberation movement   3.00

19.   50 Centavos (A) 1977. Arms. Rev: Value and
      small fish   2.00

20.   20 Centavos (A) 1977   1.25

CAYMAN ISLANDS

A British colony comprising three islands in the West Indies.

1. 25 Dollars 1972. Queen Elizabeth II. Rev: Conjoined heads of Queen and Prince Philip. (Royal wedding anniversary) 65.00
2. 25 Dollars (G) 1972 150.00

5. 1 Dollar 1972– . Rev: Flower 17.50
6. 50 Cents 1972– . Rev: Fish 12.50

7. 25 Cents (C-N) 1972– . Rev: Schooner 1.00
8. 10 Cents (C-N) 1972– . Rev: Turtle .50

9. 5 Cents (C-N) 1972– . Rev: Lobster .25
10. 1 Cent (Br) 1972– . Rev: Thrush .15

11. 100 Dollars (G) 1974. Bust of Winston Churchill. Rev: Arms. (100th anniversary of statesman's birth) 275.00
12. 25 Dollars 1974 65.00

3. 5 Dollars 1972– . Rev: Arms, value. Issued in proof only 35.00

4. 2 Dollars 1972– . Rev: Silver heron. In proof only 27.50

13. 100 Dollars (G) 1975–77. Bust of Queen Elizabeth II. Rev: Portraits of five queens 250.00
14. 50 Dollars 1975–77 85.00

CAYMAN ISLANDS (continued)

15. 100 Dollars (G) 1977. Elizabeth II. Rev: Supported shield. (Queen's Silver Jubilee)   200.00

NOTE: All Coronation Jubilee coins below issued in proof only

16. 100 Dollars (G) 1978. Elizabeth II. Rev: Shield, inscription. (25th anniversary of Queen's Coronation)   200.00

17. 25 Dollars 1978. Rev: St. Edward's Crown. (Coronation Jubilee)   60.00
18. 5 Dollars 1978. Rev: Arms, value. (Coronation Jubilee)   30.00
19. 2 Dollars 1978. Rev: Silver heron. (Coronation Jubilee)   25.00
20. 1 Dollar 1978. Rev: Flower. (Coronation Jubilee)   15.00
21. 50 Cents 1978. Rev: Fish. (Coronation Jubilee)   12.50
22. 25 Cents (C-N) 1978. Rev: Schooner. (Coronation Jubilee)   6.50
23. 10 Cents (C-N) 1978. Rev: Turtle. (Coronation Jubilee)   5.00
24. 5 Cents (C-N) 1978. Rev: Lobster. (Coronation Jubilee)   4.00
25. 1 Cent (Br) 1978. Rev: Thrush. (Coronation Jubilee)   2.50
26. 100 Dollars (G) 1981. Elizabeth II. Rev: Conjoined portraits of Prince Charles and Lady Diana. (Marriage of royal couple.) In proof only   150.00

CENTRAL AFRICAN REPUBLIC

Formerly part of French Equatorial Africa (q.v.), it became an independent republic in 1960. (See also Central African States.)

1. 100 Francs (N) 1971–74. Antelopes. Rev: Value   2.50
2. 100 Francs (N) 1975– . Slightly modified design for antelopes and value   2.00

CENTRAL AFRICAN STATES

A monetary union that issues coins and currency as a central bank in the name of its five member states: Cameroon, Chad, Central African Republic, Gabon and People's Republic of the Congo. (See also these countries and French Equatorial Africa under their separate listings.) The bank previously issued coins as the Central Bank of the Equatorial African States (q.v.).

1.	500 Francs (C-N) 1976. Woman and palm tree. Rev: Antelope and value	8.50
2.	100 Francs (N) 1976. Antelope. Rev: Tropical produce of five member republics	4.00
3.	50 Francs (N) 1976–77	1.50
4.	25 Francs (A-Br) 1975	1.00
5.	10 Francs (Bra) 1975	.60
6.	5 Francs (A-Bro) 1973, '75–79	.50
7.	1 Franc (A) 1974–76	.40

CEYLON

A large island in the Indian Ocean, southeast of India, Ceylon was successively conquered by the Portuguese, Dutch, and English. In 1948 Ceylon became a dominion in the British Commonwealth of Nations. When Ceylon became an independent republic in 1972, the traditional name Sri Lanka (q.v.) was officially adopted.

20 Stivers = 1 Gulden
4 Farthings = 1 Penny
100 Cents = 1 Rupee

GEORGE III   1760–1820

1.	2 Stivers (C) 1815. Head. Rev: Elephant	20.00
2.	1 Stiver (C) 1815	12.50

3.	½ Stiver (C) 1815	15.00

GEORGE IV   1820–30

4.	1 Rix Dollar 1821. Head. Rev: Elephant	45.00

5.	½ Farthing (C) 1827–30. Rev: Seated Britannia	25.00

WILLIAM IV   1830–37

6.	1½ Pence 1834–37	5.00
7.	½ Farthing (C) 1837. Rev: Seated Britannia	40.00

VICTORIA   1837–1901

8.	1½ Pence 1838–62. Head. Rev: Value	4.00
9.	½ Farthing (C) 1839–56	3.00
10.	¼ Farthing (C) 1839–53	25.00

CEYLON (continued)

New coinage: Head. Rev: Value

11.	50 Cents 1892–1900. Rev: Plant and value	8.50
12.	25 Cents 1892	7.50
13.	10 Cents 1892–1900	3.50
14.	5 Cents (C) 1870–92	10.00

15.	1 Cent (C) 1870–1901. Head. Rev: Plant and value	2.50
16.	½ Cent (C) 1870–1901	2.50
17.	¼ Cent (C) 1870–1901	2.50

EDWARD VII   1901–10

18.	50 Cents 1902–10. Crowned bust. Rev: Plant and value	8.50
19.	25 Cents 1902–10	4.00
20.	10 Cents 1902–10	2.00

21.	5 Cents (C-N) 1909, '10. Crowned bust. Rev: Value. (Square shape, rounded corners)	1.00
22.	1 Cent (Bro) 1904–10. Rev: Plant and value	2.00
23.	½ Cent (Bro) 1904–09	5.00
24.	¼ Cent (Bro) 1904	1.25

GEORGE V   1910–36

25.	50 Cents 1913–29. Type of #18	6.00

26.	25 Cents 1911–26. Crowned bust. Rev: Plant and value	1.50
27.	10 Cents 1911–28	1.25
28.	5 Cents (C-N) 1912–26. Type of #21, bust left	1.00
29.	1 Cent (Br) 1912–29. Type of #22, bust left	.90
30.	½ Cent (Br) 1912–26	.70

GEORGE VI   1936–52

Note: Coins issued 1937–1945 carry title KING AND EMPEROR OF INDIA. Coins issued in 1951 carry title KING GEORGE THE SIXTH

31.	50 Cents 1942. Crowned head. Rev: Type of #11	8.50
32.	10 Cents 1941	2.00
33.	50 Cents (N-Bra) 1943, '51. Rev: Crowned value between leaves	1.25
34.	25 Cents (N-Bra) 1943–51	.50

35.	10 Cents (N-Bra) 1944, '51. (Scalloped edge)	.40
36.	5 Cents (N-Bra) 1942–45. Rev: Type of #21. (Square-shaped)	.30
37.	2 Cents (N-Bra) 1944, '51. (Scalloped edge)	.15
38.	1 Cent (Bro) 1937–45. Rev: Type of #22. (Round)	.50
39.	½ Cent (Bro) 1937, '40	1.00

ELIZABETH II   1952–

40.	5 Rupees 1957. Animals in circular pattern. Rev: Inscription. (2500 years of Buddhism)	20.00

CEYLON (continued)

41. 1 Rupee (C-N) 1957. Buddhist wheel. Rev: Inscription   4.00

42. 2 Cents (N-Bra) 1955–57. Head of Elizabeth II. Rev: Value. (Scalloped edge)   1.00

43. 1 Rupee (C-N) 1963–71   1.25
44. 50 Cents (C-N) 1963–71. Arms of Ceylon. Rev: Value   .75
45. 25 Cents (C-N) 1963–71   .40

46. 10 Cents (N-Bra) 1963–71. (Scalloped)   .25
47. 5 Cents (N-Bra) 1963–71. (Square)   .20
48. 2 Cents (A) 1963–71. (Scalloped)   .15
49. 1 Cent (A) 1963–71. (Round)   .15

50. 2 Rupees (C-N) 1968. Statue of old Buddhist king. Rev: Value. (F.A.O. issue)   6.50

CHAD

This former territory in French Equatorial Africa became a republic in 1960. (See also Central African States.)

1. 100 Francs (N) 1971–75. Antelope. Rev: Value   4.00
2. 100 Francs (N) 1975. New inscription   4.00

95

CHILE

The Spaniards began the conquest of Chile toward the middle of the 16th century. Chile remained a Spanish colony until 1818, when it became a republic, thanks to the liberating efforts of San Martín and O'Higgins.

Early issues under Spanish rule bear the name of the reigning Spanish monarch. The designs are similar to those of other Spanish-American issues.

The Santiago mint mark appears as $\overset{O}{S}$ in the legend. Some of the famous gold doubloons (eight escudos) were issued at the Santiago mint. They are valued at $1000 or more.

$$8 \ Reales = 1 \ Peso \ or \ Piece\text{-}of\text{-}Eight$$
$$10 \ Centavos = 1 \ Decimo$$
$$100 \ Centavos = 1 \ Peso$$
$$100 \ Centesimos = 1 \ Escudo$$

Gold doubloon (8 escudos) 1805   1000.00

CHARLES III   1759–88

1.	8 Reales 1773–89. Bust. Rev: Spanish arms	600.00
2.	2 Reales 1773–89	50.00
3.	½ Real 1773–89	40.00

CHARLES IV   1788–1808

4.	8 Reales 1790, '91. Bust of Charles III. Rev: Arms	850.00

5.	4 Reales 1789–91	350.00
6.	2 Reales 1789–91	20.00
7.	1 Real 1789–91	20.00
8.	½ Real 1789–91	20.00
9.	¼ Real 1790–91	30.00

10.	8 Reales 1792–1808. Bust of Charles IV. Rev: Arms	275.00
11.	4 Reales 1792–1808	100.00
12.	2 Reales 1792–1808	40.00
13.	1 Real 1792–1808	17.50
14.	½ Real 1792–1808	15.00
14a.	¼ Real 1792–95	20.00
15.	¼ Real 1796–1808. Castle. Rev: Lion	30.00

FERDINAND VII   1808–17

16.	4 Reales 1808–15. Bust of Charles IV. Rev: Arms	140.00
17.	2 Reales 1808–09	35.00
18.	1 Real 1808–17	20.00
19.	½ Real 1808–17	15.00

20.	8 Reales 1808, '09. Plain head. Rev: Arms	225.00

CHILE (continued)

24.	1 Peso 1817–34. Volcano. Rev: Column	120.00
25.	2 Reales 1834	50.00
26.	1 Real 1834	35.00
27.	½ Real 1833, '34	30.00
28.	¼ Real 1832, '34. Value on both sides	50.00

21.	8 Reales 1810, '11. Laureate head	200.00
21a.	2 Reales 1810, '11	35.00

29.	8 Reales 1839–49. Arms. Rev: Condor break-ing chain	135.00
30.	2 Reales 1843, '52	20.00
31.	1 Real 1836–50	25.00
32.	½ Real 1838–51	40.00

22.	8 Reales 1812–17. Draped bust	165.00

33.	1 Peso 1853–62. Condor with shield	60.00
33a.	1 Peso 1867–91. New condor design	25.00

22a.	2 Reales 1812–17	20.00
23.	¼ Real 1808–18. Castle. Rev: Lion	30.00

34.	50 Centavos 1853–72. Flying condor	20.00
35.	20 Centavos 1852–93	5.00
36.	1 Decimo 1852–94	3.00
37.	½ Decimo 1851–94	4.00

38.	1 Centavo 1835, '51–53. Star. Rev: Value	7.50
39.	½ Centavo 1835, '51–53	5.00
40.	1 Peso 1895–97, 1902–05, '10. Condor on mountain peak. Rev: Value in wreath	20.00
41.	1 Peso 1915, '17, '21–32. Reduced size	10.00
42.	50 Centavos 1902–06	10.00
43.	20 Centavos 1895–1900, 1906–20	3.00
44.	10 Centavos 1896–1920	2.00
45.	5 Centavos 1896–1919	1.00

57.	1 Peso (S) 1932; (C-N) 1933, '40	3.50
58.	20 Centavos (C-N) 1920–41	2.00
59.	10 Centavos (C-N) 1920–41	1.00
60.	5 Centavos (C-N) 1920–38	1.25

46.	2½ Centavos (C) 1886–1908. Republic head. Rev: Value	7.00
47.	2 Centavos (C) 1878–95, 1919	6.50
48.	1 Centavo (C) 1878–1904, '08, '19	2.50
49.	½ Centavo (C) 1883–94	5.00

61.	1 Peso (C) 1942–54; (A) 1954–58. Bust of Bernardo O'Higgins. Rev: Value	.50
62.	50 Centavos (C) 1942	3.00
63.	20 Centavos (C) 1942–53	.40

NOTE: Assay and size of coins vary from year to year

50.	100 Pesos (G) 1926, '32, '46–63. Head of Republic with coiled hair. Rev: Arms	425.00
51.	50 Pesos (G) 1926–74	225.00

64.	10 Pesos (A) 1956–59. Flying condor. Rev: Value	1.00
65.	5 Pesos (A) 1956	.75

CURRENCY REVALUATION

100 Centesimos = 1 Escudo

52.	20 Pesos (G) 1896–1917, '26, '58–61	250.00
53.	10 Pesos (G) 1896, 1901	175.00
54.	5 Pesos (G) 1898, 1900	140.00
55.	5 Pesos 1927. Condor on mountain peak	30.00
56.	2 Pesos 1927	10.00

66.	10 Centesimos (A-Br) 1960–70. Flying condor. Rev: Value	.50
67.	5 Centesimos (A-Br) 1961–70	.35
68.	2 Centesimos (A-Br) 1964–70	.25
69.	1 Centesimo (A) 1960–63	.50
70.	½ Centesimo (A) 1962–63	.50

CHILE (continued)

71.   5 Escudos (C-N) 1971, '72; (A) 1972– .
       Lautaro, famous Indian, on horseback. Rev:
       Arms and value   .75

72.   1 Escudo (C-N) 1971, '72. José Miguel Carrera,
       military dictator 1811–13   .50

73.   50 Centesimos (A-Br) 1971. Manuel Rodriguez,
       freedom fighter   .35
74.   20 Centesimos (A-Br) 1971. José Manuel Bal-
       maceda, President of Republic 1886–91   .25

75.   10 Centesimos (A-Br) 1971. Bernardo O'Hig-
       gins, first governor of independent Chile,
       1818–23   .35

76.   100 Escudos (N-Bra) 1974–75. Condor. Rev:
       Value in wreath   1.00
77.   50 Escudos (N-Bra) 1974–75. (Dodecagonal
       planchet)   .75
78.   10 Escudos (A) 1974–75   .60

MONETARY REFORM

79.   1 Peso (C-N) 1975. Portrait of Bernardo O'Hig-
       gins. Rev: Value   .25

80.   50 Centavos (C-N) 1975–78; (A-Br) 1978– .
       Type of #77   .20
81.   10 Centavos (A-Br) 1975–76; (A) 1976– .
       (Dodecagonal planchet)   .15
82.   5 Centavos (A-Br) 1975–76; (A) 1976– .
       (Dodecagonal planchet)   .10
83.   1 Centavo (A) 1975   .10

84.   10 Pesos (C-N) 1976. Winged victory with bro-
       ken chains. Rev: Value. (3rd anniversary of
       overthrow of Allende government)   2.00
85.   5 Pesos (C-N) 1976   1.00
86.   1 Peso (C-N) 1976–78. Portrait of Bernardo
       O'Higgins, new inscription, LIBERTADOR.
       Rev: Value   .30
87.   1 Peso (A-Br) 1978–   .25
88.   50 Pesos (A-Br) 1981– . O'Higgins. Rev: Value   2.00
89.   10 Pesos (N-Bra) 1981– . Winged Victory with
       broken chains. Rev: Value   .35

CHINA

After thousands of years of existence the Chinese Empire came to an end in 1911 and was succeeded by a republic. Years of war, unrest, and civil strife followed, until by 1949 the Chinese Communists had complete control of the mainland. All that was left to the Chinese Nationalists was the island of Formosa (Taiwan, q.v.).

Prior to 1875 the coinage of China consisted of brass "cash" money, silver passing only by weight. Silver coins of the principal nations of the world were in circulation, each piece being verified by the "chop" or mark of the merchant passing them.

During the time of the Empire, coins were issued by the various provinces in the denominations shown on coins Nos. 1–10. The name of the issuing province and the denomination are identified in English on every legend. (Each province issued some—but not necessarily all—of the denominations.) The general design of these coins is a Chinese inscription on the obverse, with a dragon and an English legend on the reverse. Most of these coins were issued during the period 1896–1911.

In addition to issues under the Empire, there were some later issues by the individual provinces during the Chinese Republic. These are similar in design and value to the issues of the Republic.

> 10 Cash = 1 Cent
> 100 Cents = 1 Dollar
> 1 Dollar = 0.72 Tael, or 7 Mace
>   and 2 Candareens
> 10 Candareens = 1 Mace
> 10 Mace = 1 Tael

3.	20 Cents (1 Mace and 4.4 Candareens)	20.00
4.	10 Cents (7.2 Candareens)	15.00
5.	5 Cents (3.6 Candareens)	3.00
6.	20 Cash (C or Bra)	12.50

7.	10 Cash (C or Bra)	2.00
8.	5 Cash (C or Bra)	1.25
9.	2 Cash (C or Bra)	1.00

10.	1 Cash (C or Bra)	.65

PROVINCIAL ISSUES UNDER THE EMPIRE

1.	Dollar (7 Mace and 2 Candareens)	100.00
2.	50 Cents (3 Mace and 6 Candareens)	60.00

REPUBLIC   1911–49

11.	Dollar 1912. Bust of Sun Yat-sen. Rev: Inscription. (Election as Provisional President)	150.00

CHINA (continued)

12. Dollar 1912. Bust of Li Yuan-hung in uniform
    and military cap   300.00

15. Dollar 1914–21. Bust of Yuan Shi-kai in pro-
    file. (Regular-issue, non-commemorative
    coin struck in great numbers)   25.00

13. Dollar 1912. Bust of Li Yuan-hung without cap.
    (Election as Vice-President)   120.00

16. 20 Cash (C or Bra) 1912. Crossed flags   5.00
17. 10 Cash (C or Bra) 1912   3.00
18. 5 Cash (C or Bra) 1912   2.50

19. 1 Cent [10 Cash] (Bra or Bro) 1916. Wreath of
    barley. (Center hole)   3.00
20. ½ Cent [5 Cash] (Bra or Bro) 1916   2.50

14. Dollar 1912. Bust of Yuan Shi-kai (President
    1912–16) with plumed hat   275.00

21. Dollar 1916. Type of #14. Rev: Dragon. (Pres.
    Yuan's proclamation declaring himself Em-
    peror of China)   350.00

CHINA (continued)

22.   Dollar 1921. Bust of Hsu Shih-chang. Rev: Bamboo-covered Pavilion. (Election as President)   500.00

23.   Dollar 1923. Bust of Tsao Quan in military uniform. (Election as President)   450.00
24.   Dollar 1923. Bust of Tsao Quan in civil dress   400.00

25.   Dollar 1923. Dragon and phoenix. (Entire issue rejected and not placed in circulation because of imperial symbol of dragon and phoenix)   500.00
26.   20 Cents 1926   12.50
27.   10 Cents 1926   12.50

28.   Dollar 1924. Bust of Tuan Chi-sui. (Peaceful unification of country and election as President)   225.00

29.   Dollar 1928. (Kwei Chow Province). Automobile   1000.00

30.   Dollar 1929–32. Bust of Sun Yat-sen in military uniform. Rev: Chinese junk, birds, sun, and value. (Withdrawn issue)   300.00

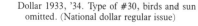

31.   Dollar 1933, '34. Type of #30, birds and sun omitted. (National dollar regular issue)   40.00

CHINA (continued)

32.	20 Cents (N) 1936–39; (C-N) 1942. Bust of Sun Yat-sen. (Ancient *Pu*—"spade money")	2.00
33.	10 Cents (N) 1936–39; (C-N) 1940–41	1.25
34.	5 Cents (N) 1936–39; (C-N) 1940–41	1.00

35.	1 Cent (Bra or Bro) 1936–40. Spade. Rev: Sun	.75
36.	½ Cent (Bra or Bro) 1936	2.00

PEOPLE'S REPUBLIC OF CHINA
(Communist China)

1.	5 Fen (A) 1955– . Arms. Rev: Value	1.50
2.	2 Fen (A) 1956–	1.00
3.	1 Fen (A) 1955–	1.00

4.	35 Yuan 1979. Arms. Rev: Boy and girl tending flower symbolizing aspirations of Chinese people. (UNICEF; International Year of Child)	50.00
5.	1 Yuan (C-N) 1980– . Arms. Rev: Great Wall of China, value	1.25
6.	5 Jiao (C-Z) 1980– . Arms. Rev: Value	.75
7.	2 Jiao (C-Z) 1980–	.50
8.	1 Jiao (C-N) 1980–	.25

COLOMBIA

Conquered by the Spanish Conquistadors during the first half of the sixteenth century, the colony, known as New Granada, gained its independence in 1819. Curiously enough, Colombia is the only country named for Christopher Columbus.

The early colonial issues bear the name of the reigning Spanish monarch. Designs are similar to those of other Spanish-American mints. The mint mark for Santa Fe de Bogotá is "NR" in the legend on the reverse. The mint mark for Popayan is "P" or "PN" in the legend. On coins of the republic the mint mark is "Ba."

> 8 Reales = 1 Peso or Piece-of-Eight
> 10 Centavos = 1 Decimo
> 100 Centavos = 1 Peso

Gold doubloon (8 escudos) 1769

NOTE: Below are Spanish-American coins struck at Popayan mint

CHARLES IV   1788–1808

1.	2 Reales 1793–1800. Bust. Rev: Arms	300.00
2.	1 Real 1792–1804	50.00
3.	½ Real 1795–1801	35.00
4.	¼ Real 1796–1808. Castle. Rev: Lion	25.00

FERDINAND VII   1808–24

5.	8 Escudos (G) 1808–20. Bust of Charles IV. Rev: Arms	850.00
6.	4 Escudos (G) 1818, '19	1250.00
7.	2 Escudos (G) 1808–19	350.00
8.	1 Escudo (G) 1808–20	200.00
9.	8 Reales 1810–20. Bust of Charles IV	1000.00

10.	2 Reales 1810–23	60.00

11.	1 Real 1810–19	65.00
12.	½ Real 1810–19	85.00

13.	¼ Real 1810–17. Castle. Rev: Lion	25.00

UNITED PROVINCES OF NEW GRANADA   1815–19

14.	8 Reales 1819, '20. Indian head. Rev: Pomegranate	125.00
15.	2 Reales 1815, '21	50.00
16.	1 Real 1813, '21	50.00
17.	½ Real 1814, '21	40.00

18.	¼ Real 1814, '15, '20, '21. Liberty cap. Rev: Pomegranate	60.00

REPUBLIC OF COLOMBIA   1820–36

19.	8 Reales 1834–36. Fasces between cornucopias. Rev: Value	120.00
20.	1 Real 1827–36	15.00
21.	½ Real 1834–36	30.00

22.	¼ Real 1826–36. Cornucopia	15.00

COLOMBIA (continued)

REPUBLIC OF NEW GRANADA   1837–58

23.	8 Reales 1837, '47. Shield of arms. Rev: Value	60.00
24.	8 Reales 1839–46. Condor flying above cornucopia	40.00

25.	2 Reales 1839–45, '47–53	15.00
26.	1 Real 1837–47, '51–53. Pomegranate	17.50
27.	½ Real 1838–47, '50–53	12.50
28.	¼ Real 1837–58	10.00

29.	10 Reales 1847–51. Condor. Rev: Value (several varieties)	60.00
30.	1 Peso 1855–58. Type of #29	40.00
31.	2 Decimos 1854–58. Shield	8.00

32.	1 Decimo (C) 1847, '48	7.50
32a.	1 Decimo 1853–58. Cornucopias	7.50
33.	½ Decimo (C) 1847, '48. Type of #32	7.50
33a.	½ Decimo 1853–58. Type of #32a	7.00

GRANADINE CONFEDERATION   1859–61

34.	1 Peso 1859–62. Condor. Rev: Value	45.00

35.	2 Reales 1862. Pointed shield	17.50
36.	1 Decimo 1859, '60. Pomegranate	12.50
37.	½ Decimo 1860, '61	30.00
38.	¼ Decimo 1860, '61	20.00

UNITED STATES OF COLOMBIA   1862–86

39.	1 Peso 1862–6. Condor above arms	40.00

40.	1 Peso 1871. Liberty head. Rev: Value	85.00
41.	5 Decimos (50 Centavos) 1868–86	10.00
42.	2 Decimos (20 Centavos) 1866, '67, '70–85	10.00
43.	1 Decimo (10 Centavos) 1863–86	6.00
44.	½ Decimo (5 Centavos) 1863–85	7.50
45.	¼ Decimo (2½ Centavos) 1863–81. Pomegranate	6.00

46.	2½ Centavos (C-N) 1881, '86; (C) 1885	.75
47.	1¼ Centavos (C-N) 1874	7.50

REPUBLIC OF COLOMBIA   1887–

48.	50 Centavos (5 Decimos). Liberty head 1887–1908	10.00
48a.	50 Centavos 1887. Head of Soledad Roman (wife of President Rafael Nunez)	45.00

49.	20 Centavos 1897	5.00
50.	10 Centavos 1897	6.00
51.	5 Centavos (C-N) 1886–1902. Head facing left. Rev: Value	1.00
51a.	5 Centavos 1902. Rev: Cornucopias	3.50

52.	50 Centavos 1892. Bust of Columbus	17.50
53.	5 Pesos (G) 1913–19. Workman cutting stone	175.00
53a.	2½ Pesos (G) 1913	125.00
54.	10 Pesos (G) 1919–24. Bolívar head. Rev: Arms	250.00
55.	5 Pesos (G) 1919–30	175.00
56.	2½ Pesos (G) 1919–28	120.00

57.	50 Centavos 1912–33. Bolívar head. Rev: Arms	17.50
58.	20 Centavos 1911–42	8.50
59.	10 Centavos 1911–42	5.00

60.	5 Centavos (C-N) 1917–50. Liberty head. Rev: Value	2.50
61.	2 Centavos (C-N) 1918–47	1.25
62.	1 Centavo (C-N) 1918–48; (N-St) 1952–58	.20

63.	50 Centavos 1947, '48. Bolívar	17.50

64.	20 Centavos 1945–51. Santander	3.50
65.	10 Centavos 1945–52. Santander	4.50

66.	20 Centavos 1953. Bolívar	3.00

67.	1 Peso 1956. Building. Rev: Wreath. (200th anniversary of Popayan mint)	35.00

68. 50 Centavos (C-N) 1958–66. Head of Bolívar to
   right. Rev: Arms 1.00
69. 20 Centavos (C-N) 1956–66 ..... .50

83. 1 Peso (C-N) 1967. Head of Bolívar. Rev:
   Value. (Decagonal planchet) 1.50

70. *73.*

70. 10 Centavos (C-N) 1952–66. Indian head ..... .50
71. 5 Centavos (Br) 1942–66. Liberty cap in
   wreath. Rev: Value ..... .35
72. 2 Centavos (Br) 1948–50 ..... 7.50
73. 2 Centavos (A-Br) 1952–65. Liberty head ..... .35
74. 1 Centavo (Br) 1942–66. Liberty cap in wreath.
   Rev: Value ..... .25

84. 50 Centavos (N-St) 1967–69. Head of Santander.
   Rev: Value ..... .85
85. 20 Centavos (N-St) 1967–69 ..... .50
86. 10 Centavos (N-St) 1967–69 ..... .25

75. 50 Centavos (C-N) 1960. Type of #68, but
   "1810–1960" below head. (1810 uprising) 17.50
76. 20 Centavos (C-N) 1960. Type of #69, but
   "1810–1960" 8.50
77. 10 Centavos (C-N) 1960. Type of #70, but
   "1810–1960" 5.00
78. 5 Centavos (Br) 1960. Type of #71, but
   "1810–1960" 7.50
79. 2 Centavos (A-Br) 1960. Type of #73, but
   "1810–1960" 3.50
80. 1 Centavo (Br) 1960. Type of #74, but
   "1810–1960" 8.50

87. 5 Centavos (C-St) 1967– . Type of #71 ..... .25
88. 1 Centavo (C-St) 1967 ..... .20

81. 50 Centavos (C-N) 1965. Head of Jorge Eliecer
   Gaitan. Rev: Arms. (Political leader assassi-
   nated in 1948) 1.50
82. 20 Centavos (C-N) 1965 ..... .75

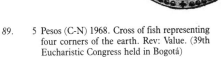

89. 5 Pesos (C-N) 1968. Cross of fish representing
   four corners of the earth. Rev: Value. (39th
   Eucharistic Congress held in Bogotá) 5.00

COLOMBIA (continued)

90. 50 Centavos (Ni-St) 1970– . Head of Santander.
    Rev: Value. (Dodecagonal planchet)   .50
91. 20 Centavos (Ni-St) 1969– . (Round planchet)   .25
92. 10 Centavos (Ni-St) 1969–   .20

93. 5 Pesos (Ni-St) 1971. Emblem. Rev: Value.
    (Sixth Pan-American Games in Cali)   4.00

94. 1 Peso (C-N) 1974–79. Bust of Bolívar. Rev:
    Value   .40

95. 2 Pesos (C-N) 1977–78; (Bro) 1977. Bolívar.
    Rev: Value   .50

96. 25 Centavos (A-Bro) 1979   .35
97. 5 Pesos (N-A) 1980– . Seated female figure.
    Rev: Factory   1.50
98. 10 Pesos (C-N) 1981–   1.25

COMORO ISLANDS

Acquired by France in 1886, these islands off the coast of Africa were formally attached to the government of Madagascar in 1912. They became an autonomous overseas territory within the French Community in 1961. On Dec. 31, 1975, they became the independent Republic of the Comoros, but one of the islands, Mayotte, voted to remain French.

100 Centimes = 1 Franc

1.	5 Francs 1890 (A.H. 1308). Weapons. Star, crescent, flags	750.00
2.	10 Centimes (Bro) 1890, 1901. Inscriptions	30.00
3.	5 Centimes (Bro) 1890, 1901	25.00

4.	20 Francs (N-Bra) 1964. Liberty head. Rev: Value, conch shells and fish	1.50
5.	10 Francs (N-Bra) 1964	1.00

6.	5 Francs (A) 1964. Rev: Value and palm trees	1.00
7.	2 Francs (A) 1964	.50
8.	1 Franc (A) 1964	.35

9.	50 Francs (N) 1975. Stylized building. Rev: Value. (F.A.O. coin plan)	1.25
10.	100 Francs (N) 1977. Ship. Rev: Value. (F.A.O.)	3.00

CONGO (Kinshasa)

Once the private property of Leopold II of Belgium and then (1908) a colony, the Belgian Congo (q.v.), this territory became independent in 1960 as the Republic of the Congo. In 1971 it was renamed Zaire (q.v.).

Katanga Province

1.	5 Francs (Br) 1961. Bananas. Rev: Baluba cross	3.00
1a.	5 Francs (G) 1961	325.00
2.	1 Franc (Br) 1961	2.00

REPUBLIC

3.	10 Francs (A) 1965. Lion. Rev: Inscription	2.00

NEW CURRENCY SYSTEM

1 Lituka = 10 Francs

4.	5 Makuta (C-N) 1967–69. Portrait of Joseph Mobuto. Rev: Value	2.50

5.	1 Likuta (A) 1967. Arms. Rev: Value	1.50
6.	10 Sengi (A) 1967. Leopard. Rev: Value	1.00

CONGO, PEOPLE'S REPUBLIC

An independent republic since 1960, formerly a territory in French Equatorial Africa.

1.	100 Francs (N) 1971– . Antelopes. Rev: Value	5.00

COOK ISLANDS

A self-governing group of 15 islands in the South Pacific under New Zealand administration. They were discovered by Captain James Cook on his second voyage in 1773.

1.   1 Dollar (C-N) 1970. Queen Elizabeth II. Rev: Capt. James Cook and sailing ship (200th anniversary of Cook's first voyage)   30.00

2.   1 Dollar (C-N) 1972– . Rev: Tangaroa, Polynesian god   17.50

3.   50 Cents (C-N) 1972– . Rev: Bonito   1.75

4.   20 Cents (C-N) 1972– . Rev: Tern   1.00

5.   10 Cents (C-N) 1972– . Rev: Oranges   .65

6.   5 Cents (C-N) 1972– . Rev: Hibiscus   .50

7.   2 Cents (Br) 1972– . Rev: Pineapples   .50

8.   1 Cent (Br) 1972– . Rev: Taro leaf   .35

15.   16.

16. 200 Dollars (G) 1978. Rev: Captain Cook wading
ashore. (Bicentennial of discovery of islands)   275.00

9. 7½ Dollars 1973, '74. Rev: Portrait of Captain
James Cook, with map and ship. (200th anniversary of discovery of Hervey Islands)   50.00
10. 2½ Dollars 1973, '74. Rev: Two ships, map of
globe. (Cook's second Pacific voyage)   30.00

17. 200 Dollars (G) 1979. Rev: Pacific flora and
fauna. (Legacy of Captain Cook)   275.00
18. 2½ Dollars 1979. Rev: Birds. (Cook Islands Conservation Day)   25.00
19. 50 Cents (C-N) 1979. Rev: Fish. (F.A.O. coin
plan)   4.00
20. 50 Dollars (G) 1981. Elizabeth II. Rev: Crowned
emblem. (Wedding of Prince Charles and
Lady Diana.) Issued in proof only   85.00

11. 2 Dollars 1973. Rev: Queen seated holding
sceptre. (20th anniversary of coronation)   20.00

12. 100 Dollars (G) 1974. Rev: Sir Winston Churchill, flag and Houses of Parliament in background   350.00

13. 50 Dollars (G) 1974   150.00

14. 100 Dollars (G) 1975. Rev: Sailing ship, portraits
of King George III and James Cook. (200th
anniversary of Cook's second Pacific voyage)   175.00

15. 250 Dollars (G) 1978. Rev: Captain Cook. (250th
anniversary of Cook's birth)   300.00

COSTA RICA

After Costa Rica gained its independence from Spain, it was a part of Mexico for a short time. Then it joined the Central American Federation, eventually becoming an independent republic.

8 Reales = 1 Peso or Piece-of-Eight
100 Centimos = 1 Colon
100 Centavos = 1 Peso

MEMBER OF CENTRAL AMERICAN FEDERATION

NOTE: Early issues carry the mint mark "CR"

1.	8 Reales 1831. Mountains and sun. Rev: Tree	3000.00
2.	2 Reales 1848–49	250.00
3.	1 Real 1831–50	60.00

4.	1 Real 1846–47, '49–50. Female bust. Rev: Coffee plant	30.00
5.	½ Real 1831–49. Type of #1	35.00
6.	¼ Real 1845. Three mountains. Rev: Tree	85.00

NOTE: During the period circa 1850 small coins of England, the United States and some other countries were counterstamped with a lion surrounded by HABILITADA POR EL GOBIERNO in a small circle, as in #6a

6a.	2 Reales (British coin, 1 Shilling; head of Victoria. Rev: Value in wreath). Lion counterstamp	20.00

REPUBLIC OF COSTA RICA

7.	¼ Peso 1850–55. Arms. Rev: Tree	25.00
8.	⅛ Peso 1850–55	25.00
9.	¹⁄₁₆ Peso 1850–55	30.00
10.	50 Centavos 1865–75, '80–90	25.00
11.	25 Centavos 1864–75, '86–93	8.00
12.	10 Centavos 1865–75, '86–92	12.50
13.	5 Centavos 1865–75, '85–92	6.00
14.	1 Centavo (C-N) 1865–68, '74	10.00
15.	20 Colones (G) 1897–1900. Head of Columbus. Rev: Arms	400.00
16.	10 Colones (G) 1897–1900	200.00

17.	5 Colones (G) 1899–1900	150.00
18.	2 Colones (G) 1900, '01, '15–28	120.00
19.	50 Centimos 1902–03. Arms. Rev: Value	40.00
20.	10 Centimos 1905–14	4.00
21.	5 Centimos 1905–14	5.00
22.	10 Centimos (Bra or Bro) 1917–47. Rev: Value in wreath	1.00
23.	5 Centimos (Bra or Bro) 1917–47	3.00
24.	2 Centimos (C-N) 1903	5.00

BANK ISSUES

25.	2 Colones (C-N) 1948; (St) 1954; (C-N) 1961–	1.00
26.	1 Colon (C-N) 1935–48; (St) 1954; (C-N) 1961–	.65
27.	50 Centimos (C-N) 1935–48, '65–	.35
28.	25 Centimos (C-N) 1935–48; (Bra) 1944–46; (Br) 1945; (C-N) 1967–78; (St) 1980–	.25
29.	10 Centimos (C-N) 1951; (St) 1953–	.20
30.	5 Centimos (Bra) 1942–47; (C-N) 1951; (St) 1953–78; (Bra) 1979–	.15

NOTE: 1935 coins were issued by the Banco Internacional de Costa Rica ("B.I.C.R." at bottom of reverse); 1937–48 coins by the Banco Nacional de Costa Rica ("B.N.C.R."); 1951– coins by the Banco Central de Costa Rica ("B.C.C.R.")

31.   20 Colones (N) 1975. Arms. Rev: Flower arrangement. (25th anniversary of Central
Bank)   5.00

32.   10 Colones (N) 1975. Rev: Tree. (Central Bank)   3.00

33.   5 Colones (N) 1975. Rev: Flowers. (Central
Bank)   2.00

34.   100 Colones 1979. Arms. Rev: Baby chicks in
nest. (International Year of Child)   30.00

CRETE

This Mediterranean island off the coast of Greece had one of the most remarkable civilizations of ancient times. It became a department of Greece in 1898 and was united with Greece ten years later.

100 Lepta = 1 Drachma

PRINCE GEORGE OF GREECE
(High Commissioner 1898–1906)

1.	5 Drachmas 1901. Head. Rev: Crowned arms on mantle	175.00

2.	2 Drachmas 1901	75.00
3.	1 Drachma 1901	40.00
4.	50 Lepta 1901	25.00

5.	20 Lepta (C-N) 1900 Crown. Rev: Value in wreath	12.50
6.	10 Lepta (C-N) 1900	10.00
7.	5 Lepta (C-N) 1900	10.00

8.	2 Lepta (Bro) 1900–01	15.00
9.	1 Lepton (Bro) 1900–01	12.50

CUBA

The largest island in the West Indies. After centuries of Spanish rule, Cuba became an independent republic under the terms of the treaty that ended the Spanish-American War. Since Jan. 1, 1959 Cuba has been led by Fidel Castro, who instituted a communist-type political system.

100 Centavos = 1 Peso

PROVISIONAL GOVERNMENT

1.   Souvenir Peso 1897   50.00

REPUBLIC

2.	20 Pesos (G) 1915–16. Head of José Martí. Rev: Arms of Cuba in wreath	200.00
3.	10 Pesos (G) 1915–16	110.00
4.	5 Pesos (G) 1915–16	60.00
5.	4 Pesos (G) 1915–16	170.00
6.	2 Pesos (G) 1915–16	45.00
7.	1 Peso (G) 1915–16	125.00

8.	1 Peso 1915–16, '32–34. Star and rays. Rev: Arms in wreath	25.00
9.	40 Centavos 1915–20	10.00
10.	20 Centavos 1915–32, '48–49	2.00
11.	10 Centavos 1915–20, '48–49	1.50
12.	5 Centavos (C-N) 1915–20, '46, '60, '61; (Bra) '43. Value in star. Rev: Type of #8	.50
13.	2 Centavos (C-N) 1915–16	1.00
14.	1 Centavo (C-N) 1915–38, '46, '61; (Bra) '43	.40

15.   1 Peso 1934–39. Liberty head. Rev: Arms   50.00

16.	40 Centavos 1952. Morro Castle. Rev: Star, tree and wheel. (50th anniversary of Republic)	10.00
17.	20 Centavos 1952	3.50
18.	10 Centavos 1952	2.00

MARTI CENTENARY

19.   1 Peso 1953. Head of Martí. Rev: Rising sun   17.50

20.   50 Centavos 1953. Rev: Scroll with inscription   10.00

CUBA (continued)

21. 25 Centavos 1953. Rev: Liberty cap   8.00

22. 1 Centavo (Bra) 1953. Rev: Star in triangle   2.50

23. 1 Centavo (C-N) 1958. Rev: Star in triangle   .75

24. 40 Centavos (C-N) 1962. Bust of Camilio Cienfuegos (peasant leader). Rev: Arms   15.00

25. 20 Centavos (C-N) 1962–68. Bust of Martí. Rev: Arms. Legend PATRIA O MUERTE ("Fatherland or death")   5.00

26. 5 Centavos (A) 1963– . Arms. Rev: Value in star   1.50

27. 1 Centavo (A) 1963–   .75
28. 20 Centavos (A) 1969–   2.50

29. 10 Pesos 1975. Facade of National Bank, Havana. Rev: Arms. (25th anniversary of bank)   50.00
30. 5 Pesos 1975.   40.00
31. 10 Pesos 1980. Orbiting space ship. Rev: Shield within wreath. (First Soviet-Cuban space flight)   50.00
32. 5 Pesos 1980   40.00
33. 5 Pesos 1980. Trio of athletes within panels. Rev: Shield within wreath. (Moscow Olympics)   40.00

CURAÇAO

Curaçao, discovered by the Spaniards, became a Dutch colony in 1634. This island in the West Indies is part of the Netherland Antilles today. It is made up of two groups of islands in the Caribbean off the northern coast of Venezuela. Two of the islands, Aruba and Curaçao, have large oil refineries.

100 Cents = 1 Guilder (Gulden)

WILHELMINA 1890–1948

1.	¼ Guilder 1900. Head. Rev: Crowned arms	80.00
2.	⅒ Guilder 1901	90.00

3.	1 Rixdollar (New coinage: 2½ Guilder) 1944. Crowned arms	25.00
4.	1 Guilder 1944. Arms	55.00

5.	¼ Guilder 1944, '47. Head. Rev: Value	12.50
6.	⅒ Guilder 1944, '47, '48	8.50

7.	5 Cents (C-N) 1948. Plant. Rev: Value. (Diamond shape, rounded corners)	15.00

8.	2½ Cents (Br) 1944–48. Lion. Rev: Value	5.00
9.	1 Cent (Br) 1944, '47	3.00

CYPRUS

Cyprus, a Mediterranean island off the coast of Turkey, became British in 1878 and a crown colony in 1925. It became an independent republic within the British Commonwealth in 1960.

9 Piastres = 1 Shilling
100 Mils = 1 Pound Sterling

VICTORIA   1837–1901

1.	18 Piastres 1901. Crowned "old" bust. Rev: Crowned shield and value	275.00
2.	9 Piastres 1901	60.00
3.	4½ Piastres 1901	50.00
4.	3 Piastres 1901	65.00
5.	1 Piastre (Bro) 1879–1900. Coroneted "young" head. Rev: Value	50.00
6.	½ Piastre (Bro) 1879–1900	40.00
7.	¼ Piastre (Bro) 1879–1901	40.00

EDWARD VII   1901–10

8.	18 Piastres 1907. Crowned bust. Rev: Type of #1	300.00
9.	9 Piastres 1907	250.00
10.	1 Piastre (Bro) 1908	300.00
11.	½ Piastre (Bro) 1908	200.00
12.	¼ Piastre (Bro) 1902–08	35.00

GEORGE V   1910–36

13.	45 Piastres 1928. Crowned bust. Rev: Lions	80.00

14.	18 Piastres 1913, '21. Rev: Type of #1	60.00
15.	9 Piastres 1913, '19, '21	40.00
16.	4½ Piastres 1921	35.00
17.	1 Piastre (Br) 1922, '27, '30, '31. Crowned bust. Rev: Value	65.00

17a.	1 Piastre (C-N) 1934. Scalloped edge. Crowned bust. Rev: Value	15.00
18.	½ Piastre (Bro) 1922, '27, '30–31. (Round)	40.00
18a.	½ Piastre (C-N) 1934. (Scalloped)	10.00
19.	¼ Piastre (Bro) 1922, '26	30.00

GEORGE VI   1936–52

20.	18 Piastres 1938, '40. Crowned head. Rev: Type of #13	25.00
21.	9 Piastres 1938, '40	15.00
22.	4½ Piastres 1938	10.00

23.	1 Piastre (C-N) 1938; (Bro) 1942–46, '49. Crowned head. Rev: Type of #17a	7.50
24.	½ Piastre (C-N) 1938; (Bro) 1942–45, '49	5.00

25.	2 Shillings (C-N) 1947, '49. Type of #20	10.00
26.	1 Shilling (C-N) 1947, '49	10.00

ELIZABETH II   1952–

27.	100 Mils (C-N) 1955–57. Crowned bust. Rev: Brig	2.50

119

28.   50 Mils (C-N) 1955. Rev: Fern leaves   1.50

29.   25 Mils (C-N) 1955. Rev: Bull's head   .75

30.   5 Mils (C-N) 1955, '56. Rev: Figure of ancient
      inhabitant   .50

31.   3 Mils (Bro) 1955. Rev: Fish   .35

REPUBLIC   1963–

32.   100 Mils (C-N) 1963– . Emblem. Rev: Moufflon
      (wild sheep)   1.50

33.   50 Mils (C-N) 1963– . Rev: Bunch of grapes .75
34.   25 Mils (C-N) 1963– . Rev: Cedar branch   .40

35.   5 Mils (Br) 1963– . Rev: Ancient galley   .20
36.   1 Mil (A) 1963–72. Rev: Numeral in wreath   .20

37.   500 Mils (C-N) 1970. Double cornucopia. Rev:
      Youth holding basket of fruit. (F.A.O. coin
      plan)   5.00
37a. 500 Mils (S) 1970. Proof   150.00
38.   500 Mils (C-N) 1975, '77. Arms. Rev: Hercules
      with cornucopia   5.00
39.   50 Pounds (G) 1977. Bust of Archbishop
      Makarios. Rev: Map of Cyprus. (Memorial to
      Makarios)   350.00
40.   1 Pound (C-N) 1976. Emblem within wreath.
      Rev: Refugee camp. (Refugee commem-
      orative)   10.00
41.   500 Mils (C-N) 1978. Torch. Rev: Value, stylized
      design. (Human Rights)   5.00
41a. 500 Mils (S) 1978. (Human Rights.) Proof   100.00
42.   500 Mils (C-N) 1980. Emblem. Rev: Value over
      Olympic rings. (Moscow Olympic Games)   10.00
42a. 500 Mils (S) 1980. (Moscow Olympics.) Proof 100.00
43.   500 Mils (C-N) 1981. Emblem. Rev: Stylized
      fish, wheat vignette. (F.A.O. coin plan)   5.00
43a. 500 Mils (S) 1981. (F.A.O.) Proof   65.00

CZECHOSLOVAKIA

A republic formed from parts of the old Austro-Hungarian empire after World War I. In 1938 the country was occupied by the Germans. The Republic was reestablished in 1945. It has been a Communist republic since February 1948.

100 Haleru = 1 Koruna
1 Ducat = 77³⁄₁₀ Koruny

1.	2 Ducats (G) 1923, '29–38. Lion on shield. Rev: St. Wenceslaus. (Fifth anniversary of Republic)	400.00
2.	1 Ducat (G) 1923–39, '51	125.00
3.	20 Koruny 1933–34. Arms. Rev: Three standing figures	12.50

7.	20 Koruny 1937. Bust of Masaryk. Rev: Arms. (Death of Masaryk)	15.00

4.	10 Koruny 1928. Bust of Pres. Masaryk. Rev: Arms. (Tenth anniversary)	12.50

8.	1 Koruna (C-N) 1922–38. Lion. Rev: Kneeling female figure with sheaf of wheat	1.50
9.	50 Haleru (C-N) 1921–22, '24–27, '31. Lion. Rev: Value above wreath	1.25
10.	25 Haleru (C-N) 1933. Lion. Rev: Value	4.00
11.	20 Haleru (C-N) 1921–38. Lion. Rev: Sheaf of wheat	1.50
12.	10 Haleru (Bro) 1922–38. Lion. Rev: Bridge	1.25
13.	5 Haleru (Bro) 1923–38	1.00
14.	2 Haleru (Z) 1923–25	12.50

SLOVAKIA

This was a German puppet state set up in March 1939.

5.	10 Koruny 1930–33. Arms. Rev: Seated female figure and branch	10.00

15.	50 Koruny 1944. Bust of Tiso. Rev: Arms	15.00
16.	20 Koruny 1939. ("Election" commemorative)	37.50

6.	5 Koruny (C-N) 1925–27; (S) 1928–32 smaller planchet; (N) 1937–38. Lion. Rev: Large "5" and smelting furnace	7.50

17.	20 Koruny 1941. St. Cyril and St. Methodius. Rev: Arms	12.50
18.	10 Koruny 1944. Three figures	10.00

19. 5 Koruny (N) 1939. Head of Father Hlinka.
    Rev: Arms 8.00
20. 1 Koruna (C-N) 1940–42, '44, '45. Arms 6.50

27. 50 Koruny 1948. Rev: Standing figure. (Third
    anniversary of liberation from Germany) 8.00

21. 50 Halierov (C-N) 1940–41; (A) '43, '44; Rev:
    Value and plow 5.00

22. 20 Halierov (Br) 1940–42; (A) '42, '43. Nitra
    Castle 5.00
23. 10 Halierov (Br) 1939–42. Bratislava Castle 5.00
24. 5 Halierov (Z) 1942. Value 17.50

28. 100 Koruny 1948. Rev: Figure with wreath. (30th
    anniversary of liberation from Austria) 12.50

REPUBLIC 1945–

25. 50 Koruny 1947. Lion. Rev: Female figure 8.00

29. 100 Koruny 1949. Lion. Rev: Miner. (700th anni-
    versary of granting of mining privileges of
    Jihlava) 12.50

26. 100 Koruny 1948. Lion. Rev: Kneeling figure and
    standing figure. (600th anniversary of Charles
    University in Prague) 15.00

30. 100 Koruny 1949. Bust of Stalin. Rev: Arms.
    (Stalin's 70th birthday) 12.50
31. 50 Koruny 1949 10.00

32. 100 Koruny 1951. Bust of Klement Gottwald. Rev: Arms. (30th anniversary of Czech Communist Party) 12.50

45. 100 Koruny 1955. Four figures. (10th anniversary of liberation from Nazis) 40.00

33. 2 Koruny (C-N) 1947–48. Janosik, Czech national hero 1.50
34. 1 Koruna (C-N) 1946–47; (A) '50–53. Type of #8 1.00
35. 50 Haleru (Br) 1947–50; (A) '51–53. Type of #9 1.00
36. 20 Haleru (Br) 1947–50; (A) '51–52. Type of #11 .75
37. 1 Koruna (A-Bro) 1957–60. Rev: Kneeling figure 1.25
38. 25 Haleru (A) 1953–54. Arms. Rev: Value .50
39. 10 Haleru (A) 1953–58 .40
40. 5 Haleru (A) 1953–55 .60
41. 3 Haleru (A) 1953–54 .25
42. 1 Haler (A) 1953–60 .20

46. 50 Koruny 1955. Soldier 25.00

COMMEMORATIVE SERIES

47. 25 Koruny 1955. Soldier 12.50
48. 10 Koruny 1955. Kneeling soldier 15.00

43. 25 Koruny 1954. Soldier. Rev: Arms. (10th anniversary of Slovak uprising) 15.00
44. 10 Koruny 1954 12.50

49. 10 Koruny 1957. Willenberg commemorative. Head. Rev: Lion 20.00
50. 10 Koruny 1957. Komensky commemorative 15.00

51. 1 Korun (A-Br) 1961– . Lion on shield. Rev:
Woman planting linden tree   .60

63. 10 Korun 1966. Arms. Rev: Horseman with
falcon. (Founding of Moravia)   17.50
64. 10 Korun 1967. Arms above landscape. Rev:
University building. (500th anniversary of
University of Bratislava)   30.00

52. 50 Haleru (Br) 1963–74, (C-N) 1978– . Rev:
Value   .40
53. 25 Haleru (A) 1962–65   .40
54. 10 Haleru (A) 1961–74   .35
55. 5 Haleru (A) 1962–   .25
56. 3 Haleru (A) 1963   .30
57. 1 Haleru (A) 1962–63   .25

65. 50 Korun 1968. Arms. Rev: Female head. (50th
anniversary of Republic)   60.00
66. 25 Korun 1968. Arms. Rev: National Museum
in Prague. (150th anniversary)   25.00

58. 10 Korun 1964. Workers' hands. Rev: Lion.
(20th anniversary of Slovak uprising in 1944)   12.50

67. 10 Korun 1968. Triga. Rev: Arms. (100th anniversary of National Theatre in Prague)   25.00

59. 25 Korun 1965. Lion on shield. Rev: Girl's head
and dove. (20th anniversary end of World
War II)   15.00
60. 10 Korun 1965. Rev: Portrait of Jan Hus. (550th
anniversary of religious martyr)   30.00
61. 5 Koruny (C-N) 1966. Arms. Rev: Value over
building equipment, star   2.50
62. 3 Koruny (C-N) 1965–69. Arms. Rev: Flower,
value   1.25

68. 25 Korun 1969. Arms. Rev: Head of Jan E. Pur-
kyne. (100th anniversary of scientist's death)   17.50
69. 25 Korun 1969. Arms. Rev: Flame (25th anniversary of 1944 Slovak uprising)   40.00

CZECHOSLOVAKIA (continued)

70. 50 Korun 1970. Arms. Rev: Lenin. (100th anniversary of birth)   15.00

74. 50 Korun 1971. Arms. Rev: Head of Pavel Orszagh (pen name, Hviezdoslav). (50th anniversary of poet's death)   20.00
74a. 50 Korun 1971. Arms. Rev: Five figures with hammer and sickle. (Commemorates 50th anniversary of Czech Communist Party)   25.00

71. 25 Korun 1970. Arms. Rev: Stylized face. (50th anniversary of Slovak National Theatre)   17.50

75. 50 Korun 1972. Arms. Rev. J. V. Myslbek. (50th anniversary of sculptor's death)   17.50
76. 20 Korun 1972. Arms. Rev: Andrej Sladkovic. (100th anniversary of poet's death)   12.50

72. 25 Korun 1970. Arms. Rev: Stylized star over mountains. (25th anniversary of liberation)   12.50

77. 2 Korun (C-N) 1972– . Arms. Rev: Value   .60
78. 20 Haleru (Bra) 1972– . Arms. Rev: Value   .40
79. 10 Haleru (A) 1974. Type of #78   .25

73. 100 Korun 1971. Arms. Rev: Bust of Josef Manes. (100th anniversary of painter's death)   20.00

80. 50 Korun 1973. Armed revolutionary worker, hammer and sickle. Rev: Arms. (25th anniversary of Republic)   15.00

81. 50 Korun 1973. Josef Jungmann. Rev: Arms. (200th anniversary of writer's birth) 15.00
82. 100 Korun 1974. Bedřich Smetana. Rev: Arms. (150th anniversary of composer's birth) 20.00

83. 50 Korun 1974. Janko Jesensky. Rev: Arms (100th birthday of writer) 15.00
84. 50 Korun 1975. Stanislav Kostka Neumann. Rev: Arms. (100th anniversary of poet's birth) 17.50
85. 100 Korun 1976. Janko Kral. Rev: Arms (100th anniversary of poet's death) 30.00
86. 100 Korun 1976. Viktor Kaplan. Rev: Arms (100th anniversary of death) 30.00
87. 100 Korun 1978. Julius Fucik. Rev: Arms 25.00

88. 50 Korun 1978. Portrait of Zdenek Nejedly. Rev: Arms. (Centennial of birth of former Minister of Culture and Education) 17.50

89.

89. 100 Korun 1978. Crowned bust of King Karel IV. Rev: Arms. (600th anniversary of monarch's death) 25.00

90. 50 Korun 1978. Series of 5 coins. Rev: Arms. (650th anniversary of Kremnica Mint) 17.50
91. 100 Korun 1979. Jan Botto. Rev: Arms 17.50
92. 50 Korun 1979. Communist Party Seal. Rev: Arms. (30th anniversary of Ninth Congress) 17.50
93. 100 Korun 1980. Peter Parier. Rev: Arms. (650th anniversary of birth) 30.00
94. 100 Korun 1980. Stylized athletic symbol. Rev: Arms. (Fifth Spartakiade Games) 25.00
95. 100 Korun 1980. Bohumir Smeral. Rev: Arms 25.00
96. 500 Korun 1981. Ludovit Stur. Rev: Arms. (125th anniversary of linguist's death) 75.00
97. 100 Korun 1981. Cosmonaut. Rev: Arms. (20th anniversary of space flight) 25.00
98. 100 Korun 1981. Professor Ota Kar Spaniel. Rev: Arms 25.00
99. 100 Korun 1982. Ivan Olbracht. Rev: Arms. (Centennial of author's birth) 25.00

DANISH WEST INDIES

A group of 68 islands also known as the Virgin Islands. They became Danish territory late in the seventeenth century, and were sold to the United States in 1917 for $25,000,000.

500 Bits or 100 Cents = 5 Francs or 1 Daler

CHRISTIAN IX   1863–1906

1.	20 Francs or 4 Dalers (G) 1904, '05. Head. Rev: Seated female figure	600.00

2.	2 Francs or 40 Cents 1905. Bust. Rev: Three female figures	135.00
3.	20 Cents 1878, '79. Head. Rev: Ship	175.00
4.	1 Franc or 20 Cents 1905. Type of #2	75.00
5.	10 Cents 1878, '79. Head. Rev: Sugar cane	65.00
6.	50 Bits or 10 Cents 1905. Head. Rev: Olive branch	25.00
7.	5 Cents 1878, '79. Type of #3	75.00

8.	25 Bits or 5 Cents (N) 1905. Crowned monogram of "C9." Rev: Sickle, caduceus and trident	25.00
9.	10 Bits or 2 Cents (Bro) 1905	30.00
10.	5 Bits or 1 Cent (Bro) 1905	20.00
11.	2½ Bits or ½ Cent (Bro) 1905	25.00

FREDERICK VIII   1906–12

12.	2 Francs or 40 Cents 1907. Head. Rev: Type of #2	175.00
13.	1 Franc or 20 Cents 1907	60.00

CHRISTIAN X   1912–17

14.	5 Bits or 1 Cent (Bro) 1913. Crowned monogram of "C10." Rev: Type of #8	35.00

DANZIG

Danzig, a port on the Baltic, was a Free City during the Middle Ages. It was then of great commercial importance and enjoyed considerable prosperity. It was Polish from 1455 to 1772 and later part of the German Empire. After World War I, when it again became a Free City, at the head of the Polish Corridor, Danzig issued its own coins and stamps. In 1939 it was proclaimed part of Germany again. Today it is once more under Polish administration.

100 Pfennigs = 1 Gulden

1.	5 Gulden 1923–27; '32 (modified design). Church. Rev: Arms between lions	175.00

2.	2 Gulden 1923. Galley. Rev: Arms between lions	75.00
3.	1 Gulden 1923	35.00

4.	½ Gulden 1923, '27. Sailing vessel. Rev: Crowned crosses and value	30.00

5.	10 Pfennigs (C-N) 1923. Arms. Rev: Value	8.00
6.	5 Pfennigs (C-N) 1923, '28	7.50

7.	2 Pfennigs (Bro) 1923, '26, '37. Crowned crosses. Rev: Value	7.00
8.	1 Pfennig (Bro) 1923–37	7.50

9.	5 Gulden 1932. Grain elevator. Rev: Arms between lions	475.00
10.	2 Gulden 1932. Galley. Rev: Type of #9	200.00
11.	1 Gulden (N) 1932. Large "1." Rev: Crowned crosses	30.00
12.	½ Gulden (N) 1932	25.00

13.	10 Pfennigs (A-Bro) 1932. Codfish. Rev: Value	7.50

14.	5 Pfennigs (A-Bro) 1932. Flounder. Rev: Value	7.50

15.	10 Gulden (N) 1935. City hall. Rev: Arms between lions	650.00

16.	5 Gulden (N) 1935. Galley. Rev: Type of #15	275.00

DENMARK

The kingdom of Denmark was once much more dominant than it is today. Towards the end of the 14th century the Danes gained control of both Sweden and Norway. Sweden obtained its freedom in 1521, but Danish domination of Norway continued until 1814.

$$120 \; Skilling = 1 \; Speciedaler$$
$$96 \; Skilling = 1 \; Rigsbankdaler$$
$$16 \; Skilling = 1 \; Mark$$
$$6 \; Marks = 1 \; Daler$$
$$4 \; Marks = 1 \; Krone$$
$$100 \; Ore = 1 \; Krone$$

CHRISTIAN IV   1588–1648

1.	1 Krone 1618–24. King standing. Rev: Crown	250.00
2.	½ Krone 1618–24	100.00
3.	¼ Krone 1618	75.00
4.	Taler 1624–47. Bust. Rev: 13 shields	350.00
5.	½ Taler 1624–46	200.00

6.	8 Skilling 1606–25. Bust. Rev: Arms and value	50.00
7.	4 Skilling 1596–1645	35.00
8.	2 Skilling 1594–1621	30.00
9.	1 Skilling 1595–1621	20.00

FREDERICK III   1648–70

10.	Taler 1649–62. Bust. Rev: Shields	400.00

11.	1 Krone 1651. Armored bust. Rev: Crown	250.00
12.	½ Krone 1651	80.00

13.	4 Marks 1659. Crowned monogram. Rev: Hand and sword	300.00
13a.	4 Marks 1652–70. Rev: Arms	75.00
14.	2 Marks 1652–69	65.00
15.	Taler 1664–69. Bust. Rev: Arms	250.00
16.	4 Skilling 1667–69. Arms. Rev: Value	35.00
17.	2 Skilling 1648–70	30.00
18.	1 Skilling 1648–67	25.00

CHRISTIAN V   1670–99

19.	4 Marks 1671–94. Monogram. Rev: Arms	100.00
20.	2 Marks 1671–96	60.00
21.	1 Mark 1672–92	25.00

22.	Taler 1687–93. Draped bust. Rev: Arms	450.00
23.	½ Taler 1693. Bust. Rev: Arms in circle of shields	150.00
24.	8 Skilling 1672–97. Monogram. Rev: Value	60.00
25.	2 Skilling 1676–94	50.00
26.	1 Skilling 1676–96	40.00

FREDERICK IV   1699–1730

27.	4 Marks 1711–23. King mounted on horseback	250.00
28.	1 Krone 1725–26. Monogram. Rev: Arms	150.00

CHRISTIAN VI   1730–46

29.	4 Marks 1731, '32. Armored bust. Rev: Crown	200.00
30.	24 Skilling 1732–43. Monogram. Rev: Arms	85.00
31.	1 Skilling 1735–46	65.00

FREDERICK V   1746–66

32.	Taler 1747. King standing under canopy	300.00
33.	Taler 1764–65. Laureate bust. Rev: Oval shield	200.00
34.	24 Skilling 1750–64. Monogram. Rev: Arms	40.00
35.	8 Skilling 1763. Rev: Value	30.00
35a.	4 Skilling 1764	20.00
36.	2 Skilling 1756–61	20.00
37.	1 Skilling 1751–65	17.50

CHRISTIAN VII   1766–1808

38.	Taler 1769. Bust. Rev: Arms in ribbon	450.00
39.	Taler 1769–85. Monogram. Rev: Shield	150.00

40.	½ Taler 1769–86	125.00
41.	¼ Taler 1769	100.00
42.	1 Taler 1791–1801. Head. Rev: Crowned arms	175.00
43.	⅔ Taler 1795, '96	70.00
44.	⅓ Taler 1795–1803	70.00
45.	24 Skilling 1767, '78–83. Monogram. Rev: Arms	60.00
46.	8 Skilling 1778–95	15.00
47.	4 Skilling 1778, '83, '88, 1807	10.00
48.	2 Skilling 1778–88, 1800–07	20.00
49.	1 Skilling 1779–82	12.50

NOTE: During the reign of Christian VII a series of speciedalers was issued for the provinces of Schleswig and Holstein

50.	Speciedaler 1788–1808	200.00

DENMARK (continued)

FREDERICK VI   1808–39

60.	Rigsbankdaler 1842–48. Head. Rev: Coat of arms	150.00
61.	32 Rigsbankskilling 1842–43	75.00
62.	16 Rigsbankskilling 1842–44	75.00
63.	8 Rigsbankskilling 1843	60.00
64.	4 Rigsbankskilling 1841–42. Head. Rev: Crown	17.50
65.	3 Rigsbankskilling 1842	12.50
66.	2 Rigsbankskilling (C) 1842	125.00
67.	1 Rigsbankskilling (C) 1842	25.00
68.	½ Rigsbankskilling (C) 1842	15.00
69.	⅓ Rigsbankskilling (C) 1842	20.00

51.	Speciedaler 1813–39. Head. Rev: Shield	150.00
52.	12 Skilling (C) 1812	35.00
53.	8 Skilling 1809. Monogram. Rev: Value	10.00
54.	6 Skilling (C) 1813. Arms. Rev: Value	30.00
55.	4 Skilling (C) 1815	35.00
56.	3 Skilling (C) 1815	15.00
56a.	2 Skilling (C) 1809–11. Head. Rev: Arms	12.50

FREDERICK VII   1848–63

57.	2 Skilling (C) 1818	45.00
58.	1 Skilling 1808–09. Monogram. Rev: Value	17.50
58a.	1 Skilling (C) 1813. Head. Rev: Value	17.50

CHRISTIAN VIII   1839–48

70.	Speciedaler 1848. Head of Frederick VII. Rev: Head of Christian VIII. (Accession to throne)	300.00

59.	1 Speciedaler 1840–48. Head. Rev: Two wild men supporting arms	225.00

71.	Speciedaler 1849–54. Head. Rev: Arms	200.00

81.   2 Rigsdaler 1863. Head of Christian IX. Rev:
       Head of Frederick VII. (Accession to throne)   325.00

72.	2 Rigsdaler 1854–63. Head. Rev: Value	225.00
73.	1 Rigsdaler 1854, '55	85.00

82.   2 Rigsdaler 1864–72. Head. Rev: Value   400.00

74.	½ Rigsdaler 1854, '55	50.00
75.	16 Skilling 1854–58	35.00
76.	4 Skilling 1854–56	12.50
77.	1 Skilling (Br) 1856–63	5.00
78.	½ Skilling (Br) 1857	7.50

CHRISTIAN IX   1863–1906

83.   2 Kroner 1875–99. Head. Rev: Arms   50.00

79.	20 Kroner (G) 1873–1900. Head. Rev: Female	
	seated	225.00
80.	10 Kroner (G) 1873–1900	200.00

84.   2 Kroner 1888. (25th year of reign)   60.00

DENMARK (continued)

85. 2 Kroner 1892. (Royal golden wedding anniversary)   50.00

86. 2 Kroner 1903. Bust. Rev: Seated figure. (40th year of reign)   55.00
87. 1 Krone 1875–98. Head. Rev: Arms   25.00
88. 25 Ore 1874–1905. Head. Rev: Value, dolphin   20.00
89. 10 Ore 1874–1905   5.00
90. 5 Ore (Bro) 1874–1906. Initial. Rev: Value, dolphin   12.50
91. 2 Ore (Bro) 1874–1906   5.00
92. 1 Ore (Bro) 1874–1904   3.00

FREDERICK VIII 1906–12

93. 20 Kroner (G) 1908–12. Head. Rev: Arms   225.00
94. 10 Kroner (G) 1908–09   175.00

95. 2 Kroner 1906. Bust of Frederick VIII. Rev: Bust of Christian IX. (Accession to throne)   40.00
96. 25 Ore 1907, 11. Head. Rev: Value   20.00
97. 10 Ore 1907–12   8.00
98. 5 Ore (Bro) 1907–12. Monogram. Rev: Value   17.50
99. 2 Ore (Bro) 1907–12   3.00
100. 1 Ore (Bro) 1907–12   2.50

CHRISTIAN X 1912–47

101. 20 Kroner (G) 1913–31. Head. Rev: Arms   225.00
102. 10 Kroner (G) 1913–17   185.00

103. 2 Kroner 1912. Bust of Christian X. Rev: Head of Frederick VIII. (Accession to throne)   50.00

104. 2 Kroner 1915–16. Regular issue   40.00

105. 2 Kroner 1923. Silver wedding. Conjoined busts   30.00

106. 2 Kroner 1930. 60th birthday   35.00

DENMARK (continued)

107.	2 Kroner 1937. 25th year of rule	30.00

117.	5 Kroner (C-N) 1960–72. Head of King. Rev: Arms	3.00

108.	2 Kroner (A-Bro) 1924–41	8.00

118.	2 Kroner (A-Br) 1947–59	5.00
119.	1 Krone (A-Br) 1947–59; (C-N) 1960–72	1.00
120.	25 Ore (C-N) 1948–60. Monogram. Rev: Value	1.50

109.	2 Kroner 1945. 75th birthday	35.00

120a.	25 Ore (C-N) 1960–67. Rev: Value in wreath	.75
121.	10 Ore (C-N) 1948–60. Rev: Value	.20
121a.	10 Ore (C-N) 1960–72. Rev: Value in wreath	.20

110.	1 Krone 1915–16. Head. Rev: Dolphins	12.50
110a.	1 Krone (A-Br) 1924–41. Crowned "CX." Rev: Crown	4.00
111.	½ Krone (A-Bro) 1924–40. Crowned "CX." Rev: Crown	12.50

122.	5 Ore (Z) 1950–64; (Br) 1960–72	.50
123.	2 Ore (Z) 1948–72	.15
124.	1 Ore (Z) 1948–72	.15

112.	25 Ore (S) 1913–19; (C-N) 1920–47; (Z) 1941–45. Rev: Value, with and without center hole	2.50
113.	10 Ore (S) 1914–19; (C-N) 1920–47; (Z) 1941–45	1.25
114.	5 Ore (Bro) 1913–23; (Iron) 1918–19; (Bro) 1927–41; (A) 1941; (Z) 1942–45	.50
115.	2 Ore (Bro) 1913–23, 1926–41; (Iron) 1918–19; (A) 1941; (Z) 1942–47	.30
116.	1 Ore (Bro) 1913–23, 1926–41; (Iron) 1918–19; (Z) 1941–46	.20

125.	2 Kroner 1953. Conjoined busts. Rev: Map of Greenland	50.00

DENMARK (continued)

126. 2 Kroner 1958. Head of King. Rev: Head of Princess Margrethe. (Her 18th birthday)   20.00

130. 10 Kroner 1968. Head of King. Rev: Head of Princess Benedikte. (Wedding anniversary)   18.00

131. 25 Ore (C-N) 1966–72. Monogram. Rev: Value (Center hole)   .30

127. 5 Kroner 1960. Conjoined heads of King Frederick and Queen Ingrid. (Silver wedding commemorative)   20.00

MARGRETHE II   1972–

128. 5 Kroner 1964. (Wedding commemorative)   20.00

132. 10 Kroner 1972. Head of Margrethe II. Rev: Head of Frederick IX. (Accession to throne)   12.00

129. 10 Kroner 1967. Head of King. Rev: Conjoined heads of Princess Margrethe and Prince Henrik. (Wedding anniversary)   20.00

133. 5 Krone (C-N) 1973– . Head. Rev: Crowned shield between oak leaves   2.50

135

DENMARK (continued)

134.   1 Krone (C-N) 1973– . Head. Rev: Crowned
        shield   .50

135.   25 Ore (C-N) 1973– . Crowned monogram, oak
        branch. Rev: Value. (Center hole)   .25

136.   10 Ore (C-N) 1973– . Crowned monogram.
        Rev: Value between oak leaves   .20

137.   5 Ore (C-St) 1973– . Rev: Value   .15
138.   10 Kroner (C-N) 1979– . Head. Rev: Value
        within wreath   2.00

DJIBOUTI

The Republic of Djibouti, formerly French Somaliland and French Territory of the Afars and Issas (q.v.), was declared on June 27, 1977.

1.	100 Francs (C-N) 1977. Arms. Rev: Two camels	5.00
2.	50 Francs (C-N) 1977	4.00
3.	20 Francs (A-Bro) 1977. Rev: Sailboat	3.00
4.	10 Francs (A-Bro) 1977	2.00
5.	5 Francs (A) 1977. Rev: Antelope head	1.75
6.	2 Francs (A) 1977	1.50
7.	1 Franc (A) 1977	1.50

DOMINICAN REPUBLIC

With Haiti the Dominican Republic shares Hispaniola, a West Indies island discovered by Columbus on his 1492 voyage. After many revolts against Spanish, French, and Haitian rule, the Dominican Republic successfully revolted once and for all against Haiti in 1844.

100 Centesimos = 1 Franc
100 Centavos = 1 Peso

19.	1 Centavo (Br) 1937–61. Palm tree. Rev: Arms	.75

1.	5 Francs 1891. Liberty head. Rev: Arms	250.00
2.	1 Franc 1891	60.00
3.	50 Centesimos 1891	40.00
4.	10 Centesimos 1891. Arms. Rev: Value	15.00
5.	5 Centesimos 1891	10.00
6.	1 Peso (base silver) 1897	125.00
7.	½ Peso 1897	60.00
8.	20 Centavos 1897	25.00
9.	10 Centavos 1897	17.50

20.	30 Pesos (G) 1955. (25th year of Trujillo regime)	650.00

10.	5 Centavos (C-N) 1877. Open book. Rev: Value	30.00
11.	2½ Centavos (C-N) 1877. Cross. Rev: Value	40.00
11a.	2½ Centavos (C-N) 1882, '88. Book and cross. Rev: Value in wreath	8.00
12.	1¼ Centavos (C-N) 1882, '88	12.50
13.	1 Centavo (Bra) 1877. Date. Rev: Value	8.50

21.	1 Peso 1955. Military bust of President Trujillo. Rev: Arms. (25th year of regime)	65.00

14.	1 Peso 1939–52. Indian in feather headdress. Rev: Arms	65.00
15.	½ Peso 1937–61	20.00
15a.	½ Peso (C-N) 1967–75	2.00
16.	25 Centavos 1937–61	7.00
16a.	25 Centavos (C-N) 1967–	2.00
17.	10 Centavos 1937–61	3.00
17a.	10 Centavos (C-N) 1967–75	.75
18.	5 Centavos (C-N) 1937–74	.50
18a.	5 Centavos (Bi) 1944	20.00

22.	1 Peso 1963. Indian in feather headdress. Rev: Arms and commemorative legend. (100th anniversary of restoration of Republic)	35.00
23.	½ Peso 1963	10.00
24.	25 Centavos 1963	5.00
25.	10 Centavos 1963	2.50
26.	5 Centavos (C-N) 1963	.50
27.	1 Centavo (Br) 1963	.50

31.

28.	½ Peso (C-N) 1967–75. Indian in feather head-dress. Rev: Arms	3.00
29.	25 Centavos (C-N) 1967–74	2.00
30.	10 Centavos (C-N) 1967–75	.75
31.	1 Centavo (Br) 1968–75	.15

32. 1 Centavo (Br) 1969. Indian in feather head-dress. Rev: Arms. (F.A.O. coin plan) .60

33. 1 Peso (C-N) 1969. Arms. Rev: Fortress. (125th anniversary of independence) 12.50

34. 1 Peso 1972. Door of mint building. Rev: Arms. (25th anniversary, founding of Banco Central) 25.00

35. 30 Pesos (G) 1974. Emblem of Central American and Caribbean Games. Rev: Arms. (12th Games) 250.00

36. 1 Peso 1974. Arms of Santo Domingo on map of Dominican Republic. Rev: Arms. (12th Central American and Caribbean Games) 20.00

37. 100 Pesos (G) 1975. Arms. Rev: Indian idol. (Mining in Pueblo Viejo)

38. 10 Pesos 1975

39. 10 Pesos 1975. Arms and value with commemorative inscription. Rev: Replica of 16th century coin. (16th assembly, governors of the Inter-American Bank of Development) 20.00

40. 1 Peso (C-N) 1976. Bust of Duarte. (100th anniversary of death of statesman and revolutionary) 10.00

41.	½ Peso (C-N) 1976	2.50
42.	25 Centavos (C-N) 1976	1.50
43.	10 Centavos (C-N) 1976	1.00
44.	5 Centavos (C-N) 1976	.50
45.	1 Centavo (Bro) 1976	.50

46.	30 Pesos 1977. Arms. Rev: Central Bank, Santo Domingo. (30th anniversary of bank)	90.00
47.	1 Peso (C-N) 1978– . Arms. Rev: Bust of Duarte	3.00
48.	½ Peso (C-N) 1978–	1.25
49.	25 Centavos (C-N) 1978–	.50
50.	10 Centavos (C-N) 1978–	.20
51.	5 Centavos (C-N) 1978–	.20
52.	1 Centavo (Bro) 1978–	.15

53.	250 Pesos (G) 1979. Arms. Rev: Bust of John Paul II. (Pope's visit to Santo Domingo)	400.00
54.	100 Pesos (G) 1979. (Papal visit)	175.00
55.	25 Pesos 1979. (Papal visit)	40.00

EAST AFRICA

This area was made up of three former British protectorates, Kenya, Uganda, Tanganyika, which have become independent countries (Tanganyika as Tanzania) within the British Commonwealth. Nyasaland, also formerly part of East Africa, was a protectorate within the Federation of Rhodesia and Nyasaland until 1963, when it withdrew. In July 1964 it achieved independence as Malawi.

1 Florin = 1 Rupee
100 Cents = 1 Shilling

EAST AFRICA PROTECTORATE

VICTORIA   1837–1901

1.	1 Pice (¼ Anna) (C) 1897–99. Coroneted head. Rev: Value in scrolled circle	6.00

EAST AFRICA AND UGANDA PROTECTORATE

EDWARD VII   1901–10

2.	50 Cents 1906, '09–10. Crowned bust. Rev: Lion and mountains	8.00
3.	25 Cents 1906–10	5.00
4.	10 Cents (C-N) 1907, '10. Crown and ornaments. Rev: Elephant tusks. (Center hole)	3.00
5.	1 Cent (A) 1907–08	3.00
5a.	1 Cent (C-N) 1909–10	1.50
6.	½ Cent (A) 1908	15.00
6a.	½ Cent (C-N) 1909	10.00

GEORGE V   1910–36

7.	50 Cents 1911–19. Crowned bust. Rev: Type of #2	7.50
8.	25 Cents 1911–18	8.00
9.	10 Cents (C-N) 1911–13, '18. Type of #4	4.00
10.	5 Cents (C-N) 1913–19	2.50
11.	1 Cent (C-N) 1911–18	2.00

EAST AFRICA   1920–

12.	1 Florin 1920–21. Type of #7, larger size	25.00
13.	1 Shilling–50 Cents 1920–21	250.00
14.	25 Cents 1920–21	25.00

15.	1 Shilling 1921–25. Smaller size	8.00
16.	50 Cents–½ Shilling 1921–24	25.00
17.	10 Cents (Br) 1921–36. Type of #4	8.00
18.	5 Cents (Br) 1921–36	5.00
19.	1 Cent (Br) 1922–35	2.75

EDWARD VIII   1936

20.	10 Cents (C) 1936. Crown above center hole. Rev: Elephant tusks	3.50
21.	5 Cents (C) 1936	3.00

GEORGE VI   1936–52

22.	1 Shilling 1937–46. Crowned head. Rev: Type of #7	2.75
22a.	1 Shilling (C-N) 1948–52. ET INDIA IMPERATOR dropped from obverse	2.00

23.	50 Cents 1937–44	7.50
23a.	50 Cents (C-N) 1948–52. Type of #22a	1.50

ELIZABETH II   1952–

24.	50 Cents (C-N) 1954–63. Crowned head. Rev: Lion	1.00
25.	10 Cents (Bro) 1956. Type of #4	3.00
26.	5 Cents (Bro) 1955–63	.50
27.	1 Cent (Bro) 1954–62	.85

INDEPENDENT ISSUES

28.	10 Cents (Br) 1964. Value above center hole. Rev: Elephant tusks	.65
29.	5 Cents (Br) 1964	.40

EAST CARIBBEAN TERRITORIES

When the British Caribbean Territories (q.v.) currency grouping disbanded in 1965, the East Caribbean Territories, comprising Barbados (q.v.), Leeward Islands and Windward Islands, was founded to provide a common currency.

1. 4 Dollars (C-N) 1970. Arms. Rev: Bananas and sugar cane. Issued with common reverse design for Antigua, Barbados (q.v.), St. Kitts-Nevis-Anguilla, Dominica, Grenada, Montserrat, St. Lucia, and St. Vincent. (Inauguration of Caribbean Development Bank, F.A.O. coin plan)   Each 10.00

ECUADOR

After three centuries of Spanish rule, Ecuador was united to Colombia upon its liberation in 1819. Ecuador became an independent republic in 1836.

8 Reales = 5 Francs = 1 Dollar or Piece-of-Eight
10 Centavos = 1 Decimo
100 Centavos = 1 Sucre
25 Sucres = 1 Condor

"EL ECUADOR EN COLOMBIA"

1.	2 Reales 1833–35. Fasces. Rev: Sun above mountains	50.00

2.	1 Real 1833–35	50.00
3.	½ Real 1833, '35	55.00

REPUBLIC OF ECUADOR

4.	4 Reales 1841–43. Fasces. Rev: Sun above mountains	40.00

5.	2 Reales 1836–41	30.00
6.	1 Real 1836–40	30.00
7.	½ Real 1838, '40	50.00
8.	8 Reales 1846. Bust of Liberty. Rev: Arms	1000.00
9.	4 Reales 1855–57, '62	50.00

10.	2 Reales 1847–57, '62	30.00
11.	½ Real 1848, '49	35.00
12.	¼ Real 1849–55	40.00

13.	5 Francs 1858	450.00

NEW COINAGE

14.	1 Sucre 1884–97. Head of General Sucre	25.00
15.	½ Sucre 1884	40.00

16.	2 Decimos 1884–96, 1912–16	6.00
17.	1 Decimo 1884–1916	3.00
18.	½ Decimo 1893–1915	2.50
19.	10 Centavos (C-N) 1918–19. Arms. Rev: Value	4.00
19a.	10 Centavos (C-N) 1924. Head of Bolívar. Rev: Arms	4.00
20.	5 Centavos (C-N) 1884–86, 1909–19. Type of #19	3.00
20a.	5 Centavos (C-N) 1924. Head of Bolívar. Rev: Arms	5.00
21.	2½ Centavos (C-N) 1917	30.00

22.	2 Centavos (C) 1872; (C-N) 1909	15.00
23.	1 Centavo (C) 1872, '90; (C-N) 1884–86, 1909	15.00
24.	½ Centavo (C-N) 1884–86; (C) 1890; (C-N) 1909	12.50

ECUADOR (continued)

25.   1 Condor (G) 1928. Bust of Bolívar   200.00

26.   2 Sucres 1928, '30. Head of Sucre. Rev: Arms   4.00
27.   1 Sucre 1928, '30, '34   4.00
28.   5 Decimos (50 Centavos) 1928, '30   4.50

29.   10 Centavos (N) 1928. Bust of Bolívar   1.50
30.   5 Centavos (N) 1928. Arms. Rev: Value   1.25

31.   2½ Centavos (N) 1928   3.50
32.   1 Centavo (Bro) 1928   1.50

LAWS OF 1937–42

33.   5 Sucres 1943–44. Head of Gen. Sucre. Rev:
       Arms   5.00
34.   2 Sucres 1944   10.00

34a.   2 Sucres (C-N) 1973–75   5.00
35.   1 Sucre (N) 1937, 1946   2.50
36.   1 Sucre (C-N) 1959   1.25
37.   1 Sucre (N-St) 1964–   .60

38.   50 Centavos (N-St) 1963– . Arms. Rev: Value   .50
39.   20 Centavos (N) 1937; (Bra) 1942–44; (C-N)
       1946, 1974–75; (N-St) 1959–   .25
40.   10 Centavos (N) 1937; (Bra) 1942; (C-N) 1946;
       (N-St) 1964–   .25
41.   5 Centavos (N) 1937; (Bra) 1942–44; (C-N)
       1946; (N-St) 1970   .20

EGYPT (Modern)

In ancient times a center of civilization, Egypt was conquered by the Ottoman Turks in 1517, and remained part of the Turkish Empire for four centuries. In 1915 Egypt was detached from Turkish rule and declared a British protectorate. Egypt became an independent kingdom in 1922 and a republic in 1953. In 1958 Egypt and Syria formed the United Arab Republic. Although Syria withdrew in 1961, Egypt retained the name until 1971.

During the years of Turkish rule, all Egyptian coins carried the *Toughra*—the Sultan's calligraphic emblem (explained in the section here on Turkish coins). In the case of all Egyptian coins issued during the reign of Abdul Hamid II (1876–1909), the opening date of the reign appears together with the year of issue on the reverse. The opening year (1876) appears as 1293 in the Islamic dating system and is inscribed in Turkish figures.

In the case of Mohammed V, who ruled from 1909 to 1915, the opening date is A.H. 1327. (See the explanation of Islamic dates in the section devoted to Iran.)

1 Ochr-el-Guerche = ¹⁄₁₀ Guerche or Piastre
10 Milliemes = 1 Guerche or Piastre
100 Piastres = 1 Pound Egyptian

UNDER TURKISH RULE
ABDUL HAMID II   1876–1909

1.	20 Piastres 1876–1909. Toughra in wreath. Rev: Inscription in wreath	40.00
2.	10 Piastres 1876–1909	15.00
3.	5 Piastres 1876–1909	8.50

4.	2 Piastres 1876–1909	5.00
5.	1 Piastre 1876–1909	4.00

6.	10 Ochr-el-Guerche (1 Piastre); (C-N) 1876–1909. Toughra in wreath. Rev: Inscription in circle of stars	4.00
7.	5 Ochr-el-Guerche (C-N) 1876–1909. Toughra in closed wreath. Rev: Inscription	2.50
8.	2 Ochr-el-Guerche (C-N) 1876–1911	1.50
9.	1 Ochr-el-Guerche (N) 1876–1911	1.25

MOHAMMED V   1909–15

10.	20 Piastres 1910–12, '14. Toughra in wreath. Rev: Inscription in wreath	40.00
11.	10 Piastres 1910–12, '14	12.50
12.	5 Piastres 1910–14	7.00
13.	2 Piastres 1910–11	5.00
14.	1 Piastre 1910–11	7.00

BRITISH PROTECTORATE   1915–22
SULTAN FUAD I   1917–22

15.	10 Piastres 1920. Inscription. Rev: Inscription and value	75.00
16.	5 Piastres 1920	100.00
17.	2 Piastres 1920	150.00

INDEPENDENT KINGDOM
KING FUAD I 1922–36

18. 100 Piastres (G) 1922–30. Bust. Rev: Inscription
    in circle   200.00
19. 50 Piastres (G) 1923–30   150.00
20. 20 Piastres (G) 1923–30   100.00

28. 2½ Milliemes (C-N) 1933. (Octagonal shape)   10.00
29. 2 Milliemes (C-N) 1924, '29   2.00
30. 1 Millieme (Bro) 1924–35   2.00

31. ½ Millieme (Bro) 1924–32   15.00

FAROUK I 1936–52

32. 50 Piastres (G) 1938. Bust. Rev: Value and dates   150.00
33. 20 Piastres (G) 1938   110.00

21. 20 Piastres 1923. Civilian bust. Rev: Inscription   75.00

34. 20 Piastres 1937, '39   50.00
35. 10 Piastres 1937, '39   15.00
36. 5 Piastres 1937, '39   12.50
37. 2 Piastres 1937–42   5.00

38. 2 Piastres 1944. (Hexagonal shape)   3.00

22. 20 Piastres 1929, '33. Military bust. Rev: In-
    scription   40.00
23. 10 Piastres 1923–33. Bust. Rev: Inscription   17.50
24. 5 Piastres 1923–33   15.00
25. 2 Piastres 1923–29   7.00
26. 10 Milliemes (C-N) 1924–35   3.00
27. 5 Milliemes (C-N) 1924–35   1.25

39. 10 Milliemes (C-N) 1938, '41. Bust. Rev: In-
    scription   1.00
40. 5 Milliemes (C-N) 1938, '41   1.00
41. 2 Milliemes (C-N) 1938   1.50
42. 1 Millieme (Br) 1938–50   1.00

EGYPT (continued)

| 43. | 1 Millieme (C-N) 1938. (Center hole) | 8.00 |
| 44. | ½ Millieme (Bro) 1938. Type of #42 | 7.50 |

| 45. | 10 Milliemes (Bro) 1938, '43 (Scalloped edge). Type of #39 | 1.50 |
| 46. | 5 Milliemes (Bro) 1938, '43 | 1.25 |

REPUBLIC 1953–

| 47. | 5 Pounds (G), 1955, '57. Pharaoh in chariot. Rev: Winged sun. (3rd and 5th anniversaries of Revolution) | 1000.00 |
| 48. | 1 Pound (G) 1955, '57 | 225.00 |

| 49. | 50 Piastres 1956. Pharaoh with broken chain and Liberty torch. Rev: Winged sun. (British evacuation of Egypt) | 35.00 |

| 50. | 25 Piastres 1956. Suez Canal Co. building at Port Said. (Nationalization of Suez Canal) | 25.00 |

51.	25 Piastres 1957. (Inauguration of National Assembly)	25.00
52.	20 Piastres 1956–59. Sphinx. Rev: Value	12.50
53.	10 Piastres 1955–57	7.50

| 54. | 5 Piastres 1955–59 | 5.00 |
| 55. | 10 Milliemes (A-Br) 1954–59 | 2.50 |

| 56. | 5 Milliemes (A-Br) 1954–59 | 2.00 |
| 57. | 1 Millieme (A-Br) 1954–59 | 1.50 |

EGYPT (continued)

UNITED ARAB REPUBLIC 1958–71

58. 20 Milliemes (A-Br) 1958. Tractor wheel. Rev:
     Value. (Agricultural and Industrial Fair)   7.50

69. 5 Pounds (G) 1960. (Aswan Dam)   1000.00
70. 1 Pound (G) 1960   250.00

59. ½ Pound (G) 1958. Pharaoh in chariot. Rev:
     Winged sun. (Founding of U.A.R.)   125.00

71. 10 Pounds (G) 1964. View of Aswan High Dam.
     Rev: Inscription (Dedication of Dam).   1250.00
72. 5 Pounds (G) 1964   900.00
73. 50 Piastres 1964   20.00
74. 25 Piastres 1964   10.00
75. 10 Piastres 1964   7.50
76. 5 Piastres 1964   3.50

60. 20 Piastres 1960. Saladin type eagle. Rev: Value   20.00
61. 10 Piastres 1959, '60   7.00
62. 10 Piastres (C-N) 1967   4.00
63. 5 Piastres 1960   4.00
63a. 5 Piastres (C-N) 1967   2.00
64. 10 Milliemes (A-Br) 1960   .65
64a. 10 Milliemes (A) 1967   .65
65. 5 Milliemes (A-Br) 1960   .75
65a. 5 Milliemes (A) 1967   .65
66. 2 Milliemes (A-Br) 1962–   .25
67. 1 Millieme (A-Br) 1960–   .20

77. 5 Piastres (C-N) 1968. Globe encircled by gear.
     Rev: Value. (International Industrial Fair)   2.50
78. 5 Pounds (G) 1968. Open Koran above globe.
     (1400th anniversary of Koran)   700.00
79. 1 Pound 1968. Aswan High Dam. Rev: Value.
     (Start of power generation)   20.00

68. 25 Piastres 1960. (National Assembly)   20.00

80. 10 Piastres (C-N) 1969. Emblem. (Cairo Inter-
     national Fair)   4.00

EGYPT (continued)

81. 5 Piastres (C-N) 1969. Two arms holding
     wrenches. Rev: Value. (Handcraft Fair)   3.00

90. 10 Piastres (C-N) 1970–71. Abstract ship design
     within cogwheel. Rev: Value. (1970 date com-
     memorates Workers' Congress)   4.00

ARAB REPUBLIC OF EGYPT   1971–

82. 5 Pounds (G) 1970. Gamal Abdul Nasser. Rev:
     Value. (Death of President)   500.00
83. 1 Pound (G) 1970   200.00
84. 1 Pound (S) 1970   25.00
85. 50 Piastres 1970   15.00
86. 25 Piastres 1970   8.00
87. 1 Pound 1970. Buildings. (1000th anniversary
     of Al-Azhar University)   25.00

90a. 10 Piastres (C-N) 1972. (Cairo State Fair)   4.00

91. 5 Pounds (G) 1973. Bank building. Rev: Value.
     (75th anniversary of National Bank)   500.00
92. 1 Pound (G) 1973   200.00
93. 25 Piastres 1973   10.00
94. 5 Piastres (C-N) 1973   2.50

88. 10 Piastres (C-N) 1970. Farming scene. Rev.
     Value. (F.A.O. coin plan)   5.00

89. 10 Piastres (C-N) 1970. Bank building at sun-
     rise. Rev: Value. (50th anniversary of Egypt
     Bank)   4.00

95. 1 Pound 1973. Aswan Dam. Rev: Value.
     (F.A.O. coin plan)   25.00
96. 5 Milliemes (A) 1973   .50

149

97. 5 Piastres (C-N) 1972. Mother and child. Rev: Value. (25th anniversary of UNICEF)   3.00

98. 10 Milliemes (A-Br) 1973. Eagle. Rev: Value   .50
99. 5 Milliemes (A-Br) 1973   .35

100. 5 Piastres (C-N) 1974. Soldier. Rev: Value. (Yom Kippur War)   2.50

101. 10 Piastres (C-N) 1975. Wheat gatherer and fisherman, goddess Isis seated. (F.A.O. coin plan)   3.00

102. 5 Piastres (C-N) 1975. Bust of Nefertiti. (F.A.O. coin plan, International Women's Year)   2.00
103. 10 Milliemes (Bra) 1975. Type of #101   .50

104. 5 Milliemes (Bra) 1975   .35
105. 1 Pound 1976. Ancient goddess of agriculture. Rev: Value. (F.A.O. coin plan)   17.50
106. 1 Pound 1976. Ship passing through Suez. Rev: Value. (Reopening of Suez Canal)   17.50

107. 1 Pound 1976. Om Kalzoom, famous Egyptian singer. Rev: Value   17.50
108. 1 Pound 1976. King Faisal of Saudi Arabia. Rev: Value. (Memorializes death of Faisal)   17.50
109. 10 Piastres (C-N) 1976. (Reopening of Suez Canal)   5.00
110. 5 Piastres (C-N) 1976. Inscription, emblem. Rev: Value. (Cairo Trade Fair)   2.50
111. 10 Milliemes (Bra) 1976. (F.A.O. coin plan.) Type of #105   .75

112. 1 Pound 1977. Vignette of ancient Egyptians engaged in food production. Rev: Value. (F.A.O. coin plan)   17.50

113. 10 Piastres (C-N) 1977. (F.A.O. coin plan)   3.00

114. 5 Piastres (C-N) 1977. (F.A.O. coin plan)   2.00
115. 10 Milliemes (Bra) 1977. (F.A.O. coin plan.) Type of #112   1.00
116. 5 Milliemes (Bra) 1977. (F.A.O. coin plan.) Type of #114   .50

117. 1 Pound 1977, '79. Rayed sun over ancient Egyptian, laurel behind. Rev: Value. (Sadat's May 15, 1971 "Corrective Revolution") 17.50

126. 1 Pound 1978. Obelisk penetrating sun. Rev: Value. (25th anniversary of Ain Shams University) 17.50

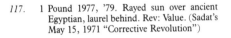

128.

130.

118. 10 Piastres (C-N) 1977, '79. ("Corrective Revolution") 2.50
119. 5 Piastres (C-N) 1977, '79 2.00
120. 10 Milliemes (Bra) 1977, '79 1.00
121. 5 Milliemes (Bra) 1977, '79 .50

127. 1 Pound 1978. Young woman botany student with microscope. Rev: Value. (F.A.O. coin plan) 17.50
128. 5 Piastres (C-N) 1978 2.00
129. 10 Milliemes (Bra) 1978 1.00
130. 1 Pound 1979. Facade of mint building. Rev: Value. (25th anniversary of Abbasia Mint) 17.50
131. 10 Piastres (C-N) 3.00

122. 1 Pound 1977. Handshake vignette within wreath. Rev: Value. (20th anniversary of Economic Union) 17.50
123. 10 Piastres (C-N) 1977 2.50
124. 1 Pound 1978. Cement works. Rev: Value. (Portland Cement Industry) 17.50

125.

125. 5 Piastres (C-N) 1978 2.00

132. 1 Pound 1979. Woman nursing child god Horus. Rev: Value. (International Year of Child, F.A.O. coin plan) 17.50
133. 5 Piastres (C-N) 1979. (International Year of Child) 2.00

151

EGYPT (continued)

134.	10 Milliemes (Bra) 1979. (International Year of Child)	1.00
135.	1 Pound 1979. Type of #117. (National Education Day)	17.50
136.	10 Piastres 1979. (National Education Day)	2.50
137.	1 Pound 1979. Agricultural vignette. Rev: Value. (Bank of Land Reform)	17.50
138.	10 Piastres (C-N) 1979. (Bank of Land Reform)	2.50
139.	1 Pound 1979. (14th century of Muhammad's Hegira ["flight"])	17.50
140.	1 Pound 1980. Anwar Sadat. Rev: Value. (Egyptian-Israeli Peace Treaty)	25.00
141.	10 Piastres (C-N) 1980. (Egyptian-Israeli Treaty)	3.00
142.	1 Pound 1980. Group of skilled workers. Rev: Value. (Honors applied professions)	17.50
143.	1 Pound 1980. Doctor. Rev: Value. (Doctor's Day)	25.00
144.	10 Piastres (C-N) 1980. (Doctor's Day)	3.00
145.	1 Pound 1980. Farm vignette. Rev: Value. (F.A.O. coin plan)	17.50
146.	10 Piastres (C-N) 1980. Farm vignette. (F.A.O.)	2.50
147.	10 Milliemes (A-Bro) 1980. Farm vignette. (F.A.O.)	.50
148.	1 Pound 1980. Upraised arm holding sheaf of wheat. Rev: Value. (1971 "Corrective Revolution")	17.50
149.	10 Piastres (C-N) 1980. ("Corrective Revolution")	3.00
150.	1 Pound 1980. Dome over scales of justice. Rev: Value. (Law Day)	17.50
151.	1 Pound 1981. Rayed sun over scientific instruments. Rev: Value. (Scientist's Day)	17.50
152.	10 Piastres 1981. (Scientist's Day)	2.50

EQUATORIAL AFRICAN STATES

A monetary union issuing coins and currency as a central bank in the name of its five member states: Cameroon and the four states of the former French Equatorial Africa (Gabon, Republic of the Congo–Brazzaville, Chad, Central African Republic). In 1974 it changed its name to the Bank of the Central African States (q.v.).

100 Centimes = 1 Franc

1.	50 Francs (C-N) 1961, '63. Three antelope heads. Rev: Value	5.00
2.	25 Francs (A-Br) 1962–74. New legend	1.25
3.	10 Francs (A-Br) 1961–74	.60
4.	5 Francs (A-Br) 1961–74	.50
5.	1 Franc (A) 1967–71	.40

6.	100 Francs (N) 1966, '68. Three antelope heads. Rev: Value	3.00

EQUATORIAL GUINEA

A new African republic made up from two former Spanish provinces, the island of Fernando Po, the mainland area of Rio Muni, and several smaller islands. Independence was gained on Oct. 12, 1968.

1. 50 Pesetas (C-N) 1969. President Macías Nguema Biyogo. Rev: Value   15.00

2. 25 Pesetas (C-N) 1969. Crossed elephant tusks. Rev: Arms and value   10.00
3. 5 Pesetas (C-N) 1969   12.50
4. 1 Peseta (A-Br) 1969   3.50

MONETARY REFORM

5. 10 Ekuele (C-N) 1975. Bust of President Macías Nguema Biyogo. Rev: Rooster   2.50

6. 5 Ekuele (C-N) 1975. Rev: Field workers   1.50
7. 1 Ekuele (Bra) 1975. Rev: Group of tools   1.00
8. 10,000 Ekuele (G) 1978. President Macías. Rev: Arms. (10th anniversary of election.) Issued in proof only   250.00
9. 5000 Ekuele (G) 1978. Rev: Central Bank at Malabo. In proof only   125.00
10. 2000 Ekuele 1978. Rev: Arms. In proof only   50.00
11. 1000 Ekuele 1978. Rev: Central Bank at Malabo. In proof only   20.00

12. 2000 Ekuele 1979. Central Bank at Malabo. Rev: Ancient discus thrower. (1980 Moscow Olympics.) In proof only   50.00

SECOND MONETARY REFORM

13. 10,000 Bipkwele (G) 1979. Dual portrait of Juan Carlos I and Queen Sofia. Rev: Arms, value. (Spanish royal couple's visit)   175.00
14. 5000 Bipkwele (G) 1979   100.00
15. 2000 Bipkwele 1979   30.00
16. 1000 Bipkwele 1979   25.00

ERITREA

Located on the northeast coast of Africa, Eritrea was an Italian colony up to World War II. Since 1950 it has been a self-governing unit of Ethiopia.

100 Centesimi = 1 Lira
100 Cents = 1 Tallero

UMBERTO I   1878–1900

1.	5 Lire 1891, '96. Head of Umberto I of Italy	300.00
2.	2 Lire 1890–96	125.00
3.	1 Lira 1890–96	100.00
4.	50 Centesimi 1890	80.00

VICTOR EMMANUEL III   1900–44

5.	1 Tallero 1918. Female bust. Rev: Crowned eagle over Italian arms (struck in style of Maria Theresa dollar, with which it was meant to compete)	175.00

ESTONIA

After years of Danish, Polish, and Swedish rule, Estonia was annexed by the Russians early in the eighteenth century. Estonia became a free country in 1918, but was reabsorbed by the U.S.S.R. in 1940.

100 Penni = 1 Mark
100 Marka = 1 Kroon
100 Senti = 1 Kroon

1.	10 Marka (N-Bro) 1925–26. Three lions. Rev: Value	25.00
2.	5 Marka (C-N) 1922; (N-Bro) 1924–26	15.00
3.	3 Marka (C-N) 1922; (N-Bro) 1925–26	12.50
4.	1 Marka (C-N) 1922; (N-Bro) 1924–26	8.50

5.	2 Krooni 1930. Tallinn castle. Rev: Arms in wreath	35.00

6.	2 Krooni 1932. Facade. Rev: Arms in wreath. (Tercentenary of University of Tartu)	75.00

7.	1 Kroon 1933. Lyre. Rev: Arms in wreath. (10th Singing Festival)	80.00

8.	1 Kroon 1934. Viking ship. Rev: Arms	35.00
9.	50 Senti (N-Bro) 1936. Three lions. Rev: Value	30.00

10.	25 Senti (N-Bro) 1928	30.00
11.	20 Senti (N-Bro) 1935	15.00
12.	10 Senti (N-Bro) 1931	12.50
13.	5 Senti (Bro) 1931	10.00
14.	2 Senti (Bro) 1934	10.00

15.	1 Sent (Bro) 1929	5.00
15a.	1 Sent (Bro) 1939. New legend	30.00

ETHIOPIA

An independent kingdom in northeast Africa. An Italian invasion of Ethiopia in 1895 resulted in disastrous defeat for the Europeans. A second Italian invasion in 1936, however, was successful and caused Emperor Haile Selassie to flee. He was restored to power in 1941.

16 Guerche = 1 Menelik Talari
100 Cents or Matoñas = 1 Talari

MENELIK II 1889–1913

1.	1 Talari 1894–1903. Crowned head. Rev: Lion	100.00
2.	½ Talari 1894–97	50.00
3.	¼ Talari 1894–1903	20.00
4.	⅛ Talari 1894	85.00
5.	¹⁄₁₆ Talari 1897–1903	8.50

HAILE SELASSIE 1930–36, 1941–74

6.	50 Matoñas or Cents (N) 1931. Crowned head. Rev: Lion	10.00
7.	25 Matoñas or Cents (N) 1931	7.00
8.	10 Matoñas or Cents (N) 1931	7.00
9.	5 Matoñas or Cents (C) 1931	10.00
10.	1 Matoña or Cent (C) 1931	7.00

11.	50 Cents 1944. Bust of Emperor. Rev: Lion	8.00
12.	25 Cents (Br) 1944	50.00
12a.	25 Cents (Br) 1944. (Scalloped edge)	1.50
13.	10 Cents (Br) 1944	.50
14.	5 Cents (Br) 1944	.35
15.	1 Cent (Br) 1944	.30

16.	50 Cents (C-N) 1976–77. Lion. Rev: Figures symbolizing Ethiopia's progressive forces	5.00

17.	25 Cents (C-N) 1976–78. Rev: Tribute to modern Ethiopian woman	5.00
18.	10 Cents (C-Z) 1976–78. Rev: Mountain nyala	3.00

19.	5 Cents (C-Z) 1976–78. Rev: Member of People's Militia	2.00
20.	1 Cent (A) 1976–78. Rev: Farmer plowing land. (F.A.O. coin plan)	1.00
21.	400 Bir (G) 1980. Stylized figure of child. Rev: Children playing. (International Year of Child.) Issued in proof only	250.00
22.	20 Bir 1980. (International Year of Child.) In proof only	50.00

FALKLAND ISLANDS

A British colony located in the South Atlantic.

1. 10 Pence (C-N) 1974– . Queen Elizabeth II.
Rev: Two seals   .75

2. 5 Pence (C-N) 1974– . Rev: Bird in flight   .40
3. 2 Pence (Br) 1974– . Rev: Gull in flight   .25

4. 1 Penny (Br) 1974– . Rev: Two penguins   .20
5. ½ Penny (Br) 1974– . Rev: Fish   .15

12. 50 Pence (C-N) 1982. Rev: Island coat of arms
superimposed on Union Jack. (Falklands' liberation from Argentine troops, 1982)   4.00
12a. 50 Pence (S) 1982. Proof   35.00

6. 50 Pence (C-N) 1977. Rev: Arms. (Queen's Silver Jubilee)   2.00
7. 10 Pounds 1979. Rev: Ducks. (Conservation
Series)   35.00
8. 5 Pounds 1979. Rev: Whale. (Conservation Series)   25.00
9. 50 Pence (C-N) 1980. Rev: Bust of Queen
Mother Elizabeth. (Queen Mother's 80th
birthday)   4.00
10. 50 Pence (C-N) 1980. Rev: Sheep   3.00
11. 50 Pence (C-N) 1981. Rev: Conjoined portraits
of Prince Charles and Lady Diana. (Marriage
of Charles and Diana)   4.00

FIJI

Made up of some 250 islands lying northeast of Australia, Fiji was annexed by Great Britain in 1874 and remained a British crown colony until 1970, when it became an independent nation within the Commonwealth.

12 Pence = 1 Shilling
2 Shillings = 1 Florin

GEORGE V   1910–36

1.	1 Florin 1934–36. Crowned bust. Rev: Shield	150.00

2.	1 Shilling 1934–36. Rev: Native boat	50.00
3.	6 Pence 1934–36. Rev: Turtle	40.00

4.	1 Penny (C-N) 1934–36. Crown. Rev: Value. (Center hole)	10.00
5.	½ Penny (C-N) 1934	20.00

EDWARD VIII   1936

6.	1 Penny (C-N) 1936. Type of #4	12.50

GEORGE VI   1936–1952

7.	1 Florin 1937–45. Crowned head. Rev: Type of #1	125.00
8.	1 Shilling 1937–43. Rev: Type of #2	10.00
9.	6 Pence 1937–43. Rev: Type of #3	7.00
10.	1 Penny (C-N) 1937–41, '45, '49–52; (Bra) 1942–43. Type of #4	5.00
11.	½ Penny (C-N) 1940–41, '49–52; (Bra) 1942–43. Type of #4, smaller size	3.00

12.	3 Pence (N-Br) 1947, 1950–52. Rev: Native hut. (Dodecagonal planchet)	12.50

ELIZABETH II   1952–

13.	1 Florin (C-N) 1957–65. Crowned head. Rev: Arms	5.00
14.	1 Shilling (C-N) 1957–65. Rev: Native boat	8.00
15.	6 Pence (C-N) 1953–67. Rev: Turtle	1.75
16.	3 Pence (N-Br) 1955–67. Rev: Native hut. (Dodecagonal planchet)	1.00
17.	1 Penny (C-N) 1954–68. Center hole	.80

18.	½ Penny (C-N) 1954	2.50

FIJI (continued)

DECIMAL COINAGE

100 Cents = 1 Dollar

19. 1 Dollar (C-N) 1969, '76. Draped bust with
    coronet. Rev: Arms   10.00

20. 20 Cents (C-N) 1969– . Rev: Tabua (native cere-
    monial object)   1.00
21. 10 Cents (C-N) 1969. Rev: Ula tavatava (throw-
    ing club)   .75

22. 5 Cents (C-N) 1969– . Rev: Lali (drum)   .35
23. 2 Cents (Bro) 1969– . Rev: Fan   .25
24. 1 Cent (Bro) 1969–76. Rev: Tanoa (wooden
    bowl)   .15
24a. 1 Cent (Bro) 1977– . Elizabeth II. Rev: Plant,
    GROW MORE FOOD. (F.A.O. coin plan)   .35

25. 1 Dollar (C-N) 1970. Rev: Great Seal of Fijian
    Kingdom. (Independence)   35.00
25a. 1 Dollar 1970. Silver proof   185.00

26. 100 Dollars (G) 1974. Rev: Cakoban, king of Fiji
    Islands until 1874. (100th anniversary of ces-
    sion to Great Britain)   350.00
27. 25 Dollars 1974   65.00

28. 50 Cents (C-N) 1975– . Rev: Native sailing ship.
    (Dodecagonal planchet)   4.00

29. 1 Cent (Bro) 1977– . Rev: Rice. (F.A.O. coin
    plan)   .40
30. 10 Dollars 1977. Elizabeth II. Rev: Arms.
    (Queen's Silver Jubilee)   75.00
31. 250 Dollars (G) 1978. Rev: Banded iguana.
    (World Wildlife Conservation Program)   600.00
32. 25 Dollars 1978. Rev: Shell. (Wildlife Conserva-
    tion)   35.00
33. 10 Dollars 1978. Rev: Bird. (Wildlife Conserva-
    tion)   25.00
34. 50 Cents (C-N) 1979   5.00
35. 200 Dollars (G) 1980. Arms. Rev: Bust of Prince
    Charles. (10th anniversary of independence)   300.00
36. 10 Dollars 1980. (Independence anniversary)   40.00
37. 50 Cents (C-N) 1980. (Independence anniver-
    sary)   7.50
38. 10 Dollars 1981. Elizabeth II. Rev: Prince
    Charles. (Marriage of Prince Charles and
    Lady Diana.) Issued in proof only   60.00

FINLAND

Finland was part of the kingdom of Sweden until 1809 when it became an autonomous Grand Duchy of the Russian Empire. Finland declared its independence in 1917 and became a republic in 1919.

100 Pennia = 1 Markka

UNDER RUSSIAN RULE

1. 20 Markkaa (G) 1878–1913. Crowned double-headed eagle. Rev: Value in wreath   375.00
2. 10 Markkaa (G) 1878–1913   325.00

3. 2 Markkaa 1865–74, 1905–08   300.00
4. 1 Markka 1864–74, '90–93, 1907–08, '15   12.50
5. 50 Pennia 1864–74, '89–93, 1907–08, '11, '15–17   5.00

6. 25 Pennia 1865–76, '89–99, 1901–17   2.50

7. 10 Pennia (C) 1865–76, '89–91, '95–99, 1900–17. Crowned monogram. Rev: Value in wreath   5.00
8. 5 Pennia (C) 1865–75, '88–92, '96–99, 1901–17   3.00
9. 1 Penni (C) 1864–76, '81–99, 1901–16   1.00

REVOLUTIONARY PERIOD   1917–18

10. 50 Pennia 1917. Double-headed eagle without crown above. Rev: Value in wreath   7.00
11. 25 Pennia 1917   3.50
12. 10 Pennia (C) 1917   10.00
13. 5 Pennia (C) 1917   7.00
14. 1 Penni (C) 1917   3.50

15. 5 Pennia (C) 1918. Three trumpets. Rev: Value. (Communist issue)   85.00

REPUBLIC   1919–

16. 200 Markkaa (G) 1926. Lion on sword. Rev: Value and sprays   1750.00
17. 100 Markkaa (G) 1926   1250.00

18. 20 Markkaa (A-Bro) 1931–39. Arms in wreath. Rev: Value in wreath   10.00
19. 10 Markkaa (A-Bro) 1928–39   12.50
20. 5 Markkaa (A-Bro) 1928–42; (Bra) '46–49; (St) '51–52   3.00
21. 1 Markka (C-N) 1921–24, '28–40; (Bro) '40–43, '49–51; (I) '43–52. Lion on sword. Rev: Value   3.00
22. 50 Pennia (C-N) 1921–40; (Bro) '40–43; (I) '43–48   2.00
23. 25 Pennia (C-N) 1921–40; (Bro) '40–43; (I) '43–45   .75

24. 10 Pennia (Bro) 1919–40   1.50

25. 10 Pennia (Bro) 1941–42; (I) '43–45. Two pine branches. Rev: Value. (Center hole)   1.50
26. 5 Pennia (Bro) 1918–40. Lion on sword. Rev: Value   1.00
27. 5 Pennia (Bro) 1941–43. Type of #25   2.00
28. 1 Penni (Bro) 1919–24. Type of #26   1.25

FINLAND (continued)

POST-WAR COINAGE

29. 200 Markkaa 1956–59. Arms. Rev: Value — 8.00
30. 100 Markkaa 1956–60 — 6.50

31. 50 Markkaa (A-Bro) 1952–62. Lion on sword. Fir tree and value — 6.50
32. 20 Markkaa (A-Bro) 1952–62 — 5.00
33. 10 Markkaa (A-Bro) 1952–62 — 4.00

34. 5 Markkaa (I) 1952, '53; (N-I) 1953–62. Arms of St. Hans. Rev: Value — 1.00
35. 1 Markka (I) 1952, '53; (N-I) 1953–62 — .50

36. 500 Markkaa 1951–52. Chain links. Rev: Value in wreath. (15th Olympiad) — 50.00

37. 1000 Markkaa 1960. Bust of J. V. Snellman (Minister of Finance in 1860). Rev: Value in wreath. (Change from ruble currency to present markkaa system) — 40.00

38. 1 Markka 1964–68. Lion on sword. Rev: Value, background of trees — 5.00
38a. 1 Markka (C-N) 1969– — .75

39. 50 Pennia (A-Bro) 1963– . Rev: Value and tree — .85
40. 20 Pennia (A-Bro) 1963– — .25
41. 10 Pennia (A-Bro) 1963– — .25
42. 5 Pennia (Bro) 1963–77; (St) 1977– . Arms of St. Hans. Rev: Value — .25
43. 1 Penni (Bro) 1963–69; (Al) 1969– — .15

44. 10 Markkaa 1967. Five flying ospreys. Rev: Construction scene. (50th anniversary of independence) — 25.00

45. 10 Markkaa 1970. Portrait of Juho Kusti Paaskivi. Rev: Value on stone slabs. (100th anniversary of statesman's birth) — 17.50

46. 10 Markkaa 1971. View of Helsinki. Rev: Six
    runners. (10th European Athletic Champion-
    ships)   17.50

47. 5 Markkaa (A-Bro) 1972– . Icebreaker within
    heptagonal field. Rev: Value, birds   2.50

48. 10 Markkaa 1975. Portrait of Urho Kekkonen.
    Rev: Trees. (75th birthday of President)   17.50
49. 10 Markkaa 1977. Standing group. Rev: Inscrip-
    tion. (60th anniversary of independence)   17.50
50. 25 Markkaa 1978. View of Lahti. Rev: Skier.
    (Winter Games at Lahti)   20.00
51. 25 Markkaa 1979. View of Turku. Rev: Stylized
    fish design. (750th anniversary of Turku)   20.00
52. 50 Markkaa 1981. Portrait of Urho Kekkonen.
    (80th birthday of President)   20.00

FRANCE

Few countries have had as stormy a history as France. Since the abolition of the monarchy in 1792, this country has had three revolutions, five republics, two empires, one restoration of the monarchy, one provisional government, and several disastrous wars.

The constitution of the Fifth Republic adopted in 1958 created a French Community made up of the French Republic (Metropolitan Departments, Overseas Departments and Territories), Member States, and former possessions which retain only special relations with the Community.

The écu was a small coin using a shield (*écu*) as a device. The gold écu was replaced by the louis d'or in 1640. The denier was a minor coin, deriving from the Roman denarius.

100 Centimes = 1 Franc
12 Deniers = 1 Sol
3 Deniers = 1 Liard

LOUIS XIII   1610–43

| 1. | 1 Ecu 1641–43. Bust. Rev: Crowned arms | 650.00 |

2.	½ Ecu 1642–43	200.00
3.	¼ Ecu 1642–43	80.00
4.	1/12 Ecu 1642–43	40.00

| 5. | 1 Denier (C). Bust. Rev: Fleur-de-lis | 15.00 |

LOUIS XIV   1643–1715

| 6. | 1 Louis d'or (G) 1644–49, 1694–1701. Bust. Rev: Fleur-de-lis | 2500.00 |

| 7. | ½ Louis d'or (G) 1644–1709. Bust. Rev: Eight "L"s in form of cross | 1250.00 |

| 8. | 1 Ecu 1643–1715. Bust. Rev: Fleur-de-lis | 225.00 |

| 9. | ½ Ecu 1643–1715 | 75.00 |

18.   1 Ecu 1716–18. Boy's head. Rev: Arms   200.00

10.	¼ Ecu 1643–1715	35.00
11.	1⁄12 Ecu 1643–1715	25.00
12.	1 Liard (C) 1648–58, 1693–1713	17.50
13.	6 Deniers (C) 1710–13. Bust. Rev: Fleur-de-lis	15.00

19.   1 Ecu 1720–40. Young bust. Rev: Arms   150.00

14.	4 Deniers (C) 1692–1708	15.00

15.	2 Deniers (C) 1696–1700	10.00

LOUIS XV   1715–74

20.	1 Ecu 1740–74. Old head. Rev: Arms	100.00
21.	½ Ecu 1716–70	35.00
22.	¼ Ecu 1715–25	20.00

16.	1 Louis d'or (G) 1716–35, '47–73. Bust. Rev: Arms	850.00
17.	½ Louis d'or (G) 1716–43	500.00
23.	24 Sols 1726	30.00

FRANCE (continued)

24.	12 Sols 1743–71	20.00
25.	6 Sols 1743–79	20.00

26.	1 Sol (C) 1719–23, '66–74. Bust. Rev: Arms	10.00
27.	½ Sol (C) 1720–23, '67–74	10.00

LOUIS XVI   1774–93

28.	Double Louis d'or (G) 1775–92	750.00

29.	1 Louis d'or (G) 1768–92. Bust. Rev: Oval shield	425.00

30.	1 Ecu 1774–92. Bust. Rev: Shield	60.00

31.	½ Ecu 1780–92	30.00
32.	⅕ Ecu 1777–90	17.50
33.	⅒ Ecu 1786–90	10.00

CONSTITUTIONAL PERIOD   1789–93

34.	12 Deniers (C or Bra) 1791–93	15.00
35.	6 Deniers (C or Bra) 1791–93	25.00
36.	3 Deniers (C or Bra) 1791–93	25.00

37.	1 Ecu 1792–93. Bust of Louis XVI. Rev: Angel	275.00

FIRST REPUBLIC   1793–1804

One of the most startling reforms ushered in by the French Revolution was a new calendar starting on September 22, 1792, the formal opening date of the new republic. There were twelve months of thirty days each (Vendémiaire, Brumaire, Frimaire, Nivôse, Pluviôse, Ventôse, Germinal, Floréal, Prairial, Messidor, Thermidor, and Fructidor) plus five feast days to fill out the year. The new era was numbered from the Year I.

38.	1 Ecu (6 Livres) 1793–94 (Years II–III). Angel	400.00

FRANCE (continued)

39. 2 Sols (Bro) 1793 (Year II). Tablet. Rev: Scales 40.00
40. 1 Sol (Bro) 1793 20.00
40a. ½ Sol (Bro) 1793 150.00

DIRECTORY 1795–1799

41. 5 Francs Years IV–VII (1795–99). Hercules group. Rev: Value 80.00

42. 2 Decimes (20 Centimes; C) Years IV–V. Head of Republic. Rev: Value in wreath 50.00
43. 1 Decime (C) Years IV–VII 7.00
44. 5 Centimes (C) Years IV–VII 4.00

45. 1 Centime (C) Years VI–VII 3.50

CONSULATE 1799–1804

46. 5 Francs Years VIII–XI (1799–1803). Hercules group, type of #41 80.00

47. 5 Francs Years XI–XII. Bare head of Bonaparte, First Consul. Rev: Value 150.00
48. 2 Francs Year XII 100.00
49. 1 Franc Years XI–XII 65.00
50. ½ Franc Years XI–XII 50.00
51. ¼ Franc Year XII 65.00
52. 1 Decime (10 Centimes; C) Years VIII–IX 7.00
53. 5 Centimes (C) Years VIII–IX 5.00
54. 1 Centime (C) Year VIII 15.00

FIRST EMPIRE
NAPOLEON 1804–14, 1815

55. 40 Francs (G) 1807–13. Laureate head 375.00
56. 20 Francs (G) 1807–15 150.00

57. 5 Francs Years XII–XIV (1804–05), 1806–07 bare head; 1807–08 laureate head. Rev: Value in wreath, REPUBLIQUE FRANÇAISE 125.00

58. 5 Francs 1809–14. Laureate head. Rev: Value,
    EMPIRE FRANÇAISE 60.00
59. 5 Francs 1815. Type of #58. (The famous
    "Hundred Days" coin struck after Napoleon's
    return from Elba) 175.00
60. 2 Francs Years XII–XIV (1804–05), 1806–14 ... 50.00
61. 1 Franc Years XII–XIV (1804–05), 1806–14 ... 25.00
62. ½ Franc Years XII–XIV (1804–05), 1806–14 ... 12.50
63. ¼ Franc Years XII–XIV (1804–05), 1806–09 ... 25.00

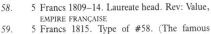

64. 10 Centimes (Billon) 1808–10. Value. Rev:
    Large "N" 4.00
65. 5 Centimes (C) 1808 .... 125.00

BOURBON RESTORATION

LOUIS XVIII   1814–15, 1815–24

66. 20 Francs (G) 1814–24 .... 175.00

67. 5 Francs 1814–15 (First Restoration). Head.
    Rev: Shield, PIECE DE 5 FRANCS 75.00

68. 5 Francs 1816–24 (Second Restoration). Bust.
    Rev: Shield 35.00
69. 2 Francs 1816–24 .... 40.00
70. 1 Franc 1816–24 .... 50.00
71. ½ Franc 1816–24 .... 80.00
72. ¼ Franc 1817–24 .... 60.00

CHARLES X   1824–30

73. 20 Francs (G) 1825–30. Bust, head right 175.00

74. 5 Francs 1824–30. Head. Rev: Arms 40.00

75.	2 Francs 1825–30	120.00
76.	1 Franc 1825–30	40.00
77.	½ Franc 1825–30	30.00
78.	¼ Franc 1825–30	10.00

LOUIS PHILIPPE 1830–48

79.	20 Francs (G) 1830–48. Bust, head left	175.00

80.	5 Francs 1830–31. Bare head. Rev: Value	30.00

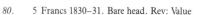

81.	5 Francs 1831–48. Laureated head	20.00
82.	2 Francs 1831–48	60.00
83.	1 Franc 1831–48	17.50
84.	½ Franc 1831–45	12.50
85.	¼ Franc 1831–45	5.00
86.	50 Centimes 1845–48	10.00
87.	25 Centimes 1845–48	6.50

SECOND REPUBLIC 1848–52

88.	20 Francs (G) 1848–49. Angel	150.00
88a.	20 Francs (G) 1849–51. Ceres	150.00

89.	10 Francs (G) 1850–51. Ceres	125.00

90.	5 Francs 1848–49. Hercules group	20.00

91.	5 Francs 1849–51. Ceres head	25.00

92.	2 Francs 1849–51	200.00
93.	1 Franc 1849–51	40.00
94.	50 Centimes 1849–51	20.00
95.	20 Centimes 1849–51	15.00

96.	1 Centime (C) 1848–51	3.00

FRANCE (continued)

97. 5 Francs 1852. Head of Louis Bonaparte as
President. Rev: Value in wreath 75.00
98. 1 Franc 1852 .... 150.00
99. 50 Centimes 1852 .... 225.00

SECOND EMPIRE
NAPOLEON III   1852–70

100. 20 Francs (G) 1853–70 150,00
101. 10 Francs (G) 1855–69 .... 80.00
102. 5 Francs (G) 1854–69 .... 80.00

103. 5 Francs 1854–59. Bare head 50.00

104. 5 Francs 1861–70. Laureate head 20.00

105. 2 Francs 1853–59. Bust. Rev: Value in wreath   400.00
105a. 2 Francs 1866–70. Type of #104 .... 25.00
106. 1 Franc 1853–64. Type of #105 .... 35.00
106a. 1 Franc 1866–70. Type of #104 .... 10.00
107. 50 Centimes 1853–63. Type of #105 ...... 30.00
107a. 50 Centimes 1864–69. Laureated bust. Rev:
Crown 10.00
108. 20 Centimes 1853–63. Type of #105 ...... 10.00
108a. 20 Centimes 1864–66. Type of #107a 12.50

109. 10 Centimes (C) 1852–65 .... 7.00
110. 5 Centimes (C) 1853–65 .... 2.50
111. 2 Centimes (C) 1853–63 .... 1.50
112. 1 Centime (C) 1853–70 .... 1.50

THIRD REPUBLIC   1870–1940

113. 20 Francs (G) 1871–98. Angel 120.00

113a. 10 Francs (G) 1889–99. Ceres 80.00

114. 5 Francs 1870–78. Hercules group 15.00

126.	1 Franc 1898–1920	5.00
127.	50 Centimes 1897–1920	3.00

128.	25 Centimes (N) 1903	2.50
128a.	25 Centimes (N) 1904–05. Rev: Fasces	1.50

115.	5 Francs 1870–71. Ceres head	65.00
116.	2 Francs 1870–95. Ceres head	20.00
117.	1 Franc 1871–95	5.00
118.	50 Centimes 1871–95	4.00

129.	10 Centimes (C) 1898–1921. Head of Republic	1.25
130.	5 Centimes (C) 1898–1921	1.00
131.	2 Centimes (C) 1898–1920. Rev: Value	2.50
132.	1 Centime (C) 1898–1920	1.50

133.	100 Francs (G) 1935–36. Head of Republic	1000.00

119.	10 Centimes (C) 1870–98. Ceres	3.50
120.	5 Centimes (C) 1871–98	2.00
121.	2 Centimes (C) 1877–97	2.50
122.	1 Centime (C) 1872–97	1.50

123.	20 Francs (G) 1899–1914. Head of Republic. Rev: Rooster	140.00
124.	10 Francs (G) 1899–1914	75.00

134.	20 Francs 1929–38. Head of Republic	20.00
135.	10 Francs (S) 1929–39; (C-N) 1945–50	1.50

125.	2 Francs 1898–1920. Sower walking	12.50

136.	5 Francs (N) 1933. Liberty head. Rev: Value	8.50

FRANCE (continued)

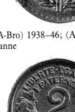

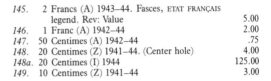

136a. 5 Francs (N) 1933–38; (A-Bro) 1938–46; (A)
1945–52. Head of Marianne   3.00

145. 2 Francs (A) 1943–44. Fasces, ETAT FRANÇAIS
legend. Rev: Value   5.00
146. 1 Franc (A) 1942–44   2.00
147. 50 Centimes (A) 1942–44   .75
148. 20 Centimes (Z) 1941–44. (Center hole)   4.00
148a. 20 Centimes (I) 1944   125.00
149. 10 Centimes (Z) 1941–44   3.00

137. 2 Francs (A-Bro) 1931–41; (A) 1941–59   .35
137a. 2 Francs (Bra) 1944. FRANCE in wreath. Rev:
Value. (Allied occupation issue)   10.00
138. 1 Franc (A-Bro) 1931–41; (A) 1941–59   .75
139. 50 Centimes (A-Bro) 1931–41; (A) 1941–47   1.00

FOURTH REPUBLIC 1946–58

150. 100 Francs (C-N) 1954–58. Liberty head. Rev:
Value   5.00

140. 25 Centimes (N) 1914–17; (C-N) 1917–38; (N-
Bro) 1938–40. (Center hole)   .75
141. 20 Centimes (Z) 1945–46   20.00
142. 10 Centimes (N) 1914; (C-N) 1917–38; (N-Br)
1938–39; (Z) 1941–46   .50
143. 5 Centimes (C-N) 1917–38; (N-Br) 1938–39   1.00

151. 50 Francs (A-Bro) 1950–58   3.50

WARTIME VICHY ISSUES

144. 5 Francs (C-N) 1941. Marshal Pétain. Rev:
Fasces and value   175.00

152. 20 Francs (A-Bro) 1950–54   3.00

153. 10 Francs (A-Bro) 1950–58   3.00

FIFTH REPUBLIC 1958–

NEW STANDARD (Heavy Franc)

100 Old Francs = 1 New Franc

154. 10 Francs 1964–73. Hercules group. Rev: Value
in wreath. (Type of Nos. 41, 90, 114)   30.00

155. 5 Francs 1960–69. Sower. Rev: Laurel branch
and value   12.50
156. 1 Franc (N) 1960–   .60
157. ½ Franc (N) 1965–   .30

158. 50 Centimes (A-Bro) 1962–64. Liberty head.
Rev: Value   1.00
159. 20 Centimes (A-Bro) 1962–   .25
160. 10 Centimes (A-Bro) 1962–   .20
161. 5 Centimes (A-Bro) 1966–   .15

162. 5 Centimes (St) 1961–64. Wheat stalk. Rev:
Value   .25
163. 1 Centime (St) 1962–   .10
164. 5 Francs (C-N) 1970– . Type of #155   5.00
165. 50 Francs 1974– . Type of #154   20.00

166. 10 Francs (C-N-A) 1974– . Modernistic map of
France. Rev: Construction scene   4.00
167. 50 Francs 1974– . Hercules group. Rev: Value in
wreath. (Type of #154, etc.)   25.00

FRENCH EQUATORIAL AFRICA

Up to 1910 this overseas territory was known as French Congo. French Equatorial Africa was made up of Gabon and Middle Congo (on the Atlantic coast) and Ubangi-Shari and Chad (q.v.; both further inland). In 1960 these areas became independent member states of the French Community, Middle Congo eventually taking the name of People's Republic of the Congo (q.v.) and Ubangi-Shari becoming the Central African Republic (q.v.).

100 Centimes = 1 Franc

1. 1 Franc (Bra) 1942; (Bro) 1943. Rooster. Rev: Cross of Lorraine   12.50

2. 50 Centimes (Bra) 1942; (Br) 1943   10.00

3. 2 Francs (A) 1948. Bust of Republic. Rev: Antelope head   4.00
4. 1 Franc (A) 1948   1.50

NOTE: In 1958 coinage was combined with that of Cameroon (q.v.)

FRENCH GUIANA

Formerly a French colony on the northeast coast of South America, it is now an overseas department in the French Community. It was used as a penal colony (including the famous Devil's Island) from about 1795 on. In 1945 this policy was discontinued and the French government removed all the prisoners.

100 Centimes = 1 Franc

1. 10 Centimes (base metal, silvered) 1818, 1846. Crowned monogram. Rev: Value   40.00

FRENCH POLYNESIA

This colony, also known as French Establishments in Oceania, is made up of 105 islands in the South Pacific. The chief ones are the Society Islands (including Tahiti), Marquesas Islands, Tubuai Islands, Tuamotu Islands, and Gambier Islands. Its full name is Overseas Territory of French Polynesia.

100 Centimes = 1 Franc

1.	5 Francs (A) 1952. Seated female figure. Rev: Island scene	7.50
2.	2 Francs (A) 1949	6.00
3.	1 Franc (A) 1949	3.00
4.	50 Centimes (A) 1949	4.00

5.	5 Francs (A) 1965– . Seated figure. Rev: Island scene, new legend	3.00
6.	2 Francs (A) 1965–	1.50
7.	1 Franc (A) 1965–	1.00
8.	50 Centimes (A) 1965	2.00

9.	50 Francs (N) 1967– . Head of Republic. Rev: Native harbor scene	7.50

10.	20 Francs (N) 1967– . Head of Republic. Rev: Native plants and flowers	4.00
11.	10 Francs (N) 1967– . Rev: Native mask	3.50
12.	100 Francs (N-Bro) 1976– . Type of #9	7.50

FRENCH SOMALILAND

This former French overseas territory, located on the Gulf of Aden in eastern Africa, in 1967 became French Territory of the Afars and Issas (q.v.). On June 27, 1977 independence was achieved; it is now the Republic of Djibouti (q.v.).

100 Centimes = 1 Franc

NOTE: Coins dated 1959 drop UNION FRANÇAISE from inscription

1.	5 Francs (A) 1948, '59, '65. Bust of Republic. Rev: Antelope head	3.00
2.	2 Francs (A) 1948, '59, '65	1.50
3.	1 Franc (A) 1948, '59, '65	1.00

4.	20 Francs (A-Bro) 1952, '65. Republic. Rev: Arabian dhow in foreground	3.00
5.	10 Francs (A-Bro) 1965	4.00

FRENCH WEST AFRICA

A former French overseas territory made up of Dahomey, French Guinea, French Sudan (now Mali), Ivory Coast, Mauritania, Niger, Senegal, and Upper Volta. During 1958–60 it was broken up into independent nations within the French Community. (See also West African States.)

100 Centimes = 1 Franc

1.	1 Franc (A-Bro) 1944. Head of Republic. Rev: Value	6.50
2.	50 Centimes (A-Bro) 1944	10.00

3.	2 Francs (A) 1948–55. Bust of Republic. Rev: Antelope head	1.00
4.	1 Franc (A) 1948–55	1.00
5.	25 Francs (A-Bro) 1956	2.50
6.	10 Francs (A-Bro) 1956	1.50
7.	5 Francs (A-Bro) 1956	1.25

NOTE: At this point coinage was unified with Togo

8.	25 Francs (A-Bro) 1957	2.00
9.	10 Francs (A-Bro) 1957	3.50

GABON

An independent republic in western Africa. (See also Central African States.)

1. 100 Francs (N) 1971, '72. Antelope. Rev. Value   3.00

THE GAMBIA

Formerly a British colony and protectorate in western Africa, the Gambia gained independence in 1965 and proclaimed a republic in 1970.

1. 4 Shillings (C-N) 1966. Draped bust of Queen Elizabeth with coronet. Rev: Crocodile   5.00

2. 2 Shillings (C-N) 1966. Rev: Head of wildebeest   2.00

3. 1 Shilling (C-N) 1966. Rev: Palm tree   1.25

4. 6 Pence (C-N) 1966. Rev: Groundnuts   .65

5. 3 Pence (N-Bra) 1966. Rev: Bush fowl   .35
6. 1 Penny (Bro) 1966. Rev: Native sailboat   .40

7.   8 Shillings (C-N) 1970. Rev: Hippopotamus   10.00
7a. 8 Shillings (S) 1970   50.00

DECIMAL COINAGE

100 Bututs = 1 Dalasi

8.   1 Dalasi (C-N) 1971. Portrait of Sir Dawda Kai-
     raba Jawara. Rev: Type of #1   5.00
9.   50 Bututs (C-N) 1971. Rev: Type of #2   1.50
10. 25 Bututs (C-N) 1971. Rev: Type of #3   1.00
11. 10 Bututs (N-Bra) 1971. Rev: Type of #5   .50
12. 5 Bututs (Bro) 1971. Rev: Type of #6   .30
13. 1 Butut (Bro) 1971–75. Rev: Type of #4   .25

14. 1 Butut (Bro) 1974. Type of #13, with FOOD FOR
     MANKIND inscription added to reverse   .25

15. 10 Dalasi 1975. Rev: Arms. (10th anniversary of
     independence)   20.00

16. 500 Dalasis (G) 1977. President Jawara. Rev:
     Wildebeest. (World Wildlife Conservation
     Program)   500.00
17. 40 Dalasis 1977. (Wildlife Conservation)   35.00
18. 20 Dalasis 1977. (Wildlife Conservation)   25.00

GERMAN EAST AFRICA

After World War I Germany lost this colony. It was divided up into three regions and mandated to Britain, Belgium and Portugal. These regions eventually became Tanzania, Rwanda and Burundi.

100 Heller = 1 Rupee

GERMAN EAST AFRICA COMPANY

1.	2 Rupees 1893–94. Helmeted Kaiser Wilhelm II. Rev: Arms	600.00
2.	1 Rupee 1890–1902	25.00
3.	½ Rupee 1891–1901	30.00
4.	¼ Rupee 1891–1901	10.00

5.	1 Pesa (C) 1890–92. German eagle. Rev: Arabic inscription	7.50

GERMAN EAST AFRICA

6.	15 Rupees (G) 1916. Elephant and mountains. Rev: German eagle	1000.00

7.	1 Rupee 1904–14. Helmeted Kaiser Wilhelm II. Rev: Value in wreath	20.00
8.	½ Rupee 1904–14	25.00
9.	¼ Rupee 1904–14	12.50

10.	10 Heller (C-N) 1908–11, '14. Crown over center hole. Rev: Value and sprays	10.00
11.	5 Heller (C-N) 1913–14	10.00

12.	5 Heller (Bro) 1908–'09. Crown. Rev: Value in wreath	30.00
13.	1 Heller (Bro) 1904–13	3.00
14.	½ Heller (Bro) 1904–06	5.00

15.	20 Heller (Bra) 1916. Crown and date. Rev: Value in wreath	12.50
15a.	20 Heller (C) 1916	15.00
16.	5 Heller (Bra) 1916	10.00

GERMAN NEW GUINEA

A German colony from 1884 to 1914, this included the northeastern part of the island of New Guinea as well as some smaller islands. Mandated to Australia in 1920, it is now part of the independent nation Papua New Guinea (q.v.; see also New Guinea).

100 Pfennigs = 1 Mark

1.	5 Marks 1894. Bird of paradise. Rev: Value	1000.00
2.	2 Marks 1894	300.00
3.	1 Mark 1894	250.00
4.	½ Mark 1894	275.00

5.	10 Pfennigs (C) 1894	100.00

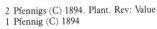

6.	2 Pfennigs (C) 1894. Plant. Rev: Value	150.00
7.	1 Pfennig (C) 1894	85.00

GERMANY

Until 1871 Germany was made up of independent states and cities which had separate rulers, laws, taxes, armies, and coinage. After these states and cities were welded into the German Empire, the issuing of new coinage was divided into two categories.

Gold coins, as well as silver coins of 2, 3 and 5 marks or more, continued to be issued by the states and cities. Coins of the states carry a portrait of the ruler on the obverse, and a crowned eagle on the reverse. (A smaller eagle is found on coins issued before 1889; a larger one on coins issued from 1891 on.) Coins issued by the Empire carry an eagle on the obverse and the value in a wreath on the reverse.

This system was maintained until 1918, when the coinage of the states and cities came to an end. (See also "Danzig," p. 128.)

100 Pfennigs = 1 Mark

GERMAN EMPIRE

1.	1 Mark 1873–87. Small eagle	10.00

2.	1 Mark 1891–1916. Large eagle	5.00
3.	50 Pfennigs 1875–78, 1896–1903	15.00
4.	½ Mark 1905–09, '11–19	3.00
5.	25 Pfennigs (N) 1909–12	12.50

6.	20 Pfennigs (S) 1873–77; (C-N) '87–88, '90, '92	10.00
7.	10 Pfennigs (C-N) 1873–76, 1888–1916; (I) 1915–22; (Z) '17–22	.50
8.	5 Pfennigs (C-N) 1874–76, 1888–1915; (I) 1915–22	.35

9.	2 Pfennigs (C) 1873–77, 1904–16	.30
10.	1 Pfennig (C) 1873–1916	.65
11.	1 Pfennig (A) 1916–18	1.00

GERMAN STATES

The coinage of the German states and cities was large and varied. Many of the pre-1800 coins are strikingly colorful pieces. (See also "Westphalia," p. 561.)

Anhalt

A duchy of central Germany, made up of Bernburg, Dessau and Cothen.

BERNBURG LINE

12.	Taler 1806, '09. Arms. Rev: Value in wreath	650.00

ALEXIUS FRIEDRICH CHRISTIAN   1796–1834

ALEXANDER CARL   1834–63

13.	Double Taler 1840–55. Head. Rev: Crowned arms in mantle	600.00
14.	Taler 1859. Head. Rev: Crowned and supported arms	100.00
15.	Mining Taler 1834. Crowned arms in mantle. Rev: Inscription	75.00

16. Mining Taler 1846–62. Crowned bear on wall. Rev. Inscription   65.00

NOTE: On the death of Alexander Carl the Bernburg territory united with Dessau

COTHEN LINE
HEINRICH 1830–47

17. Double Taler 1840. Head. Rev. Helmeted and supported arms   1250.00

NOTE: On the death of Heinrich the Cothen territory united with Dessau

DESSAU LINE
LEOPOLD FRIEDRICH 1817–71

18. Double Taler 1839–46. Head. Rev: Crowned arms in mantle   750.00
19. Taler 1858–69. Head. Rev: Crowned and supported arms   75.00
20. Taler 1863. Head. Rev: Shield in sprays. (Commemorating separation of duchies in 1603 and reunion in 1863)   80.00

FRIEDRICH I 1871–1904

21. 20 Marks (G) 1875. Head. Rev: Eagle   1000.00
22. 2 Marks 1876   300.00
23. 20 Marks (G) 1896. (25th anniversary of reign)   1000.00
24. 10 Marks (G) 1896   900.00

25. 5 Marks 1896   1100.00
26. 2 Marks 1896   300.00
27. 20 Marks (G) 1901. (70th birthday)   1000.00
28. 10 Marks (G) 1901. (70th birthday)   900.00

FRIEDRICH II 1904–18

29. 20 Marks (G) 1904. Head. Rev: Eagle   850.00

30. 5 Marks 1914. Accoladed heads of the Duke and Duchess. (Silver wedding)   250.00
31. 3 Marks 1909–11. Head. Rev: Eagle   85.00
32. 3 Marks 1914. Type of #30. (Silver wedding)   60.00
33. 2 Marks 1904. Type of #29   275.00

Baden

A grand duchy located in the southwest corner of Germany.

CARL FRIEDRICH 1738–1811

34. Taler 1803. Large head. Rev: Crowned shield in sprays   1000.00
35. Taler 1809–11. Small head. Rev: Crowned shield over sprays   600.00

CARL LUDWIG FRIEDRICH 1811–18

36. Kronen Taler 1813–19. Crowned and mantled shield. Rev: Value in wreath   250.00

LUDWIG 1818–30

37. Taler 1819–21. Head. Rev: Crowned arms in mantle   325.00
38. 2 Gulden 1821–25. Head. Rev: Crowned shield in sprays   200.00

39. Taler 1829–30. Head. Crowned arms in wreath   150.00

GERMANY: States (continued)

LEOPOLD 1830–52

40. Kronen Taler 1830–37. Head. Rev: Crowned and supported shield   125.00
41. Kronen Taler 1832. Head. Rev: Inscription. (Rare; visit of their highnesses and children to mint)   1000.00

45. Double Taler 1841–43. Head. Rev: Value in wreath   250.00
46. Double Taler 1844. Head. Rev: Statue. (Erection of statue to his father)   350.00

42. Mining Taler 1836. Head. Rev: Crown above crossed hammers   300.00

47. Double Taler 1845–52. Head. Rev: Crowned, mantled, and supported arms   300.00

43. Mining Taler 1836. Head. Rev: Griffin with shield   300.00

48. 2 Gulden 1846–52. Head. Rev: Crowned and supported arms   100.00

FRIEDRICH (Regent) 1852–56

44. Kronen Taler 1836. Head. Rev: Inscription within circle of shields of ten German states. (Commemorating a customs union of the German states)   150.00

49. Double Taler 1852–55. Head. Rev: Crowned, mantled, and supported arms   1250.00

50.	2 Gulden 1856. Head. Rev: Crowned arms supported by griffons	450.00

FRIEDRICH I   1856–1907

51.	Taler 1857–65. Head. Rev: Crowned, mantled, supported arms	75.00
52.	Taler 1865–71. Bearded head	75.00

53.	20 Marks (G) 1872–74. Head. Rev: Small eagle	225.00
54.	10 Marks (G) 1872–88	200.00
55.	5 Marks (G) 1877	225.00

56.	5 Marks 1875–88. Rev: Small eagle	75.00
57.	2 Marks 1876–88	120.00
58.	20 Marks (G) 1894–95. Head. Rev: Large eagle	150.00

59.	10 Marks (G) 1890–1901	225.00
60.	5 Marks 1891–1902	65.00
61.	2 Marks 1892–1902	75.00

62.	5 Marks 1902. (50th year of reign)	85.00
63.	2 Marks 1902	20.00
64.	10 Marks (G) 1902–07. Head with long beard. Rev: Eagle	200.00
65.	5 Marks 1902–07	65.00
66.	2 Marks 1902–07	20.00

67.	5 Marks 1906. Heads of Friedrich and Louise. (Golden wedding)	125.00
68.	2 Marks 1906	25.00
69.	5 Marks 1907. (Death of Grand Duke)	150.00
70.	2 Marks 1907	25.00

FRIEDRICH II   1907–18

71.	20 Marks (G) 1911–14. Head. Rev: Eagle	200.00
72.	10 Marks (G) 1909–13	275.00

73.	5 Marks 1908, '13	85.00
74.	3 Marks 1908–15	20.00
75.	2 Marks 1911–13	300.00

Bavaria

A kingdom in southernmost Germany.

MAXIMILIAN JOSEPH 1806–25

79. Double Taler 1839–41. Bare head. Rev: Value
    in wreath 120.00
80. Double Taler 1842–48. Bare head. Rev:
    Crowned and supported arms 115.00

76. Taler 1806–25. Bust. Rev: Arms and suppor-
    ters. (Varieties) 120.00

77. Taler 1809–25. Bare head. Rev: Crown over
    crossed mace and sword 65.00

81. 2 Gulden 1845–48 ...... 45.00

NOTE: During Ludwig's reign a series of beautiful commemorative Talers (1825–37) and Double Talers (1837–48)
was issued in addition to the regular coinage. Current
prices average $250 for Talers and $350 for Double Talers.

LUDWIG I 1825–48

MAXIMILIAN II 1848–64

82. Double Taler 1849–64. Head. Rev: Crowned
    and supported arms 160.00

83. Taler 1857–64 ...... 35.00
84. 2 Gulden 1848–56 ...... 40.00

NOTE: During Maximilian's reign commemorative
Double Talers were struck 1848–56

78. Taler 1826–37. Bare head. Rev: Crown in
    wreath 100.00

GERMANY: States (continued)

LUDWIG II   1864–86

OTTO   1886–1913

LUDWIG III 1913–18

104.	20 Marks (G) 1914. Head. Rev: Eagle	2000.00
105.	5 Marks 1914	175.00
106.	3 Marks 1914	35.00
106a.	2 Marks 1914	75.00

107.   3 Marks 1918. (Golden wedding anniversary) 10,000.00

110.	Taler 1865. Type of #108. (Second German shooting festival)	75.00
111.	Taler 1871. Type of #108. (Victory in Franco-Prussian War)	85.00
112.	20 Marks (G) 1906. Crowned and supported arms of Bremen. Rev: Eagle	800.00
113.	10 Marks (G) 1907	700.00

114.	5 Marks 1906	175.00
115.	2 Marks 1904	75.00

Bremen (Free City)

This important commercial city on the North Sea became a "free city" in 1646.

108.   Taler 1863. Inscription. Rev: Crowned and supported arms. (50th anniversary of War of Liberation)   100.00

109.   Taler 1864. Rev: Building. (Opening of new Bremen Bourse)   165.00

Brunswick (Braunschweig)

A duchy in north central Germany, famous for its remarkable coinage in the 16th, 17th and 18th centuries.

HEINRICH JULIUS 1589–1613

116.   Taler. Wild man. Rev: Arms   300.00

FRIEDRICH ULRICH   1613–34

AUGUST II   1634–66

118.   Taler. Bell over city. Rev: Arms   500.00

117.   Triple taler. Duke on horseback. Rev: Arms   3500.00

119.   1¼ Taler. Four fields with Neptune on dolphin,
       heron baiting, mine, alchemy. Rev: Fortuna
       on globe, sailing ship in background   750.00

120. Taler 1636. Duke August holding helmet. Rev:
His brothers Friedrich and George   250.00

RUDOLPH AUGUST   1666–84

121. Taler. Wild man. Rev: Arms   200.00

RUDOLPH AUGUST and ANTON ULRICH
(Joint rulers)   1685–1704

122. Broad Taler. Conjoined heads. Rev: Insignia   300.00

123. 24 Mariengroschen (½ Taler). Wild man. Rev:
Value   85.00

ANTON ULRICH   1704–14

124. Taler. Wild man. Rev: Arms   125.00
125. 24 Mariengroschen   60.00

AUGUST WILHELM   1714–31

126. Taler. Wild man. Rev: Arms   125.00
127. 24 Mariengroschen   60.00
128. 6 Mariengroschen   25.00
129. 2 Mariengroschen   17.50

LUDWIG RUDOLPH   1731–35

130. Taler. Bust. Rev: Arms   250.00

CARL I   1735–80

131. Taler   250.00
132. 24 Mariengroschen   50.00

133. 4 Mariengroschen   20.00

134. 2 Mariengroschen   17.50

KARL WILHELM FERDINAND   1780–1806

135. 16 Groschen. Arms. Rev. Value   40.00

KARL FRIEDRICH WILHELM   1815–23

NOTE: Under guardianship of George, Prince Regent and
later King (George IV) of England

136. 24 Groschen 1815–23. Crowned arms. Rev:
Value and legend   50.00

137. ¹⁄₁₂ Taler 1816–23. Running horse. Rev: Value   12.50
138. 1 Groschen 1819–21   10.00
139. 6 Pfennigs 1816–23   7.00
140. 4 Pfennigs 1823   7.00
141. 2 Pfennigs (C) 1820, '23   7.00
142. 1 Pfennig (C) 1816–23   4.00

WILHELM   1831–84

143. Double Taler 1842–55. Head. Rev: Crowned
and mantled arms   150.00

144. Double Taler 1856. Rev: Arms in wreath. (25th
year of reign)   175.00
145. Taler 1837–71. Head. Rev: Crowned and mantled arms. (Varieties)   75.00

146. 20 Marks (G) 1875. Head. Rev: Eagle   700.00

NOTE: Brunswick was governed by Prussia from
1884 to 1913

GERMANY: States (continued)

ERNST AUGUST 1913–18

147. 5 Marks, 1915. Accolated heads of Ernst August and Victoria Luise. Rev: Eagle. (Ernst August's accession to the duchy) 1500.00
148. 3 Marks 1915 850.00

152. Taler 1857–58. Bust of Franconia with towers in background. Rev: Eagle 250.00
153. Taler 1859–65. Type of #152 (no towers) 50.00

Frankfurt am Main (Free City)

Located in the Prussian province of Hesse-Nassau, Frankfurt was a free city as early as 1219.

154. 2 Gulden 1845–56. Arms of city (eagle). Rev: Value in wreath 100.00
155. 1 Gulden 1859, '61 50.00
156. ½ Gulden 1842–49 40.00

NOTE: In addition to regular coinage Frankfurt issued a series of beautiful commemorative coins 1848–63. Current prices average from $100 to $750.

Hamburg (Free City)

Located on the North Sea, Hamburg is Germany's leading port. It became a free city in the 13th century.

157. 48 Schillings 1761–63. Lion. Rev: Eagle 75.00
158. 32 Schillings 1795–96 30.00
159. 16 Schillings 1727 25.00
160. 8 Schillings 1726–97 20.00
161. 4 Schillings 1725–38 12.50
162. 2 Schillings 1727 10.00

149. Double Taler 1840–44. View of city and river. Rev: Value in wreath 200.00
150. Double Taler 1841–55. Arms (eagle). Rev: Value in wreath 165.00
151. Double Taler 1860–66. Bust of Franconia. Rev: Eagle 100.00

163. 32 Schillings 1808. City towers. Rev: Inscription 65.00

164.	20 Marks (G) 1875–89. Arms of city. Rev: Small eagle	175.00
165.	10 Marks (G) 1873–88	150.00

166.	5 Marks (G) 1877	300.00

167.	5 Marks 1875–88. Arms of city. Rev: Small eagle	40.00
168.	20 Marks (G) 1893–1913. Rev: Large eagle	150.00
169.	10 Marks (G) 1890–1913	150.00
170.	5 Marks 1891–1913	25.00
171.	3 Marks 1908–14	12.50
172.	2 Marks 1892–1914	20.00

Hannover

A kingdom located in northwest Germany. From 1714 to 1837 the kings of Hannover were also kings of England.

GEORG I   1714–27

173.	Taler 1716–27. Bust of King	225.00
174.	⅔ Taler 1715–27	50.00
175.	⅓ Taler 1716–26	20.00
176.	⅙ Taler 1726–36	17.50
177.	Taler 1717–27. Wild man and tree	85.00
178.	⅔ Taler 1717–27	35.00
179.	⅓ Taler 1718–27	15.00
180.	⅙ Taler 1720–25	10.00
181.	Taler 1718–26. St. Andrew with cross	65.00
182.	⅓ Taler 1719–24	15.00
183.	⅙ Taler 1719–24	10.00
184.	Taler 1717–27. Running horse	60.00
185.	⅔ Taler 1722–27	30.00
186.	⅓ Taler 1720–23	20.00
187.	⅙ Taler 1719–27	12.50

GEORG II   1727–60

188.	Taler 1729–51. Bust of King	150.00
189.	⅔ Taler 1727–54	40.00
190.	⅓ Taler 1729–36	20.00
191.	⅙ Taler 1727–46	20.00
192.	Taler 1727–50. Wild man and tree	50.00
193.	⅔ Taler 1727–60	30.00
194.	⅓ Taler 1731–60	12.50
195.	⅙ Taler 1730–60	12.50
196.	Taler 1727–60. St. Andrew with cross	75.00
197.	⅓ Taler 1731–58	25.00
198.	⅙ Taler 1727–59	15.00
199.	Taler 1729–60. Running horse	65.00
200.	⅔ Taler 1727–60	35.00
201.	⅓ Taler 1734–54	20.00
202.	⅙ Taler 1727–32	12.50

GEORG III   1760–1820

203.	Taler 1773–1801. Bust of King	100.00
204.	⅔ Taler 1772–1814	40.00
205.	⅓ Taler 1774–1804	25.00
206.	⅙ Taler 1773–1807	15.00
207.	Taler 1764–76. Wild man and tree	60.00
208.	⅔ Taler 1762–89	20.00
209.	⅓ Taler 1764–89	15.00
210.	⅙ Taler 1762–1804	10.00
211.	Taler 1764–76. St. Andrew with cross	80.00
212.	⅓ Taler 1764–1804	25.00
213.	⅙ Taler 1761–1804	15.00
214.	⅔ Taler 1761–1805. Crowned arms. Rev: Value	50.00
215.	½ Taler 1820. Running horse	20.00
216.	1/12 Taler 1801–16	12.50
217.	1/24 Taler 1817–18	15.00

GEORG IV   1820–30

218.	⅔ Taler 1822–29. Bust of King	50.00

219.	16 Groschen 1820–30. Running horse	35.00
220.	1/6 Taler 1821	35.00
221.	3 Groschen 1820–24	10.00
222.	1/24 Taler 1826–28. Monogram	8.50
223.	4 Pfennigs 1822–30	6.00

WILHELM IV 1830–37

224.	Taler 1834–37. Bust of King	120.00
225.	2/3 Taler 1834	150.00
226.	1/6 Taler 1834	20.00
227.	1/12 Taler 1834–37	10.00
228.	2/3 Taler 1832–33. Arms. Rev: Value	60.00
229.	16 Groschen 1830–34. Running horse	40.00
230.	1/24 Taler 1834–37	10.00
231.	4 Pfennigs 1835–37	7.50

ERNST AUGUST 1837–51

| 232. | Taler 1838–49. Head. Rev: Arms. (Varieties) | 65.00 |

GEORG V 1851–66

| 233. | Double Taler 1854–66. Head. Rev: Crowned and supported arms | 150.00 |
| 234. | Taler 1857–66. Head. Rev: Arms | 40.00 |

Hannover sympathized with Austria in the Austro-Prussian War. In revenge, the victorious Prussians formally annexed Hannover as a province of the Prussian kingdom.

Hesse

Hesse comprised a number of smaller duchies, chiefly Hesse-Cassel and Hesse-Darmstadt. Hesse-Cassel is famous as a source of mercenary soldiers, many of whom fought on the British side during the American Revolution.

Hesse-Cassel
FRIEDRICH II 1760–85

| 235. | Taler 1776–79. Head. Rev: Arms | 80.00 |

WILHELM IX   1785–1803

236. Taler 1787–1802. Head. Rev: Arms   175.00

WILHELM I   1803–21

237. Taler 1819–20. Head. Rev: Value   200.00

WILHELM II   1821–47

238. Double Taler 1840–47. Arms. Rev: Value   225.00

239. Taler 1821–22. Head. Rev: Value in wreath   225.00
240. Taler 1832–42. Arms. Rev: Value   40.00

FRIEDRICH WILHELM   1847–66

241. Double Taler 1851–55. Head. Rev: Arms   200.00
242. Taler 1851–65. Head. Rev: Arms   60.00

Hesse-Darmstadt

LUDWIG I   1790–1830

243. Taler 1809. Head. Rev: Crowned shield   450.00

244. Taler 1819. Uniformed bust. Rev: Crowned and
      mantled arms   450.00

245. Taler 1825. Head. Rev: Crowned and mantled
      arms   250.00

LUDWIG II   1830–48

246. Double Taler 1839–42. Head. Rev: Value in
      wreath   225.00
247. Double Taler 1844. Head. Rev: Crowned, sup-
      ported and mantled arms   225.00
248. Kronen Taler 1833–37. Head. Rev: Crowned
      and mantled arms   200.00

249. 2 Gulden 1845–47. Head. Rev: Shield sup-
      ported by lions   100.00

LUDWIG III   1848–77

250. Double Taler 1854. Head. Rev: Crowned, man-
      tled and supported arms   750.00

251.	2 Gulden 1848–56. Head. Rev: Arms supported by lions	100.00
252.	Taler 1857–71	75.00
253.	20 Marks (G) 1872–74. Head. Rev: Eagle	200.00

254.	10 Marks (G) 1872–77	225.00
255.	5 Marks (G) 1877	650.00

256.	5 Marks 1875–76	100.00
257.	2 Marks 1876–77	175.00

LUDWIG IV 1877–92

258.	10 Marks (G) 1878–88. Head. Rev: Small eagle	250.00
259.	5 Marks (G) 1878–88	300.00
260.	5 Marks 1888	1000.00
261.	2 Marks 1888	850.00
262.	20 Marks (G) 1892. Head. Rev: Large eagle	1000.00
263.	10 Marks (G) 1890	625.00
264.	5 Marks 1891	500.00
265.	2 Marks 1891	600.00

ERNST LUDWIG 1892–1918

266.	20 Marks (G) 1893–1911. Head. Rev: Eagle	225.00
267.	10 Marks (G) 1893–98	500.00
268.	5 Marks 1895–1900	175.00
269.	3 Marks 1910	60.00
270.	2 Marks 1895–1900	200.00

271.	5 Marks 1904. Accolated heads of Philip and Ernst Ludwig. (400th anniversary of Philip the Magnanimous)	125.00
271a.	2 Marks 1904	35.00

272.	3 Marks 1917 (25th anniversary of reign)	1250.00

Lubeck (Free City)

This Baltic port was one of the most important cities of the old Hanseatic League. From about 1500 Lubeck's commerce declined.

273.	10 Marks (G) 1901–10. Double-headed eagle. Rev: Eagle	400.00

274.	5 Marks 1904–13	275.00
275.	3 Marks 1908–14	75.00
276.	2 Marks 1901–12	85.00

Mecklenburg

Located in northeast Germany on the Baltic and made up of two duchies—Mecklenburg-Schwerin and Mecklenburg-Strelitz.

Mecklenburg-Schwerin

ADOLF FRIEDRICH 1592–1658

277.	Double taler. Head. Rev: Fortuna	150.00

277.

287. 5 Marks 1915. Busts of Friedrich Franz I and Friedrich Franz IV. (Centenary as Grand Duchy) 400.00
288. 3 Marks 1915 125.00

Mecklenburg-Strelitz
FRIEDRICH WILHELM 1860–1904

FRIEDRICH FRANZ II 1842–83
278. Taler 1848, '64, '67. Head. Rev: Crowned shield in wreath 100.00
279. 20 Marks (G) 1872. Rev: Eagle 700.00
279a. 10 Marks (G) 1872–78 750.00
280. 2 Marks 1876 300.00

FRIEDRICH FRANZ III 1883–97
281. 10 Marks (G) 1890. Head. Rev: Eagle 325.00

FRIEDRICH FRANZ IV 1897–1918
282. 20 Marks (G) 1901. Head. Rev: Eagle 1500.00
283. 10 Marks (G) 1901 1000.00
284. 2 Marks 1901 300.00

289. Taler 1870. Head. Rev: Crowned arms 60.00
290. 20 Marks (G) 1873–74. Head. Rev: Eagle 5000.00
291. 10 Marks (G) 1873–74, '80 5000.00
292. 2 Marks 1877 275.00

ADOLF FRIEDRICH 1904–14
293. 20 Marks (G) 1905. Head. Rev: Eagle 6500.00
294. 10 Marks (G) 1905 6000.00

285. 5 Marks 1904. Conjoined busts. Rev: Eagle. (Grand Duke's marriage) 125.00
286. 2 Marks 1904 40.00

295. 3 Marks 1913 500.00
296. 2 Marks 1905 400.00

Nassau

A duchy in west central Germany. Because Duke Adolph sided with Austria in the Austro-Prussian War of 1866, Prussia annexed the duchy.

WILHELM 1816–39

297. Taler 1816–25. Head. Rev: Crowned and mantled arms   500.00

298. Taler 1817. Arms. Rev: Value in wreath   650.00
299. Taler 1831–37. Head. Rev: Supported arms   325.00

ADOLPH 1839–66

300. Double Taler 1840. Head. Rev: Value in wreath   400.00

301. Double Taler 1844–54. Head. Rev: Crowned and mantled arms   400.00

302. Double Taler 1860. Head. Rev: Crowned and mantled arms   450.00

303. Taler 1859–63. Head. Rev: Crowned and supported arms   85.00
304. Taler 1864. Head. Rev: Inscription. (25th anniversary of reign)   135.00

305. 2 Gulden 1846–47. Head. Rev: Crowned arms supported by lions   150.00

Oldenburg

A duchy on the North Sea.

PAUL FRIEDRICH AUGUST 1829–53

306. Double Taler 1840. Head. Rev: Value in wreath   1250.00
307. Taler 1846. Head. Rev: Crowned shield   150.00

GERMANY: States (continued)

NICOLAUS FRIEDRICH PETER 1853–1900

308.	Taler 1858–66. Head. Rev: Crowned shield	100.00
309.	10 Marks (G) 1874. Head. Rev: Eagle	3000.00

310.	2 Marks 1891	175.00

FRIEDRICH AUGUST 1900–18

311.	5 Marks 1900–01. Head. Rev: Eagle	350.00
312.	2 Marks 1900–01	200.00

Prussia

In the 18th century this kingdom became the leading military power in Germany. Eventually Prussia took the initiative in uniting the German states in the German Empire.

FRIEDRICH II (Frederick the Great) 1740–86

313.	Taler 1764–86. Head. Rev: Eagle	75.00

FRIEDRICH WILHELM II 1786–97

314.	Taler 1786–91. Armored bust. Rev: Eagle	135.00
315.	Taler 1790–97. Bust. Rev: Supported arms	75.00

FRIEDRICH WILHELM III 1797–1840

316.	Taler 1797–1809. Bust. Rev: Shield and supporters (wild men)	75.00

317. Taler 1809–16. Head. Rev: Value in wreath   60.00

318. Taler 1816–22. Military bust. Rev: Eagle, flags,
    cannon   55.00
319. Taler 1823–40. Head. Rev: Crowned arms   55.00
320. Mining Taler 1826–28. Head. Rev: Inscription   85.00
321. Double Taler 1839–41. Head. Rev: Crowned
    and mantled arms   140.00

FRIEDRICH WILHELM IV   1840–61

326. Mining Taler 1841–60. Head. Rev: Inscription
    (varieties)   50.00

322. Double Taler 1841–56. Head. Rev: Crowned
    and mantled arms   120.00
323. Taler 1841–56   40.00
324. Double Taler 1858–59. Head. Rev: Eagle   300.00

WILHELM I   1861–88

325. Taler 1857–61   35.00

327. Taler 1861. Accolated crowned busts. Rev:
    Monograms. (Coronation issue)   35.00

| 336. | 5 Marks 1874–76. Head. Rev: Eagle | 35.00 |
| 337. | 2 Marks 1876–84 | 45.00 |

FRIEDRICH III 1888

| 338. | 20 Marks (G) 1888. Head. Rev: Eagle | 150.00 |
| 339. | 10 Marks (G) 1888 | 125.00 |

| 340. | 5 Marks 1888. Head. Rev: Eagle | 100.00 |
| 341. | 20 Marks 1888 | 35.00 |

WILHELM II 1888–1918

| 342. | 20 Marks (G) 1888–89. Head. Rev: Small eagle | 150.00 |
| 343. | 10 Marks (G) 1889 | 2500.00 |

328.	Double Taler 1861–71. Head. Rev: Eagle	375.00
329.	Taler 1861–71. Head. Rev: Eagle	35.00
330.	Mining Taler 1861–62. Head. Rev: Inscription	40.00
331.	Taler 1866. Laureate head. Rev: Eagle. (Victory in the Austro-Prussian War)	50.00

| 332. | Taler 1871. Rev: Seated female figure. (Victory in Franco-Prussian War) | 40.00 |

344.	5 Marks 1888	500.00
345.	2 Marks 1888	300.00
346.	20 Marks (G) 1890–1913. Head. Rev: Large eagle	150.00
347.	10 Marks (G) 1890–1912	100.00
348.	5 Marks 1891–1908	25.00
349.	3 Marks 1908–12	20.00
350.	2 Marks 1891–1912	17.50

| 333. | 20 Marks (G) 1871–88. Head. Rev: Eagle | 165.00 |
| 334. | 10 Marks (G) 1872–88 | 135.00 |

| 335. | 5 Marks (G) 1877–78 | 225.00 |

| 351. | 5 Marks 1901. Busts of Wilhelm II and Friedrich I. (200th anniversary of kingdom) | 50.00 |
| 352. | 2 Marks 1901 | 25.00 |

353. 3 Marks 1910. Heads of Friedrich Wilhelm III and Wilhelm II. Rev: Eagle. (Centenary of University of Berlin)   60.00

360. 20 Marks (G) 1913–15. Uniformed bust. Rev: Eagle   200.00

354. 3 Marks 1911. (Centenary of University of Breslau)   40.00

361. 5 Marks 1913–14   30.00

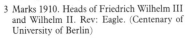

362. 3 Marks 1914   25.00

Reuss

A small state lying between Bavaria and Saxony.

ELDER LINE

HEINRICH XXII   1859–1902

355. 3 Marks 1913. King on horseback. Rev: Eagle on snake. (Centenary of the War of Liberation)   25.00
356. 2 Marks 1913   20.00
357. 3 Marks 1913. Uniformed bust, laurel branch and dates 1888–1913 below. Rev: Eagle. (25th year of reign)   25.00
358. 2 Marks 1913   20.00

363. 20 Marks (G) 1875. Head. Rev: Eagle   15,000.00

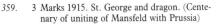

359. 3 Marks 1915. St. George and dragon. (Centenary of uniting of Mansfeld with Prussia)   250.00

364. 2 Marks 1877. Head. Rev: Small eagle   300.00

365. 2 Marks 1892, '99, 1901. Head. Rev: Large
eagle   250.00

HEINRICH XXIV 1902–18

366. 3 Marks 1909. Head. Rev: Eagle   375.00

YOUNGER LINE

HEINRICH XIV 1867–86

367. 20 Marks (G) 1881. Head. Rev: Eagle   3,500.00
368. 10 Marks (G) 1882   10,000.00
369. 2 Marks 1884   550.00

Saxon Duchies

Located west of Saxony, these duchies included Saxe-Altenburg, Saxe-Coburg-Gotha, Saxe-Meiningen, and Saxe-Weimar.

Saxe-Altenburg

ERNST 1853–1908

370. Taler 1858–69. Head. Rev: Crowned and mantled arms   100.00
371. 20 Marks (G) 1887. Head. Rev: Eagle   1750.00
372. 5 Marks 1901. Head. Rev: Eagle. (75th birthday)   650.00
373. 2 Marks 1901   400.00

374. 5 Marks 1903. (50th year of reign)   275.00

Saxe-Coburg-Gotha

ERNST II 1893–1900

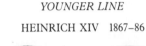

375. Double Taler 1847–54. Head. Rev: Arms   600.00
376. Taler 1846–70. Head. Rev: Arms   100.00
377. 20 Marks (G) 1872, '86. Head. Rev: Eagle   1000.00

ALFRED 1893–1900

378. 20 Marks (G) 1895. Head. Rev: Eagle   2000.00

379. 5 Marks 1895   2000.00
380. 2 Marks 1895   350.00

CARL EDWARD 1900–18

381.	20 Marks (G) 1905. Head. Rev: Eagle	1200.00
382.	10 Marks (G) 1905	1300.00
383.	5 Marks 1907	850.00
384.	2 Marks 1905	450.00

Saxe-Meiningen

GEORGE II 1866–1914

385.	Taler 1867. Head. Rev: Arms	250.00
386.	20 Marks (G) 1872, '82, '89. Head. Rev: Small eagle	7500.00
387.	20 Marks (G) 1900, '05, '10, '14. Head. Rev: Large eagle	7500.00
388.	10 Marks (G) 1890, '98, 1902, '09, '14	2500.00

389.	5 Marks 1901–02, '08. Head. Rev: Eagle	135.00
390.	3 Marks 1908, '13	100.00
391.	2 Marks 1901–02, '13	200.00

393.

392.	3 Marks 1915. (Death of Duke)	150.00
393.	2 Marks 1915	135.00

Saxe-Weimar

CARL ALEXANDER 1853–1901

394.	Double Taler 1855. Head. Rev: Arms	650.00

395.	Taler 1858–70	85.00
396.	20 Marks (G) 1892, '96. Head. Rev: Eagle	85.00
397.	2 Marks 1892. (Golden wedding anniversary)	1000.00
398.	2 Marks 1898. (80th birthday)	125.00

WILHELM ERNST 1901–18

399.	20 Marks (G) 1901. Head. Rev: Eagle	3000.00
400.	2 Marks 1901	400.00

401.	5 Marks 1903. Heads of Wilhelm Ernst and Caroline. (Marriage of Grand Duke)	225.00
402.	2 Marks 1903	55.00

403.	5 Marks 1908. Facing bust of Johann Friedrich. (350th anniversary of University of Jena)	150.00
404.	2 Marks 1908	65.00

405.   3 Marks 1910. (Second marriage of Duke)   50.00

406.   3 Marks 1915. Busts of Wilhelm Ernst and Carl
       August. (Centenary of Grand Duchy)   80.00

Saxony

Formerly a kingdom in eastern Germany. Notable for picturesque pre-1800 coinage.

407.   Taler 1500–07. Bust of Friedrich III ("the
       Wise") with cap   400.00

408.   Taler 1586–91. Bust of Christian I in armor.
       Rev: Arms   200.00

409.   Taler 1610–15. Busts of Albert, John, Ernst,
       Frederick, Wilhelm, Bernard, John Fred-
       erick, Frederick Wilhelm on obverse and re-
       verse (four to a side)   225.00

410.   Taler 1630. Johann Georg I. (Jubilee of
       Augsburg Confession)   325.00

414.	Taler 1816–23. Military bust. Rev: Arms	60.00
415.	Mining Taler 1817–23. Military bust. Rev: Arms	100.00
416.	Taler 1824–27. New bust and arms	100.00
417.	Mining Taler 1824–27. New bust and arms	85.00

418.	Taler 1827. Head. Rev: Inscription. (Death of King)	135.00
419.	Mining Taler 1827. Head. Rev: Inscription	200.00

411.	Triple Taler 1650. Johann Georg I. (Peace of Westphalia)	3500.00

ANTON   1827–36

FRIEDRICH AUGUST   1806–27

412.	Taler 1806–16. Head. Rev: Shield	75.00

413.	Mining Taler 1807–16. Head. Rev: Arms	135.00
420.	Taler 1827–36. Head. Rev: Shield	60.00

GERMANY: States (continued)

<table>
<tr><td>421.</td><td>Mining Taler 1828–36</td><td>150.00</td></tr>
<tr><td>422.</td><td>Taler 1836. Head. Rev: Shield and torches. (Death of king)</td><td>175.00</td></tr>
<tr><td>423.</td><td>Mining Taler 1836</td><td>1000.00</td></tr>
</table>

FRIEDRICH AUGUST II   1836–54

424. Double Taler 1839–54. Head. Rev: Crowned and mantled arms 165.00

<table>
<tr><td>425.</td><td>Taler 1836–38. Head. Rev: Crowned shield</td><td>100.00</td></tr>
<tr><td>426.</td><td>Mining Taler 1836–38</td><td>275.00</td></tr>
<tr><td>427.</td><td>Taler 1839–54. Head. Rev: Crowned and mantled arms</td><td>40.00</td></tr>
<tr><td>428.</td><td>Mining Taler 1841–54</td><td>100.00</td></tr>
</table>

JOHANN   1854–73

<table>
<tr><td>431.</td><td>Double Taler 1855–59. Head. Rev: Crowned and mantled arms</td><td>100.00</td></tr>
<tr><td>432.</td><td>Taler 1854–59</td><td>40.00</td></tr>
<tr><td>433.</td><td>Mining Taler 1854–58</td><td>60.00</td></tr>
<tr><td>434.</td><td>Double Taler 1861. Head. Rev: Arms supported by lions</td><td>135.00</td></tr>
<tr><td>435.</td><td>Taler 1860–71</td><td>40.00</td></tr>
</table>

436. Mining Taler 1858–71. Head. Rev: Supported arms 50.00

437. Taler 1871. Head. Rev: Victory on horseback. (Victorious conclusion of Franco-Prussian War) 60.00

<table>
<tr><td>429.</td><td>Double Taler 1854. Head. Rev: Two seated female figures. (Death of king)</td><td>300.00</td></tr>
<tr><td>430.</td><td>Taler 1854</td><td>65.00</td></tr>
</table>

438.

204

438. Double Taler 1872. Accolated busts of king and queen. Rev: Crown and inscription in wreath. (Golden wedding anniversary) — 125.00
439. 20 Marks (G) 1872–73. Head. Rev: Eagle — 150.00
440. 10 Marks (G) 1872–73 — 135.00

ALBERT 1873–1902

441. 20 Marks (G) 1874–78. Head. Rev: Small eagle — 250.00
442. 10 Marks (G) 1874–88 — 150.00
443. 5 Marks (G) 1877 — 350.00

444. 5 Marks 1875–89. Head. Rev: Small eagle — 100.00
445. 2 Marks 1876–88 — 100.00
446. 20 Marks (G) 1894–95. Head. Rev: Large eagle — 165.00
447. 10 Marks (G) 1891–1902 — 150.00
448. 5 Marks 1891–1902 — 40.00
449. 2 Marks 1891–1902 — 35.00
450. 5 Marks 1902. (Death of king) — 75.00
451. 2 Marks 1902 — 25.00

GEORG 1902–04

452. 20 Marks (G) 1903. Head. Rev: Eagle — 275.00
453. 10 Marks (G) 1903–04 — 150.00

454. 5 Marks 1903–04 — 60.00
455. 2 Marks 1903–04 — 30.00
456. 5 Marks 1904. (Death of king) — 125.00
457. 2 Marks 1904 — 30.00

FRIEDRICH AUGUST III 1904–18

458. 20 Marks (G) 1905–14. Head. Rev: Eagle — 165.00

459. 10 Marks (G) 1905–12 — 225.00

460. 5 Marks 1907–14 — 50.00
461. 3 Marks 1908–13 — 20.00
462. 2 Marks 1905–14 — 30.00

463. 5 Marks 1909. Busts of Friedrich the Pugnacious and Friedrich August III. (500th anniversary of the University of Leipzig) — 125.00

464. 3 Marks 1913. View of the monument. (Dedication of the National Battle Monument at Leipzig) — 20.00

464a. 3 Marks 1917. (400th anniversary of Reformation) — VERY RARE

Schaumburg-Lippe

A principality in north-central Germany.

ADOLF GEORG 1860–93

465. Taler 1865. Head. Rev: Arms supported by angels — 75.00

466.   20 Marks (G) 1874. Head. Rev: Eagle   RARE

GEORG 1893–1911

478.   5 Marks 1903   1750.00

467.   20 Marks (G) 1898, 1904. Head. Rev: Eagle   1750.00
468.   5 Marks 1898, 1904   1250.00
469.   2 Marks 1898, 1904   400.00
470.   3 Marks 1911. (Death of prince)   100.00

Württemberg

A kingdom in south Germany lying between Baden and Bavaria.

WILHELM I   1816–64

Schwarzburg-Rudolstadt

The principalities of Schwarzburg-Rudolstadt and Schwarzburg-Sondershausen are located between Saxony and Bavaria.

GUNTHER VICTOR   1890–1918

471.   10 Marks (G) 1898. Head. Rev: Eagle   1750.00

479.   Taler 1825–37. Head. Rev: Crowned arms in
        sprays   125.00

472.   2 Marks 1898   275.00

Schwarzburg-Sondershausen

CARL GUNTHER   1880–1909

473.   20 Marks (G) 1898. Head. Rev: Eagle   3000.00
474.   2 Marks 1896   275.00
475.   2 Marks 1905. (25th year of reign)   125.00
476.   3 Marks 1909. (Death of prince)   65.00

Waldeck-Pyrmont

A principality in west-central Germany.

FRIEDRICH   1893–1918

477.   20 Marks (G) 1903. Head. Rev: Eagle   3000.00

480.   Double Taler 1840–55. Head. Rev: Value in
        wreath   225.00
481.   2 Gulden 1845–56. Head. Rev: Helmeted and
        supported arms   100.00
482.   Taler 1857–64   75.00

GERMANY (continued)

KARL 1864–91

483. Taler 1865–70. Head. Rev: Helmeted and supported arms   85.00

484. Taler 1871. Head. Rev: Angel standing on cannon and flags. (Victorious conclusion of Franco-Prussian War)   60.00
485. 20 Marks (G) 1872–76. Head. Rev: Small eagle   175.00
486. 10 Marks (G) 1872–88   175.00
487. 10 Marks (G) 1890–91. Head. Rev: Large eagle   200.00
488. 5 Marks (G) 1877–78. Rev: Small eagle   250.00
489. 5 Marks 1874–88. Head. Rev: Eagle   50.00
490. 2 Marks 1876–88   100.00

WILHELM II 1891–1918

491. 20 Marks (G) 1894–1914. Head. Rev: Eagle   165.00
492. 10 Marks (G) 1893–1913   165.00
493. 5 Marks 1892–1913   25.00
494. 3 Marks 1908–14   15.00
495. 2 Marks 1892–1914   25.00

496. 3 Marks 1911. Heads of king and queen. Rev: Eagle. (Silver wedding)   25.00

496a. 3 Marks 1916. (25th year of reign)   RARE

GERMAN REPUBLIC

1924 COINAGE REFORM

497. 5 Marks 1927–33. Oak tree. Rev: Eagle   100.00
498. 3 Marks 1924, '25. Eagle. Rev: Value   50.00
499. 3 Marks 1931–33. Eagle and inscription. Rev: Value in oak wreath   350.00
500. 2 Marks 1925–31   17.50
501. 1 Mark 1925–27. No inscription   15.00

502. 50 Pfennigs (A-Bro) 1924, '25; (N) '27–38. Eagle in circle. Rev: Large "50"   4.00
503. 10 Reichspfennigs (A-Bro) 1924–36. Wheat stalks. Rev: Value   .75
504. 5 Reichspfennigs (A-Bro) 1924–26, '30–36.   .50

505. 4 Pfennigs (Bro) 1932. Eagle. Rev: Large "4"   10.00
506. 2 Pfennigs (Bro) 1924–36   1.00
507. 1 Pfennig (Bro) 1924–36   1.00

COMMEMORATIVE ISSUES

508. 5 Marks 1925. Knight in armor with shield. Rev: Value. (1000th year of Rhineland)   75.00
509. 3 Marks 1925   50.00

510. 3 Marks 1926. Arms. Rev: Value. (700th year of
      Lubeck as a free city)   200.00

516. 3 Marks 1927. Arms. Rev: Eagle. (400th anni-
      versary of the University of Marburg)   175.00

511. 5 Marks 1927. Ship. Rev: Eagle on shield.
      (Centenary of Bremerhaven)   500.00
512. 3 Marks 1927   200.00

517. 3 Marks 1928. Bust of Dürer. Rev: Eagle.
      (400th anniversary of death of Albrecht
      Dürer)   500.00

513. 5 Marks 1927. (450th anniversary of University
      of Tübingen). Bust of Eberhard. Rev: Eagle   500.00
514. 3 Marks 1927   125.00

518. 3 Marks 1928. Man with shield. (900th anniver-
      sary of founding of Naumburg)   200.00

515. 3 Marks 1927. Two seated crowned figures fac-
      ing each other. Rev: Value. (1000th anniver-
      sary of founding of Nordhausen)   200.00

519. 3 Marks 1928. Medieval statue. Rev: Eagle.
      (100th anniversary of Dinkelsbuhl)   850.00

GERMANY (continued)

520. 5 Marks 1929. Head of Lessing. Rev: Eagle.
(200th anniversary of birth of Lessing) 100.00
521. 3 Marks 1929 .... 40.00

522. 5 Marks 1929. Man with two shields. Rev:
Eagle. (1000th anniversary of founding of
Meissen) 125.00
523. 3 Marks 1929 .... 50.00

527. 5 Marks 1930. Zeppelin encircling world. Rev:
Eagle. (Graf Zeppelin's world flight) 100.00
528. 3 Marks 1930 .... 50.00

529. 5 Marks 1930. Eagle on bridge. Rev: Eagle on
shield. (Evacuation of the Rhineland) 125.00
530. 3 Marks 1930 .... 30.00

524. 5 Marks 1929. Head of Hindenburg. Rev:
Hand. (10th anniversary of Weimar Constitution) 85.00
525. 3 Marks 1929 .... 25.00

531. 3 Marks 1930. Walther von der Vogelweide.
Rev: Eagle on shield. (700th anniversary of
poet's death) 60.00

526. 3 Marks 1929. Eagle. Rev: Eagle. (Union of
Waldeck with Prussia) 100.00

532. 3 Marks 1931. View of city. (300th anniversary
of the rebuilding of Magdeburg) 150.00

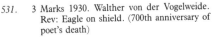

533. 3 Marks 1931. Head of Karl, Baron vom Stein.
Rev: Eagle. (Centenary of death of Stein)   175.00

541. 5 Marks 1935, '36. Bust of Hindenburg   20.00

542. 1 Mark (N) 1933–'39. Eagle. Rev: Value in
wreath   2.00
543. 50 Pfennigs (A) Eagle. Rev: Value   1.50

534. 5 Marks 1932. Head of Goethe. Rev: Eagle.
(Centenary of death of Goethe)   3000.00
535. 3 Marks 1932   100.00

LAW OF MARCH 18, 1933

544. 5 Marks 1934. Head of Schiller. (175th anniversary of birth of Friedrich Schiller)   250.00
545. 2 Marks 1934.   50.00

536. 5 Marks 1933. Bust of Luther. Rev: Eagle.
(450th anniversary of birth of Martin Luther)   200.00
537. 2 Marks 1933   50.00
538. 5 Marks 1934, '35. Potsdam Garrison Church.
Rev: Eagle   20.00

NAZI REGIME

546. 5 Marks 1936–39. Bust of Hindenburg. Rev:
Eagle and swastika   20.00
547. 2 Marks 1936–39   8.50

539. 5 Marks 1934. Type of #538, with date: 21
MARZ 1933. (Anniversary of Nazi rule)   20.00
540. 2 Marks 1934.   15.00

548. 50 Pfennig (N) 1938, '39. Eagle and swastika.
Rev: Value   50.00

GERMANY (continued)

548a. 50 Pfennig (A) 1939–44. Eagle and swastika.
  Rev: Value ... 2.50
549. 10 Pfennig (A-Br) 1936–39, (Z) '40–45 ... 1.00
550. 5 Pfennig (A-Br) 1936–39, (Z) '40–44 ... .75
551. 2 Pfennig (Br) 1936–40 ... .50
552. 1 Pfennig (Br) 1936–40, (Z) '40–45 ... .45

WESTERN OCCUPATION ZONE

553. 10 Pfennig (Z) 1945–48. Type of #549, without
  swastika ... 15.00
554. 5 Pfennig (Z) 1947–48. Type of #550, without
  swastika ... 12.50
555. 1 Pfennig (Z) 1945–46. Type of #552, without
  swastika ... 30.00

556. 50 Pfennig (C-N) 1949, 50. Girl holding plant.
  Rev: Value ... 3.00

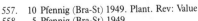

557. 10 Pfennig (Bra-St) 1949. Plant. Rev: Value ... 3.00
558. 5 Pfennig (Bra-St) 1949 ... 3.00
559. 1 Pfennig (Bro-St) 1948–49 ... 2.00

GERMAN FEDERAL REPUBLIC
(West Germany)

560. 5 Marks 1951–74. Eagle. Rev: Value ... 7.50

561. 2 Marks (C-N) 1951 ... 60.00

562. 2 Marks (C-N) 1957–71. Head of Max Planck.
  Rev: Eagle and value ... 2.50

563. 1 Mark (C-N) 1950– ... 1.00

564. 50 Pfennigs (C-N) 1950– . Girl holding plant.
  Rev: Value ... .50

211

565. 10 Pfennigs (Bra-St) 1950– . Cluster of leaves.
Rev: Value .15
566. 5 Pfennigs (Bra-St) 1950– .10
567. 2 Pfennigs (Br) 1950–68; (Br-St) 1967– .20
568. 1 Pfennig (Br-St) 1950– .20

569. 5 Marks 1952. Franconian eagle. Rev: Eagle
and value 600.00

570. 5 Marks 1955. Bust of Friedrich Schiller. Rev:
Eagle and value. (150th anniversary of poet's
death) 500.00

571. 5 Marks 1955. Wigged bust of Ludwig
Wilhelm, Margrave of Baden, 1655–1705.
Rev: Eagle and value. (300th anniversary of
birth) 500.00

572. 5 Marks 1957. Head of Baron Joseph von
Eichendorff. Rev: Eagle. (100th anniversary
of writer's death) 500.00

573. 5 Marks 1964. Head of Johann Gottlieb Fichte.
Rev: Eagle. (150th anniversary of philosopher's death) 200.00

574. 5 Marks 1966. Portrait of Gottfried Wilhelm
Leibniz. Rev: Eagle. (250th anniversary of
philosopher's death) 40.00
575. 5 Marks 1967. Conjoined heads of Wilhelm and
Alexander von Humboldt. Rev: Eagle 50.00

576. 5 Marks 1968. Bust of Friedrich Wilhelm Raif-
feisen. Rev: Arms. (150th anniversary of
banker's birth) 15.00
577. 5 Marks 1968. Bust of Johannes Gutenberg.
Rev: Arms. (400th anniversary of printer's
death) 15.00

578. 5 Marks 1968. Head of Max von Pettenkofer.
Rev: Arms. (150th anniversary of scientist's
birth) 15.00

579. 10 Marks 1969. Circle of banners. Rev: Arms.
      (1972 Olympic Games) 20.00

580. 5 Marks 1969. Head of Theodor Fontane. Rev:
      Arms. (150th anniversary of writer's birth) 15.00
581. 5 Marks 1969. Bust of Gerhard Mercator. Rev:
      Arms. (375th anniversary of cartographer's
      death) 12.50

582. 2 Marks (C-N) 1969– . Head of Konrad Ade-
      nauer. Rev: Arms 1.75

583. 5 Marks 1970. Head of Ludwig van Beethoven.
      Rev: Arms. (200th anniversary of composer's
      birth) 7.50

584. 2 Marks (C-N) 1970– . Head of Theodor
      Heuss. Rev: Arms 1.75

585. 5 Marks 1971. Parliament building in Berlin.
      Rev: Arms. (100th anniversary of German
      unification) 10.00

586. 5 Marks 1971. Initials. Rev: Arms. (500th anni-
      versary of Albrecht Dürer's birth) 10.00

587. 10 Marks 1972 (issued 1971). Two figures. Rev:
      Arms. (1972 Olympic Games) 12.50

588. 10 Marks 1972. Type of #579, except that
      inscription reads IN MÜNCHEN instead of IN
      DEUTSCHLAND 12.50

589. 10 Marks 1972. Olympic grounds. Rev: Arms. (1972 Olympic Games)   10.00

590. 10 Marks 1972. Olympic torch. Rev: Arms. (1972 Olympic Games)   10.00

591. 10 Marks 1972. Symbol of Olympic unity. Rev: Arms   12.50

592. 5 Marks 1973. Map of solar system. Rev: Arms. (500th anniversary of Copernicus' birth)   7.50

593.

593. 5 Marks 1973. Interior of St. Paul's Church in Frankfurt. Rev: Arms. (125th anniversary of Parliament of 1848)   7.50

594. 5 Marks 1974. Shield design. Rev: Arms. (25th anniversary of constitution)   7.50

595. 5 Marks 1974. Bust of Immanuel Kant. Rev: Arms. (250th anniversary of philosopher's birth)   7.50

596. 5 Marks 1975. Friedrich Ebert. Rev: Arms. (50th anniversary of President's death)   7.50

597. 5 Marks (C-N) 1975– . Modern arms. Rev: Value   3.50

598. 5 Marks 1975. Albert Schweitzer. Rev: Arms.
(100th anniversary of humanitarian's birth)   7.50

599. 5 Marks 1975. Building facades. Rev: Arms.
(European Monument Protection Year)   7.50

600. 5 Marks 1976. Half-man, half-bird creature.
Rev: Arms. (300th anniversary of death of
novelist Christoph von Grimmelshausen)   7.50
601. 5 Marks 1977. Portrait of Friedrich Gauss.
Rev: Arms. (200th anniversary of birth of
mathematician-astronomer)   7.50
602. 5 Marks 1977. Portrait of Heinrich von Kleist.
Rev: Arms. (200th anniversary of birth of
author and poet)   7.50
603. 5 Marks 1978. Gustav Stresemann. Rev: Arms.
(Centennial of birth of statesman and Nobel
Peace Prize winner)   7.50
604. 5 Marks 1978. Balthasar Neumann. Rev:
Arms. (Architect and church builder)   7.50
605. 5 Marks 1979. Pegasus. Rev: Arms. (150th anniversary of German Archeological Institute)   7.50
606. 5 Marks (C-N) 1979. Stylized atoms. Rev:
Arms. (Centennial of birth of Otto Hahn,
atomic scientist and Nobel Prize winner in
chemistry)   7.50
607. 5 Marks (C-N) 1980. Walther von der Vogelweide. Rev: Arms. (Most celebrated medieval
German poet)   7.50
608. 5 Marks (C-N) 1980. Twin spires of the Cologne Cathedral. Rev: Arms. (Centennial of
completion of Cologne Cathedral)   7.50
609. 5 Marks (C-N) 1981. Gotthold Ephraim Lessing. Rev: Arms. (200th anniversary of death
of philosopher and dramatist)   7.50

610. 5 Marks (C-N) 1981. Karl, Baron vom Stein.
Rev: Arms. (150th anniversary of death of
Prussian statesman and social reformer)   7.50

GERMAN DEMOCRATIC REPUBLIC
(East Germany)

1. 50 Pfennig (A-Br) 1950. Factory and plow. Rev:
   Value   8.00

2. 10 Pfennig (A) 1948–50. Gear and wheat ear.
   Rev: Value   5.00
3. 5 Pfennigs (A) 1948–50   3.00
4. 1 Pfennig (A) 1948–50   5.00

5. 10 Pfennig (A) 1952–53. Hammer and compass
   between wheat ears. Rev: Value   2.00
6. 5 Pfennig (A) 1952–53   1.25
7. 1 Pfennig (A) 1952–53   2.50
8. 2 Marks (A) 1957. Hammer and compass
   within wreath of wheat. Rev: Value   2.50
9. 1 Mark (A) 1956–   2.00

10. 50 Pfennig (A) 1958–   .80
11. 10 Pfennig (A) 1963–   .40
11a. 5 Pfennig (A) 1968–   .45
12. 1 Pfennig (A) 1960–   .35

13. 20 Marks 1966. Bust of Gottfried Wilhelm Leib-
    niz. Rev: Hammer and compass. (250th anni-
    versary of scholar-philosopher's death)   75.00

14. 10 Marks 1966. Bust of Karl Friedrich Schinkel.
    Rev: Hammer and compass. (125th anniver-
    sary of architect's death)   75.00
15. 20 Marks 1967. Head of Wilhelm von Hum-
    boldt. Rev: Hammer and compass. (200th
    anniversary of author's birth)   50.00

16. 10 Marks 1967. Head of Kathe Kollwitz. Rev:
    Hammer and compass. (100th anniversary of
    painter's birth)   40.00
17. 20 Marks 1968. Head of Karl Marx. Rev: Ham-
    mer and compass. (150th anniversary of
    birth)   45.00

18. 10 Marks 1968. Inscription. (500th anniversary
    of death of Johann Gutenberg, inventor and
    printer)   35.00
19. 5 Marks (C-N-Z) 1968. Head of Robert Koch.
    (125th anniversary of bacteriologist's birth)   40.00
20. 20 Marks 1969. Head of Goethe. Rev: Hammer
    and compass. (220th anniversary of writer's
    birth)   40.00

20.

21.

21. 10 Marks 1969. Meissen Pitcher. (250th anniversary of death of inventor Johann Böttger) — 30.00

28. 20 Marks 1971. Heads of Rosa Luxemburg and Karl Liebknecht, Communist leaders. (100th anniversary of Liebknecht's birth) — 40.00

29. 20 Marks (C-N-Z) 1971. Head of Ernst Thälmann. Rev: Arms. (85th anniversary of politician's birth) — 20.00

22. 5 Marks (C-N) 1969. Inscription. (20th anniversary of People's Republic) — 7.50

23. 5 Marks (C-N) 1969. Head of Heinrich Hertz. (75th anniversary of physicist's death) — 15.00

30. 20 Marks (C-N-Z) 1971. Head of Heinrich Mann. Rev: Arms. (100th anniversary of author's birth) — 25.00

31. 10 Marks 1971. Initials. Rev: Arms. (500th anniversary of Albrecht Dürer's birth) — 35.00

24. 20 Pfennig (Al-Br) 1969- . Hammer and compass. Rev: Value — .50

25. 20 Marks 1970. Head of Friedrich Engels. Rev: Arms. (150th anniversary of socialist philosopher's birth) — 40.00

32. 5 Marks (C-N-Z) 1971, '79-80. Brandenburg Gate. Rev: Arms — 6.00

33. 5 Marks (C-N-Z) 1971. Earth's path around the sun. Rev: Arms. (400th anniversary of Johannes Kepler's birth) — 12.50

26. 10 Marks 1970. Bust of Ludwig van Beethoven. Rev: Arms. (200th anniversary of composer's death) — 35.00

27. 5 Marks (C-N-Z) 1970. X-ray tube. Rev: Arms. (125th anniversary of Wilhelm Röntgen's birth) — 12.50

34.

35.

34. 20 Marks 1972. Winged snake. Rev: Arms.
(500th anniversary of birth of Lucas Cranach,
artist)   40.00
35. 20 Marks (C-N-Z) 1972. Head of Wilhelm
Pieck, first President of German Democratic
Republic. Rev: Arms   20.00

42. 20 Marks (C-N-Z) 1973. Head of Otto Gro-
tewohl. Rev: Arms   20.00

36. 20 Marks (C-N-Z) 1972. Bust of Friedrich
Schiller, author. Rev: Arms   20.00
37. 10 Marks 1972. Portrait of Heinrich Heine. Rev:
Arms. (175th anniversary of poet's birth)   35.00

43. 10 Marks (C-N-Z) 1973. Emblem of 10th annual
World Youth Game Festival. Rev: Arms   12.50

38. 10 Marks (C-N-Z) 1972. Five figures with flag.
Rev: Arms. (Buchenwald memorial)   10.00
39. 5 Marks (C-N-Z) 1972. Cathedral at Meissen.
Rev: Arms   7.50

43a. 10 Marks 1973. Bust of Bertolt Brecht, play-
wright. Rev: Arms   30.00

40. 5 Marks (C-N-Z) 1972. Musical notes,
JOHANNES BRAHMS. Rev: Arms. (75th anniversary of death of composer)   22.50
41. 20 Marks 1973. Portrait of August Bebel. Rev:
Arms. (60th anniversary of politician's death)   40.00

44. 5 Marks (C-N-Z) 1973. Glider. Rev: Arms.
(125th anniversary of birth of Otto Lilienthal,
aeronautical engineer)   12.50
45. 20 Marks 1974. Portrait of Immanuel Kant.
Rev: Arms. (250th anniversary of philosopher's birth)   40.00

46. 10 Marks 1974. Bust of Caspar David Friedrich.
Rev: Arms. (200th anniversary of artist's
birth)   50.00

51. 10 Marks 1975. Head of Albert Schweitzer. Rev:
Arms. (100th anniversary of humanitarian's
birth)   35.00

47. 10 Marks (C-N-Z) 1974. Arms and motto. Rev:
Value. (25th anniversary of G.D.R.
[D.D.R.])   12.50

52. 10 Marks (C-N) 1975. National arms of Warsaw
Pact nations. Rev: Arms. (20th anniversary of
pact)   12.50

53. 5 Marks (C-N-Z) 1975. Head of Thomas
Mann. Rev: Arms. (100th anniversary of author's birth)   12.50

48. 10 Marks 1974. Modern city. Rev: Arms. (25th
anniversary of G.D.R.)   35.00

54. 5 Marks (C-N-Z) 1975. Three conjoined heads.
Rev: Arms. (International Women's Year)   8.50

55. 10 Marks (C-N) 1976. Portrait of soldier. Rev:
Arms. (20th anniversary of National People's
Army)   12.50

49. 5 Marks (C-N-Z) 1974. Early telephone. Rev:
Arms. (100th anniversary of death of Philipp
Reis, physicist)   12.50

50. 20 Marks 1975. Musical score. Rev: Arms.
(225th anniversary of death of J.S. Bach)   30.00

56. 5 Marks (C-N-Z) 1976. Military hat, sword.
Rev: Arms. (Ferdinand von Schill, military
hero)   12.50

57. 5 Marks (C-N-Z) 1977. Bust of Friedrich Ludwig Jahn. Rev: Arms (125th anniversary of death of nationalist, patriot and gymnast) 12.50
58. 20 Marks 1976. Head of Wilhelm Liebknecht. (150th anniversary of Socialist leader) 45.00
59. 10 Marks (C-N) 1976. Bust of Carl Maria von Weber. (150th anniversary of birth of composer) 40.00
60. 10 Marks 1977. Otto von Guericke. (Physicist) 30.00
61. 20 Marks 1977. Carl Friedrich Gauss. (200th anniversary of birth of mathematician-astronomer) 45.00
62. 20 Marks 1978. Johann Gottfried von Herder (175th anniversary of death of philosopher, poet and critic) 40.00
63. 10 Marks 1978. Baron Justus von Liebig. (175th anniversary of birth of chemist) 30.00
64. 5 Marks (C-N) 1978. Bust of Friedrich Gottlieb Klopstock. (175th anniversary of death of poet) 12.50
65. 10 Marks (C-N) 1978. Satellite orbiting earth. Rev: Arms. (First joint East German–Soviet orbital flight) 15.00
66. 5 Marks (C-N) 1978. Upraised fist. Rev: Arms. (Anti-Apartheid Year) 7.50
67. 20 Marks 1979. Gotthold Ephraim Lessing standing with two dramatic figures. Rev: Arms 40.00
68. 20 Marks (C-N) 1979. Workers, factory. Rev: Arms. (30th anniversary of East German regime) 20.00
69. 10 Marks 1979. Ludwig Feuerbach. Rev: Arms. (Philosopher of naturalistic materialism) 30.00

80. 10 Marks 1982. Stylized depiction of Leipzig Gewandhaus. Rev: Arms 30.00
81. 5 Marks 1982. Children playing. Rev: Arms. (200th anniversary of birth of Friedrich Fröbel, founder of the kindergarten system) 12.50

70. 5 Marks (C-N) 1979. Albert Einstein. Rev: Arms. (Centennial of scientist's birth) 12.50
71. 20 Marks 1980. Stylized optical equipment. Rev: Arms. (75th anniversary of death of Ernst Abbe, scientist and labor reformer) 40.00
72. 10 Marks 1980. Gerhard von Scharnhorst. Rev: Arms. (225th anniversary of birth of military reformer) 30.00
73. 5 Marks (C-N) 1980. Adolph von Menzel. Rev: Arms. (75th anniversary of death of painter and illustrator) 12.50
74. 20 Marks 1981. Karl, Baron vom Stein. Rev: Arms 40.00
75. 10 Marks (C-N) 1981. Heavy military equipment. Rev: Arms. (25th anniversary of National People's Army) 15.00
76. 10 Marks 1981. Georg Hegel. Rev: Arms. (150th anniversary of philosopher's death) 30.00
77. 10 Marks (C-N) 1981. Minting symbol. Rev: Arms. (700th anniversary of Berlin Mint) 20.00
78. 5 Marks 1981. Tilman Riemenschneider. Rev: Arms. (450th anniversary of Renaissance sculptor's death) 12.50
79. 20 Marks 1982. Clara Zetkin. Rev: Arms. (Honors Communist leader and feminist) 40.00

GHANA

The former British crown colonies of the Gold Coast and British Togoland united in 1957 as the state of Ghana with dominion status in the British Commonwealth. Ghana became a republic within the Commonwealth in 1960.

100 Pesewas = 1 Cedi

1.	10 Shillings 1958. Head of Kwame Nkrumah. Rev: Star. Proof	30.00
2.	2 Shillings (C-N) 1958	2.50
3.	1 Shilling (C-N) 1958	1.00
4.	6 Pence (C-N) 1958	1.50

8.	50 Pesewas (C-N) 1965. Head of Nkrumah. Rev: Star	2.50
9.	25 Pesewas (C-N) 1965	1.75
10.	10 Pesewas (C-N) 1965	.60
11.	5 Pesewas (C-N) 1965. (Scalloped edge)	.40

5.	3 Pence (C-N) 1958. (Scalloped-edge planchet)	40.00

12.	20 Pesewas (C-N) 1967. Cocoa plant. Rev: Value	1.25
13.	10 Pesewas (C-N) 1967–	.65
14.	5 Pesewas (C-N) 1967, '73, '75	.50

15.	2½ Pesewas (C-N) 1967 (scalloped)	.40

6.	1 Penny (Bro) 1958	.35
7.	½ Penny (Bro) 1958	.25

16.	1 Pesewas (Bro) 1967. Drums. Rev: Star	.25
17.	½ Pesewa (Bro) 1967	.20

18.   1 Cedi (Bra) 1979. Shell. Rev: Arms. (Hepta-
       gonal coin)   2.00
19.   50 Pesewas (C-N) 1979. Fruit. Rev: Arms   1.75

GIBRALTAR

A British crown colony on the Rock of Gibraltar, a peninsula of southern Spain. This strategic fortress has been maintained by the British since 1704.

VICTORIA   1837–1901

1.	2 Quarts (C) 1842. Head. Rev: Castle, key below	65.00
2.	1 Quart (C) 1842	40.00
3.	½ Quart (C) 1842	20.00

ELIZABETH II   1952–

4.	1 Crown (C-N) 1967–70. Portrait of Queen Elizabeth with coronet. Rev: Castle	4.00
4a.	1 Crown (S) 1967. Proof	60.00

DECIMAL COINAGE

5.	25 New Pence (C-N) 1971. Portrait of Queen Elizabeth II. Rev: Barbary ape	5.00
5a.	25 New Pence (S) 1971. Proof	50.00

6.	25 New Pence (C-N) 1972. Rev: Conjoined arms. (Royal Silver Wedding Anniversary)	3.00
6a.	25 Pence (S) 1972. Proof	40.00

7.	100 Pounds (G) 1975. Rev: Arms, value	675.00

8.	50 Pounds (G) 1975. Rev: Our Lady of Europa	350.00
9.	25 Pounds (G) 1975. Rev: Lion with key	175.00
10.	25 New Pence (C-N) 1977. Queen Elizabeth II. Rev: Arms. (Queen's Silver Jubilee)	3.00

12.

11.	50 Pounds (G) 1980. Elizabeth II. Rev: Bust of Lord Nelson, ship. (175th anniversary of death of Nelson)	400.00
12.	1 Crown (C-N) 1980	3.00

13. 1 Crown (C-N) 1980. Elizabeth II. Rev: Por-
     trait of Queen Mother Elizabeth against Rock
     of Gibraltar. (Queen Mother's 80th Birthday)   4.00

GREAT BRITAIN

Because of its many and varied issues, British coinage is one of the most interesting and popular fields of numismatics.

$$4 \text{ Farthings} = 1 \text{ Penny}$$
$$12 \text{ Pence} = 1 \text{ Shilling (or Testoon)}$$
$$4 \text{ Pence} = 1 \text{ Groat}$$
$$2 \text{ Shillings} = 1 \text{ Florin}$$
$$5 \text{ Shillings} = 1 \text{ Crown}$$
$$20 \text{ Shillings} = 1 \text{ Pound Sterling}$$
$$= \text{(or Sovereign)}$$
$$21 \text{ Shillings} = 1 \text{ Guinea}$$

English coins were all undated prior to 1548. Many of the coins struck between 1548 and 1661 are also without dates. Up to 1662 the coinage was hand-hammered by the same methods used in ancient times. In the listings below the spelling of the monarch's name as it actually appears on coins is given in parentheses below each heading.

WILLIAM I (the Conqueror) 1066–1087
(crudely lettered PILLELMVS or variant)

Following his victory at the Battle of Hastings, Duke William of Normandy established himself on the throne of England as King William I. His coinage consisted of silver pennies in the pattern of the preceding Saxon issues.

1.   1 Penny (undated). Head. Rev: Cross   150.00

WILLIAM II 1087–1100
(PILLELMVS or variant)

The coins bear the same legends as the preceding reign but the issues of William II can be distinguished from those of William I by differences in the design and workmanship.

2.   1 Penny. Head. Rev: Cross   400.00

HENRY I 1100–1135
(hENRICVS or variant)

During this reign many coins were struck in base silver on short-weight planchets.

3.   1 Penny. Head. Rev: Cross   175.00

STEPHEN 1135–1154
(STIEFNE or variant)

Henry's daughter Matilda was away from England at the King's death, and Stephen, grandson of William the Conqueror, was confirmed as ruler. Not wishing to be ruled by a woman, the Norman nobles supported his claim. A few coins, all rare, were issued during this reign with Matilda's legends.

4.   1 Penny. Head. Rev. Cross   250.00

HENRY II 1154–1189
(hENRI or hENRICVS)

The legends are similar to those of the first Henry, but the workmanship is quite different and the reverse shows a distinctive "short cross" design. This type was continued through the reigns of Richard I and John with little change in design; all bear the name Henricus.

5.   1 Penny. Facing head. Rev: Short cross type   85.00

RICHARD I 1189–99
(hENRICVS on coins)

Richard was crusading in the Holy Land or fighting in Normandy during most of his reign. The short cross pennies with Henry's legends were continued with slight variations in the design.

6.   1 Penny. Facing head. Rev: Short cross   65.00

JOHN 1199–1216
(hENRICVS on coins)

Henry's legend and the short cross design were continued under John. His later issues are distinguished by superior workmanship.

7.   1 Penny. Facing head. Rev: Short cross   50.00

GREAT BRITAIN (continued)

HENRY III 1216–1272
(hENRICVS III or TERCI)

A new design type, the "long cross" penny, was introduced during this reign. Extending the cross to the edge of the coin was supposed to discourage clipping.

8.	1 Penny. Facing head. Rev: Short cross type	35.00

9.	1 Penny. Facing head. Rev: Long cross type	35.00

EDWARD I 1272–1307
(EDWARDVS or variant)

The "long cross" pennies continued into this reign, which also saw the introduction of a new denomination, the groat or fourpenny piece.

10.	1 Groat. Facing head. Rev: Cross	500.00
11.	1 Penny	35.00
12.	1 Halfpenny	50.00
13.	1 Farthing	60.00

EDWARD II 1307–1327
(EDWARDVS or variant)

The inscriptions on Edwardian coins do not show whether they are of the first, second or third monarch of that name. The issues may be differentiated by minor variations in design. Silver halfpennies and farthings first issued under Edward I were continued in this reign.

14.	1 Penny. Facing head. Rev: Cross	25.00

15.	1 Halfpenny	85.00
16.	1 Farthing	65.00

EDWARD III 1327–1377
(EDWARDVS or variant)

The coinage of gold was permanently established under Edward III.

17.	1 Noble (G). King standing in ship	3000.00
18.	½ Noble (G)	1500.00
19.	¼ Noble (G)	500.00
20.	1 Groat. Facing head. Rev: Cross	75.00
21.	½ Groat	30.00
22.	1 Penny	20.00
23.	1 Halfpenny	40.00
24.	1 Farthing	65.00

RICHARD II 1377–1399
(RICARD)

The larger size coins that had come into use allowed space for longer titles.

25.	1 Groat. Facing bust. Rev: Cross	225.00
26.	½ Groat	200.00
27.	1 Penny	80.00
28.	1 Halfpenny	40.00
29.	1 Farthing	150.00

HENRY IV 1399–1413
(hENRICVS or variant)

Coins of Henry IV are the scarcest of any reign with the single exception of Edward V.

30.	1 Groat. Facing bust. Rev: Cross	600.00
31.	1 Penny. Facing bust. Rev: Cross	250.00

32.	1 Halfpenny	175.00
33.	1 Farthing	450.00

GREAT BRITAIN (continued)

HENRY V   1413–1422
(hENRICVS or variant)

As on the Edwardian issues, the inscriptions do not show whether coins are of the fourth, fifth or sixth Henry. Collectors can differentiate between the issues because of minor variations in design.

34.	1 Groat. Facing bust. Rev: Cross	100.00
35.	½ Groat	75.00

36.	1 Penny	40.00
37.	1 Halfpenny	35.00
38.	1 Farthing	175.00

HENRY VI   1422–1461 and 1470–1471
(hENRICVS or variant)

Henry was deposed and imprisoned in the Tower of London for nine years during the Wars of the Roses. The gold angel was introduced during his imprisonment; specimens bearing Henry's inscription were struck during his short restoration.

39.	1 Angel (G). St. Michael slaying dragon. Rev: Cross and arms on ship	175.00
40.	1 Groat. Facing head. Rev: Cross	75.00
41.	1 Penny	25.00
42.	1 Halfpenny	25.00
43.	1 Farthing	125.00

EDWARD IV   1461–1470 and 1471–1483
(EDWARD)

Edward was forced to flee the country during the restoration of Henry VI, but the House of York was soon reestablished upon the throne.

44.	1 Groat. Facing head. Rev: Cross	65.00
45.	½ Groat	25.00
46.	1 Penny	20.00
47.	1 Halfpenny	50.00
48.	1 Farthing	RARE

EDWARD V   1483
(EDWARD)

A lad of 12, young Edward reigned only a few weeks before his uncle seized the crown and had him murdered. Small quantities of silver groats, gold angels and half angels were struck during this short period. They can be identified by a boar's-head mint mark in the legend. All coins of this reign are quite rare.

49.	1 Angel (G). St. Michael slaying dragon. Rev: Cross and arms on ship	RARE
50.	1 Groat. Facing head. Rev: Cross	2000.00

RICHARD III   1483–1485
(RICARD)

The coins of this reign show the same legends as those of Richard II.

51.	1 Groat. Facing head. Rev: Cross	225.00
52.	1 Penny	275.00

HENRY VII   1485–1509
(hENRICVS, hENRIC or SEPTIM)

English coinage was reformed under Henry. At this time the shilling first appeared (then called a testoon or teston from the Italian *testa*—head). The obverse and reverse designs are quite different from the preceding issues.

53.	1 Sovereign (G). King on throne. Rev: Arms RARE	

54.	1 Groat. Facing bust. Rev. Cross	65.00
55.	½ Groat	30.00
56.	1 Penny	40.00
57.	1 Halfpenny	60.00

58.	1 Groat. Profile issue. Rev: Quartered arms. (First coin to display royal arms)	150.00
59.	½ Groat	50.00

HENRY VIII   1509–1547
(HENRICVS VIII or variant)

Silver coins were steadily debased during this reign. The shilling finally reached a proportion of two-thirds copper to one-third silver, earning Henry the nickname "Old Coppernose."

60.	1 Groat. Profile bust. Rev: Quartered arms	75.00
61.	½ Groat	40.00
62.	1 Penny. King on throne with orb and sceptre	35.00

EDWARD VI   1547–1553
(EDWARD)

The first dated English coins were struck during Edward's reign. The silver crown of 1551 was the first of this denomination.

67.	1 Crown 1551–53. King on horseback. Rev: Shield on cross	500.00
68.	1 Halfcrown 1551–53	350.00
69.	1 Shilling 1548–51. Crowned bust to right. Rev: Shield. (Date in Roman numerals)	85.00

63.	1 Testoon or shilling. Facing bust. Rev: Arms	300.00
64.	1 Groat	85.00
65.	½ Groat	50.00
66.	1 Penny	50.00

70.	1 Shilling. Facing head. (XII in field)	65.00
71.	6 Pence. (VI in field)	100.00
72.	3 Pence. (III in field)	150.00
73.	1 Penny. Double rose	40.00

GREAT BRITAIN (continued)

MARY 1553–1554
(MARIA)

Mary's coinage is divided into two periods—coins of her own reign and of the time when she shared the throne with Philip of Spain.

74.	1 Groat. Profile portrait	100.00

PHILIP AND MARY 1554–1558
(PHILIP, MARIA)

The marriage was accomplished by proxy, and Philip spent only a few months in England during the entire joint reign.

75.	1 Shilling. Busts face to face	150.00
76.	6 Pence	125.00

ELIZABETH I 1558–1603 (ELIZABETH or ELIZAB)

Machinery was introduced into the mint for a short time during Elizabeth's reign, but opposition from the workers forced a return to hand-hammering methods. Note that various types of English coins were dated on an irregular basis until the reign of George II. Thus, many of the coins below, dated in the illustration, cannot be precisely dated as a type.

77.	1 Crown. Crowned profile portrait, with sceptre and orb	500.00
78.	1 Halfcrown	300.00

79.	1 Shilling. (Hammered coinage)	80.00

79a.	1 Shilling. (Milled coinage)	100.00

80.	6 Pence. (Hammered)	35.00
80a.	6 Pence. (Milled)	100.00
81.	1 Groat. (Hammered)	35.00
82.	1 Groat. (Milled)	150.00
83.	3 Pence. (Hammered)	25.00
84.	3 Pence. (Milled)	75.00
85.	½ Groat. (Hammered)	25.00
86.	½ Groat. (Milled)	100.00
87.	1 Penny. (Hammered)	30.00

GREAT BRITAIN (continued)

JAMES I 1603–1625
(IACOBVS)

James VI of Scotland came to the throne of England uniting the two kingdoms under one monarch.

88.	½ Laurel (G). Laureate head. Rev: Arms	750.00

92.	6 Pence	60.00
93.	½ Groat. Crowned rose. Rev: Crowned thistle	25.00
94.	1 Penny. Similar, but no crowns	20.00
95.	1 Halfpenny	25.00
96.	1 Farthing (C). Crossed sceptres and crown. Rev: Harp	25.00

CHARLES I 1625–1649
(CAROLVS or variant)

Charles declared he would defend the "Protestant religion, the laws of England and the liberties of Parliament" against his opposing faction. This inscription appears on many coins of his reign.

89.	1 Crown. King on horseback	750.00
90.	1 Halfcrown	200.00

91.	1 Shilling. Crowned profile bust	850.00

97.	1 Pound. King on horseback	2000.00
98.	1 Crown	500.00
99.	1 Halfcrown	125.00

100. 1 Shilling. Crowned profile bust   50.00

100a.	1 Shilling. Rev: Proclamation legend	125.00
101.	6 Pence	85.00
102.	3 Pence	35.00
103.	1 Penny	50.00
104.	1 Halfpenny. Rose, no legend	25.00
105.	"Richmond" Farthing (C). Crown. Rev: Crowned harp	20.00

COMMONWEALTH 1649–1660

The inscriptions on early Commonwealth coins are in English rather than Latin.

106. 1 Crown. Shield of St. George. Rev: Shields of St. George and Ireland   1250.00

107.	1 Halfcrown	250.00
108.	1 Shilling	125.00
109.	6 Pence	125.00
110.	2 Pence	50.00
111.	1 Penny	40.00
112.	1 Halfpenny. Shield of St. George. Rev: Shield of Ireland	50.00

OLIVER CROMWELL, PROTECTOR 1653–58

113.	1 Crown. Laureate bust of Oliver Cromwell. Rev: Crowned shields	750.00

114.	1 Halfcrown	800.00
115.	1 Shilling	500.00

CHARLES II 1660–1685
(CAROLVS)

The hand-hammering of coins came to an end during this reign. Milled coinage started in 1662. Symbols on the new coins denoted the source of the metal from which they were struck: an elephant (or elephant and castle)—the Africa (Guinea) Company, which had this emblem on its badge; plume—Welsh mines; rose—West English mines.

The first official coinage of copper—halfpennies and farthings—was issued during Charles's reign.

116.	1 Crown. Laureate bust. Rev: Crowned shields	175.00
117.	1 Halfcrown	100.00
118.	1 Shilling	75.00
119.	6 Pence	65.00

120. 1 Halfpenny (C). Mailed bust. Rev: Britannia
　　　seated　　　　　　　　　　　　　　　35.00
121. 1 Farthing (C)　　　　　　　　　　　　25.00

122. Maundy set: 4, 3, 2 Pence and 1 Penny　　　300.00

JAMES II　1685—1688
(IACOBVS)

The coins of this short reign are similar to Charles's
issues.

123. 1 Crown. Laureate bust. Rev: Crowned shields　300.00
124. 1 Halfcrown　　　　　　　　　　　　　　125.00

125. 1 Shilling　　　　　　　　　　　　　　100.00
126. 6 Pence　　　　　　　　　　　　　　　 85.00
127. Maundy set: 4, 3, 2 Pence and 1 Penny (uniform
　　　dates)　　　　　　　　　　　　　　　200.00

WILLIAM AND MARY　1689–1694
(GVLIELMVS ET MARIA)

Prince William of Orange and Princess Mary of England ruled jointly until Mary's death.

128. 1 Crown. Conjoined heads. Rev: Crowned
　　　shields　　　　　　　　　　　　　　　750.00
129. 1 Halfcrown　　　　　　　　　　　　　100.00

130. 1 Shilling　　　　　　　　　　　　　　100.00
131. 6 Pence　　　　　　　　　　　　　　　 75.00

GREAT BRITAIN (continued)

132.	1 Halfpenny (C). Rev: Britannia seated	35.00
133.	1 Farthing (C)	35.00
134.	Maundy set: 4, 3, 2 Pence and 1 Penny (uniform dates)	225.00

WILLIAM III 1694–1702
(GVLIELMVS)

All hand-hammered coinage remaining in circulation was called in to be recoined in the new milled style.

135.	1 Crown. Laureate bust. Rev: Crowned shields	200.00
136.	1 Halfcrown	45.00
137.	1 Shilling	30.00
138.	6 Pence	20.00
139.	1 Halfpenny (C). Rev: Britannia seated	20.00
140.	1 Farthing (C)	20.00
141.	Maundy set: 4, 3, 2 Pence and 1 Penny (uniform dates)	250.00

ANNE 1702–1714
(ANNA)

Some coins of the reign are marked VIGO to commemorate the British capture of the Spanish port of that name, along with many galleons and their cargoes of treasure from the New World. Coins so marked were struck from captured silver.

NOTE: Shields on reverse are arranged differently on coins struck prior to union with Scotland in 1707

142.	1 Crown. Draped bust. Rev: Crowned shields	350.00
143.	1 Halfcrown	75.00
144.	1 Shilling.	25.00
145.	6 Pence. Type of #136	17.50
146.	Maundy set: 4, 3, 2 Pence and 1 Penny (uniform dates)	140.00
147.	1 Farthing (C). Rev: Britannia seated	160.00

GEORGE I 1714–1727
(GEORGIVS)

None of Queen Anne's 17 children survived her, and the throne went to George Louis of Hannover. His coins show his English titles on the obverse, his German titles on the reverse.

148.

233

NOTE: Coins of this reign minted from silver supplied by the South Sea Company are marked "SSC" on reverse

148.	5 Guineas (G) Laureate head. Rev: Shields	3500.00
149.	1 Guinea (G)	650.00
150.	1 Half Guinea (G)	500.00
151.	1 Quarter Guinea (G)	200.00
152.	1 Crown. Laureate bust	500.00
153.	1 Crown. Similar, with "SSC" on reverse	650.00
154.	1 Halfcrown. Type of #152	200.00
155.	1 Halfcrown. Type of #153	250.00

156.   157.

156.	1 Shilling. Type of #152	50.00
157.	1 Shilling. Type of #153	25.00
158.	6 Pence. Type of #152	60.00
159.	6 Pence. Type of #153	30.00

165.	1 Crown 1732–41. Young head. Rev: Shields	500.00
166.	1 Crown 1746–51. Old bust	600.00
167.	1 Crown. Similar; LIMA below bust	750.00
168.	1 Halfcrown 1731–42. Young head	100.00
169.	1 Halfcrown 1743–51. Old bust	80.00
170.	1 Halfcrown. Similar; LIMA below bust	50.00
171.	1 Shilling 1727–41. Young head	25.00
172.	1 Shilling 1743–58. Old bust	20.00
173.	1 Shilling. Similar; LIMA below bust	25.00
174.	6 Pence 1728–41. Young head	30.00
175.	6 Pence 1743–58. Old bust	10.00
176.	6 Pence. Similar; LIMA below bust	17.50
177.	Maundy set: 4, 3, 2 Pence and 1 Penny (uniform dates)	150.00

160.	1 Halfpenny (C). Rev: Britannia seated	12.50
161.	1 Farthing (C)	12.50
162.	Maundy set: 4, 3, 2 Pence and 1 Penny (uniform dates)	225.00

GEORGE II 1727–1760
(GEORGIVS)

Coins of this reign marked LIMA were struck from captured Spanish-American silver.

163.	1 Guinea (G)	600.00
164.	1 Half Guinea (G)	375.00

178.	1 Halfpenny (C) 1727–39. Young head. Rev: Britannia seated	10.00
179.	1 Halfpenny (C) 1740–54. Old head	10.00
180.	1 Farthing (C) 1727–40. Young head	8.00
181.	1 Farthing (C) 1741–54. Old head	6.50

GREAT BRITAIN (continued)

GEORGE III 1760–1820
(GEORGIVS)

The copper twopenny piece weighing a full two ounces made its only appearance in 1797. The coins were so large and heavy they were known as "cartwheels."

182.	1 Guinea (G)	250.00
183.	1 Half Guinea (G)	175.00
184.	⅓ Guinea (7 Shillings) (G)	150.00
185.	¼ Guinea (G)	175.00

186.	1 Guinea (G). "Spade" reverse	225.00
187.	1 Half Guinea (G) "Spade" reverse	175.00

191. Emergency issue 1800—Spanish Dollar countermarked with George III head in oval. (Official value 4 Shillings 9 Pence) 135.00

191a. Emergency issue 1800—Similar, with octagonal countermark 175.00

188.	1 Shilling 1787. Laureate bust. Rev: Shields	30.00

189.	6 Pence 1787	17.50
190.	Maundy set: 4, 3, 2 Pence and 1 Penny 1792–1800 (uniform dates)	135.00

192. Emergency issue 1800—Spanish 4 Reales countermarked with George III head 125.00

GREAT BRITAIN (continued)

193. Bank Dollar 1804. Laureate bust. Rev: Britannia seated   250.00

194. 3 Shillings Bank Token 1811–16. Rev: Value in
wreath   60.00
195. 18 Pence Bank Token 1811–16   30.00

198. 2 Pence (C) 1797. (Second copper issue—the
famous "Cartwheel")   50.00
199. 1 Penny (C) 1797. ("Cartwheel")   25.00
200. 1 Halfpenny (C) 1797. ("Cartwheel"—Issued
in proof only)   200.00
201. 1 Farthing (C) 1797 ("Cartwheel"—In proof
only)   200.00

196. 1 Halfpenny (C) 1770–75. Rev: Britannia
seated. (First copper issue)   17.50
197. 1 Farthing (C) 1771–75   15.00

202. 1 Halfpenny (C) 1799. (Third copper issue)   10.00
203. 1 Farthing (C) 1799   15.00

204.	1 Penny (C) 1806–07. (Fourth copper issue)	10.00
205.	1 Halfpenny (C) 1806–07	5.00

206.	1 Farthing (C) 1806–07	7.50

NEW STYLE COINAGE 1816–20

207.	1 Sovereign (G) 1817–20. Head. Rev: St. George and dragon	450.00

208.	½ Sovereign (G) 1817–20. Rev: Shields	200.00

209.	1 Crown 1818–20. Head. Rev: St. George and dragon	125.00

210.	1 Halfcrown 1816–17. "Bull" head. Rev: Crowned shield	35.00
211.	1 Halfcrown 1817–20. "Small" head	35.00
212.	1 Shilling 1816–20. "Bull" head	10.00
213.	6 Pence 1816–20	10.00
214.	Maundy set: 4, 3, 2 Pence and 1 Penny 1817–20 (uniform dates)	100.00

GEORGE IV 1820–1830
(GEORGIUS)

Pistrucci's famous sculpture of St. George and dragon first appeared in 1817 and continued under George IV.

215.	1 Sovereign (G) 1821–25. Laureate head. Rev: St. George and dragon	400.00
216.	1 Sovereign (G) 1825–30. Bare head. Rev: Crowned shield	375.00
217.	1 Half Sovereign (G) 1825–28	350.00

218.	1 Crown 1821–22. Laureate head. Rev: St. George and dragon	150.00

219.	1 Halfcrown 1821–29. Head. Rev: Crowned shield	40.00
220.	1 Shilling 1821–25. Laureate head. Rev: Crowned shield	20.00

GREAT BRITAIN (continued)

221.	1 Shilling 1825–29. Bare head. Rev: Lion on crown	7.50
222.	6 Pence 1821–26. Type of #220	15.00
223.	6 Pence 1826–29. Type of #221	12.50
224.	Maundy set: 4, 3, 2 Pence and 1 Penny 1822–30 (uniform dates)	65.00

235.	1 Penny (C) 1831–37. Bare head. Rev: Britannia seated	25.00
236.	1 Halfpenny (C) 1831–37	10.00
237.	1 Farthing (C) 1831–37	6.00

VICTORIA 1837–1901
(VICTORIA)

Four distinct heads appeared on the coins in the course of this, the longest reign of any British ruler.

FIRST ISSUE (YOUNG AND GOTHIC HEAD TYPE)

225.	1 Penny (C) 1825–27. Rev: Britannia seated	15.00
226.	1 Halfpenny (C) 1825–27	8.00
227.	1 Farthing (C) 1821–30	3.50

238.	1 Sovereign (G) 1838–74. Rev: Shield	175.00
239.	1 Sovereign (G) 1871–85. Rev: St. George and dragon	165.00
240.	1 Half Sovereign (G) 1838–85. Rev: Shield	125.00

WILLIAM IV 1830–1837
(GULIELMUS)

One set of designs served for the coinage of this reign, in contrast to the variety of types issued under the Georges.

228.	1 Sovereign (G) 1831–37. Head. Rev: Crowned shield	400.00
229.	1 Half Sovereign (G) 1834–37	250.00

230.	1 Halfcrown 1834–37. Bare head. Rev: Crowned arms in canopy	75.00

241.	1 Crown 1844–47. Rev: Crowned arms	125.00
242.	1 Halfcrown 1839–87	35.00

231.	1 Shilling 1834–37. Rev: Crowned value in wreath	15.00
232.	6 Pence 1831–37	12.50
233.	1 Groat 1836–37. Rev: Britannia seated	7.50
234.	Maundy set: 4, 3, 2 Pence and 1 Penny 1831–37 (uniform dates)	125.00

243.	1 Shilling 1838–87. Rev: Value in wreath	7.50
244.	6 Pence 1838–87	5.00
245.	1 Groat 1838–56. Rev: Britannia seated	7.50
246.	Maundy set: 4, 3, 2 Pence and 1 Penny 1838–87 (uniform dates)	65.00

GREAT BRITAIN (continued)

247. 1 Crown 1847. Crowned head. Rev: Shields. (Gothic lettering) 1750.00

248. 1 Florin 1849. Crowned bust. ("Godless Florin"—words "*Dei Gratia*"omitted) 75.00

249. 1 Florin 1852–87. (Gothic lettering) 30.00

250. 1 Penny (C) 1841–59. Rev: Britannia seated 7.50
251. 1 Halfpenny (C) 1838–59 4.00
252. 1 Farthing (C) 1838–60 4.00

SECOND ISSUE (JUBILEE TYPE)
(Obverse: Veiled bust of Queen with crown)

253. 1 Sovereign (G) 1887–92. Rev: St. George and dragon 150.00

254. 1 Half Sovereign (G) 1887–93. Rev: Shield 120.00

255. 1 Crown 1887–92 45.00

256. 1 Double Florin (4 Shillings) 1887–90. Rev: Shields 30.00
257. 1 Halfcrown 1887–92. Rev: Crowned square shield 15.00
258. 1 Florin 1887–92. Type of #256 12.50

GREAT BRITAIN (continued)

259. 1 Shilling 1887–89. Small head. Rev: Crowned
    shield in garter   7.50
260. 1 Shilling 1889–92. Large head   6.00
261. 6 Pence 1887. Rev: Shield in garter   3.50
262. 6 Pence 1887–93. Rev: Value in wreath   4.00
263. Maundy set: 4, 3, 2 Pence and 1 Penny 1888–92
    (uniform dates) .   55.00

272. 1 Shilling 1893–1901   6.00
273. 6 Pence 1893–1901. Rev: Value in wreath   3.50
274. Maundy set: 4, 3, 2 Pence and 1 Penny
    1893–1901 (uniform dates)   50.00

264. 1 Penny (Bro) 1860–94. Young head. Rev: Bri-
    tannia seated. (Size reduced from #250)   4.00
265. 1 Halfpenny (Bro) 1860–94   3.00
266. 1 Farthing (Bro) 1860–95   1.75

275. 1 Penny (Bro) 1895–1901. Rev: Britannia
    seated   2.50
276. 1 Halfpenny (Bro) 1895–1901   1.75
277. 1 Farthing (Bro) 1895–1901   1.25

THIRD ISSUE (OLD HEAD TYPE)
(Obverse: Draped bust with veil over large crown)

EDWARD VII   1901–1910
(EDWARDVS)

A new interpretation of Britannia not seen again on English coins appeared on Edward's florins. The obverse of all types is the bare head of the king.

278. 1 Sovereign (G) 1902–10. Rev: St. George and
    dragon   125.00
279. 1 Half Sovereign (G) 1902–10   120.00

267. 1 Sovereign (G) 1893–1901. Rev: St. George
    and dragon   150.00
268. 1 Half Sovereign (G) 1893–1901   120.00

269. 1 Crown 1893–1900   40.00
270. 1 Halfcrown 1893–1901. Rev: Crowned shield   17.50
271. 1 Florin 1893–1901. Rev: Three shields   12.50

280. 1 Crown 1902   125.00
281. 1 Halfcrown 1902–10. Rev: Crowned shield   30.00

282. 1 Florin 1902–10. Rev: Britannia standing   17.50

283. 1 Shilling 1902–10. Rev: Lion on crown   7.50
284. 6 Pence 1902–10. Rev: Value in wreath   4.00
285. 3 Pence 1902–10   2.00

286. Maundy set: 4, 3, 2 Pence and 1 Penny 1902–10
      (uniform dates)   40.00

290. 5 Pounds 1911 (G). Rev: St. George and
      dragon. Proof   RARE
291. 2 Pounds 1911 (G). Proof   RARE
292. 1 Sovereign (G) 1911–25   125.00
293. 1 Half Sovereign (G) 1911–15   120.00

287. 1 Penny (Bro) 1902–10. Rev: Britannia seated   5.00
288. 1 Halfpenny (Bro) 1902–10   3.00
289. 1 Farthing (Bro) 1902–10   1.50

294. 1 Crown 1927–34, '36. Rev: Crown   175.00

GEORGE V   1910–1936
(GEORGIVS)

The high price of silver forced the debasement of coinage to an alloy half silver and half base metal. However, all silver denominations struck between 1920 and 1927 were base silver.

The obverse of all types is the bare head of the king.

295. 1 Crown 1935 (Silver Jubilee). Rev: Modernistic St. George and dragon   40.00

241

GREAT BRITAIN (continued)

302.   304.

EDWARD VIII   1936
(EDWARDVS)

Dies with Edward's portrait were cut and brass 3-pence pieces dated 1937 already struck when the King abdicated in December, 1936. The coins were subsequently melted down, but a few reached the hands of collectors and are now very rare. Coins bearing Edward's name (but not his portrait) were issued in British West Africa, East Africa, Fiji and New Guinea.

GEORGE VI   1936–1952
(GEORGIVS)

In 1947 a new metal, an alloy of 75 percent copper and 25 percent nickel, replaced the already debased silver being used for coins. Two differently designed shillings were issued simultaneously during this reign, one with an English reverse, the other with a Scottish reverse in tribute to the ancestry of the Queen Consort, Elizabeth.

The obverse of all types is the bare head of the king. Coins issued after 1948 drop the title IND. IMP. on reverse.

313. 1 Crown 1937. Rev: Crowned arms   35.00

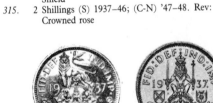

314. 1 Halfcrown (S) 1937–46; (C-N) '47–48. Rev:
      Shield   7.50
315. 2 Shillings (S) 1937–46; (C-N) '47–48. Rev:
      Crowned rose   2.00

316. 1 Shilling (S) 1937–46; (C-N) '47–48. Rev: En-
      glish crest   3.50
317. 1 Shilling (S) 1937–46; (C-N) '47–48. Rev:
      Scottish crest   3.50

318. 6 Pence (S) 1937–46; (C-N) '47–48. Rev:
      Crowned monogram ("GRI")   3.00
319. 3 Pence 1937–45. Rev: Shield on rose   2.00

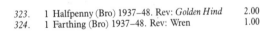

320. Maundy set: 4, 3, 2 Pence and 1 Penny 1937–48
      (uniform dates)   75.00

321. 3 Pence (N-Bra) 1937–48. Rev: Thrift plant.
      (Dodecagonal planchet)   2.00

322. 1 Penny (Bro) 1937–48. Rev: Britannia seated   2.50

323. 1 Halfpenny (Bro) 1937–48. Rev: *Golden Hind*   2.00
324. 1 Farthing (Bro) 1937–48. Rev: Wren   1.00

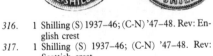

325. 1 Crown (C-N) 1951. Rev: St. George and
      dragon. (Festival of Britain)   25.00
326. 1 Halfcrown (C-N) 1949–51.   10.00

327.	2 Shillings (C-N) 1949–51. Type of #315	7.50
328.	1 Shilling (C-N) 1949–51. Type of #316	4.00
329.	1 Shilling (C-N) 1949–51. Type #317	4.00

337.   Crown (C-N) 1953. Queen on horseback. Rev: Crown with shields. (Coronation)   15.00

330.	6 Pence (C-N) 1949–52. Rev: Crown over new monogram	4.00
331.	3 Pence (N-Bra) 1949–52. Type of #321	6.00
332.	1 Penny (Bro) 1949–51. Type of #322	3.50
333.	1 Halfpenny (Bro) 1949–52. Type of #323	2.50
334.	1 Farthing (Bro) 1949–52. Type of #324	1.25
335.	Maundy set: 4, 3, 2 Pence and 1 Penny 1949–52 (uniform dates)	80.00

ELIZABETH II   1952–
(ELIZABETH)

A special crown piece was issued honoring Elizabeth's coronation. The design is reminiscent of the coins of Edward VI, James I and Charles I showing the sovereign mounted on horseback.

The words BRITT: OMN in the legend on the obverse disappeared after 1953.

338.   Crown (C-N) 1960. Laureate head of the Queen   20.00

336.   Sovereign (G) 1957–68. Laureate head of the Queen. Rev: St. George and the dragon   150.00

339.	Halfcrown (C-N) 1953–67. Rev: Crowned arms	5.00
340.	Florin (C-N) 1953–67. Rev: Double rose within circle, outer border of radiating thistles, shamrocks and leeks	4.50

337.

341.   *342.*

341.	Shilling (C-N) 1953–66. Rev: English arms	1.50
342.	Shilling (C-N) 1953–66. Rev: Scottish arms	1.25

343. 6 Pence (C-N) 1953–67. Rev: Garland of inter-
laced rose, thistle, shamrock and leek   .65
344. 3 Pence (N-Bra) 1953–67. Rev: Chained portcullis. (Dodecagonal planchet)   .50

345. Penny (Bro) 1953, 1961–67. Rev: Britannia
seated   .50

346. Halfpenny (Bro) 1953–67. Rev: *Golden Hind*   .40
347. Farthing (Bro) 1953–56. Rev: Wren   2.00
348. Maundy set: 4, 3, 2 Pence and 1 Penny 1953–
(uniform dates)   80.00

349. Crown (C-N) 1965. Rev: Portrait of Sir Winston
Churchill   3.00

DECIMAL COINAGE

100 New Pence = 1 Pound

350. 50 New Pence (C-N) 1969– . Draped bust with
coronet. Rev: Britannia. (Heptagonal
planchet)   2.00

351. 10 New Pence (C-N) 1968– . Rev: Crowned lion   .75

352. 5 New Pence (C-N) 1968– . Rev: Crowned
thistle   .45
353. 2 New Pence (Bro) 1971– . Rev: Three feathers   .25

354. 1 New Penny (Bro) 1971– . Rev: Portcullis   .15

355. ½ New Penny (Bro) 1971– . Rev: Crown   .10

360. 5 Pounds (G) 1980. Bust of Elizabeth II with
      coronet. Rev: Type of #336. Issued in proof
      only   1300.00
361. 2 Pounds (G) 1980. In proof only   250.00
362. 25 New Pence (C-N) 1980. Elizabeth II. Rev:
      Small bust of Queen Mother Elizabeth within
      circle of banners. (Queen Mother's 80th
      birthday)   2.00
363. 1 Crown (C-N) 1981. Elizabeth II. Rev: Con-
      joined portraits of Prince Charles and Lady
      Diana. (Marriage of Charles and Diana)   3.00
364. 20 New Pence (C-N) 1982. Elizabeth II. Rev:
      Crowned double rose. (Heptagonal planchet)   1.25

356. 25 New Pence (C-N) 1972. Rev: Crowned mono-
      gram. (Royal Silver Wedding Anniversary)   2.50

357. 50 New Pence (C-N) 1953. Rev: Hands grasped
      in circle. (English entry into Common Mar-
      ket)   3.50
358. 1 Sovereign (G) 1974– . Rev: Type of #336   150.00

359. 1 Crown (C-N) 1977. Queen on horseback.
      Rev: Bird on pedestal, crown above. (Silver
      Jubilee of Queen Elizabeth)   5.00

BRITISH TRADE DOLLARS

From 1895 through 1935, Great Britain issued these trade coins in the Far East. These were struck at the Bombay and Calcutta mints in India and the Royal Mint in London. Bombay has a tiny "B" mint mark on center prong of trident; Calcutta a "C" below Britannia's feet; London has no mint mark.

1.   1 Dollar 1895–1935. Britannia standing with spear and shield; date and value. Rev: Chinese and Malay inscriptions   30.00

GREECE (Modern)

In ancient times Greece produced the finest civilization known to history (see appendix, "Ancient Greece"). After being conquered by the Turks in the 15th century, Greece did not regain full independence until 1830. Following World War I and a disastrous campaign against Turkey, it became a republic in 1925. In 1935 the monarchy was restored. After World War II an attempt by the Communists to seize power was defeated. The Greek monarch was forced into exile by a military coup in 1967, and a republic was established in 1973.

100 Lepta = 1 Drachma

OTTO 1831–63

1.	5 Drachmai 1833. Head. Rev: Crowned arms	200.00
2.	1 Drachma 1832–51	100.00
3.	½ Drachma 1833–55	75.00
4.	¼ Drachma 1833–55	80.00

5.	10 Lepta (C) 1833–57. Crowned arms. Rev: Value in wreath	35.00
6.	5 Lepta (C) 1833–57	25.00
7.	2 Lepta (C) 1832–57	30.00
8.	1 Lepton (C) 1832–57	65.00

GEORGE I 1863–1913

9.	20 Drachmai (G) 1884	200.00
10.	10 Drachmai (G) 1876. Head. Rev: Value in wreath	500.00

11.	5 Drachmai 1875–76. Old head. Rev: Crowned arms with mantle	65.00

12.	2 Drachmai 1868–73, '83. Young head. Rev: Crowned arms with mantle	50.00

13.	2 Drachmai 1911. Old head. Rev: Thetis on sea horse	25.00
14.	1 Drachma 1868–74, '83. Type of #11	17.50
15.	1 Drachma 1910–11. Type of #13	20.00
16.	50 Lepta 1874, '83. Young head. Rev: Crown	30.00
17.	20 Lepta 1874, '83	5.00

18.	20 Lepta (C-N) 1893–95. Crown Rev: Value in wreath	1.50
19.	10 Lepta (C-N) 1894–95	1.50
20.	5 Lepta (C-N) 1894–95	1.50

21.	10 Lepta (C) 1869–82. Young head. Rev: Value in wreath	7.50
22.	5 Lepta (C) 1869–82	4.00
23.	2 Lepta (C) 1869, '78	20.00
24.	1 Lepton 1869–70, '78	15.00

25.	20 Lepta (N) 1912. Inscription and shield. Rev: Athena and olive. (Center hole)	7.50
26.	10 Lepta (N) 1912. Inscription and crown. Rev: Owl and value. (Center hole)	5.00
27.	5 Lepta (N) 1912	4.50

GREECE (continued)

GEORGE I 1863–1913
CONSTANTINE 1913–17, 1920–22
ALEXANDER 1917–20
GEORGE II 1922–23

28. 10 Lepta (A) 1922. Crown. Rev: Value and spray 12.50

REPUBLIC 1924–35

29. 20 Drachmai 1930. Head of Poseidon. Rev:
Prow of galley 35.00

30. 10 Drachmai 1930. Head of Demeter. Rev:
Wheat stalk 60.00

31. 5 Drachmai (N) 1930. Phoenix. Rev: Value in
wreath 17.50

32. 2 Drachmai (C-N) 1926. Head of Athena. Rev:
Inscription 17.50
33. 1 Drachma (C-N) 1926 7.50
34. 50 Lepta (C-N) 1926 7.50
35. 20 Lepta (C-N) 1926 8.50

RESTORATION OF MONARCHY

GEORGE II 1935–47
PAUL I 1947–64

36. 20 Drachmai 1960–65. Bust of King Paul. Rev:
Moon goddess emerging from sea 15.00
37. 10 Drachmai (N) 1959–65. Rev: Crowned arms 3.50

38. 5 Drachmai (C-N) 1954–65 6.00
39. 2 Drachmai (C-N) 1954–65 7.50
40. 1 Drachma (C-N) 1954–65 .75
41. 50 Lepta (C-N) 1954–65 4.00

42. 20 Lepta (A) 1954–71. Crown over center hole in
wreath. Rev: Spray and value .35
43. 10 Lepta (A) 1954–71 .25
44. 5 Lepta (A) 1954–71 1.00

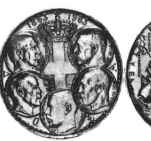

45. 30 Drachmai 1963. Heads of the five kings of
Greek Dynasty. Rev: Map of Greece. (100th
anniversary of dynasty) 20.00

GREECE (continued)

CONSTANTINE II   1964–73

61.   20 Drachmai (C-N) 1973. Moon goddess on
horseback. Rev: Arms, value   5.00

46.   30 Drachmai 1964. Wedding commemorative   17.50

REPUBLIC   1973–

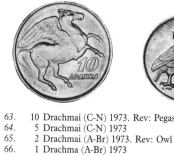

62.   20 Drachmai (C-N) 1973. Arms. Rev: Athena   4.00

47.   10 Drachmai (C-N) 1966. Head of King. Rev:
Arms   5.00
48.   5 Drachmai (C-N) 1966–70   2.50
49.   2 Drachmai (C-N) 1966–70   1.25
50.   1 Drachma (C-N) 1966–70   .40
51.   50 Lepta (C-N) 1966–70   .25

63.   10 Drachmai (C-N) 1973. Rev: Pegasus   4.00
64.   5 Drachmai (C-N) 1973   3.00
65.   2 Drachmai (A-Br) 1973. Rev: Owl   1.50
66.   1 Drachma (A-Br) 1973   1.25

67.   50 Lepta (A-Br) 1973. Rev: Leaf design   .35
68.   20 Lepta (A) 1973. Rev: Olive branch   .25
69.   10 Lepta (A) 1973. Rev: Trident with dolphins   .20
70.   5 Drachmai (N-Br) 1975. Aristotle. Rev: Value   1.25
71.   2 Drachmai (A-Br) 1975. Georgios Ka-
raiskakis, national hero. Rev: Guns, value   .60
72.   1 Drachma (A-Br) 1975. Konstantinos Kan-
aris, national hero. Rev: Warship, value   .40
73.   50 Lepta (A-Br) 1975. Markos Botsaris, national
hero. Rev: Value   .35
74.   20 Lepta (A) 1975. Redesigned arms. Rev:
Horse's head from fourth century coin   .25
75.   10 Lepta (A) 1975. Rev: Bull from fourth century coin   .20

52.   100 Drachmai 1967 (issued 1970). Arms and
value. Rev: Soldier and phoenix. (1967 revolution)   125.00
53.   100 Drachmai (G) 1967 (issued 1970)   1200.00
54.   50 Drachmai 1967 (issued 1970)   55.00
55.   20 Drachmai (G) 1967 (issued 1970)   400.00
56.   10 Drachmai (C-N) 1971, '73. Head of King.
Rev: Arms   5.00
57.   5 Drachmai (C-N) 1971, '73   3.50
58.   2 Drachmai (C-N) 1971, '73   1.50
59.   1 Drachma (C-N) 1971, '73   1.50
60.   50 Lepta (C-N) 1971, '73   .50

76. 20 Drachmai (C-N) 1976. Head of Pericles. Rev:
     Temple   3.50

77. 10 Drachmai (C-N) 1976. Head of Democritus.
     Rev: Sun and stars   1.75
78. 20 Lepta (A) 1976. Arms. Rev: Horse's head   .25
79. 10 Lepta (A) 1976. Rev: Pawing bull   .20
80. 50 Drachmai (C-N) 1980. Rev: Value   7.50
81. 100 Drachmai 1978. Athena. Rev: Value. (50th
     anniversary of Bank of Greece)   75.00

GREENLAND

A large island off the northeast coast of North America, Greenland lies mostly within the Arctic Circle. It had been a Danish colony for a long time; in 1953 it became part of the Danish Commonwealth.

100 Ore = 1 Krone

1.	5 Kroner (A-Bro) 1944. Polar bear. Rev: Crowned arms	75.00
2.	1 Krone (A-Bro) 1926	20.00
3.	50 Ore (A-Bro) 1926	15.00
4.	25 Ore (C-N) 1926	10.00
4a.	25 Ore (C-N) 1926. (Center-hole planchet)	25.00

5.	1 Krone (A-Bro) 1957, (C-N) 1960, '64. Crowned shields of Denmark and Greenland	25.00

GUADELOUPE

A group of islands in the West Indies, discovered by Columbus in 1493. Subsequently Guadeloupe became a French colony. In 1946 it became an overseas department of France.

100 Centimes = 1 Franc

1.	1 Franc (C-N) 1903, '21. Head of native. Rev. Palm	40.00
2.	50 Centimes (C-N) 1903, '21	30.00

GUATEMALA

After being conquered by Spain in 1524, Guatemala remained a colony until 1821, when it gained its independence. Then, after being a part of Mexico for a brief time, it became part of the Central American Federation, 1825–38. Since then it has been an independent republic.

Early issues under Spanish rule bear the name of the reigning monarch. Designs are similar to those of other Spanish-American mints. The original Guatemala mint mark was "G" in the legend. Upon the rebuilding of the city of Guatemala after the earthquake of 1773, it was renamed New Guatemala and the mint mark became "NG."

100 Centavos or 8 Reales = 1 Peso
100 Centavos = 1 Quetzal

CHARLES III   1760–88

1.	8 Reales 1760–72. Pillar type	225.00

2.	8 Reales 1772–89. Bust type	150.00

3.	4 Reales 1760–85	125.00
4.	2 Reales 1772–87	40.00
5.	1 Real 1772–87	27.50

CHARLES IV   1788–1808

6.	8 Reales 1789. Bust of Charles III	140.00

7.	8 Reales 1791–1808. Bust of Charles IV	150.00
8.	4 Reales 1789–1807	75.00
9.	2 Reales 1789–1807	20.00
10.	1 Real 1790–1807	17.50
11.	½ Real 1790–1804	17.50

12.	¼ Real 1796–1801. Castle. Rev: Lion	20.00

FERDINAND VII   1808–22

13.	8 Reales 1808–12. Bust of Charles IV	100.00

GUATEMALA (continued)

REPUBLIC OF GUATEMALA

14.	8 Reales 1814–22. Bust of Ferdinand VII	65.00
15.	4 Reales 1809–21	75.00
16.	2 Reales 1809–21	30.00
17.	1 Real 1808–21	17.50
18.	½ Real 1809–21	17.50
19.	¼ Real 1809–21. Castle. Rev: Lion	25.00

24.	1 Peso 1859–71 (Varieties). Head of Pres. Rafael Carrera. Rev: Arms	35.00
25.	4 Reales 1860–67	20.00

CENTRAL AMERICAN REPUBLIC

26.	2 Reales 1860–69	12.50
27.	1 Real 1859–69	8.00
28.	½ Real 1859–69	12.50

NOTE: Nos. 24–28 may be found countermarked with an "R" in a circle indicating that they have been recoined

29.	¼ Real 1861–69. Lion. Rev: Value	17.50

30.	2 Reales 1872–73. Cartouche with inscription. Rev: Value in wreath	7.50
31.	1 Real 1872–78	8.50
32.	½ Real 1872–79	7.50

20.	8 Reales 1824–48. Mountain range. Rev: Tree	100.00
21.	1 Real 1824–28	35.00
22.	½ Real 1824	25.00

23.	¼ Real 1824–50	12.50
33.	¼ Real 1872–89. Mountain range. Rev: Value	4.00

GUATEMALA (continued)

34.   1 Peso 1882, '89. Liberty head. Rev: Arms   80.00

35.   1 Peso 1872–97. Republic seated. Rev: Arms   25.00
36.   4 Reales 1873–94   15.00
37.   2 Reales 1879–99   8.50
38.   1 Real 1879–1900   4.00
39.   ½ Real 1879–99   3.00
40.   ¼ Real 1887–93. Mountain range. Rev: Lion   3.50

41.   1 Centavo (Bro) 1871. Mountain range. Rev:
        Value   8.50
42.   1 Centavo (Bro) 1881. Arms. Rev: Value   10.00

43.   1 Real (C-N) 1900–12. Republic seated. Rev:
        Arms   1.25
44.   ½ Real (C-N) 1900–01   .80
45.   ¼ Real (C-N) 1900–01. Mountain range   .65

46.   5 Pesos (A-Bro) 1923. Bust of Barrios. Rev:
        Value   6.50

47.   1 Peso (A-Bro) 1923. Bust of Granados. Rev:
        Value   3.50

48.   50 Centavos (A-Bro) 1922. Sun. Rev: Value in
        circle   10.00

REFORM OF NOV. 26, 1924

49.   20 Quetzales (G) 1926. Arms. Rev: Quetzal on
        pillar   1000.00
50.   10 Quetzales (G) 1926   800.00
51.   5 Quetzales (G) 1926   450.00

52.   1 Quetzal 1925   2500.00

53.	½ Quetzal 1925	90.00
54.	¼ Quetzal 1925	45.00

55.	25 Centavos 1943. National palace. Rev: Quetzal, on map	25.00
56.	10 Centavos 1925–38, '43–49. Type of #52	3.50
57.	5 Centavos 1925–38, '43–49	1.50

58.	2 Centavos (Bra) 1932. Arms. Rev: Value	12.50
59.	1 Centavo (Bro) 1925, '29; (Bra) 1932–48	2.50
60.	½ Centavo (Bra) 1932, '46	2.00

NOTE: In 1977 minor changes were made in arms design of Nos. 61, 62, 63 and 64

61.	25 Centavos 1950–59, smaller head 1960–64. Native. Rev: Arms	10.00
61a.	25 Centavos (N-Bra) 1965–	1.50

62.	10 Centavos 1949–64. Quiriga column. Rev: Arms	1.50
62a.	10 Centavos (N-Bra) 1965–	.30

63.	5 Centavos 1950–64. Ceiba tree. Rev: Arms	1.50
63a.	5 Centavos (N-Bra) 1965–	.20

64.	1 Centavo (Bra) 1949– . Fray Bartolome de las Casas. Rev: Arms	.15

65.	50 Centavos 1962, '63. Orchid (the White Nun, the national flower). Rev: Arms	17.50

GUERNSEY

This English Channel island is a British possession. On its coins until 1949 the name is spelled in the French manner: "Guernesey."

8 Doubles = 1 Penny

1a.

1.	8 Doubles (C) 1834–58. Arms in wreath. Rev: Value in wreath	10.00
1a.	8 Doubles (Bro) 1864–1949	3.50
2.	4 Doubles (C) 1830–58	15.00
2a.	4 Doubles (Bro) 1864–1949	4.00
3.	2 Doubles (C) 1858	30.00
3a.	2 Doubles (Bro) 1868–1929	8.50
4.	1 Double (C) 1830	7.50
4a.	1 Double (Bro) 1868–1938	3.00

5.	8 Doubles (Bro) 1956–66. Lily. Rev: Arms	3.00

6.	4 Doubles (Bro) 1956–66. Lily. Rev: Arms	4.00

7.	3 Pence (C-N) 1956. Cow. Rev: Arms	4.00
7a.	3 Pence (C-N) 1959, '66. (Double thickness planchet)	2.00

8.	10 Shillings (C-N) 1966. Portrait of Queen Elizabeth II with coronet. Rev: Portrait of William the Conqueror. (900th anniversary of Norman Conquest)	7.50

DECIMAL COINAGE

9.	50 New Pence (C-N) 1969– . Arms. Rev: Native hat. (Heptagonal planchet)	2.50

10.	10 New Pence (C-N) 1968– . Arms. Rev: Guernsey cow	1.00
11.	5 New Pence (C-N) 1968– . Arms. Rev: Lily	.50

12.	2 New Pence (Bro) 1971. Arms. Rev: Sark Mill	.35

13.	1 New Pence (Bro) 1971. Arms. Rev: Gannet	.25
14.	½ New Penny (Bro) 1971. Arms. Rev: Value	.20

15.	25 New Pence (C-N) 1972. Eros. Rev: Arms	
	(Royal Silver Wedding Anniversary)	10.00
15a.	25 New Pence (S) 1972. Proof	40.00
16.	25 Pence (C-N) 1977. Portrait of Elizabeth II.	
	(Queen's Silver Jubilee)	5.00
16a.	25 Pence (S) 1977. Proof	40.00
17.	25 Pence (C-N) 1978. Elizabeth II. Rev: Arms.	
	(Queen's Royal Visit)	4.00
17a.	25 Pence (S) 1978. Proof	40.00
18.	25 Pence (C-N) 1980. Elizabeth II. Rev: Bust of	
	Queen Mother Elizabeth. (Queen Mother's	
	80th birthday)	4.00
18a.	25 Pence (S) 1980. Proof	40.00
19.	1 Crown (S) 1981. Elizabeth II. Rev: Conjoined	
	portraits of Prince Charles and Lady Diana.	
	(Marriage of Charles and Diana). Issued in	
	proof only	75.00
20.	1 Pound (C-N-Z) 1981. Sprays. Rev: Arms	4.00

GUINEA

Guinea, on the west coast of Africa, was the only French colony there to reject the new French Constitution in 1958. It became the independent Republic of Guinea in 1958.

2.

1. 25 Francs (A-Bro) 1959. Bust of President Sékou Touré. Rev: Value, legend LE 2 OCTOBRE 1958. (1958 independence) 25.00
2. 10 Francs (A-Bro) 1959 .... 17.50

3. 5 Francs (A-Bro) 1959 .... 12.50

5.

4. 25 Francs (C-N) 1962– . Bust of President Sékou Touré. Rev: Value 12.50
5. 10 Francs (C-N) 1962 .... 7.50
6. 5 Francs (C-N) 1962. Head, type of #4 ...... 4.00
7. 1 Franc (C-N) 1962. Head, type of #5 .... 2.00

DECIMAL COINAGE

100 Cauris = 1 Syli

8. 5 Sylis (A) 1971. Native head. Rev: Value, motto 6.50

9. 2 Sylis (A) 1971. Bust facing left. Rev: Value 6.50

10. 1 Syli (A) 1971. Bust facing front. Rev: Value 6.50

11. 50 Cauris (A) 1971. Cowry shell. Rev: Value 7.50
12. 2000 Sylis (G) 1977. Bust of President Sékou Touré. Rev: Arms 275.00

GUYANA

The former British crown colony called British Guiana on the northeastern coast of South America became an independent state within the British Commonwealth on May 26, 1966. A republic was proclaimed in 1970. The nation is rich in diamond and aluminum deposits.

16. 100 Dollars (G) 1977. El Dorado gathering in the Golden Sheaves. Rev: Arms — 175.00

1. 50 Cents (C-N) 1967. Arms. Rev: Value — 1.50
2. 25 Cents (C-N) 1967– — .80
3. 10 Cents (C-N) 1967 — .40

4. 5 Cents (Bra) 1967. Floral design. Rev: Value — .30
5. 1 Cent (Bra) 1967– — .20

6. 1 Dollar (C-N) 1970. Head of Cuffy, leader of 1763 slave revolt. Rev: Cow and grain. (F.A.O. coin plan) — 6.00
7. 100 Dollars (G) 1976. Kneeling figure of fabled ancient Indian, the Golden Man. Rev: Arms — 1.75
8. 10 Dollars 1976 (C-N). Head of Cuffy, leader of slave revolt — 35.00
9. 5 Dollars (C-N). Head of Critchlow, revolutionary labor union leader — 30.00
10. 1 Dollar (C-N) 1976. Caiman, South American crocodile — 6.00
11. 50 Cents (C-N) 1976– . Conje pheasant — 3.50
12. 25 Cents (C-N) 1976– . Harpy eagle — 2.00
13. 10 Cents (C-N) 1976– . Sakiwinka monkey — .60
14. 5 Cents (C-N) 1976– . Jaguar — .40
15. 1 Cent (Br) 1976– . Seacow — .30

HAITI

Haiti is the western third of the island San (or Santo) Domingo or Hispaniola, located between Cuba and Puerto Rico. The island was discovered in 1492 by Columbus. In 1697 it passed from Spanish to French control, and became France's richest colony. A revolt under Toussaint L'Ouverture in 1801 assured Haiti's independence.

100 Centimes or Cents = 1 Gourde or Franc

HENRI CHRISTOPHE   1806–11

1.	1 Centime (C) 1807. Facing bust in uniform and cocked hat. Rev: Value	350.00

PRESIDENT BOYER   1818–43

2.	100 Centimes *An* 26, 27, 30 (1829–33). Head. Rev: Arms	40.00
3.	50 Centimes *An* 25–30	20.00
4.	25 Centimes *An* 15–24	20.00
5.	12 Centimes *An* 24	40.00
5a.	6 Centimes *An* 15	50.00

6.	2 Centimes (C) 1828–42. Fasces. Rev: Value in wreath	7.50
7.	1 Centime (C) 1828–42	5.00

8.	6 Centimes (C) 1846	12.50

GENERAL REPUBLICAN ISSUES

9.	1 Gourde 1881–95. Draped head of Republic. Rev: Arms	35.00
10.	50 Centimes 1882–95	10.00
11.	20 Centimes 1881–95	5.00
12.	10 Centimes 1881–94	2.50
13.	2 Centimes (Bro) 1881	5.00
13a.	2 Centimes (Bro) 1886–94. Arms. Rev: Value	3.00
14.	1 Centime (Bro) 1881	5.50
14a.	1 Centime (Bro) 1886–95. Type of #13a	4.00

15.	50 Centimes (C-N) 1907–08. Bust of Pres. Alexis. Rev: Arms	5.00
16.	20 Centimes (C-N) 1907–08	4.00
17.	10 Centimes (C-N) 1906, '07	3.00
18.	5 Centimes (C-N) 1904–06	2.50

PRESIDENT ESTIME   1946–50

19.	10 Centimes (C-N) 1949. Head of Pres. Estime. Rev: Arms	.65
20.	5 Centimes (C-N) 1949	.50

261

HAITI (continued)

PRESIDENT MAGLOIRE   1951–56

21.	20 Centimes (N-S) 1956. Head of the President.	
	Rev: Arms	1.50
22.	10 Centimes (N-S) 1953	.50
23.	5 Centimes (N-S) 1953	.35

PRESIDENT FRANÇOIS DUVALIER   1957–71

24.	20 Centimes (N-S) 1970. Head of President.	
	Rev: Arms	1.00
25.	10 Centimes (N-S) 1958–70	.50
26.	5 Centimes (N-S) 1958–70	.35

PRESIDENT J. C. DUVALIER   1971–

27.	50 Centimes (C-N) 1972, '75. Head of President.	
	Rev: Arms. (F.A.O. coin plan)	1.50
28.	20 Centimes (C-N) 1972, '75	.75
29.	10 Centimes (C-N) 1975	.50
30.	5 Centimes (C-N) 1975	.25
31.	500 Gourdes (G) 1977. Map of Europe. Rev: Arms. (20th anniversary of European Common Market)	200.00
32.	500 Gourdes (G) 1977. Olympic Torch. Rev: Arms. (1980 Moscow Olympics)	200.00

HAWAIIAN ISLANDS

An archipelago about a thousand miles long in the Pacific, discovered by Captain James Cook in 1778, the islands were often visited in the 19th century by American whalers and missionaries. In 1898 Hawaii was annexed as a territory by the United States.

In 1959 Hawaii became the 50th state in the Union. One effect, numismatically, was an enormous rise in the valuation of its early coins.

KAMEHAMEHA III   1825–54

1.	1 Cent (C) 1847. Facing bust. Rev: Value in wreath	325.00

KALAKAUA I   1874–1891

2.	1 Dollar 1883. Head. Rev: Crowned arms	400.00

3.	½ Dollar 1883	175.00
4.	¼ Dollar 1883	75.00
5.	1 Dime 1883. Head. Rev: Value in wreath	100.00

HONDURAS

After becoming a Spanish colony early in the 16th century, Honduras gained its freedom in 1821. For several years it was part of Mexico, and from 1825 to 1838 one of the states in the Central American Federation. Since then it has been an independent republic.

8 Reales = 1 Dollar = 1 Peso
100 Centavos = 1 Peso or 1 Lempira

STATE OF HONDURAS

1.	8 Reales 1856–61. Mountains. Rev: Tree	35.00
2.	4 Reales 1849–57	25.00
3.	2 Reales 1832–55	17.50
4.	1 Real 1832–51	25.00
5.	½ Real 1832–33	25.00

REPUBLIC OF HONDURAS

6.	50 Centavos 1871. Feathered crown over pyramid. Rev: Tree	25.00
7.	25 Centavos 1871	15.00
8.	10 Centavos 1871	75.00
9.	5 Centavos 1871	RARE

10.	1 Peso 1881–1904. Liberty standing. Rev: Arms	75.00
11.	50 Centavos 1883–1908	25.00

12.	25 Centavos 1883–1913	8.00
13.	10 Centavos 1883–1900. Arms. Rev: Value	27.50
14.	5 Centavos 1883–1902	25.00

15.	2 Centavos (Bro) 1908–20	5.00
16.	1 Centavo (Bro) 1881–1920	6.00
17.	½ Centavo (Bro) 1881–91	40.00

DECREE OF APRIL 6, 1926

18.	1 Lempira 1931–37. Arms. Rev: Head of Indian chief Lempira	17.50
19.	50 Centavos 1931–51	8.50
19a.	50 Centavos (C-N) 1967, '78	1.00
19b.	50 Centavos (C-N) 1973. (F.A.O. coin plan)	2.00
20.	20 Centavos 1931–58	2.50
20a.	20 Centavos (C-N) 1967–	1.00

21.	10 Centavos (C-N) 1932–67; (Bra) 1976. Arms. Rev: Value in wreath	1.00
22.	5 Centavos (C-N) 1931–56, '72; (Bra) 1975	.50
23.	2 Centavos (Bro) 1939–56; (Bro-St) 1974	.50
24.	1 Centavo (Bro) 1935–57; (Bro-St) 1974	.35

25.	50 Centavos (C-N) 1973. Type of #19, with PRO-DUZCAMOS MAS ALIMENTOS obverse inscription	1.50

HONG KONG

A British crown colony located on a peninsula and island at the mouth of the Canton River in southeast China. Hong Kong was captured by the Japanese in December 1941, and returned to British control after the end of World War II.

100 Cents = 1 Dollar

VICTORIA 1837–1901

1.	1 Dollar 1866–68. Coroneted bust. Rev: English and Chinese inscription	80.00
2.	½ Dollar 1866–67	375.00

3.	50 Cents 1890–94. Crowned bust. Rev: English value	40.00
4.	20 Cents 1866–98. Rev: Chinese value	20.00
5.	10 Cents 1863–1901	3.00
6.	5 Cents 1866–1901	2.00

7.	1 Cent (C) 1863–1901. Crowned bust. Chinese inscription in circle	2.00

8.	1 Mil (Br) 1863–66. (Center hole)	4.00

EDWARD VII 1901–10

9.	50 Cents 1902–05. Crowned bust. Rev: Value in English and Chinese	40.00
10.	20 Cents 1902–05	75.00
11.	10 Cents 1902–05	7.50
12.	5 Cents 1903–05	3.00
13.	1 Cent (Bro) 1902–05. Rev: Type of #7	2.00

GEORGE V 1910–36

14.	10 Cents (C-N) 1935–36. Crowned bust. Rev: Type of #9	3.00
15.	5 Cents (S) 1932–33; (C-N) 1935	3.50
16.	1 Cent (Br) 1919–26	3.00
16a.	1 Cent (Br) 1931–34. (Smaller planchet)	1.50

GEORGE VI 1936–52

17.	50 Cents (C-N) 1951. Crowned head. Rev: Type of #8	5.00
18.	10 Cents (N) 1937–39; (N-Bra) '48–51	.75
19.	5 Cents (N) 1937–41; (N-Bra) '49, '50	.65

ELIZABETH II 1952–

20.	1 Dollar (C-N) 1960–75. Crowned bust of Queen. Rev: Lion holding globe	1.50

21.	50 Cents (C-N) 1958–75; (N-Bra) 1977–	.50
22.	10 Cents (N-Bra) 1955–	.25
23.	5 Cents (N-Bra) 1958–	.15

24.	1000 Dollars (G) 1975. Rev: Arms. (Royal visit)	550.00
25.	2 Dollars (C-N) 1975– . Rev: Type of #20. (Scalloped planchet)	2.00
26.	20 Cents (Bra) 1975. Rev: Type of #21. (Scalloped planchet)	.25

27.	1000 Dollars (G) 1976. Rev: Dragon	550.00
28.	5 Dollars (C-N) 1976–79. Rev: Type of #20. (Decagonal planchet)	2.50
29.	1000 Dollars (G) 1977. Rev: Snake	550.00
30.	1000 Dollars (G) 1978. Rev: Horse	550.00
31.	1000 Dollars (G) 1979. Rev: Goat	550.00
32.	1000 Dollars (G) 1980. Rev: Monkey	550.00
33.	5 Dollars (C-N) 1980– . Rev: Value	2.50
33a.	1 Dollar (C-N) 1978. Type of #33	1.50
34.	1000 Dollars (G) 1981. Rev: Cockerel	550.00
35.	1000 Dollars (G) 1982. Rev: Dog	550.00

HUNGARY

This eastern European country was conquered by Austria and Turkey in the 16th century. Eventually all of Hungary was incorporated into the Austrian Empire. The dual monarchy for Austria-Hungary started in 1867 and lasted until the end of World War I. After the end of World War II, Hungary became a People's Republic.

100 Kreuzer = 1 Florin
100 Filler = 1 Korona = 1 Pengo = 1 Forint

MARIA THERESA   1740–80

1.	Taler 1741–80. Head. Rev: Madonna and child	100.00

JOSEPH II   1780–90

2.	1 Taler 1781–99	60.00

LEOPOLD II   1790–92

3.	1 Taler 1790	650.00

FRANCIS (II, 1792–1806; I, 1806–35)

Francis was the last Holy Roman Emperor, Francis II (1792–1806). From 1806 to his death in 1835 he was Francis I, Emperor of Austria.

4.	1 Taler 1792–1833. Head. Rev: Madonna and child	175.00

FERDINAND I   1835–48

5.	1 Taler 1837, '39. Head. Rev: Madonna and child	500.00

FRANZ JOSEPH   1848–1916

6.	1 Florin 1868–92. Laureate head. Rev: Shield in several varieties	12.00
7.	20 Kreuzer 1868–72	15.00
8.	10 Kreuzer 1868–88	7.50
9.	1 Kreuzer (C) 1868–92	2.50
10.	5/10 Kreuzer (C) 1882	5.00

11.	5 Korona 1900–09. Head. Rev: Angels holding crown	35.00

12.	5 Korona 1907. Rev: Coronation scene. (Jubilee issue)	40.00

13.	2 Korona 1912–14	8.50
14.	1 Korona 1892–1916. Rev: Crown over value	6.00

15.	20 Filler (N) 1892–1914. Crown. Rev: Value in wreath	2.50
16.	10 Filler (N) 1892–95, 1906, '08–14; (N-Bra) 1915–16	.75
17.	2 Filler (Bro) 1892–1915	.50
18.	1 Filler (Bro) 1892–1906	.50

HORTHY REGENCY 1920–44

19.	2 Pengo 1929–39. Madonna	8.50

20.	1 Pengo 1926–39. Arms. Rev: Value	3.50
21.	50 Filler (C-N) 1926–40. Crown. Rev: Value	1.50
22.	20 Filler (C-N) 1926–40	1.00
23.	10 Filler (C-N) 1926–40	.65
24.	2 Filler (Bro) 1926–40	.50
25.	1 Filler (Bro) 1926–39	.75

26.	5 Pengo 1930. Bust of Admiral Horthy. Rev: Hungarian arms. (10th year of Horthy regency)	17.50

27.	2 Pengo 1935. Three figures. Rev: Hungarian arms (University of Budapest commemorative)	12.50

28.	2 Pengo 1935. Bust of Rakoczi. Rev: Hungarian arms. (Rakoczi commemorative)	10.00

29.	2 Pengo 1936. Bust of Liszt. Rev: Hungarian arms. (Liszt commemorative)	10.00

30.	5 Pengo 1938. Bust of St. Stephen. (900th anniversary of death of St. Stephen)	25.00

HUNGARY (continued)

31. 5 Pengo 1939. Bust of Admiral Horthy 17.50

WORLD WAR II ISSUES

32. 5 Pengo (A) 1943. Bust of Admiral Horthy. (Admiral Horthy's 75th birthday) 5.00

33. 5 Pengo (A) 1945. Parliamentary buildings 4.00
34. 2 Pengo (A) 1941–43. Hungarian arms. Rev: Value 1.00
35. 1 Pengo (A) 1941–44 .50
36. 20 Filler (St) 1941–44. Crown. Rev: Value. (Center hole) .75
37. 10 Filler (St) 1940–42 .50
38. 2 Filler (St) 1940–42; (Z) '43–44 1.00

PEOPLE'S REPUBLIC 1946–

39. 5 Forint 1946. Head of Kossuth. Rev: Hungarian arms 20.00

39a. 5 Forint 1947. (Thinner planchet) 6.50
40. 2 Forint (A) 1946–47. Hungarian arms 3.50
41. 1 Forint (A) 1946–47 2.50

42. 20 Filler (Bro-A) 1946–50. Three ears of wheat. Rev: Value 1.00

43. 10 Filler (C-A) 1946–47. Dove of peace. Rev: Value .65
44. 2 Filler (Bro) 1946–47. Hungarian arms. Rev: Value .50

COMMEMORATIVE ISSUES

45. 20 Forint 1948. Head of Tancsics. (Revolution of 1848) 15.00

46. 10 Forint 1948. Head of Szechenyi. (Commemorating Revolution of 1848) 15.00
47. 5 Forint 1948. Head of Petöfi. (Revolution of 1848) 10.00

48. 25 Forint 1956. Parliament building. (10th year
of monetary system)   35.00

49. 20 Forint 1956. Bridge   30.00
50. 10 Forint 1956. Museum   20.00
51. 2 Forint (C-N) 1950–56. Five-pointed star with
rays, hammer and wheat ear below. Rev:
Value in wreath   1.50

52. 1 Forint (A) 1949–52. Rev: Value in spray   .85

53. 2 Forint (C-N) 1957–61; (C-N-Z) 1962–67.
Arms. Rev: Value   .85
54. 1 Forint (A) 1957–   .50

55. 50 Filler (A) 1948, 1953–66   .50
56. 20 Filler (A) 1953–66. Wheat ears   .25
56a. 20 Filler (A) 1967– . (Smaller planchet)   .25

57. 10 Filler (A) 1950–66. Dove   .25
57a. 10 Filler (A) 1967– . (Smaller planchet)   .20
58. 5 Filler (A) 1948– . Head   .15

59. 2 Filler (A) 1950– . (Center hole)   .10

60. 50 Forint 1961. Head of Franz Liszt. (150th anniversary of musician's birth)   35.00
61. 25 Forint 1961   25.00
62. 50 Forint 1961. Head of Béla Bartók. (80th anniversary of musician's birth)   35.00
63. 25 Forint 1961   25.00

64. 50 Forint 1966. Head of Miklos Zrinyi. Rev:
Allegorical scene. (400th anniversary of patriot's death)   35.00
65. 25 Forint 1966   25.00

68.

66. 100 Forint 1967. Head of Zoltán Kodály. Rev:
     Peacock. (85th anniversary of musician's
     birth)   37.50
67. 50 Forint 1967   17.50
68. 25 Forint 1967   15.00

69. 5 Forint (C-N-Z) 1967–68. Kossuth (type of
     #39, smaller planchet). Rev: New arms   2.00

70. 50 Filler (Al) 1967. Charles Bridge. Rev: Value   .50

75. 100 Forint 1970. Female figure. Rev: Arms, value
     in wreath. (25th anniversary of Liberation)   25.00
76. 50 Forint 1970   15.00

77. 2 Forint (Bra) 1970– . Arms. Rev: Value   .75

71. 100 Forint 1968. Head of Dr. Semmelweis. (150th
     anniversary of physician's birth)   25.00
72. 50 Forint 1968   17.50

78. 10 Forint (N) 1971– . Female figure. Rev: Value,
     small arms   2.50

73. 100 Forint 1969. Worker waving flag. (50th anni-
     versary of Republic)   35.00
74. 50 Forint 1969   20.00

79. 5 Forint (N) 1971– . Louis Kossuth, national
     hero. Rev: Arms   1.50

80. 100 Forint 1972. Two signs, joined. Rev: Arms,
value. (100th anniversary of city of Budapest)   25.00

83. 100 Forint 1973. Head of Sándor Petöfi, poet,
with inscription "We boldly defended our
country!" (125th anniversary of Revolution of
1848)   25.00

84. 50 Forint 1973. Bust of Petöfi. Rev: Ribbon,
value   15.00

81. 100 Forint 1972. Portrait of King Stephen I. Rev:
Monogram. (1000th anniversary, birth of first
king of Hungary)   25.00

82. 50 Forint 1972. King Stephen I on horseback.
Rev: Copy of silver denar   15.00

85. 100 Forint 1974. Arms. Rev: Coins of member
nations, Council of Mutual Economic As-
sistance. (25th anniversary of Council)   30.00

HUNGARY (continued)

86. 100 Forint 1974. Symbols of industry. Rev: Arms, value. (50th anniversary of Hungarian National Bank)   25.00

87. 50 Forint 1974. Bank building. Rev: Small arms, value. (50th anniversary of Hungarian National Bank)   15.00

88. 200 Forint 1975. Dove over bridge. Rev: Arms, value. (30th anniversary of Liberation)   35.00
89. 200 Forint 1975. Abstract design. Rev: Graph. (150th anniversary of Academy of Science)   35.00
90. 200 Forint 1976. Ferenc Rakoczi II. (300th anniversary of national hero's death)   35.00
91. 200 Forint 1976. Milhaly Munkacsy, painter   35.00
92. 200 Forint 1976. Pal Szinyei Merse, painter   35.00
93. 200 Forint 1976. Gyula Derkovits, painter   35.00
94. 200 Forint 1977. Adam Manyoki. Rev: Arms   35.00
95. 200 Forint 1977. Tivadar C. Kosztka. Rev: Arms   35.00
96. 200 Forint 1977. Jozsef Rippl-Ronai   35.00
97. 200 Forint 1977. Inscription upon museum facade. Rev: Eagle. (175th anniversary of National Museum, Budapest)   35.00

98. 200 Forint 1978. Minting vignette. Rev: Flower. (First Hungarian gold forint)   35.00

99. 200 Forint 1979. Child with ball. Rev: Abstract design based on children's drawings. (International Year of Child)   35.00

100. 200 Forint 1979. Half-length bust of Gabor Bethlen. Rev: Arms. (350th anniversary of death of Transylvanian prince)   35.00

101. 500 Forint 1980. Ice Skaters. Rev: Olympic symbol. (13th Winter Olympics, Lake Placid)   65.00
102. 200 Forint 1980. Winter Olympics   35.00

103. 100 Forint (N) 1980. Two astronauts above globe. Rev: Arms. (First Hungarian-Soviet space flight)   12.50

104. 500 Forint 1981. Béla Bartók. Rev: Music sheet. (Composer's birth centennial)   40.00

107. 500 Forint 1981. Soccer match. Rev: Official emblem of World Cup Soccer 1982. (1982 World Cup, Madrid, Spain)   40.00

105. 100 Forint (N) 1981. Female figure. Rev: Symbolic sheaf of wheat. (World Food Day)   10.00

106. 10 Forint (N) 1981. Type of #78. (F.A.O. coin plan)   3.00

108. 500 Forint 1981. Figure of player delivering a shot. Rev: Schematic design of soccer field. (1982 World Cup)   40.00

109. 100 Forint 1981. Portraits of the two great poets of
Bulgaria and Hungary, Hristo Botev and
Sándor Petöfi. Rev: Arms. (1300th anniver-
sary of Bulgaria)   15.00

ICELAND

An island in the North Atlantic, about 800 miles northwest of the British Isles. It was settled by Vikings about 870, and was first a Norwegian and then a Danish colony. The Althing, the Icelandic parliament and supreme court, was founded in 930. Iceland became an independent republic in 1944.

CHRISTIAN X OF DENMARK   1912–44

1.	2 Kronur (A-Bro) 1925–40. Arms. Rev: Value	7.50
2.	1 Krona (A-Bro) 1925–40	3.00
3.	25 Aurar (C-N) 1922–40; (Z) 1942	5.00
4.	10 Aurar (C-N) 1922–40; (Z) 1942	10.00

5.	5 Aurar (Bro) 1926–42. Monogram. Rev: Value	2.50
6.	2 Aurar (Bro) 1926–42	2.50
7.	1 Eyrir (Bro) 1926–42	2.50

COMMEMORATIVE ISSUE
(of outstanding interest)

NOTE: This is for the one-thousandth anniversary of the Althing. Values appear on the edges of coins.

8.	10 Kronur 1930. King of Thule seated. Rev: Shield with supporters	250.00
9.	5 Kronur 1930. Ulfliot the Lawmaker. Rev: Interlocked dragons	150.00
10.	2 Kronur 1930. Seated figure. Rev: Icelandic Cross with designs in angles	65.00

REPUBLIC   1944–

11.	10 Kronur (C-N) 1967– . Arms. Rev: Value	.35
12.	5 Kronur (C-N) 1969–	.20
13.	2 Kronur (A-Bro) 1946; (N-Bra) 1958– . Arms. Rev: Value	.50
14.	1 Krona (A-Bro) 1946; (N-Bra) 1957–75; (A) 1976–80; (C-N) 1981	.20
15.	50 Aurar (N-Bra) 1969–74; (Bro) 1981–	.30
16.	25 Aurar (C-N) 1946–	.20
17.	10 Aurar (C-N) 1946–69; (A) 1970–74	.20
18.	5 Aurar (Bro) 1946–66	.60
19.	1 Eyrir (Bro) 1946–66	.50

20.	500 Kronur (G) 1961. Head of Jon Sigurdsson (Iceland's national hero). Rev: Arms. (150th anniversary of his birth)	350.00

21.	50 Kronur (N) 1968. Parliament building. (50th anniversary of sovereignty)	5.00

22.	50 Kronur (C-N) 1970– . Parliament building. Rev: Value	1.25

23.10,000 Kronur (G) 1974. Man in ship. Rev: Round
shield, quartered, with bird, dragon, bull and
giant. (1100th anniversary of first settlement)   350.00

24. 1000 Kronur 1974. Two men with fire. Rev:
Shield. (1100th anniversary of first settlement)   20.00

25. 500 Kronur 1974. Woman leading heifer. Rev:
Shield. (1100th anniversary of first settlement)   15.00
26.   5 Kronur (C-N) 1981– . Two dolphins. Rev:
Round shield   1.25
27.   1 Krona (C-N) 1981– . Dolphin. Rev: Shield   .75
28.   50 Aurar (Br) 1981–   .50
29.   10 Aurar (Br) 1981–   .30
30.   5 Aurar (Br) 1981–   .30

INDIA

This vast subcontinent was once the proudest possession of the British Empire. Today it is divided into two parts: India (Bharat), which is mainly Hindu in population; and Pakistan (q.v.), which is mainly Muslim. India became a republic within the British Commonwealth in 1950. Pakistan is now a republic.

3 Pies = 1 Pice
4 Pice = 1 Anna
16 Annas = 1 Rupee
15 Rupees = 1 Mohur

BRITISH INDIA

WILLIAM IV   1830–37

1.	1 Rupee 1835. Head. Rev: Value in English and Persian in wreath, with legend EAST INDIA COMPANY	30.00
2.	½ Rupee 1835	35.00
3.	¼ Rupee 1835	20.00

VICTORIA   1837–1901

4.	1 Rupee 1840. Young head, with legend VICTORIA QUEEN. Rev: Type of #1	15.00
5.	½ Rupee 1840	10.00
6.	¼ Rupee 1840	7.50
7.	2 Annas 1841	5.00

8.	1 Rupee 1862–76. Crowned bust, with legend VICTORIA QUEEN. Rev: Type of #1	15.00
9.	½ Rupee 1862–76	12.50
10.	¼ Rupee 1862–76	5.00
11.	2 Annas 1862–76	4.00
12.	½ Anna (C) 1862–76	5.00
13.	¼ Anna (C) 1862–76	3.00

14.	½ Pice (C) 1862	2.00
15.	¹⁄₁₂ Anna (C) 1862–76	1.50

16.	1 Rupee 1877–1901. Crowned bust, with legend VICTORIA EMPRESS. Rev: Value in scroll border	12.50
17.	½ Rupee 1877–99	15.00
18.	¼ Rupee 1877–1901	7.50
19.	2 Annas 1877–1901	3.50
20.	½ Anna (C) 1877. Rev: Value in dotted circle and floral scroll	20.00
21.	¼ Anna (C) 1877–1901	1.50
22.	½ Pice (C) 1885–1901	2.50
23.	¹⁄₁₂ Anna (C) 1877–1901	2.50

EDWARD VII   1901–10

24.	1 Rupee 1903–10. Head. Rev: Crowned value between sprays	12.50
25.	½ Rupee 1905–10	7.50
26.	¼ Rupee 1903–10	4.00
27.	2 Annas 1903–10	2.50

28.	1 Anna (C-N) 1907–10. Crowned bust. Rev: Value in scroll. (Scalloped edge)	1.50
29.	¼ Anna (C) 1903–06; (Br) 1906–10. Bare head. Rev: Type of #20. (Round)	1.50
30.	½ Pice (C) 1903–06; (Br) 1906–10	5.00
31.	¹⁄₁₂ Anna (C) 1903–06; (Br) 1906–10	1.50

GEORGE V   1910–36

32.	1 Rupee 1911–22. Crowned bust. Rev: Value in scroll	12.50
33.	½ Rupee 1911–36	6.50
34.	¼ Rupee 1911–35	3.00
35.	2 Annas 1911–17	4.00
36.	8 Annas (C-N) 1919, '20. Rev: Large "8"	7.50

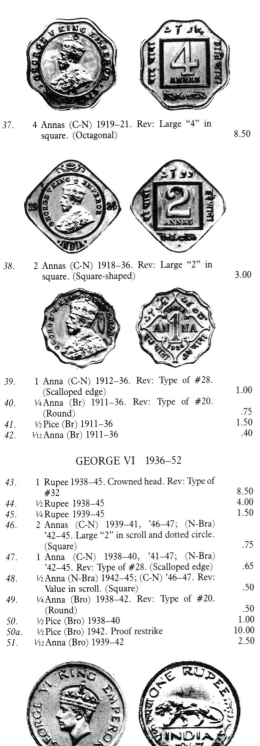

37.   4 Annas (C-N) 1919–21. Rev: Large "4" in square. (Octagonal)   8.50

38.   2 Annas (C-N) 1918–36. Rev: Large "2" in square. (Square-shaped)   3.00

39.   1 Anna (C-N) 1912–36. Rev: Type of #28. (Scalloped edge)   1.00
40.   ¼ Anna (Br) 1911–36. Rev: Type of #20. (Round)   .75
41.   ½ Pice (Br) 1911–36   1.50
42.   ¹⁄₁₂ Anna (Br) 1911–36   .40

GEORGE VI 1936–52

43.   1 Rupee 1938–45. Crowned head. Rev: Type of #32   8.50
44.   ½ Rupee 1938–45   4.00
45.   ¼ Rupee 1939–45   1.50
46.   2 Annas (C-N) 1939–41, '46–47; (N-Bra) '42–45. Large "2" in scroll and dotted circle. (Square)   .75
47.   1 Anna (C-N) 1938–40, '41–47; (N-Bra) '42–45. Rev: Type of #28. (Scalloped edge)   .65
48.   ½ Anna (N-Bra) 1942–45; (C-N) '46–47. Rev: Value in scroll. (Square)   .50
49.   ¼ Anna (Bro) 1938–42. Rev: Type of #20. (Round)   .50
50.   ½ Pice (Bro) 1938–40   1.00
50a.   ½ Pice (Bro) 1942. Proof restrike   10.00
51.   ¹⁄₁₂ Anna (Bro) 1939–42   2.50

52.   1 Rupee (N) 1947. Rev: Tiger   7.50

53.   ½ Rupee (N) 1946–47   3.50
54.   ¼ Rupee (N) 1946–47   3.00

55.   1 Pice (Bro) 1943–47. Crown and date. Rev: Floral scroll. (Center hole)   .65

REPUBLIC OF INDIA (Bharat)

56.   1 Rupee (N) 1950–54. Asoka pillar, three lions on pedestal. Rev: Value   6.00
57.   ½ Rupee (N) 1950–56   2.00
58.   ¼ Rupee (N) 1950–56   1.50
59.   2 Annas (C-N) 1950–55. Rev: Brahman bull. (Square)   1.25

60.   1 Anna (C-N) 1950–55. (Scalloped edge)   1.00

61.   ½ Anna (C-N) 1950–55. (Square)   .75

62.   1 Pice (Br) 1950 (thick planchet), 1951–55 (thin planchet)   .50

INDIA (continued)

100 Naya Paise = 1 Rupee

63.	1 Rupee (N) 1962–70. Asoka pillar. Rev: Value	2.50
64.	50 Naya Paisa (N) 1960–63	1.25
65.	25 Naya Paise (N) 1957–63	1.00
66.	10 Naya Paise (C-N) 1957–63. (Scalloped)	.75
67.	5 Naya Paise (C-N) 1957–63. (Square)	.50
68.	2 Naya Paise (C-N) 1957–63 (Scalloped)	.25
69.	1 Naya Paise (Bro) 1957–61; (N-Bra) 1962–63. (Round)	.20

70.	1 Rupee (N) 1964. Portrait of Jawaharlal Nehru. Rev: Asoka pillar and value. (Memorial coin)	2.50
71.	50 Paise (N) 1964	1.25

72.	50 Paise (N) 1964–71. Asoka pillar. Rev: Numeral of value	.75
73.	25 Paise (N) 1964–68; (A-Bro) 1968–71	.50
74.	10 Paise (C-N) 1964– . (Scalloped)	.35
75.	5 Paise (C-N) 1964–67; (A) 68–71. (Square)	.25

76.	3 Paise (Al) 1964–71. (Hexagonal planchet)	.15
77.	2 Paise (C-N) 1964; (A) 1965– . (Scalloped)	.10
78.	1 Paisa (N-Bra) 1964. (Round)	.15
79.	1 Paisa (A) 1965– . (Square)	.10

80.	20 Paise (N-Bra) 1968– . Rev: Lotus flower	.30
81.	10 Paise (N-Bra) 1968–71. Type of #74	.25

82.	10 Rupees 1969, '70. Head of Mahatma Gandhi. Rev: Asoka pillar. (100th anniversary of birth)	20.00
83.	1 Rupee (N) 1969, '70	1.50
84.	50 Paise (N) 1969, '70	.75
85.	20 Paise (A-Br) 1969, '70	.50

86.	10 Rupees 1970, '71. Lotus blossom. Rev: Asoka pillar. (F.A.O. coin plan)	20.00
87.	20 Paise (A-Br) 1970, '71	.50

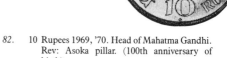

88.	10 Paise (A) 1971– . Asoka pillar in floral border. Rev: Value in border. (Scalloped planchet)	.30

INDIA (continued)

103.   1 Rupee (C-N) 1975. Asoka Pillar. Rev: Value,
      wheat. (Type of #63)   1.50

104.   10 Paise (Al) 1975. Type of #101. (F.A.O.;
      scalloped planchet)   .35

89.   10 Rupees 1972. Two youths holding flag. Rev:
      Asoka pillar and value. (25th anniversary of
      independence)   20.00
90.   50 Paise (C-N) 1972   .75
91.   50 Paise (C-N) 1972– . Asoka pillar. Rev: Value   .35
92.   25 Paise (C-N) 1972–   .30
93.   5 Paise (A) 1972– . Asoka pillar. Rev: Value.
      (Square planchet)   .15
94.   3 Paise (A) 1972– . (Hexagonal planchet)   1.50

95.   20 Rupees 1973. Wheat around motto. Rev:
      Asoka pillar, value. (F.A.O. coin plan)   35.00
96.   10 Rupees 1973   20.00
97.   50 Paise (C-N) 1973   1.50

105.   50 Rupees (C-N) 1977. Symbols for saving, edu-
      cation, welfare, medical help, industry and
      agriculture. Rev: Asoka pillar between leg-
      ends. (F.A.O.)   20.00
106.   10 Rupees (C-N) 1977 (F.A.O)   5.00

98.   50 Rupees 1974. Family planning symbol. Rev:
      Asoka pillar, value. (F.A.O.)   30.00
99.   10 Rupees (C-N) 1974   10.00
100.   10 Paise (A) 1974. (Scalloped planchet)   .35

107.

107a.

107.   10 Paise (Al) 1977. (F.A.O.)   2.50
107a.   5 Paise (Al) 1977. (F.A.O.)   1.50
108.   50 Rupees 1978. Asoka Pillar. Rev: House; sym-
      bols of agriculture; FOOD & SHELTER FOR ALL.
      (F.A.O.)   17.50
109.   10 Rupees 1978. Type of #108   5.00
110.   10 Paise (C-N) 1978. Type of #108   .25
111.   50 Rupees 1979. Rev: Emblem within wreath.
      (International Year of Child)   17.50
112.   10 Rupees 1979. (International Year of Child)   5.00
113.   10 Paise (C-N) 1979. (International Year of
      Child)   .25

101.   50 Rupees 1975. Woman in sari with ear of
      wheat, dam in background. Rev: Asoka pillar,
      value. (F.A.O.)   30.00
102.   10 Rupees (C-N) 1975   10.00

114. 100 Rupees 1980. Rev: Woman using modern ap-
     pliances. (Rural Women's Advancement)   30.00
115. 10 Rupees 1980. (Rural Women's Advancement)   5.00
116. 10 Paise (C-N) 1980. (Rural Women's Advance-
     ment.) Issued in proof only   10.00
117. 100 Rupees 1981. Rev: Stylized agricultural
     scene. (World Food Day; F.A.O. coin plan)   30.00

INDIA (continued)

INDIAN STATES

NOTE: Coins listed below are representative of issues of the individual states. (See also "Bhutan," p. 56.)

Bengal

5.	1 Mohur (G) 1750–1820	175.00

Alwar

1.	1 Rupee 1877–82, '91. Crowned bust of Victoria. Rev: Value and inscription	25.00

Bikanir

6.	1 Rupee 1892–97. Crowned bust of Victoria. Rev: Value and inscription	25.00
7.	¼ Anna 1895	15.50
8.	½ Pice 1894	15.50

9.	1 Mohur (G) 1937. Bust of Rajah Sri Ganga Singhji. Rev: Inscription. (50th year of reign)	375.00

Bahawalpur

2.	¼ Anna (C) 1940. Bust of Raja Sadiq Mohammed V in fez. Rev: Toughra	2.50
3.	½ Pice (C) 1940	2.00

10.	1 Rupee 1937. Bust of Rajah Sri Ganga Singhji. (50th year of reign)	30.00

Baroda

4.	2 Paisas (Bro) 1940–50. Inscription. Rev: Hoof and sword	5.00

Bombay

11.	Double Pice (C) 1804. Arms of East India Co. Rev: Balance	17.50

INDIA (continued)

Dewas

NOTE: Senior branch and junior branch are indicated by
S.B. and J.B. on reverse.

12.	¼ Anna (C) 1888. Crowned bust of Victoria. Rev: Value and inscription	25.00
13.	¹⁄₁₂ Anna (C) 1888	25.00

Dhar

14.	¼ Anna (C) 1887. Crowned bust of Victoria. Rev: Value and inscription	20.00
15.	½ Pice (C) 1887	15.00
16.	¹⁄₁₂ Anna (C) 1887	12.50

Gwalior

17.	¼ Anna (C) 1929; (reduced size) 1942. Bust of Rajah Jivaji III in turban. Rev: Arms with supporters	2.50

Hyderabad

18.	1 Rupee A.H. 1321–43 (1903–24). Palace gateway. Rev: Inscription	17.50
19.	½ Rupee (N) A.H. 1366 (1948)	2.50
20.	¼ Rupee (N) A.H. 1366–68	1.00
21.	⅛ Rupee (N) A.H. 1366–68	.50
22.	1 Anna (Bro) 1942–48. (Square planchet)	.35

23.	2 Pai (Bro) 1943–48. Inscriptions. (Center hole)	.75

Indore

24.	¼ Anna (C) 1886–1902. Seated bull.	4.00
25.	½ Anna (C) 1935. Bust of Yeshwant Rao Holkar	7.50
26.	¼ Anna (C) 1935	6.50

Jaipur

27.	1 Anna (N-Bro) 1944. Bust of Man Singh II	1.00

INDIA (continued)

Jaora

28.	2 Paisas (C) 1893–94. Inscription	12.50
29.	1 Paisa (C) 1893–96	10.00

Kutch

30.	5 Kori 1936. Native inscription IN THE NAME OF EDWARD VIII	15.00
31.	1 Kori 1936	5.00
32.	3 Dokda (C) 1936	17.50

33.	5 Kori 1947. Castle towers and inscription. Rev: Trident, crescent, dagger and inscription	250.00

Madras

34.	1 Rupee 1758–1811. Native inscription. (Crude, thick planchet)	20.00

35.	1 Rupee 1811–22. Native inscription. (Round, milled planchet)	25.00

36.	1 Pagoda (G) 1808–15. Pagoda. Rev: The god Swami	250.00
37.	½ Pagoda 1807–08	250.00
38.	¼ Pagoda 1807–08	75.00

Mewar Udaipur

39.	Rupee 1932. Hills and inscription in floral border. Rev: Inscription	15.00

Sailana

40.	¼ Anna (C) 1908. Head of Edward VII	25.00
41.	¼ Anna (C) 1912. Head of George V	17.50

Travancore

42.	1 Chuckram (C) 1938. Bust of Rajah Bala Rama Varma in plumed hat. Rev: Conch shell in floral border	6.50
43.	½ Rupee 1936–45. Rev: Conch shell	10.00
44.	8 Cash (C). Conch shell. Rev: Monogram	2.00
45.	4 Cash (C)	1.00
46.	1 Cash (C)	.75

INDO-CHINA

The states in this, the easternmost area of the Southeast Asian peninsula, were united under a French protectorate, the Union of Indo-China, until 1946. Laos and Cambodia became independent in 1949 and 1953 respectively. Vietnam gained temporary independence in 1945, but it was not until 1954 that the French pulled out completely. (See separate listings for subsequent histories of these nations.)

100 Centimes = 1 Piastre = 1 Franc
1 Xu = 1 Centime
10 Haos = 1 Piastre
1 Dong = 1 Piastre

FRENCH COCHIN-CHINA

1.	1 Piastre 1879–85. Republic seated. Rev: Value in wreath. Proof	RARE
2.	50 Centimes 1879–85	200.00
3.	20 Centimes 1879, '84–85	125.00
4.	10 Centimes 1879, '84–85	75.00

5.	1 Centime (Br) 1879–85. Rev: Value in circle	25.00
6.	2 Sapeque (Br) 1879–85. (Square center hole)	20.00

FRENCH INDO-CHINA

7.	1 Piastre 1885–1928. Republic seated. Rev: Value in wreath	25.00
8.	50 Centimes 1885–1936	7.50
9.	20 Centimes 1885–1937	5.00
10.	10 Centimes 1885–1937	4.00
11.	1 Centime (Br) 1885–94	4.00

12.	2 Sapeque (Br) 1887–1902. (Square center hole)	10.00

13.	1 Piastre 1931. Liberty head. Rev: Value	25.00

14.	5 Centimes (C-N) 1923–38; (N-Bra) 1938, '39. Head and cornucopias. Rev: Value. (Center hole)	1.50

15.	1 Centime (Bro) 1896–1939. Seated figures. Rev: Value in Chinese. (Center hole)	3.00

16.	½ Centime (Br) 1935–40. Liberty cap and "RF." Rev: Value. (Center hole)	2.00
16a.	½ Centime (Z) 1939, '40	RARE

17. 20 Centimes (N) 1939; (C-N) 1939–41 Inscription REPUBLIQUE FRANÇAISE, bust of Liberty. Rev: Rice plants and value   2.50
18. 10 Centimes (N) 1939–40; (C-N) 1939–41   2.00

19. 1 Piastre (N-Bro) 1946–47. Inscription UNION FRANÇAISE, bust of Liberty. Rev: Rice plants and value   17.50

20. 50 Centimes (C-N) 1946. Republic seated. Rev: Value   12.50

21. 20 Centimes (A) 1945. Bust of Liberty. Rev: Rice plants and value   4.00
22. 10 Centimes (A) 1945   3.00
23. 5 Centimes (A) 1946   1.50

INDONESIA

This republic is made up of Java, Sumatra, most of Borneo, Celebes and 3000 other islands, all formerly part of the Netherlands East Indies (q.v.). It came into existence in 1949. Netherlands New Guinea, now known as West Irian, was added in 1963.

100 Sen = 1 Rupiah

1.   50 Sen (C-N) 1952–57. Indonesian. Rev: Value   .75

2.   50 Sen (A) 1958–61. Bird. Rev: Value   .75
3.   25 Sen (A) 1952–57. Bird. Rev: Value   .75
4.   10 Sen (A) 1951–57   .75

5.   5 Sen (A) 1951–54. (Holed center)   .65
6.   1 Sen (A) 1952   1.00

7.   50 Rupiah (C-N) 1971. Bird of paradise. Rev: value   1.50

8.   25 Rupiah (C-N) 1971. Crowned pigeon. Rev: Value   .75

9.   10 Rupiah (C-N) 1971. Cotton and rice with value. Rev: Value. (F.A.O. coin plan)   .50
10.   5 Rupiah (A) 1970. Long-tailed bird. Rev: Value   .75

11.   2 Rupiah (A) 1970. Rice and cotton with value. Rev: Value   .35
12.   1 Rupiah (A) 1970. Bird with fanlike tail. Rev: Value   .25

13.   100 Rupiah (C-N) 1973. Longhouse. Rev: Value   1.50

14.   100,000 Rupiah (G) 1974. Komodo dragon. Rev: Arms. (Conservation commemorative)   650.00

INDONESIA (continued)

15. 5000 Rupiah 1974. Orangutan. Rev: Arms (Conservation) 50.00

19. 100 Rupiah (C-N) 1978. Longhouse. Rev: "Tree of Life" agricultural symbol. (F.A.O. coin plan) 1.50
20. 10 Rupiah (A) 1979. National savings symbol. Rev: Value. (F.A.O. coin plan) .... .50
21. 5 Rupiah (A) 1979. Family planning symbol. Rev: Value. (F.A.O. coin plan) .... .40

16. 2000 Rupiah 1974. Javan tiger. Rev: Arms (Conservation) 35.00

17. 10 Rupiah (Bra-St) 1974. National savings symbol. Rev: Value. (F.A.O. coin plan) .... .50

18. 5 Rupiah (A) 1974. Family planning symbol. Rev: Value. (F.A.O.) .... .50

INDONESIA (continued)

Riau

This archipelago, a province of Indonesia, lies between Sumatra and Singapore.

1.	50 Sen (A) 1962. Bust of President Sukarno. Rev: Value in wreath, lettered edge KEP-ULAUAN RIAU	3.50
2.	25 Sen (A) 1962	3.00
3.	10 Sen (A) 1962	2.25

4.	5 Sen (A) 1962	1.50
5.	1 Sen (A) 1962	2.00

Irian Jaya (West Irian)

Formerly Netherlands New Guinea, this area was not included in the Republic of Indonesia established in 1949 when the Netherlands withdrew. Under an agreement reached in 1962, Indonesia won control of West Irian, following a brief period of U.N. administration.

1.	50 Sen (A) 1962 Bust of President Sukarno. Rev: Value and wreath, reeded edge	4.00
2.	25 Sen (A) 1962	3.00
3.	10 Sen (A) 1962. (Plain edge)	2.50
4.	5 Sen (A) 1962. (Plain edge)	2.00
5.	1 Sen (A) 1962. (Plain edge)	2.50

IRAN

This country, located in western Asia on the Persian Gulf, was known as Persia until 1935. The Persians had one of the mightiest empires of ancient times. In 1906 a constitutional monarchy was established. In 1979 the Shah was deposed and the Islamic Republic of Iran founded. Iran is economically important for its large oil reserves.

10 Krans = 1 Toman
100 Dinars = 1 Ryal or Rial

GENERAL TYPE

1.	5 Krans 1878–1928. Lion with sword. Rev: Inscription	25.00
2.	2 Krans 1878–1928	12.50
3.	1 Kran 1878–1928	7.50
4.	½ Kran 1878–1927	10.00
5.	¼ Kran 1878–1924	10.00

MOZAFAR-ED-DIN SHAH   1896–1907

6.	2 Krans 1904. Bust. Rev: Lion	30.00

AHMED SHAH   1909–25

7.	2 Krans 1919. Bust. Rev: Lion	300.00

RIZA SHAH PAHLEVI   1925–41

8.	2 Krans 1927–29. Bust in uniform	25.00

LAW OF 1937 (S.H. 1315)

9.	50 Dinars (A-Bro) S.H. 1315–22. Lion with sword	2.00
10.	10 Dinars (A-Bro) S.H. 1315–21	2.00
11.	5 Dinars (A-Bro) S.H. 1315–21	2.00

MOHAMMED RIZA PAHLEVI   1942–79
LAW OF 1944 (S.H. 1323)

12.	10 Rials S.H. 1323–26. Lion with sword	15.00
13.	5 Rials S.H. 1322–28	6.00
14.	2 Rials S.H. 1322–30	2.50
15.	1 Rial S.H. 1322–25	2.00

LAW OF 1954 (S.H. 1333)

16.	10 Rials (C-N) S.H. 1335–44	3.00
17.	5 Rials (C-N) S.H. 1333–56. Lion with sword	1.50
18.	2 Rials (C-N) S.H. 1333–56	1.50
19.	1 Rial (C-N) S.H. 1333–54	1.00
20.	50 Dinars (A–Bro) S.H. 1333–54; (Bra-St) A.D. 1975–77	.50

21.	10 Rials (C-N) 1966–77. Head of Shah. Rev: Lion with sword	2.50

22.	10 Rials (C-N) 1969. Rev: F.A.O. inscription	2.50
23.	20 Rials (C-N) 1971–77. Type of #21	1.50

24. 1 Rial (C-N) 1971–73. Head of Shah. Rev: Lion with sword, inscription. (F.A.O. coin plan)   .35

25. 20 Rials (C-N) 1974. Rev: Stylized star. (Seventh Asian Games in Teheran)   1.00

26. 20 Rials (C-N) 1976. Mohammed Riza Pahlevi. Rev: Arms. (50th anniversary of Pahlevi rule)   1.00
27. 10 Rials (C-N) 1976   .75

28. 5 Rials (C-N) 1976. Arms. Rev: Value   .40
29. 2 Rials (C-N) 1976   .40
30. 1 Rial (C-N) 1976   .25
31. 50 Dinars (Bra) 1976   .15
32. 20 Rials (C-N) 1979. Religious symbols. Rev: Value. (1400th anniversary of Muhammad's Hegira ["flight"])   7.50
33. 20 Rials (C-N) 1979– . Inscription. Rev: Value within wreath   3.50
34. 10 Rials (C-N) 1979. Stylized design. Rev: Value within wreath. (First anniversary of Islamic revolution)   5.00
35. 10 Rials (C-N) 1979– . Inscription. Rev: Value within wreath   3.50
36. 5 Rials (C-N) 1979–   2.00
37. 2 Rials (C-N) 1979–   1.75

38. 1 Rial (C-N) 1979–   1.50
39. 1 Rial (C-N) 1979. Mosque of Omar, Jerusalem. Rev: Value   1.50

IRAQ

Until World War I part of the Turkish Empire and known as Mesopotamia, Iraq became a British mandate in 1920. The mandate ended in 1932, when Iraq became independent. It was a monarchy from 1921 until 1958 when an army revolt resulted in the assassination of King Faisal II and the creation of a republic.

1000 Fils or 20 Dirhem or 5 Riyals =
1 Pound or 1 Dinar

FAISAL I 1921–33

1.	200 Fils or 1 Riyal 1932. Head. Rev: Arabic inscription	65.00
2.	50 Fils or 1 Dirhem 1931–33	12.50
3.	20 Fils 1931–33	10.00
4.	10 Fils (N) 1931–33. Scalloped edge	7.50
5.	4 Fils (N) 1931–33	6.50
6.	2 Fils (Bro) 1931–33. Type of #1	4.00
7.	1 Fil (Bro) 1931–33	3.00

GHAZI I 1933–39

8.	50 Fils or 1 Dirhem 1937–38. Head. Rev: Arabic inscription	7.50
9.	20 Fils 1938	6.00
10.	10 Fils (N) 1937–38; (Bro or C-N) 1938. Scalloped edge	5.00
11.	4 Fils (C-N) 1938; (Bro) 1938; (N) 1938–39	1.00
12.	1 Fil (Bro) 1936–38. Round	1.00

FAISAL II 1939–58
(Regency 1939–53)

13.	10 Fils (Bro) 1943. Young head. Rev: Arabic inscription. (Scalloped edge)	12.50
14.	4 Fils (Bro) 1943	12.50

15.	100 Fils 1953–55. Older head. Rev: Arabic inscription	20.00
16.	50 Fils 1953, '55. (Reduced planchet)	10.00
17.	20 Fils 1953, '55. (Reduced)	10.00
18.	10 Fils (C-N) 1953. (Scalloped edge)	1.50
19.	4 Fils (C-N) 1953. (Scalloped edge)	1.50
20.	2 Fils (Br) 1953. (Round)	3.00
21.	1 Fil (Bro) 1953	1.00

REPUBLIC 1958–

22.	100 Fils 1959. Emblem of Republic. Rev: Value	5.00
23.	50 Fils 1959	4.00
24.	25 Fils 1959	1.50
25.	10 Fils (C-N) 1959. (Scalloped edge)	1.00
26.	5 Fils (C-N) 1959	1.00
27.	1 Fil (Br) 1959. (Decagonal planchet)	1.00

28.	50 Fils (C-N) 1969– Palm trees. Rev: Crossed branches	.75
29.	25 Fils (C-N) 1969–75	.45
30.	10 Fils (C-N) 1967–71; (St) 1971–75. (Scalloped)	.40
31.	5 Fils (C-N) 1967–71; (St) 1971–75	.30
32.	100 Fils (C-N) 1970–75	1.00
33.	250 Fils (N) 1970. Type of #28, with added reverse inscription. (F.A.O. coin plan)	6.50

34.	5 Dinars (G) 1971. Two soldiers. Rev: Value. (50th anniversary of Iraqi army)	325.00

35.	1 Dinar 1971	40.00
36.	500 Fils 1971	20.00

37. 250 Fils (N) 1971. Dove in flight over mountains. Rev: Value. (1st anniversary of peace with Kurds)   12.50

38. 1 Dinar 1972. Type of #28 with added reverse inscription. (25th anniversary of Central Bank)   40.00

39. 250 Fils (N) 1972   15.00

40. 250 Fils (N) 1972. Type of #28 with added reverse inscription. (25th anniversary of Al Baath political party)   15.00

46. 1 Dinar 1977. Canal. Rev: Value and inscription. (First anniversary, Tharthat-Euphrates Canal.) Issued in proof only   50.00

47. 1 Dinar 1979. Child within circle. Rev: Value, inscription. (International Year of Child.) In proof only   40.00

48. 1 Dinar 1980. Stylized religious symbols. Rev: Value. (1400th anniversary of Muhammad's Hegira.) In proof only   40.00

49. 250 Fils (N) 1980. Saddam Hussein. Rev: Value, inscription   4.00

50. 250 Fils (N) 1981. Agricultural scene. Rev: F.A.O. emblem, inscription. (F.A.O. coin plan; octagonal shape)   4.00

41. 1 Dinar 1973. Oil tanker, rising sun. Rev: Value and inscription. (Nationalization of petroleum industry)   40.00

42. 500 Fils (N) 1973. Oil tank. Rev: Value and inscription. (Nationalization of petroleum industry)   20.00

43. 250 Fils (N) 1973. Torch between storage tanks and oil rig. Rev: Value and inscription. (Nationalization of petroleum industry)   12.50

44. 10 Fils (C-N) 1975. Three palms. Rev: Value. (F.A.O. coin plan)   1.00

45. 5 Fils (C-N) 1975   .50

IRELAND (Eire)

An independent republic. All coins of Ireland picture a harp on the obverse. Coins issued 1928–38 read SAORSTAT EIREANN; those from 1939 to date, EIRE. Denominations are the same as Great Britain's.

7.	Halfpenny (Bro) 1928–67. Rev: Sow and piglets	1.00
8.	Farthing (Bro) 1928–66. Rev: Woodcock	1.25

9.   10 Shillings 1966. Padraig H. Pearse. Rev: Memorial statue in Dublin. (50th anniversary of 1916 Easter Uprising)   10.00

1.	Half Crown 1928–43. Harp. Rev: Horse	15.00
1a.	Half Crown (C-N) 1951–67	2.00

DECIMAL COINAGE

2.	Florin 1928–43. Rev: Salmon	10.00
2a.	Florin (C-N) 1951–68	1.50
3.	Shilling 1928–42. Rev: Bull	6.00
3a.	Shilling (C-N) 1951–68	2.00

10.	50 Pence (C-N) 1970– . Harp. Rev: Woodcock. (Heptagonal planchet)	1.75
11.	10 Pence (C-N) 1969– . Harp. Rev: Salmon	.40
12.	5 Pence (C-N) 1969– . Harp. Rev: Bull	.25

NOTE: All 1971 decimal coins also struck in special proof editions

4.	6 Pence (N) 1928–40; (C-N) 1942–69. Rev: Wolfhound	2.00
5.	3 Pence (N) 1928–40; (C-N) 1942–68. Rev: Hare	3.00
6.	Penny (Bro) 1928–68. Rev: Hen and chicks	1.00
13.	2 Pence (Bro) 1971– . Harp. Stylized bird	.25
14.	1 Penny (Bro) 1971–	.15
15.	½ Penny (Bro) 1971–	.10

ISLE OF MAN

Located in the Irish Sea, this island had been held by the Romans, Irish and Scandinavians before coming under British rule. After being privately held by the Earls of Derby and the Dukes of Atholl it passed to the British Crown. An interesting feature of the island's coinage is the triquetrum—"a three-legged device of booted and spurred human legs bent at the knee as though running, and joined at the hip to form a radiating design."

12 Pence = 1 Shilling
25 New Pence = 1 Crown

EARLS OF DERBY

1.	Penny (C) 1709, '33. The Stanley crest. Rev: Triquetrum	60.00
2.	Halfpenny (C) 1709, '33	75.00

DUKES OF ATHOLL

3.	Penny (C) 1758. Crowned monogram	50.00
4.	Halfpenny (C) 1758	50.00

GEORGE III   1760–1820

5.	Penny (C) 1786. Laureated head. Rev: Triquetrum	50.00
6.	Halfpenny (C) 1786	20.00
7.	Penny (C) 1798, 1813. Laureated head. Rev: Triquetrum. ("Cartwheel" type)	30.00

8.	Halfpenny (C) 1798, 1813	20.00

VICTORIA   1837–1901

9.	Penny (C) 1839. Young head. Rev: Triquetrum	35.00
10.	Halfpenny 1839	25.00
11.	Farthing 1839	25.00

ELIZABETH II   1952–

12.	5 Pounds (G) 1965. Queen Elizabeth II. Rev: Arms in shield. (200th anniversary, acquisition of Isle of Man)	850.00
13.	1 Pound (G) 1965	200.00
14.	½ Pound (G) 1965	125.00

15.	1 Crown (CN) 1970. Draped bust of Queen Elizabeth with coronet. Rev: Tailless Manx cat	12.50

ISLE OF MAN (continued)

DECIMAL COINAGE

23.	5 Pounds (G) 1973, '77. Rev: Viking on horseback	850.00
24.	2 Pounds (G) 1973, '77	350.00
25.	1 Sovereign (G) 1973, '77	150.00
26.	½ Sovereign (G) 1973, '77	100.00

16. 50 New Pence (C-N) 1971– . Draped bust of Queen Elizabeth II. Rev: Viking ship   4.00

17. 10 New Pence (C-N) 1971– . Rev: Triquetrum   1.00
18. 5 New Pence (C-N) 1971– . Rev: Tower of Refuge   1.00

27.	1 Crown (C-N) 1974. Rev: Bust of Winston Churchill. (100th anniversary of statesman's birth)	5.00
28.	1 Crown (S) 1974. Proof	35.00
29.	25 Pence (C-N) 1975. Rev: Manx cat	4.00
29a.	1 Crown (C-N) 1976. Rev: Bust of George Washington. (Bicentennial of American independence)	5.00
29b.	1 Crown (C-N) 1976. Rev: Tram. (Centennial of horse-drawn tram)	5.00

19. 2 New Pence (Bro) 1971–75. Rev: Two falcons   .65
20. 1 New Penny (Bro) 1971–75. Rev: Ring chain pattern   .25
21. ½ New Penny (Bro) 1971–75. Rev: Cushag (national flower)   .20

30. 5 Pence (C-N) 1976– . Rev: Laxey water wheel superimposed on map   .35

31. 2 Pence (Br) 1976– . Rev: Bird in flight over map   .15
32. 1 Penny (Bro) 1976– . Rev: Mountain goat superimposed on map   .10
33. ½ Penny (Br) 1976– . Rev: Fish superimposed on map   .10

22. 25 New Pence (C-N) 1972. Rev: Conjoined arms. (Royal Silver Wedding Anniversary)   10.00
22a. 25 New Pence (S) 1972. Proof   50.00

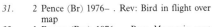

297

ISLE OF MAN (continued)

34. 1 Crown (C-N) 1977. Rev: Triquetrum within triple crown. (Queen's Silver Jubilee)   10.00
35. 1 Crown (C-N) 1977. Rev: Crowned royal monogram within wreath. (Queen's Jubilee Appeal)   5.00

36. 1 Crown (C-N) 1978. Rev: Two falcons. (25th anniversary of Queen's coronation)   5.00
37. 1 Crown (C-N) 1979. Rev: Triquetrum within circle of eight coins. (300th anniversary of Manx coinage)   5.00

39.

40.

39. 1 Crown (C-N) 1979. Rev: English "cog," a vintage broad-beamed warship   5.00
40. 1 Crown (C-N) 1979. Rev: Flemish carrack   5.00

38. 1 Crown (C-N) 1979. Rev: Viking longship. (Millennium of Tynwald Court)   5.00

41.

42.

41. 1 Crown (C-N) 1979. Rev: Royalist soldier and English man-of-war   5.00
42. 1 Crown (C-N) 1979. Rev: Cameo portrait of Sir Hillary above lifeboat   5.00
43. 1 Crown (C-N) 1980. Rev: Jockey on race horse. (Centennial of English Derby)   5.00

44.

45.

48. 1 Crown (C-N) 1980. Rev: Bust of Queen Mother Elizabeth wearing tiara. (Queen Mother's 80th Birthday) 5.00

49.

50.

51.

52.

46.

47.

44. 1 Crown (C-N) 1980. Rev: Triquetrum within circle of winter-sports athletes. (1980 Lake Placid Winter Olympics) 5.00

45. 1 Crown (C-N) 1980. Rev: Triquetrum within circle of athletes, runner at top. (1980 Moscow Olympics) 5.00

46. 1 Crown (C-N) 1980. Rev: Triquetrum, circle of athletes, javelin thrower at top. (Moscow Olympics) 5.00

47. 1 Crown (C-N) 1980. Rev: Triquetrum, circle of athletes, judo match at top. (Moscow Olympics) 5.00

49. 1 Crown (C-N) 1981. Rev: Bust of Prince Philip, Duke of Edinburgh. (Duke of Edinburgh's "Award Scheme" and 60th birthday) 5.00

50. 1 Crown (C-N) 1981. Rev: Crowned monogram within wreath 5.00

51. 1 Crown (C-N) 1981. Rev: Swimmers at bottom 5.00

52. 1 Crown (C-N) 1981. Rev: Cyclist, climber, sailor 5.00

53.   1 Crown (C-N) 1981. Rev: Bust of Louis Braille and vignette of Braille alphabet for blind. (International Year of Disabled)   5.00

54.   1 Crown (C-N) 1981. Rev: Bust of Ludwig van Beethoven against musical motif. (International Year of Disabled)   5.00

55.   1 Crown (C-N) 1981. Rev: Bust of Sir Douglas Bader. (International Year of Disabled)   5.00

56.   50 Pence (C-N) 1981. Rev: Peel Harbor, boats under full sail. (Christmas issue; heptagonal planchet)   3.00

57.   20 Pence (C-N) 1982. Rev: Montage of arms and armor from Middle Ages. (Heptagonal planchet)   2.50

58.   5 Pounds (G) 1982. Elizabeth II. Rev: Type of #23, with countermark of baby's crib (honors birth of Prince William, son of Prince Charles and Princess Diana)   850.00

59.   2 Pounds (G) 1982   350.00

60.   1 Sovereign (G) 1982   150.00

61.   ½ Sovereign (G) 1982   100.00

ISRAEL

As a result of action by the United Nations, Israel came into existence as an independent republic in May 1948. Previously it was part of the British mandate of Palestine.

1000 Pruta = 1 Israeli Pound (Lira)

NOTE: In Nos. 1–15 both traditional Jewish dates and Western dates are given (see chart p. 305).

1. 25 Mils (A) 5708–09 (1948–49). Cluster of grapes, "Israel" in Hebrew above, Arabic below. Rev: Value in olive wreath   50.00

2. 500 Pruta 5709 (1949). Pomegranates. Rev: Value in olive wreath   40.00

3. 250 Pruta 5709 (1949). Wheat ears. Rev: Value in olive wreath, "H" mint mark at bottom   30.00
3a. 250 Pruta (C-N) 5709 (1949). (No mint mark)   6.50

4. 100 Pruta (C-N) 5709, '15 (1949, '55). Palm tree with date clusters   7.50
4a. 100 Pruta (N-St) 5714 (1954). (Smaller planchet)   7.50

5. 50 Pruta (C-N) 5709, '14 (1949, '54). Vine leaf   7.50
5a. 50 Pruta (N-St) 5714 (1954). (Slightly smaller planchet)   6.50

6. 25 Pruta (C-N) 5709 (1949). Cluster of grapes   3.50
6a. 25 Pruta (N-St) 5714 (1954)   7.50

7.   7b.

7a.

7. 10 Pruta (Bro) 5709 (1949). Amphora with two handles. Rev: Value in olive wreath   4.00
7a. 10 Pruta (A) 5712 (1952). Jug with one handle. (Scalloped-edge planchet)   5.00
7b. 10 Pruta (A) 5717 (1957); (C-A) 5717 (1957). (Round planchet)   7.50

8. 5 Pruta (Bro) 5709 (1949). Lyre. Rev: Value in olive wreath   5.00

9. 1 Pruta (A) 5709 (1949). Anchor. Rev: Value in olive wreath   3.50

ISRAEL (continued)

COMMEMORATIVE ISSUES

10. 1 Pound (C-N) 5723–27 (1963–67). Menorah.
     Rev: Value   3.50
11. ½ Pound (C-N) 5723–39 (1963–79)   2.00

16. 5 Pounds 1958. Stylized menorah. Rev: Value.
     (10th anniversary of Israel's independence)   50.00

12. 25 Agorot (A-Bro) 5720–38 (1960–78). Lyre.
     Rev: Value   1.25
12a. 25 Agorot (C-N) 5731–39 (1971–79)   1.00

13. 10 Agorot (A-Bro) 5720–37 (1960–77). Palm
     tree with date clusters   1.00
13a. 10 Agorot (C-N) 5731–38 (1971–78); (A)
     5737–40 (1977–80)   1.00

17. 1 Pound (C-N) 1958. (Chanukah—"Festival of
     Lights")   12.50

14. 5 Agorot (A-Bro) 5720–35 (1960–75). Pome-
     granates   .75
14a. 5 Agorot (C-N) 5731–37 (1971–77); (A)
     5736–39 (1976–79)   .75

18. 5 Pounds 1959. Dancers. Rev: Value. (11th an-
     niversary of Israel's independence—"In-
     gathering of the Exiles" in Hebrew)   75.00

19. 20 Pounds (G) 1960. Head of Theodor Herzl.
     Rev: Menorah. (100th anniversary of birth of
     founder of Zionism)   850.00

15. 1 Agora (A) 5720–40 (1960–80). Barley ears.
     (Scalloped edge planchet)   .25

20. 5 Pounds 1960. (Theodor Herzl commemorative)   65.00

21. 1 Pound (C-N) 1960. (50th anniversary of founding of Deganya, the first kibbutz)   15.00

22. 1 Pound (C-N) 1960. Woman with lamb. Rev: Hadassah Medical Center in Jerusalem. (Henrietta Szold commemorative)   150.00

23. 5 Pounds 1961. Ark containing six rolls of the Torah. (Bar Mitzvah commemorative)   150.00

24. 1 Pound (C-N) 1961. Charging elephant and warriors. (Heroism and sacrifice commemorative)   50.00

25. ½ Pound (C-N) 1961, '62. Reproduction of ancient Jewish half shekel. Rev: Value. (Feast of Purim)   40.00

26. 100 Pounds (G) 1962. Head of Chaim Weizmann. Rev: Menorah. (10th anniversary of death of Israel's first president.) Proof   1000.00

27. 50 Pounds (G) 1962. Proof   650.00

31. 1 Pound (C-N) 1963. North African Chanukah
    lamp   150.00

28. 5 Pounds 1962. (Industrialization of Negev)   200.00

32. 50 Pounds [Lirot] (G) 1964. Pomegranate and
    double cornucopia. Rev: Menorah. (10th an-
    niversary of Bank of Israel)   1000.00

29. 1 Pound (C-N) 1962. Early Italian menorah   150.00

33. 5 Pounds 1964. Museum buildings. Rev: An-
    cient pillar. (16th anniversary of Museum of
    Israel)   150.00

30. 5 Pounds 1963. Ancient galley. Rev: Smoke-
    stack of modern ship. (Honors seafaring)   750.00

34. 5 Pounds 1965. Parliament (Knesset) building
    in Jerusalem. Rev: Menorah and value. (17th
    anniversary of Knesset building)   85.00

ISRAEL (continued)

JEWISH AND GREGORIAN CALENDARS

תש״ח	-	5708(1948)
תש״ט	-	5709(1949)
תשי״ב	-	5712(1952)
תשי״ד	-	5714(1954)
תשט״ו	-	5715(1955)
תשי״ז	-	5717(1957)
תש״ך	-	5720(1960)
תשכ״א	-	5721(1961)
תשכ״ב	-	5722(1962)
תשכ״ג	-	5723(1963)
תשכ״ד	-	5724(1964)
תשכ״ה	-	5725(1965)

© 1964 Fred Bertram (Miami, Fla.)

NOTE: The dates on Israeli coins are according to the Jewish calendar, figured from the time of Adam. The year 1965, for example, is 5725. Israeli commemorative coins show Christian era dates in Arabic numerals, but regular issue coins carry only Hebrew dates in Hebrew characters per the above chart.

36. 10 Pounds 1967. Wailing Wall of Temple of Solomon in Jerusalem. Rev: Emblem of Israel Defense Forces. (Victory in Six Day War) 35.00

37. 5 Pounds 1967. Lighthouse. Rev: Large numeral. (10th anniversary of port of Eilat) 75.00

35. 5 Pounds 1966. Modernistic design of Hebrew words. Rev: Inscription and value. (18th anniversary of independence) 60.00

38. 1 Pound (C-N) 1967– . Pomegranates. Rev: Value and inscription 2.00

305

39. 10 Pounds 1968. View of Jerusalem. Rev: Facade of Temple of Solomon. (Reunification of city and 20th anniversary of Israel)   50.00

42. 10 Pounds 1970. Stylized plow. Rev: Campus building. (Centenary of Mikveh Israel School)   35.00

40. 10 Pounds 1969. Hebrew letters for *Shalom* ("Peace"). Rev: Military memorial, helmet. (21st anniversary of independence)   50.00

43. 10 Pounds 1971. Cogwheel rotating molecule. Rev: Atomic reactor building at Nahal Sorek. (23rd anniversary of independence)   50.00

41. 10 Pounds 1970–72. Tablets of Law. Rev: Arms. (*Pidyon ha-ben* coin for ceremony of redemption of first-born child; reverse design differs slightly each year)   35.00

44. 100 Pounds (G) 1971. Sun behind bars. Rev: Value, small menorah   800.00

45. 10 Pounds 1971   35.00

46. 10 Pounds 1972, Stylized jet. Rev: Value with rocket for numeral 1. (24th anniversary of independence)   40.00

47. 5 Pounds 1972. Russian menorah. Rev: Value   25.00

48. 200 Pounds (G) 1973. Final paragraph of Declaration of Israeli Independence with signatures. Rev: Arms and value. (25th anniversary of independence)   650.00
49. 100 Pounds (G) 1973   300.00
50. 50 Pounds (G) 1973   175.00
51. 10 Pounds 1973   25.00

52. 10 Pounds 1973–74. Offering tray with five replicas of shekels. Rev: Arms and value. (*Pidyon ha-ben* coin; reverse design differs slightly each year)   25.00

53. 5 Pounds 1973. Babylonian menorah. Rev: Value   15.00

54. 500 Pounds (G) 1974. Head of Ben Gurion in incuse panel. Rev: Arms   650.00
55. 25 Pounds 1974   35.00

56. 10 Pounds 1974. Menorah from Damascus. Rev: Value   30.00

57. 10 Pounds 1974. Torah scroll. Rev: Value, arms. (Preservation of Hebrew language)   30.00

58. 500 Pounds (G) 1975. Value. Rev: Star design. (25th anniversary of Israeli bond program)   500.00
59. 25 Pounds 1975   30.00

60. 10 Pounds 1975. Menorah from Holland. Rev: Value in pentagon   30.00

61. 25 Pounds 1976. Menorah between olive branches. Rev: Five pomegranate stalks. (*Pidyon ha-ben* coin)   30.00

62. 10 Pounds 1976. Menorah from the U.S. Rev: Value   75.00

63. 25 Pounds 1977. Value. Rev: Stylized view of old Jerusalem, BROTHERHOOD IN JERUSALEM. (29th anniversary of independence)   30.00
64. 25 Pounds 1977. Value over menorah. (*Pidyon ha-ben*)   30.00

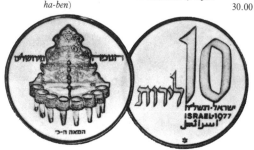

65. 10 Pounds (C-N) 1977. Menorah. "Chanukah-Jerusalem." Open-style *mem*   15.00
66. 10 Pounds (C-N) 1977. Closed-style *mem*   35.00
67. 1000 Pounds (G) 1978. Value. Rev: Olive tree. (30th anniversary of independence.) Issued in proof only   450.00
68. 50 Pounds 1978. (30th anniversary of independence)   25.00
69. 25 Pounds (C-N) 1978. Chanukah   12.50

70. 5 Pounds (C-N) 1978–79. Lion. Rev: Value. (Lion design adapted from ancient seal of King Jeroboam II, found by German archeologist, 1904)   2.00
71. 100 Pounds 1979. Value over menorah. Rev: Egyptian Chanukah lamp   15.00

72.   73.

72. 5000 Pounds (G) 1980. Menorah, inscription, value. Rev: Olive branches, PEACE. (Israeli-Egyptian Peace Treaty) — 450.00
73. 200 Pounds 1980 — 60.00
74. 1 Pound (C-N) 1980. (25th anniversary of Bank of Israel) — 5.00
75. ½ Pound (N) 1980 — 2.00
76. 25 Agorot (N) 1980 — 1.50
77. 10 Agorot (N) 1980 — 1.50
78. 5 Agorot (N) 1980 — 1.50
79. 1 Agora (N) 1980 — 1.25

NEW MONETARY SYSTEM   FEBRUARY 24, 1980

1 New Agora = 10 Old Agorot
1 Lira = 10 New Agorot
1 Sheqel = 10 Lirot

80. 500 Sheqalim (G) 1980. Bust of Zeev Jabotinsky. Rev: Menorah over value. In proof only — 450.00
81. 25 Sheqalim 1980. Zeev Jabotinsky — 60.00
82. 1 Sheqel 1980. Corfu chanukah menorah — 25.00
83. ½ Sheqel (C-N) 1980– . Lion. Value — .25
84. 10 New Agorot (Bro) 1980– . Rev: Value — .15
85. 5 New Agorot (Al) 1980– . Menorah. Rev: Value — .15
86. 1 New Agora (Al) 1980– . Palm tree with date clusters. Rev: Value — .15
87. 10 Sheqalim (G) 1981. Type of #89. (33rd anniversary of independence) — 400.00
88. 5 Sheqalim (C-A-N) 1981. Cornucopia. Rev: Value — 2.00

89. 2 Sheqalim (S) 1981. Open book, all characters of Hebrew alphabet. Rev: Value, menorah. (33rd anniversary of independence) — 40.00

90. 1 Sheqel 1981. Polish Chanukah menorah — 25.00
91. 10 Sheqalim (G) 1982. Bust, Baron Edmond de Rothschild (1845–1934), international financier. Rev: Value, inscription — 400.00
92. 2 Sheqalim (S) 1982. Baron de Rothschild — 40.00

ITALIAN SOMALILAND

This area, located on the northeast coast of Africa along
the Indian Ocean, joined with British Somaliland in 1960
to become the Somali Republic (q.v.).

100 Bese = 1 Rupia
100 Centesimi = 1 Lira or 1 Somalo

VICTOR EMMANUEL III   1900–44

1.	1 Rupia 1910, '12–15, '19–21. Head. Rev: Crowned value and Arabic inscription	125.00
2.	½ Rupia 1910, '12–13, '15, '19	100.00
3.	¼ Rupia 1910, '13	75.00

4.	4 Bese (Bro) 1909–10, '13, '21, '23–24. Bust. Rev: Arabic inscription over value	55.00
5.	2 Bese (Bro) 1909–10, '13, '21 '23–24	35.00
6.	1 Besa (Bro) 1909–10, '13, '21	30.00

7.	10 Lire 1925. Crowned bust. Rev: Coroneted arms	200.00
8.	5 Lire 1925	150.00

ITALY

Until the complete unification of Italy in 1860, the principal coin-issuing areas were:

1. The Kingdom of the Two Sicilies—the island of Sicily and "Naples" (southern part of the Italian peninsula);
2. Papal States (central Italy);
3. Tuscany (west-central Italy);
4. Venice (northeast Italy); and
5. Sardinia (northwest Italy and the island of Sardinia).

The house of Savoy, rulers of Sardinia, eventually became the reigning family of the new kingdom of Italy.

100 Centesimi = 1 Lira
120 Grani or 12 Tari = 1 Piastre
1 Scudo = 97 Cents (U.S.) approx.

Naples and Sicily
(after 1816 Kingdom of the
Two Sicilies)

CHARLES II of Spain (Habsburg) 1665–1700

1.	1 Scudo 1684. Bust. Rev: Crown over hemispheres	350.00
2.	½ Scudo 1683. Bust. Rev: Seated figure	150.00

PHILIP V of Spain (Bourbon) 1700–13

3.	1 Scudo 1702. Bust. Rev: Sun above globe	300.00
4.	½ Scudo 1701–02	125.00

CHARLES III (VI of Holy Roman Empire; Habsburg) 1713–34

5.	120 Grani 1731. Bust. Rev: Crowned arms	200.00
6.	60 Grani 1732	125.00
7.	24 Grani 1730	65.00

CHARLES IV (Bourbon) 1734–59

8.	120 Grani 1734–53. Bust. Rev: Seated female	250.00
9.	60 Grani 1734–38	150.00

FERDINAND IV of Naples (III of Sicily) 1759–1825
(First Period: 1759–99)

Charles IV succeeded to the Spanish throne in 1759, becoming Charles III of Spain. He abdicated his Italian throne in favor of Ferdinand, his eight-year-old son. Hence the title HISPANIAR INFANS—the Infante of Spain—which appears on most of Ferdinand's coins.

Until 1816 the Kingdom had two separate parts governed by the same king. Thus Ferdinand was Ferdinand IV of Naples and Ferdinand III of Sicily. His reign occurred in four periods, the first of which was 1759–99.

10.	120 Grani 1791. Conjoined heads. Rev: Zodiac encircling sun and earth	300.00

11.	30 Tari 1791 (Sicily)	1500.00

311

ITALY: Naples and Sicily (continued)

11. Rev.

12.   120 Grani 1784–96. Head. Rev: Arms   150.00

13.   10 Tornesi (C) 1798   40.00

NEAPOLITAN REPUBLIC 1799

In 1799 the French captured Naples and established the
short-lived Neapolitan Republic.

14.   1 Piastre (12 Carlini). Liberty. Rev: Value   250.00
15.   ½ Piastre   150.00

FERDINAND IV   (Second Period: 1799–1805)

In 1805 Ferdinand was forced by Napoleon to flee from
Naples and go to the island of Sicily. Coins issued subsequently for Sicily alone have a distinctive eagle reverse.

16.   120 Grani 1800, '02. Head. Rev: Crowned arms   100.00

17.   120 Grani 1805. Head in circle. Rev: Crowned
        spade-shaped shield   100.00
18.   6 Tornesi (C) 1799–1803   40.00
19.   4 Tornesi (C) 1799–1800   25.00
20.   1 Tornese (C) 1804   20.00
21.   1 Piastre (12 Tari) 1801–04. Bust. Rev:
        Crowned eagle   75.00
22.   1 Piastre (12 Tari) 1805–10. Rev: Eagle in
        wreath   100.00

ITALY: Naples and Sicily (continued)

23.	10 Grani (C) 1814–15. Radiate head. Rev: Corn ear and cornucopia	60.00
24.	5 Grani (C) 1814–16. Rev: Security seated	40.00

25.	2 Grani (C) 1814–15. Rev: Pegasus	35.00
26.	1 Grano (C) 1814–15. Rev: Grapes	25.00

JOSEPH BONAPARTE   1806–08

28.	12 Carlini (1 Piastre) 1809–10. Head. Rev: Value in wreath	400.00

29.	5 Lire 1812–13. Head. Rev: Crowned arms in canopy	400.00
30.	2 Lire 1812–13. Rev: Value in wreath	150.00
31.	1 Lira 1812–13	50.00
32.	½ Lira 1813	40.00

FERDINAND IV   (Third Period: 1815–16)

After the French were driven out and Murat was executed, Ferdinand IV was restored to the throne of Naples.

27.	120 Grani (1 Piastre) 1806–08. Head. Rev: Arms	300.00

(After the removal of the Spanish royal family from Madrid, Joseph Bonaparte was transferred to Madrid as King of Spain. His brother-in-law Joachim Murat, one of Napoleon's marshals, became King of Naples.)

33.	120 Grani 1815–16. Bust. Rev: Arms	150.00

34.	60 Grani 1816	65.00	50.	2 Tornesi (C) 1825–26	12.50
35.	1 Carlino 1815–16	20.00	51.	1 Tornese (C) 1827	15.00

FERDINAND (Fourth Period, as FERDINAND I 1816–25)

In 1816 Ferdinand welded the two kingdoms, Naples and Sicily, into a single state and took the title of Ferdinand I, King of the Two Sicilies.

36.	120 Grani (1 Piastre) 1817–18. Crowned head. Rev: Arms	100.00
37.	60 Grani 1818	75.00
38.	1 Carlino 1818	35.00
39.	10 Tornesi (C) 1819	20.00
40.	8 Tornesi (C) 1817–18	30.00
41.	5 Tornesi (C) 1817–19	30.00
42.	4 Tornesi (C) 1817	30.00
43.	1 Tornese (C) 1817–18	12.50

FRANCIS I 1825–30

44.	120 Grani (1 Piastre) 1825–28. Head. Rev: Crowned arms	100.00
45.	60 Grani 1826	120.00
46.	2 Carlini 1826	50.00
47.	1 Carlino 1826	17.50

48.	10 Tornesi (C) 1825. Head. Rev: Legend	25.00
49.	5 Tornesi (C) 1827	12.50

FERDINAND II 1830–59

52.	120 Grani (1 Piastre) 1831–39. "Smooth" face type. Rev: Arms	85.00

53.	120 Grani (1 Piastre) 1840–59. Bearded face type. Rev: Arms	75.00
54.	60 Grani 1832–58	85.00
55.	1 Tari 1832–59	17.50
56.	1 Carlino 1832–56	17.50
57.	½ Carlino 1836–53	25.00
58.	10 Tornesi (C) 1831–59	20.00
59.	5 Tornesi (C) 1831–58	20.00
60.	3 Tornesi (C) 1833–54	35.00
61.	2 Tornesi (C) 1835–59	15.00
62.	1½ Tornesi (C) 1832–54	15.00
63.	1 Tornese (C) 1832–58	15.00
64.	½ Tornese (C) 1833–54	12.50

FRANCIS II 1859–61

65.	120 Grani (1 Piastre) 1859. Head. Rev: Crowned arms	125.00
66.	1 Tari 1859	35.00
67.	10 Tornesi (C) 1859	17.50
68.	2 Tornesi (C) 1859	17.50

ITALY (continued)

Papal States

This region, with its core in Rome, was under the temporal rule of the Popes for many centuries. Papal rule came to an end in 1870, and has since then been limited to the comparatively small area of Vatican City (q.v.).

Papal coinage has a long and interesting history, and the coins are rich in colorful symbolism. The Pope's Tiara, or triple crown, is frequently seen. It symbolizes the Pope's triple function as teacher, lawgiver and judge. A ship represents the Church; an anchor signifies faith.

Another important device is the intertwining of the Greek letters X and P, the beginning letters of Christ's name, which sound as CH (as in Scottish "loch") and R. This is known as the Chrismon. A fish represents Christianity; a lion stands for Christ or St. Mark; crossed keys are a reference to the "Keys of the Kingdom of Heaven."

URBAN VIII   1623–44

CLEMENT VIII   1592–1605

69.	1 Testone 1593–1600. S. PETRUS. Arms, bust	200.00
70.	1 Giulio 1598–1600. SINE CLADE. Arms	100.00
71.	1 Grosso. SUB TUUM PRAES. Arms	50.00
72.	½ Grosso 1595–1600. VIRGO CLEMENS. Arms	35.00

SEDE VACANTE   1605

73.	1 Giulio 1605. S. PAULUS ALMA. Arms	125.00

PAUL V   1605–21

74.	1 Testone 1610–15. S. PAULUS ALMA. Bust and arms	200.00
75.	1 Giulio	100.00
76.	½ Grosso. SALVA NOS. Bust and arms	35.00

SEDE VACANTE   1621

77.	1 Giulio 1621. STATUIT SUPRA. Arms	200.00

GREGORY XV   1621–23

78.	½ Grosso. SUB TUUM. Bust and arms	60.00

79.	1 Scudo 1634–43. Bust. St. Michael battling Lucifer	650.00
80.	1 Scudo 1635–43. Bust. Pope kneeling before St. Michael	650.00
81.	1 Scudo 1643. TE MANE TE. Bust. Saints Peter and Paul	600.00
82.	1 Testone 1625–43. VULT DEUS. Bust and arms	200.00
83.	1 Giulio 1625–32. Saints Peter and Paul. Arms	125.00
84.	1 Grosso 1625. QUI INGRED. Arms and bust	50.00
85.	½ Grosso 1625–32	30.00

INNOCENT X   1644–55

86.	1 Scudo. 1646–52. Christ blessing St. Peter	650.00

315

87.	1 Scudo 1650. Bust. Holy Year Issue. ANNO IUBILEI	650.00
88.	1 Giulio 1650. ANNO IUBILEI. Arms	125.00
89.	1 Grosso 1650	75.00
90.	½ Grosso 1650–51. APER. ET CLAUS. Arms	40.00

SEDE VACANTE   1655

91.	1 Scudo 1655. Arms and dove	500.00
92.	1 Grosso 1655. INUNDE AMOREM CORDIBUS ROMA	100.00

ALEXANDER VII   1655–67

93.	1 Scudo. St. Peter in clouds. St. Thomas and beggar	600.00

94.	1 Testone. NEC CITRA NEC. Arms	100.00
95.	1 Giulio. VIRGO CONCIPIET. Arms	50.00
96.	1 Grosso. HILAREM DATOREM. Arms	40.00
97.	½ Grosso. TEMPERATO SPLEN. Arms	25.00

SEDE VACANTE   1667

98.	1 Scudo 1667. Arms and dove	500.00
99.	1 Testone 1667. DA RECTA SAPERE	100.00
100.	1 Giulio 1667	75.00

CLEMENT IX   1667–69

101.	1 Scudo. Arms. Throne of St. Peter	650.00
102.	1 Testone. AUXILIUM DE SANC. Arms	100.00
103.	1 Giulio 1667	50.00
104.	2 Grossi 1667–69. Saint holding key	40.00
105.	1 Grosso 1667	25.00
106.	½ Grosso 1667	25.00

SEDE VACANTE   1669–70

107.	1 Scudo 1669. Arms and dove	500.00
108.	1 Giulio 1669. ILLUXIT ILLUCESCAT. Holy Spirit with tongue of fire	50.00
109.	1 Grosso 1669	40.00
110.	½ Grosso 1669	25.00

CLEMENT X   1670–76

111.	1 Scudo 1671–72. Bust. Mercy and Charity standing	600.00

112.	1 Scudo 1675. Bust or arms. Opening of Holy Door	650.00
113.	1 Scudo 1675. Bust or arms. Holy Door closed	600.00
114.	1 Testone 1670–75. COLLES FIVENT. Bust and arms	100.00
115.	1 Giulio 1670–75. IN PORTIS OPERA. Bust and arms	50.00
116.	1 Grosso 1670–75. PORTO COELI. Bust and arms	40.00
117.	½ Grosso 1670–75. HAEC PORTA. Bust and arms	25.00

SEDE VACANTE   1676

118.	1 Scudo 1676. Arms and dove	500.00
119.	1 Grosso 1676. MENTES TUORUM. Arms	50.00
120.	½ Grosso 1676. DOCEBIT VOS. Arms	25.00

INNOCENT XI   1676–89

121.	1 Scudo 1676. Bust. St. Matthew on clouds writing gospel	500.00

122.	1 Scudo 1677. Bust or arms. St. Peter's Basilica	650.00

123.	1 Scudo 1678. Bust. Christ and apostles in boat	800.00

124.	1 Scudo 1680–81. Arms. St. Peter on throne	500.00
125.	1 Scudo 1683–84. Bust or arms. Rev: Inscription	450.00
126.	½ Scudo 1676–89. AVARUS NON. Arms	100.00
127.	1 Testone 1676–89. MELIUS EST. Arms	75.00
128.	1 Giulio 1676–88. GRESSUS MEOS. Arms	40.00
129.	1 Grosso 1676–88. SACROSAN BASIL. Arms	25.00
130.	½ Grosso 1676–88. NOCET MINUS. Arms	20.00

SEDE VACANTE   1689

131.	1 Scudo 1689. Arms and dove	400.00
132.	1 Testone 1689. ACCENDE LUMEN. Arms	100.00
133.	1 Giulio 1689. UBI VULT SPIRAT. Arms	50.00
134.	1 Grosso 1689	40.00
135.	½ Grosso 1689	25.00

ALEXANDER VIII   1689–91

136.	1 Scudo 1690–91. Bust. The Church personified, standing	600.00
137.	1 Testone 1689–91. SANCTI BRUN. Bust	150.00
138.	1 Giulio 1689–90. SANCTUS PAUL. Arms	50.00
139.	½ Grosso 1689. SANCTUS PETRUS. Arms	35.00

SEDE VACANTE   1691

140.	1 Testone 1691. DOCEBIT ET SUG. Arms	125.00

INNOCENT XII   1691–1700

141.	1 Scudo 1692. Bust. Throne of St. Peter	700.00

147.	1 Scudo 1699. Bust. Jews gathering manna in the desert	750.00
148.	1 Scudo 1699. Bust. Holy Door opened. (Jubilee Year.)	500.00
149.	½ Scudo 1692–1700. NON SIBI SED. Bust. Arms	125.00
150.	1 Testone 1692–1700. IPSE EST PAX. Arms	75.00
151.	1 Giulio 1691–1700. PECCATA EC. Arms	50.00
152.	1 Grosso 1691–99. EGENO SPES. Bust and arms	25.00
153.	½ Grosso 1691–99. PORTEA AUREA. Arms	20.00

SEDE VACANTE 1700

154.	1 Scudo 1700. Arms and dove	500.00
155.	1 Testone 1700. VADO ET VENIO. Arms	100.00

CLEMENT XI 1700–21

156.	1 Scudo 1700. Bust. Holy Door closed. Jubilee Year	500.00
157.	1 Scudo 1702. Bust. St. Clement seated on clouds	450.00
158.	1 Scudo 1703. Arms. Church of St. Theodore	500.00

142.	1 Scudo 1692–93. Bust. St. Michael hurling thunderbolts at Satan	650.00
143.	1 Scudo 1693. Bust. Children at breast of Charity	450.00
144.	1 Scudo 1694. Bust. Peace seated at altar	600.00

145.	1 Scudo 1696–97. Bust. Pope presiding at consistory	650.00

146.	1 Scudo 1698. Bust. St. Peter preaching	750.00
159.	1 Scudo 1704. Arms. Infant Jesus in temple	650.00

160. 1 Scudo 1706. Bust or arms. Pope seated on
throne   650.00
161. 1 Scudo 1706. Bust. St. Peter in boat   750.00
162. 1 Scudo 1707. Bust. St. Clement praying before
lamb   650.00
163. 1 Scudo 1707–09. Arms. Inscription   350.00

164. 1 Scudo 1711. Arms. Bridge of Civita Cas-
tellana   750.00

165. 1 Scudo 1713. Arms. View of Pantheon piazza   750.00
166. 1 Scudo 1713. Arms. Fountain and obelisk   600.00
167. 1 Scudo 1715. Bust. Arms   400.00
168. ½ Scudo 1706–15. Arms and bust   100.00

169. 1 Testone 1700–07   60.00

170. 1 Giulio 1700–07. NOLI LABORARE. Arms and
bust   30.00
171. 1 Grosso 1701. PAUPERI POR. Arms   25.00
172. ½ Grosso 1701. DA ET ACCEPE. Arms   20.00

INNOCENT XIII   1721–24

173. ½ Scudo. CUM EXULTATIONE. Arms   75.00
174. 1 Giulio 1721. SACROSAN BASILIC. Arms   40.00
175. 1 Grosso 1721–23. ERIGIT ELISOS. Arms   25.00

BENEDICT XIII   1724–30

176. 1 Testone 1725. FOENERATUR DOMI. Arms   75.00
177. 1 Giulio 1724–28. IN CARITATE Arms   25.00
178. 1 Grosso 1724–29. BENEFAC HUMILI. Arms   20.00

SEDE VACANTE   1730

179. 1 Giulio 1730. LUMEN SEMITIS. Arms   50.00

CLEMENT XII   1730–40

180. ½ Scudo 1736. DECUS PATRIAE. Bust and arms   100.00
181. 1 Testone 1733–36. URBE NOBILITATE. Bust and
arms   50.00
182. 1 Giulio 1730–35. ABUNDET IN GLO. Bust and
arms   25.00
183. 1 Grosso 1730–39. IN CIBOS PAUP. Arms   20.00

SEDE VACANTE   1740

184. 1 Giulio 1740. VENI SANCTE. Arms   50.00
185. 1 Grosso 1740. ILLUMINET CORDA. Arms   50.00

BENEDICT XIV   1740–58

186. 1 Scudo 1753–54. Bust. The Church seated on
cloud   350.00
187. ½ Scudo 1752–54. CURABANTUR OM. Bust   150.00
188. 1 Testone 1756. PRINCIPIS URBIS. Arms   50.00

189.	2 Giulio 1753–57. MDCCLVII. Bust	25.00
190.	1 Giulio 1741. SACROSANC BASIL. Arms	20.00
191.	1 Grosso 1740–50. UT ALAT EOS. Arms	20.00
192.	1 Baiocco (C) 1740–58. Arms. Value	12.50
193.	½ Baiocco (C) 1740–55	10.00
194.	1 Quattrino (C) 1740–56	7.50

SEDE VACANTE   1758

195.	1 Scudo 1758. Arms and dove	300.00
196.	½ Scudo 1758. UBI VUIT SPIRAT. Arms	150.00
197.	2 Giulio 1758	50.00
198.	1 Grosso 1758	25.00

CLEMENT XIII   1758–69

199.	1 Scudo 1759. Arms. The Church seated on clouds	500.00
200.	½ Scudo 1759–60. SUPRA FIRMAM. Bust and arms	250.00
201.	1 Testone 1761–67. S. PETRUS S.P. Arms	60.00
202.	2 Giulio 1760–65. OBLECTAT IUSTOS. Bust	30.00
203.	1 Grosso 1758–67. UTERA QUASI. Arms	25.00
204.	1 Baiocco (C) 1758–59. Arms. Value	25.00
205.	½ Baiocco (C) 1758–60	20.00
206.	1 Quattrino (C) 1758–59	20.00

SEDE VACANTE   1769

207.	½ Scudo 1769. VENI SANCTE. Arms	200.00
208.	2 Giulio 1769	50.00
209.	1 Giulio 1769	40.00

CLEMENT XIV   1769–74

210.	½ Scudo 1773. S. PETRUS, S. PAULUS. Arms	150.00
211.	1 Testone 1770–73	50.00
212.	2 Giulio 1769–73. FIAT PAX IN. Arms	25.00
213.	1 Grosso 1769–74	20.00

SEDE VACANTE   1774–75

214.	½ Scudo 1774. VENI LUMEN. Arms	125.00
215.	2 Giulio 1774	50.00

PIUS VI   1775–99

216.	1 Scudo 1780. Arms. The Church seated on clouds	100.00
217.	½ Scudo 1775–96. AUXILIUM DE. Bust and arms	65.00
218.	1 Testone 1785–96. SANCTUS PETRUS. Arms	50.00
219.	1 Giulio 1775. MUNDI REVERTUN. Arms	25.00
220.	1 Grosso 1775–83. APERUIT CUNCTIS. Arms	20.00
221.	5 Baiocchi (C) 1797–99. SANCTA DEI GENETRIX	20.00

222.	2½ Baiocchi (C) 1795–97. St. Peter	20.00
223.	2 Baiocchi (C) 1795–97. Arms. Value	10.00

224.	1 Baiocco (C)	6.50
225.	½ Baiocco (C)	6.50
226.	1 Quattrino (C)	6.50

PIUS VII   1800–23

227.	1 Scudo 1800–18. Arms or bust. The Church seated on clouds	150.00
228.	½ Scudo 1800–17. AUXILIUM DE. Arms	175.00
229.	1 Testone 1802–04. St. Peter and St. Paul. Arms	100.00
230.	2 Giulio 1816–18	50.00
231.	1 Giulio 1816–18	40.00
232.	1 Grosso 1815–17. PAUPERI POR. Arms	35.00
233.	1 Baiocco (C) 1801–17. Arms. Value	25.00
234.	½ Baiocco (C) 1801–22	20.00
235.	1 Quattrino (C) 1801–22	10.00

SEDE VACANTE   1823

236.	1 Scudo 1823. Arms of Cardinal Barthelemy Paca. The Church seated on clouds	200.00
237.	½ Scudo 1823	150.00
238.	2 Giulio 1823. Arms. Madonna in clouds	125.00

LEO XII   1823–29

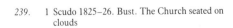

239.	1 Scudo 1825–26. Bust. The Church seated on clouds	250.00

240.	½ Baiocco (C) 1825–27. Arms. Value	50.00
241.	1 Quattrino (C) 1825–28	20.00

SEDE VACANTE 1829

242.	1 Scudo 1829. Arms. The Church seated on clouds	300.00
243.	½ Scudo 1829. AUXILIUM DE. Arms	150.00

PIUS VIII 1829–30

244.	1 Scudo 1830. Bust. St. Peter and St. Paul	350.00
245.	1 Testone 1830. ISTI SUNT. Bust	75.00
246.	1 Baiocco (C) 1829. Arms. Value	50.00
247.	½ Baiocco (C) 1829	25.00
248.	1 Quattrino (C) 1829	15.00

SEDE VACANTE 1830–31

249.	1 Scudo 1830. Arms and dove	300.00
250.	30 Baiocchi	100.00

GREGORY XVI 1831–46

251.	1 Scudo 1831–34. Bust. Presentation of the infant Jesus in the temple	175.00
252.	1 Scudo 1835–46. Bust. Value and date	150.00
253.	50 Baiocchi 1832–46	75.00
254.	30 Baiocchi 1834–46	50.00
255.	20 Baiocchi 1834–46	50.00
256.	10 Baiocchi 1836–46	25.00
257.	5 Baiocchi 1835–46	20.00
258.	1 Baiocco (C) 1831–45. Arms. Value and date	20.00
259.	½ Baiocco (C) 1831–45	7.50
260.	¼ Baiocco (C) 1831–44	7.50

SEDE VACANTE 1846

261.	1 Scudo 1846. Arms and dove	250.00

PIUS IX 1846–78

262.	1 Scudo 1846–56. Bust. Value and date	100.00
263.	50 Baiocchi 1850–57	85.00
264.	20 Baiocchi 1848–66	25.00
265.	10 Baiocchi 1847–65	25.00
266.	5 Baiocchi 1847–66	25.00

267.	5 Baiocchi (C) 1849–54. Arms. Value	25.00
268.	2 Baiocchi (C) 1848–53	15.00
269.	1 Baiocco (C) 1846–53	12.50
270.	½ Baiocco (C) 1847–52	7.50
271.	1 Quattrino (C) 1851, '54	12.50

SECOND COINAGE: LIRE SYSTEM
(Last coinage of States of the Church)

272.	5 Lire 1867, '70. Bust. Value	200.00
273.	2½ Lire 1867	125.00
274.	2 Lire 1866–70	50.00
275.	1 Lira 1866–69	15.00
276.	10 Soldi 1866–69	10.00
277.	5 Soldi 1866–67	10.00
278.	4 Soldi (C) 1866–69	15.00
279.	2 Soldi (C) 1866–67	10.00
280.	1 Soldo (C) 1866–67	8.50
281.	½ Soldo (C) 1866–67	7.50
282.	1 Centesimo (C) 1866–68	12.50

Tuscany (Etruria)

The duchy of Tuscany in west-central Italy existed from the 11th to the 19th century. From the 16th until the mid-18th century it was conferred on the Medici family. At that time the duchy passed to the house of Lorraine-Habsburg.

The coins of Tuscany may be identified by the distinctive coat of arms or by the ETR, ETRVR, or ETRVRIAE in the legend on the obverse.

289.

FERDINAND DE MEDICI   1587–1608

283.	1 Scudo 1587–95. Bust. Rev: Draped arms	600.00

COSIMO II   1608–21

284.	1 Scudo 1609–20. Bust in spiked crown	350.00

FERDINAND II   1621–70

285.	1 Scudo 1621–63. Bust. Rev: St. John	400.00

COSIMO III   1670–1723

288.	1 Scudo 1684–1707. Arms and titles. Rev: Rosebush	400.00
289.	1 Scudo 1707–23. Bare head. Rev: Crown over castle	350.00

FRANCIS III   1737–65

290.	1 Scudo 1742–65. Bust. Rev. Arms	150.00
291.	½ Scudo 1738–48	100.00

PETER LEOPOLD   1765–90

292.	1 Scudo 1766–90. Bust (several varieties). Rev: Arms	150.00
293.	½ Scudo 1777–87	100.00

FERDINAND III   1790–1801

294.	1 Francescone 1793–1801. Bare head. Rev: Crowned arms	100.00

LOUIS I   1801–03

286.	1 Scudo 1676–94. Bare head. Rev: St. John baptizing	300.00

289 Rev.

287.	1 Scudo 1683–98. Head in spiked crown. Rev: View of Leghorn	350.00

295.	1 Francescone 1801–03. Head. Rev: Crowned arms	150.00

CHARLES LOUIS AND MARIE LOUISE   1803–07

296.   Broad 10 Lire 1803–07 (value on edge of coin:
       DIECI LIRE). Conjoined busts. Rev: Crowned
       arms   125.00
297.   5 Lire 1803 (value on edge: CINQUE LIRE)   175.00

298.   1 Francescone 1803–07. Busts facing each
       other   150.00
299.   1 Lira 1803–06. Crowned arms. Rev: Value   80.00

305.   ½ Francescone 1827–34   60.00

FERDINAND III (Restoration)   1814–24

300.   1 Francescone 1814–24. Head. Rev: Crowned
       arms   100.00

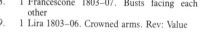

306.   1 Fiorino 1826–58. Head. Rev: Lily   40.00
307.   ½ Fiorino 1827. Crowned arms. Rev: Value   50.00
308.   ¼ Fiorino 1827   85.00

301.   ½ Francescone 1820–23   65.00
302.   1 Lira 1821–23. Head. Rev: Value   50.00
303.   10 Lire 1821–23   12.50

309.   1 Paolo 1831–53. Head. Rev: Crowned arms   50.00
310.   ½ Paolo 1832–59   25.00
311.   10 Quattrini (Bi) 1826–58   25.00
312.   5 Quattrini (Bi) 1826–30   40.00
313.   3 Quattrini (C) 1826–57   20.00
314.   1 Quattrino (C) 1827–57   25.00

LEOPOLD II   1824–59

PROVISIONAL GOVERNMENT   1859

315.   1 Fiorino 1859. Lion with banner. Rev: Arms of
       mint master   75.00
316.   5 Centesimi 1859. Crowned arms. Rev: Value   35.00
317.   2 Centesimi 1859   20.00
318.   1 Centesimo 1859   50.00

304.   1 Francescone 1826–59. Head. Rev: Crowned
       arms   100.00

ITALY (continued)

Venice

This city built on 118 islands was once one of the great commercial powers of Europe. The Venetian Republic was headed by a doge and a council. Napoleon's invasion of 1797 brought the Republic to an end. He soon handed Venice over to the Austrians. In 1848 a Venetian revolt against Austrian rule led to a short-lived republic. Then in 1866 Austria's defeat at the hands of Prussia made it possible for Venice to be incorporated into the Kingdom of Italy.

The winged lion (symbol of St. Mark, patron saint of Venice) appears on most Venetian coins. It was not until the middle of the 18th century that dates began to appear on Venetian coins. The names of the reigning doges are an aid to identifying Venetian coins.

321.	Giovanni Bembo 1615–18. 1 Scudo. Cross and lion	350.00
322.	Antonio Prioli 1618–23. 1 Scudo	200.00
323.	½ Scudo	80.00
324.	Francesco Contarini 1623–24. 1 Scudo	250.00
325.	¼ Scudo	100.00
326.	Giovanni Cornaro I 1624–29. ½ Scudo	100.00
327.	¼ Scudo	50.00
328.	Nicolo Contarini 1630–31. 1 Scudo	200.00
329.	Francesco Erizzo 1631–46. 1 Scudo	150.00
330.	½ Scudo	75.00
331.	¼ Scudo	50.00
332.	Francesco Molino 1646–55. 1 Scudo	150.00
333.	¼ Scudo	50.00
334.	⅛ Scudo	60.00

319.   10 Ducats (G) (undated). Doge kneeling before St. Mark. Rev: Christ   RARE

335.	Domenico Contarini 1659–75. 1 Scudo	125.00
336.	½ Scudo	150.00
337.	¼ Scudo	50.00
338.	⅛ Scudo	50.00
339.	Ludovico Contarini 1676–84. 1 Scudo	175.00
340.	¼ Scudo	100.00
341.	⅛ Scudo	40.00
342.	Francesco Morosini 1688–94. 1 Scudo. Doge kneeling	175.00
343.	½ Scudo	80.00
344.	¼ Scudo	50.00
345.	Silvestro Valiero 1694–99. 1 Scudo	125.00
346.	½ Scudo	50.00
347.	¼ Scudo	40.00

320.   1 Ducat (G)   350.00

348.	Ludovico Mocenigo II 1700–09. 1 Scudo	175.00
349.	Giovanni Cornaro II 1709–22. 1 Scudo	150.00
350.	½ Scudo	75.00
351.	⅛ Scudo	40.00
352.	Carlo Ruzzini 1732–34. 1 Scudo	175.00
353.	¼ Scudo	40.00
354.	Ludovico Pisani 1735–41. 1 Scudo	175.00
355.	¼ Scudo	40.00
356.	Pietro Grimani 1741–52. 1 Scudo	175.00
357.	½ Scudo	60.00
358.	¼ Scudo	25.00
359.	15 Marchetti 1749	20.00
360.	10 Marchetti 1749	20.00
361.	5 Marchetti 1749	20.00
362.	Francesco Loredano 1752–62. 1 Scudo 1756. Female head. Rev: Lion	175.00
363.	Marco Foscarini 1762–63. 1 Scudo. Doge kneeling. Rev: Lion	250.00
364.	½ Scudo	100.00

DEMOCRATIC REPUBLIC   1797–98

378.   10 Lire 1797. Liberty standing. Rev: Value and date   500.00

PROVISIONAL REPUBLIC   1848

379.   5 Lire 1848. Lion on base. Rev: Value in wreath   300.00

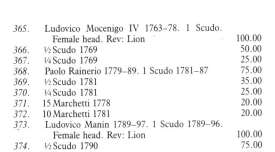

365.	Ludovico Mocenigo IV 1763–78. 1 Scudo. Female head. Rev: Lion	100.00
366.	½ Scudo 1769	50.00
367.	¼ Scudo 1769	25.00
368.	Paolo Rainerio 1779–89. 1 Scudo 1781–87	75.00
369.	½ Scudo 1781	35.00
370.	¼ Scudo 1781	25.00
371.	15 Marchetti 1778	20.00
372.	10 Marchetti 1781	20.00
373.	Ludovico Manin 1789–97. 1 Scudo 1789–96. Female head. Rev: Lion	100.00
374.	½ Scudo 1790	75.00
375.	¼ Scudo 1789	35.00
376.	10 Marchetti 1789–91	20.00
377.	5 Marchetti 1789	20.00

380.	5 Lire 1848. Lion on plain ground	300.00
381.	15 Centesimi (C) 1849. Lion. Rev: Value	25.00
382.	5 Centesimi (C) 1849	20.00
383.	3 Centesimi (C) 1849	20.00
384.	1 Centesimo (C) 1849	35.00

REPUBLICS SET UP BY NAPOLEON

(Subalpine Republic through Lucca, pp. 326–27; see
also pp. 312–13.)

Subalpine Republic (Milan)   1798–1802

385.   5 Francs 1801–02 (Years IX, X). France and
Italy standing. Rev: Value and date in wreath   175.00

Ligurian Republic (Genoa)   1798–1805

386.   8 Lire 1798–1804. Liberty and Equality standing. Rev: Liberty Cap above Genoese arms   250.00
387.   4 Lire 1798–99   125.00
388.   2 Lire 1798   400.00
389.   1 Lira 1798   125.00

Cisalpine Republic   1797–1802

390.   1 Scudo Anno VIII (1800). France seated, Republic standing. Rev: Value and date in
wreath   500.00

391.   30 Soldi Anno IX (1801). Bust of Republic. Rev:
Value in wreath   150.00

Italian Republic   1802–05

392.   1 Soldo 1804. Balance. Rev: Value in wreath   100.00
393.   ½ Soldo 1804   75.00

Kingdom of Italy   1805–14

NAPOLEON, EMPEROR AND KING

394.   5 Lire 1807–14. Bare head. Rev: Crowned arms
in canopy   150.00

395.	2 Lire 1807–14	50.00
396.	1 Lire 1808–14	35.00
397.	15 Soldi 1808–14	40.00
398.	10 Soldi 1808–14	10.00
399.	5 Soldi 1808–14	10.00
400.	1 Soldo (C) 1807–14	10.00
401.	3 Centesimi (C) 1807–13	10.00
402.	1 Centesimo (C) 1807–13	10.00

Roman Republic 1798–99

403.	1 Scudo 1798–99. Liberty standing holding fasces and spear. Rev: Value in wreath	325.00

404.	2 Baiocchi 1798–99. Fasces. Rev: Value	30.00

Parma
MARIE LOUISE 1815–47

405.	5 Lire 1815, '32. Diademed head. Rev: Crowned arms in canopy	600.00

406.	2 Lire 1815	300.00
407.	1 Lira 1815	75.00
408.	10 Soldi 1815, '30. Rev: Crowned monogram	40.00
409.	5 Soldi 1815, '30	30.00

Lucca
ELISA BONAPARTE AND FELIX BACCIOCCHI 1805–08

410.	5 Francs 1805–08. Accolated busts. Rev: Value in wreath	150.00
411.	1 Franc 1806–08	40.00
412.	5 Centesimi (C) 1806	30.00
413.	3 Centesimi (C) 1806	30.00

CHARLES LOUIS OF BOURBON 1815–47

414.	2 Lire 1837. Bare head. Rev: Crowned arms	150.00
415.	1 Lira 1834, '37–38. Rev: Value in wreath	40.00
416.	10 Soldi 1833, '38	40.00
417.	5 Soldi (composition metal: S-C) 1833, '38. Crowned arms. Rev: Value	12.50
418.	2 Soldi (comp: S-C 1835)	25.00
419.	1 Soldo (C) 1826, '41. Crowned monogram	15.00
420.	½ Soldo (C) 1826, '35. Crown	15.00
421.	5 Quattrini (C) 1826	15.00
422.	2 Quattrini (C) 1826. Arms	15.00
423.	1 Quattrino (C) 1826. Title	15.00

Lombardy (Provisional Government) 1848

424.	5 Lire 1848. Italia standing. Rev: Value	150.00

ITALY (continued)

Sardinia

In 1720 Sardinia passed to the house of Savoy. The kingdom continued to be ruled by Savoy descendants until 1861, when the King of Sardinia, Victor Emmanuel II, became King of Italy.

CHARLES EMMANUEL III   1760–73

425.	1 Scudo 1755–69. Bust. Rev: Crowned arms in oval shield	175.00
426.	½ Scudo 1755–70	150.00
427.	¼ Scudo 1755–59	15.00
428.	⅛ Scudo 1755–70	7.50
429.	20 Soldi 1742–47. Head. Crowned arms and value	35.00
430.	10 Soldi 1742	20.00

VICTOR AMADEUS III   1773–96

431.	1 Scudo 1773. Bust. Rev: Crowned arms	RARE
432.	½ Scudo 1773–93	350.00
433.	¼ Scudo 1773–91	300.00
434.	5 Soldi (C) 1794–96. Bust. Rev: Mauritius	40.00
435.	1 Soldo (C) 1782–85. Rev: Monogram	75.00
436.	½ Soldo (C) 1781–87	75.00

CHARLES EMMANUEL IV   1796–1802

437.	½ Scudo 1797. Bust. Rev: Crowned arms	350.00

VICTOR EMMANUEL I   1802–21

438.	5 Lire 1816–21. Bare head. Rev: Crowned arms	400.00

CHARLES FELIX   1821–31

439.	5 Lire 1821–31. Bare head. Rev: Crowned arms	125.00
440.	2 Lire 1823–31	60.00
441.	1 Lira 1823–30	40.00
442.	50 Centesimi 1823–31	30.00
443.	25 Centesimi 1829–30	30.00

444.	5 Centesimi (C) 1826. Arms. Rev: Value	12.50
445.	3 Centesimi (C) 1826	10.00
446.	1 Centesimo (C) 1826	7.50

CHARLES ALBERT   1831–49

447.	5 Lire 1831–49. Bare head. Rev: Crowned arms	120.00
448.	2 Lire 1832–49	75.00
449.	1 Lira 1831–49	40.00
450.	50 Centesimi 1832–47	35.00
451.	25 Centesimi 1832–37	50.00
452.	5 Centesimi (C) 1842	12.50
453.	3 Centesimi (C) 1842	7.50
454.	1 Centesimo (C) 1842	7.50

VICTOR EMMANUEL II   1849–61

455.	5 Lire 1850–61. Bare head. Rev: Crowned arms	250.00
456.	2 Lire 1850–60	225.00
457.	1 Lira 1850–60	40.00
458.	50 Centesimi 1850–60	25.00

ITALY (continued)

KINGDOM OF ITALY

The modern state of Italy came into being with the unification in 1860, under Victor Emmanuel II of Sardinia. Later, though still a kingdom, the country was controlled by Mussolini and his Fascist Party from the 1920's until World War II. Following Italy's defeat, the King abdicated, and Italy became a republic in 1946.

100 Centesimi = 1 Lira

VICTOR EMMANUEL II   1861–78

459.	5 Lire 1861. Head. Rev: Crowned arms, legend FIRENZE MARZO 1861. (Accession to throne)	650.00
460.	5 Lire 1861–78. Head. Rev: Crowned arms	30.00
461.	2 Lire 1861–63	35.00
462.	1 Lira 1861–67	10.00
463.	50 Centesimi 1861–67	10.00
464.	20 Centesimi 1863–67	7.50

465.	10 Centesimi (C) 1862–67. Head. Rev: Value in wreath	5.00
466.	5 Centesimi (C) 1861–67	2.00
467.	2 Centesimi (C) 1861–67	2.00
468.	1 Centesimo (C) 1861–67	2.00

UMBERTO I   1878–1900

469.	5 Lire 1878–79. Bare head. Rev: Crowned arms	100.00

470.	2 Lire 1881–99	12.50
471.	1 Lira 1883–1900	10.00
472.	50 Centesimi 1889, '92	75.00

473.	20 Centesimi (C-N) 1894–95. Crown. Rev: Value	2.00
474.	10 Centesimi (C) 1893–94. Head. Rev: Value	7.50
475.	5 Centesimi (C) 1895–96	12.50
476.	2 Centesimi (C) 1895–1900	1.50
477.	1 Centesimo (C) 1895–1900	1.50

VICTOR EMMANUEL III   1900–46

478.	20 Lire (G) 1902–05. Bust. Rev: Crowned eagle	350.00

479.	5 Lire 1901. Bust. Rev: Type of #478. (Highest degree of rarity)	VERY RARE
480.	2 Lire 1901–07	30.00
481.	1 Lira 1901–07	12.50
482.	25 Centesimi (N) 1902–03. Crowned eagle. Rev: Value in wreath	30.00
483.	2 Centesimi (C) 1903–08. Bust. Rev: Value	2.00
484.	1 Centesimo (C) 1902–08	3.00

485.	50 Lire (G) 1911. Head. Rev: Allegorical figures, a factory, prow of a ship. (50th anniversary of kingdom)	1000.00
486.	5 Lire 1911	350.00
487.	2 Lire 1911	25.00
488.	10 Centesimi (Bro) 1911	12.50

ITALY (continued)

489. 100 Lire (G) 1912, '26–27. Bust. Rev: Female and plow   1500.00
490. 50 Lire (G) 1912, '26–27   750.00
491. 20 Lire (G) 1912, '26–27   350.00
492. 10 Lire (G) 1912, '26–27   1500.00

498. 5 Centesimi (Bro) 1908–18. Rev: Figure on prow of galley   2.00
499. 2 Centesimi (Bro) 1908–17   2.00
500. 1 Centesimo (Bro) 1908–18   2.00

501. 100 Lire (G) 1923. Head. Rev: Fasces. (First anniversary of Fascist government)   1500.00
502. 20 Lire (G) 1923   500.00
503. 2 Lire (N) 1923–27. Bust. Rev: Fasces   10.00

493. 5 Lire 1914. Military bust. Rev: Quadriga   1500.00
494. 2 Lire 1908–17   10.00
495. 1 Lira 1908–17   5.00

504. 1 Lira 1921–28. Italia seated. Rev: Value in wreath   3.50

496. 50 Centesimi (N) 1919–35. Rev: Chariot drawn by lions   7.50

505. 10 Centesimi (Bro) 1919–37. Head. Rev: Bee   2.50

497. 20 Centesimi (N) 1908–35. Classical head   3.00

506. 5 Centesimi (Bro) 1919–37. Head. Rev: Wheat ear   1.50

ITALY (continued)

REVALUATION OF LIRA, REDUCED SIZE

507. 100 Lire (G) 1931–33. Head. Rev: Italia on prow   250.00

508. 50 Lire (G) 1931–33. Bust. Rev: Man carrying
fasces   200.00

509. 20 Lire 1927–28. Head. Rev: Seated and standing figures   200.00

510. 10 Lire 1926–30. Head. Rev: Biga   50.00

511. 5 Lire 1926–30. Head. Rev: Eagle on fasces   8.50

512. 20 Lire 1928. Helmeted head. Rev: Fasces and
lion's head. (10th anniversary of end of World
War I)   350.00

513. 100 Lire (G) 1936. Head. Rev: Man with sword,
walking   RARE

514. 50 Lire (G) 1936. Head. Rev: Eagle above, two
medallions below   RARE

515. 20 Lire 1936. Head. Rev: Quadriga   1000.00

ITALY (continued)

516.   10 Lire 1936. Head. Rev: Italia on prow of galley   35.00
517.   5 Lire 1936–37. Head. Rev: Seated mother and
       children   20.00

518.   2 Lire (N) 1936–38; (St) '39–43. Head. Rev:
       Eagle   25.00
519.   1 Lira (N) 1936–38; (St) '39–43   2.00

520.   50 Centesimi (N) 1936; (St) '39–43. Head. Rev:
       Eagle in flight   1.50
521.   20 Centesimi (N) 1936; (St) '39–43. Head. Rev:
       Head and fasces   3.00

522.   10 Centesimi (Bro) 1936–39; (A-Bro) '39–43.
       Head. Rev: Arms and fasces   3.00

523.   5 Centesimi (Bro) 1936–39; (A-Bro) '39–43.
       Head. Rev: Eagle   1.50

ITALIAN REPUBLIC   1946–

524.   10 Lire (A) 1946–50. Pegasus. Rev: Olive   7.50

525.   5 Lire (A) 1946–50. Liberty head. Rev: Bunch
       of grapes   6.50

526.   2 Lire (A) 1946–50. Plowman. Rev: Wheat   5.00

527.   1 Lira (A) 1946–50. Ceres head. Rev: Orange
       branch   3.00

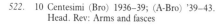

528. 500 Lire 1958–71. Peasant girl. Rev: Ships   12.50

ITALY (continued)

529. 100 Lire (St) 1955–   1.00
530. 50 Lire (St) 1954–   1.00

531. 20 Lire (A-Bro) 1957–59; 1969– . Rev: Oak
     leaves. (Plain edge)   .50

532. 10 Lire (A) 1951– . Plow. Rev: Wheat   .50

533. 5 Lire (A) 1951– . Rudder. Rev: Dolphin   .50

534. 2 Lire (A) 1953– . Bee   .75
535. 1 Lira (A) 1951– . Scales   1.00

536. 500 Lire 1961. (Italian unification)   17.50

537. 500 Lire 1965. Portrait of Dante Alighieri. Rev:
     Flames of the Inferno. (700th anniversary of
     great poet's birth)   15.00

538. 1000 Lire 1970. Bust of Concordia. Rev: Geometric
     design, value. (100 years of Rome as a capital
     city)   25.00

539. 500 Lire 1974. Bust of Marconi. Rev: Map. (100th
     anniversary of inventor's birth)   20.00

540. 100 Lire (St) 1974. Portrait of Guglielmo Mar-
     coni. Rev: Antenna. (100th anniversary of
     inventor's birth)   3.00
541. 200 Lire (Bro) 1977– . Liberty head. Rev: Value
     within cogwheel   2.00

542. 100 Lire (St) 1979. Liberty head. (F.A.O. coin
     plan)   2.50
543. 200 Lire (Al-Br) 1980. Rev: Mother and child.
     (International Women's Year; F.A.O. coin
     plan)   1.50
544. 200 Lire (Al-Br) 1981   1.00
545. 100 Lire (St) 1981. Anchor motif. Rev: Facade of
     building. (Centennial of Livorno Naval Acad-
     emy)   3.00

JAMAICA

The largest and most valuable island in the British West Indies, Jamaica was discovered by Columbus in 1494 and became a British colony in 1670. It became an independent state within the British Commonwealth in 1962.

4 Farthings = 1 Penny

VICTORIA   1837–1901

1.	1 Penny (C-N) 1869–1900. Coroneted head. Rev: Arms	15.00
2.	Half Penny (C-N) 1869–1900	10.00
3.	1 Farthing (C-N) 1880–1900	7.50

EDWARD VII   1901–10

NOTE: Issues of 1902–03 have horizontal shading lines on the reverse, 1904–10 have vertical lines

4.	1 Penny (C-N) 1902–10. Crowned bust of King. Rev: Arms	10.00
5.	Half Penny (C-N) 1902–10	8.00
6.	1 Farthing (C-N) 1902–10	4.00

GEORGE V   1910–36

7.	1 Penny (C-N) 1914–28. Crowned bust. Rev: Arms	5.00

8.	Half Penny (C-N) 1914–28	4.00
9.	1 Farthing (C-N) 1914–34	3.50

GEORGE VI   1936–52

NOTE: Coins issued after 1948 drop "Emperor of India" from their legend. The 1937 coins have smaller heads.

10.	1 Penny (N-Bra) 1937. Small crowned head. Rev: Arms	8.00
10a.	1 Penny (N-Bra) 1938–52. Large crowned head	3.00
11.	Half Penny (N-Bra) 1937. Small head	7.50
11a.	Half Penny (N-Bra) 1938–52. Large head	2.50
12.	1 Farthing (N-Bra) 1937. Small head	7.50
12a.	1 Farthing (N-Bra) 1938–52. Large head	1.50

ELIZABETH II   1952–

13.	1 Penny (N-Bra) 1953–63. Crowned head. Rev: Arms	.75
14.	Half Penny (N-Bra) 1955–63	.65

15.	1 Penny (N-Bra) 1964–67. Crowned head. Rev: New arms	.50
16.	Half Penny (N-Bra) 1964–66	.35

JAMAICA (continued)

17. 5 Shillings (C-N) 1966. Arms. Rev: Inscription. (8th British Empire and Commonwealth Games) — 5.00

18. 1 Penny (N-Bra) 1969. Crowned head. Rev: Arms, "1869–1969" (100th anniversary of Jamaican coinage) — 1.00
19. ½ Penny (N-Bra) 1969 — 1.00

DECIMAL COINAGE

20. 1 Dollar (C-N) 1969– . Sir Alexander Bustamante. Rev: Arms. (First Prime Minister) — 8.50

21. 25 Cents (C-N) 1969– . Arms. Rev: Swallow tail hummingbird — 1.00

22. 20 Cents (C-N) 1969– . Arms. Rev: Blue mahoe trees — 1.00
23. 10 Cents (C-N) 1969– . Arms. Rev: Lignum vitae tree — .50

24. 5 Cents (C-N) 1969– . Arms. Rev: Crocodile — .25
25. 1 Cent (Bro) 1969– . Arms. Rev: Edible ackee plant — .25

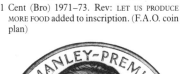

26. 1 Cent (Bro) 1971–73. Rev: LET US PRODUCE MORE FOOD added to inscription. (F.A.O. coin plan) — .35

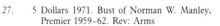

27. 5 Dollars 1971. Bust of Norman W. Manley, Premier 1959–62. Rev: Arms — 50.00

28. 20 Dollars (G) 1972. Map of Jamaica, three
     ships. Rev: Arms. (10th anniversary of inde-
     pendence)   200.00

31.   10 Dollars (C-N) 1974. Sir Henry Morgan, Lieu-
      tenant Governor 1674. Rev: Arms   25.00
31a. 10 Dollars (S) 1974. Proof   50.00
31b. 5 Dollars (C-N) 1974– . Type of #30.   7.50

32.   100 Dollars (G) 1975. Bust of Christopher Colum-
      bus. Rev: Arms   175.00

29.   10 Dollars 1972. Busts of Alexander Bustamante
      and Norman W. Manley, map of Jamaica.
      Rev: Arms. (10th anniversary of indepen-
      dence)   35.00

33.   10 Dollars 1975. Bust of Columbus, ship in
      background. Rev: Arms   40.00

34.   1 Cent (A) 1975, '76. Type of #26. (F.A.O. coin
      plan; dodecagonal planchet)   .35

30.   5 Dollars 1972– . Head of Manley. Rev: Arms   17.50

JAMAICA (continued)

35. 100 Dollars (G) 1976. Bust of Admiral Nelson
     with map and ship. Rev: Arms 200.00
36. 10 Dollars (C-N) 1976 .... 35.00
36a. 10 Dollars (S) 1976. Proof 50.00

37. 50 Cents (C-N) 1976– . Bust of Marcus Garvey,
     philosopher. Rev: Arms 7.50

38. 20 Cents (C-N) 1976. Three trees over value.
     (F.A.O. coin plan) 3.00

39. 10 Dollars (C-N) 1977. Bust of Admiral George
     Rodney. Rev: Arms 25.00
39a. 10 Dollars (S) 1977. Proof 30.00

40. 25 Dollars 1978. Elizabeth II on throne. Rev:
     Arms. (Jubilee of coronation) 100.00

41. 10 Dollars (C-N) 1978. Heads in a circle. Rev:
     Arms. (Jamaican unity) 25.00
41a. 10 Dollars (S) 1978. Proof 30.00

39.

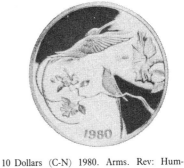

45.   10 Dollars (C-N) 1980. Arms. Rev: Hummingbirds   20.00

45a.   10 Dollars (S) 1980. Proof   35.00

46.   10 Dollars 1980. Arms. Rev: Map of Caribbean. (10th anniversary of Caribbean Development Bank)   35.00

47.   250 Dollars (G) 1981. Dual portrait of Prince Charles and Lady Diana. (Wedding of royal couple.) In proof only   250.00

48.   10 Dollars 1981. (Royal wedding.) In proof only   35.00

49.   10 Dollars (C-N) 1981. American crocodile. Rev: Arms   20.00

49a.   10 Dollars (S) 1981. Proof   35.00

NOTE: Nos. 50–58 issued also in proof

42.   10 Dollars (C-N) 1979. Arms. Rev: Homerus swallowtail butterflies   20.00

42a.   10 Dollars (S) 1979. Proof   30.00

43.   10 Dollars 1979. Arms. Rev: Standing child. (International Year of Child.) Issued in proof only   35.00

44a.

50.   10 Dollars 1982. Mongoose. Rev: Arms   35.00

51.   5 Dollars 1982. Norman Manley   17.50

52.   1 Dollar (C-N) 1982. Sir Alexander Bustamente   4.00

53.   50 Cents (C-N) 1982. Marcus Garvey   2.50

54.   25 Cents (C-N) 1982. Native flora-fauna design   2.00

55.   20 Cents (C-N) 1982   1.50

56.   10 Cents (C-N) 1982   1.00

57.   5 Cents (C-N) 1982   .75

58.   1 Cent (Br) 1982   .50

44.   250 Dollars (G) 1980. Group of athletes in circle. Rev: Arms. (1980 Moscow Olympics)   250.00

44a.   25 Dollars 1980. (1980 Moscow Olympics.) In proof only   100.00

JAPAN

The feudal system was prolonged in Japan until well into the 19th century. Contact with Westerners was discouraged. In 1854 Commodore Perry forced the opening of trade relations with the Western world. From then on Japan was modernized and industrialized until it took its place among the great powers.

10 Rin = 1 Sen
100 Sen = 1 Yen

1.	1 Yen 1870. Coiled dragon. Rev: Rayed sun	300.00
2.	50 Sen 1870–71	30.00
3.	20 Sen 1870–71	15.00
4.	10 Sen 1870	20.00
5.	5 Sen 1870–71	150.00

6.	Trade Dollar 1875–77. Dragon. Rev: Value in wreath. Inscription in English: 420 GRAINS, TRADE DOLLAR, .900 FINE	650.00

7.	1 Yen 1874–1914. Coiled dragon. Rev: Value in wreath. In English: 416 ONE YEN 900	35.00
8.	50 Sen 1873–1905	15.00
9.	20 Sen 1873–1905	5.00
10.	10 Sen 1873–1906	3.00
11.	5 Sen 1873–1880	12.00
11a.	1 Sen (Bro) 1873–88	2.00

12.	50 Sen 1906–17. Rayed sun. Rev: Value in wreath	10.00
13.	20 Sen 1906–11	4.00
14.	10 Sen 1907–17	2.50
15.	5 Sen (C-N) 1897–1905	5.00
16.	2 Sen (Bro) 1873–84	2.50

17.	1 Sen (Bro) 1898–1915	2.50
18.	½ Sen (Bro) 1873–88	2.00

19.	50 Sen 1922–37. Rayed sun. Rev: Value between birds of longevity	5.00

20.	10 Sen (C-N) 1920–32. Eight-petaled flower around center hole	.50
21.	5 Sen (C-N) 1917–32	1.00

22.	1 Sen (Bro) 1916–38. Kiri crest. Value in circle	1.50
23.	5 Rin (Bro) 1916–19	3.00

JAPAN (continued)

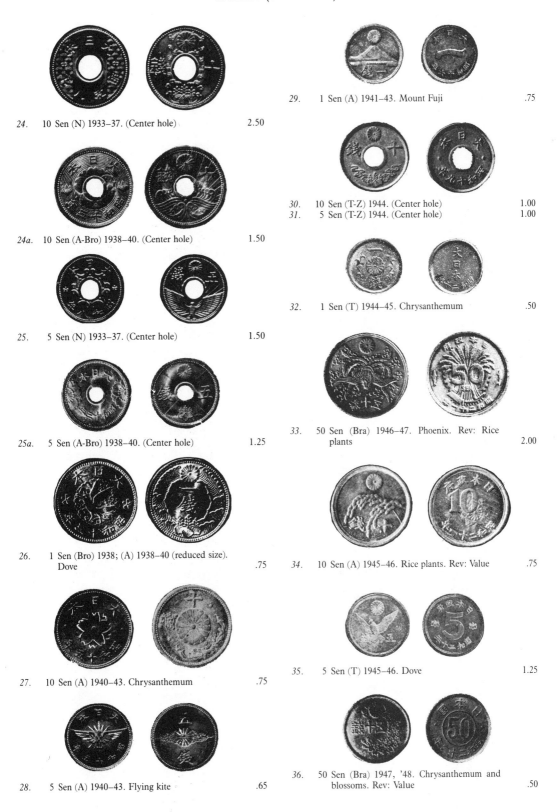

24. 10 Sen (N) 1933–37. (Center hole)   2.50

24a. 10 Sen (A-Bro) 1938–40. (Center hole)   1.50

25. 5 Sen (N) 1933–37. (Center hole)   1.50

25a. 5 Sen (A-Bro) 1938–40. (Center hole)   1.25

26. 1 Sen (Bro) 1938; (A) 1938–40 (reduced size). Dove   .75

27. 10 Sen (A) 1940–43. Chrysanthemum   .75

28. 5 Sen (A) 1940–43. Flying kite   .65

29. 1 Sen (A) 1941–43. Mount Fuji   .75

30. 10 Sen (T-Z) 1944. (Center hole)   1.00
31. 5 Sen (T-Z) 1944. (Center hole)   1.00

32. 1 Sen (T) 1944–45. Chrysanthemum   .50

33. 50 Sen (Bra) 1946–47. Phoenix. Rev: Rice plants   2.00

34. 10 Sen (A) 1945–46. Rice plants. Rev: Value   .75

35. 5 Sen (T) 1945–46. Dove   1.25

36. 50 Sen (Bra) 1947, '48. Chrysanthemum and blossoms. Rev: Value   .50

JAPAN (continued)

37.   5 Yen (Bra) 1948–49. Dove in circle. Rev:
      Building   3.00

38.   1 Yen (Bra) 1948–50. Blossoms. Rev: Value   1.00

39.   100 Yen 1957–58. Phoenix   5.00

40.   50 Yen (N) 1955–58. Blossom   4.00

41.   100 Yen 1959–66. Rice plant   5.00

42.   50 Yen (N) 1959–66. (Center hole)   3.50

43.   10 Yen (Bro) 1951– . Palace. Rev: Value   .40

44.   5 Yen (Bra) 1949– . (Center hole)   .30

45.   1 Yen (A) 1955–   .10

1964 OLYMPIC GAMES COMMEMORATIVES

46.   1000 Yen 1964. Mount Fuji, surrounded by cherry
      blossoms. Rev: Olympic emblem of five inter-
      locking rings   50.00

47.   100 Yen 1964. Flaming Olympic torch and em-
      blem. Rev: Value   5.00

48.   100 Yen (C-N) 1967– . Cherry blossoms. Rev:
      Value   .75

49. 50 Yen (C-N) 1967– . (Center hole)   .35

50. 100 Yen (C-N) 1970. Mount Fuji. Rev: Expo '70
     emblem. (1970 World Exposition)   5.00

51. 100 Yen (C-N) 1972. Olympic torch. Rev: Value,
     rings. (Winter Olympic Games 1972)   5.00

52. 100 Yen (C-N) 1975. Gate of Shurei. Rev: Value.
     (International Sea Expo at Okinawa)   4.00

53. 100 Yen (C-N) 1976. Imperial Palace. Rev: Chry-
     santhemum. (50th anniversary of Emperor
     Hirohito's reign)   4.00

JERSEY

This Channel island is a British possession.

VICTORIA 1837–1901

1. 1/13 Shilling (C) 1841–61; (Bro) 1866–71. Head.
   Rev: Ornamented shield ... 15.00

2. 1/26 Shilling (C) 1841–61; (Bro) 1866–71 ... 12.50
3. 1/52 Shilling (C) 1841 ... 65.00
4. 1/12 Shilling (Bro) 1877–94. Head. Rev: Blunt
   shield ... 2.50
5. 1/24 Shilling (Bro) 1877–94 ... 5.00
6. 1/48 Shilling (Bro) 1877 ... 50.00

EDWARD VII 1901–1910

7. 1/12 Shilling (Bro) 1909. Crowned bust. Rev:
   Pointed shield ... 15.00
8. 1/24 Shilling (Bro) 1909 ... 20.00

GEORGE V 1910–36

9. 1/12 Shilling (Bro) 1911, '13, '23. Crowned bust.
   Rev: Type of #7 ... 7.50
10. 1/12 Shilling (Bro) 1923, '26, '31, '33, '35. Rev:
    Blunt shield ... 10.00
11. 1/24 Shilling (Bro) 1911, '13, '23. Type of #9 ... 12.50
12. 1/24 Shilling (Bro) 1923, '26, '31, '33, '35. Type of
    #10 ... 10.00

GEORGE VI 1936–1952

13. 1/12 Shilling (Bro) 1937, '46, '47. Crowned head.
    Rev: Type of #10 ... 3.00
14. 1/24 Shilling (Bro) 1937, '46, '47 ... 8.00

15. 1/12 Shilling (Bro) 1949–52. Type of #13, with
    inscription LIBERATED 1945. (Liberation
    penny) ... 2.50

ELIZABETH II 1952–

16. 1/12 Shilling (Bro) 1954. Crowned bust. Rev: Type
    of #13, with inscription LIBERATED 1945 ... 7.50
17. 1/4 Shilling (N-Bra) 1957 ... 2.00
18. 1/12 Shilling (Bro) 1957, '64 ... 1.00

19. 1/12 Shilling (Bro) 1960. (King Charles II 300th
    year commemorative—1660–1960) ... 1.50
20. 1/4 Shilling (N-Bra) 1964. (Dodecagonal
    planchet) ... 1.50
21. 5 Shillings (C-N) 1966. Crowned bust. Rev:
    Arms, dates "1066–1966." (Battle of Hast-
    ings) ... 4.00
22. 1/4 Shilling (N-Bra) 1966. (Dodecagonal
    planchet) ... 1.00
23. 1/12 Shilling (Br) 1966. (Round) ... 3.00

DECIMAL COINAGE

24. 50 New Pence (C-N) 1969– . Draped bust with
    coronet. Rev: Arms. (Heptagonal planchet) ... 2.25

25. 10 New Pence (C-N) 1968– ... 1.00
26. 5 New Pence (C-N) 1968– ... .50
27. 2 New Pence (Bro) 1971– ... .50
28. 1 New Penny (Bro) 1971– ... .40
29. 1/2 New Penny (Bro) 1971– ... .30
30. 25 Pence (C-N) 1977. Rev: Harbor scene. (Silver
    Jubilee of Queen Elizabeth) ... 2.50
31. 2 Pounds 1981. Rev: Conjoined portraits of
    Prince Charles and Lady Diana. (Marriage of
    Charles and Diana.) Issued in proof only ... 75.00
32. 1 Pound (C-N) 1981. Rev: Crowned shield. (Bi-
    centennial of Battle of Jersey) ... 4.00

JORDAN

An Arab kingdom since 1946. After being part of the Turkish Empire for several centuries, this area became a British mandate after World War I, receiving independence in 1946.

100 Fils = 1 Dinar or 1 Pound Sterling

ABDULLA IBN AL HUSSEIN 1946–51

1.	100 Fils (C-N) 1949. Crowned shield and Arabic inscription. Rev: Value in English	3.00
2.	50 Fils (C-N) 1949	2.00
3.	20 Fils (C-N) 1949	1.00
4.	10 Fils (Bro) 1949	1.00
5.	5 Fils (Bro) 1949	.75
6.	1 Fil (Bro) 1949	.75

HUSSEIN I 1952–

7.	100 Fils (C-N) 1955–65. Crowned shield. Rev: Value	3.00
8.	50 Fils (C-N) 1955–65	1.50
9.	20 Fils (C-N) 1964–65	5.00
10.	10 Fils (Bro) 1955–67	1.00
11.	5 Fils (Bro) 1955–67	1.00
12.	1 Fil (Bro) 1955–65	2.00
13.	100 Fils (C-N) 1968– . Head of King. Rev: Inscription	3.00
14.	50 Fils (C-N) 1968–	1.00
15.	25 Fils (C-N) 1968–	.75
16.	10 Fils (Bro) 1968–	.50
17.	5 Fils (Bro) 1968–	.30
18.	1 Fil (Bro) 1968–	.50

19.	¼ Dinar (C-N) 1969. Head of King. Rev: Olive tree (F.A.O. coin plan)	5.00
20.	¼ Dinar (C-N) 1970. Rev: Without F.A.O. inscription	4.00

21.	25 Dinars (G) 1977. Bust of King. Rev: Crowned shield. (25th anniversary of Hussein's reign)	325.00

22.	3 Dinars 1977. Bust of King. Rev: Bird and flower. (Conservation series)	50.00
23.	2½ Dinars. 1977. Rev: Deer. (Conservation series)	35.00

24.	¼ Dinar (C-N) 1977. Head of King. Rev: Petra temple. (Silver Jubilee of Hussein)	1.50
25.	½ Dinar (C-N) 1980. (A.H. 1400). Bust of Hussein. Rev: Sun rays over mosque. (1400th anniversary of Islam)	10.00

26.	3 Dinars 1981. Bust of Hussein. Rev: Two children gazing at Palace of Culture, "Hussein Youth City," Amman. (International Year of Child)	40.00

KENYA

Formerly a British protectorate and then colony on the east coast of Africa astride the Equator, Kenya became an independent state within the British Commonwealth in December 1963, and a republic the following year.

1.	2 Shillings (C-N) 1966–68. President Jomo Kenyatta. Rev: Arms	1.50
2.	1 Shilling (C-N) 1966–68	1.00
3.	50 Cents (C-N) 1966–68	1.00
4.	25 Cents (C-N) 1966, '67	.50
5.	10 Cents (N-Bra) 1966–68	.40
6.	5 Cents (N-Bra) 1966–68	.30
7.	2 Shillings (C-N) 1969– . Head of Kenyatta within legend. Rev: Arms	1.50
8.	1 Shilling (C-N) 1969–	1.00
9.	50 Cents (C-N) 1969–	.75
10.	25 Cents (C-N) 1969–	.50
11.	10 Cents (N-Bra) 1969–	.40
12.	5 Cents (N-Bra) 1969–	.30

13.	5 Shillings (Bra) 1973. (10th anniversary of independence; nonagonal planchet)	5.00

KIAOCHOW

Pre–World War I German-leased territory in northeast China.

1.	10 Cents (C-N) 1909. German eagle. Rev: Chinese inscription	25.00
2.	5 Cents (C-N) 1909	10.00

KOREA

Located on a peninsula between the Yellow Sea and the Sea of Japan, Korea was annexed by the Japanese in 1910, liberated at the end of World War II and divided into North Korea (under Communist influence) and South Korea (under Western influence). The status quo was maintained through the Korean War.

$$100 \; Fun = 1 \; Yang$$
$$100 \; Chon = 1 \; Won$$

EMPEROR TAI 1863–97

1.	10 Mun (C) 1888. Dragon in circle. Rev: Value	175.00
2.	5 Mun (C) 1888	80.00

3.	5 Yang 1892. Dragon in circle. Rev: Value in wreath	750.00
4.	1 Yang 1892–98	80.00
5.	¼ Yang (C-N) 1892–1901	10.00
6.	5 Fun (C) 1892–1902	7.50
7.	1 Fun (C) 1892–96	25.00

UNDER JAPANESE INFLUENCE

8.	½ Won 1905–06. Dragon in circle, value in English	75.00
8a.	½ Won 1907–08. (Reduced weight)	65.00
9.	20 Chon 1905–06	25.00
9a.	20 Chon 1907–10. (Reduced weight)	20.00
10.	10 Chon 1906	12.50
10a.	10 Chon 1907–10. (Reduced size)	10.00

11.	5 Chon (N) 1905–07. Phoenix	12.50
12.	1 Chon (Bro) 1905–06	10.00
12a.	1 Chon (Bro) 1907–10. (Reduced size)	7.50
13.	½ Chon (Bro) 1906	7.50

13a.	½ Chon (Bro) 1907–10. (Reduced size)	10.00

South Korea

14.	100 Hwan (C-N) 1959. Head of President Rhee. Rev: Peacocks and value	4.00

15.	50 Hwan (N-Bra) 1959, '61. Armor-clad war galley	2.00

16.	10 Hwan (Bro) 1959, '61. Rose (national flower)	.50

17.	10 Won (Bro) 1966– . Prabhutaratna pagoda. Rev: Value	.35

18.	5 Won (Bro) 1966– . 16th century armor-clad tortoise war galley. Rev: Value	.20

19.	1 Won (Bro) 1966, '67; (A) 1968– . Rose of Sharon. Rev: Value	.20

KOREA (continued)

20. 100 Won (C-N) 1970– . Portrait of Admiral Yi
Sun Sin. Rev: Value   1.50

21. 50 Won (C-N) 1972– . Wheat. Rev: Value.
(F.A.O. coin plan)   1.00

22. 100 Won (C-N) 1975. Independence Arch. Rev:
Female figure with flag. (30th anniversary of
Liberation)   1.50
23. 500 Won (C-N) 1978. Rifleman. Rev: Stylized
emblem. (42nd World Shooting Championships)   5.00
24. 500 Won (S) 1978. Rider. Rev: Type of #23.
(Shooting Championships)   25.00
25. 20,000 Won 1981. Arms, value. Rev: Military group.
(First anniversary of Fifth Republic)   140.00
26. 100 Won (C-N) 1981. Korean flag. Rev: Hibiscus. (First anniversary of Fifth Republic)   4.00

North Korea

1. 10 Chon (A) 1959. Arms. Rev: Value   7.50
2. 5 Chon (A) 1959, '74   5.00
3. 1 Chon (A) 1959, '70   4.00

KUWAIT

Oil-rich Arab sheikhdom on the Persian Gulf.

1000 Fils = 1 Dinar

SHEIKH ABDULLAH AL SALIMAL SABAH

1. 100 Fils (C-N) 1961– . Dhow, Arab sailing ship.
    Rev: Value. (Arabic legend changes slightly
    after 1961) 1.50
2. 50 Fils (C-N) 1961– .... .75
3. 20 Fils (C-N) 1961– .... .60
4. 10 Fils (N-Bra) 1961– .... .35
5. 5 Fils (N-Bra) 1961– .... .25
6. 1 Fil (N-Bra) 1961– .... .15

7. 2 Dinar (S-Ni) 1976. Portrait of present and
    former rulers. Rev: Oil derrick, dhow, for-
    tress, ocean waves. (15th anniversary of Na-
    tional Day of State) 30.00

LAOS

Laos became an independent constitutional monarchy in 1949. In 1954 the nation was divided, with the Pathet Lao in control in the north. Then, on Dec. 3, 1974, the Pathet Lao took over the whole country, and the Lao People's Democratic Republic was proclaimed. Laos today is strongly influenced by the Socialist Republic of Vietnam.

1. 50 Centimes (A-Mg) 1952 .... 2.50

2. 20 Centimes (A-Mg) 1952 .... 1.50

3. 10 Centimes (A-Mg) 1952 .... 1.25

People's Democratic Republic of Laos 1975–

100 Att = 1 Kip

4. 50 Att (Al) 1980– . Star within arms. Rev: Value ... 2.00
5. 20 Att (Al) 1980– 1.50
6. 10 Att (Al) 1980– 1.25

LATVIA

After becoming part of Russia in the 18th century, Latvia achieved its independence in 1918. The U.S.S.R. absorbed Latvia in 1940.

100 Santimu = 1 Lats

1.	50 Santimu (N) 1922. Arms. Rev: Figure at tiller of boat	15.00
2.	20 Santimu (N) 1922. Arms. Rev: Value above wheat ear	10.00
3.	10 Santimu (N) 1922	10.00

4.	5 Santimi (Bro) 1922. Arms. Rev: Value	10.00
5.	2 Santimi (Bro) 1922–32	7.50
6.	1 Santims (Bro) 1922–35	7.00

7.	5 Lati 1929, 1931–32. Native girl. Rev: Arms with supporters	35.00

8.	2 Lati 1925–26. Arms with supporters. Rev: Value in wreath	15.00
9.	1 Lats 1924	12.50
10.	2 Santimi (Bro) 1937–39. Arms. Rev: Value	15.00
11.	1 Santims (Bro) 1937–39	10.00

LEBANON

Lebanon, just south of Turkey on the Mediterranean coast, was formerly part of the Turkish Empire. It became an independent state in 1920, was a French Mandate 1920–1, and has been a republic since 1926. Recently it has been torn by civil war.

100 Piastres = 1 Lira or Pound

1.	50 Piastres 1929, '33, '37. Cedar of Lebanon. Rev: Cornucopia	35.00
2.	25 Piastres 1929, '33, '37	40.00
3.	10 Piastres 1929	25.00

4.	5 Piastres (A-Bro) 1924. Cedar. Rev: Arabic inscription	20.00
5.	2 Piastres (A-Bro) 1924	25.00

6.	5 Piastres (A-Bro) 1925–40. Cedar. Rev: Galley	7.50
7.	2 Piastres (A-Bro) 1925	30.00

8.	1 Piastre (C-N) 1925–37; (Z) 1940	3.00
9.	½ Piastre (C-N) 1934, '36; (Z) 1941	7.50

10.	2½ Piastres (A-Bro) 1940. Inscription. Rev: Inscription and lions. (Center hole)	5.00

LEBANON (continued)

11. 50 Piastres 1952. Cedar. Rev: Value in wreath — 4.00
12. 25 Piastres (A-Bro) 1952, '61. Cedar. Rev: Value
and leaves — 2.00

13. 10 Piastres (A) 1952. Cedar. Rev: Lion's head — 10.00

14. 5 Piastres (A) 1952. Cedar. Rev: Sailing vessel — 3.00
15. 10 Piastres (A-Bro) 1955; (C-N) 1961. Cedar.
Rev: Sailing ship (design varies) — 1.00
16. 5 Piastres (A) 1954. Cedar. Rev: Wreath — 1.25
16a. 5 Piastres (A-Bro) 1955, '61. Rev: Lion's head — .30
17. 2½ Piastres (A-Bro) 1955. (Center hole) — .25
18. 1 Piastre (A-Bro) 1955 — .25
19. 50 Piastres (N) 1968– . Cedar, BANQUE DU LIBAN.
Rev: Value in wreath — .60
20. 25 Piastres (N-Bra) 1968– — .40
21. 10 Piastres (N-Bra) 1968– — .20
22. 5 Piastres (N-Bra) 1968– — .15

23. 1 Livre (N) 1968. Cedar. Rev: Fruit (F.A.O.
coin plan) — 2.50

24. 1 Livre (N) 1975. Cedar. Rev: Value — 1.00

25. 5 Livres (N) 1978. Cedar. (F.A.O. coin plan) — 3.00
26. 400 Livres (G) 1980. Stylized design, inscription.
Lake Placid Winter Olympics symbol. Issued
in proof only — 500.00
27. 10 Livres (S) 1980. (Lake Placid Winter Olympics.) In proof only — 40.00
28. 1 Livre (C-N) 1980. (Lake Placid Winter Olympics) In proof only — 15.00

351

LIBERIA

An independent republic on the southwest coast of Africa, Liberia was founded in 1822 by the American Colonization Society.

100 Cents = 1 Dollar

1. 1 Cent (C) 1833. Native and palm tree. Rev: Inscription. (Token of American Colonization Society) 30.00

2. 2 Cents (C) 1847, '62. Liberty head. Rev: Palm tree 30.00
3. 1 Cent (C) 1847, '62 .... 35.00

4. 50 Cents 1896, 1906. Female head. Rev: Value in wreath 50.00
5. 25 Cents 1896, 1906 .... 30.00
6. 10 Cents 1896, 1906 .... 20.00
7. 2 Cents (Bro) 1896, 1906 .... 12.50
8. 1 Cent (Bro) 1896, 1906 .... 15.00

9. 2 Cents (Bra) 1937; (C-N) 1941. Elephant. Rev: Palm tree 1.50
10. 1 Cent (Bra) 1937; (C-N) 1941 .... 3.00
11. ½ Cent (Bra) 1937; (C-N) 1941 .... .65

13.

12. 1 Dollar, 1961–62. Head of native girl. Rev: Value and wreath 25.00
12a. 1 Dollar (C-N) 1966– 3.50
13. 50 Cents 1960, '61 .... 10.50
13a. 50 Cents (C-N) 1966– 2.00
14. 25 Cents 1960, '61 .... 7.50
14a. 25 Cents (C-N) 1966– 1.50
15. 10 Cents 1960, '61 .... 3.00
15a. 10 Cents (C-N) 1966– 1.50

16. 5 Cents (C-N) 1960– . Elephant. Rev: Coastal scene 1.50
17. 1 Cent (Bro) 1960– 1.00

18. 5 Dollars 1973– . Map, African elephant. Rev: Arms 30.00
19. 25 Cents (C-N) 1976. Bust of President Tolbert. Rev: Native woman with basket of food on her head. (F.A.O. coin plan) 3.50

352

20.	100 Dollars (G) 1977. Bust of Joseph J. Roberts. Rev: Arms. (130th anniversary of independence)	250.00
21.	100 Dollars (G) 1979. Bust of President William R. Tolbert. Rev: Arms. (Organization of African Unity Summit Conference)	250.00
22.	100 Dollars (G) 1979. African elephant. Rev: Arms. (African Unity Summit)	250.00

LIBYA

Located on the northern coast of Africa. In 1911 Libya fell under Italian control, but after World War II, in 1951, it became an independent kingdom. In September 1969 a military junta took power, establishing a socialist republic.

10 Milliemes = 1 Piastre

IDRIS I   1951–69

1.	2 Piastres (C-N) 1952. Head. Rev: Crowned inscription and wreath	2.00
2.	1 Piastre (C-N) 1952	1.00
3.	5 Milliemes (Bro) 1952	.75
4.	2 Milliemes (Bro) 1952	.50
5.	1 Millieme (Bro) 1952	.35

6.	100 Milliemes (C-N) 1965. Crowned arms. Rev: Value	3.50

7.	50 Milliemes (C-N) 1965 (scalloped)	3.00
8.	20 Milliemes (C-N) 1965, '70 (round)	1.00
9.	10 Milliemes (C-N) 1965, '70	.75
10.	5 Milliemes (Ni-Bra) 1965 (scalloped)	.35
11.	1 Millieme (Ni-Bra) 1965 (round)	.25

MONETARY REFORM

100 Dirhams = 1 Dinar

12.	100 Dirhams (C-N) 1975. Arms. Rev: Value within wreath	3.00
13.	50 Dirhams (C-N) 1975	2.00
14.	20 Dirhams (C-N-St) 1975	1.50
15.	10 Dirhams (C-N-St) 1975	1.00
16.	5 Dirhams (Br-St) 1975	.65
17.	1 Dirham (Br-St) 1975	.65

LIECHTENSTEIN

A small principality of 62 square miles in central Europe, lying between Austria and Switzerland.

100 Heller = 1 Krone
100 Rappen = 1 Franken

PRINCE JOHN II   1858–1929

1.	1 Taler 1862. Head of Johann II. Rev: Arms	1750.00

2.	20 Kronen (G) 1898. Head. Rev: Arms	RARE
3.	10 Kronen (G) 1900	RARE

4.	5 Kronen 1900–15. Head. Rev: Arms and value	250.00
5.	2 Kronen 1912, '15	30.00
6.	1 Krone 1900–15	15.00
7.	5 Franken 1924. Type of #4	800.00
8.	2 Franken 1924	125.00
9.	1 Franken 1924	100.00
10.	½ Franken 1924	135.00

PRINCE FRANZ I   1929–1938

11.	20 Franken (G) 1930. Bust. Rev: Arms	1250.00
12.	10 Franken (G) 1930	1000.00

PRINCE FRANZ JOSEF II   1938–

13.	20 Franken (G) 1946. Head. Rev: Arms	325.00
14.	10 Franken (G) 1946	275.00

15.	100 Franken (G) 1952. Busts of Franz Josef II and Princess Gina. Rev: Arms	RARE
16.	50 Franken (G) 1956	350.00
17.	25 Franken (G) 1956	300.00

LITHUANIA

Lithuania had its golden age in the 15th century, when it was about three times the size of Poland. Later on, greatly reduced, it became part of Russia. After World War I Lithuania enjoyed a brief period of independence. In 1940 it was made part of the U.S.S.R.

100 Centu = 1 Litas

1.	5 Litai 1925. Horseman. Rev: Value	30.00
2.	2 Litai 1925	17.50
3.	1 Litas 1925	15.00
4.	50 Centu (A-Bro) 1925. Horseman	15.00
5.	20 Centu (A-Bro) 1925	12.50
6.	10 Centu (A-Bro) 1925	10.00
7.	5 Centai (A-Bro) 1925	7.50
8.	1 Centas (A-Bro) 1925	10.00

9.	10 Litu 1936. Head of Vytautas. Rev: Horseman	50.00
10.	5 Litai 1936. Dr. Jonas Basanavicius. Rev: Horseman	30.00

11.	5 Centai (Bro) 1936. Horseman	10.00
12.	2 Centai (Bro) 1936	10.00
13.	1 Centas (Bro) 1936	8.50

14.	10 Litu 1938. Head of President Smetona. (20th anniversary of founding of state)	65.00

LUXEMBOURG

A tiny country that borders on Belgium, France and Germany. In the 14th and 15th centuries several counts of Luxembourg were elected Holy Roman Emperor. During World War II, Luxembourg was occupied by the Germans and eventually freed by American troops.

100 Centimes = 1 Franc

WILLIAM III   1849–90

1.	10 Centimes (Bro) 1854–70. Arms. Rev: Value	7.50
2.	5 Centimes (Bro) 1854–70	12.50
3.	2½ Centimes (Bro) 1854–70	7.50

ADOLPHE   1890–1905

4.	10 Centimes (C-N) 1901. Head. Rev: Value	2.50
5.	5 Centimes (C-N) 1901	2.50
6.	2½ Centimes (Bro) 1901. Type of #3	4.00

WILLIAM IV   1905–12

7.	5 Centimes (C-N) 1908. Head. Rev: Value	2.50
8.	2½ Centimes (Bro) 1908. Arms. Type of #3	5.00

MARIE ADELAIDE   1912–19

9.	25 Centimes (Z) 1916. (Center hole)	10.00
10.	10 Centimes (Z) 1915	7.50
11.	5 Centimes (Z) 1915	7.50

12.	25 Centimes (I) 1919. Arms. Rev: Value	15.00
13.	10 Centimes (I) 1918	10.00
14.	5 Centimes (I) 1918	7.50

CHARLOTTE   1919–1964

15.	25 Centimes (I) 1920–22. Type of #12	10.00
16.	10 Centimes (I) 1921–23	10.00
17.	5 Centimes (I) 1921–22	8.50

18.	10 Francs 1929. Head. Rev: Arms	25.00
19.	5 Francs 1929	12.50

20.	2 Francs (N) 1924. Puddler	7.50
21.	1 Franc (N) 1924–35	2.00
22.	50 Centimes (N) 1930–41	2.00
23.	25 Centimes (C-N) 1927, 1938; (Br) 1930 Arms. Rev: Value	3.00
24.	10 Centimes (C-N) 1924. Monogram. Rev: Value	2.50
25.	5 Centimes (C-N) 1924	2.50
26.	10 Centimes (Bro) 1930. Head. Rev: Value	2.00
27.	5 Centimes (Bro) 1930	1.50

28.	1 Franc (C-N) 1939. Standing figure. Rev: Monogram	5.00

LUXEMBOURG (continued)

600TH ANNIVERSARY OF JOHN THE BLIND

37.	5 Francs (C-N) 1962	1.00

JEAN 1964–

38.	100 Francs 1964. Head of Grand Duke. Rev: Arms	30.00
39.	1 Franc (C-N) 1965– . Head. Rev: Value	.20

29.	100 Francs 1946. King John mounted. Rev: Head of Prince	35.00
30.	50 Francs 1946	20.00
31.	20 Francs 1946	15.00

40.	10 Francs (N) 1971– . Head. Rev: Value	.75

32.	5 Francs (N) 1949. Head. Rev: Value	3.00
33.	1 Franc (C-N) 1946–47; (reduced size) 1952– . Puddler. Rev: Monogram and value	.50
34.	25 Centimes (Bro) 1946–47; (A) 1954– . Arms. Rev: Value	.15

41.	5 Francs (C-N) 1971. Head. Rev: Value	.50
42.	20 Francs (Bro) 1980– . Head of Grand Duke. Rev: Value	1.75

35.	250 Francs 1963. Head of ruler. Rev: Ancient castle. (1000th anniversary of city of Luxembourg)	100.00
36.	100 Francs 1963. Rev: Arms and value	25.00

MACAO

A Portuguese colony for 400 years located at the mouth of the Canton River in China.

100 Avos = 1 Pataca

1.	5 Patacas 1952. Arms of Macao. Rev: Portuguese arms in cross	12.50
1a.	5 Patacas 1971. (Smaller planchet)	8.50
2.	1 Pataca 1952	7.50
2a.	1 Pataca (N) 1968–75; (C-N) 1980– . (Larger planchet)	2.00
3.	50 Avos (C-N) 1952	2.00
3a.	50 Avos (C-N) 1972. (Larger planchet)	1.25

4.	10 Avos (Bro) 1952. Arms of Macao. Rev: Value in Chinese	1.50
4a.	10 Avos (N-Bra) 1967–	.25
5.	5 Avos (Bro) 1952	3.00
5a.	5 Avos (N-Bra) 1967	.50

6.	20 Patacas 1974. Chinese junk under bridge. Rev: Arms. (Opening of Macao-Taipa Bridge)	20.00
7.	500 Patacas (G) 1978. Facade of ruins of San Paulo. Rev: Racing car. (25th anniversary of Grand Prix)	200.00
8.	100 Patacas (C-N) 1978. (Grand Prix)	50.00
8a.	100 Patacas (S) 1978. Proof	75.00
9.	500 Patacas (G) 1979. Arms. Rev: Goat. (Chinese New Year)	200.00

10.	1000 Patacas (G) 1980. Arms. Rev: Monkey. (Chinese New Year)	350.00
11.	500 Patacas (G) 1980. Rev: Monkey. (Chinese New Year)	200.00

12.	1000 Patacas (G) 1981. Rev: Cockerel. (Chinese New Year)	350.00
13.	500 Patacas (G) 1981. Rev: Cockerel. (Chinese New Year)	200.00

15.

14.	1000 Patacas (G) 1982. Rev: Chinese pug dog (Chinese New Year)	350.00
15.	100 Patacas (S) 1982. (Chinese New Year)	75.00

MADAGASCAR

This large island off the southeast coast of Africa became the Democratic Republic of Madagascar in 1975. See also "Malagasy" below.

100 Centimes = 1 Franc

1.	1 Franc (Bro) 1943. Rooster. Rev: Cross of Lorraine	35.00
2.	50 Centimes (Bro) 1943	10.00
3.	20 Francs (A-Bro) 1953. Republic. Rev: Map and value	2.50
4.	10 Francs (A-Bro) 1953	2.00
5.	5 Francs (A) 1953. Rev: Cattle	1.50

6.	2 Francs (A) 1948	1.50
7.	1 Franc (A) 1948, '58	1.25

NEW CURRENCY

5 Francs = 1 Ariary

8.	20 Ariary (N) 1978– . Star, value within wreath. Rev: Wheat field. (F.A.O. coin plan)	5.00
9.	10 Ariary (N) 1978– . Rev: Farmer. (F.A.O. coin plan)	4.00

MADEIRA ISLANDS

An archipelago in the Atlantic, southwest of Portugal. The islands were officially discovered by the Portuguese in the early part of the 15th century, though they appeared on maps before that time. Administratively the islands are part of the Funchal district of Portugal.

MARY II   1828–53

1.	20 Reis (C) 1842, '52. Crowned arms. Rev: Value (Roman numerals) in wreath	25.00

2.	10 Reis (C) 1842–52	35.00
3.	5 Reis (C) 1850	65.00

MALAGASY

A large island off the southeast coast of Africa. Formerly the French Overseas Territory of Madagascar, and previously a French colony, it became the Republic of Malagasy in 1958, achieving full independence within the French Community in March 1960. In 1975 it became the Democratic Republic of Madagascar. See also "Madagascar" above.

1.	5 Francs (St) 1966–72. Flower. Rev: Head of longhorn steer and value	.75
2.	2 Francs (St) 1965–74	.40

3.	1 Franc (St) 1965–79	.30

4.	20 Francs (A-Bro) 1970–76. Zebu ox head, coffee flower. Rev: Cotton flower. (F.A.O. coin plan)	1.50
5.	10 Francs (A-Bro) 1970–76. Rev: Vanilla flower	1.00

MALAWI

Malawi is the name the former British Protectorate of Nyasaland adopted in 1963 when it withdrew from the Federation of Rhodesia and Nyasaland, of which it had been a member since 1953. It became an independent state in July 1964 and a republic within the British Commonwealth in July 1966.

1. ½ Crown (C-N) 1964. Head of Prime Minister
   Dr. Hastings Banda. Rev: Arms   3.50
2. 1 Florin (Ni) 1964. Rev: Elephants   2.50

3. 1 Shilling (N) 1964. Rev: Ears of corn   1.50
4. 6 Pence (N) 1964. Rev: Rooster   .75

5. 1 Crown (N-Bra) 1966. Rev: Arms. (Republic
   Day)   10.00

6. 1 Penny (Bro) 1967. Value and date. Rev: Value   1.00

DECIMAL COINAGE

100 Tambala = 1 Kwacha

7. 1 Kwacha (C-N) 1971. Head of Prime Minister
   Dr. Hastings Banda. Rev: Arms   6.00
8. 20 Tambala (C-N) 1971. Rev: Elephants   1.50
9. 10 Tambala (C-N) 1971. Rev: Ears of corn   .75

10. 5 Tambala (C-N) 1971. Rev: Purple heron   .50
11. 2 Tambala (C-N) 1971– . Rev: Bird of paradise   .25
12. 1 Tambala (Bro) 1971– . Rev: Rooster   .15

13. 10 Kwacha 1974. Rev: Small arms, map within
    broken chain. (10th anniversary of indepen-
    dence)   35.00
14. 10 Kwacha 1975. Rev: Eagle with rising sun and
    waves. (10th anniversary of Reserve Bank)   35.00

15. 250 Kwacha (G) 1978. Rev: Male and female nyala. (World Wildlife Conservation Program) ... 500.00
16. 10 Kwacha 1978. (Wildlife Conservation) ... 40.00

MALAYA and BRITISH BORNEO

Malaya, including the former Straits Settlement on the Malay Peninsula, became a sovereign member of the British Commonwealth as the Federation of Malaya in 1957. In 1963 it joined with the State of Singapore (q.v.) and the former colonies of British North Borneo (now Sabah) and Sarawak to form the Federation of Malaysia (q.v.). The Sultanate of Brunei decided not to join the Federation but to use the same coins.

100 Cents = 1 Dollar

British North Borneo

1.	1 Cent (Bro) 1882–96, 1907	10.00
2.	½ Cent (Bro) 1885–91, 1907. Arms. Rev: Value in wreath	12.50

3.	5 Cents (C-N) 1903–41. Arms and supporters. Rev: Value in dotted circle	4.00
4.	2½ Cents (C-N) 1903, '20	10.00
5.	1 Cent (C-N) 1904–41	3.00
5a.	25 Cents 1929	20.00

Malaya

GEORGE VI 1936–52

6.	20 Cents (S) 1939–45; (C-N) '48–50. Crowned head. Rev: Value in dotted circle	2.50
7.	10 Cents (S) 1939–45; (C-N) '48–50	2.00
8.	5 Cents (S) 1939–45; (C-N) '48–50	1.00

9.	1 Cent (Bro) 1939–45. (Square-shaped)	1.00
10.	½ Cent (Bro) 1940	3.00

Malaya and British Borneo

ELIZABETH II 1952–

11.	50 Cents (C-N) 1954–61. Crowned head. Rev: Type of #1	5.00
12.	20 Cents (C-N) 1954–61	2.00
13.	10 Cents (C-N) 1953–61	1.50
14.	5 Cents (C-N) 1953–61	1.25

15.	1 Cent (Bro) 1956–66. (Square-shaped)	.50

16.	1 Cent (Bro) 1962. Crossed daggers. Rev: Value	.40

MALAYSIA

Malaya, including the former Straits Settlements on the Malay Peninsula, became a sovereign member of the British Commonwealth as the Federation of Malaya in 1957. In 1963, the eleven states of Malaya joined with Sabah (former British North Borneo), Sarawak and the State of Singapore to form the Federation of Malaysia. In 1965 Singapore (q.v.) withdrew from the Federation.

100 Sen = 1 Ringgit Dollar

1.	50 Sen (C-N) 1967– . Bank Negara Malaysia in Kuala Lumpur, coat of arms at side. Rev: Value	1.00
2.	20 Sen (C-N) 1967–	.45
3.	10 Sen (C-N) 1967–	.30
4.	5 Sen (C-N) 1967–	.20
5.	1 Sen (Bro) 1967–73; (C-St) 1973–80; (C-N) 1980– . Issued in proof only	.15

6.	1 Dollar (C-N) 1969. Head of Sultan. Rev: Value. (10th anniversary of Central Bank)	3.00
6a.	1 Dollar 1969	100.00

7.	100 Dollars (G) 1971. Head of Abdul Rahman. Rev: Bank Negara Malaysia, arms in background	350.00
8.	5 Dollars (C-N) 1971	5.00

9.	1 Dollar (C-N) 1971. Rev: Value	3.00

10.	1 Dollar (C-N) 1972. Arms of city of Kuala Lumpur. Rev: Value. (First anniversary of status as city)	3.00
11.	500 Dollars (G) 1976. Arms. Rev: Tapir	700.00
12.	25 Dollars 1976. Rev: Rhinoceros hornbill	40.00
13.	15 Dollars 1976. Rev: Seladang	35.00
14.	25 Dollars 1976. Map of Malaysia, emblem. Rev: Value. (25th Anniversary of Employee Provident Fund)	25.00
15.	1 Dollar (C-N) 1976. Emblem, collage of faces. (Employee Provident Fund)	1.50
16.	1 Dollar (C-N) 1976. Abdul Rahman within circle of flags. Rev: Supported shield. (Third Five-Year Plan)	1.50
17.	1 Dollar (C-N) 1977. Abdul Rahman. Rev: Supported shield. (20th year of independence)	1.50
18.	1 Dollar (C-N) 1977. Rubber-working. Rev: Value. (100th anniversary of natural rubber production)	1.50
19.	1 Dollar (C-N) 1977. Symbol of athletics. Rev: Supported shield. (Ninth Southeast Asian Games)	1.50
20.	1 Dollar (C-N) 1979. Bank Negara Malaysia. Rev: Value. (Central Bank's 20th anniversary)	1.50
20a.	1 Dollar (S) 1979–80. Issued in proof only	25.00
22.	1 Dollar (C-N) 1981. Stylized religious symbols. Rev: Value. (Commemorates 15 centuries of Islam)	3.00

MALAYSIA (continued)

23. 1 Dollar (C-N) 1981. Tun Hussein Onn. Rev:
     Value   3.00

MALDIVE ISLANDS

Formerly a British protected state of coral atolls in the
Indian Ocean, independence was achieved in 1965, and a
republic proclaimed in 1968.

100 Lari = 1 Rupee (Rufiyaa)

1. 50 Lari (N-Bra) 1960. Arms. Rev: Value   3.00
2. 25 Lari (N-Bra) 1960   2.00
3. 10 Lari (N-Bra) 1960. Scalloped edge   1.50
4.   5 Lari (N-Bra) 1960, '70   .75
5.   2 Lari (Bro) 1960; (A) 1970. (Square-shaped)   .75
6.   1 Larin (Bro) 1960; (A) 1970. Round   .50
7. 20 Rufiyaa 1977. Rev: Value between bonito and
       bluefin tuna. (F.A.O. coin plan)   20.00

8.   5 Rufiyaa (C-N) 1977. Rev: Value and bonito
        fish. (F.A.O. coin plan)   10.00
9.   25 Rufiyaa 1978. Fishing boat. Rev: Arms.
        (F.A.O. coin plan)   25.00
10. 100 Rufiyaa 1979. Farm workers. Rev: Arms.
        (F.A.O. coin plan.) Issued in proof only   35.00
11. 100 Rufiyaa 1980. Wheat. Rev: Arms. (F.A.O.
        coin plan)   20.00

MALI

In 1958 the French Sudan, formerly part of French West Africa, became the autonomous Sudanese Republic. With Senegal it formed the Mali Federation in 1959. When Senegal withdrew in 1960 to form an independent Republic, Mali retained the new name.

1.	25 Francs (A) 1961. Lion. Rev: Value	6.00
2.	10 Francs (A) 1961. Horse	3.00

3.	5 Francs (A) 1961–62. Hippopotamus head. Rev: Value	2.00
4.	100 Francs (N-Bra) 1975. Three stalks of maize. Rev: Value. (F.A.O. coin plan)	3.00
5.	50 Francs (N-Bra) 1975–77. Millet bush. Rev: Value. (F.A.O. coin plan)	2.50
6.	25 Francs (A) 1976. Millet bush. (F.A.O. coin plan)	1.50
7.	10 Francs (A) 1976. (F.A.O. coin plan)	1.25

MALTA

This island in the Mediterranean was a British crown colony from 1814 to September 1964, when it became an independent state within the British Commonwealth. A peculiarity of its coinage is a ⅓ farthing denomination.

1.	⅓ Farthing (C) 1827. Head of George IV. Rev: Britannia	15.00
2.	⅓ Farthing (C) 1835. Head of William IV	20.00
3.	⅓ Farthing (C) 1844. Head of Victoria	50.00
4.	⅓ Farthing (Bro) 1866–85. Rev: Crowned value in wreath	15.00

5.	⅓ Farthing (Bro) 1902. Head of Edward VII	12.50
6.	⅓ Farthing (Bro) 1913. Head of George V	12.50

DECIMAL COINAGE

7.	50 Pounds (G) 1972. Arms. Rev: Statue of Neptune	600.00

8.	20 Pounds (G) 1972. Rev: National bird	250.00
9.	10 Pounds (G) 1972. Rev: Stone stove	150.00
10.	5 Pounds (G) 1972. Rev: Map, torch	75.00

11.	2 Pounds 1972. Rev: Fort St. Angelo	25.00
12.	1 Pound 1972. Rev: Portrait of Manwel Dimech, politician	15.00

13.	50 Cents (C-N) 1972– . Three allegorical figures. Rev: Value. (Decagonal planchet)	4.00

14.	10 Cents (C-N) 1972– . Barge. Rev: Value	1.50
15.	5 Cents (C-N) 1972– . Altar. Rev: Value	.75

16.	2 Cents (C-N) 1972– . Helmeted head. Rev: Value	.50
17.	1 Cent (Bro) 1972– . St. George Cross. Rev: Value	.40
18.	5 Mils (A) 1972– . Lampstand. Rev: Value. (Scalloped planchet)	.30

19. 3 Mils (A) 1972– . Bee on honeycomb. Rev: Value. (Scalloped planchet)   .30
20. 2 Mils (A) 1972– . Maltese Cross. Rev: Value   .30

21. 50 Pounds (G) 1973. Arms. Rev: Castle   350.00
22. 20 Pounds (G) 1973. Rev: Fountain   150.00
23. 10 Pounds (G) 1973. Rev: Watchtower   100.00

29. 4 Pounds 1974. Rev: Door of Cottonera   25.00
30. 2 Pounds 1974. Portrait of Giovanni Francesco Abela, historian   15.00

24. 2 Pounds 1973. Rev: View of Il-Bieb Ta'l-Imdina   25.00
25. 1 Pound 1973. Rev: Temi Zammit, Maltese historian   15.00

31. 50 Pounds (G) 1975. New arms. Rev: Stone balcony   350.00
32. 20 Pounds (G) 1975. Rev: Crab   150.00
33. 10 Pounds (G) 1975. Rev: Maltese falcon   100.00

26. 50 Pounds (G) 1974. Rev: Likeness of first Maltese coin   350.00
27. 20 Pounds (G) 1974. Rev: Boat   150.00
28. 10 Pounds (G) 1974. Rev: National flower   85.00

34. 4 Pounds 1975. Rev: St. Agatha's Tower at Qammieh   25.00
35. 2 Pounds 1975. Rev: Portrait of Alfonso M. Galea, writer and philanthropist   15.00

369

36.	50 Pounds (G) 1976. Statue of Neptune. Rev: Arms	300.00
37.	20 Pounds (G) 1976. Storm petrel	150.00
38.	10 Pounds (G) 1976. Swallowtail butterfly	80.00
39.	4 Pounds 1976. Arms. Rev: Gate	17.50
40.	2 Pounds 1976. Arms. Rev: Bust of Guze Ellul Mercer	12.50
41.	100 Pounds (G) 1977. Sculpture, *Les Gavroches*. Rev: Arms	500.00
42.	50 Pounds (G) 1977. Pottery	300.00
43.	25 Pounds (G) 1977. Ancient coin	175.00
44.	5 Pounds 1977. Arms. Rev: Windmill	30.00
45.	2 Pounds 1977. Arms. Rev: Bust of Luigi Preziosi	12.50
46.	1 Pound 1977. Arms. Rev: Dog	10.00
47.	1 Pound 1979. Arms. Rev: Island held within hands. (Departure of British military from Malta)	10.00

48.	5 Pounds 1981. Arms. Rev: Children playing hopscotch. (UNICEF, International Year of Child)	30.00
49.	2 Pounds 1981. Arms. Rev: Fishing boat. (F.A.O. coin plan)	12.50

MANCHUKUO

Located in northeastern China. From 1932 to 1945 Manchukuo was a puppet state under Japanese influence. In 1945 China resumed sovereignty over Manchukuo.

100 Li = 10 Fen = 1 Chiao

1.	1 Chiao (C-N) 1933–39. Lotus flower. Rev: Value between dragons	7.50
2.	5 Fen (C-N) 1933–39	5.00

3.	1 Fen (Bro) 1933–39. Flag. Rev: Value in wreath	7.50
4.	5 Li (Bro) 1933–39	25.00

5.	1 Chiao (C-N) 1940. Winged horses. Rev: Value in wreath	15.00

6.	10 Fen (A) 1940–43. Value. Rev: Inscription	7.50

7.	5 Fen (A) 1940–44	7.50

8.	1 Fen (A) 1939–43	7.50
9.	1 Fen (A) 1943–44. Type of #6	10.00

MARTINIQUE

This island, one of the Windward group in the West Indies, was discovered by Columbus and first colonized by the French in 1635. It is now an overseas department of metropolitan France.

100 Centimes = 1 Franc

1.	1 Franc (C-N) 1897, 1922. Bust of native woman. Rev: Value in wreath	15.00
2.	50 Centimes (C-N) 1897, 1922	12.00

MAURITANIA

This former French colony became independent in 1960. Until 1973 Mauritania employed the West African States joint currency.

55 Khoum = 1 Ouguiya

1.	20 Ouguiya (C-N) 1973. Star over crescent with date palm and millet. Rev: Value; Arabic legend	2.00
2.	10 Ouguiya (C-N) 1973	1.25
3.	5 Ouguiya (C-N-A) 1973	.75
4.	1 Ouguiya (C-N-A) 1973	.50
5.	⅕ Ouguiya (A) 1973	.25

MAURITIUS

This British crown colony is an island in the Indian Ocean about 700 miles east of Madagascar. Mauritius was originally settled by the Dutch, then seized by the French, and finally became British territory during the Napoleonic wars. In 1968 it became an independent nation within the British Commonwealth.

100 Cents = 1 Rupee

VICTORIA 1837–1901

1.	20 Cents 1877–99. Diademed head. Rev: Value in circle	6.00
2.	10 Cents 1877–97	5.00
3.	5 Cents (Bro) 1877–97	7.50

4.	2 Cents (Bro) 1877–97	5.00
5.	1 Cent (Bro) 1877–97	4.00

GEORGE V 1910–36

6.	1 Rupee 1934. Crowned bust. Rev: Arms	15.00

7.	½ Rupee 1934. Rev: Stag	10.00
8.	¼ Rupee 1934. Rev: Crowned rose and other ornaments	7.50

9.	5 Cents (Bro) 1917, '20–24. Rev: Value in circle	15.00
10.	2 Cents (Bro) 1911–12, '17, '20–24	7.50
11.	1 Cent (Bro) 1911–24	7.50

GEORGE VI 1936–52

NOTE: Coins issued after 1948 drop "Emperor" from the legend

12.	1 Rupee (S) 1938; (C-N) '50–51. Crowned head. Rev: Type of #6	7.50
13.	½ Rupee (S) 1946; (C-N) '50–51	5.00
14.	¼ Rupee (S) 1938, '46; (C-N) '50–51	4.00
15.	10 Cents (C-N) 1947, '52. Rev: Value. (Scalloped edge)	5.00
16.	5 Cents (Bro) 1942–45. Rev: Type of #9	4.00
17.	2 Cents (Bro) 1943–52	3.00
18.	1 Cent (Bro) 1943–52	2.00

ELIZABETH II 1952–

19.	1 Rupee (C-N) 1956– . Crowned head. Rev: Arms	1.50
20.	½ Rupee (C-N) 1965– . Rev: Stag	1.00
21.	¼ Rupee (C-N) 1960–	1.00

22.	10 Cents (C-N) 1954– . (Scalloped edge)	1.50
23.	5 Cents (Bro) 1956–	.50
24.	2 Cents (Bro) 1953–	.35
25.	1 Cent (Bro) 1953–	.25

26. 200 Rupees (G) 1971. Rev: Two figures in native
     scene. (Third anniversary of independence)   375.00

32. 25 Rupees 1977. Rev: Cane cutter. (Queen's Sil-
     ver Jubilee)   20.00
33. 1000 Rupees (G) 1978. Rev: Parliament building.
     (10th anniversary of independence)   300.00
34. 25 Rupees 1978. (Independence anniversary)   25.00
35. 10 Rupees (C-N) 1981. Rev: Dual portraits of
     Prince Charles and Lady Diana. (Marriage of
     Charles and Diana)   5.00

27. 10 Rupees (C-N) 1971. Rev: Dodo bird. (Third
     anniversary of independence)   5.00
28. 10 Rupees (S) 1971. Proof   400.00

29. 1000 Rupees (G) 1975. Rev: Flycatcher. (Conser-
     vation)   350.00

30. 50 Rupees 1975. Rev: Kestrel. (Conservation)   50.00
31. 25 Rupees 1975. Rev: Butterfly   30.00

MEXICO

During the centuries of Spanish rule, Mexico's rich silver mines were one of the chief sources of the famous Spanish Dollars or Pieces of Eight (8 Reales).

The first coins to be struck at the Mexican mint appeared during the reign of Charles and Joanna. Up to the reign of Ferdinand VII, all coins were struck at the Mexico City mint and bear the mint mark M̃.

Mexico is now a republic.

100 Centavos = 1 Peso

CHARLES AND JOANNA 1521–56

1.   4 Reales. Two pillars, PLVS VLTRA. Rev: Crowned and quartered arms   275.00

2.   2 Reales   100.00
3.   1 Real   50.00
4.   ½ Real. Large KI. Rev: Two pillars   35.00

PHILIP II 1556–98

5.   8 Reales. Crowned shield. Rev: Quartered
      arms   250.00
6.   4 Reales   150.00
7.   2 Reales   50.00
8.   1 Real   40.00

9.   ½ Real. Monogram. Rev: Arms   40.00

NOTE: The preceding coins are of the round type, though usually crude and irregular. During the following reign "cob money" came into use. This type of money was made by cutting off sections from crudely rolled silver bars and then striking the coins from crude dies by means of a hammer.

PHILIP III 1598–1621

10.   8 Reales 1600–18 (Crude "cob" type)   200.00

PHILIP IV 1621–65

11.   8 Reales 1621–65. (Planchets usually square
      cut)   150.00

12.	4 Reales 1631–39	125.00
13.	2 Reales 1641	65.00
14.	1 Real 1622	40.00

CHARLES II   1665–1700

15.	8 Reales 1667–99. (Finer dies)	1000.00
16.	4 Reales 1679–89	375.00
17.	½ Real. CAROLVS in monogram. Rev: Arms	200.00

PHILIP V   1700–46

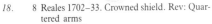

| 18. | 8 Reales 1702–33. Crowned shield. Rev: Quartered arms | 175.00 |
| 19. | 4 Reales 1721 | 150.00 |

| 20. | 8 Reales 1732–47. Two globes between pillars. Rev: Crowned arms | 150.00 |

| 21. | 4 Reales 1732–47 | 175.00 |

| 22. | 2 Reales 1732–46 | 65.00 |

23.	1 Real 1732–47	40.00
24.	½ Real 1709–43. PHILIP V in monogram	35.00
25.	½ Real 1733–47. Pillar type	20.00

FERDINAND VI   1746–59

26.	8 Reales 1747–60. Pillar type	150.00
27.	4 Reales 1746–60	200.00
28.	2 Reales 1747–60	50.00
29.	1 Real 1747–59	40.00
30.	½ Real 1747–60	25.00

CHARLES III   1759–88

32.

31.	8 Reales 1760–72. Pillar type	125.00
32.	4 Reales 1760–70	175.00
33.	2 Reales 1760–71	25.00
34.	1 Real 1760–69	20.00
35.	½ Real 1760–71	15.00

36.	8 Reales 1772–89. Bust. Rev: Crowned arms	75.00
37.	4 Reales 1772–89	85.00
38.	2 Reales 1772–89	17.50
39.	1 Real 1772–89	15.00
40.	½ Real 1772–89	12.50

CHARLES IV   1788–1808

41.	8 Reales 1789–90. Bust of Charles III. Rev: Arms	85.00

42.	4 Reales 1789–90	100.00
43.	2 Reales 1789–90	35.00
44.	1 Real 1789–90	20.00
45.	½ Real 1789–90	17.50

46.	8 Reales 1791–1808. Bust of Charles IV. Rev: Crowned arms	50.00
47.	4 Reales 1791–1808	85.00
48.	2 Reales 1791–1808	20.00

49.	1 Real 1791–1808	12.50

50.	½ Real 1791–1808	10.00

51.	¼ Real 1796–1808. Castle. Rev: Lion	30.00

MEXICO (continued)

FERDINAND VII 1808–21

NOTE: Prior to this reign all coins had been struck at the Mexico City mint with the mint mark M̊. During the reign of Ferdinand VII Mexican mints were established at Chihuahua (CA); Durango (D or Do); Guadalajara (Ga); Guanajuato (Go); Zacatecas (Z or Zs). In the period 1811–14, during the revolution led by General Morelos, many provisional issues were struck (copper and silver).

52.	8 Reales 1808–11. Large armored bust	75.00
53.	4 Reales 1808–12	200.00
54.	2 Reales 1808–11	20.00
55.	1 Real 1808–13	20.00
56.	½ Real 1808–14	7.50
57.	¼ Real 1808–16. Castle. Rev: Lion	30.00

58.	8 Reales 1812–21. Small draped bust	65.00
59.	4 Reales 1813–21	350.00
60.	2 Reales 1812–21	17.50
61.	1 Real 1814–21	20.00
62.	½ Real 1815–21	10.00

FIRST EMPIRE 1822–23
AGUSTIN I (ITURBIDE)

63.	8 Reales 1822. Small head. Rev: Eagle	175.00

64.	8 Reales 1822–23. Large head	175.00

65.	2 Reales 1822–23	100.00
66.	1 Real 1822–23	250.00
67.	½ Real 1822–23	45.00

MEXICO (continued)

REPUBLIC 1823–1864

NOTE: Republican coinage was interrupted for a while by the reign of Maximilian during 1864–67

68.	8 Reales 1823–24. Hook-neck eagle facing left. Rev: Liberty cap and rays	175.00

69.	2 Reales 1824	50.00
70.	1 Real 1824	RARE
71.	½ Real 1824	85.00

72.	8 Reales 1825–69. Eagle facing right	25.00
73.	4 Reales 1825–69	30.00
74.	2 Reales 1825–69	10.00
75.	1 Real 1825–69	5.00
76.	½ Real 1825–69	7.50
77.	¼ Real (C) 1829–36	7.50
78.	⅛ Real (C) 1829–35	10.00
79.	¹⁄₁₆ Real (C) 1831–33	25.00

80.	⅛ Real (C) 1841–61. Liberty seated	12.50

EMPIRE OF MAXIMILIAN 1864–67

81.	1 Peso 1866–67. Head. Rev: Arms	65.00
82.	50 Centavos 1866	50.00
83.	10 Centavos 1864–66. Eagle. Legend: IMPERIO MEXICANO	35.00
84.	5 Centavos 1864–66	50.00

85.	1 Centavo (C) 1864	60.00

REPUBLIC 1867–

NOTE: Metric system adopted 1869

86.	1 Peso 1869–73. Eagle. Rev: Balance scale	30.00
87.	50 Centavos 1869–95	15.00
88.	25 Centavos 1869–92	10.00

378

89.	20 Centavos 1898–1914. Eagle. Rev: Value and wreath	10.00
90.	10 Centavos 1867–1919	3.50
91.	5 Centavos 1867–69. Rev: Liberty cap and rays	40.00
91a.	5 Centavos 1869–1905	3.00
91b.	5 Centavos (N) 1905–14. (Larger planchet)	4.00
92.	1 Centavo (C) 1869–98	4.00
92a.	1 Centavo (Br) 1899–1905. (Smaller planchet)	4.00

NOTE: During the period 1913–16 there were many revolutionary issues by various cities and states

93.	8 Reales 1869–97. Eagle. Rev: Liberty cap and rays	25.00

94.	5 Centavos (C-N) 1882, '83. Bow, arrows and club. Rev: Value	2.50
95.	2 Centavos (C-N) 1882–83	2.00
96.	1 Centavo (C-N) 1882, '83	2.00

97.	1 Peso 1898–1909. Eagle. Rev: Liberty cap and rays. (Type of #93)	25.50

98.

98.	1 Peso 1910–14. Liberty on horseback. Rev: Eagle	40.00

99.	50 Centavos 1905–45	10.00
100.	20 Centavos 1919–43	3.00
101.	10 Centavos 1925–35	2.50

102.	20 Centavos (Bro) 1920, '35. Eagle. Rev: Value in wreath	15.00
103.	10 Centavos (Bro) 1919–35	25.00
104.	5 Centavos (Bro) 1914–35	10.00
105.	2 Centavos (Bro) 1905–41	7.50
106.	1 Centavo (Bro) 1905–49	1.00

107.	1 Peso 1918–45. Eagle. Liberty cap above value	15.00

108.	2 Peso 1921. Winged victory. Rev: Eagle. (100th anniversary of independence from Spain)	200.00

MEXICO (continued)

109. 50 Pesos (G) 1921–47. Eagle. Rev: Winged victory. (100th anniversary of independence)　　750.00

118. 1 Peso 1947–49. Eagle. Rev: Head of Morelos　　8.50

110. 20 Pesos (G) 1917–59. Eagle. Rev: Aztec calendar stone　　325.00

111. 10 Pesos (G) 1905–59. Eagle. Rev: Head of Hidalgo　　175.00
112. 5 Pesos (G) 1905–55　　100.00
113. 2½ Pesos (G) 1918–48　　50.00

114. 2 Pesos (G) 1919–48. Eagle. Rev: Value　　45.00

119. 5 Pesos 1950. Locomotive, palm trees and rising sun. Rev: Eagle. (Opening of Southeast Railroad)　　40.00

115. 10 Centavos (C-N) 1936–46. Eagle. Rev: Value　　1.50
116. 5 Centavos (C-N) 1936–42　　1.50

120. 1 Peso (Bi) 1950. Eagle. Rev: Bust of General Morelos　　5.00

117. 5 Pesos 1947, '48. Eagle. Rev: Head of Cuauhtemoc　　30.00

121. 50 Centavos (Bi) 1950, '51. Eagle. Rev: Cuauhtemoc　　2.50

122.   25 Centavos (Bi) 1950–53. Eagle. Rev: Balance   1.25

123.   5 Centavos (Bro) 1942–55. Eagle. Rev: Dona
        Josefa Ortiz de Dominguez   .50
123a. 5 Centavos (C-N) 1950   3.50

124.   5 Pesos 1951–54. Head of Hidalgo in wreath.
        Rev: Eagle   20.00

126.   10 Pesos 1955, '56. Head of Hidalgo, INDEPEN-
        DENCIA Y LIBERTAD legend. Rev: Eagle   30.00
127.   5 Pesos 1955–57   15.00

128.   10 Pesos 1957. Head of Juarez. Rev: Eagle.
        (100th anniversary of Mexican Constitution)   40.00
129.   5 Pesos 1957   15.00
130.   1 Peso (Bi) 1957   17.50

125.   5 Pesos 1953. Bust of Hidalgo, cathedral in
        background. Rev: Eagle. (200th anniversary
        of Hidalgo's birth)   25.00

131.   5 Pesos 1959. Head of Venustiano Carranza.
        Rev: Eagle. (100th anniversary of birth of
        former Mexican president)   15.00
132.   10 Pesos 1960. Portraits of Hidalgo and Madero.
        Rev: Eagle. (150th anniversary of War for
        Independence and 50th anniversary of later
        revolutionary period)   30.00

133. 1 Peso (Bi) 1957–67. Morelos. Rev: Eagle — 2.00

140. 25 Pesos 1968. Ancient Mayan athlete. Rev: Eagle. (Olympic Games) — 20.00

134. 50 Centavos (Bro) 1955–59. Eagle. Rev: Cuauhtemoc — 1.50
134a. 50 Centavos (C-N) 1964–69. (Smaller planchet) — .25

141. 1 Peso (C-N) 1970– . Head of Morelos. Rev: Redesigned arms — .50
142. 50 Centavos (C-N) 1970– . Type of #134, new reverse design — .30
143. 20 Centavos (Bro) 1970–74. Type of #136, new reverse design — .40
144. 5 Centavos (Bra) 1970– . Type of #138, new eagle design. (Smaller planchet) — .15
145. 1 Centavo (Bra) 1970–73. Type of #139, new eagle design. (Smaller planchet) — 1.00

135. 25 Centavos (C-N) 1964–66. Eagle. Rev: Madero — .35
136. 20 Centavos (Bro) 1943–55. Eagle. Rev: Pyramid of the Sun — 3.00
136a. 20 Centavos (Bro) 1955–71. Redesigned eagle — .50

146. 5 Pesos (C-N) 1971–78. Head of Guerrero. Rev: Arms — 1.00
147. 25 Pesos 1972. Bust of Juarez — 15.00

137. 10 Centavos (Bro) 1955–67. Eagle. Rev: Juarez — .50
138. 5 Centavos (Bra) 1954–69. Eagle. Rev: Dona Josefa — .25

139. 1 Centavo (Bra) 1950–69. Eagle. Rev: Wheat ear — .25

148. 10 Pesos (C-N) 1974– . Head of Hidalgo. (Heptagonal planchet) — 2.00
149. 20 Centavos (C-N) 1974– . Bust of Madero — .50
150. 100 Pesos 1977– . Rev: Eagle — 15.00

151.   20 Pesos (C-N) 1980– . Rev: Eagle   1.25

MONACO

With an area of about 470 acres, Monaco, an independent principality, is the smallest country in the world. It is located on the Mediterranean coast of France.

100 Centimes = 1 Franc

LOUIS II   1922–49

1.	2 Francs (A-Bro) 1924, '26. Bowman. Rev: Value and arms	50.00
2.	1 Franc (A-Bro) 1924, '26	35.00
3.	50 Centimes (A-Bro) 1924, '26	35.00

4.	5 Francs (A) 1945. Head. Rev: Arms	7.50
5.	2 Francs (A) 1943; (A-Bro) 1945. No date appears	5.00
6.	1 Franc (A) 1943; (A-Bro) 1945. No date appears	3.50
7.	20 Francs (C-N) 1947. Bust. Rev: Arms	8.50

8.	10 Francs (C-N) 1946	6.50

RAINIER III   1949–

9.	100 Francs (C-N) 1950. Head. Rev: Rider	30.00
10.	50 Francs (A-Bro) 1950	15.00

11.	20 Francs (A-Bro) 1950, '51. Head. Rev: Arms	5.00
12.	10 Francs (A-Bro) 1950, '51	3.00

13.	100 Francs (A-Bro) 1956. New head. Rev: Arms	10.00

14.	5 New Francs 1960, '66	15.00

15.	1 New Franc (N) 1960–	2.00
16.	½ Franc (N) 1965– . Rev: Shield and crown	.75

17.	50 Centimes (A-Br) 1962–	2.00
18.	20 Centimes (A-Br) 1962–	1.00
19.	10 Centimes (A-Br) 1962	.75

MONACO (continued)

20. 10 Francs 1966. Conjoined heads of Prince Rainier and Princess Grace. Rev: Arms and value. (10th wedding anniversary)   50.00
20a. 200 Francs (G) 1966   600.00
20b. 5 Centimes (C-N, A) 1976–   4.00
20c. 1 Centime (St) 1976– . Crowned shield/value, date   3.50

21. 10 Francs 1966. Head of Charles III (1856–89). Rev: Arms. (Centennial of foundation of Monte Carlo)   50.00

22. 5 Francs (C-N) 1971– . Head of Prince Rainier. Rev: Monograms, value   3.00

23. 50 Francs 1974. Bust of Prince Rainier. Rev: Four crowned monograms forming cross. (25th anniversary of reign)   60.00

24. 10 Francs (C-N-A) 1974. Head of Prince Rainier. Rev: Monograms over crowned arms. (25th anniversary of reign)   12.50
25. 10 Francs (C-N-A) 1975– . Type of #24, but regular issue   5.00

MONGOLIA

This large area in northeast Asia, also known as Outer Mongolia, declared its independence from China in 1921, and became the Mongolian People's Republic in 1924 on the death of its ruler. The separation from Nationalist China became complete in 1946. A part of northwest Mongolia is an autonomous province within the U.S.S.R. Coins listed here were struck in Leningrad.

100 Mung = 1 Tugrik

1.	1 Tugrik 1925. Buddhist symbols. Rev: Value in wreath	30.00
2.	50 Mung 1925	20.00
3.	20 Mung 1925; (C-N) 1937	7.50
4.	15 Mung 1925; (C-N) 1937	6.50

5.	10 Mung 1925; (C-N) 1937	7.50
6.	5 Mung (C) 1925; (A-Bro) 1937	7.50
7.	2 Mung (C) 1925; (A-Bro) 1937	5.00
8.	1 Mung (C) 1925; (A-Bro) 1937	5.00
9.	20 Mung (N) 1945. Arms. Rev: Value in wreath	15.00
10.	15 Mung (N) 1945	10.00
11.	10 Mung (N) 1945	10.00

12.	5 Mung (A-Bro) 1945	10.00
13.	2 Mung (A-Bro) 1945	7.50
14.	1 Mung (A-Bro) 1945	10.00
15.	20 Mung (A) 1959. Arms. Rev: Value	10.00
16.	15 Mung (A) 1959	7.50
17.	10 Mung (A) 1959	5.00

18.	5 Mung (A) 1959. (Center hole)	5.00
19.	2 Mung (A) 1959	4.00
20.	1 Mung (A) 1959	4.00

21.	50 Mung (C-N) 1970. Arms. Rev: Value	7.50
22.	20 Mung (C-N) 1970	5.00
23.	15 Mung (C-N) 1970	5.00
24.	10 Mung (C-N) 1970	5.00

25.	5 Mung (A) 1970. Arms. Rev: Value	5.00
26.	2 Mung (A) 1970	4.00
27.	1 Mung (A) 1970	4.00

28.	1 Tugrik (A-Bro) 1971. Statue of Suche-Bator. Rev: Arms. (50th anniversary of Republic)	20.00
28a.	1 Tugrik (C-N) 1971	20.00

29.	10 Tugrik (C-N) 1974. Arms. Rev: State Bank building. (50th anniversary, founding of State Bank)	40.00
30.	50 Tugrik 1976. Arms. Rev: Camel. (World Wildlife Conservation Program)	40.00
31.	25 Tugrik 1976. Rev: Mountain goat. (Wildlife Conservation)	25.00

32. 750 Tugrik (G) 1980. Arms. Rev: Two dancing
     children. (International Year of Child.) Issued
     in proof only   350.00
33.   25 Tugrik 1980. Arms. (International Year of
     Child.) In proof only   50.00

MONTENEGRO

A Balkan kingdom which was incorporated into the new state of Yugoslavia after World War I. In 1941 Montenegro was again set up as an independent state, and at the end of World War II it became part of the Yugoslav People's Republic.

100 Para = 1 Perper

NICHOLAS I   1860–1918

1.	20 Perpera (G) 1910. Head. Rev: Arms on mantle in wreath	600.00
2.	10 Perpera (G) 1910	500.00

3.	5 Perpera 1909, '12, '14	175.00
4.	2 Perpera 1910, '14	35.00
5.	1 Perper 1909, '12, '14	20.00

6.	20 Para (N) 1906, '08, '13, '14. Crowned two-headed eagle. Rev: Value	15.00
7.	10 Para (N) 1906–14	12.50

8.	2 Pare (Bro) 1906–14	15.00
9.	1 Para (Bro) 1906, '14	20.00

MOROCCO

This North African monarchy was a French protectorate, 1912–56. It has been a constitutional monarchy since 1962. The franc standard was adopted in 1920.

500 Mazunas = 1 Ryal or 1 Piastre
100 Centimes = 1 Franc

MOULAY ABDUL AZIZ 1894–1908 (A.H. 1311–26)
MOULAY HAFID 1908–12 (A.H. 1326–30)
MOULAY YOUSSEF 1912–27 (A.H. 1330–45)

1.	1 Ryal 1881–1919 (A.H. 1299–1337). Arabic inscriptions in double circle. Rev: Six-pointed star with date	35.00
2.	½ Ryal 1881–1919 (A.H. 1299–1337)	25.00
3.	¼ Ryal 1881–1919 (A.H. 1299–1337)	17.50
4.	10 Mazunas (Bro) A.H. 1320–23. Arabic inscription and date in circle with Grecian ornamental border. Rev: Value in Arabic with similar circle	7.50

5.	5 Mazunas (Bro) A.H. 1320–23	7.50
6.	2 Mazunas (Bro) A.H. 1320–21	10.00
7.	1 Mazuna (Bro) A.H. 1320–21	10.00

8.	10 Centimes (Bro) A.H. 1330, '40. Lobed triangle with date. Rev: Five-pointed star with value	2.50
9.	5 Centimes (Bro) A.H. 1330, '40	3.00

10.	2 Centimes (Bro) A.H. 1330	5.00
11.	1 Centime (Bro) A.H. 1330	7.50

12.	1 Franc (N) 1921–24. Five-pointed star in circle and Moorish design. Rev: Value in French in Moorish design	3.50
13.	50 Centimes (N) 1921–24	5.00
14.	25 Centimes (N-Bro) 1921–26. Six-pointed star in circle and Moorish design. Rev: Value in French in Moorish design. (Center hole)	6.50

SIDI MOHAMMED BEN YOUSSEF 1927–53
(A.H. 1345–72)

15.	20 Francs 1929, '34 (A.H. 1347, '52). Lobed triangle with date in circle and Moorish design. Rev: Value in French in square inside six-pointed star and Moorish design	30.00
16.	10 Francs 1929, '34. (A.H. 1347, '52)	10.00
17.	5 Francs 1929, '34. (A.H. 1347, '52)	5.00
18.	20 Francs (C-N) 1947 (A.H. 1366)	3.00
19.	10 Francs (C-N) 1947 (A.H. 1366)	2.00
20.	5 Francs (A-Bro) 1946 (A.H. 1365)	2.50
21.	2 Francs (A-Bro) 1945 (A.H. 1364). Double six-pointed star. Rev: Value	2.50
22.	1 Franc (A-Bro) 1945 (A.H. 1364)	2.00
23.	50 Centimes (A-Bro) 1945 (A.H. 1364)	1.50

24.	200 Francs 1953 (A.H. 1372). Small five-pointed star within large six-pointed star in Moorish design. Rev: Value in French and Arabic inside dotted circle and Moorish design	12.50
25.	100 Francs 1953 (A.H. 1372)	7.50

26.	50 Francs (A-Bro) 1952 (A.H. 1371). Type of #15	2.00
27.	20 Francs (A-Bro) 1952 (A.H. 1371). Six-pointed star and date. Rev: Value in French and Arabic	1.50
28.	10 Francs (A-Bro) 1952 (A.H. 1371)	1.00
29.	5 Francs (A) 1951 (A.H. 1370)	.75
30.	2 Francs (A) 1951 (A.H. 1370)	.75
31.	1 Franc (A) 1951 (A.H. 1370)	.50

MOHAMMED V 1955–61
(New title of Sidi Mohammed Ben Youssef)
100 Francs = 1 Dirham

32.	500 Francs 1956. Head of the King. Rev: Star	25.00
33.	1 Dirham 1960. Rev: Arms	5.00

MULAI HASSAN II 1961–

34.	5 Dirhams 1965. Portrait of King. Rev: Arms	12.50
35.	1 Dirham (C-N) 1965–69	1.50

MONETARY REFORM
100 Centimes = 1 Dirham

36.	1 Dirham (N) 1974, '78. Head of King. Rev: Arms	1.50
37.	50 Centimes (N) 1974, '78	1.00
38.	20 Centimes (Bra) 1974, '78	.75

39.	10 Centimes (Bra) 1974, '78. Arms. Rev: Sun and sunflowers. (F.A.O. coin plan)	.50

40.   5 Centimes (Bra) 1974–78. Arms. Rev: Fish
      and boat wheel. (F.A.O. coin plan)   .50

41.   1 Centime (A) 1974–75. Arms. Rev: Value   .25

42.   5 Dirhams (C-N) 1975. Head of King. Rev:
      Value, turnip, dam. (F.A.O. coin plan)   7.50
43.   50 Dirhams 1975. Rev: Arms. (Independence)   50.00

44.   50 Dirhams 1975. Rev: Woman's hand on dial.
      (International Women's Year)   45.00
45.   50 Dirhams 1976–78. Rev: Agricultural symbol.
      (First anniversary of Green March)   40.00
46.   5 Dirhams (C-N) 1980. Rev: Arms   5.00

MOZAMBIQUE

A Portuguese colony in southeastern Africa (also known as Portuguese East Africa) until 1975, when years of guerilla warfare led to independence.

1.	10 Escudos 1936. Blunt shield. Rev: Portuguese arms on cross	25.00
2.	5 Escudos 1935	15.00
3.	2½ Escudos 1935	12.50

4.	1 Escudo (C-N) 1936. Blunt shield. Rev: Value	15.00
5.	50 Centavos (C-N) 1936	12.50

6.	20 Centavos (Bro) 1936	7.50
7.	10 Centavos (Bro) 1936	7.50

8.	20 Escudos 1952–66; (C-N) 1968–70. Crowned shield. Rev: Portuguese arms in cross	10.00
9.	10 Escudos 1938–66; (C-N) 1968–70	8.50

10.	5 Escudos 1938–65; (C-N) 1969–73	1.50
11.	2½ Escudos 1938–51; (C-N) 1952–73	1.25

12.	1 Escudo (Bro) 1945; (N-Br) 1950, '51; (Br) 1953–74. Crowned shield. Rev: Value	1.25
13.	50 Centavos (Bro) 1945; (N-Br) 1950–51; (Br) 1953–73; (C-N) 1973–75	1.00
14.	20 Centavos (Bro) 1941–73	.75
15.	10 Centavos (Bro) 1942–61	.65

16.	20 Escudos (N) 1971. Blunt shield. Rev: Portuguese arms	5.00

MONETARY REFORM 1975

100 Centavos = 1 Metical

17.	1 Metica (C-N) 1975. Issued in proof only	25.00
18.	20 Meticais (C-N) 1980– . Arms	5.00
19.	10 Meticais (C-N) 1980–	4.00
20.	5 Meticais (A) 1980–	3.00
21.	2½ Meticais (C-N) 1980–	2.50
22.	1 Metical (Bra) 1980– . Rev: Seated woman	2.00
23.	50 Centavos (A) 1980–	1.25

NEPAL

An independent state lying between Tibet and India. Most Nepalese coins are dated according to the Samvat system. Nepalese coins with Samvat dates 1989–2001 are equivalent to 1932–44.

100 Paisa = 1 Rupee

1.	1 Rupee (C-N) 1953–54. Head of Tribhubana Bira Bikrama	5.00
2.	50 Paisa (C-N) 1953–54	4.00

3.	25 Paisa (C-N) 1953–57. Knife in front of mountain scene. Rev: Mountains and rising sun	5.00
4.	10 Paisa (Bro) 1953–55	2.00
5.	5 Paisa (Bro) 1953–57. Hand of Buddha. Rev: Crossed ears of corn	2.00

6.	1 Rupee (C-N) 1955– . Trident in inner circle. Rev: Sword and ornamental design	3.00
7.	50 Paisa (C-N) 1954–	1.50
8.	25 Paisa (C-N) 1958–	1.00

18.

9.	1 Rupee (G) 1956. Plumed crown. Rev: Value. (Coronation of Mahendra)	400.00
10.	1 Rupee (C-N) 1956	3.00
11.	½ Rupee (G) 1956	200.00
12.	50 Paisa (C-N) 1956	2.50
13.	25 Paisa (C-N) 1956	2.00
14.	⅙ Paisa (G) 1956	100.00
15.	10 Paisa (Bro) 1956	2.50

16.	5 Paisa (Bro) 1956	2.50
17.	2 Paisa (Bra) 1956	2.00
18.	1 Paisa (Bra) 1956	2.00

19.	4 Paisa (Bra) 1955. (Center hole)	3.00
20.	2 Paisa (Bra) 1953–57. Type of #3	2.00

21.	10 Paisa (Bro) 1957–66. Trident. Rev: Value	1.00
22.	5 Paisa (Bro) 1957–66	1.00
23.	2 Paisa (Bra) 1957–66	1.00
24.	1 Paisa (Bra) 1957–65	.75

25.	10 Paisa (Bra) 2023–28 (1966–72). Mountains. Rev: Yak	1.00
26.	5 Paisa (A) 2023– . (1966–)	.50

27.	2 Paisa (A) 2023– . (1966–). Rev: Dapha bird	.30
28.	1 Paisa (A) 2023– . (1966–). Rev: Lali guras flower	.20

29.	10 Rupees 1968. Head of King Mahendra. Rev: Trident and gear. (F.A.O. coin plan)	12.50

30. 10 Paisa (Bra) 1971. Wheat. Rev: Yak. (F.A.O. coin plan) .50

31. 10 Paisa (Bra) 1972– . Mountains. Rev: Value .40

32. 25 Rupees 1974. Crown. Rev: Sword. (Coronation of Birendra) 17.50
33. 1 Rupee (C-N) 1974– 2.00
34. 50 Paisa (C-N) 1974– 1.25
35. 25 Paisa (C-N) 1974– .75
36. 10 Paisa (A) 1974– .60
37. 5 Paisa (A) 1974– .50
38. 1 Paisa (A) 1974– .25

39. 10 Rupees 1974. Parents and children with fruit and vegetables. Rev: Value. (F.A.O. coin plan) 12.50

40. 5 Paisa (A) 1974. Irrigation sluices. Rev: Value. (F.A.O. coin plan) 1.00
41. 20 Rupees 1975. Conjoined busts of King and Queen. Rev: Value in wreath with dove and feminine symbol. (F.A.O. coin plan, commemorates International Women's Year) 12.50
42. 1 Rupee (C-N) 1976 2.50

43. 10 Paisa (Bra) 1976. Stylized agricultural symbol. Rev: Value. (F.A.O. coin plan) .35
44. 20 Paisa (Bra) 1978. Trident in inner circle. Rev: Value 1.00

45. 100 Rupees 1979. Bust of King Birendra Bihram. Rev: Boy and girl filling jar from water tap. (International Year of Child) 40.00
46. 50 Rupees 1979. Trident in inner circle. Rev: Open scroll. (Publicizes education for village women) 25.00
47. 20 Rupees 1979. (International Year of Child) 10.00
48. 20 Paisa (Bra) 1979. (International Year of Child) 1.00
49. 10 Paisa (Bra) 1979. (International Year of Child) .35
50. 10 Paisa (Bra) 1979. (Education for village women) .35
51. 2 Paisa (A) 1979. (Education for village women) .35
52. 5 Rupees (C-N) 1980. Rev: Trident in inner circle. (Publicizes advancement for rural women; F.A.O. coin plan) 4.00
53. 50 Rupees 1981. (International Year of Disabled Persons) 20.00
54. 5 Rupees (C-N) 1981. (National Bank Silver Jubilee) 5.00
55. 2 Rupees (C-N) 1981. Trident in inner circle. Rev: Agricultural vignette. (World Food Day; F.A.O. coin plan) 1.50
56. 50 Paisa (C-N) 1981. (World Food Day) 1.00
57. 50 Paisa (C-N) 1981. (International Year of Disabled Persons) 1.50

NETHERLANDS

Originally ruled by the Austrian and then the Spanish Habsburgs, the seven northern provinces of the Low Countries achieved their freedom after a long revolt which started in 1568. During the heyday of Napoleon's power, the Netherlands came under his control. However, the House of Orange returned to the throne in 1813 and has reigned ever since.

During the period 1600–1795, coins were struck by the various cities and provinces. The coins in this series that were struck under Spanish kings usually have the Spanish arms.

100 Cents = 1 Guilder (Gulden)

Campen (Campine, Kempen)

1.	Ducatoon 1648. Warrior over arms. Rev: Lion	200.00

Gelderland (Gelria)
[GEL in legend]

2.	Ducatoon 1699. Standing warrior. Rev: Arms	175.00

Holland
[HOL in legend]

3.	Guilder 1713–94	65.00

Overyssel (Transisulania)
[TRANSI in legend]

4.	Ducatoon 1612. Bust of Philip III of Spain	200.00

Utrecht (Trajectum)
[TRA in legend]

5.	Ducatoon 1760. Warrior on horse	200.00

Westfrisia
[WESTFRI in legend]

6.	Ducatoon 1677. Warrior over arms	250.00

NETHERLANDS (continued)

Zeeland
[ZEL in legend]

7. Ducatoon 1690. Warrior and arms   200.00

Zwolle

8. Ducatoon 1619. Eagle and arms   200.00

BATAVIAN REPUBLIC 1795–1806

9. Ducatoon 1795–1806. Warrior standing with shield. Rev: Crowned shield   200.00
10. 3 Guilders 1795–1801. Nederlandia standing. Rev: Crowned shield   125.00
11. 1 Guilder 1795–1800   75.00

KINGDOM OF HOLLAND 1806–10
LOUIS BONAPARTE 1806–10

12. 50 Stivers 1808   5000.00

KINGDOM OF THE NETHERLANDS
WILLIAM I 1813–1840

13. Ducat (G) 1814–40. Knight in armor. Rev: Tablet   400.00

NOTE: Trade coins of the type of #13 were struck from 1586–1937

14. 10 Guilders (G) 1818–1840   1500.00
15. 5 Guilders (G) 1826–27   850.00
16. 3 Guilders 1817–32. Bare head. Rev: Crowned shield   1250.00
17. 1 Guilder 1818–40   500.00
18. ½ Guilder 1818–30   800.00
19. 25 Cents 1819–30. Crowned "W". Rev: Crowned shield   125.00
20. 10 Cents 1818–28   100.00
21. 5 Cents 1818–28   200.00

22. 1 Cent (C) 1819–37   65.00
23. ½ Cent (C) 1819–37   65.00

WILLIAM II 1840–49

	10 Guilders (G) 1842	RARE
	5 Guilders (G) 1843	RARE

26.	2½ Guilders 1841–49. Bare head. Rev: Crowned shield	125.00
27.	1 Guilder 1842–49	100.00
28.	½ Guilder 1847, '48	200.00
29.	25 Cents 1848, '49	100.00
30.	10 Cents 1848, '49	200.00
31.	½ Cent (C) 1841–47. Crowned "W"	100.00

WILLIAM III 1849–90

32.	10 Guilders (G) 1850–89	150.00
33.	5 Guilders (G) 1850, '51	RARE

34.	2½ Guilders 1849–74	60.00
35.	1 Guilder 1850–66	100.00
36.	½ Guilder 1857–68	80.00
37.	25 Cents 1849–90	375.00
38.	10 Cents 1849–90	100.00
39.	5 Cents 1850–87	15.00
40.	2½ Cents (C) 1877–86. Lion. Rev: Value	25.00
41.	1 Cent (C) 1860–77. Crowned monogram. Rev: Crowned shield	25.00
41a.	1 Cent (C) 1877–84. Type of #40	15.00
42.	½ Cent (C) 1850–77. Type of #41	50.00
42a.	½ Cent (C) 1878–86. Type of #40	15.00

WILHELMINA 1890–1948

43.	10 Guilders (G) 1892–97. Head of girl	350.00
44.	10 Guilders (G) 1898. Young head	RARE

45.	10 Guilders (G) 1911–17. Middle-aged head	135.00
45a.	5 Guilders (G) 1912	450.00
46.	10 Guilders (G) 1925–33. Bare head	150.00

47.	2½ Guilders 1929–40	25.00

TYPES OF LOWER DENOMINATIONS

Type I	1890–97. Girl's head with flowing hair
Type II	1898–1909. Young head with coronet
Type III	1910–1920. Middle-aged head
Type IV	1921–1945. Old head

48.	1 Guilder 1892–1945	15.00
49.	½ Guilder 1898–1930	10.00
50.	25 Cents (S) 1892–1945, (N) 1948	3.00
51.	10 Cents (S) 1892–1945, (N) 1948	4.00

52.	5 Cents (C-N) 1913–40. Orange branch. Rev: Value. Square shape	15.00
53.	2½ Cents (Bro) 1890–1906, 1912–41. Lion. Rev: Value	7.50
54.	1 Cent (Bro) 1892–1941	3.00
55.	½ Cent (Bro) 1891–1940	5.00

NETHERLANDS (continued)

JULIANA 1948–80

56. 2½ Guilders 1959–66. Head. Rev: Crowned
    arms   15.00
56a. 2½ Guilders (N) 1969–   1.50

57. 1 Guilder 1954–67   4.00
57a. 1 Guilder (N) 1967–   1.00

58. 25 Cents (N) 1950– . Head. Rev: Value   .40
59. 10 Cents (N) 1950–   .25
60. 5 Cents (Bro) 1950–   .15
61. 1 Cent (Bro) 1950–   .15

62. 10 Guilders 1970. Head of Juliana. Rev: Head of
    Queen Wilhelmina. (25th anniversary of lib-
    eration from German occupation)   30.00

63. 10 Guilders 1973. Head of Juliana. Rev:
    Crowned arms. (25th anniversary of reign)   30.00

64. 2½ Guilders (N) 1979. Head of Juliana. Rev:
    Value within inscription. (400th anniversary
    of Union of Utrecht)   3.00

BEATRIX 1980–

65. 2½ Guilders (N) 1980. Dual portrait of Queens
    Juliana and Beatrix. Rev: Crowned shield.
    (Investiture of Queen Beatrix)   3.00
66. 1 Guilder (N) 1980   1.50

67. 50 Guilders 1982. Head of Beatrix. Rev: Stylized
    Dutch lion and American eagle. (200th anni-
    versary of establishment of diplomatic rela-
    tions between United States and Netherlands)   35.00

NETHERLANDS ANTILLES

A group of six Dutch West Indies islands, including Curaçao and Aruba. Since 1950 they have been organized as a part of the kingdom of the Netherlands, with considerable powers of self-government.

100 Cents = 1 Guilder (Gulden)

1. 1 Guilder 1952–70. Head of Queen Juliana.
    Rev: Crowned shield   15.00
2. ¼ Guilder 1954–70. Rev: Value   10.00
3. ¹⁄₁₀ Guilder 1954–70   6.00

4. 5 Cents (C-N) 1957–70. Orange branch in circle. Rev: Value. (Square planchet)   7.50
5. 2½ Cents (Bro) 1956–65. Lion. Rev: Value   3.00
6. 1 Cent (Bro) 1952–70   1.50
7. 2½ Guilders 1964. Head of Queen Juliana. Rev: Crowned shield   20.00
7a. 2½ Guilders (N) 1979–80   6.50

8. 1 Guilder (N) 1970–80. Head of Queen Juliana. Rev: Crowned shield   2.50

9. 25 Cents (N) 1970– . Crowned shield. Rev: Value   1.00
10. 10 Cents (N) 1970–   .75

11. 5 Cents (N) 1971–   (Square planchet)   .50
12. 2½ Cents (Bro) 1970–78; (A) 1979–   .50
13. 1 Cent (Bro) 1970–78; (A) 1979–   .35

14. 25 Guilders 1973. Head of Queen Juliana. Rev: Queen and Prince Bernhard in carriage. (25th anniversary of reign)   50.00

15. 200 Guilders (G) 1976. Rev: American ship *Andrew Doria*   165.00
16. 25 Guilders 1976. (Round planchet)   50.00

17. 200 Guilders (G) 1977. Queen Juliana. Rev: Peter Stuyvesant standing. (U.S. Bicentennial; octagonal shape)   200.00
18. 25 Guilders 1977. Peter Stuyvesant   150.00
19. 100 Guilders (G) 1978. Queen Juliana. Rev: Bust of Willem I. (150th anniversary of National Bank)   135.00
20. 10 Guilders 1978. Queen Juliana. Rev: Crowned shield. (National Bank)   25.00
21. 50 Guilders (G) 1979. Rev: Crowned and opened scroll. (75th anniversary of Royal Covenant)   75.00

NETHERLANDS ANTILLES (cont.)

22.   25 Guilders 1979. Rev: Group of dancing children. (International Year of Child)   60.00
23.   300 Guilders (G) 1980. Rev: Crowned shields. (Abdication of Queen Juliana; square planchet)   175.00
24.   50 Guilders 1980. Queen Beatrix. Rev: Crowned shields. (Investiture of Queen Beatrix)   50.00
25.   2½ Guilders (N) 1980– . Queen Beatrix. Rev: Crowned shield   3.00
26.   1 Guilder (N) 1980–   1.50
27.   50 Guilders 1982. Queen Beatrix. Rev: Figure with Dutch and American flags. (200th anniversary of Dutch-American friendship.) Issued in proof only   75.00

NETHERLANDS EAST INDIES

An archipelago in the southwest Pacific which achieved independence in 1949 as the United States of Indonesia (q.v.), bringing Dutch rule to an end.

100 Cents = 1 Guilder (Gulden)

WILHELMINA 1890–1948

1.   1 Ducat (G) 1901–37. Knight. Rev: Inscription. (Trade coin)   85.00
2.   ¼ Guilder 1890–1945. Crowned shield. Rev: Javanese and Malay inscriptions   3.50
3.   1⁄10 Guilder 1891–1945   5.00

4.   5 Cents (C-N) 1913, '21–22. Crown in wreath. (Center hole)   5.00
5.   2½ Cents (C or Bro) 1896–1945. Crowned shield in circle. Rev: Inscription in circle   2.50
6.   1 Cent (C or Bro) 1896–1945   2.50
7.   ½ Cent (C or Bro) 1902–45   2.00

NEW BRUNSWICK

Part of Nova Scotia when it was ceded to England by France, New Brunswick became a separate province in 1784. It was one of the original provinces of the Dominion of Canada created in 1867.

1.	Penny (Bro) 1843, '54. Rev: Sailing vessel	12.50
2.	Halfpenny (Bro) 1843, '54	7.50
3.	20 Cents 1862, '64. Head of Victoria. Rev: Crowned value	40.00
4.	10 Cents 1862, '64	100.00
5.	5 Cents 1862, '64	85.00

6.	1 Cent (Bro) 1861, '64. Rev: Crowned date in circle and value	10.00
7.	Half Cent (Bro) 1861	125.00

NEW CALEDONIA

This Pacific island, northeast of Australia, is a French overseas territory.

100 Centimes = 1 Franc

1.	5 Francs (A) 1952, '79. Seated female figure. Rev: Tropical bird	1.00
2.	2 Francs (A) 1949; (A-Bro) 1971–	.50
3.	1 Franc (A) 1949, 1972– ; (A-Bro) 1971	.35
4.	50 Centimes (A) 1949–	2.00

5.	50 Francs (N) 1967– . Head of Republic. Rev: Native hut	2.50

6.	20 Francs (N) 1967– . Rev: Three cattle heads	1.50

7.	10 Francs (N) 1967– . Rev: Native sailboat	1.00
8.	100 Francs (N-Bro) 1976, '79. Republic (head). Rev: Native hut	7.50

NEWFOUNDLAND

A large island located in the Gulf of St. Lawrence. Discovered by Sebastian Cabot in 1497, Newfoundland was England's first colony. By vote of its inhabitants, Newfoundland became part of the Dominion of Canada in 1948.

100 Cents = 1 Dollar
VICTORIA 1837–1901

1.	2 Dollars (G) 1865–88. Bust. Rev: Value	250.00
2.	50 Cents 1870–1900. Bust. Rev: Value	15.00
3.	20 Cents 1865–1900	25.00
4.	10 Cents 1865–96	30.00

5.	5 Cents 1865–96	25.00
6.	1 Cent (Bro) 1865–96	7.50

EDWARD VII 1901–10

7.	50 Cents 1904, '07–09. Crowned bust. Rev: Value in scrolled circle	20.00
8.	20 Cents 1904	80.00
9.	10 Cents 1903–04	20.00
10.	5 Cents 1903–04, '08	10.00
11.	1 Cent (Bro) 1904, '07, '09	8.50

GEORGE V 1910–36

12.	50 Cents 1911, '17–19. Crowned bust. Rev: Value in scrolled circle	10.00
13.	25 Cents 1917, '19	8.50
14.	20 Cents 1912	15.00
15.	10 Cents 1912, '17, '19	20.00
16.	5 Cents 1912, '17, '19, '29	5.00

17.	1 Cent (Bro) 1913, '17, '19–20, '29, '36	3.50

GEORGE VI 1936–52

18.	10 Cents 1938–47. Bust. Rev: Value	5.00
19.	5 Cents 1938–47	3.00

20.	1 Cent (Bro) 1938–44, '47. Rev: Pitcher plant	2.00

NEW GUINEA

This large island north of Australia contains Indonesian West Irian (formerly Netherlands New Guinea) on the west, and the Australian Trusteeship of New Guinea and Papua on the east. In 1975 the Australian territory became an independent nation under the name Papua New Guinea (q.v.). The coins illustrated below are of the Australian Territory of New Guinea.

12 Pence = 1 Shilling
GEORGE V 1910–36

1.	1 Shilling 1935–36. Crowned maces crossed. Rev: Cross made of ornaments. (Holed center)	7.50

2.	1 Penny (C-N) 1929	650.00
3.	1 Halfpenny (C-N) 1929	650.00

4.	6 Pence (C-N) 1935. Crown, date and inscription "G.R.I." Rev: Eight-pointed circle. (Holed center)	17.50
5.	3 Pence (C-N) 1935. Rev: Square inside four-pointed circle	15.00

EDWARD VIII 1936

6.	1 Penny (C) 1936. Crown, native ornament, and inscription E.R.I. Rev: Native ornament. (Holed center)	5.00

GEORGE VI 1936–52

7.	1 Shilling 1938, '45. Type of #1	5.00
8.	6 Pence (C-N) 1943. Type of #4	15.00
9.	3 Pence (C-N) 1944. Type of #5	10.00
10.	1 Penny (C) 1938, '44. Type of #6	6.50

A group of islands in the southwest Pacific Ocean, the New Hebrides was a condominium administered jointly by Great Britain and France. It gained its independence in 1980 as Vanuatu (q.v.).

1.	100 Francs 1966, '79. Head of Republic. Rev: Carved post	20.00
2.	50 Francs (N) 1972, '79	4.00

3.	20 Francs (C-N) 1967–79. Rev: Carved head	2.00
4.	10 Francs (C-N) 1967–79	1.00

5.	5 Francs (N-Bra) 1970–79. Rev: Buff-bellied flycatcher (native bird)	2.00
6.	2 Francs (N-Bra) 1970–79	.50
7.	1 Franc (N-Bra) 1970–79	.75
8.	500 Francs 1979. Value. Rev: Mother nursing child. (International Year of Child)	35.00

NEW ZEALAND

New Zealand has been a self-governing dominion since 1907.

> 4 Crowns = 1 Pound Sterling
> 12 Pence = 1 Shilling
> 2 Shillings = 1 Florin
> 20 Shillings = 1 Pound Sterling

GEORGE V 1910–36

1.   1 Crown 1935. Crown bust of King. Rev: Maori and Captain William Hobson, Territory's first governor. (25th year of reign of George V; also Waitangi Treaty of 1840 which brought islands under British sovereignty)   4000.00

2.   ½ Crown (2½ Shillings) 1933–35. Rev: Arms   40.00

3.   1 Florin (2 Shillings) 1933–36. Rev: Kiwi bird   30.00
4.   1 Shilling 1933–35. Rev: Maori warrior   17.50

5.   6 Pence 1933–36. Rev: Huia bird   12.50
6.   3 Pence 1933–36. Rev: War clubs   10.00

GEORGE VI 1936–52

NOTE: All obverses of these types show bare head of King. Coins issued after 1948 drop "Emperor" from legend

7.   ½ Crown (S) 1937–46; (C-N) '47–51. Head. Rev: Type of #2   17.50
8.   1 Florin (S) 1937–46; (C-N) '47–51. Rev: Type of #3   10.00
9.   1 Shilling (S) 1937–46; (C-N) '47–52. Rev: Type of #4   10.00
10.   6 Pence (S) 1937–46; (C-N) '47–52. Rev: Type of #5   3.00
11.   3 Pence (S) 1937–46; (C-N) '47–52. Rev: Type of #6   2.00

12.   1 Penny (Bro) 1940–52. Rev: Tui bird   4.00

13.   1 Halfpenny (Bro) 1940–52. Rev: Tiki   2.50

14.   ½ Crown 1940. (Commemorative). Rev: Maori woman   50.00

15.   1 Crown 1949. Rev: Leaf with four stars. (Proposed royal visit)   30.00

ELIZABETH II 1952–

16. 1 Crown (C-N) 1953. Head. Rev: Crowned
     monogram above Maori design 25.00

17. 1 Half Crown (C-N) 1953–65. Rev: Arms 6.50
18. 1 Florin (C-N) 1953–65. Rev: Kiwi bird 3.00

19. 1 Shilling (C-N) 1953–65. Rev: Maori warrior 2.00
20. 6 Pence (C-N) 1953–65. Rev: Huia bird 1.50
21. 3 Pence (C-N) 1953–65. Rev: War clubs 1.00

22. 1 Penny (Bro) 1953–65. Rev: Tui bird 1.00
23. 1 Halfpenny (Bro) 1953–65. Rev: Tiki .75

DECIMAL COINAGE

24. 1 Dollar (C-N) 1967–76. Portrait of Queen
     Elizabeth. Rev: Arms 5.00

25. 50 Cents (C-N) 1967– . Rev: Sailing ship En-
     deavour 1.50
26. 20 Cents (C-N) 1967– . Rev: Kiwi bird .75

27. 10 Cents (C-N) 1967– . Rev: Maori carved head .50
27a. 10 Cents (C-N) 1970– . Rev: Without ONE SHILL-
     ING inscription .50
28. 5 Cents (C-N) 1967– . Rev: Tuatara lizard .30

29. 2 Cents (Bro) 1967– . Rev: Kowhai flowers .25
30. 1 Cent (Bro) 1967– . Rev: Fern leaf .15

31. 1 Dollar (C-N) 1969. Rev: Bust of Captain James Cook, map and sailing ship. (200th anniversary of discovery) — 6.50
32. 50 Cents (C-N) 1969. Type of #25 with edge inscribed COOK BI-CENTENARY 1769–1969 — 3.50

33. 1 Dollar (C-N) 1970. Rev: View of Mount Cook. (Royal visit) — 6.50

34. 1 Dollar (C-N) 1974. Rev: Eight running figures supporting emblem — 7.50
34a. 1 Dollar (S) 1974. (Proof issue) — 100.00

35. 1 Dollar (C-N) 1974. Rev: Kotuku bird, rising sun. (New Zealand Day) — 15.00

36. 1 Dollar (C-N) 1977. Rev: Treaty House, Waitangi. (Waitangi Day) — 10.00
36a. 1 Dollar (S) 1977. Proof — 75.00
37. 1 Dollar (C-N) 1978. Rev: Island parliament. (Silver Jubilee of Queen's Coronation) — 7.50
37a. 1 Dollar (S) 1978. Proof — 40.00
38. 1 Dollar (C-N) 1979. Rev: Crowned shield — 5.00
38a. 1 Dollar (S) 1979. Proof — 35.00
39. 1 Dollar (C-N) 1980. Rev: Bird on branch — 5.00
39a. 1 Dollar (S) 1980. Proof — 40.00
40. 1 Dollar (C-N) 1981. Rev: Crossed branches. (Queen's Royal Visit) — 4.00
40a. 1 Dollar (S) 1981. Proof — 35.00

NICARAGUA

A Spanish colony for three centuries, Nicaragua gained its independence in 1821. For a while it became part of Mexico and then joined the Central American Federation, finally breaking away to become an independent republic.

100 Centavos = 1 Cordoba

REPUBLIC OF NICARAGUA

1. 20 Centavos 1880, '87. Arms. Rev: Value in wreath — 15.00
2. 10 Centavos 1880, '87 — 10.00
3. 5 Centavos 1880–87; (C-N) 1898–99 — 8.50
4. 1 Centavo (C-N) 1878. Coroneted arms with flags. Rev: Value in wreath — 25.00

5. 1 Cordoba 1912. Bust of Francisco de Cordoba. Rev: Rays over mountains — 100.00
6. 50 Centavos 1912, '29 — 30.00
7. 25 Centavos 1912–36 — 10.00
8. 10 Centavos 1912–36 — 3.50
9. 5 Centavos (C-N) 1912–40. Arms. Rev: Value in wreath — 2.00
10. 1 Centavo (Bro) 1912–40; (Bra) 1943 — 2.00
11. ½ Centavo (Bro) 1912–37 — 3.50

12. 50 Centavos (C-N) 1939–74 — 1.00
13. 25 Centavos (C-N) 1939–74 — .50
14. 10 Centavos (C-N) 1939–72 — .35
15. 5 Centavos (C-N) 1946–72 — .15

16. 1 Cordoba (C-N) 1972. Type of #5, smaller planchet — 2.00

17. 10 Centavos (A) 1974. Map. Rev: Value. (F.A.O. coin plan) — .50
17a. 10 Centavos (A) 1974; (C-N) 1975–78. (Regular coinage) — .35

18. 5 Centavos (A) 1974. Arms. Rev: Value. (F.A.O. coin plan) — .25
18a. 5 Centavos (A) 1974. (Regular coinage) — .25
19. 100 Cordobas 1975. Arms. Rev: Astronaut and colonial girl. (Commemorates U.S. Bicentennial) — 50.00
20. 50 Cordobas 1975. Rev: Liberty Bell. (U.S. Bicentennial) — 25.00
21. 5 Cordobas (C-N) 1980– . Value. Rev: Bust of Sandino — 5.00
22. 1 Cordoba (C-N) 1980– — 2.00
23. 50 Centavos (C-N) 1980– — 1.00

NIGERIA

Formerly part of British West Africa, Nigeria became an independent Federation within the British Commonwealth in 1960.

ELIZABETH II 1952–

1. 2 Shillings (C-N) 1959. Crowned head of Elizabeth. Rev: Flowers 2.50

2. 1 Shilling (C-N) 1959–62. Rev: Palm branches 2.00

3. 6 Pence (C-N) 1959. Rev: Cacao beans 1.00

4. 3 Pence (N-Bra) 1959. Rev: Flowers. (Dodecagonal planchet) .75

5. 1 Penny (Bro) 1959–61. Six-pointed star. (Center hole) .75
6. ½ Penny (Bro) 1959 .50

DECIMAL COINAGE

100 Kobo = 1 Naira

7. 25 Kobo (C-N) 1973. Arms. Rev: Peanuts 1.50

8. 10 Kobo (C-N) 1973. Rev: Palm trees .75
9. 5 Kobo (C-N) 1973. Rev: Cacao beans .60

10. 1 Kobo (Bro) 1973. Rev: Oil rigs .50
11. ½ Kobo (Bro) 1973. Rev: Value .30

407

NORWAY

From 1387 to 1814 Norway was united with Denmark. Coins issued during that period bear the bust and name of the reigning Danish monarch. From 1814 to 1905 Norway was united with Sweden, and coins issued during that period bear the bust and name of the reigning Swedish monarch.

The Norwegian arms (lion rampant with battle-axe) appear on the obverse or reverse of almost every Norwegian coin.

120 Skilling = 1 Speciedaler
100 Ore = 1 Krone

CHRISTIAN IV   1588–1648

1.	Taler 1628–48. Crowned bust. Rev: Lion	200.00
2.	½ Taler 1628–48	175.00
3.	¼ Taler 1628–48	100.00
4.	⅛ Taler 1628–46	100.00

5.	8 Skilling 1641–44. Lion. Rev: Value	25.00
6.	4 Skilling 1641–44	25.00
7.	2 Skilling 1641–48	12.50
8.	1 Skilling 1643–48	10.00

FREDERICK III   1648–70

9.	Taler 1649–69. Crowned bust. Rev: Lion	250.00
10.	½ Taler 1649–69	350.00
11.	¼ Taler 1649–55	150.00

12.	⅛ Taler 1649–65	150.00

13.	2 Marks 1649–69. Monogram. Rev: Lion	65.00
14.	16 Skilling—1 Mark 1649–69	50.00
15.	8 Skilling 1649–65	65.00
16.	2 Skilling 1649–70. Lion. Rev: Value	25.00
17.	1 Skilling 1649–68	20.00

CHRISTIAN V   1670–99

18.	Taler 1670–74. Crowned or laureate bust. Rev: Lion	750.00
19.	½ Taler 1671–75	400.00
20.	4 Marks 1670–99. Monogram. Rev: Value	150.00
21.	2 Marks 1670–98	65.00

22.	16 Skilling 1670–99. Lion. Rev: Value	65.00
23.	8 Skilling 1670–75	25.00
24.	2 Skilling 1670–99	20.00
25.	1 Skilling 1670–82	20.00

FREDERICK IV   1699–1730

26.	2 Skilling 1700–25. Monogram. Rev: Lion	25.00

CHRISTIAN VI   1730–46

27.	6 Marks 1732–33. Armored bust. Rev: Lion	650.00
28.	24 Skilling 1736–46. Monogram. Rev: Lion	50.00
29.	8 Skilling 1730–35. Lion. Rev: Value	40.00

FREDERICK V   1746–66

30.	6 Marks 1749. Laureate bust. Rev: Lion	650.00
31.	24 Skilling 1746–63. Monogram. Rev: Lion	65.00

CHRISTIAN VII   1766–1808

32.	Speciedaler 1781–86. Hercules standing	1000.00
33.	1 Rigsdaler 1788. Armored bust. Rev: Lion	1250.00
34.	24 Skilling 1773–83. Monogram. Rev: Lion	75.00
35.	12 Skilling 1798–1801	40.00
36.	1 Skilling (C) 1771. Monogram. Rev: Value	20.00
37.	½ Skilling (C) 1771	20.00

UNITED WITH SWEDEN 1814–1905

CHARLES XIII 1814–18

38.	8 Skilling 1817. Lion. Rev: Value	35.00

CHARLES XIV JOHN
(Jean Baptiste Jules Bernadotte) 1818–44

39.	Speciedaler 1819–36, '44. Head. Rev: Lion	500.00
40.	½ Speciedaler 1819–36, '44	300.00
41.	24 Skilling 1819–36. Lion. Rev: Value	200.00
42.	8 Skilling 1819, '25, '27	50.00
43.	4 Skilling 1825, '42	20.00
44.	2 Skilling (C) 1822–36	50.00
45.	1 Skilling (C) 1819–37	25.00
46.	½ Skilling (C) 1837–41	15.00

OSCAR I 1844–59

47.	Speciedaler 1846–57. Head. Rev: Lion	450.00

48.	½ Speciedaler 1846–55	300.00
49.	24 Skilling 1845–55	60.00

50.	12 Skilling 1845–56	35.00

CHARLES XV 1859–72

51.	Speciedaler 1861–69. Head. Rev: Lion	1000.00

52.	½ Speciedaler 1861–65	400.00
53.	24 Skilling 1861–65	150.00
54.	12 Skilling 1861–65	250.00
55.	4 Skilling 1871. Lion. Rev: Value	20.00
56.	3 Skilling 1868, '73	25.00
57.	2 Skilling (C) 1870, '71	10.00
58.	1 Skilling (C) 1870	10.00
59.	½ Skilling (C) 1863, '67	7.50

OSCAR II 1872–1905

60.	20 Kroner (G) 1876–1902. Head. Rev: Lion	450.00
61.	10 Kroner (G) 1877–1902	750.00
62.	2 Kroner 1878–1904. Head. Rev: Lion	85.00
63.	1 Krone 1875–1904	35.00
64.	50 Ore 1874–1904	50.00
65.	25 Ore 1876, 1896–1904. Lion. Rev: Value	25.00
66.	10 Ore 1874–1903. Monogram. Rev: Value	20.00

67.	5 Ore (Bro) 1875–1902	10.00
68.	2 Ore (Bro) 1876–1902	5.00
69.	1 Ore (Bro) 1876–1902	5.00

INDEPENDENT KINGDOM 1905–

HAAKON VII 1905–57

70. 20 Kroner (G) 1910. Crowned bust. Rev: St. Olaf standing   450.00
71. 10 Kroner (G) 1910   450.00

72. 2 Kroner 1906–07. Lion. Rev: Legend commemorating independence   50.00

73. 2 Kroner 1908–17. Head. Rev: Lion and shields   40.00
73a. 1 Krone 1908–17   35.00

74. 2 Kroner 1914. Standing figure. Rev: Lion. (Centenary of constitution)   40.00

75. 50 Ore 1909–19. Head. Rev: Lion in shield   12.50

76. 25 Ore 1909–19. Lion. Rev: Crowned monogram   15.00

77. 10 Ore 1909–19. Crowned monogram. Rev: Value   10.00
78. 5 Ore (Bro) 1908–16, '21–41, '51–57; (I) '17–20   3.50
79. 2 Ore (Bro) 1909–15, '21–40, '46–57; (I) '17–20   3.00
80. 1 Ore (Bro) 1908–15, '21–41, '46–57; (I) '18–21   1.50

81. 1 Krone (C-N) 1925–51. Four crowned monograms around center hole   2.00

82. 50 Ore (C-N) 1920–23. Four crowned monograms. Rev: Arms. (With or without center hole)   15.00
83. 25 Ore (C-N) 1921–23. Crowned monogram. Rev: Lion. (With or without center hole)   12.50
84. 10 Ore (C-N) 1920–23. Crowned monogram. Rev: Value   15.00

NORWAY (continued)

85. 50 Ore (C-N) 1926–41, '45–49. Rev: Crown,
     value   3.00
86. 25 Ore (C-N) 1924–40, '46–50   1.50

98. 5 Ore (Bro) 1958–73. Moose   .30

87. 10 Ore (C-N) 1924–41, '45–51. Crown. Rev:
     Value. (Center hole)   1.00

99. 2 Ore (Bro) 1958–72. Chicken   .75
100. 1 Ore (Bro) 1958–72. Squirrel   .30

88. 50 Ore (Z) 1941–45. Lion in shield. Rev: Value.
     (Nazi occupation issue)   15.00
89. 25 Ore (Z) 1943–45   10.00
90. 10 Ore (Z) 1941–45   5.00
91. 5 Ore (Z) 1941–45   5.00
92. 2 Ore (Z) 1943–45   3.00
93. 1 Ore (I) 1941–45   2.00

101. 10 Kroner 1964. Lion on shield. Rev: Building.
     (Signing of constitution in 1814)   20.00

OLAV V   1957–

94. 1 Krone (C-N) 1958–73. Horse   .75

102. 5 Kroner (C-N) 1963–73. Bare head of King.
     Rev: Shield   2.50

95. 50 Ore (C-N) 1958–73. Dog   .75
96. 25 Ore (C-N) 1958–73. Bird   .50

97. 10 Ore (C-N) 1958–73. Bee   .35

103.

103. 25 Kroner 1970. Conjoined heads of King Haakon and King Olav. Rev: Monogram and inscription. (25th anniversary of liberation from wartime occupation)   25.00

104. 5 Kroner (C-N) 1974– . Head of King Olav. Rev: Crowned shield with lion   1.50

105. 1 Krone (C-N) 1974– . Head. Rev: Crown, value   .50

106. 50 Ore (C-N) 1974– . Crowned shield with lion. Rev: Value   .40

107. 25 Ore (C-N) 1974– . Four crowned monograms. Rev: Value   .25

108. 10 Ore (C-N) 1974– . Crowned monogram. Rev: Value   .20

109. 5 Ore (Bro) 1974– . Lion. Rev: Value   .10

110. 5 Kroner (C-N) 1975. Sailing ship. Rev: Lion. (150th anniversary of emigration to U.S.)   5.00

111. 5 Kroner (C-N) 1975. Seated figure striking coin with hammer. Rev: Crowned arms. (100th anniversary of decimal coinage)   5.00

112. 5 Kroner (C-N) 1978. Sword between crowned emblems. Rev: Lion. (350th anniversary of Norwegian Army)   4.00

113. 50 Kroner 1978. Plain head of Olav V. Rev: Sceptre, signature, dates. (King's 75th birthday)   25.00

114. 200 Kroner 1980. Village & steeples. Rev: Lion. (35th anniversary of liberation from Nazi Germany)   50.00

NOVA SCOTIA

Located on the east coast of Canada, Nova Scotia, formerly known as Acadia, was ceded to the British by the French in 1713. It is one of the original provinces of the Dominion of Canada.

1.	Penny (C) 1824, '32. Laureated head of George IV	6.00

2.	Halfpenny (C) 1823–24, '32	6.00
3.	Penny (C) 1840, '43. Head of Victoria	6.00
4.	Halfpenny (C) 1840, '43	4.00
5.	Penny (C) 1856. Rev: Maple leaves	6.00
6.	Halfpenny (C) 1856	6.00

7.	1 Cent (C) 1861–62, '64	5.00
8.	Half Cent (C) 1861, '64	8.00

OMAN

An independent sultanate at the southeastern tip of the Arabian peninsula, called Muscat and Oman until 1970.

200 Baizas = 1 Maria Theresa Dollar

SA'ID-BEN TAIMUR   1932–70

1.	½ Riyal 1948, '61, '62. Arms. Rev: Arabic inscription	12.50

2.	50 Baizas (C-N) 1940. (Scalloped edge)	15.00

3.	20 Baizas (C-N) 1940. (Square planchet)	12.50
3a.	20 Baizas (C-N) 1946. (Scalloped edge)	5.00
4.	10 Baizas (C-N) 1940. (Round)	7.50

5.	5 Baizas (N) 1946. (Scalloped edge)	3.00

5a.	5 Baizas (C-N) 1962. Arms. Rev: Native sailing craft. (Round planchet)	2.00
6.	3 Baizas (Bro) 1961. Arms. Rev: Value	1.50
7.	2 Baizas (C-N) 1946. (Square planchet)	2.00

OMAN (continued)

QABUS BIN SA ID 1970–
MONETARY REFORM

1000 Baizas = 1 Riyal

19.   1 Omani Riyal 1978. Arms. Rev: Fish. (F.A.O. coin plan)   12.50

8.	100 Baizas (C-N) 1970. Arms. Rev: Value	2.00
9.	50 Baizas (C-N) 1970	1.50
10.	25 Baizas (C-N) 1970	1.00
11.	10 Baizas (Bro) 1970	.50
12.	5 Baizas (Bro) 1970	.35
13.	2 Baizas (Bro) 1970	.30

20.   ½ Omani Riyal 1978. Rev: Lemon. (F.A.O. coin plan)   5.00

14.   10 Baizas (Bro) 1975. Two palms on island. Rev: Value. (F.A.O. coin plan)   2.00

15.   16.

17.   18.

15.	50 Baizas (C-N) 1975	1.50
16.	25 Baizas (C-N) 1975	1.00
17.	10 Baizas (Br) 1975	.75
18.	5 Baizas (Br) 1975	.50

PAKISTAN

In the partition of British India in 1947, Pakistan was formed out of predominantly Moslem areas into a self-governing dominion within the British Commonwealth of Nations. Subsequently it changed its status to that of republic within the same framework.

$$3 \text{ Pies} = 1 \text{ Pice}$$
$$4 \text{ Pice} = 1 \text{ Anna}$$
$$16 \text{ Annas} = 1 \text{ Rupee}$$

1.	1 Rupee (N) 1948–49. Toughra in wreath. Rev: Star and crescent in wreath	3.50
2.	½ Rupee (N) 1948–51.	1.50
3.	¼ Rupee (N) 1948–51.	1.00
4.	2 Annas (N) 1948–51. (Square-shaped)	.50
5.	1 Anna (N) 1948–52. (Scalloped edge)	.40
6.	½ Anna (C-N) 1948–51. (Square-shaped)	.35
7.	1 Pice (Bro) 1948–52. (Center hole)	.25
8.	2 Annas (C-N) 1953–59. (Square planchet)	1.00

9.	1 Anna (C-N) 1953–59. Star and crescent, Toughra below. Rev: Value. (Scalloped edge)	.75
10.	½ Anna (N-Bra) 1953–58. (Square planchet)	.50
11.	1 Pice (N-Bra) 1953–59. (Round planchet)	.35
12.	1 Pie (Bro) 1951–56	.35

NEW DECIMAL SYSTEM COINAGE

$$100 \text{ Paisa} = 1 \text{ Rupee}$$

13.	50 Paisa (N) 1964–69. Star and crescent, Toughra below. Rev: Value	1.00

13a.	50 Paisa (C-N) 1969–74 (redesigned reverse); (C-N) 1975– (redesigned obverse and rev.)	.50
14.	25 Paisa (N) 1964–67	.50
14a.	25 Paisa (C-N) 1967–74 (redesigned reverse); (C-N) 1975– (redesigned obv. and rev.)	.25

15.	10 Paisa (C-N) 1961–63. (Some 1961 coins show denomination as Pice; scalloped edge)	.50
15a.	10 Paisa (C-N) 1964–74. Bengali legend. Rev: Numeral "10"	.25

16.   16a.

16.	5 Paisa (C-N) 1961–63. Rev: Sailing craft with value on sail. (Square planchet)	.35
16a.	5 Paisa (C-N) 1964–74. Bengali legend. Rev: Numeral "5" superimposed on sail	.15
17.	2 Paisa (Bro) 1964–66; (A) 1966– . Rev: Value. (Scalloped edge)	.15
18.	1 Paisa (Bro) 1961–63. Rev: Value between ears of wheat	.25
18a.	1 Paisa (Bro) 1964–65; (N-Bra) 1965, '66; (A) 1967–73. Bengali legend. Rev: Numeral "1"	.15

19.	10 Paisa (A) 1974–79. Rev: Value in circle of wheat. (F.A.O. coin plan; scalloped planchet)	.50

20.	5 Paisa (A) 1974–. Rev: Value between sugar plants. (F.A.O. coin plan; square planchet)	.75

21.	2 Paisa (A) 1974–76. Rev: Value between millet plants. (F.A.O. coin plan; scalloped edge)	.50
22.	1 Paisa (A) 1974– . Rev: Value between cotton plants. (F.A.O.)	.20
23.	100 Rupees 1976. Head of Mohammed Ali Jinnah. Rev: Crescent. (100th anniversary of birth of "Great Leader," founding father of Pakistan)	30.00
24.	100 Rupees 1977. Islamic Summit Minar (tower). Rev: Legends. (Islamic Summit Conference of 1974, completion of commemorative tower in 1977)	35.00

415

PAKISTAN (continued)

25. 1 Rupee (C-N) 1977. Head of A. M. Iqbal.
    Rev: Value above wreath. (Birth of poet)   3.00
26. 1 Rupee (C-N) 1980. Star and crescent. Rev:
    Inscription within wreath. (1400th anniver-
    sary of Muhammad's Hegira [flight])   2.50
27. 1 Rupee (C-N) 1981. Star and crescent. Rev:
    Stylized symbols of grain. (World Food Day)   2.00

PALESTINE

An area in the Middle East on the Mediterranean mandated to Great Britain after World War I. The mandate
came to an end in 1948 when the United Nations created
the independent state of Israel (q.v.).

1000 Mils = 1 Pound

1. 100 Mills 1927–42. Olive sprig. Rev: Value   30.00
2. 50 Mils 1927–42   20.00

3. 20 Mils (C-N) 1927–41; (Bro) '42–44 Wreath.
    Rev: Value. (Center hole)   25.00
4. 10 Mils (C-N) 1927–42, '46; (Bro) '42–43. (Cen-
    ter hole)   12.50

5. 5 Mils (C-N) 1927–41, '46; (Bro) '42–44. (Cen-
    ter hole)   6.50

6. 2 Mils (Bro) 1927–46. Inscription. Rev: Olive
    sprig   6.50

7. 1 Mil (Bro) 1927–46   5.00

PANAMA

For centuries Panama was part of the Spanish colony of New Granada, and later a part of Colombia. Panama became independent in 1903.

100 Centesimos = 1 Balboa

1.	50 Centesimos 1904–05. Bust of Balboa. Rev: Arms	30.00
2.	25 Centesimos 1904	20.00
3.	10 Centesimos 1904	15.00
4.	5 Centesimos 1904	7.50

5.	2½ Centesimos 1904. (So-called "Panama Pill")	15.00

5a.	2½ Centesimos (C-N) 1929	3.50
6.	½ Centesimo (C-N) 1907	2.00
7.	5 Centesimos (C-N) 1929–32. Arms. Rev: Value	5.00
8.	2½ Centesimos (C-N) 1907, '16	3.00

LAW OF 1930

9.	1 Balboa 1931, '34, '47. Bust of Balboa. Rev: Female figure and arms	7.50

10.	½ Balboa 1930, '32–34, '47, '62. Rev: Arms	4.00
11.	¼ Balboa 1930–34, '47, '62	2.00

12.	⅒ Balboa 1930–34, '47, '62	1.00
13.	2½ Centesimos (C-N) 1940. Rev: Value	2.00
14.	1¼ Centesimos (Bro) 1940	2.00

15.	1 Centesimo (Bro) 1935, '37. Head of Urraca. Rev: Value and spray	3.00

DECREE OF 1953: FIFTIETH ANNIVERSARY OF REPUBLIC

16.	1 Balboa 1953. Bust of Balboa, CINCUENTENARIO inscription. Rev: Female figure	25.00
17.	½ Balboa 1953. Rev: Arms	5.00
18.	¼ Balboa 1953	15.00
19.	⅒ Balboa 1953	2.00
20.	1 Centesimo (Bro) 1953. Head of Urraca. Rev: Value. CINCUENTENARIO inscription	1.00
21.	1 Balboa 1966– . Type of #10	10.00
22.	½ Balboa 1961, '62	5.00
22a.	½ Balboa (clad 40% silver) 1966–	2.00
23.	¼ Balboa 1961, '62	2.00
23a.	¼ Balboa (C-N clad copper) 1966–	.75
24.	⅒ Balboa 1961, '62	1.00
24a.	⅒ Balboa (C-N clad copper) 1966–	.25

25.	5 Centesimos (C-N) 1961– . Arms. Rev: Value	.20
26.	1 Centesimo (Bro) 1961– . Type of #20, without CINCUENTENARIO	.25

27.   5 Balboas 1970. Arms. Rev: Discus thrower. (11th Central American and Caribbean Games)   35.00

32.   500 Balboas (G) 1975–77. Balboa kneeling. Rev: Arms. (500th anniversary of explorer's birth)   800.00

28.   20 Balboas 1971. Simón Bolívar. Rev: Arms. (150th anniversary of independence)   100.00
29.   20 Balboas 1972– . Without commemorative inscription   85.00

33.   100 Balboas (G) 1975–77. Bust of Balboa. Rev: Arms   175.00

34.   5 Balboas 1975– . Belisario Porras, former president. Rev: Arms   30.00

30.   5 Balboas 1972. Hand holding rice. Rev: Arms. (F.A.O. coin plan)   30.00
31.   2½ Centesimos (C-N) 1974   .20

35.   1 Balboa 1975– . Type of #33   12.50

36. 50 Centesimos (C-N) 1975– . Ferdinand de Lesseps, canal promoter. Rev: Arms   3.00
37. 25 Centesimos (C-N) 1975– . Justo Arosemena, former president   2.50

43. 75 Balboas (G) 1978. Arms. Rev: Flags. (75th anniversary of independence)   175.00
44. 1 Balboa (C-N) 1978. (75th anniversary of independence)   10.00

38. 10 Centesimos (C-N) 1975– . Manuel E. Amador, creator of national flag   2.00
39. 5 Centesimos (C-N) 1975– . Carlos Finlay, physician and biologist   2.00

45. 10 Balboas (N) 1978. Arms. Rev: Map of Isthmus of Panama. (Ratification of Panama Canal Treaty with U.S.)   20.00
45a. 10 Balboas (S) 1978. Proof   40.00

40. 2½ Centesimos (C-N) 1975– . Victoriano Lorenzo, Indian leader   1.00
41. 1 Centesimo (Bro) 1975– . Urraca, Indian leader   .50

46. 200 Balboas (Pl) 1979. Arms. Rev: Panamanian flag, map. (Implementation of Panama Canal Treaty)   300.00

42. 500 Balboas (G) 1978. Arms. Rev: Western Hemisphere. (30th anniversary of Organization of American States)   800.00

47. 10 Balboas 1979. Arms. Rev: Panamanian flag over ship in canal. (Implementation of Panama Canal Treaty.) Issued in proof only   50.00

PANAMA (continued)

48. 5 Balboas 1979– . Arms. Rev: Map of Panama, flag planted in Canal. (Implementation of Panama Canal Treaty.) In proof only ... 35.00
49. 100 Balboas (G) 1980. Arms. Rev: Bust of Ferdinand de Lesseps. (Centennial of beginning of Panama Canal) ... 175.00
50. 20 Balboas 1980. Arms. Rev: Simón Bolívar on horseback. (150th anniversary of his death) ... 150.00
51. 20 Balboas (G) 1981. Arms. Rev: Figure-of-eight butterfly. In proof only ... 75.00
52. 20 Balboas 1982. Arms. Rev: Armored standing figure of Balboa. (Balboa's discovery of Pacific.) In proof only ... 150.00

PAPUA NEW GUINEA

Papua New Guinea is comprised of the formerly separate territories of Papua and New Guinea.

100 Toea = 1 Kina

1. 100 Kina (G) 1975. Bust of Prime Minister Somare. Rev: Bird of paradise, value. (Independence) ... 200.00

2. 10 Kina (C-N) 1975– . Arms (bird of paradise). Rev: Bird of paradise ... 75.00
2a. 10 Kina (S) 1975– . Proof ... 55.00

3. 5 Kina (C-N) 1975, '76. Arms. Rev: Eagle ... 50.00
3a. 5 Kina (S) 1975– . Proof ... 25.00

4. 1 Kina (C-N) 1975– . Emblem of Bank of Papua New Guinea. Rev: Crocodiles. (Center hole)   3.50

NOTE: #4 is first Papua New Guinean coin with center hole

5. 20 Toea (C-N) 1975– . Arms. Rev: Cassowary (flightless bird)   2.50

6. 10 Toea (C-N) 1975– . Rev: Spotted cuscus   2.00
7. 5 Toea (C-N) 1975– . Rev: Plateless turtle   1.00

8. 2 Toea (Bro) 1975– . Rev: Butterfly cod   .35
9. 1 Toea (Bro) 1975– . Rev: Butterfly   .25

10. 100 Kina (G) 1976. Crest of Bank of PNG. Rev: Arms, string of coins. (First anniversary of independence)   200.00

11. 10 Kina (C-N) 1977. Elizabeth II. Rev: Arms. (Queen's Silver Jubilee). Also in silver proof   50.00

12. 100 Kina (G) 1979. Arms. Rev: "Four faces of nation"   200.00
13. 100 Kina (G) 1980. Arms. Rev: Stylized native art. (South Pacific Festival of Arts)   200.00
14. 100 Kina (G) 1980. Arms. Rev: Flag over map of Papua New Guinea. (Fifth anniversary of independence)   200.00
15. 100 Kina (G) 1981. Head of Prime Minister Sir Julius Chan. Rev: Bird of paradise   200.00

16. 5 Kina 1981. Arms. Rev: Boy with freshly caught fish. (International Year of Child)   20.00

PARAGUAY

Paraguay is a landlocked country which became a Spanish colony in the 16th century. For 150 years the Jesuits ran the country and protected the native Guarani Indians from extermination by the Spaniards and Portuguese. Since 1811, when Paraguay gained its independence from Spain, the country has been ruled by dictatorships and has taken part in several costly wars.

100 Centavos = 100 Centesimos = 1 Peso
100 Centimos = 1 Guarani

1.	¹/₁₂ Real (C) 1845. Lion. Rev: Fraction	50.00
2.	4 Centesimos (C) 1870. Star in wreath. Rev: Value	35.00
3.	2 Centesimos (C) 1870	25.00
4.	1 Centesimo (C) 1870	25.00

5.	1 Peso 1889. Seated lion. Rev: Star	200.00
6.	20 Centavos (C-N) 1900, '03	12.50
7.	10 Centavos (C-N) 1900, '03	10.00
8.	5 Centavos (C-N) 1900, '03	10.00

9.	10 Pesos (C-N) 1939. Star in wreath. Rev: Value	10.00
10.	5 Pesos (C-N) 1939	20.00
11.	2 Pesos (C-N) 1925; (A) 1938	5.00
12.	1 Peso (C-N) 1925; (A) 1938	3.00
13.	50 Centavos (C-N) 1925; (A) 1938	5.00
14.	20 Centavos (C-N) 1908	20.00
15.	10 Centavos (C-N) 1908	50.00
16.	5 Centavos (C-N) 1908	30.00

17.	50 Centimos (A-Bro) 1944–51. Lion. Rev: Value	3.50
18.	25 Centimos (A-Bro) 1944–51. Flower	2.00

19.	10 Centimos (A-Bro) 1944–47. Orchid	1.25
20.	5 Centimos (A-Bro) 1944–47. Flower	.75
21.	1 Centimo (A-Bro) 1944–50. Flower	1.25

22.	50 Centimos (A-Bro) 1953. Lion. Rev: Value. (Scalloped-edge planchet)	2.50
23.	25 Centimos (A-Bro) 1953	2.00
24.	15 Centimos (A-Bro) 1953	1.50
25.	10 Centimos (A-Bro) 1953	1.00

26.	300 Guaranies 1968. President Stroessner. Rev: Arms	25.00
27.	50 Guaranies (St) 1974. Bust of Marshal Estigarribia Rev: Dam, value	3.00
28.	10 Guaranies (St) 1974. Bust of General Eugenio Garay. Rev: Cow, value	1.00
29.	5 Guaranies (St) 1974. Woman. Rev: Cotton plant, value	.50
30.	1 Guarani (St) 1974. Soldier. Rev: Tobacco plant, value	.35

PARAGUAY (continued)

31.   10 Guaranies (St) 1978. General Garay. Rev: Cow, inscription. (F.A.O. coin plan)   .35
32.   5 Guaranies (St) 1978. Woman. Rev: Cotton plant, inscription. (F.A.O. coin plan)   .50
33.   1 Guarani (St) 1978. Soldier. Rev: Tobacco plant, inscription. (F.A.O. coin plan)   .35

PERU

Prior to the Spanish Conquest, Peru was the setting for a remarkably advanced civilization—that of the Incas. In 1532 Francisco Pizarro, perhaps the greediest and most bloodthirsty of all the conquistadors, began the subjugation of the Incas. Peru achieved its independence from Spain in 1824.

8 Reales = 1 Dollar = 1 Piece-of-Eight
100 Centimos = 1 Real
100 Centavos = 1 Sol
10 Soles = 1 Libra

CHARLES II   1665–1700

1.	8 Reales 1683, '92. Cross, arms. Rev: Pillars	300.00

2.	2 Reales 1672, '83, '97	125.00

3.	1 Real 1686–95	65.00

PHILIP V   1700–46

4.	8 Reales 1730	200.00
5.	4 Reales 1730	325.00
6.	2 Reales 1716–42	50.00
7.	1 Real 1707–44	35.00

FERDINAND VI   1746–59

8.	8 Reales 1755–59. Crowned arms. Rev: Globes between pillars; mint mark in legend	200.00
9.	2 Reales 1755–58	75.00
10.	1 Real 1753–59	100.00
11.	½ Real 1756–59	50.00

CHARLES III   1759–88

12.	8 Reales 1764–72. Pillar type	200.00
13.	2 Reales 1762–72	75.00

14.	1 Real 1763–72	60.00
15.	½ Real 1762–70	40.00

16.	8 Reales 1779–88. Laureate bust. Rev: Crowned arms between pillars	60.00
17.	4 Reales 1780–88	100.00
18.	2 Reales 1773–88	20.00
19.	1 Real 1773–88	15.00
20.	½ Real 1779–88	20.00

CHARLES IV   1788–1808

21.	8 Reales 1789, '90. Bust of Charles III	100.00
22.	4 Reales 1790	150.00
23.	2 Reales 1789–91	20.00
24.	1 Real 1789–91	15.00
25.	½ Real 1789–91	15.00
26.	8 Reales 1791–1808. Bust of Charles IV	50.00

27.	4 Reales 1795–1808	75.00

28.	2 Reales 1791–1808	15.00

29.	1 Real 1791–1808	15.00
30.	½ Real 1791–1808	12.50
31.	¼ Real 1792, '93	50.00

32.	¼ Real 1794–1808. Castle. Rev: Lion	25.00

FERDINAND VII   1808–24

33.	8 Reales 1809–12. Unusual laureate bust (peculiar to Lima mint)	50.00
34.	4 Reales 1810	150.00
35.	2 Reales 1810–12	25.00
36.	1 Real 1811	30.00
37.	½ Real 1810–12	20.00
38.	8 Reales 1812–24. Draped laureate bust	50.00

39.	4 Reales 1813–21	65.00
40.	2 Reales 1813–21	12.50
41.	1 Real 1813–23	17.50
42.	½ Real 1812–21	20.00

43.	¼ Real 1813–23. Castle. Rev: Lion	40.00

REPUBLIC OF PERU

44.	8 Reales 1822, '23. Column between standing figures of Virtue and Justice. Rev: Arms	150.00
45.	8 Reales 1825–55. Liberty standing with shield. Rev: Arms. (Varieties)	65.00
46.	4 Reales 1843–55	30.00

47.	2 Reales 1825–56	17.50
48.	1 Real 1826–61	25.00
49.	½ Real 1826–60	17.50

50.	¼ Real (C) 1822, '23; (S) 1826–56. Llama. Rev: Value	12.50
51.	⅛ Peso (C) 1823	15.00
52.	50 Centavos 1858, '59. Liberty seated. Rev: Arms	50.00
53.	25 Centavos 1859	50.00

54.	1 Libra (G) 1898–1930. Indian head. Rev: Arms	175.00
55.	½ Libra (G) 1902–08	85.00
56.	⅕ Libra (G) 1906–30	50.00

57.	1 Sol 1864–1916, 1923–35. Liberty seated	25.00
58.	½ Sol 1864–65, 1907–17, '22–35	10.00
59.	⅕ Sol 1863–1916	7.50
60.	1 Dinero (⅒ Sol) 1864–1913, 1916	5.00
61.	½ Dinero 1863–1917	4.00
62.	20 Centavos (C-N) 1879. Sun. Rev: Value	20.00

62a.	20 Centavos (C-N) 1918–41. Liberty head	2.00
63.	10 Centavos (C-N) 1879, '80. Type of #62	12.50
63a.	10 Centavos (C-N) 1918–41	1.25
64.	5 Centavos (C-N) 1879, '80. Type of #62	7.50
64a.	5 Centavos (C-N) 1918–41	2.50

65.	2 Centavos (Bro) 1863–1900, 1917–49. Sun	1.25
66.	1 Centavo (Bro) 1863–1949	1.50

67.	50 Soles (G) 1930–31, '67–69. Head of the Inca Manco Capac. Rev: Inca symbol	650.00
68.	1 Sol (Bra) 1943–65. Arms. Rev: Value	1.00

69.	½ Sol (Bra) 1935–65	.75
70.	20 Centavos (Bra) 1942–65. Liberty head	.50
71.	10 Centavos (Bra) 1942–65	.25
72.	5 Centavos (Bra) 1942–65	.35
73.	2 Centavos (Z) 1950–58. Sun	1.25
74.	1 Centavo (Z) 1950–65	2.00

SPECIAL BULLION ISSUE

75.	100 Gold Soles (G) 1950–69. Seated Liberty. Rev: Arms	900.00
76.	50 Gold Soles (G) 1950–69	500.00
77.	20 Gold Soles (G) 1950–69	200.00

78.	20 Centavos (A-Bro) 1954. Head of Castilla. Rev: Value	20.00
79.	10 Centavos (A-Bro) 1954	15.00
80.	5 Centavos (A-Bro) 1954	10.00

81.	20 Soles 1965. Replica of obverse of 8 reales coin of type struck at Lima mint in 1565. Rev: Arms. (400th anniversary of mint)	10.00
82.	1 Sol (Bra) 1965	1.00
83.	½ Sol (Bra) 1965	.75
84.	25 Centavos (Bra) 1965	.50
85.	10 Centavos (Bra) 1965	.50
86.	5 Centavos (Bra) 1965	.40

87.	20 Soles 1966. Arms. Rev: Our Lady of Victory, Lima statue. (Centenary of Spanish bombardment of Callao)	35.00

88.	1 Sol (Bra) 1966– . Arms. Rev: Vicuna and value	.50
89.	½ Sol (Bra) 1966	.40

90.	25 Centavos (Bra) 1966–75. Arms. Rev: Cantuta flower	.50
91.	10 Centavos (Bra) 1966–75	.25
92.	5 Centavos (Bra) 1966–75	.25

93.	10 Soles (C-N) 1969. Arms. Rev: Stylized fish	2.50
94.	5 Soles (C-N) 1969. Arms. Rev: Inca design	1.25

95.	50 Soles 1971. Tupac Amaru, Indian hero. Rev: Arms. (150th anniversary of independence)	25.00
96.	10 Soles (C-N) 1971	5.00
96a.	5 Soles (C-N) 1971	1.75

97a.

97. 10 Soles (C-N) 1972– . Without commemorative
   inscription   1.50
97a. 5 Soles (C-N) 1972–75   .75

98. 100 Soles 1973. Chrysanthemums, value. Rev:
   Arms. (100 years of trade relations between
   Japan and Peru)   25.00

99. 200 Soles 1974–77. Heads of J. Chavez and
   J. Quinones, airplane pioneers. Rev: Arms   25.00

100. 5 Soles (C-N) 1975–77. Tupac Amaru. Type of
    #97, smaller   1.00
101. 1 Sol (Bra) 1975– . Arms. Rev: Value   .50
102. ½ Sol (Bra) 1975–77   .50
103. 20 Centavos (Bra) 1975   .30
104. 10 Centavos (Bra) 1975   .20

105. 1000 Soles (C-N) 1976. Facade of National Con-
    gress. Rev: Arms   6.00
106. 400 Soles 1976. Obverse similar to #99. Rev:
    Monument. (150th anniversary of Battle of
    Ayacucho)   30.00

NOTE: Nos. 107–14 commemorate centenary of
War of Pacific. All have reverse arms designs

107.
   100,000 Soles (G) 1979. Admiral Miguel Grau   750.00
108.
   100,000 Soles (G) 1979. Colonel Francisco Bolognese 750.00
109.
   100,000 Soles (G) 1979. Colonel Andres A. Caceras   750.00
110.
   50,000 Soles (G) 1979. Alfonso Ugarte   375.00
111.
   50,000 Soles (G) 1979. Francisco Calderon   375.00
112.
   50,000 Soles (G) 1979. Captain Elias Aguirre   375.00
113.
   5,000 Soles (S) 1979. Battle of Iquique   65.00
114.
   1,000 Soles (S) 1979. Battle of Iquique   15.00

THE PHILIPPINES

The Republic of the Philippines comprises 7000 islands in the southwest Pacific. They were under Spanish rule from the 16th century until the Spanish-American War in 1898, when they passed to the United States. The Philippines gained partial freedom in 1935 and complete independence in 1946.

100 Centimos = 1 Peseta
100 Centavos = 1 Peso

UNDER SPAIN
ISABELLA II 1833–68

1.	4 Pesos (G) 1861–68. Laureated head. Rev: Crowned arms between pillars	325.00
2.	2 Pesos (G) 1861–68	200.00
3.	1 Peso (G) 1861–68	175.00
4.	50 Centimos 1865–68	75.00
5.	20 Centimos 1864–68	25.00
6.	10 Centimos 1864–68	50.00

ALFONSO XII 1874–85

7.	50 Centimos 1880–85. Head. Rev: Type of #1	30.00
8.	20 Centimos 1880–85	25.00
9.	10 Centimos 1880–85	12.50

ALFONSO XIII 1886–1898

10.	1 Peso 1897. Head. Rev: Type of #1	75.00

UNDER THE UNITED STATES

11.	1 Peso 1903–06. Standing female figure representing "Filipinas," Mayon volcano in background. Rev: U.S. arms	30.00
11a.	1 Peso 1907–12. (Reduced-size planchet)	20.00

12.	50 Centavos 1903–06	20.00
12a.	50 Centavos 1907–21 (Reduced)	17.50
13.	20 Centavos 1903–06	7.50
13a.	20 Centavos 1907–29 (Reduced)	5.00
14.	10 Centavos 1903–06	5.00
14a.	10 Centavos 1907–35 (Reduced)	3.50

15.	5 Centavos (C-N) 1903–28. Workman with anvil, Mayon volcano	5.00
15a.	5 Centavos (C-N) 1930–35. (Reduced)	15.00
16.	1 Centavo (Bro) 1903–36	5.00
17.	½ Centavo (Bro) 1903–08	4.00

COMMONWEALTH OF THE PHILIPPINES
1935–46

18.	1 Peso 1936. Busts of Pres. Roosevelt and Pres. Quezon. Rev: Arms of Commonwealth	200.00
19.	1 Peso 1936. Busts of Gov. Gen. Murphy and Pres. Quezon	200.00

20.	50 Centavos 1936. Facing busts of Gov. Murphy and Pres. Quezon	100.00

REPUBLIC OF THE PHILIPPINES
1946–

21. 50 Centavos 1944–45. Female figure and vol-
    cano. Rev: Philippine arms with eagle above   1.25
22. 20 Centavos 1937–45   1.00
23. 10 Centavos 1937–45   .75
24. 5 Centavos (C-N) 1937–41; (N-S) 1944–45.
    Workman and volcano   .20
25. 1 Centavo (Bro) 1937–44   .30

26. 1 Peso 1947. Bust of Gen. MacArthur. Rev:
    Shield. (MacArthur Commemorative)   7.50
27. 50 Centavos 1947   3.00

28. 50 Centavos (C-N) 1958–64. Standing figure.
    Rev: Arms   1.00
29. 25 Centavos (C-N) 1958–66   .50
30. 10 Centavos (C-N) 1958–66   .35
31. 5 Centavos (Bra) 1958–66. Seated figure   .20
32. 1 Centavo (Bra) 1958–63   .10

33. 1 Peso 1961. Head of Dr. José Rizal. (Centen-
    nial commemorative)   10.00
34. ½ Peso 1961. Rizal   3.00

35. 1 Peso 1963. Head of Andres Bonifacio. Rev:
    Arms. (100th anniversary of birth of national
    hero)   6.00

36. 1 Peso 1964. Head of Apolinario Mabini. Rev:
    Arms. (100th anniversary of birth of national
    hero)   6.00

37. 1 Peso 1967. Broken sword in flames. Rev:
    Arms. (25th anniversary of Bataan March)   6.00

FILIPINO HEROES ISSUES

38. 50 Sentimos (C-N-Z) 1967. Head of Marcelo H.
    del Pilar. Rev: Arms. (Legends in Tagalog)   .50

39. 25 Sentimos (C-N-Z) 1967– . Head of Juan Luna. Rev: Arms .35
40. 10 Sentimos (C-N-Z) 1967– . Head of Francisco Baltazar. Rev: Arms .25

41. 5 Sentimos (C-Z) 1967– . Head of Melchora Aguino .15
42. 1 Sentimo (A) 1967– . Head of Chief Lapu-lapu .15

43. 1 Piso 1969. Head of Emilio Aguinaldo. Rev: Arms. (100th anniversary of general's birth) 25.00

44. 1 Piso (N) 1970. Bust of Pope Paul VI. Rev: Bust of Ferdinand Marcos. (Papal visit) 3.00
44a. 1 Piso (S) 1970 20.00
44b. 1 Piso (G) 1970 650.00

45. 1 Piso (C-N) 1972–74. Bust of José Rizal. Rev: Arms 1.50

46. 25 Piso 1974. Bank building. Rev: Arms (25th anniversary of Central Bank of the Philippines) 25.00
47. 1000 Piso (G) 1975. Bust of Marcos. Rev: Arms. (3rd anniversary of New Society Program) 250.00

48. 50 Piso 1975. Bust of President Marcos. Rev: Arms 40.00
49. 25 Piso 1975. Bust of Aguinaldo, president of first Philippine Republic 20.00
50. 5 Piso (N) 1975. Type of #48 10.00

51. 1 Piso (C-N) 1975– . Bust of Rizal, author and patriot 1.25
52. 25 Sentimos (C-N) 1975– . Bust of Luna, artist and patriot .50

53. 10 Sentimos (C-N) 1975– . Bust of Baltasar, poet .25
54. 5 Sentimos (C-Z) 1975– . Bust of Aquino, patriot. (Scalloped planchet) .25
55. 1 Sentimo (A) 1975– . Bust of Lapulapu, warrior chief. (Square planchet) .25

60. 25 Piso 1977. Arms. Rev: Banawie rice terraces   35.00

56. 1500 Piso (G) 1976. Four logos of international
    banking organizations. Rev: Map. (Interna-
    tional Monetary Fund—World Bank meet-
    ing)   500.00
57. 50 Piso 1976   65.00
58. 25 Piso 1976. Young woman holding rice. Rev:
    Arms. (F.A.O. coin plan)   25.00

62.

61. 1500 Piso (G) 1978. View of the new mint, Manila.
    Rev: Arms. (Inauguration of Manila Security
    Printing Plant, Gold Refinery & Mint)   425.00
62. 50 Piso 1977. (Inauguration of new mint; variant
    design)   50.00

63. 50 Piso 1978. Arms. Rev: Bust of Manuel L.
    Quezon. (Centennial of president's birth)   40.00

59. 5000 Piso (G) 1977. Conjoined busts of President
    and Mrs. Marcos. Rev: Presidential seal.
    (Fifth anniversary of "New Society")   1750.00

64. 25 Piso 1978. Arms. Rev: Monument. (Quezon
    birth centennial)   30.00

65. 50 Piso 1979. Arms. Rev: Child (International
     Year of Child)   50.00
66. 25 Piso 1979. Building. Rev: United Nations
     symbol. (U.N. Conference on Trade and De-
     velopment)   30.00
67. 2500 Piso (G) 1980. Bust of General Douglas Mac-
     Arthur. Rev: MacArthur and staff wading
     ashore on Luzon. (Centennial of MacArthur's
     birth)   500.00
68. 25 Piso 1980. (MacArthur centennial)   30.00

POLAND

Towards the end of the 18th century the Kingdom of Poland was divided up by Russia, Austria and Prussia. After World War I Poland became an independent country, only to lose its freedom once more in 1940. After World War II Poland became a "People's Republic" under Russian domination. (See also "Danzig.")

24 Groschen = 1 Taler
100 Groszy = 1 Zloty

SIGISMUND III   1587–1632

1.	Taler 1587–1632. Crowned bust with sword. Rev: Arms	250.00
2.	½ Taler 1587–1632	125.00
3.	¼ Taler 1587–1632	65.00

4.	6 Groschen 1587–1632. Crowned bust in ruff collar	30.00

5.	3 Groschen 1587–1632	15.00
6.	1 Groschen 1587–1632	12.50

VLADISLAV IV   1632–48

7.	Taler 1633–44. Crowned bust holding sword and orb	225.00

JOHN CASIMIR   1648–69

8.	Taler 1648–69. Three-quarter crowned bust. Rev: Arms	300.00

JOHN III SOBIESKI   1674–96

8a.	Orte 1679	35.00

AUGUST II   1697–1733

9.	Taler 1697–1733. Laureate bust. Rev: Arms	200.00

AUGUST III   1733–63

10.	Taler 1733–63. Crowned bust. Rev: Arms	175.00

STANISLAUS AUGUST   1764–95

11.	Taler 1764–95. Bust. Rev: Arms	175.00

POLAND (continued)

POLISH REPUBLIC 1918–39

12.	50 Groszy (N) 1923. Eagle. Rev: Value in wreath	1.50
13.	20 Groszy (N) 1923	1.50
14.	10 Groszy (N) 1923	1.25
15.	5 Groszy (Bro) 1923–38. Eagle. Rev: Value on scroll	1.25
16.	2 Groszy (Bro) 1923–38	1.00
17.	1 Grosz (Bro) 1923–38	1.25

24. 5 Zlotych 1930. Flags and inscription. Rev: Eagle. (Centenary of Revolution of 1830)   35.00

18. 20 Zlotych (G) 1925. Head of Boleslaus I. Rev: Eagle   75.00
19. 10 Zlotych (G) 1925   50.00

25.	10 Zlotych 1932–33. Female head. Rev: Eagle	15.00
26.	5 Zlotych 1932–34	7.50
27.	2 Zlote 1932–34	3.50

20. 5 Zlotych (1925). Seated and standing figures. Rev: Eagle. (One of the rarest of modern coins)   500.00
21. 2 Zlote 1924–25. Peasant girl. Rev: Eagle   20.00
22. 1 Zloty 1924–25   7.50

28. 10 Zlotych 1933. Bust of Jan Sobieski. Rev: Eagle. (250th anniversary of relief of siege of Vienna)   30.00
29. 10 Zlotych 1933. Bust of Traugutt. Rev: Eagle. (70th anniversary of 1863 insurrection)   30.00

30. 10 Zlotych 1934. Head of Pilsudski. Rev: Eagle. (20th anniversary of Rifle Corps' entry into field in 1914)   25.00

23. 5 Zlotych 1928–32. Winged figure. Rev: Eagle   35.00

POLAND (continued)

30a. 10 Zlotych 1934–39. Head of Pilsudski. (Regular issue, no badge under eagle) 15.00
31.   5 Zlotych 1934. (Rifle Corps) 15.00
31a. 5 Zlotych 1934–36. (Regular issue) 7.50
32.   2 Zlote 1934–36 .... 10.00

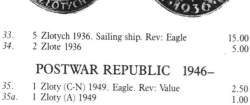

33. 5 Zlotych 1936. Sailing ship. Rev: Eagle 15.00
34. 2 Zlote 1936 .... 5.00

POSTWAR REPUBLIC 1946–

35. 1 Zloty (C-N) 1949. Eagle. Rev: Value 2.50
35a. 1 Zloty (A) 1949 .... 1.00

36. 50 Groszy (C-N) 1949 .... 2.00
36a. 50 Groszy (A) 1949 .... 1.00
37. 20 Groszy (C-N) 1949 .... 1.00
37a. 20 Groszy (A) 1949 .... .75
38. 10 Groszy (C-N) 1949 .... 1.00
38a. 10 Groszy (A) 1949 .... .75
39.   5 Groszy (Bro) 1949 .... 1.00
39a. 5 Groszy (A) 1949 .... 1.00
40.   2 Groszy (A) 1949 .... .35
41.   1 Grosz (A) 1949 .... .20

42. 10 Zlotych (C-N) 1959, '65. Head of Copernicus. Rev: Eagle 5.00
42a. 10 Zlotych (C-N) 1967–69. (Smaller planchet) 2.50
43. 10 Zlotych (C-N) 1959–66. Head of Kosciuszko. Rev: Eagle 4.00
43a. 10 Zlotych (C-N) 1969–73. (Smaller planchet) 2.50

44. 5 Zlotych (A) 1958– . Fisherman and net 1.00
45. 2 Zlote (A) 1958–74. Eagle. Rev: Value .... .75
46. 1 Zloty (A) 1957– .... .75
47. 50 Groszy (A) 1957– .... .60
48. 20 Groszy (A) 1957– .... .45
49. 10 Groszy (A) 1961– .... .25

50. 10 Zlotych (C-N) 1964. Crowned head of King Casimir the Great. Rev: Polish eagle. (600th anniversary of Jagiello University in Cracow) 5.00
50a. 10 Zlotych (C-N) 1964. Type of #50 with incuse legends 5.00

51. 10 Zlotych (C-N) 1965. Nike with sword. Rev: Eagle. (Warsaw's 700th anniversary) 4.00

52. 10 Zlotych (C-N) 1965. Commemorative column. Rev: Eagle. (Warsaw's 700th anniversary) 4.00
53. 10 Zlotych (C-N) 1966. Type of #52 with edge inscription. (200th anniversary of Warsaw Mint) 4.00

436

54. 100 Zlotych 1966. Obv: Eagle. Rev: Figures of Mieszko and Dabrowka, first king and queen. (1000th anniversary of Polish state) 25.00

55. 10 Zlotych (C-N) 1967. Portrait of General Karol Swierczewski Walter. Rev: Polish eagle. (20th anniversary of death) 3.00

56. 10 Zlotych (C-N) 1967. Portrait of Marie Curie. Rev: Polish eagle. (100th anniversary of scientist's birth) 3.00

57. 10 Zlotych (C-N) 1968. Eagle. Rev: xxv and soldier. (25th anniversary of People's Army) 3.00

58.

58. 10 Zlotych (C-N) 1969. Eagle. Rev: Sheaf of grain. (25th anniversary of People's Republic) 3.00

59. 10 Zlotych (C-N) 1970. Eagle. Rev: Arms of former German provinces. (25th anniversary of annexation of western and northern provinces) 1.75

60. 10 Zlotych (C-N) 1971. Fish with wheat superimposed. Rev: Arms, value. (F.A.O. coin plan) 3.00

61. 10 Zlotych (C-N) 1971. Monument in Katowice, Silesia. Rev: Arms. (50th anniversary of Third Silesian Uprising) 3.00

62. 50 Zlotych 1972–74. Head of Chopin. Rev: Arms, value 20.00

63.

63. 10 Zlotych (C-N) 1972. Aerial view of Gdynia-Gdansk (formerly Danzig). Rev: Arms, value. (50th anniversary of seaport)   3.00

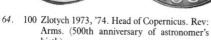

64. 100 Zlotych 1973, '74. Head of Copernicus. Rev: Arms. (500th anniversary of astronomer's birth)   25.00

65. 20 Zlotych (C-N) 1973, '74, '76. Field of wheat, silo in background. Rev: Arms within band   3.00

66. 200 Zlotych 1974. Map, plaque superimposed. Rev: Arms. (30th anniversary of republic)   15.00

67. 100 Zlotych 1974. Marie Curie with rays of radium. Rev: Arms. (40th anniversary of physicist's death)   25.00

68. 20 Zlotych (C-N) 1974. Marceli Nowotko, first secretary of Polish Communist Party. Rev: Arms   3.00

69. 20 Zlotych (C-N) 1974. Legend within half cogwheel, half wheel. Rev: Arms (25th anniversary of East European Communist bloc trade partnership)   3.00

70. 200 Zlotych 1975. Conjoined busts of soldiers. Rev: Arms. (30th anniversary, end of World War II)   25.00

71. 100 Zlotych 1975. Royal Castle in Warsaw. Rev: Arms   25.00

72. 100 Zlotych 1975. Helena Modrzejewska, actress   25.00

73. 100 Zlotych 1975. Ignacy Paderewski, composer and pianist   25.00

74. 10 Zlotych (C-N) 1975, '76. Bust of Adam Mickiewicz. Rev: Arms. (120th anniversary of poet's death)   3.00
75. 10 Zlotych (C-N) 1975, '76. Bust of Boleslaw Prus, novelist   3.00

76. 2 Zlotych (A) 1975–79. Eagle. Rev: Value, wheat   1.00
77. 20 Zlotych (C-N) 1975. Profile of woman. Rev: Arms. (International Women's Year)   3.00
78. 500 Zlotych (G) 1976. Bust of Tadeusz Kosciuszko. Rev: Arms. (U.S. Bicentennial)   650.00
79. 100 Zlotych (S) 1976. Kosciuszko. (U.S. Bicentennial)   25.00
80. 500 Zlotych (G) 1976. Bust of Casimir Pulaski. Rev: Arms. (U.S. Bicentennial)   650.00
81. 100 Zlotych (S) 1976. Pulaski. (U.S. Bicentennial)   25.00
82. 200 Zlotych 1976. Olympic rings and flame. Rev: Arms. (21st Olympic Games at Montreal)   15.00
82a. 200 Zlotych 1976. Proof   20.00
83. 2000 Zlotych (G) 1977. Head of Frederic Chopin, composer   300.00

84. 100 Zlotych 1977. European bison. Rev: Arms. (Environmental protection)   25.00
85. 100 Zlotych 1977. Henryk Sienkiewicz, writer   25.00
86. 100 Zlotych 1977. Wladyslaw Reymont, writer   25.00
87. 100 Zlotych 1977. Wawel Castle, Krakow   25.00
88. 100 Zlotych 1978. Adam Mickiewicz, poet   25.00
89. 100 Zlotych 1978. Moose. Rev: Arms. (Environmental protection)   25.00
90. 100 Zlotych 1978. Janusz Korczak, medical doctor and World War II hero   25.00
91. 100 Zlotych 1978. Beaver. Rev: Arms. (Environmental protection)   25.00
92. 2000 Zlotych (G) 1979. Nicolaus Copernicus   200.00
93. 2000 Zlotych (G) 1979. Marie Curie   200.00

95.

94. 200 Zlotych 1979. Mieszko I   25.00
95. 50 Zlotych (C-N) 1979. Mieszko I   7.50
96. 100 Zlotych 1979. Henryk Wieniawski, violinist   25.00
97. 100 Zlotych 1979. Ludwig Zamenhof, philologist   25.00
98. 100 Zlotych 1979. European wildcat. (Environmental protection)   25.00
99. 100 Zlotych 1979. Red deer. (Environmental protection)   25.00
100. 2000 Zlotych (G) 1980. Boleslaus I   200.00
101. 200 Zlotych 1980. Boleslaus I   25.00
102. 50 Zlotych (C-N) 1980. Boleslaus I   5.00
103. 2000 Zlotych (G) 1980. Ski jumper in midflight. Rev: Arms. (13th Winter Olympic Games at Lake Placid, N.Y.)   200.00
104. 200 Zlotych (S) 1980. Ski jumper. (Winter Olympics)   25.00
105. 100 Zlotych 1980. Olympic rings and runner. Rev: Arms. (1980 Moscow Olympics)   20.00
106. 200 Zlotych 1980. Casimir I   25.00
107. 50 Zlotych (C-N) 1980. Casimir I   5.00

108. 100 Zlotych 1980. *Dar Pomorza* sailing ship. (Ship's 50th year of service)   20.00
109. 100 Zlotych 1980. Jan Kochanowski, poet   20.00
110. 100 Zlotych 1980. Chicken. (Environmental protection)   20.00
111. 200 Zlotych (S) 1981. Boleslaus II ("Boleslaus Smialy")   40.00
112. 50 Zlotych (C-N) 1981. Boleslaus II   5.00

113. 100 Zlotych (S) 1981. General Broni Wladyslaw
    Sikorski   20.00
114. 50 Zlotych (C-N) 1981. General Sikorski   5.00
115. 100 Zlotych 1981. Rev: Horse. (Environmental
    protection)   20.00
116. 50 Zlotych (C-N) 1981. Rev: Stylized symbols of
    grain. (World Food Day)   5.00

PORTUGAL

Despite Portugal's small size, it managed to build up the third largest colonial empire of modern times. Profiting by the country's long Atlantic coastline, Portuguese mariners ventured further and further until they founded a vast empire for the mother country. Portugal was a monarchy until 1910, when it became a republic. (See also Madeira Islands.)

1000 Reis = 1 Crown
100 Centavos = 1 Escudo

JOHN V 1706–50

1.	8 Escudos or "Johanna" (G) 1723–32. Bust. Rev: Arms	2500.00
2.	4 Escudos or "Half Johanna" (G) 1723–50	1500.00

3.	400 Reis 1706–50. Type of #19	65.00
4.	200 Reis 1719–49	30.00
5.	100 Reis (undated)	15.00

JOSEPH I 1750–77

6.	400 Reis 1750–75	25.00
7.	200 Reis 1750–75	30.00
8.	100 Reis (undated)	20.00

MARY I AND PETER III 1777–86

9.	400 Reis 1778–86	75.00

10.	200 Reis 1778–82	30.00
11.	100 Reis (undated)	20.00
12.	50 Reis (undated)	10.00

MARY I 1786–99

13.	400 Reis 1786–99	75.00
14.	300 Reis 1794	25.00
15.	200 Reis 1786–99	50.00
16.	150 Reis 1794–98	20.00
17.	100 Reis (undated)	15.00
18.	50 Reis (undated)	10.00

JOHN (Prince) 1799–1801

19.	400 Reis 1799–1801. Crowned square shield. Rev: Cross with motto, IN HOC SIGNO VINCES	60.00
20.	120 Reis (undated)	15.00
21.	60 Reis (undated)	12.50
22.	80 Reis (undated). Value in Roman numerals (LXXX). Rev: Cross of St. George	10.00
23.	40 Reis (undated). Value in Roman numerals (XXXX)	8.50

JOHN (Prince Regent) 1802–16

24.	400 Reis 1802–16. Type of #19	30.00
25.	200 Reis 1806–16	100.00
26.	120 Reis (undated)	10.00
27.	60 Reis (undated)	5.00

28.	80 Reis (undated). Value: LXXX	15.00
29.	40 Reis (undated). Value: XXXX	10.00

PORTUGAL (continued)

54. 400 Reis 1833–37. Crowned square shield   30.00

30.	40 Reis (Bro) 1811–16. Bust. Rev: Crowned oval shield	10.00
31.	10 Reis (C) 1803–13. Crowned arms. Rev: Value in wreath	5.00
32.	5 Reis (C) 1804–14	5.00
33.	3 Reis (C) 1804	15.00

JOHN VI (King) 1816–26

34.	400 Reis 1818–25. Crowned square shield on globe	100.00
35.	200 Reis 1818–22	85.00
36.	120 Reis (undated)	25.00
37.	60 Reis (undated)	5.00
38.	80 Reis (undated). Value: LXXX	15.00
39.	40 Reis (undated). Value: XXXX	7.50
40.	40 Reis (C) 1817–25	7.50

41.	10 Reis (C) 1818–25	5.00
42.	5 Reis (C) 1818–24	10.00

PETER IV 1826–28

43.	400 Reis 1826–27. Crowned square shield	100.00
44.	40 Reis (Bro) 1826–28. Bust. Rev: Type of #30	17.50

MICHAEL I 1828–33

45.	400 Reis 1828–34. Crowned square shield	125.00
46.	200 Reis 1829–30	80.00
47.	120 Reis (undated)	25.00
48.	60 Reis (undated)	15.00
49.	80 Reis (undated). Value: LXXX	40.00
50.	40 Reis (undated) Value: XXXX	25.00
51.	40 Reis (Bro) 1828–34. Crowned arms. Rev: Value in wreath	7.50
52.	10 Reis (C) 1829–33	5.00
53.	5 Reis (C) 1829	8.00

55.	1000 Reis 1836–45. Diademed bust. Rev: Crowned arms with mantle	125.00
56.	500 Reis 1836–53	25.00
57.	200 Reis 1836–48. Rev: Value	30.00
58.	100 Reis 1836–53	10.00
59.	10 Reis (C) 1830–53. Crowned arms. Rev: Value	5.00
60.	5 Reis (C) 1830–53	5.00

PETER V 1853–61

61.	500 Reis 1854–59. Head. Rev: Crowned arms with mantle	30.00
62.	200 Reis 1854–61. Rev: Value	10.00
63.	100 Reis 1854–61	7.50
64.	50 Reis 1855, '61. Rev: Crowned date	8.00

LOUIS I 1861–89

65.	500 Reis 1863–89. Head. Crowned arms in wreath	15.00
66.	200 Reis 1862–88. Rev: Value	7.50

67.	100 Reis 1864–89	6.00
68.	50 Reis 1862–89. Rev: Crowned date	7.50

69.	20 Reis (C) 1867–74. Crowned arms. Rev: Value in wreath	7.50
69a.	20 Reis (Bro) 1882–86. Bust. Rev: Value in wreath	2.50
70.	10 Reis (C) 1867–74	5.00
70a.	10 Reis (Bro) 1882–86. Type of #69a	2.50
71.	5 Reis (C) 1867–79	5.00
71a.	5 Reis (Bro) 1882–86. Type of #69a	2.50
72.	3 Reis (C) 1868–75	7.50

CHARLES I   1889–1908

73.	1000 Reis 1899. Head. Rev: Crowned arms with mantle	30.00
74.	500 Reis 1891–1908. Rev: Arms in wreath	15.00
75.	200 Reis 1891–1903	12.50
76.	100 Reis 1890–98	15.00
77.	50 Reis 1893. Rev: Crowned date	15.00
78.	100 Reis (N) 1900. Crowned arms. Rev: Value	4.00
79.	50 Reis (N) 1900	4.00
80.	20 Reis (C) 1891–92. Head. Rev: Value in wreath	4.00
81.	10 Reis (C) 1891–92	3.00
82.	5 Reis (C) 1890–1906	3.00

83.	1000 Reis 1898. Conjoined busts. Rev: Cross with motto, IN HOC SIGNO VINCES. (Nos. 83, 84 and 85 commemorate 400th anniversary of discovery of route to Indies)	35.00
84.	500 Reis 1898	20.00
85.	200 Reis 1898	15.00

MANUEL II   1908–10

86.	500 Reis 1908–09. Head. Rev: Crowned arms in wreath	15.00

87.	200 Reis 1909. Rev: Crowned value in wreath	7.50
88.	100 Reis 1909–10	7.50

89.	1000 Reis 1910. Head. Rev: Crowned shield. (Centenary of Peninsular War)	60.00
90.	500 Reis 1910	35.00

91.	500 Reis 1910. Head. Figures with shield. (Marquis de Pombal Commemorative)	30.00

REPUBLIC   1910–26

92.	1 Escudo 1914, dated 1910. Rev: Arms in wreath. (Founding of Republic)	35.00

93. 1 Escudo 1915–16. Republic head. Rev: Type
     of #92   25.00
94. 50 Centavos 1912–16   12.50
95. 20 Centavos 1913, '16   12.50
96. 10 Centavos 1915   5.00

97. 1 Escudo (A-Bro) 1924, '26. Republic with flag.
     Rev: Arms   5.00
98. 50 Centavos (A-Bro) 1924–26   2.50

99.   20 Centavos (C-N) 1920–22; (Bro) 1924, '25.
      Republic head. Rev: Value   2.00
100. 10 Centavos (C-N) 1920–21; (Bro) 1924–40   1.50
101. 5 Centavos (Bro) 1924–27   3.00
102. 5 Centavos (Bro) 1920–22. Arms. Rev: Value   3.50
103. 4 Centavos (Bro) 1917, '19. Republic head.
      Rev: Value   1.50
104. 2 Centavos (Bro) 1918–21. Type of #102   1.50
105. 1 Centavo (Bro) 1917–22   1.25

NEW STATE 1926–

106. 10 Escudos 1928. Mounted knight. Rev: Shield
      with cross. (Battle of Ourique, fought in
      1139)   30.00

107. 10 Escudos 1932–48. Caravel. Rev: Arms over
      value   20.00
108. 5 Escudos 1932–51   7.50
109. 2½ Escudos 1932–51   5.00

110. 20 Escudos 1960. Rev: Arms. (500th anniver-
      sary, death of Prince Henry the Navigator)   50.00
111. 10 Escudos 1960   25.00
112. 5 Escudos 1960   40.00

113. 20 Escudos 1953. Seated figure. Rev: Shield
      with quinas cross over globe   25.00
114. 10 Escudos 1954–55. Sailing ship   15.00

115. 5 Escudos (C-N) 1963– . Sailing ship. Rev:
      Shield with quinas cross   .85
116. 2½ Escudos (C-N) 1963–   .40

117. 1 Escudo (N-Bro) 1927–68. Head of Republic.
      Rev: Arms and value   .50

118. 50 Centavos (N-Bro) 1927–68 .50

119. 20 Centavos (Bro) 1942–68. Quinas cross. Rev:
Value .30
120. 10 Centavos (Bro) 1942–69 .25

121. 20 Escudos 1966. Bridge. Rev: Arms (New Salazar Bridge at Lisbon) 10.00

122. 50 Escudos 1968. Bust of Pedro Alvares Cabral.
Rev: Arms. (500th anniversary of birth of
discoverer of Brazil) 15.00

123. 50 Escudos 1969. Vasco da Gama. Rev: Arms.
(500th anniversary of explorer's birth) 15.00

124.

124. 50 Escudos 1969. Marshal Carmona. Rev:
Arms. (100th anniversary of former president's birth) 17.50

125. 1 Escudo (Bro) 1969–79. Quinas cross. Rev:
Value. (N-Bra) 1981– . (Reduced) .25
126. 50 Centavos (Bro) 1969– .15
127. 20 Centavos (Bro) 1969–74 .20

128. 50 Escudos 1971. Tree. Rev: Quinas cross.
(125th anniversary of Bank of Portugal) 17.50
129. 10 Escudos (C-N) 1971–74. Type of #115 1.50

130. 10 Centavos (A) 1971–77. Type of #119, value in
numerals .20

131. 50 Escudos 1972. Angel standing within lyre.
Rev: Arms. (400th anniversary of publication
of "Os Lusiadas") 17.50

132. 250 Escudos 1976. Arms and value. Rev: Abstract
design, commemorative date (1974 Day of the
Revolution) 30.00

133. 100 Escudos 1979. Rev: Abstract design, commemorative date 10.00

445

PORTUGAL (continued)

134. 25 Escudos (C-N) 1977– . Republic head. Rev:
     Quinas cross, value   1.50

136.

135. 25 Escudos (C-N) 1977. Bust of Alexandre Her-
     culano. Rev: Quinas cross. (Centenary of
     death of Herculano, considered Portugal's
     greatest modern historian)   3.00
136. 5 Escudos (C-N) 1977. Alexandre Herculano   1.50
137. 2 Escudos (C-N) 1977. Alexandre Herculano   1.00

PORTUGUESE GUINEA

A Portuguese overseas province on the west coast of
Africa. It was discovered by the Portuguese in 1446, and
remained a colony until 1974, when it became the independent republic of Guinea-Bissau.

100 Centavos = 1 Escudo

1. 1 Escudo (N-Bro) 1933. Head of Republic.
   Rev: Arms and value   8.50
2. 50 Centavos (N-Bro) 1933   10.00
3. 20 Centavos (Bro) 1933. Head of Republic
   (young head). Rev: Value   4.00
4. 10 Centavos (Bro) 1933   2.00
5. 5 Centavos (Bro) 1933   7.50

6. 1 Escudo (Bro) 1946. Crowned shield. Rev:
   Value. (500th anniversary, discovery of Portuguese Guinea)   1.50
7. 50 Centavos (Bro) 1946   2.00
8. 20 Escudos 1952. Arms. Rev: Crowned shield   7.50
9. 10 Escudos 1952   4.00
10. 2½ Escudos (C-N) 1952   2.00
11. 50 Centavos (Bro) 1952. Crowned shield. Rev:
    Value   1.00

12. 10 Escudos (C-N) 1973. Type of #9   4.00
13. 5 Escudos (C-N) 1973   1.75
14. 1 Escudo (Bro) 1973. Type of #6   7.50
15. 20 Centavos (Bro) 1973. Type of #3   4.50
16. 10 Centavos (A) 1973   3.50

PORTUGUESE INDIA

This former Portuguese overseas province, made up of Goa, Daman and Diu, was held by the Portuguese for 400 years. In December 1961 India invaded and annexed this area.

16 Tangas = 1 Rupia
100 Centavos = 1 Escudo

1.	1 Rupia 1912. Head of Republic. Rev: Value in wreath	35.00
2.	1 Rupia 1935. Arms on cross. Rev: Shield over value	20.00
3.	½ Rupia 1936	25.00
4.	4 Tangas (C-N) 1934. Shield over date. Rev: Arms over value	15.00
5.	2 Tangas (C-N) 1934	12.50

6.	1 Tanga (Bro) 1934	12.50
7.	1 Rupia (S) 1947. Arms on cross over date. Rev: Crowned shield over value	17.50
8.	½ Rupia (C-N) 1947–52. Crowned shield over date. Rev: Value	5.00
9.	¼ Rupia (C-N) 1947–52	3.00
10.	1 Tanga (Bro) 1947	2.00
10a.	1 Tanga (Bro) 1952. (Smaller planchet)	2.50

NEW MONETARY SYSTEM   1958

11.	6 Escudos (C-N) 1959. Arms on cross. Shield	5.00
12.	3 Escudos (C-N) 1958, '59	3.00
13.	1 Escudo (C-N) 1958, '59	2.50
14.	60 Centavos (C-N) 1958	2.00

15.	30 Centavos (Bro) 1958–59. Shield. Rev: Value	2.00
16.	10 Centavos (Bro) 1958–61	1.50

PRINCE EDWARD ISLAND

A former crown colony in the Gulf of St. Lawrence, Prince Edward Island became a province of the Dominion of Canada in 1873.

1.	1 Cent (Bro) 1871. Head of Victoria. Rev: Trees	25.00

PUERTO RICO

A former possession of Spain, this island was ceded to the United States after the Spanish-American War. It is now a self-governing Commonwealth of the United States.

1.	1 Peso 1895. Young head of Alfonso XIII of Spain. Rev: Spanish arms	600.00
2.	40 Centavos 1896	400.00
3.	20 Centavos 1895	75.00
4.	10 Centavos 1896	75.00
5.	5 Centavos 1896	30.00

QATAR and DUBAI

In 1966, Qatar and Dubai set up a joint currency, the rial. Except for the joint currency they are separate nations.

Qatar is an independent sheikhdom on the Persian Gulf. Dubai, on the southern shore of the Persian Gulf, is one of seven semi-independent sheikhdoms in the United Arab Emirates (formerly Trucial States) in the region. Great Britain is responsible for the foreign affairs of both states.

1.	50 Dirhem (C-N) 1966. Gazelle. Rev: Inscription	2.00
2.	25 Dirhem (C-N) 1966, '69	1.25
3.	10 Dirhem (Bro) 1966	.75
4.	5 Dirhem (Bro) 1966; (A) 1969	.65

QATAR

Qatar declared its independence in 1971.

1.	50 Dirhem (C-N) 1973, '78. Native dhow. Rev: Value	1.50
2.	25 Dirhem (C-N) 1973, '76	1.00
3.	10 Dirhem (Bro) 1972, '73	.75
4.	5 Dirhem (Bro) 1973, '78	.50
5.	1 Dirhem (Bro) 1973	.35

REUNION

Reunion, an island in the Indian Ocean slightly more than 400 miles east of Madagascar, was settled by the French in 1646. It is an overseas department in the French Community.

100 Centimes = 1 Franc

2.

1.	1 Franc 1896. Mercury head. Rev: Value	75.00
2.	50 Centimes 1896	65.00

3.	2 Francs (A) 1948–73	2.50
4.	1 Franc (A) 1948–73	1.00

5.	5 Francs (A-Bro) 1955–73	1.50
6.	100 Francs (N) 1964–73. Liberty head with winged cap. Rev: Arms	3.50

7.	50 Francs (N) 1962–73	4.00
8.	20 Francs (A-Bro) 1955–73	2.50
9.	10 Francs (A-Bro) 1955–73	2.00

RHODESIA AND NYASALAND

The Central African Federation of Rhodesia and Nyasaland, 1953–1963, comprised Southern Rhodesia (which became Rhodesia, a republic, in 1970 and is now Zimbabwe), Northern Rhodesia (Zambia since 1964) and Nyasaland (Malawi since 1963). (See these under separate listings.)

12 Pence = 1 Shilling
20 Shillings = 1 Pound

SOUTHERN RHODESIA

GEORGE V 1910–1936

1.	½ Crown (2½ Shillings) 1932–36. Crowned bust. Rev: Crowned arms	35.00

2:	2 Shillings 1932, '34–36. Rev: Antelope	60.00
3.	1 Shilling 1932–36. Rev: Stonebird	25.00

4.	6 Pence 1932–36. Rev: Axes	30.00
5.	3 Pence 1932–36. Rev: Three spears	25.00

6.	1 Penny (C-N) 1934–36. Crowned rose. Rev: Value. (Center hole)	15.00
7.	½ Penny (C-N) 1934, '36	20.00

GEORGE VI 1936–52

NOTE: Coins issued after 1948 drop "Emperor" from obverse legend

8.	½ Crown 1937–46. Crowned head. Rev: Crowned arms	35.00
8a.	½ Crown (C-N) 1947–52	15.00
9.	2 Shillings 1937–46. Rev: Antelope	35.00
9a.	2 Shillings (C-N) 1947–52	10.00
10.	1 Shilling 1937–46. Rev: Stonebird	30.00
10a.	1 Shilling (C-N) 1947–52	10.00
11.	6 Pence 1937–46 Rev: Axes	20.00
11a.	6 Pence (C-N) 1947–52	7.50
12.	3 Pence 1937–46. Rev: Three spears	12.50
12a.	3 Pence (C-N) 1947–52	6.50
13.	1 Penny (C-N) 1937–42; (Bro) 1942–52. Rev: Crowned rose	5.00
14.	½ Penny (C-N) 1938–39; (Bro) 1942–52	6.00

ELIZABETH II 1952–

15.	Crown 1953. Head. Rev: Portrait of Rhodes and arms. (Rhodes Commemorative Crown)	30.00
16.	½ Crown (C-N) 1954. Crowned head. Rev: Type of #8	85.00

17.	2 Shillings (C-N) 1954. Rev: Type of #9	350.00
18.	1 Penny (Bro) 1954. Rev: Type of #6	85.00
19.	½ Penny (Bro) 1954	50.00

RHODESIA AND NYASALAND

20. ½ Crown (C-N) 1955–57. Head. Rev: Arms   20.00

21. 2 Shillings (C-N) 1955–57. Rev: Eagle holding fish in talons   12.50
22. 1 Shilling (C-N) 1955–57. Rev: Antelope   7.50

23. 6 Pence (C-N) 1955–63. Rev: Lioness   5.00
24. 3 Pence (C-N) 1955–64. Rev: Flower   2.00

25. 1 Penny (Bro) 1955–63. Two elephants, crown above. Rev: Value and ornaments. (Center hole)   2.00
26. ½ Penny (Bro) 1955–64. Two giraffes and crown. Rev: Type of #30. (Center hole)   1.25

RHODESIA

27.

NOTE: In Nos. 27–30, reverses show dual values of sterling and decimal systems

27. ½ Crown or 25 Cents (C-N) 1964. New portrait of Queen Elizabeth with coronet. Rev: Antelope   10.00

28. 2 Shillings or 20 Cents (C-N) 1964. Rev: Stonebird   4.00
29. 1 Shilling or 10 Cents (C-N) 1964. Rev: Arms   2.50
30. 6 Pence or 5 Cents (C-N) 1964. Rev: Lily   1.50

31. 3 Cents (C-N) 1968. Rev: Three spearheads   1.50

REPUBLIC

32. 2½ Cents (C-N) 1970. Arms. Rev: Spears   1.00
33. 1 Cent (Bro) 1970–76. Arms. Rev: Value   .35
34. ½ Cent (Bro) 1970–72. Arms. Rev: Value   .35

35. 5 Cents (C-N) 1973. Rev: Lily   .65
35a. 5 Cents (C-N) 1975–76. Smaller arms, inscription change   .65
36. 25 Cents (C-N) 1975–77. Rev: Antelope   3.00
37. 20 Cents (C-N) 1975–76. Rev: Stonebird   2.00
38. 10 Cents (C-N) 1975–76. Rev: Value   1.50

RUMANIA

In the 19th century Rumania was formed from the Turkish provinces of Moldavia and Walachia. The country suffered heavily in both world wars. After World War II Rumania became a "People's Republic" in the Russian orbit.

100 Bani = 1 Leu

CAROL I 1866–1914

1.	50 Lei (G) 1906. Bust in uniform. Rev: Carol on horseback	500.00
2.	25 Lei (G) 1906. Bust in uniform. Rev: Crowned eagle	375.00
3.	12½ Lei (G) 1906	250.00
4.	5 Lei 1880–84, 1901. Head. Rev: Crowned arms on mantle	50.00

5.	5 Lei 1906. Young head. Rev: Older bearded head. (40th jubilee)	125.00
6.	2 Lei 1881–1901, 1910–14. Bearded head	10.00

7.	1 Leu 1870–1901, 1906, 1910–14	8.50

8.	50 Bani 1881–1901. Rev: Value in wreath	5.00
8a.	50 Bani 1910–14. Rev: Crowned olive branch	5.00
9.	20 Bani (C-N) 1900 Crown. Rev: Value	8.50
9a.	20 Bani (C-N) 1905, '06. Center hole	3.50
10.	10 Bani (C-N) 1900. Type of #9	3.50

10a.	10 Bani (C-N) 1905, '06. Center hole	3.00
11.	5 Bani (C-N) 1900. Type of #9	2.50
11a.	5 Bani (C-N) 1905, '06. Center hole	2.50
12.	2 Bani (C) 1900. Head. Rev: Arms	3.00
13.	1 Ban (C) 1900	2.50

FERDINAND I 1914–27

14.	25 Lei (G) 1922. Crowned bust of Ferdinand. Rev: Crowned bust of Queen Marie	400.00
15.	20 Lei (G) 1922. Laureated head. Rev: Arms	400.00

16.	2 Lei (C-N) 1924. Arms. Rev: Value	3.00
17.	1 Leu (C-N) 1924	3.00
18.	50 Bani (A) 1921. Center hole	5.00
19.	25 Bani (A) 1921. Center hole	5.00

MIHAI I 1927–30 (First Reign)

20.	20 Lei (N-Bra) 1930. Head. Rev: Four figures	10.00
21.	5 Lei (N-Bra) 1930. Head. Rev: Crowned arms	8.50

RUMANIA (continued)

CAROL II 1930–40

22.	250 Lei 1935. Head. Rev: Arms	40.00
23.	250 Lei 1939–40. Head to right. Rev: Value	20.00
24.	100 Lei (S) 1932	35.00
25.	100 Lei (N) 1936–38. Head to left. Rev: Arms	12.50

26.	50 Lei (N) 1937–38. Helmeted head	10.00
27.	20 Lei (N-Bra) 1930. Bare head	8.50
28.	10 Lei (N-Bra) 1930	5.00
29.	1 Leu (Bra) 1938–41. Crown. Rev: Value	1.00

MIHAI I 1941–47 (Second Reign)

30.	500 Lei 1941. King kneeling	25.00
31.	500 Lei 1944. Bare head. Rev: Arms	12.50
31a.	500 Lei (Bra) 1945	10.00
32.	200 Lei 1942. Head. Rev: Arms	10.00
32a.	200 Lei (Bra) 1945. Head. Rev: Value	8.50
33.		
	100,000 Lei 1946	25.00
34.	25,000 Lei 1946	15.00

35.	10,000 Lei (Bra) 1947	15.00
36.	2,000 Lei (Bra) 1946	7.50
37.	500 Lei (A) 1946	15.00

38.	5 Lei (A) 1947. Head. Rev: Value	12.50
39.	2 Lei (Bro) 1947. Arms. Rev: Value	5.00
40.	1 Leu (Bra) 1947	5.00
41.	50 Bani (Bra) 1947. Crown. Rev: Value	5.00

PEOPLE'S REPUBLIC 1947–

42.	20 Lei (A) 1951. Arms. Rev: Value	35.00

43.	5 Lei (A) 1948–51	5.00
44.	2 Lei (A-Bro) 1950–51; (A) 1951, '52. Agricultural products. Rev: Value	5.00
45.	1 Leu (A-Bro) 1949–51; (A) 1951, '52. Oil derrick. Rev: Value	4.00
46.	50 Bani (C-N) 1955–56. Arms. Rev: Workman	3.00
47.	25 Bani (C-N) 1952–55. Rev: Value	2.50
48.	10 Bani (C-N) 1952–56	1.00
49.	5 Bani (A-Bro) 1952–57	2.00
50.	3 Bani (A-Bro) 1952–53	1.00
51.	1 Ban (A-Bro) 1952–54	.65

52.	3 Lei (N-St) 1963. Arms. Rev: Oil refinery	3.00

53.	1 Leu (N-St) 1963. Rev: Tractor in field	2.50
54.	25 Bani (N-St) 1960	1.50
55.	15 Bani (N-St) 1960	1.00
56.	5 Bani (N-St) 1963	.65

57.	3 Lei (N-St) 1966– . Type of #52, with obverse inscription REPUBLICA SOCIALISTA ROMANIA	1.50
58.	1 Leu (N-St) 1966. Type of #53, new obverse inscription	1.00
59.	25 Bani (N-St) 1966. Type of #54, new obverse inscription	1.00
60.	15 Bani (N-St) 1966; (A) 1975. Type of #55, new obverse inscription	.50
61.	5 Bani (N-St) 1966; (A) 1975. Type of #56, new obverse inscription	.50

453

RUSSIA (U.S.S.R.)

Only one quarter of Russia lies in Europe, yet it is the largest country in that continent. Russia was ruled by the Romanov dynasty from 1613 to 1917. The Communist regime came into power in November 1917, changing the country's name to the Union of Soviet Socialist Republics.

100 Kopecks = 1 Rouble
10 Roubles = 1 Chervonetz

PETER I ("the Great")   1689–1725

1.	1 Rouble 1704–06. Young boy bust in armor. Rev: Eagle	400.00
2.	1 Rouble 1707–25. Laureate head	300.00

3.	½ Rouble 1699–1725	75.00
4.	¼ Rouble 1701–13	50.00
5.	2 Kopecks (C) 1723–25. Arms	30.00
6.	1 Kopeck (C) 1703–19. St. George	20.00

CATHERINE I   1725–27

7.	1 Rouble 1725–27. Bust. Rev: Eagle	200.00
8.	½ Rouble 1726–27	100.00
9.	¼ Rouble 1726	60.00
10.	5 Kopecks (C) 1726–27. Arms. Rev: Cross	25.00
11.	1 Kopeck (C) 1726–27. St. George	20.00

PETER II   1727–30

12.	1 Rouble 1727–29. Armored bust. Rev: Monogram	200.00

13.	½ Rouble 1727–29	100.00
14.	¼ Rouble 1727	50.00
15.	5 Kopecks (C) 1728–30. Arms. Rev: Cross	35.00
16.	1 Kopeck (C) 1728–29. St. George. Rev: Value	20.00

ANNA   1730–40

17.	1 Rouble 1730–40. Bust. Rev: Eagle	175.00

RUSSIA (continued)

18.	½ Rouble 1731–40	50.00
19.	¼ Rouble 1730–40	40.00
20.	½ Kopeck (C) 1730–40. Arms. Rev: Value	25.00

PETER III   1761–62

IVAN III   1740–41

21.   1 Rouble 1741. Laureate bust. Rev: Eagle   750.00

27a.   1 Rouble 1762. Bust   300.00

ELIZABETH   1741–61

CATHERINE II ("the Great")   1762–96

22.	1 Rouble 1741–61. Bust. Rev: Eagle	150.00
23.	½ Rouble 1742–61	100.00
24.	¼ Rouble 1743–58	25.00
25.	5 Kopecks (C) 1757–61. Arms. Rev: Value	25.00

28.   1 Rouble 1762–96. Crowned bust. Rev: Eagle   100.00

26.	2 Kopecks (C) 1757–61. St. George	20.00
27.	1 Kopeck (C) 1757–61. St. George	17.50

29.	½ Rouble 1762–96	75.00
30.	¼ Rouble 1764–96	50.00

RUSSIA (continued)

35.	1 Rouble 1802–25. Double eagle. Rev: Crowned inscription in wreath	40.00
36.	½ Rouble 1802–25	40.00
37.	¼ Rouble 1802–10	80.00
38.	20 Kopecks 1810–25	10.00
39.	10 Kopecks 1802–25	10.00
40.	5 Kopecks 1811–25	10.00

31.	5 Kopecks (C) 1766–80. Arms (Siberia). Rev: Monogram	50.00
32.	2 Kopecks (C) 1764–80	30.00
33.	1 Kopeck (C) 1766–80	25.00

PAUL I   1796–1801

41.	5 Kopecks (C) 1802–10. Double eagle. Rev: Value	30.00
42.	2 Kopecks (C) 1802–25	7.50
43.	1 Kopeck (C) 1804–25	10.00
44.	½ Kopeck (C) 1804–25	12.50
45.	¼ Kopeck (C) 1803–10	65.00

34.	1 Rouble 1791–1801. Tablet. Rev: Monogram	100.00

RUSSIA (continued)

NICHOLAS I   1825–55

46. 1½ Roubles 1835–36. Head of Czar. Rev: Heads
     of Czarina and 7 children   RARE
47. 1½ Roubles 1839. Head of Alexander I. Rev:
     Memorial   1250.00

50.	1 Rouble 1839. Head of Alexander I. Rev: Borodino monument	275.00
51.	½ Rouble 1826–55. Type of #48	15.00
52.	25 Kopecks 1827–55	10.00
53.	20 Kopecks 1826–55	8.00
54.	10 Kopecks 1826–55	8.00
55.	5 Kopecks 1826–55	7.50
56.	10 Kopecks (C) 1830–39	35.00
57.	5 Kopecks (C) 1830–39, '49–55	12.50
58.	3 Kopecks (C) 1849–55	7.50
59.	2 Kopecks (C) 1826–39, '49–55	5.00
60.	1 Kopeck (C) 1826–39	10.00
61.	½ Kopeck (C) 1827–28	12.50

48. 1 Rouble 1826–55. Double eagle. Rev: Inscription on wreath   40.00

49. 1 Rouble 1834. Type of #47   200.00

62.	3 Kopecks (C) 1839–47. Monogram. Rev: Value	15.00
63.	2 Kopecks (C) 1839–47	7.50
64.	1 Kopeck (C) 1839–55	5.00
65.	½ Kopeck (C) 1839–55	6.00
66.	¼ Kopeck (C) 1839–53	8.00

RUSSIA (continued)

ALEXANDER II 1855–81

67.	1 Rouble 1859. Head of Nicholas I. Rev: Memorial	200.00
68.	1 Rouble 1856–81	30.00
69.	½ Rouble 1856–81	17.50
70.	25 Kopecks 1856–81	15.00
71.	20 Kopecks 1856–81	7.50
72.	15 Kopecks 1860–81	5.00
73.	10 Kopecks 1856–81	5.00
74.	5 Kopecks 1856–81	8.00
75.	5 Kopecks (C) 1856–81	10.00
76.	3 Kopecks (C) 1856–81	7.50
77.	2 Kopecks (C) 1856–81	5.00
78.	1 Kopeck (C) 1855–81. Monogram	3.00
79.	½ Kopeck (C) 1855–81	6.00
80.	¼ Kopeck (C) 1855–81	6.50

ALEXANDER III 1881–94

81.	1 Rouble 1883. Head. Rev: Regalia. (Coronation)	80.00
82.	1 Rouble 1882–85. Double eagle. Rev: Value	30.00
82a.	½ Rouble 1882–85.	80.00
83.	1 Rouble 1886–94. Head. Rev: Double eagle	65.00
84.	½ Rouble 1886–94	30.00
85.	25 Kopecks 1882–94	35.00
86.	20 Kopecks 1882–93. Type of #82	5.00
87.	15 Kopecks 1882–93	4.00
88.	10 Kopecks 1882–94	3.00
89.	5 Kopecks 1882–93	3.00
90.	3 Kopecks (C) 1882–94	6.00
91.	2 Kopecks (C) 1882–94	4.00
92.	1 Kopeck (C) 1882–94	2.00
93.	½ Kopeck (C) 1881–94. Monogram	5.00
94.	¼ Kopeck (C) 1881–94	5.00

NICHOLAS II 1894–1917

95.	10 Roubles (G) 1895–1911. Head. Rev: Double eagle	175.00
96.	5 Roubles (G) 1895–1911	85.00

97.	1 Rouble 1896. Head. Rev: Regalia in wreath. (Coronation)	100.00

98.	1 Rouble 1895–1915. Type of #96	30.00
99.	½ Rouble 1895–1914	15.00
100.	¼ Rouble 1895–1901	20.00
101.	20 Kopecks 1901–17. Double Eagle. Rev: Value	3.00
102.	15 Kopecks 1896–1916	3.00
103.	10 Kopecks 1895–1916	2.00
104.	5 Kopecks (S) 1897–1915; (C) 1911–16	3.00
105.	3 Kopecks (C) 1895–1916	2.50
106.	2 Kopecks (C) 1895–1916	2.50
107.	1 Kopeck (C) 1895–1916	1.25
108.	½ Kopeck (C) 1894–1916. Monogram	1.50
109.	¼ Kopeck (C) 1894–1916	3.00

COMMEMORATIVE ROUBLES

110.	1 Rouble 1898. Head of Alexander I. Rev: Monument	450.00

458

111. 1 Rouble 1912. Head of Alexander III. Rev:
Statue of Alexander III   1000.00

115. 1 Rouble 1924. Two workers. Rev: Hammer
and sickle in wreath   35.00
116. 50 Kopecks 1921–22. Type of #114   15.00

112. 1 Rouble 1912. Crowned double eagle. Rev:
Inscription. (Centenary of victory over
Napoleon)   350.00

117. 50 Kopecks 1924–27. Blacksmith. Rev: Type of
#115   12.50

118. 20 Kopecks 1921–30. Value in wreath. Rev:
Hammer and sickle in wreath   6.50
119. 15 Kopecks 1921–30   5.00
120. 10 Kopecks 1921–30   4.00

113. 1 Rouble 1913. Heads of Nicholas II and
Michael Feodorovich. Rev: Crowned double
eagle. (Tercentenary of the Romanov dynasty)   50.00

121. 20 Kopecks (C-N) 1931–34. Hammer and sickle
in wreath. Rev: Workman holding shield with
value   4.00
122. 15 Kopecks (C-N) 1931–34   3.50
123. 10 Kopecks (C-N) 1931–34   3.00

U.S.S.R. 1917–

124. 20 Kopecks (C-N) 1935–57. Hammer and sickle
in wreath. Rev: Value in panel inside of
wreath   3.00

114. 1 Rouble 1921–24. Value in star. Rev: Hammer
and sickle   40.00

125. 15 Kopecks (C-N) 1935–57   3.00
126. 10 Kopecks (C-N) 1935–57   2.00

459

127. 5 Kopecks (A-Bro) 1926–57. Hammer and
     sickle in wreath. Rev: Value in wreath 4.00
128. 3 Kopecks (A-Bro) 1926–57 .... 3.00
129. 2 Kopecks (A-Bro) 1926–57 .... 2.00
130. 1 Kopeck (A-Bro) 1926–57 .... 2.50

NOTE: Varying numbers of ribbons on wreaths of above
issues signify the number of states in the Soviet Union at
the time of issue

NEW STANDARD

1 New Rouble = 10 Old Roubles

131. 1 Rouble (C-N) 1961– . Hammer and sickle in
     wreath. Rev: Value in wreath 3.00
132. 50 Kopecks (C-N) 1961– 1.50
133. 20 Kopecks (C-N) 1961– .... .75
134. 15 Kopecks (C-N) 1961– .... .75
135. 10 Kopecks (C-N) 1961– .... .50
136. 5 Kopecks (A-Bro) 1961– .... .50
137. 3 Kopecks (A-Bro) 1961– .... .50
138. 2 Kopecks (A-Bro) 1961– .... .30
139. 1 Kopeck (A-Bro) 1961– .... .25

140. 1 Rouble (C-N-Z) 1965. Statue of soldier.
     Rev: Arms. (20th anniversary of end of
     World War II) 7.50

141. 1 Rouble (C-N-Z) 1967. Lenin standing, ham-
     mer and sickle in background. Rev: Arms.
     (50th anniversary of Socialist Revolution) 5.00
142. 50 Kopecks (C-N-Z) 1967 .... 2.50

143. 20 Kopecks (C-N-Z) 1967. Cruiser *Aurora* 2.00
144. 15 Kopecks (C-N-Z) 1967. Man and woman
     holding hammer and sickle 1.50

145. 10 Kopecks (C-N-Z) 1967. Rocket 1.25

146. 1 Rouble (C-N-Z) 1970. Head of Lenin. Rev:
     Arms. (100th anniversary of birth) 5.00
147. 10 Roubles (G) 1975. Farmer sowing seeds; fac-
     tory and rising sun in background (same de-
     sign as 1923 issue) 150.00

148. 1 Rouble (C-N-Z) 1975. Statue of "Mother-
     land." Rev: Arms, value. (30th anniversary of
     end of World War II) 7.50
149. 1 Rouble (C-N-Z) 1977. Lenin. (60th anniver-
     sary of Socialist Revolution) 6.50

RUSSIA (continued)

NOTE: Nos. 150–92 commemorate the 1980 Moscow
Olympic Games

150. 150 Roubles (Pl) 1977. Building within wreath
over Olympic symbol. Rev: Arms   350.00

151. 100 Roubles (G) 1977. Arms. Rev: Stylized emblem over Olympic symbol   250.00

152. 10 Roubles 1977. Map of Soviet Union. Rev:
Arms   20.00

153.

154.   155.

153. 10 Roubles 1977. Kremlin. Rev: Arms   20.00
154. 5 Roubles 1977. City view of Kiev. Rev: Arms   10.00
155. 5 Roubles 1977. City view of Leningrad. Rev:
Arms   10.00

156.   157.

156. 5 Roubles 1977. City view of Minsk. Rev:
Arms   10.00
157. 5 Roubles 1977. City view of Tallinn. Rev:
Arms   10.00
158. 1 Rouble (C-N) 1977. Stylized emblem over
Olympic symbol. Rev: Arms   5.00
159. 150 Roubles (Pl) 1978–79. Discus thrower. Rev:
Arms   350.00
160. 100 Roubles (G) 1978. Sports complex. Rev:
Arms   250.00

161. 100 Roubles (G) 1978. Athletic stadium. Rev:
Arms   250.00

162. 10 Roubles 1978. Cyclist. Rev: Arms   20.00
163. 10 Roubles 1978. Rowers. Rev: Arms   20.00

461

177.

164.	10 Roubles 1978. Horsemen. Rev: Arms	20.00
165.	10 Roubles 1978. Athlete over Olympic stadium. Rev: Arms	20.00

176.	10 Roubles 1979. Boxers. Rev: Arms	20.00
177.	10 Roubles 1979. Wrestlers. Rev: Arms	20.00

166.	5 Roubles 1978. Sprinter. Rev: Arms	10.00
167.	5 Roubles 1978. Swimmer. Rev: Arms	10.00
168.	5 Roubles 1978. Athlete, stadium. Rev: Arms	10.00
169.	5 Roubles 1978. Steeplechase. Rev: Arms	10.00
170.	1 Rouble (C-N) 1978. Rev: Arms	5.00
171.	150 Roubles (Pl) 1979. Quadriga. Rev: Arms	350.00
171a.	150 Roubles (Pl) 1979. Ancient Greek marble statue of wrestlers. Rev: Arms	350.00
172.	100 Roubles (G) 1979. Stadium. Rev: Arms	250.00

178.   10 Roubles 1979. Standing athlete. Rev: Arms   20.00

173.	100 Roubles (G) 1979. Arms. Rev: Universal Sports Hall, Moscow	250.00
174.	10 Roubles 1979. Basketball players. Rev: Arms	20.00
175.	10 Roubles 1979. Volleyball players. Rev: Arms	20.00

179.	5 Roubles 1979. Weightlifter. Rev: Arms	10.00
180.	5 Roubles 1979. Hammer throw. Rev: Arms	10.00
181.	1 Rouble (C-N) 1979. Moscow skyscrapers. Rev: Arms	5.00
182.	1 Rouble (C-N) 1979. Rev: Arms	5.00
183.	150 Roubles (Pl) 1980. Nude athletes marching. Rev: Arms	300.00
184.	100 Roubles (G) 1980. Olympic flame. Rev: Arms	250.00
185.	10 Roubles 1980. Wrestlers. Rev: Arms	20.00
186.	10 Roubles 1980. Tug-of-war. Rev: Arms	20.00
187.	5 Roubles 1980. Archer. Rev: Arms	10.00
188.	5 Roubles 1980. Gymnast. Rev: Arms	10.00
189.	5 Roubles 1980. Horsemen. Rev: Arms	10.00
190.	5 Roubles 1980. Standing athlete. Rev: Arms	10.00
191.	1 Rouble (C-N) 1980. Equestrian figure. Rev: Arms	5.00
192.	1 Rouble (C-N) 1980. Olympic flame. Rev: Arms	5.00

176.

193.   1 Rouble (C-N) 1981. Arms. Rev: Cosmonaut.
     (20th anniversary of first manned space flight)   5.00

194.   1 Rouble (C-N) 1981. Handshake vignette.
     Rev: Arms. (Russian-Bulgarian friendship)   5.00

RWANDA

Formerly part of the Belgian U.N. Trusteeship of Ruanda-Urundi, it became an independent republic in July 1962.

1. 10 Francs (C-N) 1964. Head of Kayibanda. Rev:
   Arms 2.00
2. 5 Francs (Bro) 1964, '65 .... 1.25
3. 1 Franc (C-N) 1964, '65 .... .75

4. 1 Franc (A) 1969. Head of Kayibanda. Rev:
   Arms .... .35

5. 2 Francs (A) 1970. Native pouring coffee. Rev:
   Arms (F.A.O. coin plan) 2.00

6. ½ Franc (A) 1970. Inscription. Rev: Value .... .65

7. 200 Francs 1972. Two men with flag. Rev: Farmer
   in rice field. (F.A.O. coin plan; 10th anniversary of independence) 17.50

8. 10 Francs (C-N) 1974. Plant. Rev: Arms 2.00

9. 5 Francs (Bro) 1974–77. Coffee plant. Rev:
   Arms 1.00
10. 1 Franc (A) 1974, '77. Rice plant. Rev: Arms .50

11. 50 Francs (Bra) 1977. Tree branch. Rev: Arms
    and coffee plant 3.00

12. 20 Francs (Bra) 1977. Palm leaves and banana.
    Rev: Arms 2.00

RWANDA AND BURUNDI

A common currency was issued by the two provinces during the transitional period 1960–64.

1.   1 Franc (Bra) 1960–64. Lion. Rev. Value   1.50

SAARLAND

Part of the French Zone of Occupation after World War II, this territory, bounded by France and Luxembourg, was returned to Germany in 1959 and is now a state within the German Federal Republic.

1.   50 Franken (A-Bro) 1954. Factory, smokestacks,
      shield and coalpit. Rev: Value   15.00
2.   20 Franken (A-Bro) 1954   5.00

3.   10 Franken (A-Bro) 1954   5.00

4.   100 Franken (C-N) 1955. Arms within wheel-
      shaped design. Rev: Type of #1   10.00

ST. HELENA

This island in the South Atlantic is a British colony.

1.   Half Penny (C) 1821. Arms. Rev: Value   7.50

2.   25 Pence (C-N) 1973. Queen Elizabeth II. Rev:
      Sailing ship. (300th anniversary of charter)   2.00
2a.   25 Pence (S) 1973. Proof   30.00
3.   25 Pence (C-N) 1977. Rev: View of island.
      (Queen's Silver Jubilee)   3.00
3a.   25 Pence (S) 1977. Proof   30.00

4.   1 Crown (C-N) 1978. Rev: Crowned cameo
      portrait. (Coronation Silver Jubilee)   3.00
4a.   1 Crown (S) 1978. Proof   30.00
5.   25 Pence (C-N) 1980. Rev: Cameo portrait of
      Queen Mother Elizabeth over island view.
      (Queen Mother's 80th birthday)   3.00
5a.   25 Pence (S) 1980. Proof   30.00
6.   25 Pence (C-N) 1981. Rev: Crowned cameo por-
      traits of Prince Charles and Lady Diana.
      (Royal couple's marriage)   3.00
6a.   25 Pence (S) 1981. Proof   40.00

465

ST. PIERRE and MIQUELON

A group of eight small islands south of Newfoundland. This is the only possession of France in North America today. The islands were first settled by the French about 1660.

100 Centimes = 1 Franc

1.	2 Francs (A) 1948. Head of the Republic. Rev: Fishing vessel	7.50
2.	1 Franc (A) 1948	5.00

EL SALVADOR

After three centuries of Spanish rule, this Central American country declared its independence of Spain in 1821. For a while Salvador was part of Mexico and then of the Central American Federation, eventually becoming an independent republic.

Due to the scarcity of coinage in Salvador during the early 19th century, the arms of Salvador were sometimes countermarked on whatever coins came into the country.

100 Centavos = 1 Peso or 1 Colon

1.	1 Peso 1892. Flag. Rev: Arms	175.00
2.	50 Centavos 1892	75.00

3.	1 Peso 1892–1914. Head of Columbus. Rev: Arms	25.00
4.	50 Centavos 1892–94	20.00

5.	20 Centavos 1892. Arms. Rev: Value in wreath	40.00
6.	10 Centavos 1892	125.00
7.	5 Centavos 1892, '93	17.50

8.	25 Centavos 1911. Arms. Rev: Value in wreath	12.50
9.	10 Centavos 1911	7.50
10.	5 Centavos 1911	10.00

11.	25 Centavos 1914. New arms. Rev: Value	12.50
12.	10 Centavos 1914	7.50
13.	5 Centavos 1914	6.50

14.	10 Centavos (C-N) 1921–72. Head of Francisco Morazan. Rev: Value	1.00
14a.	10 Centavos (German silver) 1952	2.00
15.	5 Centavos (C-N) 1915–	1.00
15a.	5 Centavos (German silver) 1944–52	1.50
16.	3 Centavos (C-N) 1889–1915	7.50
17.	1 Centavo (C-N) 1889–1940; (Bro) 1942–	1.25
18.	25 Centavos 1943, '44	6.50

19.	1 Colon 1925. Busts of Pedro de Alvarado and Pres. Quinonez. Rev: Arms in wreath. (400th anniversary of San Salvador)	250.00

20.	50 Centavos 1953. Head of Pres. Morazan. Rev: Value in wreath	7.50
21.	25 Centavos 1953	4.00

22.	50 Centavos (N) 1970. Head of Morazan. Rev: Value	1.00
23.	25 Centavos (N) 1970–77	.50
24.	3 Centavos (N-Bro) 1974. Type of #16	1.50
25.	2 Centavos (N-Bro) 1974	1.00

26.	250 Colones (G) 1977. Arms. Rev: Sun over mountains. (18th Annual Governors' Assembly)	350.00
27.	25 Colones (S) 1977. Type of #26.	35.00

SAN MARINO

A tiny republic in Italy, 38 square miles in size, which, according to traditional accounts, has maintained its freedom since the fourth century A.D.

100 Centesimi = 1 Lira

1.	5 Lire 1898. Standing saint. Rev: Crowned arms	275.00
2.	2 Lire 1898–1906. Rev: Value in wreath	65.00
3.	1 Lira 1898–1906	35.00
4.	50 Centesimi 1898	30.00
5.	10 Centesimi (C) 1875, '93–94	15.00
6.	5 Centesimi (C) 1864, '69, '94	10.00

7.	20 Lire (G) 1925. Three towers. Rev: Standing saint	1250.00
8.	10 Lire (G) 1925	850.00

9.	20 Lire 1931–38. Crown over three feathers. Rev: Half figure of St. Marinus	200.00

10.	10 Lire 1931–38. Crowned arms. Rev: Female half figure	25.00

11.	5 Lire 1931–38. Helmeted head. Rev: Plow	20.00
12.	10 Centesimi (Bro) 1935–38. Crowned arms. Rev: Value	8.50
13.	5 Centesimi (Bro) 1935–38	5.00

14.	500 Lire 1972. Three towers. Rev: Mother holding child	25.00

15.	100 Lire (St) 1972. Towers with feathers. Rev: Saint Marinus in boat	5.00

16.	50 Lire (St) 1972. Rev: Roman lady kneeling to Saint Marinus	5.00

17.	20 Lire (A-Bro) 1972. Rev: Garibaldi climbing Mount Titano	3.00
18.	10 Lire (A) 1972. Rev: Cow nursing calf	2.50

19.	5 Lire (A) 1972. Bust of Saint Marinus facing left. Rev: Value over arms	2.00
20.	2 Lire (A) 1972. Bust facing right	2.00
21.	1 Lira (A) 1972. Bust facing left	2.00

22.

22. 500 Lire 1973. Crowned arms in shield. Rev:
Woman holding dove   20.00

23. 100 Lire (St) 1973. Crowned arms in shield. Rev:
Ship passing Pillars of Hercules   2.50

24. 50 Lire (St) 1973. Rev: Woman holding sword
and balance   2.50
25. 20 Lire (A-Bro) 1973. Rev: Man carrying old
man and child   2.50

26. 10 Lire (A) 1973. Rev: Man with shield and
torch   2.00
27. 5 Lire (A) 1973. Rev: Five faces in boat   2.00

28. 2 Lire (A) 1973. Rev: Pelican feeding young
with blood   1.50
29. 1 Lira (A) 1973. Rev: Woman with flag   1.50

30. 2 Scudi (G) 1974. Arms. Rev: Saint Marinus   175.00
31. 1 Scudo (G) 1974   85.00

32.

32. 500 Lire 1974. Three towers with feathers. Rev:
Two doves   17.50

33. 100 Lire (St) 1974. Rev: Goat   2.50

34. 50 Lire (St) 1974. Rev: Rooster   2.50
35. 20 Lire (A-Bro) 1974. Rev: Lobster   2.50

36. 10 Lire (A) 1974. Rev: Bee. (F.A.O. coin plan)   1.00
37. 5 Lire (A) 1974. Rev: Porcupine   2.00

38. 2 Lire (A) 1974. Rev: Ladybug   1.50
39. 1 Lira (A) 1974. Rev: Ant   1.50

40. 500 Lire 1975. Arms. Rev: Three gulls   15.00

41. 100 Lire (St) 1975. Rev: Dog and cat   3.00

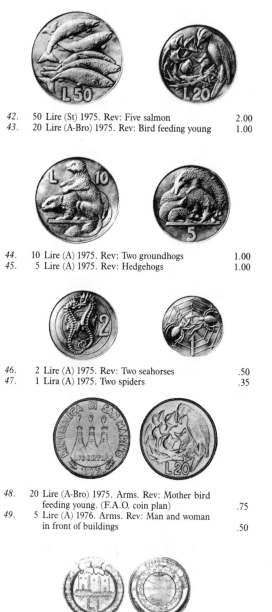

42. 50 Lire (St) 1975. Rev: Five salmon 2.00
43. 20 Lire (A-Bro) 1975. Rev: Bird feeding young 1.00

44. 10 Lire (A) 1975. Rev: Two groundhogs 1.00
45. 5 Lire (A) 1975. Rev: Hedgehogs 1.00

46. 2 Lire (A) 1975. Rev: Two seahorses .50
47. 1 Lira (A) 1975. Two spiders .35

48. 20 Lire (A-Bro) 1975. Arms. Rev: Mother bird
feeding young. (F.A.O. coin plan) .75
49. 5 Lire (A) 1976. Arms. Rev: Man and woman
in front of buildings .50

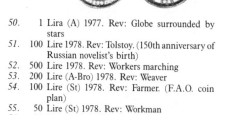

50. 1 Lira (A) 1977. Rev: Globe surrounded by
stars .50
51. 100 Lire 1978. Rev: Tolstoy. (150th anniversary of
Russian novelist's birth) 25.00
52. 500 Lire 1978. Rev: Workers marching 20.00
53. 200 Lire (A-Bro) 1978. Rev: Weaver 2.00
54. 100 Lire (St) 1978. Rev: Farmer. (F.A.O. coin
plan) 2.50
55. 50 Lire (St) 1978. Rev: Workman 1.00
56. 20 Lire (A-Bro) 1978. Rev: Workman .50
57. 10 Lire (A) 1978. Rev: Workman .40
58. 5 Lire (A) 1978. Rev: Street sweeper .30
59. 2 Lire (A) 1978. Rev: Lathe operator .25
60. 1 Lira (A) 1978 .20

61. 1000 Lire 1979. Rev: Female head against mountain backdrop. (European unity) 25.00
62. 500 Lire 1979. Rev: Biga 20.00
63. 200 Lire (A-Bro) 1979. (F.A.O. coin plan) 2.00
64. 100 Lire (St) 1979 2.50
65. 50 Lire (St) 1979. Rev: Bell 1.00
66. 20 Lire (A-Bro) 1979 .50
67. 10 Lire (A) 1979 .50
68. 5 Lire (A) 1979 .40
69. 2 Lire (A) 1979 .35
70. 1 Lira (A) 1979 .30
71. 1000 Lire 1980. Rev: St. Benedict. (1500th anniversary of saint's birth) 25.00

NOTE: Nos. 72–80 commemorate the
1980 Moscow Olympic Games

72. 500 Lire 1980. Three towers, Olympic symbols.
Rev: Ancient boxers 22.50
73. 200 Lire (A-Bro) 1980. Rev: Wrestlers 2.00
74. 100 Lire (St) 1980. Rev: Ancient archer 1.50
75. 50 Lire (St) 1980. Rev: Water sports 1.50
76. 20 Lire (St) 1980. Rev: Gymnast .75
77. 10 Lire (A) 1980. Rev: Steeplechase .50
78. 5 Lire (A) 1980. Rev: Runner .40
79. 2 Lire (A) 1980. Rev: Athlete .35
80. 1 Lira (A) 1980. Rev: Lady gymnast .30
81. 1000 Lire 1981. Rev: Aeneas on horseback.
(2000th anniversary of Vergil's death) 25.00
82. 500 Lire 1981. Rev: Flute player. (Vergil's death) 15.00
83. 500 Lire 1981. Rev: Standing figure. (Vergil's
death) 15.00

NOTE: Nos. 84–92 commemorate World Food Day
(F.A.O. coin plan)

84. 500 Lire 1981. Rev: Child's head 15.00
85. 200 Lire (A-Bro) 1981. Rev: Livestock 2.00
86. 100 Lire (St) 1981 1.50
87. 50 Lire (St) 1981 1.50
88. 20 Lire (St) 1981 .75
89. 10 Lire (St) 1981 .50
90. 5 Lire (A) 1981. Rev: Sheep .40
91. 2 Lire (A) 1981 .35
92. 1 Lira (A) 1981 .30

SÃO TOMÉ AND PRÍNCIPE

Located in the Gulf of Guinea off the west coast of Africa, this pair of islands remained a Portuguese province for 500 years. The Democratic Republic of São Tomé and Príncipe was proclaimed on July 12, 1975.

100 Centavos = 1 Escudo

14.	20 Centavos (Bro) 1962	2.00
14a.	20 Centavos (Bro) 1971. (Smaller planchet)	.50
15.	10 Centavos (Bro) 1962; (A) 1971	1.00

NEW STATE 1926–

1.	50 Centavos (N-Bro) 1929. Bust of the Republic. Rev: Arms above value	20.00
2.	20 Centavos (N-Bro) 1929	12.50
3.	10 Centavos (N-Bro) 1929	10.00
4.	10 Escudos 1939. Arms on cross over date. Rev: Crowned shield over value	60.00
5.	5 Escudos 1939, '48	15.00
6.	2½ Escudos 1939, '48	20.00

7.	1 Escudo (C-N) 1939; (N-Bro) 1948. Crowned shield. Rev: Value	10.00
8.	50 Centavos (N-Bro) 1948	15.00
9.	10 Escudos 1951. Crowned shield over value. Rev: Arms over date	25.00

10.	5 Escudos 1951	25.00
11.	2½ Escudos 1951; (C-N) 1962, '71	2.50
12.	1 Escudo (C-N) 1951. Similar to #7	50.00
12a.	1 Escudo (Bro) 1962, '71	2.00
13.	50 Centavos (C-N) 1951; (Bro) 1962	2.00
13a.	50 Centavos (Bro) 1971. (Larger planchet)	.50

16.	50 Escudos 1970. Quinas cross. Rev: Arms between dates. (500th anniversary of discovery)	15.00

17.	20 Escudos (N) 1971. Emblem within shield. Rev: Arms of Portugal	7.50

18.	10 Escudos (C-N) 1971. Crowned shield over value. Rev: Arms over date	6.50
19.	5 Escudos (C-N) 1971	2.00

DEMOCRATIC REPUBLIC OF SÃO TOMÉ AND PRÍNCIPE

DECIMAL COINAGE

100 Centimos = 1 Dobra

20.	250 Dobras 1977. Arms. Rev: Mother and child	30.00
21.	250 Dobras 1977. Arms. Rev: U.N. emblem, map of Africa, arms. ("World Unity")	30.00
22.	250 Dobras 1977. Rev: Group of fictional characters. ("Folklore")	30.00
23.	250 Dobras 1977. Rev: Group of five figures around emblem. ("World Friendship")	30.00
24.	250 Dobras 1977. Rev: Group of 12 figures around globe. ("World Population")	30.00

SÃO TOMÉ AND PRÍNCIPE (continued)

25. 20 Dobras (C-N) 1977. Arms. Rev: Plants, inscription. (F.A.O. coin plan)   3.00

26. 10 Dobras (C-N) 1977. Rev: Rooster. (F.A.O.)   2.00
27. 5 Dobras (C-N) 1977. Rev: Ears of corn. (F.A.O.)   1.25

28. 2 Dobras (C-N) 1977. Rev: Goats. (F.A.O.)   1.00
29. 1 Dobra (Bra) 1977. Rev: Cacao plant. (F.A.O.)   .50
30. 50 Centimos (Bra) 1977. Rev: Fish, plants. (F.A.O.)   .35

SARAWAK

Occupying part of the island of Borneo, Sarawak in 1841 was granted by the Sultan of Brunei to James Brooke, an Englishman, who had helped him quiet a revolt in the province. In 1888 both Brunei and Sarawak became British protectorates. In 1946 they were given the status of a British crown colony and in 1963 became part of the Federation of Malaysia.

100 Cents = 1 Dollar

JAMES BROOKE   1841–68

1. 1 Cent (C) 1863. Head. Rev: Value in wreath   15.00
2. ½ Cent (C) 1863   50.00
3. ¼ Cent (C) 1863   65.00

CHARLES BROOKE   1868–1917

4. 50 Cents 1900, '06. Head. Rev: Value in roped circle   65.00

5. 20 Cents 1900–15   35.00
6. 10 Cents 1900–15   20.00
7. 5 Cents 1900–15   25.00
8. 1 Cent (C) 1870–91. Rev: Value in wreath   12.50
8a. 1 Cent (C) 1892–97. (Center hole)   10.00
9. ½ Cent (C) 1870–96   15.00
10. ¼ Cent (C) 1870–96   22.50

CHARLES VYNER BROOKE   1917–46

11. 50 Cents 1927. Head. Rev: Type of #4   30.00
12. 20 Cents 1920, '27   20.00
13. 10 Cents 1920   30.00
14. 5 Cents 1920   40.00
15. 10 Cents (C-N) 1920, '27, '34. Rev: Value in wreath   7.50
16. 5 Cents (C-N) 1920, '27   5.00
17. 1 Cent (C-N) 1920   12.50
18. 1 Cent (Bro) 1927–41. Rev: Value in wreath   7.50
19. ½ Cent (Bro) 1933   5.00

SAUDI ARABIA

An Arab kingdom, formerly part of the Turkish Empire. It is made up of the former Sultanate of Nejd and the Kingdom of Hejaz.

HEJAZ

5 Riyals = 1 Dinar

HUSSEIN IBN ALI 1916–24

1.	1 Dinar (G) 1923 (A.H. 1342). Arabic inscriptions	225.00
2.	1 Riyal 1923 (A.H. 1342)	75.00

3.	½ Riyal 1923 (A.H. 1342)	175.00
4.	¼ Riyal 1923 (A.H. 1342)	65.00

SAUDI ARABIA

5 Halala = 1 Ghirsh
20 Ghirsh = 1 Riyal
40 Riyals = 1 Guinea

SAUD IBN ABDUL AZIZ 1953–64

5.	1 Riyal 1928–30. (A.H. 1346–48). Arabic inscription with swords and palm trees	50.00
6.	1 Guinea (G) 1957–58	200.00

7.	1 Riyal 1955 (A.H. 1374). Type of #5	12.50
8.	½ Riyal 1955	8.50
9.	¼ Riyal 1955	5.00

10.	4 Ghirsh (C-N) 1957–59 (A.H. 1376–78)	1.50
11.	2 Ghirsh (C-N) 1957–60	1.00
12.	1 Ghirsh (C-N) 1957–59	.50

13.	1 Halala (Bro) 1964	.50

FAISAL 1964–75

14.	50 Halala (C-N) 1972 (A.H. 1392). Arabic inscription with palm tree over swords. Rev: Value	1.50
15.	25 Halala (C-N) 1972	3.00
16.	10 Halala (C-N) 1972	1.00
17.	5 Halala (C-N) 1972	.65

19.

18.	50 Halala (C-N) 1972. Type of #14, F.A.O. inscription on reverse. (F.A.O. coin plan)	2.50
19.	25 Halala (C-N) 1973	1.50

KHALID 1975–82

20.	100 Halala (C-N) 1976 (A.H. 1396). Arabic inscription with palm tree over swords. Rev: Value	2.00
21.	50 Halala (C-N) 1977– . Type of #14	1.25
22.	25 Halala (C-N) 1977–	1.00
23.	10 Halala (C-N) 1977–	.85
24.	10 Halala (C-N) 1978. Type of #18	1.00

SERBIA

Formerly a Balkan kingdom; incorporated into the new state of Yugoslavia after World War I.

40 Paras = 1 Dinar

MICHAEL III   1860–68

1. 10 Paras (C) 1868. Head. Crowned value in
   wreath   15.00
2. 5 Paras (C) 1868   20.00
3. 1 Para (C) 1868   17.50

MILAN OBRENOVICH IV   1882–89
(Prince   1868–82)

4. 5 Dinars 1879. Head. Rev: Crowned value in
   wreath   75.00

5. 2 Dinars 1875, '79   25.00
6. 1 Dinar 1875, '79   17.50
7. 50 Paras 1875, '79   15.00
8. 10 Paras (C) 1879   10.00
9. 5 Paras (C) 1879   8.50

10. 20 Paras (C-N) 1883–84. Crowned double eagle.
    Rev: Value   10.00
11. 10 Paras (C-N) 1883–84   7.50
12. 5 Paras (C-N) 1883–84   8.50

ALEXANDER I   1889–1903

13. 2 Dinars 1897. Head. Rev: Crowned value in
    wreath   25.00
14. 1 Dinar 1897   15.00

PETER I   1903–18

15. 5 Dinars 1904. Two heads. Rev: Crowned arms
    in mantle. (Centenary of Karageorgeviches)   100.00
16. 2 Dinars 1904, '12, '15. Head. Rev: Crowned
    value in wreath   15.00
17. 1 Dinar 1904, '12, '15   7.50
18. 50 Paras 1904, '12, '15   6.50

19. 20 Paras 1912, '17. Crowned double eagle. Rev:
    Value   7.50
20. 10 Paras (C-N) 1912, '17   5.00
21. 5 Paras (C-N) 1904, '12, '17   4.00
22. 2 Paras (Bro) 1904   10.00

SEYCHELLES

A group of 92 islands in the Indian Ocean, about 800 miles off the east African coast. Formerly an English crown colony, Seychelles gained independence in 1976. It is a member of the British Commonwealth.

100 Cents = 1 Rupee

GEORGE VI 1936–1952

1.	1 Rupee 1939. Crowned head. Rev: Value	40.00
2.	½ Rupee 1939	50.00
3.	25 Cents 1939, '43–44	35.00
4.	25 Cents (C-N) 1951	12.50

5.	10 Cents (N-Bro) 1939, '43–44; (C-N) '51. Rev: Value	12.50

6.	5 Cents (Bro) 1948. Rev: Value in circle	1.50
7.	2 Cents (Bro) 1948	1.25
8.	1 Cent (Bro) 1948	1.00

ELIZABETH II 1952–

9.	1 Rupee (C-N) 1954–74. Crowned head. Rev: Type of #1	2.00
10.	½ Rupee (C-N) 1954–74	1.25
11.	25 Cents (C-N) 1954–74	1.25

12.	10 Cents (N-Bra) 1953–74	1.25
13.	5 Cents (Bro) 1964–71. Rev: Type of #6	1.50
14.	2 Cents (Bro) 1959–69	2.50
15.	1 Cent (Bro) 1959–69	2.00

16.	5 Cents (A) 1972, '75. Rev: Cabbage head, scalloped planchet. (F.A.O. coin plan)	.50

17.	1 Cent (A) 1972. Rev: Cow's head. (F.A.O. coin plan)	.35

18.	5 Rupees (C-N) 1972. Rev: Palm tree, sailing ship and turtle. (Heptagonal planchet)	4.00
18a.	5 Rupees (S) 1972, '74. Proof	60.00

19.	10 Rupees (C-N) 1974. Rev: Turtle	7.50
19a.	10 Rupees (S) 1974. Proof	35.00
20.	1000 Rupees (G) 1976. Bust of President James R. Mancham. Rev: Giant tortoise. (Declaration of Independence)	300.00
21.	10 Rupees (C-N) 1976. (Independence)	7.50
21a.	10 Rupees (S) 1976. Proof	25.00
22.	5 Rupees (C-N) 1976. (Independence; heptagonal planchet)	5.00
22a.	5 Rupees (S) 1976. Proof	20.00
23.	1 Rupee (C-N) 1976. (Independence)	3.00
23a.	1 Rupee (C-N) 1976. Proof	10.00

24.   50 Cents (C-N) 1976. (Independence)   2.50
24a. 50 Cents (C-N) 1976. Proof   7.50
25.   25 Rupees 1977. Bust of President Mancham.
        Rev: Cross over orb. (Elizabeth II's Silver
        Jubilee)   20.00

26.   10 Rupees (C-N) 1977–78. Arms. Rev: Turtle.
        (F.A.O. coin plan)   4.00

27.   5 Rupees (C-N) 1977–78. Rev: Coconut tree.
        (Heptagonal planchet)   1.50
28.   1 Rupee (C-N) 1977–78. Rev: Seashell   1.25

29.   50 Cents (C-N) 1977–78. Rev: Flowers   1.00
30.   25 Cents (C-N) 1977–78. Rev: Bird perched on
        tree   .75

31.   10 Cents (N-Bro) 1977–78. Rev: Jumping sail-
        fish. (F.A.O. coin plan; dodecagonal
        planchet).   .50
32.   5 Cents (A) 1977–78. Rev: Red snapper.
        (F.A.O. coin plan; scalloped-edge octagon)   .35
33.   1 Cent (A) 1977–78. Rev: Fish, seaweed   .25
34. 100 Rupees 1978. Arms. Rev: Birds in flight.
        (World Wildlife Conservation Program)   35.00
35.   50 Rupees 1978. Rev: Fish. (Conservation Pro-
        gram)   25.00

36.   50 Rupees 1980. Arms. Rev: Group of children.
        (International Year of Child)   30.00
37.   10 Rupees 1981. Arms. Rev: Farmer. (World
        Food Day)   35.00
38.   5 Cents (A) 1981. Rev: Tree. (World Food Day)   .75

SIERRA LEONE

Formerly a British colony and protectorate on the west coast of Africa, Sierra Leone became an independent member of the Commonwealth in 1961 and a republic in 1971.

1.	1 Dollar 1791. Lion. Rev: Clasped hands	1250.00
2.	50 Cents 1791	250.00
3.	20 Cents 1791	150.00
4.	10 Cents 1791, '96, 1805	75.00
5.	1 Penny (Bro) 1791	40.00
5a.	1 Cent (Bro) 1791, '96	40.00

6.   1 Leone (C-N) 1964–76. Head of Sir Milton Margai, late Prime Minister and founder of the state. Rev: Arms supported by lions   20.00

7.	20 Cents (C-N) 1964– . Rev: Lion	1.00
8.	10 Cents (C-N) 1964– . Rev: Value	.75
9.	5 Cents (C-N) 1964– . Rev: Cottonwood tree	.50

10.	1 Cent (Bro) 1964– . Rev: Palm branches	.35
11.	½ Cent (Bro) 1964– . Rev: Bonga fish	.25

REPUBLIC   1971–

12.   50 Cents (C-N) 1972– . Head of Dr. Siaka Stevens. Rev: Arms   3.00

13.	1 Leone (C-N) 1974. Rev: Lion in mountain scene	4.00
13a.	1 Leone (S) 1974. Proof	25.00
14.	2 Leones (C-N) 1976. Head of Dr. Siaka Stevens. Rev: Peasant in field. (Heptagonal planchet, F.A.O. coin plan)	5.00
15.	5 Golde (G) 1980. Head of Dr. Siaka Stevens. Rev: Map of Africa. (Organization of African Unity Summit Conference, Freetown)	250.00
16.	1 Leone (C-N) 1980 (O.A.U. Summit)	4.00
16a.	1 Leone (S) 1980. Proof	35.00

SINGAPORE

An island off the southern tip of the Malay Peninsula. This former British colony achieved self-government in 1959; in September 1963 it joined the Federation of Malaysia, of which it was a member until August 1965, when it withdrew. It remains a member of the British Commonwealth.

1.	1 Dollar (C-N) 1967– . Lion. Rev: Value	2.00

2.	50 Cents (C-N) 1967– . Lionfish	1.00
3.	20 Cents (C-N) 1967– . Swordfish	.50

4.	10 Cents (C-N) 1967– . Seahorse	.35
5.	5 Cents (C-N) 1967– . Snakebird	.25

6.	1 Cent (Bro) 1967– . Apartment building	.20

7.	150 Dollars (G) 1969. Arms. Rev: Raffles Lighthouse. (150th anniversary, founding of Singapore)	400.00

8.	5 Cents (A) 1971. Pomfret, a native fish. Rev: Rice plant, value. (F.A.O. coin plan)	.50

9.	10 Dollars 1972. Arms. Rev: Eagle	35.00
9a.	10 Dollars 1973, '77. Rev: SINGAPORE inscription right side up	20.00

10.	5 Dollars 1973. Arms. Rev: Stadium, interlocked circles emblem. (Seventh South East Asia Peninsular Games)	20.00

11. 500 Dollars (G) 1975. Arms. Rev: Roaring lion.
(10th anniversary of Republic) 650.00
12. 250 Dollars (G) 1975. Rev: Four hands clasped.
(10th anniversary of Republic) 325.00

13. 100 Dollars (G) 1975. Rev: Modern housing project. (10th anniversary of Republic) 150.00

17a.

17. 10 Dollars 1978–79 Arms. Rev: Communica-
tions satellites 20.00
17a. 10 Dollars (N) 1980. Type of #17. 10.00

14. 10 Dollars 1975. Rev: Ship in harbor. (10th anniversary of Republic) 25.00
15. 1 Dollar 1975. Type of #1 35.00
16. 10 Dollars 1977. Arms. Rev: Map of Southeast
Asia. (10th anniversary of Association of
Southeast Asian Nations [A.S.E.A.N.]) 20.00

18. 50 Dollars 1980–81. Arms. Rev: Stylized vignette of monetary symbols of various nations. (Singapore as world financial center.) 50.00
19. 10 Dollars 1981. Rev: Rooster. (Chinese New
Year) 10.00

20. 10 Dollars 1982. Rev: Dog. (Chinese New Year) 10.00
21. 5 Dollars 1982. Arms. Rev: Singapore skyline.
(Honors city as leader in Asian banking) 10.00
21a. 5 Dollars 1982. Proof 20.00

SOLOMON ISLANDS

A British protectorate located east of New Guinea, the Solomon Islands were granted self-government in 1975.

1. 100 Dollars (G) 1978   175.00

2. 30 Dollars (S-G) 1975. Arms. Rev: Cuscus   40.00

3. 1 Dollar (C-N) 1977– . Queen. Rev: Nuso-Nuso head used as war canoe figurehead   2.00

4. 20 Cents (C-N) 1977– . Rev: Traditional design with four monkeys   .50
5. 10 Cents (C-N) 1977– . Rev: Sea spirit   .30

6. 5 Cents (C-N) 1977– . Rev: Native mask   .25
7. 2 Cents (Bro) 1977– . Rev: Eagle perched on war club   .25
8. 1 Cent (Bro) 1977– . Rev: Native food bowl. (F.A.O. coin plan)   .20

9. 100 Dollars (G) 1978. Queen Elizabeth II. Rev: Arms. (Attainment of sovereignty)   200.00

10. 5 Dollars (C-N) 1978– . Rev: Bokolo (fossilized clam shell)   20.00
10a. 5 Dollars (S) 1977– . Proof   40.00

11. 5 Dollars 1978. Queen Elizabeth II. Rev: Supported crown. (Queen's Coronation Silver Jubilee)   25.00

12. 10 Dollars (C-N) 1979– . Rev: Frigate bird   25.00
12a. 10 Dollars (S) 1979– . Proof   40.00
13. 100 Dollars (G) 1980. Rev: Stylized native art 100.00
14. 100 Dollars (G) 1981. Rev: Shark   150.00

480

SOMALI REPUBLIC

This nation, on the northeast coast of Africa along the Indian Ocean, used to be two colonies, Italian Somaliland (q.v.) and the British Somaliland Protectorate. Following World War II Italian Somaliland became an Italian trusteeship known as Somalia. In 1960 it merged with British Somaliland to form the Somali Republic.

100 Centesimi = 1 Somalo (Scellino, Shilling)

SOMALIA

1.	1 Somalo 1950. Star over lioness. Rev: Value in circle	5.00
2.	50 Centesimi 1950	5.00

3.	10 Centesimi (Bro) 1950. Elephant head. Rev: Star over value	1.50
4.	5 Centesimi (Bro) 1950	1.00
5.	1 Centesimo (Bro) 1950	.50

REPUBLIC

6.	1 Scellino (C-N) 1967. Arms. Rev: Value	1.50
7.	50 Centesimi (C-N) 1967, '75	1.00
8.	10 Centesimi (Bra) 1967, '75	.50
9.	5 Centesimi (Bra) 1967, '75	.40
10.	5 Shillings (C-N) 1970. Cow, goat, sheep and produce. Rev: Arms. (F.A.O. coin plan)	5.00
11.	1 Scellino (C-N) 1976. Arms. Rev: Lamb (F.A.O. coin plan)	1.50
12.	50 Centesimi (C-N) 1976. Rev: Fruit, maize, wheat	1.00
13.	10 Centesimi (A) 1976. Type of #11. (Dodecagonal planchet)	.25
14.	5 Centesimi (A) 1976. Type of #12. (Dodecagonal planchet)	.20
15.	10 Shillings (C-N) 1979. Arms. (10th anniversary of Republic)	5.00

SOUTH AFRICA

SOUTH AFRICAN REPUBLIC

The South African Republic was formed in 1853 by the Boers who lived in the Transvaal. In 1877 Great Britain annexed the Transvaal, but the Boers regained their independence in 1883. Their defeat in the Boer War put an end to the South African Republic in 1902.

12 Pence = 1 Shilling

PRES. S. J. PAUL KRUGER   1883–1902

1.	5 Shillings 1892 (two varieties). Head of Kruger. Rev: Arms	350.00
2.	2½ Shillings 1892–97	30.00
3.	2 Shillings 1892–97	40.00
4.	1 Shilling 1892–97. Rev: Value in wreath	30.00

5.	6 Pence 1892–97	20.00
6.	3 Pence 1892–97	15.00

7.	1 Penny (Bro) 1892–94, '98	10.00

UNION OF SOUTH AFRICA

In 1910 the Cape of Good Hope, Natal and the Orange Free State (and later Transvaal) were formed into the Union of South Africa, a self-governing dominion of the British Commonwealth. In 1961 it became the Republic of South Africa and withdrew from the British Commonwealth.

GEORGE V   1910–36

1.	2½ Shillings 1923–36. Crowned bust. Rev: Arms or crowned arms	65.00

2.	1 Florin (2 Shillings) 1923–36	65.00
3.	1 Shilling 1923–36. Rev: Hope standing	40.00

Note: After 1930 spelling becomes "Suid Afrika"

4.	6 Pence 1923–24. Rev: Value in wreath	50.00
4a.	6 Pence 1925–36. Rev: Six bundles of sticks around a flower	40.00
5.	3 Pence 1923–25. Rev: Value in wreath	40.00
5a.	3 Pence 1925–36. Rev: Three bundles	30.00

6.	1 Penny (Bro) 1923–36. Rev: Ship	12.50
7.	½ Penny (Bro) 1923–36	40.00

8.	¼ Penny (Bro) 1923–31. Rev: Two sparrows	15.00

SOUTH AFRICA (continued)

GEORGE VI   1936–52

NOTE: Coins issued after 1948 drop "Imperator" from
obverse legends

9.   1 Sovereign (G) 1952. Head. Rev: Springbok   150.00
10. ½ Sovereign (G) 1952   120.00

11. 5 Shillings 1947. Rev: Springbok. (Royal visit)   25.00
12. 5 Shillings 1948–50   30.00
13. 5 Shillings 1951 ("5s" on reverse)   30.00

14. 5 Shillings 1952. Rev: Ship. (300th anniversary
of founding of Cape Town by Jan van
Riebeeck)   25.00

15. 2½ Shillings 1937–52. Rev: Crowned arms   20.00
16. 2 Shillings 1937–52. Rev: Arms   15.00

17. 1 Shilling 1937–52. Rev: Hope standing   12.50
18. 6 Pence 1937–52. Rev: Six bundles of sticks
around a flower   10.00
19. 3 Pence 1937–52. Three bundles of sticks
around a flower   6.00
20. 1 Penny (Bro) 1937–52. Rev: Ship   3.50

21. ½ Penny (Bro) 1937–52   4.00
22. ¼ Penny (Bro) 1937–52. Rev: Two birds   2.50

ELIZABETH II   1952–

23. 1 Sovereign (G) 1953–60. Head. Rev: Arms   200.00
24. ½ Sovereign (G) 1953–60   175.00

25. 5 Shillings 1953–59. Rev: Springbok   25.00
26. 2½ Shillings 1953–60. Rev: Crowned arms   25.00
27. 2 Shillings 1953–60. Rev: Arms   12.50
28. 1 Shilling 1953–60. Rev: Hope standing   10.00
29. 6 Pence 1953–60. Rev: Six bundles of sticks
around a flower   5.00
30. 3 Pence 1953–60. Rev: Three bundles of sticks
around a flower   5.00

31.	1 Penny (Bro) 1953–60. Rev: Sailing ship	4.00
32.	½ Penny (Bro) 1953–60	4.00
33.	¼ Penny (Bro) 1953–60. Rev: Two sparrows	2.50

34.	5 Shillings 1960. Rev: Parliament buildings. (50th anniversary of Union)	25.00

REPUBLIC OF SOUTH AFRICA
CURRENCY REVALUATION
100 Cents = 1 Rand

35.	2 Rands (G) 1961– . Bust of Jan van Riebeeck. Rev: Springbok	150.00
36.	1 Rand (G) 1961–	80.00

37.	50 Cents 1961–64. Rev: Springbok	20.00

38.	20 Cents 1961–64. Rev: Coat of arms	7.50
39.	10 Cents 1961–64. Rev: Hope with anchor	5.00

40.	5 Cents 1961–64. Rev: Five bundles of sticks around a flower	2.50
41.	2½ Cents 1961–64. Rev: Flower	8.00

42.	1 Cent (Bra) 1961–64. Rev: Pioneer covered wagon	2.50
43.	½ Cent (Bra) 1961–64. Rev: Two sparrows	1.50

44.	1 Rand 1965–68. Bust of Jan van Riebeeck, SOUTH AFRICA. Rev: Springbok	15.00
44a.	1 Rand 1965–68. Type of #44, but SUID AFRIKA	15.00

NOTE: In listings 45–48, the first coin listed bears a legend in English, the *a* coin bears an Afrikaans inscription; from 1970 on, all coins bear dual language inscriptions

45.	50 Cents (N) 1965–69. Rev: Native flowers	3.00
45a.	50 Cents (N) 1965–69	3.00
46.	20 Cents (N) 1965–69. Rev: Protea plant	1.50
46a.	20 Cents (N) 1965–69	1.50
47.	10 Cents (N) 1965–69. Rev: Aloe plant	.75
47a.	10 Cents (N) 1965–69	.75

48.	5 Cents (N) 1965–69. Rev: Blue crane	.50
48a.	5 Cents (N) 1965–69	.50
49.	2 Cents (Bro) 1965–69. Rev: Black wildebeest	.25

49a.	2 Cents (Bro) 1965–69	.25
50.	1 Cent (Bro) 1965–69. Rev: Two sparrows	.20
50a.	1 Cent (Bro) 1965–69	.20

51.	1 Rand 1967. Bust of Hendrik Frensch Verwoerd, SOUTH AFRICA. Rev: Springbok	12.50
51a.	1 Rand 1967. Type of #51, but SUID AFRIKA	12.50
52.	50 Cents (N) 1968. Bust of Dr. Charles R. Swart, South Africa. Rev: Native flower	2.00
52a.	50 Cents (N) 1968. Type of #52, but SUID AFRIKA	2.00
53.	20 Cents (N) 1968. Rev: Protea plant	2.00
53a.	20 Cents (N) 1968	2.00
54.	10 Cents (N) 1968. Rev: Aloe plant	2.00
54a.	10 Cents (N) 1968	2.00
55.	5 Cents (N) 1968. Rev: Blue crane	1.00
55a.	5 Cents (N) 1968	1.00
56.	2 Cents (Br) 1968. Rev: Black wildebeest	.25
56a.	2 Cents (Br) 1968	.25
57.	1 Cent (Br) 1968. Rev: Two sparrows	.15
57a.	1 Cent (Br) 1968	.15
58.	1 Rand 1969. Bust of Dr. T. E. Donges. Rev: Arms. (Late President-elect)	12.50
58a.	1 Rand 1969. Type of #58, but SUID AFRIKA	12.50
59.	1 Rand 1970– . New arms, dual language inscription	4.50
60.	50 Cents (N) 1970– . Rev: Native flower	1.00
61.	20 Cents (N) 1970– . Rev: Protea plant	.75
62.	10 Cents (N) 1970– . Rev: Aloe plant	.50
63.	5 Cents (N) 1970– . Rev: Blue crane	.35
64.	2 Cents (Br) 1970– . Rev: Black wildebeest	.20
65.	1 Cent (Br) 1970– . Rev: Two sparrows	.15
66.	½ Cent (Br) 1970–	.10

67.	1 Rand 1974–78. Arms. Rev: Front door of Pretoria Mint, surrounded by four coin designs from the past. (50th anniversary of South African Mint)	15.00
68.	50 Cents (N) 1976. Former State President J. J. Fouche. Rev: Lily	2.50
69.	20 Cents (N) 1976	1.00
70.	10 Cents (N) 1976	.35
71.	5 Cents (N) 1976	.25

72.	2 Cents (Br) 1976	.25
73.	1 Cent (Br) 1976	.15
74.	½ Cent (Br) 1976	1.00
75.	1 Rand (N) 1977– . Arms. Rev: Shield	2.00
76.	1 Rand (N) 1979. Rev: Springbok	2.00
76a.	1 Rand (S) 1979. Proof	25.00
77.	50 Cents (N) 1979	2.00
78.	20 Cents (N) 1979	1.00
79.	10 Cents (N) 1979	.35
80.	5 Cents (N) 1979	.25
81.	2 Cents (Br) 1979	.25
82.	1 Cent (Br) 1979	.15
83.	½ Cent (Br) 1979	1.50

SOUTH ARABIA

On the shores of the Gulf of Aden and the Arabian Sea, this country is made up of the former British Protectorate of South Arabia, the former colony of Aden, and certain surrounding islands, which took the name People's Republic of Southern Yemen upon achieving complete independence in November 1967, and is now known as the Democratic Republic of Yemen (q.v.).

1.	50 Fils (C-N) 1964. Emblem. Rev: Dhow, Arab sailing ship	2.00
2.	25 Fils (C-N) 1964	1.00

3.	5 Fils (Bro) 1964. Rev: Crossed daggers	1.00
4.	1 Fils (Bro) 1964	.50

SPAIN

The 18th century was the period of Spain's most extensive coinage. Coins were struck in both Spanish and Spanish-American mints. The exact country of origin may be determined by examining the reverse side of the coin.

In the case of coins originating in Spain, the legend on the reverse reads HISPANIARUM REX ("King of the Spains"). The mint mark appears in the field of the coin to the left of the shield. Principal Spanish mints were those at Madrid (M), Seville (S), Segovia (an aqueduct).

As for Spanish-American coins, the legend on the reverse reads HISPANIARUM ET IND. REX ("King of the Spains and the Indies"). Many of the earlier issues (beginning with the reign of Philip V) are of the "pillar and globe design," which was struck only in the New World. On the later bust-type coins the mint marks appear in the legend on the reverse. The chief Spanish-American mints were: Guatemala (G or NG); Peru (L or LIMA in monogram); Mexico (M̂); Bolivia (P or PTS in monogram); Chile (Ŝ); Colombia (P or PN; NR).

| 9. | 1 Cuarto (C). Crowned "Y." Rev: Crowned pillars | 25.00 |

PHILIP II (PHILIPPVS) 1556–98

NOTE: Coins of this reign struck prior to 1586 are undated and are rarer than others

| 10. | 8 Reales. Shield. Rev: Quartered arms | 300.00 |

11.	4 Reales	100.00
12.	2 Reales	50.00
13.	1 Real	30.00
14.	½ Real	25.00

15.	8 Maravedis (C). Castle. Rev: Lion	35.00
16.	4 Maravedis (C)	25.00
17.	2 Maravedis (C)	20.00

PHILIP III 1598–1621

18.	8 Reales. Shield. Rev: Quartered arms	350.00
19.	4 Reales	200.00
20.	2 Reales	100.00
21.	1 Real	30.00
22.	½ Real	40.00

---

4 Cuartos = 1 Real
16 Maravedis = 1 Real = 1 Piece of Eight
1 Escudo = 2 Reales
100 Centimos = 1 Real = 1 Escudo = 1 Peseta

FERDINAND V AND ISABELLA I   1474–1504
(FERDINANDVS ET ELISABET)
FERDINAND V   1504–16

1.	8 Reales. Arms. Rev: Sheaf of arrows	500.00
2.	4 Reales	200.00
3.	2 Reales	60.00
4.	1 Real	35.00
5.	2 Cuartos (C). Castle. Rev: Lion	20.00
6.	1 Cuarto (C)	25.00
7.	1 Cuarto (C)	35.00

CHARLES AND JOANNA   1516–56
(CAROLVS ET IOHANA)

| 8. | 1 Real | 30.00 |

SPAIN (continued)

23.	8 Maravedis (C). Castle. Rev: Lion	40.00
24.	4 Maravedis (C)	30.00
24a.	2 Maravedis (C)	25.00

PHILIP IV   1621–65

| 25. | 50 Reales 1628. Arms | RARE |
| 26. | 8 Reales 1623–62. Shield. Rev: Quartered arms | 350.00 |

27.	4 Reales 1651–60	250.00
28.	2 Reales 1628–52	50.00
29.	1 Real 1652	25.00
30.	½ Real 1651	35.00

31.	16 Maravedis (C) 1660–65. Head. Rev: Arms	35.00
32.	8 Maravedis (C) 1661–65	25.00
33.	4 Maravedis (C) 1661–65	20.00
34.	2 Maravedis (C) 1661–65	15.00

CHARLES II   1665–1700

35.	8 Reales 1682–97. Shield. Rev: Quartered arms	250.00
36.	4 Reales 1683–88	125.00
37.	2 Reales 1686	25.00
38.	1 Real 1674–87	25.00
39.	½ Real 1686	35.00
40.	2 Maravedis (C) 1680–96. Castle. Rev: Lion	25.00

| 41. | 2 Maravedis (C) 1688. Head. Rev: Crowned "double C" monogram | 17.50 |

CHARLES of Habsburg as CHARLES III of Spain

In 1700 Philip of Bourbon was declared King of Spain as Philip V. However, the Habsburgs, ruling family of Austria, had their own candidate, Archduke Charles (later Holy Roman Emperor Charles VI). In 1703 in Vienna and in 1706 in Madrid he was declared King of Spain. But in the War of the Spanish Succession, which started in 1703, Charles was defeated. He renounced his claim to the Spanish throne in 1714.

| 42. | 2 Reales 1701–14. Crowned CAROLUS. Rev: Arms | 20.00 |

PHILIP V   1700–46

NOTE: The familiar "pillar-type" coins that were first issued in this reign were struck in large numbers at various Spanish-American mints; they were not issued in Spain proper

SPAIN (continued)

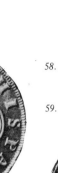

58.   1 Maravedi (C) 1746–47   15.00

CHARLES III   1759–88

59.   8 Reales 1762. Shield. Rev: Quartered arms. (Last year of issue for this type)   350.00

43.	8 Reales 1704–40. Shield. Rev: Quartered arms	300.00
44.	4 Reales 1718	200.00
45.	2 Reales 1717–37	25.00
46.	1 Real 1726–41	20.00
47.	½ Real 1726–41	30.00

60.	4 Reales 1761	75.00
61.	2 Reales 1760–70	25.00
62.	1 Real 1761	35.00

48.   6 Maravedis or Sesena (C) 1709–12. Arms. Rev: Crowned "V" (for Valencia)   40.00

49.   3 Maravedis (C) 1710–11   35.00

50.   4 Maravedis (C) 1718–46. Lion seated with sceptre, sword, and globe. Rev: Crowned shield   35.00

51.   2 Maravedis (C) 1718–46   20.00

52.   1 Maravedi (C) 1718–20   17.50

LOUIS I (LUIS)   1724

53.   8 Reales 1724. Shield. Rev: Quartered arms   750.00

FERDINAND VI   1746–59

54.   2 Reales 1754–88. Shield. Rev: Quartered arms   20.00

55.   1 Real 1750, '51   17.50

56.   ½ Real 1747–58   20.00

57.   2 Maravedis (C) 1750. Shield. Rev: Seated lion   35.00

63.	8 Reales 1772–88. Bust right. Rev: Arms	275.00
64.	4 Reales 1773–81	60.00
65.	2 Reales 1772–85	25.00
66.	1 Real 1774–85	30.00
67.	½ Real 1773–88	17.50

68.   8 Maravedis (C) 1772–88. Bust right. Rev: Ornate arms   15.00

69.	4 Maravedis (C) 1772–88	12.50
70.	2 Maravedis (C) 1772–87	15.00
71.	1 Maravedi (C) 1772–87	25.00

CHARLES IV   1788–1808

72.	8 Reales 1788–1808. Draped bust. Rev: Arms	225.00
73.	4 Reales 1791–1807	50.00
74.	2 Reales 1789–1808	20.00
75.	1 Real 1793–1808	30.00
76.	½ Real 1789–1803	30.00

77.	8 Maravedis (C) 1789–1808	17.50
78.	4 Maravedis (C) 1790–1808	12.50
79.	2 Maravedis (C) 1789–1808	8.50
80.	1 Maravedi (C) 1793–1802	25.00

FRENCH OCCUPATION
JOSEPH BONAPARTE   1808–13

81.	8 Reales 1809–10. Head. Rev: Arms	300.00
82.	20 Reales (Vellon-base silver) 1808–13	100.00

83.	10 Reales (Vellon) 1810–13	100.00
84.	4 Reales (Vellon) 1808–13	35.00
85.	2 Reales (Vellon) 1813	100.00
86.	1 Real (Vellon) 1813	50.00

87.	8 Maravedis (C) 1810–13	25.00

BOURBON RESTORATION
FERDINAND VII   1814–33
NOTE: Coins dated 1808–14 were struck in Spain during Ferdinand's exile in France

88.	8 Reales 1808–13. Bare head. Rev: Arms	150.00

89.	8 Reales 1809–30. Laureate bust. Rev: Arms	85.00
90.	4 Reales 1809–33	50.00
91.	2 Reales 1810–33	20.00
92.	1 Real 1811–32	20.00
93.	½ Real 1812–32	20.00

94.	8 Maravedis (C) 1812–33. Head. Rev: Ornate arms	10.00

95.	4 Maravedis (C) 1812–33	10.00
96.	2 Maravedis (C) 1812–33	7.50
97.	1 Maravedi (C) 1824	25.00

CONSTITUTIONAL COINAGE

104.	20 Reales 1856–64. Diademed head. Rev: Arms	75.00
105.	10 Reales 1840–65. Varieties as above	50.00
106.	4 Reales 1835–64	25.00
107.	2 Reales 1836–63	25.00
108.	1 Real 1839–64	17.50

98.	20 Reales (Vellon) 1821–23. New plain head. Rev: Arms and pillars	100.00
99.	10 Reales (Vellon) 1821. Rev: RESELLADO re-struck over other coins	20.00
100.	4 Reales (Vellon) 1822–32. Rev: Arms	30.00
101.	8 Maravedis (C) 1823–33. Rev: Ornate arms	6.00

109.	8 Maravedis (C) 1835–50. Bare head. Rev: Arms in angles of cross	17.50
110.	4 Maravedis (C) 1838–45	17.50
111.	2 Maravedis (C) 1840–48	10.00
112.	1 Maravedi (C) 1842	50.00
113.	2 Escudos 1865–68. Diademed head. Rev: Arms	100.00
114.	1 Escudo 1867–68	35.00
115.	40 Centimos 1864–68	20.00
116.	20 Centimos 1864–68	25.00
117.	10 Centimos 1864–68	35.00
118.	5 Centimos (C) 1867–68	15.00
119.	2½ Centimos (C) 1867–68	10.00
120.	1 Centimo (C) 1868	15.00
121.	½ Centimo (C) 1866–68	15.00

ISABELLA II   1833–68

102.	20 Reales 1834–50. Young head with upswept hair. Rev: Crowned arms in collar of the Fleece	150.00

PROVISIONAL GOVERNMENT   1868–70

103.	20 Reales 1850–55. New style head. Rev: Arms between pillars	100.00

122.	5 Pesetas 1869–70. Hispania reclining. Rev: Crowned arms between pillars	40.00

123.	2 Pesetas 1869–70	35.00
124.	1 Peseta 1869–70	40.00
125.	50 Centimos 1869–70	100.00
126.	20 Centimos 1869–70	650.00
127.	10 Centimos (C) 1870. Lion. Rev: Hispania	3.00
128.	5 Centimos (C) 1870	2.00
129.	2 Centimos (C) 1870	1.50
130.	1 Centimo (C) 1870	2.50

AMADEO I   1871–73

131.	5 Pesetas 1871. Bearded head. Rev: Crowned arms	35.00

ALFONSO XII   1874–85

132.	5 Pesetas 1875–81. Bare head. Rev: Crowned arms between pillars	30.00
133.	5 Pesetas 1882–85	30.00
134.	2 Pesetas 1879–84	25.00
135.	1 Peseta 1876–85	25.00
136.	50 Centimos 1880–85	12.50
137.	10 Centimos (C) 1877–79	10.00
138.	5 Centimos (C) 1877–79	5.00

ALFONSO XIII   1885–1931

139.	5 Pesetas 1888–92. Baby head. Rev: Arms	20.00
140.	5 Pesetas 1892–94. Child head. Rev: Arms	25.00
141.	5 Pesetas 1896–99. Youthful head	25.00
142.	2 Pesetas 1889–94. Varieties as above	30.00

143.	2 Pesetas 1905. Uniformed bust. Rev: Crowned arms between pillars	25.00
144.	1 Peseta 1889–1905. Varieties as above	20.00
145.	½ Peseta 1889–1910. Varieties as above	5.00
146.	50 Centimos 1926. Mature head. Rev: Crowned arms	12.50

147.	25 Centimos (N-Bra) 1925. Galleon. Rev: Value	4.00

148.	25 Centimos (C-N) 1927. Crown, hammer and olive branch. Rev: Value and sprays. (Center hole)	2.50
149.	2 Centimos (Bro) 1904–12. Uniformed bust. Rev: Crowned shield	1.00
150.	1 Centimo (Bro) 1906–13	2.50

REPUBLIC   1931–39

151.	1 Peseta 1933. Seated figure. Rev: Arms between pillars	17.50

152.	25 Centimos (N-Bro) 1934. Woman holding branch. Rev: Value. (Center hole)	10.00

SPAIN (continued)

153. 1 Peseta (Bra) 1937. Female head. Rev: Value
and grape spray   3.00

CIVIL WAR 1936–39

154. 50 Centimos (Bro) 1937. Seated figure. Rev:
Value   3.50

155. 25 Centimos (Bro) 1938. Chains. Rev: Value.
(Center hole)   15.00

156. 5 Centimos (I) 1937. Hispania head. Rev: Value   3.00

NATIONALIST GOVERNMENT 1937–
GEN. FRANCISCO FRANCO 1937–75

157. 25 Centimos (C-N) 1937. Sun and arrows. Rev:
Shield, value and spray   2.50

158. 10 Centimos (A) 1940–53. Horseman with
lance. Rev: Eagle over shield   2.50
159. 5 Centimos (A) 1940–53   2.00

160. 1 Peseta (A-Bro) 1944. Arms. Rev: Value   7.50

161. 5 Pesetas (N) 1949–51. Head of Gen. Franco.
Rev: Arms   2.50

162. 50 Pesetas (C-N) 1957–75. Rev: Eagle and
shield   4.00
163. 25 Pesetas (C-N) 1957–75   1.00
164. 5 Pesetas (C-N) 1957–75   2.00

165. 2½ Pesetas (A-Bro) 1953–71. Rev: Coat of arms   3.00
166. 1 Peseta (A-Bro) 1947–67   1.25

167. 50 Centimos (C-N) 1949–65. Value. Rev: Arrows. (Center hole)   1.50
168. 10 Centimos (A) 1959. Head. Rev: Value   .50

169. 100 Pesetas 1966–70. Head of Gen. Franco. Rev: Crowned arms   10.00
170.   1 Peseta (A-Bro) 1966–75. Rev: Arms   1.00

171. 50 Centimos (A-Mg) 1966. Rev: Laurel branch   1.00

JUAN CARLOS I   1975–

172. 100 Pesetas (C-N) 1975–76. King Juan Carlos. Rev: Old arms   3.00

173. 50 Pesetas (C-N) 1975–76. Rev: New arms   2.00
174. 25 Pesetas (C-N) 1975–76. Rev: Crown   1.75
175. 5 Pesetas (C-N) 1975–76. Rev: Old arms   .75
176. 50 Centimos (A) 1975–76. Rev: Laurel sprig   1.00

NOTE: Nos. 177–182 commemorate 1982 World Cup Soccer Games

177. 100 Pesetas (C-N) 1980–81. Head of Juan Carlos. Rev: Soccer ball, value   3.50
178. 50 Pesetas (C-N) 1980–82   2.50
179. 25 Pesetas (C-N) 1980–82   2.00
180. 5 Pesetas (C-N) 1980–82   1.50
181. 1 Peseta (Al-Br) 1980–82   1.00
182. 50 Centimos (Al) 1980   .75

SRI LANKA

A large island in the Indian Ocean, southeast of India, Sri Lanka was formerly known as Ceylon (q.v.). Successively conquered by the Portuguese, Dutch and English, in 1948 it became a dominion in the British Commonwealth of Nations. When Ceylon became an independent republic in 1972, the traditional name Sri Lanka was officially adopted.

100 Cents = 1 Rupee

1.	1 Rupee (C-N) 1972, '75–78. New arms of Republic. Rev: Value	1.00

2.	50 Cents (C-N) 1972, '75, '78	1.00
3.	25 Cents (C-N) 1975, '78	.30
4.	10 Cents (N-Bra) 1975; (A) 1978	.35
5.	5 Cents (N-Bra) 1975; (A) 1978	.25
6.	2 Cents (A) 1975–78. (Scalloped planchet)	.35
7.	1 Cent (A) 1975, '78	.20
8.	1 Rupee (C-N) 1976. Statue of old Buddhist king. Rev: Value. (F.A.O. coin plan)	.15
9.	5 Rupees (C-N) 1976. Building. Rev: Value. (Non-aligned nations conference)	4.00
10.	2 Rupees (C-N) 1976	2.00

11.	1 Rupee (C-N) 1978. Bust of President J. R. Jayewardene. Rev: Arms. (Inauguration of new president)	3.00

STRAITS SETTLEMENTS

This former British crown colony in Asia was dissolved in 1946. It included Singapore; the Federation of Malaysia now contains many of these states.

100 Cents = 1 Dollar

VICTORIA 1837–1901

1.	50 Cents 1886–1901. Coroneted head. Rev: Value	40.00
2.	20 Cents 1871–1901	8.50
3.	10 Cents 1871–1901	6.00
4.	5 Cents 1871–1901	5.00
5.	1 Cent (C) 1872–1901	8.50
6.	½ Cent (C) 1872–89	7.50
7.	¼ Cent (C) 1872–1901	8.50

EDWARD VII 1901–10

8.	1 Dollar 1903–04, 1907–09. Crowned bust. Rev: Value in Malay and Chinese in ornamental panels	30.00
9.	50 Cents 1902–08. Rev: Value in circle	15.00
10.	20 Cents 1902–10	7.50
11.	10 Cents 1902–10	5.00
12.	5 Cents 1902–03, 1910	5.00

GEORGE V 1910–36

13.	1 Dollar 1919, '20. Type of #8	15.00
14.	50 Cents 1920–21. Type of #9, bust facing left	7.50
15.	20 Cents 1916–35	5.00
16.	10 Cents 1916–27	5.00
17.	5 Cents 1918–35	2.50
17a.	5 Cents (C-N) 1920, '27	7.50

18.	1 Cent (C) 1919–20, 26. Crowned bust. Rev: Value in double circle. (Square-shaped, rounded corners)	5.00
19.	½ Cent (C) 1916. (Round-shaped)	8.50
20.	½ Cent (C) 1932. Type of #18	4.00
21.	¼ Cent (C) 1916. Type of #19	7.50

SUDAN

An independent nation south of Egypt (formerly Anglo-Egyptian Sudan).

10 Milliemes (Millim) = 1 Piastre (Ghirsh)

2.

1. 20 Piastres (C-N) 1967–69. Camel and rider. Rev. Value. Proof 15.00
2. 10 Piastres (C-N) 1956–71. Camel and rider. Rev: Value 2.50
3. 5 Piastres (C-N) 1956–71 ..... 1.00
4. 2 Piastres (C-N) 1956–71 ..... 1.00

5. 10 Milliemes (Bro) 1956–71. (Scalloped edge) 1.00
6. 5 Milliemes (Bro) 1956–71 ..... .75
7. 2 Milliemes (Bro) 1956–71 ..... .50
8. 1 Millieme (Bro) 1956–71. (Round) ..... .35

9. 25 Piastres (C-N) 1968. (F.A.O. coin plan) 15.00

10. 10 Piastres (C-N) 1971–75. New arms. Rev: Value. (Second anniversary of revolution) 1.50

11. 5 Piastres (C-N) 1971, '75 ..... 1.25
12. 2 Piastres (C-N) 1971, '75 ..... .75
13. 10 Milliemes (Bro) 1971 ..... .50
13a. 10 Milliemes (Bra) 1975 ..... .75
14. 5 Milliemes (Bro) 1971 ..... .75
14a. 5 Milliemes (Bra) 1975 ..... .50

15. 50 Piastres (C-N) 1972. Arms. Rev: Farmer plowing. (F.A.O. coin plan) 6.50

16. 10 Milliemes (Bro) 1972. Arms. Rev: Value. (Scalloped planchet) 1.00

17. 5 Milliemes (Bro) 1972, '73. Arms. Rev: Value. (F.A.O. coin plan) ..... .50

17a.

18.

17a. 50 Ghirsh (C-N) 1976. Rev: Symbolic tree in cartouche. (Commemorates establishment of Arab Fund for Social and Economic Development) 6.50
18. 10 Piastres (C-N) 1976. Type of #10, new legend on obverse. (F.A.O. coin plan) 2.00

SUDAN (continued)

19. 5 Piastres (C-N) 1976. (20th anniversary of independence) — 1.00

20. 2 Piastres (C-N) 1976 — .75
21. 10 Milliemes (Bra) 1976 — .50
22. 5 Milliemes (Bra) 1976 — .50

23. 50 Ghirsh (C-N) 1977. Rev: Cogwheel design. (Eighth anniversary of 1969 revolt) — 6.50
24. 1 Pound (C-N) 1978. Arms. Rev: Stylized agricultural design. (Honors rural women; F.A.O. coin plan) — 4.00
25. 50 Pounds (G) 1980. Arms. Rev: Mosques. (1400th anniversary of Islam) — 250.00
26. 25 Pounds (G) 1980 — 150.00
27. 10 Pounds 1980 — 35.00
28. 5 Pounds 1980 — 20.00
29. 50 Pounds (G) 1981. Arms. (25th year of independence) — 175.00

30. 5 Pounds 1981. Arms. Rev: Children tossing ball, Mahdi's Tomb in background. (International Year of Child) — 35.00

SURINAM

This former Dutch colony on the northeast coast of South America was organized in 1954 as a part of the Kingdom of the Netherlands, with considerable powers of self-government. It achieved full independence on November 25, 1975.

JULIANA 1948–80

1. 1 Cent (Bro) 1957–60. Lion. Rev: Value — 4.00

2. 1 Guilder 1962. Head of Queen. Rev: Arms — 10.00
3. 25 Cents (C-N) 1962– . Arms. Rev: Value — 1.00
4. 10 Cents (C-N) 1962– — .50

5. 5 Cents (N-Bro) 1962–72; (A) 1976. (Square planchet) — .50
6. 1 Cent (Bro) 1962–72; (A) 1974– . (Round) — .30
7. 25 Guilders 1976. Supported shield. Rev: Banner against sun rays. (First anniversary of independence) — 30.00
8. 10 Guilders 1976. (Independence anniversary) — 20.00

BEATRIX 1980–

9. 25 Guilders 1981. Liberty triumphant. Rev: Revolutionary movement vignette. (First anniversary of revolution) — 30.00

SWAZILAND

Located in southeastern Africa, Swaziland has been an independent nation within the British Commonwealth since 1968.

1.   1 Lilangeni (C-N) 1974, '79. Bust of King Sobhuza II. Rev: Mother and child   6.00

2.   50 Cents (C-N) 1974–75, '79. Rev: Arms   3.00

3.   20 Cents (C-N) 1974–75, '79. Rev: Elephant. (Scalloped planchet)   1.50

4.   10 Cents (C-N) 1974, '79. Rev: Sugar cane. (Scalloped planchet)   1.00
5.   5 Cents (C-N) 1974–75, '79. Rev: Lusekwane flower. (Scalloped planchet)   .50

6.   2 Cents (Bro) 1974, '79. Rev: Pine trees. (Square planchet)   .35
7.   1 Cent (Bro) 1974, '79. Rev: Pineapple. (Dodecagonal planchet)   .25

8.

8.   1 Lilangeni (C-N) 1975. Type of #1, added rev. inscription. (F.A.O. coin plan and International Women's Year)   6.00

9.   10 Cents (C-N) 1975. Type of #4, added rev. inscription. (F.A.O.)   1.00

10.   2 Cents (Bro) 1975. Type of #6, added rev. inscription. (F.A.O.)   .35
11.   1 Cent (Bro) 1975. Type of #7, added rev. inscription. (F.A.O.)   .25
12.   1 Lilangeni (C-N) 1976. King Sobhuza II. Rev: Mother and child. (F.A.O.)   6.00

13.   250 Emalangeni (G) King Sobhuza II. Rev: Tusked African elephant. (60th year of reign)   300.00
14.   25 Emalangeni 1981. Rev: Purple-crested lourie bird on branch. (60th year of reign)   30.00
15.   2 Emalangeni (C-N) 1981. Rev: Calla lilies. (60th year of reign)   5.00
15a.   2 Emalangeni (S) 1981. Proof   25.00
16.   1 Lilangeni (C-N) 1981. Rev: Woman with stalks. (F.A.O. coin plan)   6.00
17.   20 Cents (C-N) 1981. Rev: Plants. (F.A.O. coin plan; scalloped-edge planchet)   1.50

SWEDEN

Established as a separate kingdom after Gustavus Vasa led a successful revolt in 1521 to drive out the Danes. From 1814 to 1905 the Swedish monarchs were also kings of Norway. Swedish arms are three crowns on a shield.

8 Ore = 1 Mark
8 Marks = 1 Daler
96 Ore = 48 Skilling = 1 Rigsdaler
100 Ore = 1 Krona

GUSTAVUS I (GUSTAVUS VASA) 1523–60

1.   Taler 1540–59. Half-length figure with sword.
      Rev: Figure of Christ   1500.00

JOHN III 1568–92

2.   Taler 1569–92   1000.00

CHARLES IX 1604–11

3.   20 Marks 1606–11   1750.00

GUSTAVUS II (GUSTAVUS ADOLPHUS) 1611–32

4.   Taler 1615–32. Bust. Rev: Christ   1250.00

499

SWEDEN (continued)

| 6a. | 1 Ore (Bro) 1638–53. Arms. Rev: Arrows | 150.00 |

CHARLES XI   1660–97

5. Taler 1632. ("Purim" taler; commemorates victory at Leipzig) 600.00

CHRISTINA   1632–54

6. Taler 1632–52. Three-quarter facing figure of queen. Rev: SALVATOR MUNDI 1000.00

| 7. | 8 Marks 1664–96. Bust. Rev: Arms | 500.00 |
| 8. | 4 Marks 1664–96 | 250.00 |

6a.

9.	2 Marks 1661–96	150.00
10.	1 Mark 1663–97	125.00
11.	5 Ore 1667–94. Linked "C"s. Rev: Crowns	50.00
12.	2 Ore 1664–69. C.R.S. crowned	40.00
13.	1 Ore 1668–72. Charles XI crowned	10.00
14.	½ Ore 1661–64. Arms. Rev: Lion	135.00

SWEDEN (continued)

CHARLES XII 1697–1718

20.	1 Daler (C) 1718. IVPITER	25.00
21.	1 Daler (C) 1718. Father Time with scythe and infant, SATVRNVS	25.00
22.	1 Daler (C) 1718. Sun god, PHOEBVS	25.00

23.	1 Daler (C) 1718. War god, MARS	30.00
24.	1 Daler (C) 1718. MERCVRIVS	25.00
25.	1 Daler (C) 1719. Hope with anchor	50.00

ULRICA ELEONORA 1718–20

26.	1 Ore (C) 1719–20. Three crowns. Rev: Crossed arrows on shield. (Struck over De Gortz dalers)	15.00

FREDERICK I 1720–51

15.	Taler 1707. Bust. Rev: Arms	1000.00

BARON DE GORTZ DOLLARS

After the Swedish army under Charles XII had been defeated by Czar Peter I of Russia, the almost-bankrupt Swedish government called in all silver coins and replaced them with a new issue of copper coins struck at Stockholm.

16.	1 Daler (C) 1715. Crown. Rev: Value	25.00

17.	1 Daler (C) 1716. Svea seated, PUBLICA FIDE	35.00
18.	1 Daler (C) 1717. Warrior with sword and shield, WETT OCH WAPEN	25.00
19.	1 Daler (C) 1718. Warrior and lion, FLINK OCH FARDIG	25.00

27.	Taler 1721. Bust and medallion portraits of Gustavus Vasa and Gustavus Adolphus. (200th anniversary of Reformation)	1250.00

501

28.	Taler 1721–51. Bust and shield	350.00
29.	10 Ore 1739–51. Crossed "F"s	75.00
30.	5 Ore 1722–51	35.00
31.	2 Ore (C) 1743–50. Arrows	15.00

| 32. | 1 Ore (C) 1720–50 | 12.50 |
| 33. | ½ Ore (C) 1720–21 | 25.00 |

ADOLPHUS FREDERICK   1751–71

| 34. | Taler 1751–71. Head. Rev: Crowned shield | 160.00 |

35.	½ Taler 1752–68	500.00
36.	5 Ore 1751–67. Crowns	50.00
37.	2 Ore (C) 1751–68	25.00
38.	1 Ore (C) 1751–68	25.00

GUSTAVUS III   1771–92

| 39. | 1 Rigsdaler 1771–82. Head and shield | 200.00 |
| 40. | ⅔ Rigsdaler 1776–80 | 85.00 |

41.	⅓ Rigsdaler 1776–89	50.00
42.	⅙ Rigsdaler 1776–90	30.00
43.	1/12 Rigsdaler 1777–79	25.00
44.	1/24 Rigsdaler 1777–83	15.00
45.	2 Ore (C) 1777. Arrows	50.00
46.	1 Ore (C) 1772, '78	12.50

GUSTAVUS IV (GUSTAVUS ADOLPHUS) 1792–1809

47.	1 Rigsdaler 1792–1807. Head. Rev: Arms	200.00
48.	⅓ Daler 1798–1800	400.00
49.	⅙ Daler 1800–09	30.00

| 50. | 1 Skilling (C) 1802–05. Crowned monogram | 10.00 |

SWEDEN (continued)

51.	½ Skilling (C) 1802–09	6.00
52.	¼ Skilling (C) 1802–08	4.00
53.	1/12 Skilling (C) 1802–08	3.50

CHARLES XIII   1809–18

54.	1 Rigsdaler 1812–18. Head. Rev: Arms	550.00
55.	⅓ Daler 1813–14	350.00
56.	⅙ Daler 1809–17	150.00
57.	1/12 Daler 1811. Monogram. Rev: Shield	100.00
58.	1/24 Daler 1810–16	30.00
59.	1 Skilling 1812–17. Monogram. Rev: Arrows	20.00
60.	½ Skilling 1815–17	15.00
61.	¼ Skilling 1817	35.00

62.	1/12 Skilling 1812	7.50

CHARLES XIV JOHN
(Jean Baptiste Jules Bernadotte)   1818–44

63.	1 Rigsdaler 1821. Bust and medallion portraits of Gustavus Vasa, Gustavus II Adolphus, and Frederick I. (300th anniversary of Reformation)	750.00

64.	1 Rigsdaler 1818–42. Head. Rev: Arms and value	350.00
65.	½ Daler 1831–36	200.00
66.	¼ Daler 1830–36	85.00
67.	⅛ Daler 1830–37	35.00
68.	1/12 Daler 1831–33	45.00
69.	1/16 Daler 1835–36	30.00

70.	1 Skilling (C) 1819–43	17.50
71.	½ Skilling (C) 1819–32	8.00
72.	¼ Skilling (C) 1819–33	5.00
73.	⅙ Skilling (C) 1830–44	4.00

OSCAR I   1844–59

74.	1 Rigsdaler 1844–59. Head. Rev: Arms and supporters	200.00
75.	½ Daler 1845–52	200.00
76.	¼ Daler 1846–52	125.00
77.	1/16 Daler 1845–55	15.00
78.	1/32 Daler 1852–53	12.50

SWEDEN (continued)

79. 50 Ore 1857. Head. Rev: Value   125.00
80. 25 Ore 1855–59   30.00
81. 10 Ore 1855–59   20.00

82. 2 Skilling (C) 1844–55. "Banco" head. Rev:
Arrows   50.00
83. 1 Skilling (C) 1844–55   25.00
84. ⅔ Skilling (C) 1844–55   20.00
85. ⅓ Skilling (C) 1844–55. Crowned monogram   7.50
86. ⅙ Skilling (C) 1844–55   5.00

87. 5 Ore (C) 1857–58   25.00
88. 2 Ore (C) 1856–58   10.00
89. 1 Ore (C) 1856–58   5.00
90. ½ Ore (C) 1856–58. Monogram   3.00

CHARLES XV   1859–72

91. 4 Rigsdaler 1861–71. Head. Rev: Arms   200.00
92. 2 Rigsdaler 1862–71   450.00
93. 1 Rigsdaler 1860–71   150.00
94. 50 Ore 1862. Value in wreath   RARE

95. 25 Ore 1862–71   35.00
96. 10 Ore 1861–71   15.00
97. 5 Ore (C) 1860–72   17.50
98. 2 Ore (C) 1860–72   10.00
99. 1 Ore (C) 1860–72   5.00
100. ½ Ore 1867. Monogram   25.00

OSCAR II   1872–1907

101. 20 Kronor (G) 1873–1902. Head. Rev: Crowned
arms   350.00
102. 10 Kronor (G) 1873–1901   150.00
103. 5 Kronor (G) 1881–86, 1901. Rev: Value   175.00

104. 2 Kronor 1876–1907. Head to right. Rev:
Arms   30.00

105. 2 Kronor 1897. Crowned bust. Silver jubilee of
reign. Rev: Arms   25.00

106.	2 Kronor 1907. Conjoined busts of Oscar II and Sophia. Golden wedding	25.00
107.	1 Krona 1875–1907. Type of #104	17.50
108.	50 Ore 1875–1907. Monogram. Rev: Value	20.00
109.	25 Ore 1874–1907	4.00
110.	10 Ore 1872–1907	4.00
111.	5 Ore (Bro) 1874–1907	4.00
112.	2 Ore (Bro) 1874–1907	3.00
113.	1 Ore (Bro) 1874–1907	1.50

GUSTAV V   1907–50

114.	20 Kronor (G) 1925. Head to right. Rev: Crowned arms	850.00
115.	5 Kronor (G) 1920. Head to right. Rev: Value	200.00
116.	2 Kronor 1910–40	12.50

119.	5 Kronor 1935. Head. Rev: Arms. 500th anniversary of Parliament (Riksdag)	25.00

117.	2 Kronor 1921. Head of Gustavus Vasa. Rev: Arms. 400th year of political liberty	25.00

120.	2 Kronor 1938. Head to left. Rev: Ship. (300th anniversary of Swedish settlement in Delaware; reverse similar to U.S. 1936 Delaware commemorative, p. 541, #44)	20.00
121.	1 Krona 1910–42. Head. Rev: Arms	7.50
122.	50 Ore 1911–19, '27–39. Crowned arms. Rev: Value	7.50
122a.	50 Ore (N-Bro) 1920–24, '40–47. Crowned monogram. Rev: Value	6.50
123.	25 Ore 1910–19, '27–41	5.00
123a.	25 Ore (N-Bro) 1921, '40–47. Type of #122a	5.00
124.	10 Ore 1909–19, '27–42	4.00
124a.	10 Ore (N-Bro) 1920–25, '40–47. Type of #122a	3.00

118.	2 Kronor 1932. Bust of Gustavus II Adolphus. Rev: Inscription on panel: "Third centenary of death"	30.00

125.	5 Ore (Bro) 1909–42, '50; (I) 1917–19, '42–50. Monogram. Rev: Value	2.50
126.	2 Ore (Bro) 1909–42, '50; (I) 1917–19, '42–50	2.00
127.	1 Ore (Bro) 1909–42, '50; (I) 1917–19, '42–50	1.00

505

SWEDEN (continued)

NEW SILVER COINAGE

128. 2 Kronor 1942–50. Older head. Rev: Arms   7.50
129. 1 Krona 1942–50   6.00

130. 50 Ore 1943–50. Crown. Rev: Value   6.00
131. 25 Ore 1943–50   4.00
132. 10 Ore 1942–50   2.00

GUSTAV VI ADOLF   1950–73

133. 5 Kronor 1952. Head. Rev: Monogram. King's
70th birthday   75.00
134. 5 Kronor 1954, '55, '71. Head. Rev: Arms   7.50

135. 2 Kronor 1952–66   6.00
135a. 2 Kronor (C-N) 1968–71   1.25
136. 1 Krona 1952–68   3.00
136a. 1 Krona (C-N clad) 1968–73   .65

137. 50 Ore 1952–61. Crown. Rev: Value   12.50
138. 25 Ore 1952–61   5.00
139. 10 Ore 1952–62   2.50

140. 5 Ore (Bro) 1952–71. Incuse crown. Rev: Value   .35
141. 2 Ore (Bro) 1952–71   .25
142. 1 Ore (Bro) 1952–71   .20

143. 5 Kronor 1959. Head of King. Rev: Four men.
(Sesquicentennial of Swedish form of government)   27.50

144. 5 Kronor 1962. Head of King. Rev: Athena
with owl. (80th birthday commemorative)   100.00

SWEDEN (continued)

145. 50 Ore (C-N) 1962–73. Crowned monogram.
 Rev: Value .35
146. 25 Ore (C-N) 1962–73 .25
147. 10 Ore (C-N) 1962–73 .15

148. 5 Kronor 1966. Head of King. Rev: Tablet.
 (100th anniversary, two-chamber system of
 Parliament) 7.00

149. 10 Kronor 1972. Rev: Royal signature. (90th
 birthday of King) 10.00

150. 5 Kronor (C-N) 1972, '73. Rev: Crowned arms 2.00

151. 5 Ore (Bro) 1972, '73. Three crowns. Rev:
 Value .10

CARL XVI GUSTAF 1973–

152. 50 Kronor 1975. Three crowns, value. Rev:
 Torch, uplifted hands. (Constitutional reform) 20.00

153. 5 Kronor (C-N) 1976. Head of King Carl. Rev:
 Flag 3.00

154. 1 Krona (C-N) 1976. Head facing left. Rev:
 Arms 1.00
155. 50 Ore (C-N) 1976. Crowned monogram. Rev:
 Value .50
156. 25 Ore (C-N) 1976 .40
157. 10 Ore (C-N) 1976 .40
158. 5 Ore (Bro) 1976 .30

159. 50 Kronor 1976. Royal couple. Rev: Crowned
 arms. (June 19, 1976 wedding) 20.00
160. 200 Kronor 1980. Plain head of King Carl. Rev:
 Elaborate inscription. (Swedish Law of Royal
 Succession) 50.00

SWITZERLAND

Switzerland has been independent since 1386. Prior to 1850 the individual cantons issued their own coinage. Representative coins of these issues are listed.

4 Kreutzers = 1 Batz = 10 Centimes
100 Centimes or Rappens = 1 Franc

SWISS CANTONS
Appenzell

1.	4 Franken 1812, '16. Arms. Rev: Warrior with tablet	700.00
2.	2 Franken 1812	225.00
3.	1 Batzen (Bi) 1808, '16. Arms. Rev: Value	35.00

Argau (Argovie)

4.	4 Franken 1812. Arms. Rev: Warrior	700.00
5.	1 Batzen (Bi) 1805–16. Arms. Rev: Value	30.00

Basel

6.	5 Batzen 1809–10. Arms. Rev: Value	50.00
7.	1 Batzen (Bi) 1805–10	30.00

Bern

8.	1 Thaler 1798, 1823, '35. Arms. Rev: Warrior	450.00
9.	40 Batzen. Counterstamped on French écu	200.00
10.	½ Thaler 1835. Arms. Rev: Warrior	200.00
11.	1 Batzen (Bi) 1754–1826. Arms. Rev: Value in wreath	17.50

Freyburg (Fribourg)

12.	4 Franken 1823. Arms. Rev: Warrior	650.00
13.	1 Batzen (Bi) 1806–30. Arms. Rev: Value	25.00

Geneva (Genève)

14.	1 Thaler 1794. Liberty head	250.00

15.	5 Francs 1848. Arms. Rev: Value	250.00
16.	25 Centimes (Bi) 1839, '44	17.50
17.	10 Centimes (Bi) 1839, '44	11.50
18.	5 Centimes (Bi) 1840	15.00
19.	4 Centimes (Bi) 1839	25.00
20.	2 Centimes (Bi) 1839	25.00
21.	1 Centime (Bi) 1839	15.00

Graubunden (Grisons)

22.	10 Batzen 1825. Arms. Rev: Value	350.00
23.	5 Batzen 1807, '20, '26	125.00

Luzern (Lucerne)

24.	4 Franken 1813–14. Arms. Rev: Warrior	275.00
25.	1 Batzen 1803–13	20.00

St. Gall

26.	1 Taler 1621. Bear standing	200.00

Solothurn (Soleure)

27.	4 Franken 1813. Arms. Rev: Warrior	850.00
28.	1 Batzen (Bi) 1805–26. Arms. Rev: Value	25.00

Ticino (Tessin)

29.	4 Franchi 1814. Arms. Rev: Warrior	550.00

Vaud

30.	5 Batzen 1826–31. Arms. Rev: Cross	35.00

31.	1 Batzen (Bi) 1826–34	17.50

Zurich

32.	40 Batzen 1813. Arms. Rev: Motto	250.00

33.	8 Batzen 1810, '14	75.00
34.	1 Kreuzer (Bi) 1842. Arms. Rev: Value in wreath	10.00

HELVETIAN CONFEDERATION 1850–

35.	5 Francs 1850–74. Helvetia seated. Value in wreath	200.00
36.	2 Francs 1850, '57, '60, '62–63	100.00
37.	1 Franc 1850–57, '60–61	65.00
38.	½ Franc 1850–51	125.00

39.	5 Francs 1888–1916. Diademed head of Helvetia. Rev: Shield and value in wreath	175.00

SWITZERLAND (continued)

SHOOTING FESTIVAL COINS
(Nos. 40–56)
NOTE: These were intended primarily as prizes but also were used in general circulation for a brief time; the denomination is 5 francs

40.   GRAUBUNDEN 1842   500.00

41.   GLARUS 1847   1500.00

42.   SOLOTHURN 1855   1250.00

43.   BERN 1857   325.00

44.   ZURICH 1859   250.00

45.   NIDWALDEN 1861   150.00

46.   LA CHAUX-DE-FONDS 1863   200.00

47.   SCHAFFHAUSEN 1865   125.00

48.	SCHWYZ 1867	125.00
52.	LAUSANNE 1876	80.00
49.	ZUG 1869	150.00
53.	BASEL 1879	75.00
50.	ZURICH 1872	125.00
54.	FRIBOURG (FREYBURG) 1881	75.00
51.	ST. GALL 1874	100.00
55.	LUGANO 1883	75.00

56.   BERN 1885   75.00

60.   5 Francs 1939. Kneeling figure shooting. Rev: Motto. (Luzern [Lucerne] Shooting Festival)   75.00

57.   5 Francs 1922–28. Bust of "William Tell." Rev: Shield   125.00

61.   5 Francs 1939. Farm scene above, clasped hands below. Rev: Shield and inscription. (Zurich Exposition)   75.00

COMMEMORATIVE ISSUES

58.   5 Francs 1934. Swiss Guard. Rev: Crowned arms in wreath. (Fribourg Shooting Festival)   80.00

62.   5 Francs 1939. Male figure. Rev: Helvetian cross. (Laupen commemorative)   350.00
63.   5 Francs 1941. Three figures swearing oath. Rev: Helvetian cross and inscription. (650 years of Confederation)   80.00

59.   5 Francs 1936. Kneeling female figure. Rev: Inscription. (Premium for Armament Fund)   45.00

64.   5 Francs 1944. Male figure. Rev: Helvetian cross and inscription. (500th anniversary of Battle of St. Jakob an der Birs)   80.00
65.   5 Francs 1948. Woman and child. Rev: Helvetian cross. (Centenary of Swiss constitution)   30.00

SWITZERLAND (continued)

66. 20 Francs (G) 1897–1949. Peasant girl. Rev:
    Shield — 165.00
67. 10 Francs (G) 1911–22 — 100.00
68. 5 Francs 1931–69. Type of #57, but smaller — 10.00
68a. 5 Francs (C-N) 1968– — 4.00

78. 5 Francs (C-N) 1974. Three women with Swiss
    cross. Rev: Value and dates. (100th anniver-
    sary of constitution) — 10.00

69. 2 Francs 1874–1967. Helvetia standing, border
    of stars. Rev: Value in wreath — 7.50
69a. 2 Francs (C-N) 1968– — 1.50
70. 1 Franc 1875–1967 — 4.00
70a. 1 Franc (C-N) 1968– — .50
71. ½ Franc 1875–1967 — 3.00
71a. ½ Franc (C-N) 1968– — .35

79. 5 Francs (C-N) 1975. Hands around inscrip-
    tion. Rev: Value. (European Monument Pro-
    tection Year) — 8.50
80. 5 Francs (C-N) 1976. Three armored pikemen.
    Rev: Value. (500th anniversary, Battle of
    Murten Castle) — 8.50
81. 5 Francs (C-N) 1977. Head of Johann Heinrich
    Pestalozzi, founder of modern elementary ed-
    ucation. Rev: Value — 7.50
82. 5 Francs (C-N) 1978. Head of Henri Dunant,
    founder of Red Cross in 1862. Rev: Value — 7.50
83. 5 Francs (C-N) 1979. Head of Albert Einstein.
    Rev: Value. (Centennial of scientist's birth) — 7.50
84. 5 Francs (C-N) 1979. Mathematical equation.
    Rev: Value. (Einstein centennial) — 7.50

72. 20 Centimes (N) 1881–1938; (C-N) 1939-
    Head of Helvetia — .25
73. 10 Centimes (C-N) 1879–1915, 1919–31,
    1940– ; (Bra) 1918, '19; (N) 1932–39 — .15
74. 5 Centimes (C-N) 1879–1917, 1919–31,
    1940– ; (Bra) 1918; (N) 1932–41 — .10

75. 2 Centimes (Bro) 1948–74. Helvetian cross — .15
76. 1 Centime (Bro) 1948– — .15

85. 5 Francs (C-N) 1980. Value. Rev: Head of Fer-
    dinand Hodler, Swiss painter — 7.50

77. 5 Francs 1963. Nurse standing between two
    bandaged men. Rev: Value (Red Cross cen-
    tennial) — 20.00

86.

SYRIA

86. 5 Francs (C-N) 1981. Stylized design, STANS 1481. Rev: Value. (500th anniversary of Stans Convention, which brought peace to Swiss cantons)   7.50

87. 5 Francs (C-N) 1982. Gotthard railroad vignette. Rev: Value. (Gotthard railroad centenary)   7.50

Originally a part of the Turkish Empire, Syria was a French mandate, with some self-government, from 1920 to 1943. In 1944 Syria became an independent republic. With Egypt, it was part of the United Arab Republic from 1958 until 1961.

100 Piastres = 1 Lira (Pound)

FRENCH MANDATE 1920–1943

1.	50 Piastres 1929–37	30.00
2.	25 Piastres 1929–38	20.00
3.	10 Piastres 1929	17.50
4.	5 Piastres (A-Bro) 1926–40	8.50
5.	2 Piastres (A-Bro) 1926	25.00

6. 1 Piastre (N-Bro) 1929–36; (Z) 1940. (Center hole)   6.50

INDEPENDENT REPUBLIC 1944–

7.	1 Pound (G) 1950	185.00
8.	½ Pound (G) 1950	80.00

9.	1 Lira 1950	12.50
10.	50 Piastres 1947	12.50
11.	25 Piastres 1947	10.00
12.	10 Piastres (C-N) 1948, '56	4.00
13.	5 Piastres (C-N) 1948, '56	3.00
14.	2½ Piastres (C-N) 1948, '56	1.50

UNITED ARAB REPUBLIC ISSUES

15.	50 Piastres 1958. Eagle. Rev: Value in gear	12.50
16.	25 Piastres 1958	6.50

SYRIA (continued)

17.	50 Piastres 1959. Eagle with two stars on shield. Rev: Value within inscription. (Founding of Republic)	12.50
18.	10 Piastres (A-Bro) 1960. Eagle. Rev: Value	1.25
19.	5 Piastres (A-Bro) 1960	.75

29. 1 Pound (N) 1972. Arms. Rev: Hand holding torch over map. (25th anniversary of Socialist Party)   2.50

20. 2½ Piastres (A-Bro) 1960   .65

SYRIAN ARAB REPUBLIC

| 30. | 50 Piastres (N) 1972. Rev: Value over torch (25th anniversary of Socialist Party) | 1.50 |
| 31. | 25 Piastres (N) 1972. Rev: Lighted altar. (25th anniversary of Socialist Party) | 1.25 |

21.	1 Pound (N) 1968, '71. Arms: Rev: Inscription in panel	1.50
22.	50 Piastres (N) 1968	1.25
23.	25 Piastres (N) 1968	1.00
24.	10 Piastres (A-Bro) 1962, '65. Rev: Value	.65
25.	5 Piastres (A-Bro) 1962, '65	.35
26.	2½ Piastres (A-Bro) 1962, '65	.35

32.	1 Pound (N) 1976. (F.A.O. coin plan)	1.75
33.	50 Piastres (N) 1976	1.25
34.	25 Piastres (N) 1976	1.00
35.	10 Piastres (Bra) 1976	.50
36.	5 Piastres (Bra) 1976	.40
37.	1 Pound (N) 1978. Arms. Rev: Bust of General Hafez al Assad. (Re-election of the president)	10.00
38.	1 Pound (C-N) 1979. Arms. Rev: Inscription in panel	1.50
39.	50 Piastres (C-N) 1979	1.25
40.	25 Piastres (C-N) 1979	.50
41.	10 Piastres (A-Br) 1979	.40
42.	5 Piastres (A-Br) 1979	.35

27. 1 Pound (N) 1968. Arms. Rev: Wheat stalks. (F.A.O. coin plan)   2.50

28. 5 Piastres (Bra) 1971. Arms. Rev: Wheat. (F.A.O. coin plan)   .65

TAIWAN (Nationalist China)

Taiwan has been Chinese since the 16th Century, except for 50 years of Japanese rule (1895–1945). In 1949 the Nationalists under Chiang Kai-shek fled to Taiwan, which they administer to the present day.

10 Chiao = 1 Yuan

1.   5 Chiao 1949. Bust, Sun Yat-sen. Rev: Map   6.00

2.   2 Chiao (A) 1950   .50
3.   1 Chiao (Bro) 1949, (A) 1955   .35

4.   1 Dollar (C-N) 1960– . Plum flower. Rev: Orchid (50th anniversary of Republic)   .75

5.   100 Yuan 1965. Head of Dr. Sun Yat-sen. Rev: Running deer. (100th anniversary of birth)   25.00
6.   50 Yuan 1965   20.00

7.   10 Yuan (C-N) 1965. Rev: Mausoleum at Nanking   5.00
8.   5 Yuan (C-N) 1965   6.50

9.

9.   1 Yuan or dollar (C-N) 1966. Head of Chiang Kai-shek. Rev: Inscription. (80th birthday)   1.25

10.   5 Chiao or 50 Fen (Bra) 1967–78. Mayling orchid. Rev: Inscription   1.00
10a.   5 Chiao or 50 Fen (Bro) 1982– . Type of #10 (Smaller planchet)   .75

11.   1 Chiao (A) 1967. Simple Heart orchid   .50

12.   1 Yuan (C-N-Z) 1969. Plum flower. Rev: Farm girl and tractor. (F.A.O. coin plan)   1.25

13.   5 Yuan (C-N) 1970–   Head of Chiang Kai-shek. Rev: Value   1.00
14.   5 Yuan (C-N) 1970–78. Head of Dr. Sun Yat-sen. Rev: Value within wreath   .75
14a.   5 Yuan (C-N) 1982– . Sun Yat-sen. Type of #14. (Smaller planchet)   .50
15.   10 Yuan (C-N) 1982– . Head of Dr. Sun Yat-sen. Rev: Value within wreath   1.00

TANZANIA

The Republic of Tanganyika and the People's Republic of Zanzibar (q.v.) federated in April 1964, and adopted the name United Republic of Tanzania in October 1964. Tanganyika, formerly part of German East Africa, a British mandate after World War I, and a U.N. Trust Territory after World War II, became an independent state in 1961 and a republic within the British Commonwealth in 1962. Zanzibar, a small island in the Indian Ocean 20 miles off the coast of East Africa, was proclaimed a People's Republic in January 1964, after becoming an independent state within the Commonwealth in 1963.

1.	1 Shilling (C-N) 1966– . Head of Pres. Nyerere. Rev: Freedom torch	1.00

2.	50 Cents (C-N) 1966– . Rev: Rabbit	1.00

3.	20 Cents (N-Bro) 1966– . Rev: Ostrich	.30
4.	5 Cents (Bro) 1966– . Rev: Sailfish	.20

5.	5 Shillings (C-N) 1971. Head of President Nyerere. Rev: Value surrounded by food crops and cow. (F.A.O. coin plan; 10th anniversary of independence)	3.00

6.	5 Shillings (C-N) 1972, '73. Type of #5, without commemorative legend (F.A.O. coin plan)	2.50

7.	1500 Shillings (G) 1974. Rev: Leopard	500.00

8.	50 Shillings 1974. Rev: Rhinoceros	40.00

9.	25 Shillings 1974. Rev: Giraffes	25.00
10.	5 Shillings (C-N) 1978. Head of President Nyerere. Rev: Tractor. (F.A.O. coin plan)	4.00

THAILAND

A kingdom on the Indo-Chinese peninsula in Asia, formerly known as Siam.

64 Atts = 1 Tical
100 Satangs or 8 Fuangs = 1 Tical

EARLY BULLET MONEY   1824–80

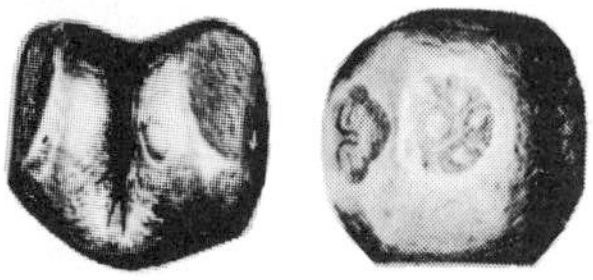

1.	4 Ticals	250.00
2.	2 Ticals	225.00
3.	1 Tical	15.00
4.	½ Tical	20.00
5.	¼ Tical	10.00
6.	⅛ Tical	10.00
7.	¹⁄₁₆ Tical	25.00
8.	¹⁄₃₂ Tical	35.00

P'RA CHOM KLAO MONGKUT   1851–68

9.	2 Ticals 1860. Crown with three umbrellas and leaf scrolls. Rev: Elephant in center of ornamental design	250.00
10.	1 Tical	35.00
11.	½ Tical	65.00
12.	¼ Tical	25.00
13.	⅛ Tical	12.50
14.	¹⁄₁₆ Tical	40.00

15.	⅛ Fuang (T alloy)	6.00
16.	¹⁄₁₆ Fuang (T alloy)	6.00
17.	½ Fuang (C)	20.00
18.	¼ Fuang (C)	30.00

P'RA PARAMIN MAHA CHULALONGKORN
1868–1910

19.	1 Tical. Type of #9, but without leaf scrolls	25.00
20.	¼ Tical	10.00
21.	⅛ Tical	6.50

22.	1 Tical 1868–1907. Bust. Rev: Arms with supporters	15.00
23.	¼ Tical 1868–1909	20.00
24.	⅛ Tical 1868–1908	5.00
25.	¹⁄₁₆ Fuang (T alloy). Type of #19	20.00
26.	4 Atts (C). Crowned monogram. Rev: Value in wreath	25.00
27.	2 Atts (C)	5.00
28.	1 Att (C)	4.00
29.	½ Att (C)	3.00

30.	20 Satangs (C-N) 1897. Three-headed elephant. Rev: Value in wreath	20.00
31.	10 Satangs 1897 (C-N)	30.00
32.	5 Satangs 1897 (C-N)	12.50
33.	2½ Satangs 1897 (C-N)	6.50

34.	10 Satangs (N) 1908. Name and value. Rev: Date and ornamental design of #9. (Center hole)	3.00
35.	5 Satangs (N) 1908–09	7.50

36.	2 Atts (Bro) 1887–1905. Bust. Rev: Allegorical figure of Siam seated	5.00
37.	1 Att (Bro) 1887–1905	4.00
38.	½ Att (Bro) 1887–1905	4.00

THAILAND (continued)

P'RA PARAMIN MAHA VAJIRAVUDH 1910–25

39.	1 Tical 1910, '13–18. Bust. Rev: Three-elephant design	15.00
40.	½ Tical 1915–21	10.00
41.	¼ Tical 1915–25	6.50
42.	10 Satangs (N) 1910–21. Type of #34	2.50
43.	5 Satangs (N) 1910–21	2.50
44.	1 Satang (Bro) 1910–24	2.00

P'RA PARAMIN MAHA PRAJADHIPOK 1925–33

45.	½ Tical 1929. Bust in uniform. Rev: Elephant	20.00
46.	¼ Tical 1929	10.00
47.	5 Satangs (C-N) 1926. Type of #34	2.50
48.	1 Satang (Bro) 1926–29	1.50

ANANDA MAHIDOL 1933–46

49.	20 Satangs (T) 1945. Ornamental designs. (Center hole)	3.00
50.	10 Satangs (N) 1935, '37; (S) '41; (T) 1942, '44, '45	2.00
51.	5 Satangs (N) 1935–37; (S) '41; (T) 1942, '44, '45	2.00
52.	1 Satang (T) 1942, '44	.50
52a.	1 Satang (Br) 1935–39. Type of #34	2.00
53.	½ Satang (Bro) 1937	1.50

54.	50 Satangs (T) 1946. Young bust. Rev: Arms	50.00
55.	10 Satangs (T) 1946	4.00
56.	5 Satangs 1946	2.50

57.	50 Satangs 1946. Older bust. Rev: Type of #54	4.00
58.	25 Satangs 1946	3.00
59.	10 Satangs 1946	2.00
60.	5 Satangs 1946	1.00

PHUMIPHOL ADULYADET 1946–

100 Satangs = 1 Baht

61.	50 Satangs (A-Bro) 1950. Bust of King in uniform. Rev: Arms	4.00
62.	25 Satangs (A-Bro) 1954–56	3.50
63.	10 Satangs (T) 1950–73; (A-Bro) 1950	1.25
64.	5 Satangs (T) 1950–73; (A-Bro) 1950	.75

65.	1 Baht (C-N) 1957–60. Bust of King with three medals on uniform. Rev: Arms	1.50
66.	50 Satangs (A-Bro) 1957	.30
67.	25 Satangs (A-Bro) 1957; (Bra) 1977	.60
68.	10 Satangs (A-Bra or Bro) 1957–	.60
69.	5 Satangs (A-Bra or Bro) 1957	.30
70.	1 Baht (C-N) 1961. Heads of King and Queen. Rev: Arms	1.50
71.	1 Baht (C-N) 1962. Bust of King (does not divide legend)	1.50

72.	20 Bahts 1963. Bust of King. Rev: Royal emblems below royal umbrella. (King's 36th birthday)	25.00

519

73.   1 Baht (C-N) 1963. Rev: Royal insignia   1.50

74.   1 Baht (C-N) 1966. Conjoined busts of King
       and Queen. Rev: Sunstar and inscription.
       (Fifth Asian Games)   1.50

75.   600 Bahts (G) 1968. Bust of Queen Sirikit. Rev:
       Crowned monogram. (Queen's 36th birth-
       day)   300.00
76.   300 Bahts (G) 1968   150.00
77.   150 Bahts (G) 1968   85.00

78.   1 Baht (C-N) 1970. Type of #74, reverse in-
       scription updated. (Sixth Asian Games)   1.50

79.   800 Bahts (G) 1971. Bust of King. Rev: Crowned
       insignia. (25th year of reign)   400.00
80.   400 Bahts (G) 1971   200.00
81.   10 Bahts 1971   6.00

82.   50 Bahts 1971. Bust of King. Rev: Buddhist
       Wheel of Law. (20th anniversary of World
       Fellowship of Buddhists)   30.00

83.   5 Bahts (C-N) 1972. Bust of King. Rev: Mythi-
       cal Garuda bird. (Nonagonal planchet)   2.00
83a.   5 Bahts (C-N) 1977, '79. (Round)   1.25
84.   1 Baht (C-N) 1972. Bust of Prince Va-
       jiralongkorn. Rev: Crowned monogram   1.50

85.   1 Baht (C-N) 1972. Bust of King. Rev: Plough-
       ing ceremony. (F.A.O. coin plan)   1.50
86.   1 Baht (C-N) 1973. Rev: Emblem of World
       Health Organization. (25th anniversary of
       W.H.O.)   1.50

87.   50 Bahts 1974. Conjoined portraits of Kings P'ra
       Chom Klao Mongkut and P'ra Paramin Maha
       Chulalongkorn. Rev: Symbols of Chakri dy-
       nasty. (100th anniversary of National Mu-
       seum in Bangkok)   30.00
88.   1 Baht (C-N) 1974. Bust. Rev: Garuda bird   1.25

THAILAND (continued)

89. 2500 Bahts (G) 1975. Bust. Rev: Swallow (Conservation commemorative) 650.00

90. 100 Bahts 1975. Rev: Stag 35.00
91. 50 Bahts 1975. Rev: Rhinoceros 30.00

92. 1 Baht (C-N) 1975. Conjoined busts of King and Queen. Rev: Symbol of South East Asian Peninsular Games. (Commemorates eighth S.E.A.P. Games) 1.50
93. 150 Bahts 1975. Portrait of Somdej Phra Sri Nakharintra. Rev: "S" monogram in shape of lotus bud. (75th birthday of King's mother) 30.00
94. 150 Bahts 1977. Man and boy sowing rice. Rev: Elephant and cub. (F.A.O. coin plan) 35.00
95. 1 Baht (C-N) 1977. Rev: Seated woman holding rice stalk. (F.A.O.) .... .75

96. 150 Baht (S) 1977. Dual portrait of Crown Prince Vajiralong and Princess Soamsawali. Rev: Royal insignia. (Royal Wedding) 25.00
97. 10 Baht (N) 1977. (Royal Wedding) 2.00

98. 150 Baht (S) 1977. Princess Soamsawali. Rev: Royal insignia. (Princess' graduation) 25.00
99. 10 Baht (N) 1977. (Princess' graduation) 2.00
100. 1 Baht (C-N) 1977. (Princess' graduation) .... .65

101. 150 Baht (S) 1977. Bust of Princess Sirindhorn. Rev: Royal insignia. (Investiture of Princess Sirindhorn) 25.00
102. 1 Baht (C-N) 1977. (Investiture of Princess Sirindhorn) .... .65
103. 150 Baht 1978. Bust of Rama IX. Rev: Orchid arrangement. (Ninth World Orchid Conference, Bangkok) 25.00

105.

104. 150 Baht 1978. Bust of Crown Prince. Rev: Royal insignia. (Graduation of Crown Prince) 25.00
105. 1 Baht (C-N) 1978. (Crown Prince's graduation) .... .65

107.

106. 5 Baht (C-N) 1978. Dual royal portrait. Rev: Rayed sun within wreath. (Eighth Asian Games, Bangkok) 1.50
107. 1 Baht (C-N) 1978. (Eighth Asian Games) .... .65
108. 300 Baht 1979. Bust of Princess Chulabhorn. Rev: Royal insignia. (Princess' graduation) 35.00
109. 10 Baht (N) 1979. (Princess Chulabhorn's graduation) 2.00
110. 2 Baht (C-N) 1979. (Princess' graduation) 1.00
111. 200 Baht 1979. Royal baby. Rev: Inscription. (Royal Cradle Ceremony) 30.00
112. 5 Baht (C-N) 1979. (Royal Cradle Ceremony) 1.50
113. 10 Baht (N) 1980. Bust of Queen Mother. Rev: Triple royal insignia. (80th birthday of King's mother) 2.00
114. 5 Baht (C-N) 1980. (Queen Mother's 80th birthday) 1.50

115. 600 Baht 1980. Bust of Queen. Rev: Agricultural vignette (F.A.O. coin plan)   35.00

116. 5 Baht (C-N) 1980. Bust of Queen. Rev: Agricultural vignette. (F.A.O. coin plan)   1.50

117. 10 Baht (N) 1980. Bust of Rama IX. Rev: Buddhist symbol. (30th anniversary of Buddhist Fellowship)   2.00

118. 600 Baht 1981. Bust of Rama VI. Rev: Royal emblem. (Birth centennial of Rama VI)   35.00

This mountainous country which lies between China and India has a vaguely defined status. For more than two centuries it has been claimed by China. Overrun by the Chinese Communist Army in 1951, shaken by revolution against the Chinese in 1959, it was made an autonomous region of the People's Republic of China in 1965.

10 Shokay = 1 Srang
1 Tangka = 1½ Shokang

119. 600 Baht 1981. Dual bust of Rama IX, as young and as older man. Rev: Royal insignia. (35th anniversary of reign)   35.00

120. 10 Baht (C-N) 1981. (35th anniversary of reign)   2.00

121. 5 Baht (C-N) 1981. (Rama VI birth centennial)   1.50

122. 600 Baht 1982. Dual royal bust. Rev: Royal insignia. (Bicentennial of Bangkok)   40.00

1. 1 Rupee 1903   75.00

2. 10 Srang 1948–49   20.00

3. 5 Srang 1946–48   12.50

4. 5 Shokang (C) 1947–53   6.00

5. 3 Shokang (C) 1946   20.00

TIMOR

This Indonesian island formerly was divided into two parts. The eastern end was a Portuguese Overseas Territory with its own coinage, while the western end, previously Dutch-controlled, became part of the Republic of Indonesia in 1949. In December 1975, the Indonesians overran the eastern end of the island.

100 Avos = 1 Pataca
100 Centavos = 1 Escudo

1.	50 Avos 1945, '48, '51. Arms on cross. Rev: Value above spray	20.00
2.	20 Avos (N-Bro) 1945. Bust of Republic. Rev: Arms	30.00

3.	10 Avos (Bro) 1945, '48, '51. Quinas cross	4.00
4.	6 Escudos 1958. Arms on cross above date. Rev: Crowned shield	17.50
5.	3 Escudos 1958	8.50

6.	1 Escudo (C-N) 1958	5.00
7.	60 Centavos (C-N) 1958	3.50
8.	30 Centavos (Bro) 1958. Crowned shield. Rev: Value	2.50
9.	10 Centavos (Bro) 1958	5.00
10.	10 Escudos 1964. Arms on cross above date. Rev: Crowned shield	12.50

11.	10 Escudos (C-N) 1970	5.00
12.	5 Escudos (C-N) 1970	3.00
13.	2½ Escudos (C-N) 1970	2.50

14.	1 Escudo (Bro) 1970. Crowned shield. Rev: Value	1.25
15.	50 Centavos (Bro) 1970	1.00
16.	20 Centavos (Bro) 1970	.65

TOGO

A former German colony on the west coast of Africa, Togo became a French mandate after World War I and is now an independent republic and member of the West African States currency group (q.v.).

100 Centimes = 1 Franc

1.	2 Francs (A-Bro) 1924–25. Head of the Republic. Rev: Value	20.00
2.	1 Franc (A-Bro) 1924–25	17.50
3.	50 Centimes (A-Bro) 1924–26	12.50

4.	2 Francs (A) 1948. Bust of the Republic. Rev: Value and antelope head	30.00
5.	1 Franc (A) 1948	25.00
6.	5 Francs (A-Bro) 1956. Bust of Republic. Rev: Antelope	7.50

TONGA

Also known as the Friendly Islands, situated in the South Pacific Ocean, this is a fully independent kingdom and a member of the Commonwealth of Nations.

100 Seniti = 1 Pa'anga

8.   2 Pa'anga (C-N) 1967. Head of King Taufa'ahau Tupou IV. Rev: Arms. (Coronation commemorative) 12.50
9.   1 Pa'anga (C-N) 1967 .... 7.50
10. 50 Seniti (C-N) 1967 .... 5.00
11. 20 Seniti (C-N) 1967 .... 3.00
12. 2 Pa'anga (C-N) 1968– . Head of King, different inscription. Rev: Arms 5.00

1.   1 Pa'anga (C-N) 1967. Head of Queen Salote Tupou III. Rev: Arms 7.50
2.   50 Seniti (C-N) 1967 .... 2.50
3.   20 Seniti (C-N) 1967 .... 2.00

13. 1 Pa'anga (C-N) 1968– 4.00
14. 50 Seniti (C-N) 1968 .... 3.00
15. 20 Seniti (C-N) 1968– 1.00
16. 10 Seniti (C-N) 1968– . Rev: Value .... .75
17. 5 Seniti (C-N) 1968– .... .25
18. 2 Seniti (Bro) 1968– . Rev: Turtle .... .20
19. 1 Seniti (Bro) 1968 .... .20
20. 50 Seniti (C-N) 1974. Type of #14 (Dodecagonal planchet) 3.00
21. 1 Seniti (Bra) 1974. Type of #19 .... .25

4.   10 Seniti (C-N) 1967. Rev: Value .... .75
5.   5 Seniti (C-N) 1967 .... .50

6.   2 Seniti (Bro) 1967. Rev: Turtle .... .50
7.   1 Seniti (Bro) 1967 .... .35

22. 2 Pa'anga (C-N) 1975, '77. Bust of King (type of #23). Rev: Livestock and produce. (F.A.O. coin plan) 7.50

23.   1 Pa'anga (C-N) 1975. Rev: 100 coconut trees.
(F.A.O. coin plan)   6.50

31.   2 Pa'anga (C-N) 1978. Military bust of King
Taufa'ahau Tupou IV. Rev: Type of #22.
(King's 60th birthday; F.A.O. coin plan)   10.00
32.   2 Pa'anga (C-N) 1979–80. Rev: Whale. (Sea
Resource Management; F.A.O. coin plan)   15.00
33.   2 Pa'anga (C-N) 1981. (World Food Day;
F.A.O. coin plan)   5.00
34.   50 Seniti 1981. Rev: Fruit. (F.A.O. coin plan)   2.00

24.   50 Seniti (C-N) 1975, '77–78. Rev: 50 fish.
(F.A.O. coin plan; dodecagon)   2.50
25.   20 Seniti (C-N) 1975, '77–79. Rev: 20 bees and
beehive. (F.A.O.)   1.50

26.   10 Seniti (C-N) 1975, '77–79. Rev: 10 cows.
(F.A.O. coin plan)   1.00
27.   5 Seniti (C-N) 1975, '77–79. Hen and 4 chicks.
Rev: Bunch of bananas. (F.A.O.)   .50

28.   2 Seniti (Bro) 1975, '77–79. 2 watermelons.
Rev: Symbol of World Population Year.
(F.A.O.)   .50
29.   1 Seniti (Bro) 1975, '79. Ear of maize. Rev: Sow
(F.A.O.)   .25
30.   1 Pa'anga (C-N) 1977. Rev: Coconut trees.
(F.A.O.)   5.00

TRINIDAD AND TOBAGO

These islands in the British West Indies were discovered by Columbus and settled by the Spanish, who ceded them to Great Britain in 1802. They became one colony in 1889 and an independent member state of the British Commonwealth in 1962.

1.	50 Cents (C-N) 1966–71. Arms. Rev: Value	2.00
2.	25 Cents (C-N) 1966–73	1.00
3.	10 Cents (C-N) 1966–73	.50
4.	5 Cents (Bro) 1966–73	.40
5.	1 Cent (Bro) 1966–73	.40

6.	1 Dollar (N) 1969, '79. Arms. Rev: Value and cocoa branch. (F.A.O.)	8.50
7.	1 Dollar (C-N) 1970–71. Arms. Rev: Value	8.50

8.	5 Dollars 1971– . Arms. Rev: Scarlet ibis	20.00

9.

9.	10 Dollars 1972. Antique map. Rev: Arms over inscription. (10th anniversary of independence)	40.00
10.	5 Dollars 1972. Type of #8 with added inscription	30.00

11.	1 Dollar (C-N) 1972. Arms over inscription. Rev: Native cocorico bird	8.50

12.	50 Cents (C-N) 1972. Type of #1. Rev: Redesigned lettering, commemorative inscription	2.50
13.	25 Cents (C-N) 1972	1.00
14.	10 Cents (C-N) 1972	.75
15.	5 Cents (Bro) 1972	.50
16.	1 Cent (Bro) 1972	.35
17.	10 Dollars 1973– . Type of #9, without commemorative inscription	30.00
18.	10 Dollars (C-N) 1973–	30.00
19.	1 Dollar (C-N) 1973– . Type of #11, without commemorative inscription	7.50

20.	50 Cents (C-N) 1973– . Arms. Rev: Steel drums	2.00
21.	25 Cents (C-N) 1974– . Arms. Rev: Chaconia flower, value	.65

22.	10 Cents (C-N) 1974– . Rev: Hibiscus flower	.40
23.	5 Cents (Bro) 1974– . Rev: Bird of paradise	.25
24.	1 Cent (Bro) 1974– . Rev: Balisier bird	.10

TRINIDAD AND TOBAGO (continued)

25. 100 Dollars (G) 1976. Arms. Rev: Two scarlet
    ibises 80.00
26. 25 Dollars 1980. Arms. Rev: Flag, map of Carib-
    bean. (10th anniversary of Caribbean De-
    velopment Bank.) Issued in proof only 30.00
27. 100 Dollars (G) 1981. Arms. Rev: Flowers. (Fifth
    anniversary of republic) 185.00
28. 10 Dollars (C-N) 1981. Rev: Antique map.
    (Fifth anniversary of republic) 15.00
28a. 10 Dollars (S) 1981. Proof 25.00
29. 10 Dollars (C-N) 1982. Arms. Rev: Flag. (20th
    anniversary of independence) 15.00
29a. 10 Dollars (S) 1982. Proof 25.00
30. 5 Dollars (C-N) 1982. Arms. Rev: Scarlet ibis.
    (Independence) 10.00
30a. 5 Dollars (S) 1982. Proof 20.00

TRISTAN DA CUNHA

A small cluster of volcanic islands located in the South
Atlantic about midway between South Africa and South
America, Tristan da Cunha became a dependency of the
British colony of St. Helena in 1938.

1. 25 Pence (C-N) 1977. Elizabeth II. Rev: Ship.
    (Queen's Silver Jubilee) 4.00
1a. 25 Pence (S) 1977. Proof 25.00
2. 1 Crown (C-N) 1978. Rev: Crowned cameo
    portrait of Elizabeth II. (Coronation Jubilee) 4.00
2a. 1 Crown (S) 1978. Proof 25.00
3. 1 Crown (C-N) 1980. Rev: Queen Mother Eliz-
    abeth. (Queen Mother's 80th birthday) 4.00
3a. 1 Crown (S) 1980. Proof 30.00
4. 1 Crown (C-N) 1981. Rev: Dual cameo portrait
    of Prince Charles and Lady Diana. (Royal
    couple's wedding) 4.00
4a. 1 Crown (S) 1981. Proof 40.00

527

TUNISIA

Tunisia became a French protectorate in 1881. It now has independent status.

100 Centimes = 1 Franc

FIRST ISSUE

1.	20 Francs (G) 1901–28. French inscription. Rev: Arabic inscription	50.00
2.	2 Francs 1891–1916. French inscription. Rev: Arabic inscription	12.50
3.	1 Franc 1891–1918	8.50
4.	50 Centimes 1891–1917	8.50

5.	10 Centimes (Bro) 1891–93, 1903–17. French inscription. Rev: Arabic inscription	3.50
6.	5 Centimes (Bro) 1891–93, 1903–17	2.00
7.	2 Centimes (Bro) 1891	6.00
8.	1 Centime (Bro) 1891	10.00

NEW STANDARD

NOTE: Nos. 9, 10 and 11 were never placed in general circulation

9.	100 Francs (G) 1930, '32, '34. French inscription. Rev: Arabic inscription	200.00
10.	20 Francs 1930, '32, '34. French inscription. Rev: Arabic inscription	100.00

11.	10 Francs 1930, '32, '34	100.00

12.	20 Francs 1935. French inscription. Rev: Arabic inscription	25.00
13.	10 Francs 1935	12.50
14.	5 Francs 1935–36	10.00

NOTE: Nos. 15, 16 and 17 were never placed in general circulation because of the outbreak of World War II; most of the coins were melted down

15.	20 Francs 1939. French inscription. Rev: Arabic inscription	50.00
16.	10 Francs 1939	15.00
17.	5 Francs 1939	10.00

18.	2 Francs (A-Bro) 1921–46. French and Arabic inscriptions	2.50
19.	1 Franc (A-Bro) 1921–46	1.00
20.	50 Centimes (A-Bro) 1921–46	1.00

21.	25 Centimes (N-Bro) 1919–38. French inscription. Rev: Arabic inscription. (Center hole)	3.50
22.	5 Francs (A-Bro) 1946. Type of #15	7.50
23.	20 Centimes (Z) 1942–46	20.00
24.	10 Centimes (Z) 1942–46	4.00

27.

25.	100 Francs (C-N) 1950–57. Arabic inscription. Rev: French inscription	8.50
26.	50 Francs (C-N) 1950–57	2.00
27.	20 Francs (C-N) 1950–57	2.00
28.	5 Francs (C-N) 1954–58	.40

29. 100 Milliemes (Bra) 1960– . Arabic legend in circle. Rev: Value in circle of leaves 2.00
30. 50 Milliemes (Bra) 1960– 1.25
31. 20 Milliemes (Bra) 1960– ..... .75
32. 10 Milliemes (Bra) 1960– ..... .60

33. 5 Milliemes (A) 1960– . Tree. Rev: Value ..... .50
34. 2 Milliemes (A) 1960– ..... .30
35. 1 Millieme (A) 1960– ..... .25

36. ½ Dinar (N) 1968. Head of President Bourguiba. Rev: Value 7.50

37. 1 Dinar 1970. Rev: Man harvesting dates. (F.A.O. coin plan) 12.50
38. 5 Dinars 1976. Head of President Bourguiba. Rev: Value. (20th year of independence) 35.00

39. 1 Dinar (C-N) 1976. Rev: Girl harvesting olives. (F.A.O. coin plan) 10.00

40. ½ Dinar (C-N) 1976. Rev: Stylized agricultural theme; ear of wheat, three oranges. (F.A.O. coin plan) 10.00

TURKEY

At the height of its power the empire of the Ottoman Turks stretched from Hungary to the Indian Ocean, and from northern Africa to central Asia. In the days of its decline, during the 19th century, the empire lost one province after another. World War I left Turkey with only Asia Minor and a much smaller area in Europe. In 1921 a revolt deposed the last Sultan, and Turkey became a republic.

All Turkish coins under the sultanate carry the Toughra, the Sultan's calligraphic emblem, on the obverse. In most cases the value appears right under the Toughra. On the bottom of the reverse appears the date on which the reigning Sultan began his rule. (The dates follow the Islamic system of beginning with A.D. 622 as the year 1. This is explained in the section on dating systems, p. 10.) At the top of the reverse appears the year of the then current Sultan's reign when the coin was issued.

40 Paras = 1 Piastre
100 Piastres = 1 Lira or Pound
100 Kurus = 1 Lira

COINS ISSUED 1839–1921

1.	500 Piastres (G). Toughra. Rev: Inscription in wreath	750.00
2.	250 Piastres (G)	400.00
3.	100 Piastres (G)	150.00
4.	50 Piastres (G)	80.00
5.	25 Piastres (G)	65.00

6.	20 Piastres (A.H. 1261–1336)	25.00
7.	10 Piastres (A.H. 1261–1331)	15.00
8.	5 Piastres (A.H. 1261–1331)	7.50
9.	2 Piastres (A.H. 1261–1336)	5.00
10.	1 Piastre (A.H. 1261–1329)	3.00
11.	40 Paras (C or Bi) (A.H. 1261–1340)	5.00
12.	20 Paras (C or Bi) (A.H. 1261–1334)	7.50
13.	10 Paras (C or Bi) (A.H. 1261–1334)	5.00
14.	5 Paras (C or Bi) (A.H. 1261–1334)	4.00
15.	1 Para (C or Bi) (A.H. 1261–1278)	4.00

REPUBLIC 1922–

16.	500 Piastres (G) 1926–29. Star and crescent. Rev: Inscription in wreath	750.00
17.	250 Piastres (G) 1927–28	450.00
18.	100 Piastres (G) 1926–28	225.00
19.	50 Piastres (G) 1927–28	125.00
20.	25 Piastres (G) 1925–29	85.00
21.	25 Piastres (N) 1925–28. Wheat spray and inscription. Rev: Oak spray and inscription	10.00
22.	10 Piastres (A-Bro) 1924–26	5.00
23.	5 Piastres (A-Bro) 1924–26	2.00
24.	2½ Piastres [100 Paras] (A-Bro) 1926–27	2.50

LAW OF JUNE 7, 1933
(All coins use Gregorian calendar)

25.	100 Kurus 1934. Head of Kemal Ataturk. Rev: Value, star and crescent	35.00
26.	1 Lira 1937–39. New head of Kemal Ataturk. Rev: Value, star and crescent	25.00
27.	50 Kurus 1935–37	10.00
28.	25 Kurus 1935–37	8.50
29.	1 Lira 1940–41. Head of Ismet Inonu. Rev: Star and crescent and value	20.00
30.	25 Kurus (N-Bro) 1943–46. Star and crescent. Rev: Value	2.00

31.	10 Kurus (C-N) 1935–40	1.50
32.	5 Kurus (C-N) 1935–43	1.50
33.	1 Kurus (C-N) 1935–37	1.00
34.	1 Kurus (C-N) 1938–42. Star and crescent. Rev: Value. (Scalloped edge)	1.50
35.	10 Paras (A-Bro) 1940–42	1.25

TURKEY (continued)

36. 1 Lira 1947–48. Star and crescent. Rev: Value in wreath — 6.00
37. 50 Kurus 1947, '48 — 5.00
38. 25 Kurus (Bra) 1948–56. Type of #30 — 1.00
39. 10 Kurus (Bra) 1949–56 — .50
40. 5 Kurus (Bra) 1949–57 — 1.25
41. 2½ Kurus (Bra) 1948–51 — 1.00
42. 1 Kurus (Bra) 1947–51 — .75

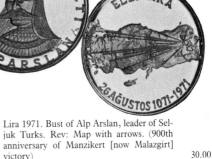

43. 10 Lira 1960. Head of Ataturk. Rev: Emblems of Revolution. (Armed forces' overthrow of Menderes government, May 27, 1960) — 20.00

44. 2½ Lira (St) 1960– . Figure of Ataturk. Rev: Value between wheat and daphne branches — 1.00
45. 1 Lira (C-N) 1957; (St) 1959– . Ataturk — .60

46. 25 Kurus (St) 1959– . Peasant woman with sack on shoulder. Rev: Value — .45
47. 10 Kurus (Bro) 1958–74. Star and crescent. Rev: Wheat — .40
48. 5 Kurus (Bro) 1958–74. Rev: Oak branch — .25
49. 1 Kurus (Bro) 1961–63; (Bro) 1963–74. Rev: Olive branch and value — .20
50. 25 Lira 1970. Bust of Kemal Ataturk. Rev: National Assembly Building. (50th anniversary of Assembly) — 25.00
51. 2½ Lira (Ac) 1970. Ataturk on tractor. Rev: Value. (F.A.O. coin plan) — 1.25

52. 50 Lira 1971. Bust of Alp Arslan, leader of Seljuk Turks. Rev: Map with arrows. (900th anniversary of Manzikert [now Malazgirt] victory) — 30.00

53. 50 Kurus (St) 1971– . Girl in native headdress — .35

54. 10 Kurus (Bro) 1971–74. Ataturk on tractor. Rev: Wheat, value. (F.A.O. coin plan) — .35

55. 50 Lira 1972. General on horseback. Rev: Battle scene. (50th anniversary of war between Turkey and Greece) — 25.00

56. 500 Lira (G) 1973. Bust of Ataturk. Rev: Star within flower, comet's tail. (50th anniversary of Republic) — 175.00

531

TURKEY (continued)

57. 100 Lira 1973. Front and side views of Ataturk on
    pedestal. Rev: Type of #56 .... 35.00
58. 50 Lira 1973 .... 25.00

59. 5 Lira (St) 1974– . Ataturk on horseback. Rev:
    Value 1.25
60. 10 Kurus (A) 1975– . Type of #47 .... .20
61. 5 Kurus (A) 1975– . Type of #48 .... .15
62. 1 Kurus (A) 1975– . Type of #49 .... .10
63. 10 Kurus (A) 1975. Type of #54. (F.A.O. coin
    plan) 1.00

64. 5 Kurus (A) 1975. Head of woman. Rev: Oak
    branch. (F.A.O.) .... .65

65. 5 Lira (C-S) 1976. Woman nursing child. Rev:
    Value. (International Women's Year) 6.00
66. 10 Kurus (A) 1976. Rev: Wheat stalks. (F.A.O.) 5.00
67. 5 Kurus (A) 1976. Rev: Oak leaves .... .75

68. 50 Lira 1977. Family and wheat. Rev: Value.
    (F.A.O.) 20.00
69. 5 Lira (Chrome-St) 1977 .... 5.00
70. 2½ Lira (Chrome-St) 1977 .... 2.50
71. 25 Lira 1977. Wheat stalks. Rev: Value. (F.A.O.
    coin plan) 20.00
72. 150 Lira 1978. Ataturk on tractor. Rev: Value.
    (F.A.O. coin plan) 35.00
73. 5 Lira (St) 1978. (F.A.O. coin plan.) Type of
    #72 .... 10.00
74. 2½ Lira (St) 1978. Woman nursing child.
    (F.A.O. coin plan) 5.00
75. 1 Lira (St) 1978. Type of #74 .... 3.00
76. 50 Kurus (St) 1978. Type of #72 .... 1.50
77. 200 Lira 1978. Bust of Mevlana Celaleddin-i
    Rumi. Rev: Mosque 40.00
78. 150 Lira 1978. Soccer player. Rev: World map.
    (World Soccer Championships, Argentina) 60.00

79. 150 Lira 1979. Head of Woman. Rev: Value.
    (F.A.O. coin plan) 35.00
80. 5 Lira (St) 1979. Type of #79 .... 10.00
81. 2½ Lira (St) 1979. Type of #79 .... 5.00
82. 1 Lira (St) 1979. Type of #72 .... 2.00
83. 50 Kurus (St) 1979. Type of #72 .... 1.25
84. 1 Kurus (Bro) 1979. Obv: Type of #79. Rev:
    Value 6.00
85. 500 Lira 1980. Type of #74 .... 40.00
86. 5 Lira (St) 1980. Rev: Value. (F.A.O. coin
    plan) 8.00
87. 2½ Lira (St) 1980. Type of #83 .... 4.00
88. 1 Lira (St) 1980. Type of #78 .... 1.50
89. 50 Kurus (St) 1980. Type of #79 .... 1.00
90. 10 Kurus (Bro) 1980. Type of #79 .... .50
91. 5 Kurus (Bro) 1980. Type of #87 .... 2.00
92. 100 Lira (C-N) 1982. Soccer player. Rev: Inscrip-
    tion and date. (World Soccer Championships,
    Madrid) 10.00

TURKS AND CAICOS ISLANDS

A British crown colony made up of two groups of small islands at the southeast end of the Bahamas.

1. 1 Crown (C-N) 1969. Draped bust of Queen Elizabeth wearing a coronet. Rev: Arms   5.00

2.   5.

2. 100 Crowns (G) 1974. Bust of Churchill. Rev: Arms, value. (100th anniversary of statesman's birth)   200.00
3. 50 Crowns (G) 1974   100.00
4. 20 Crowns 1974   40.00
5. 100 Crowns (G) 1975. Bust of Queen Elizabeth II. Rev: Globe showing orbits of John Glenn and Scott Carpenter   225.00
6. 50 Crowns (G) 1975. Rev: Bust of Columbus with ships   150.00
7. 25 Crowns (G) 1975. Rev: Arms   65.00
8. 20 Crowns 1975. Type of #6   50.00
9. 10 Crowns 1975. Type of #5   25.00
10. 5 Crowns 1975. Rev: Turk's Head cactus   15.00
11. 1 Crown (C-N) 1975. Rev: Map   5.00
12. 50 Crowns (G) 1976. Rev: Facing portraits of King George III and George Washington, flags above. (U.S. Bicentennial)   150.00
13. 20 Crowns 1976   40.00
14. 50 Crowns (G) 1977. Rev: Crown and date in wreath. (Queen's Silver Jubilee)   100.00

15a.

15. 100 Crowns (G) 1978. Rev: Two field athletes. 11th Commonwealth Games, Edmonton, Alberta, Canada)   200.00
15a. 20 Crowns 1978. (Commonwealth Games)   40.00

16. 100 Crowns (G) 1980. Rev: Bust of Louis, Earl Mountbatten, World War II hero and mentor of Prince Charles   200.00
17. 20 Crowns 1980. Type of #16, larger   35.00
18. 10 Crowns 1980   25.00
19. 5 Crowns 1980   15.00
20. 100 Crowns (G) 1981. Conjoined portraits of Prince Charles and Lady Diana. (Marriage of royal couple)   225.00

TUVALU

Composed of nine clusters of coral islands in the South Pacific, Tuvalu, formerly part of the British colony, the Gilbert and Ellice Islands, gained its independence in 1978. It is a member of the Commonwealth of Nations.

1.	1 Dollar (C-N) 1976– . Queen. Rev: Turtle	5.00

2.	50 Cents (C-N) 1976– . Rev: Octopus	3.00

3.	20 Cents (C-N) 1976– . Rev: Flying fish	1.50
4.	10 Cents (C-N) 1976– . Rev: Crab	1.00

5.	5 Cents (Bro) 1976– . Rev: Tiger shark	.50
6.	2 Cents (Bro) 1976– . Rev: Sting ray	.40
7.	1 Cent (Bro) 1976– . Rev: Cowrie shell	.30
8.	5 Dollars 1976. Rev: Catamaran. Proof	25.00
9.	10 Dollars 1979. Rev: Sailing ship. (First anniversary of independence)	25.00

10.	10 Dollars 1980. Rev: Bust of Queen Mother Elizabeth wearing tiara. (Queen Mother's 80th birthday)	25.00
11.	10 Dollars 1981. Rev: Head of Prince Philip, Duke of Edinburgh. (Duke of Edinburgh Award Scheme)	25.00
12.	5 Dollars (C-N) 1981. Rev: Interlocked monograms of Prince Charles and Lady Diana. (Marriage of Charles and Diana)	7.50

UGANDA

A former British protectorate in East Africa, Uganda became internally self-governing in 1962 and a fully independent state within the British Commonwealth in October of that year.

1.	2 Shillings (C-N) 1966. Arms. Rev: Crane and mountains	2.00
2.	1 Shilling (C-N) 1966–	1.00
3.	50 Cents (C-N) 1966–	.40

4.	20 Cents (Bro) 1966–74. Elephant tusks. Rev: Value	.50
5.	10 Cents (Bro) 1966–	.25
6.	5 Cents (Bro) 1966–	.20

7.	5 Shillings (C-N) 1968. Cow and calf. Rev: Arms. (F.A.O. coin plan)	5.00

8.	5 Shillings (C-N) 1972. Type of #1. (Heptagonal planchet)	5.00

11.

9.	1000 Shillings (S) 1981. Arms. Rev: Dual portrait of Prince Charles and Lady Diana. (Marriage of royal couple.) Issued in proof only	200.00
10.	100 Shillings (S) 1981. (Royal wedding.) In proof only	50.00
11.	10 Shillings (C-N) 1981. (Royal wedding)	7.50

535

UNITED ARAB EMIRATES

A group of seven oil-rich sheikhdoms on the Persian Gulf.

100 Fils = 1 Dinar

1.   1 Dinar (C-N) 1973. Carafe. Rev: Value   2.00

2.   50 Fils (C-N) 1973. Oil derricks   2.00

3.   25 Fils (C-N) 1973. Antelope   .75
4.   10 Fils (Bro) 1973. Dhow (Arab sailboat)   1.00

5.   5 Fils (Bro) 1973. "Bareface" fish. (F.A.O. coin
        plan)   .35
6.   1 Fil (Bro) 1973. Date palms. (F.A.O.)   .25
7.   50 Dirhams 1980. Value, inscription. Rev: Two
        children. (International Year of Child)   35.00

UNITED STATES OF AMERICA

NOTE: Dealers have classified U.S. coins into eight different conditions, and values are so dependent upon these conditions that it is impossible within the scope of this book to cover all. (A whole book could be written on U.S. coins, and it has been—namely, Reinfeld's *Coin Collector's Handbook*; it can be consulted for more information.) Unlike others in this book, this section is organized according to coin denomination.

HALF CENTS   1793–1857

1.	Liberty Cap type (C) 1793–97	600.00
2.	Draped Bust type (C) 1800–08	80.00
3.	Turban Head type (C) 1809–36	65.00
4.	Braided Hair type (C) 1840–57	75.00

LARGE CENTS   1793–1857

5.	Chain type (C) 1793	4000.00
6.	Wreath type (C) 1793	1750.00
7.	Liberty Cap type (C) 1793–96	200.00
8.	Draped Bust type (C) 1796–1807	175.00
8a.	Turban Head type (C) 1808–14	250.00
9.	Coronet type (C) 1816–39	25.00
10.	Braided Hair type (C) 1839–57	20.00

SMALL CENTS   1793–

11.	Flying Eagle type (C-N) 1857–58	30.00
12.	Indian Head type (C-N) 1859–64; (Bro) 1864–1909; struck at San Francisco mint 1908–09	4.00
13.	Lincoln Head type (Bro) 1909–42, '46– ; (St) '43; (C) '44–45	.15

TWO CENTS   1864–73

14.	Shield type (Bro) 1864–73	15.00

THREE CENTS   1851–89

15.	Liberty Head type (N) 1865–89	12.50

16.	Star type (S) 1851–73	25.00

FIVE CENTS   1866–

17.	Shield type (N) 1866–83	20.00
18.	Liberty Head type (N) 1883–1912	6.50
19.	Buffalo (or Indian Head) type (N) 1913–38	2.00
20.	Jefferson type (N) 1938–42, '46– ; (Silver alloy) '42–45	.20

HALF DIMES   1794–1873

21.	Bust (or Liberty Head) type 1794–1837	50.00

22.	Liberty Seated type 1837–73	15.00

DIMES   1796–

23.	Bust 1796–1837	50.00
24.	Liberty Seated type 1837–91	20.00
25.	Liberty Head type 1892–1916	15.00
26.	Mercury Head type 1916–45	2.00
27.	Roosevelt type 1946–64; (C-N) 1965–	.25

TWENTY CENTS   1875–78

28.	Liberty Seated type 1875–78	150.00

QUARTERS 1796–

29.	Bust type 1796–1838	100.00

30.	Liberty Seated type 1838–91	40.00
31.	Liberty Head (Barber) type 1892–1916	35.00
32.	Liberty Standing type 1916–30	35.00
33.	Washington type 1932–64; (C-N) 1965–	.50
33a.	Bicentennial type (C-N) 1976	.75

HALF DOLLARS 1794–

34.	Bust type 1794–1839	35.00

35.	Liberty Seated type 1839–91	35.00
36.	Liberty Head (Barber) type 1892–1915	60.00
37.	Liberty Standing type 1916–47	12.50
38.	Franklin type 1948–1963	7.00

39.	Kennedy type 1964–70; (C-N) 1971–	1.00
39a.	Bicentennial type (C-N) 1976	2.50

SILVER DOLLARS 1794–1935

40.	Bust type 1794–1804	650.00
41.	Liberty Seated type 1840–73	175.00

42.	Liberty Head type (Morgan) 1878–1921	17.50
43.	Peace type 1921–35	20.00

43a.	Eisenhower type (C-N) 1971–78	5.00
43b.	Eisenhower type (silver clad) 1971–76. (Non-circulating, for collector's only)	12.50

43c.	Susan B. Anthony type (C-N) 1979–81	2.00

GOLD DOLLARS 1849–89

44.	Liberty Head type (G) 1849–54	375.00

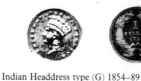

45.	Indian Headdress type (G) 1854–89	250.00

QUARTER EAGLES ($2.50) 1796–1829

46.	Liberty Cap type (G) 1796–1807	2500.00
47.	Turban Head type (G) 1808–34	2750.00
48.	Ribbon type (G) 1834–39	400.00
49.	Coronet type (G) 1840–1907	200.00

50.	Indian Head Incuse type (G) 1908–29	200.00

UNITED STATES OF AMERICA (continued)

THREE-DOLLAR GOLD PIECES 1854–89

51.	Indian Headdress type (G) 1854–89	750.00

HALF EAGLES ($5.00) 1795–1929

52.	Bust type (G) 1795–1834	1100.00
53.	Ribbon type (G) 1834–38	400.00
54.	Coronet type (G) 1839–1908	200.00
55.	Indian Head Incuse type (G) 1908–29	225.00

EAGLES ($10) 1795–1933

56.	Bust type (G) 1795–1804	2500.00

57.	Coronet type (G) 1838–1907	300.00

58.	Indian Head type (G) 1907–33	500.00

DOUBLE EAGLES ($20)

59.	Coronet type (G) 1850–1907	650.00

 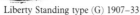

60.	Liberty Standing type (G) 1907–33	700.00

SILVER COMMEMORATIVE COINS

Note: These are half dollars unless otherwise stated

1.	Columbian Exposition 1892–93	35.00

2.	Isabella Quarter 1893	600.00

3.	Lafayette Dollar 1900	1750.00

4.	Panama-Pacific Exposition 1915	900.00

539

UNITED STATES OF AMERICA (continued)

5.	Illinois Centennial 1918	100.00
6.	Maine Centennial 1920	125.00

18.	California Diamond Jubilee 1925	175.00
19.	Fort Vancouver Centennial 1925	700.00

7.	Pilgrim Tercentenary 1920–21	75.00
8.	Missouri Centennial (with star) 1921	900.00
9.	Missouri Centennial (no star) 1921	850.00
10.	Alabama Centennial (with "2X2") 1921	500.00
11.	Alabama Centennial (no "2X2") 1921	400.00
12.	Grant Memorial (with star) 1922	875.00
13.	Grant Memorial (no star) 1922	150.00

20.	Sesquicentennial of American Independence 1926	75.00

14.	Monroe Doctrine Centennial 1923	75.00
15.	Huguenot-Walloon Tercentenary 1924	135.00

21.	Oregon Trail Memorial 1926, '33–34, '36–39	175.00
22.	Vermont Sesquicentennial 1927	325.00

16.	Lexington-Concord Sesquicentennial 1925	100.00

23.	Hawaiian Sesquicentennial 1928	1750.00
24.	Maryland Tercentenary 1934	200.00

17.	Stone Mountain Memorial 1925	40.00

25.	Texas Centennial 1934–38	150.00

| 26. | Daniel Boone Bicentennial 1934–38 | 175.00 |

27.	Connecticut Tercentenary 1935	300.00
28.	Arkansas Centennial 1935–39	100.00
29.	Hudson, N.Y. Sesquicentennial 1935	850.00
30.	California-Pacific Exposition 1935–36	125.00

31.	Old Spanish Trail 1935	1200.00
32.	Rhode Island Tercentenary 1936	200.00
33.	Cleveland, Great Lakes Exposition 1936	125.00
34.	Wisconsin Territorial Centennial 1936	250.00
35.	Cincinnati Musical Center 1936	550.00

| 36. | Long Island Tercentenary 1936 | 100.00 |
| 37. | York County, Maine Tercentenary 1936 | 250.00 |

| 38. | Bridgeport, Conn. Centennial 1936 | 200.00 |

39.	Lynchburg, Va. Sesquicentennial 1936	250.00
40.	Elgin, Ill. Sesquicentennial 1936	300.00
41.	Albany, N.Y. Charter 1936	350.00

| 42. | San Francisco–Oakland Bay Bridge 1936 | 150.00 |
| 43. | Columbia, S.C. Sesquicentennial 1936 | 425.00 |

| 44. | Delaware Tercentenary 1936 | 300.00 |

| 45. | Battle of Gettysburg 1936 | 325.00 |
| 46. | Norfolk, Va. Bicentennial 1936 | 500.00 |

| 47. | Roanoke Island, N.C. 1937 | 200.00 |

| 48. | Battle of Antietam 1937 | 500.00 |
| 49. | New Rochelle, N.Y. 1938 | 500.00 |

50.   Iowa Centennial 1946   115.00

6.   Panama-Pacific Exposition ($50; round) 1915 40,000.00

51.   Booker T. Washington Memorial 1946–51   20.00
52.   Geo. W. Carver—B. T. Washington 1951–54   20.00
53.   George Washington 250th Birthday Anniver-
            sary 1982–   10.00
53a.   George Washington Birthday. Proof. 1982– . 12.00

GOLD COMMEMORATIVE COINS

NOTE: These are dollars unless otherwise stated

1.   Louisiana Purchase (Jefferson) 1903   1000.00
2.   Louisiana Purchase (McKinley) 1903   1000.00

7.   Panama-Pacific Exposition ($50; octagonal)
            1915   30,000.00

3.   Lewis and Clark Exposition 1904–05   2000.00

8.   McKinley Memorial 1916–17   850.00

4.   Panama-Pacific Exposition 1915   1100.00

9.   Grant Memorial (with star) 1922   1650.00
10.   Grant Memorial (no star) 1922   1650.00

5.   Panama-Pacific Exposition ($2.50) 1915   2750.00

11.   Philadelphia Sesquicentennial ($2.50) 1926 750.00

1984 LOS ANGELES OLYMPICS
COMMEMORATIVE COINS

1. 1 Dollar (S) 1983. Ancient Greek discus
    thrower. Rev: Eagle's head. (1984 Los An-
    geles Olympic Games.) Issued in proof only —
2. 1 Dollar (S) 1984. Sculpture facing Los Angeles
    Memorial Coliseum. Rev: Full eagle. In proof
    only —
3. 10 Dollars (G) 1984. Olympic torch runners.
    Rev: Traditional U.S. eagle design. In proof
    only —

    NOTE: #3 is first U.S. gold coin issued since 1933.
    Its price will vary according to bullion market.

URUGUAY

For centuries Uruguay was the scene of a struggle between the Spaniards and Portuguese, with the Spaniards maintaining the upper hand. The eventual freedom from Spain that was achieved only plunged the country into new chaos. Finally in 1828, with the help of Great Britain, Uruguay was established as an independent republic, a buffer state between Argentina and Brazil.

100 Centesimos = 1 Peso

1.	1 Peso 1844. Arms. Rev: Value	600.00

2.	1 Peso 1877–95	50.00
3.	50 Centesimos 1877–94	20.00
4.	20 Centesimos 1877, '93	10.00
5.	10 Centesimos 1877, '93	8.50

6.	40 Centesimos (C) 1844, '57. Sun. Rev: Value	20.00
7.	20 Centesimos (C) 1840–55, '57	25.00
8.	5 Centesimos (C) 1840–55, '57; (C-N) 1901–41	2.00
9.	4 Centesimos (C) 1869	12.50
10.	2 Centesimos (C) 1869; (C-N) 1901–41	2.00
11.	1 Centesimo (C) 1869; (C-N) 1901–36	2.00

12.	1 Peso 1917. Bust of Artigas. Rev: Arms	65.00
13.	50 Centesimos 1916, '17	25.00
14.	20 Centesimos 1920	15.00

1930 CENTENARY

15.	5 Pesos (G) 1930. Head of Artigas. Rev: Value	250.00

16.	20 Centesimos 1930. Seated Liberty	25.00

17.	10 Centesimos (A-Bro) 1930, '36. Liberty head. Rev: Jaguar	20.00

NEW SILVER COINAGE

18.	1 Peso 1942. Head of Artigas. Rev: Jaguar	17.50
19.	50 Centesimos 1943	10.00
20.	20 Centesimos 1942. Liberty head	7.50

21. 5 Centesimos (Bro) 1944–51. Sun. Rev: Value   4.00
22. 2 Centesimos (Bro) 1943–51   2.50

23. 20 Centesimos 1954. Artigas. Rev: Value   6.00

24. 10 Centesimos (C-N) 1953–59   1.00
25. 5 Centesimos (C-N) 1953–   .20
26. 2 Centesimos (C-N) 1953–   .15
27. 1 Centesimo (C-N) 1953–   .15

28. 10 Pesos 1961. Gaucho. Rev: Value. (150th anniversary, revolution against Spain)   15.00
29. 1 Peso (C-N) 1960. Head of Artigas. Rev: Arms and value   1.50
30. 50 Centesimos (C-N) 1960   1.00
31. 25 Centesimos (C-N) 1960   .75

32. 10 Centesimos (N-Bra) 1960– . Rev: Value   .50
33. 5 Centesimos (N-Bra) 1960–   .50
34. 2 Centesimos (N-Bra) 1960   .40

35.

35. 10 Pesos (A-Bro) 1965. Bust of Artigas. Rev: Arms   1.00
36. 5 Pesos (A-Bro) 1965   1.00
37. 1 Peso (A-Bro) 1965   .50

38. 10 Pesos (N-Bra) 1968. Bust of Artigas. Rev: Ceibo flower   .75
39. 5 Pesos (N-Bra) 1968   .50
40. 1 Peso (N-Bra) 1968   .35

41. 1000 Pesos 1969. Modern sun. Rev: Modern art design. (F.A.O. coin plan)   25.00
41a. 1000 Pesos (Bro) 1969   50.00

42. 10 Pesos (A-Bro) 1969. Sun-face. Rev: Ceibo flower   .65
43. 5 Pesos (A-Bro) 1969   .35
44. 1 Peso (A-Bro) 1969   .25
45. 50 Pesos (C-N) 1970. Arms. Rev: Wheat spikes   2.00
46. 20 Pesos (C-N) 1970   1.00

47.

47. 50 Pesos (C-N) 1971. José Enrique Rodo. Rev: Quill. (100th anniversary of philosopher's birth) 2.50

48. 100 Pesos (C-N) 1973. Head of Artigas. Rev: Value, laurel branch 3.50

49. 5 New Pesos (C-N-Z) 1975. Bust of Artigas in panel. Rev: Flag and lance. (150th anniversary of independence) 10.00
49a. 5 New Pesos (C-A) 1976. Bust of Zabala. Rev: Shield. (250th anniversary of Montevideo) 10.00

50. 1 New Peso (A-Bro) 1976–78. Bust of Artigas. Rev: Value. (Dodecagonal planchet) .75

51. 50 Centesimos (A-Bro) 1976–78. Scales. Rev: Value. (Dodecagonal planchet) .30
52. 20 Centesimos (A-Bro) 1976–78. Fort of Montevideo. (Dodecagonal planchet) .20
53. 10 Centesimos (A-Bro) 1976–78. Horse. (Dodecagonal planchet) .20

54. 5 Centesimos (A) 1977–78. Bull. Rev: Value. (Dodecagonal planchet) .25

55.
56.

55. 2 Centesimos (A) 1977–78. Radiant sunface. Rev: Value. (Dodecagonal planchet) .20
56. 1 Centesimo (A) 1977. Radiant sunface. Rev: Value. (Dodecagonal planchet) .15
57. 10 New Pesos (C-N) 1980– . Bust of Artigas. Rev: Value 2.00
58. 5 New Pesos (C-N) 1980– . Flag. Rev: Value 1.50
59. 1 New Peso (C-N) 1980– . Flag. Rev: Value .75

VANUATU

The New Hebrides Anglo-French condominium (q.v.) gained its independence in 1980 as Vanuatu, but still remains under the protection of Britain and France.

1. 10,000 Vatu (G) 1981. Obverse (English): Native warrior, ivory tusk. Rev. (French): Coconut trees, value. (First anniversary of independence)   400.00
2.   50 Vatu (C-N) 1981. Obv. (English): Type of #1. Rev. (French): Natives tending taro crops   5.00
2a.   50 Vatu (S) 1981. Proof   35.00

VATICAN CITY

One-sixth of a square mile in area and located just outside Rome, Vatican City houses the Vatican Palace. The papal city has its own coinage and postage stamps, as well as its own newspaper and broadcasting station. (See previous coins of the Papacy under "Italy: Papal States").

100 Centesimi = 1 Lira

POPE PIUS XI   1922–39

1.   100 Lire (G) 1929–35. Bust. Rev: Christ standing   400.00
2.   100 Lire (G) 1936–37. Reduced size   375.00

3.   10 Lire 1929–37. Bust. Rev: Seated madonna holding child   35.00
4.   5 Lire 1929–37. Rev: St. Peter in boat   25.00

5.   2 Lire (N) 1929–37. Arms. Rev: Good Shepherd with lamb   15.00
6.   1 Lira (N) 1929–37. Rev: Virgin standing   12.50

7.   50 Centesimi (N) 1929–37. Rev: Archangel Michael   12.50
8.   20 Centesimi (N) 1929–37. Rev: Bust of St. Paul   10.00

9.   10 Centesimi (Bro) 1929–37. Rev: Bust of St. Peter   10.00
10.   5 Centesimi (Bro) 1929–37. Rev: Olive spray   10.00

SEDE VACANTE   1939

11.   10 Lire 1939. Arms of Cardinal Pacelli. Rev: Dove   50.00
12.   5 Lire 1939   40.00

POPE PIUS XII   1939–58

13.   100 Lire (G) 1939–41. Bust. Rev: Type of #1   400.00

14.	10 Lire 1939–41. Bust. Rev: Type of #3	40.00
15.	5 Lire 1939–41. Rev: Type of #4	25.00
16.	2 Lire (N) 1939; (St) '40–41. Rev: Type of #5	8.50
17.	1 Lira (N) 1939; (St) '40–41. Rev: Type of #6	7.50
18.	50 Centesimi (N) 1939; (St) '40–41. Rev: Type of #7	6.50
19.	20 Centesimi (N) 1939; (St) '40–41. Rev: Type of #8	5.00
20.	10 Centesimi (Bro) 1939–41. Rev: Type of #9	20.00
21.	5 Centesimi (Bro) 1939–41. Rev: Type of #10	20.00

31.	10 Lire (A) 1947–49. Bust. Rev: Caritas	10.00
32.	5 Lire (A) 1947–49	7.50
33.	2 Lire (A) 1947–49. Rev: Justice	20.00
34.	1 Lira (A) 1947–49	15.00

22.	100 Lire (G) 1942–49. Bust. Rev: Caritas	375.00
23.	10 Lire 1942–46	100.00
24.	5 Lire 1942–46	50.00
25.	2 Lire (St) 1942–46. Arms. Rev: Justice	5.00
26.	1 Lira (St) 1942–46	6.50

35.	100 Lire (G) 1950 (Holy Year issue). Bust of Pope in tiara. Rev: Pope opening Holy Door	400.00
36.	10 Lire (A) 1950. Bust facing right. Rev: Gate of Heaven	7.50

27.	50 Centesimi (St) 1942–46	6.50
28.	20 Centesimi (St) 1942–46	6.50

37.	5 Lire (A) 1950. Bust facing left	7.50
38.	2 Lire (A) 1950. Bust facing right. Rev: Dove and dome of St. Peter's	10.00

29.	10 Centesimi (Bra) 1942–46. Bust. Rev: Dove	50.00
30.	5 Centesimi (Bra) 1942–46	40.00

39.	1 Lira (A) 1950. Arms. Rev: Holy Door	12.50
40.	100 Lire (G) 1951–58. Bust to right. Rev: Caritas	650.00
41.	100 Lire (St) 1955–58. Head to left. Rev: Fides	6.00
42.	50 Lire (St) 1955–58. Head to right. Rev: Spes	6.50

43. 20 Lire (A-Bro) 1957–58. Head to left. Rev:
    Caritas   4.00
44. 10 Lire (A) 1951–58. Bust facing left. Rev:
    Prudentia   1.00

51. 500 Lire 1959–62. Bust. Rev: Arms   40.00
52. 100 Lire (St) 1959–62. Rev: Fides   3.00
53. 50 Lire (St) 1959–62. Rev: Spes   3.00
54. 20 Lire (A-Bro) 1959–62. Rev: Caritas   4.00
55. 10 Lire (A) 1959–62. Rev: Prudentia   4.00
56. 5 Lire (A) 1959–62. Rev: Iustitia   5.00
57. 2 Lire (A) 1959–62. Arms. Rev: Fortitudo   15.00
58. 1 Lira (A) 1959–62. Rev: Temperantia   7.50

45. 5 Lire (A) 1951–58. Bust facing right. Rev:
    Justice   1.50
46. 2 Lire (A) 1951–58. Female figure. Rev: Arms   2.00
47. 1 Lira (A) 1951–58. Female figure. Rev: Arms   2.00

59. 500 Lire 1962. Pope with tiara. Rev: Pope presid-
    ing at meeting of Council. (Ecumenical Coun-
    cil commemorative)   30.00
60. 100 Lire (St) 1962. Bust of Pope   4.00
61. 50 Lire (St) 1962   3.00

48. 500 Lire 1958 (20th year commemorative). Bust.
    Rev: Arms   30.00

SEDE VACANTE 1958

62. 20 Lire (A-Bro) 1962. Rev: Dove   3.00
63. 10 Lire (A) 1962   3.00

49. 500 Lire 1958. Dove. Rev: Arms   15.00

POPE JOHN XXIII 1959–63

64. 5 Lire (A) 1962   4.00

50. 100 Lire (G) 1959. Robed bust of Pope. Rev:
    Papal arms   RARE

65. 2 Lire (A) 1962. Papal arms. Rev: Dove   5.00
66. 1 Lira (A) 1962   5.00

VATICAN CITY (continued)

SEDE VACANTE 1963

67. 500 Lire 1963. Arms of Cardinal Masella. Rev: Dove and value 30.00

PAUL VI 1963–78

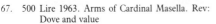

68. 500 Lire 1963–65. Bust of the Pope. Rev: Papal arms 30.00

69. 100 Lire (St) 1963–65. Rev: Fides (Faith) 5.00

70. 50 Lire (St) 1963–65. Rev: Spes (Hope) 3.00
71. 20 Lire (A-Bro) 1963–65. Rev: Caritas (Charity) 4.00
72. 10 Lire (A) 1963–65. Rev: Prudentia (Prudence) 4.00
73. 5 Lire (A) 1963–65. Rev: Iustitia (Justice) 2.50
74. 2 Lire (A) 1963–65. Papal arms. Rev: Fortitudo (Fortitude) 4.00

75. 1 Lira (A) 1963–65. Rev: Temperantia (Temperance) 7.50

76. 500 Lire 1966. Head of Pope wearing mitre. Rev: Good Shepherd carrying a sheep 30.00
77. 100 Lire (St) 1966 .... 5.00
78. 50 Lire (St) 1966 .... 3.00
79. 20 Lire (A-Bro) 1966 .... 2.50
80. 10 Lire (A) 1966 .... 2.50
81. 5 Lire (A) 1966 .... 3.50
82. 2 Lire (A) 1966 .... 3.00
83. 1 Lira (A) 1966 .... 5.00

84. 500 Lire 1967. Bust of the Pope. Rev: Heads of St. Peter and St. Paul. (5th year of reign) 30.00

85. 100 Lire (St) 1967. Rev: St. Peter on throne 5.00

86. 50 Lire (St) 1967. Rev: St. Paul on horseback 4.00
87. 20 Lire (A-Bro) 1967. Type of #84 .... 3.00

88. 10 Lire (A) 1967. Rev: Papal keys 3.00
89. 5 Lire (A) 1967. Rev: Crossed keys 3.00

90. 2 Lire (A) 1967. Rev: Type of #88   3.00
91. 1 Lira (A) 1967. Rev: Type of #89   2.00

92. 500 Lire 1968. Bust of the Pope. Rev: Wheat spikes. (F.A.O. coin plan)   15.00

93. 100 Lire (St) 1968. Rev: Feeding the hungry. (F.A.O.)   3.00
94. 50 Lire (St) 1968. Rev: Blessing of growing plants. (F.A.O.)   3.00
95. 20 Lire (A-Bro) 1968. Rev: Type of #92   1.50
96. 10 Lire (A) 1968. Rev: Type of #93   1.50
97. 5 Lire (A) 1968. Rev: Type of #94   3.00
98. 2 Lire (A) 1968. Rev: Type of #93   3.00
99. 1 Lira (A) 1968. Rev: Type of #92   2.00

100. 500 Lire 1969. Head of Pope wearing mitre. Rev: Negroid angel   15.00

101. 100 Lire (St) 1969. Rev: Oriental angel   3.00
102. 50 Lire (St) 1969. Rev: Caucasian angel   3.00
103. 20 Lire (A-Bro) 1969. Rev: Type of #102   1.50
104. 10 Lire (A) 1969. Rev: Type of #101   2.00

105. 5 Lire (A) 1969. Rev: Type of #100   2.00
106. 2 Lire (A) 1969. Rev: Type of #101   3.00
107. 1 Lira (A) 1969. Rev: Type of #100   1.00

108. 500 Lire 1970–74. Papal arms. Rev: Grain and grapes   7.50

109. 100 Lire (St) 1970–74. Rev: Dove with olive branch   3.00

110. 50 Lire (St) 1970–74. Rev: Olive branch   2.00
111. 20 Lire (A-Bro) 1970–74. Rev: Deer   1.00

112. 10 Lire (A) 1970–74. Rev: Fish   1.50
113. 5 Lire (A) 1970–74. Rev: Pelican   2.00

114. 2 Lire (A) 1970–74. Rev: Lamb   3.00
115. 1 Lira (A) 1970–74. Rev: Palm branches   2.00

116. 500 Lire 1975. Papal arms. Rev: Embrace of prodigal son and father. (Holy year)   25.00

117. 100 Lire (St) 1975. Papal arms. Rev: Design symbolizing baptism   5.00

118. 50 Lire (St) 1975. Rev: Design symbolizing peace within the Lord   3.00
119. 20 Lire (A-Bro) 1975. Rev: Design symbolizing man's confidence in the Lord   2.00

120. 10 Lire (A) 1975. Rev: Ark   2.50
121. 5 Lire (A) 1975. Rev: Woman of Bethany   1.50

122. 2 Lire (A) 1975. Rev: Reconciliation of brothers   2.50
123. 1 Lira (A) 1975. Rev: Design symbolizing faith of afflicted   1.50

NOTE: Nos. 124–33 have papal arms on obverse

124. 500 Lire 1977   15.00
125. 50 Lire (St) 1977   1.50
126. 500 Lire 1978   15.00
127. 200 Lire (A-Bro) 1978   4.00
128. 100 Lire (St) 1978   2.00

129. 50 Lire (St) 1978   1.50
130. 20 Lire (A-Bro) 1978   1.75
131. 10 Lire (A) 1978   1.50
132. 5 Lire (A) 1978   1.25

SEDE VACANTE 1978

133. 500 Lire 1978. Rev: Dove and value. (Death of Paul VI)   15.00

POPE JOHN PAUL I 1978

134. 1000 Lire 1978. Bust of Pope John Paul I. Rev: Arms   35.00

SEDE VACANTE 1978

135. 500 Lire 1978. Arms, SEPTEMBER 1978. Rev: Dove and value. (Death of John Paul I)   15.00

POPE JOHN PAUL II 1978–

NOTE: Nos. 136–47 have bust of Pope John Paul II on obverse, in varying forms

136. 500 Lire 1979, '80. Rev: Arms   15.00
137. 200 Lire (A-Bro) 1979, '80   3.00
138. 100 Lire (St) 1979, '80   1.50
139. 50 Lire (St) 1979, '80   1.00
140. 20 Lire (A-Bro) 1979, '80   1.50
141. 10 Lire (A) 1979, '80   1.50
142. 500 Lire 1981   15.00

143. 200 Lire (A-Bro) 1981   3.00
144. 100 Lire (St) 1981   1.50
145. 50 Lire (St) 1981   1.00
146. 20 Lire (A-Bro) 1981   1.50
147. 10 Lire (A) 1981   1.50

VENEZUELA

A Spanish colony for three centuries, Venezuela was a part of New Granada when it threw off the Spanish yoke in 1811. In 1830 Venezuela finally became an independent state.

100 Centavos = 8 Reales = 1 Peso
100 Centimos = 1 Bolivar

REPUBLIC OF VENEZUELA

1.	5 Reales 1858. Liberty head. Rev: Value	650.00
2.	2 Reales 1858	300.00
3.	1 Real 1858	250.00
4.	½ Real 1858	700.00

5.	1 Centavo (C) 1843, '52, '58, '62, '63. Liberty head	20.00
6.	½ Centavo (C) 1843, '52	20.00
7.	¼ Centavo (C) 1843, '52	20.00

UNITED STATES OF VENEZUELA

1 Venezolano = 10 Reales (fineness .835)

8.	1 Venezolano 1876. Bolívar head. Rev: Arms	650.00
9.	50 Centavos (5 Reales) 1873, '74, '76	150.00
10.	20 Centavos 1874, '76	75.00
11.	10 Centavos 1874, '76	85.00
12.	5 Centavos 1874, '76	50.00

5 Bolivares = 10 Reales (fineness .900)

13.	2½ Centavos (C-N) 1876, '77. Arms. Rev: Value	15.00
14.	1 Centavo (C-N) 1876, '77	15.00
15.	20 Bolivares (G) 1879–1905, 1910–12. Bolívar head	165.00

16.	10 Bolivares (G) 1930	125.00
17.	5 Bolivares 1879, 1886–89, 1900–36. Bolívar head. Rev: Arms	40.00
18.	2 Bolivares 1879, 1887–89, '94, 1900–45	15.00
19.	1 Bolivar 1879, 1886–89, '93, 1900–45	10.00
20.	½ Bolivar (50 Centimos) 1879, 1886–89, '93, 1900–46	7.50
21.	¼ Bolivar 1894, 1900–48	5.00
22.	12½ Centimos (C-N) 1896, 1925–38; (Bra) 1944; (C-N) 1945–48	2.00

REPUBLIC OF VENEZUELA

23.	2 Bolivares 1960–65. Head of Bolívar.	10.00
23a.	2 Bolivares (N) 1967	2.50
24.	1 Bolivar 1954–65	3.00
24a.	1 Bolivar (N) 1967	1.00
24b.	1 Bolivar (C-N) 1977. Rev: Modified shield	1.00
25.	50 Centimos 1954, '60	2.00
25a.	50 Centimos (N) 1965	1.00
26.	25 Centimos 1954, '60	2.50
26a.	25 Centimos (N) 1965	.50
26b.	25 Centimos (N) 1977–78. Value under arms	.35

27.	12½ Centimos (C-N) 1958–69. Arms. Rev: Value	.75
28.	5 Centimos (C-N) 1958	.35
29.	10 Centimos (C-N) 1971. Arms. Rev: Value	.35
30.	5 Centimos (C-N) 1964–71	.25
30a.	5 Centimos (C-St) 1974–77. Modified arms, value	.20

31.	10 Bolivares 1973. Head of Bolívar in incuse panel. Rev: Arms in panel. (100th anniversary of Bolívar's appearance on coinage)	35.00

VENEZUELA (continued)

32a.

32.	5 Bolivares (N) 1973. Type of #23	7.50
32a.	5 Bolivares (N) 1977–78. Value under arms	7.50

33.	1000 Bolivares (G) 1975. Arms. Rev: Cock	650.00
34.	50 Bolivares 1975. Rev: Armadillo	50.00
35.	25 Bolivares 1975. Rev: Jaguar	35.00
36.	500 Bolivares (G) 1975. Head of Bolívar in incuse panel. Rev: Oil rigs. (Nationalization of oil industry)	400.00
37.	100 Bolivares 1980. Bust of Bolívar. Rev: Monument. (150th anniversary of independence)	65.00
38.	75 Bolivares 1980. Bust of Bolívar. Rev: Mule. (150th anniversary of independence)	50.00

VIETNAM

Became two states in 1954; the two Vietnams were united as the Socialist Republic of Vietnam in 1976.

SOUTH VIETNAM
100 Xu (Su) = 1 Dong

1.	50 Xu (A-Mg) 1953	20.00
2.	20 Su (A-Mg) 1953	3.00
3.	10 Su (A-Mg) 1953	2.00

4.	1 Dong (C-N) 1960. Head of President Ngo Dinh-Diem. Rev: Rice stalks	1.25
5.	50 Su (A-Mg) 1960, '63	1.25

6.	10 Dong (C-N) 1964; (N-St) 1968, '70. Rice stalks. Rev: Value	1.00

7.	5 Dong (C-N) 1966; (N-St) 1971. (Scalloped-edge planchet)	1.25
8.	1 Dong (C-N) 1964; (N-St) 1971. (Round planchet)	1.00
9.	20 Dong (N-St) 1968. Farmer in rice paddy. Rev: Value	2.50

10.

VIETNAM (continued)

10.   20 Dong (St) 1968. F.A.O. inscription   3.00

11.   1 Dong (A) 1971. Type of #6, with F.A.O.
inscription   1.00

12.   10 Dong (Bra-St) 1974. Two peasants. Rev:
Value. (F.A.O. coin plan)   1.00

NORTH VIETNAM

100 Xu = 1 Hao = 1 Dong

1.   2 Dong (Bro) 1946. Ho Chi Minh. Rev: Star in
wreath   100.00

2.   1 Dong (A) 1946. Ho Chi Minh. Rev: Value   100.00

3.   5 Hao (A) 1946. Incense burner. Rev: Value in
star (value raised or incuse)   35.00

4.   20 Xu (A) 1945. Star. Rev: Value   100.00

5.   5 Xu (A) 1958. Arms. Rev: Value. (Center
hole)   5.00
6.   2 Xu (A) 1958   4.00
7.   1 Xu (A) 1958   4.00

SOCIALIST REPUBLIC OF VIETNAM

1.   1 Dong (A) 1976. Arms, value   30.00
2.   5 Hao (A) 1976   8.00
3.   2 Hao (A) 1976   6.00
4.   1 Hao (A) 1976   6.00
5.   5 Xu (A) 1976. (Center hole)   6.00
6.   2 Xu (A) 1976. (Center hole)   5.00
7.   1 Xu (A) 1976. (Center hole)   5.00

VIZCAYAN REPUBLIC

Spanish province on the Bay of Biscay, autonomous during the Civil War of 1936–37.

1.	2 Pesetas (N) 1937. Head of Republic. Rev: Value in wreath	10.00
2.	1 Peseta (N) 1937	7.50

WEST AFRICAN STATES

Former French colonies in this area joined together for coinage purposes: Dahomey (now Benin), Upper Volta, Ivory Coast, Mauritania, Niger, Senegal, and Togo, each now autonomous.

1.	10 Francs (A-Bro) 1959– . Antelope head. Rev: Native design	.50
2.	5 Francs (A-Bro) 1960–	.30
3.	1 Franc (A-Bro) 1961–	.20

4.	100 Francs (N) 1967– . Native design. Rev: Value	2.00
5.	25 Francs (A-Bro) 1970–78. Type of #1	1.00

6.	500 Francs 1972. Native design. Rev: Shields of member nations. (10th anniversary of monetary union)	60.00

7.	50 Francs (C-N) 1972– . Native design. Rev: Value. (F.A.O. coin plan)	1.50

557

WEST AFRICAN STATES (continued)

8.	1 Franc (St) 1976– . Native design. Rev: Value	.20
9.	25 Francs (Al-Br) 1980. Native design, value. Rev: Native farmer. (F.A.O. coin plan)	3.00
10.	10 Francs (Bra) 1981. Rev: Farm workers. (F.A.O. coin plan)	1.50

WESTERN SAMOA

This group of four islands in the South Pacific Ocean was a German colony until after World War I, when it became a New Zealand mandate. Under New Zealand U.N. trusteeship from 1945 on, it achieved independence within the British Commonwealth on January 1, 1962. New Zealand continues to represent Western Samoa in foreign affairs.

1.	1 Tala (C-N) 1967. Portrait of Malietoa Tanumafili II. Rev: Arms	5.00
2.	50 Sene (C-N) 1967	2.00
3.	20 Sene (C-N) 1967	1.00
4.	10 Sene (C-N) 1967	.50

5.	5 Sene (C-N) 1967. Rev: Value in wreath	.35
6.	2 Sene (Bro) 1967	.25
7.	1 Sene (Bro) 1967	.20

8.	1 Tala (C-N) 1969. Robert Louis Stevenson lying in bed. Rev: Arms. (75th anniversary of writer's death)	6.00

9. 1 Tala (C-N) 1970. James Cook. Rev: Type of
    #8. (200th anniversary of Cook's voyages)   7.50

13. 1 Tala (C-N) 1974. Head of Malietoa Tan-
    umafili II. Rev: Coconut palm   8.50

10. 1 Tala (C-N) 1970. Pope Paul VI. (Papal visit)   7.50

14. 50 Sene (C-N) 1974. Rev: Banana tree   4.00
15. 20 Sene (C-N) 1974. Rev: Breadfruit   2.00

11. 1 Tala (C-N) 1972. Sailing ship. (Roggeveen's
    discovery of Samoa)   10.00

16. 10 Sene (C-N) 1974. Rev: Taro leaves   1.00
17. 5 Sene (C-N) 1974. Rev: Pineapple   .65

18. 2 Sene (Bro) 1974. Rev: Cocoa pods   .35
19. 1 Sene (Bro) 1974. Rev: Coconut   .25
20. 1 Tala (C-N) 1976. Rev: Weightlifter. (1976
     Montreal Olympics)   6.00
20a. 1 Tala (S) 1976. Proof   40.00
21. 1 Tala (C-N) 1976. Rev: Pony Express rider.
     (U.S. Bicentennial)   6.00
21a. 1 Tala (S) 1976. Proof   50.00
22. 1 Tala (C-N) 1977. Rev: Charles A. Lindbergh
     and *Spirit of St. Louis*. (50th anniversary of
     transatlantic flight)   6.00

12. 1 Tala (C-N) 1974. Boxers. (10th British Com-
    monwealth Games)   8.50

22a. 1 Tala (S) 1977. Proof   50.00

23.　1 Tala (C-N) 1977. Rev: Cameo portrait of Elizabeth II over Samoan village. (Queen's Silver Jubilee)　6.00
23a.　1 Tala (S) 1977. Proof　50.00

32.　10 Tala 1981. Rev: Franklin D. Roosevelt in wheelchair. (International Year of Disabled Persons)　50.00
33.　1 Tala (C-N) 1981. (Franklin D. Roosevelt)　6.00

24.　1 Tala (C-N) 1978. Rev: Three runners. (11th Commonwealth Games)　6.00
24a.　1 Tala (S) 1978. Proof　50.00

34.　10 Tala 1981. Rev: Dual portrait of Prince Charles and Lady Diana. (Marriage of royal couple)　50.00
35.　1 Tala (C-N) 1981. (Charles and Diana)　6.00
36.　10 Tala (C-N) 1982. Rev: Javelin thrower. (British Commonwealth Games)　10.00
36a.　10 Tala (S) 1982. Proof　42.00

25.　1 Tala (C-N) 1978. Rev: Portrait of Kingsford Smith, airplane, map of Pacific. (50th anniversary of first transpacific flight)　6.00
25a.　1 Tala (S) 1978. Proof　50.00
26.　10 Tala 1979. Rev: Captain Cook, sailing ship. (200th anniversary of Cook's death)　30.00
27.　1 Tala 1979 (C-N). (Captain Cook)　6.00
27a.　1 Tala 1979 (S). Proof　25.00
28.　10 Tala 1980. Rev: Coconut palm, FOOD FOR ALL. (F.A.O. coin plan)　30.00
29.　1 Tala (C-N) 1980. (F.A.O. coin plan)　6.00

30.　10 Tala 1980. Rev: Hurdlers. (1980 Moscow Olympics)　30.00
31.　1 Tala (C-N) 1980. (Moscow Olympics)　6.00

WESTPHALIA

After the Peace of Tilsit in 1807 Napoleon Bonaparte created the Kingdom of Westphalia from several German territories and set up his brother Jerome as king. Jerome lost his throne in 1813 and the territories were re-distributed.

100 Centimes = 1 Frank

JÉRÔME BONAPARTE   1807–13

1.	5 Franken 1808, '09. Laureated head. Rev: Value in wreath	1000.00
2.	2 Franken 1808	300.00
3.	1 Frank 1808	225.00
4.	½ Frank 1808	150.00
5.	20 Centimes (Bi) 1810–12. Crowned monogram ("HN" for "Hieronymus Napoleon") in wreath. Rev: Value	25.00
6.	10 Centimes (Bi) 1808–12	20.00

7.	5 Centimes (C) 1808–12	15.00
8.	3 Centimes (C) 1808–12	12.50
9.	2 Centimes (C) 1808–12	12.50
10.	1 Centime (C) 1809–12	10.00

YEMEN ARAB REPUBLIC

An Arab kingdom on the Red Sea until 1962, when it became a republic.

2 Halala = 1 Bogach
40 Bogaches = 1 Imadi = 1 Riyal

1.	1 Riyal (Imadi) 1948–61 (A.H. 1367–80). Arabic inscriptions	30.00
2.	½ Imadi 1948–60	15.00
3.	¼ Imadi 1948–58	12.50
4.	⅛ Imadi 1948–61. (Pentagonal planchet)	10.00
5.	¹⁄₁₆ Imadi 1948–55. (Pentagon)	7.50
6.	1 Bogach (Bro) 1949–60	4.00
7.	1 Halala (Bro) 1949–62	3.00
8.	1 Bogach (A) 1955–57	5.00

9.	1 Halala (A) 1955–57	5.00

REPUBLIC 1962–

10.	1 Riyal 1963. (A.H. 1382) Arabic inscription. Rev: Two laurel branches	20.00
11.	20 Bogaches 1963	10.00
12.	10 Bogaches 1963	5.00
13.	5 Bogaches 1963	3.00
14.	2 Bogaches (A-Bro) 1963	2.00
15.	1 Bogach (A-Bro) 1963	1.00

16.	½ Bogach (A-Bro) 1963	1.00

17.	¼ Riyal 1963. Coffee tree above dam. Rev: Arabic inscription	30.00
18.	⅓ Riyal 1963	10.00
19.	¹⁄₁₀ Riyal 1963	7.50
20.	¹⁄₂₀ Riyal 1963	6.00

21.	1 Bogach (Bro) 1963–65. Hand holding torch. Rev: Arabic inscription	3.00
22.	1 Halala (Bro) 1963	1.50

23.	½ Bogach (Bro) 1963. Star between lines. Rev: Value as fraction	10.00
24.	1 Halala (Bro) 1963. Rev: Value written out	7.50

DECIMAL COINAGE

100 Fils = 1 Riyal

25.	50 Fils (C-N) 1974– . Arms. Rev: Value	2.00
25a.	50 Fils (C-N) 1974. (F.A.O. coin plan)	2.00
26.	25 Fils (C-N) 1974–	1.50
26a.	25 Fils (C-N) 1974. (F.A.O.)	1.00
27.	10 Fils (Bra) 1974–	1.00
27a.	10 Fils (Bra) 1974. (F.A.O.)	1.00
28.	5 Fils (Bra) 1974–	.75
28a.	5 Fils (Bra) 1974. (F.A.O.)	.75
29.	1 Fil (A) 1974–	.50
30.	10 Riyals 1976. Olympic design. Rev: Arms. (1976 Olympic Games)	40.00
31.	1 Riyal (C-N) 1976– . Arms. Rev: Value	5.00

YEMEN ARAB REPUBLIC (continued)

32.	1 Riyal (C-N) 1978. Rev: Value, inscription. (F.A.O. coin plan)	6.00
33.	1 Fil (A) 1978. Rev: Value, inscription. (F.A.O.)	2.50

YEMEN, DEMOCRATIC REPUBLIC

Formerly South Arabia (q.v.) under British rule; gained independence in 1967; became People's Democratic Republic of Yemen in 1970.

1.	5 Fils (Bro) 1971. Emblem. Rev: Crossed daggers	2.00
2.	5 Fils (Al) 1973. Value, date. Rev: Lobster	1.00
3.	2½ Fils 1973	.35
4.	5 Dinars 1977	25.00
5.	250 Fils (C-N) 1977	3.00
6.	50 Fils (C-N) 1977	2.00
7.	25 Fils (C-N) 1977	1.50

YUGOSLAVIA

The Kingdom of Serbs, Croats and Slovenes was formed after World War I from Serbia, Montenegro and parts of the former Austro-Hungarian Empire, but did not take the name Yugoslavia until 1929. After World War II, in 1945, Yugoslavia became a republic headed by Marshal Tito, who had led the resistance against the invading Germans. Although a Communist state, it remained outside the Soviet orbit. It took the name Socialist Federal Republic of Yugoslavia in 1963 when a new constitution was adopted. (See also "Serbia.")

100 Para = 1 Dinar

ALEXANDER I   1921–34

1. 20 Dinars (G) 1925. Head. Crowned value in
    wreath   225.00
2. 1 Ducat (G) 1931–34. Rev: Eagle   150.00

3. 50 Dinars 1932. Head. Rev: Crowned double
    eagle   60.00
4. 20 Dinars 1931–33   20.00
5. 10 Dinars 1931–32   15.00

6. 2 Dinars (N-Bro) 1925. Head. Rev: Crowned
    value in wreath   5.00
7. 1 Dinar (N-Bro) 1925   4.00
8. 50 Para (N-Bro) 1925   4.00

9. 25 Para (N-Bro) 1920. Crowned, mantled arms.
    Rev: Value   6.00
10. 10 Para (Z) 1920   7.50
11. 5 Para (Z) 1920   50.00

PETER II   1934–45

12. 50 Dinars 1938. Head facing right. Rev:
    Crowned double eagle   15.00

13. 20 Dinars 1938. Head facing left   15.00

14. 10 Dinars 1938. Head facing right. Rev:
    Crowned value in wreath   7.50

15. 2 Dinars (A-Bro) 1938. Crown. Rev: Value   25.00
16. 1 Dinar (A-Bro) 1938   4.00
17. 50 Para (A-Bro) 1938   4.00

18. 25 Para (A-Bro) 1938 (Center hole). Crowned
    wreath. Rev: Value   8.50

564

PEOPLE'S REPUBLIC 1945–

19. 5 Dinars (Z) 1945; (A) 1953, '63. Arms. Rev:
     Value 1.50
20. 2 Dinars (Z) 1945; (A) 1953, '63 .... .50
21. 1 Dinar (Z) 1945; (A) 1953, '63 .... .35

22. 50 Para (Z) 1945; (A) 1953 .... .25

23. 50 Dinars (A-Bro) 1955, '63. Heads of two work-
     ers, male and female. Rev: Arms 5.00

24. 20 Dinars (A-Bro) 1955, '63. Head of male
     worker 3.00
25. 10 Dinars (A-Bro) 1955, '63. Head of female
     worker 2.00

REVALUATION 1965

26. 1 Dinar (C-N) 1965, '68. Arms. Rev: Value,
     stars 1.00
27. 50 Para (A-Bro) 1965– .... .75
27a. 5 Para (A-Bro) 1965 .... .30
28. 20 Para (A-Bro) 1965– . Arms. Rev: Value .... .30
29. 10 Para (A-Bro) 1965– .... .20
30. 5 Para (A-Bro) 1965 .... .15

31. 5 Dinars (C-N) 1970. Arms. Rev: Value
     (F.A.O. coin plan) 2.00
32. 2 Dinars (C-N) 1970 .... 1.50

33. 5 Dinars (C-N) 1971– . Arms. Rev: Value .... .60
34. 2 Dinars (C-N) 1971– .... .40
35. 1 Dinar (C-N) 1973– .... .40

36.   53.

36. 5 Dinars (C-N-Z) 1975. Arms. Rev: Value, in-
     scription. (30th anniversary, end of World
     War II) 2.50
37. 200 Dinars 1977. Bust of President Tito (Josip
     Broz). Rev: Arms, value, dates. (Marshal
     Tito's 85th birthday) 30.00
38. 5000 Dinars (G) 1979. Bust of President Tito. Rev:
     Administration building. (Eighth Mediter-
     ranean Games at Split) 750.00
39. 2500 Dinars (G) 1979. Rev: Athletic stadium ... 400.00
40. 2000 Dinars (G) 1979. Rev: Indoor stadium 250.00
41. 1500 Dinars (G) 1979. Rev: Gymnastic rings ... 185.00
42. 400 Dinars 1979. Rev: Building 100.00
43. 350 Dinars 1979 .... 85.00
44. 300 Dinars 1979 .... 75.00
45. 250 Dinars 1979 .... 60.00
46. 150 Dinars 1979 .... 35.00
47. 100 Dinars 1979 .... 35.00
48. 1000 Dinars 1980. Bust of Tito. Rev: Facade of
     building. (Vukovar Congress) 75.00
49. 500 Dinars 1980. (Vukovar Congress) 40.00
50. 1000 Dinars 1980. Bust of Tito. Rev: Arms. (Death
     of Tito) 50.00
51. 1000 Dinars 1981. Table tennis. Rev: Arms 60.00
52. 500 Dinars 1981. Table tennis 35.00
53. 500 Dinars 1982. Emblem of XIV Winter Olym-
     pic Games, arms and value. Rev: Snow
     sports. (One of eighteen proof coins issued
     commemorating 1984 games at Sarajevo) 40.00

ZAIRE

The Republic of the Congo (q.v.; formerly the Belgian Congo, q.v.) changed its name to the Republic of Zaire in 1971.

100 Makuta = 1 Zaire

1. 20 Makuta (C-N) 1973, '76. Portrait of President Mobutu with hat. Rev: Arm holding torch   10.00

2. 10 Makuta (C-N) 1973, '76. Portrait of President Mobutu. Rev: Arms   5.00

3. 5 Makuta (C-N) 1977. President Mobutu. Rev: Value   1.25
4. 100 Zaires (G) 1975. President Mobutu. Rev: Leopard. (World Wildlife Conservation Program)   750.00
5. 5 Zaires 1975. President Mobutu. Rev: Antelope. (Wildlife Conservation)   60.00
6. 2½ Zaires 1975. President Mobutu. Rev: Baboon. (Wildlife Conservation)   35.00

ZAMBIA

Formerly Northern Rhodesia in the Federation of Rhodesia and Nyasaland (q.v.), which dissolved in 1963, Zambia became an independent republic within the British Commonwealth in 1964.

1. 2 Shillings (C-N) 1964. Arms. Rev: Oribi buck   5.00

2. 1 Shilling (C-N) 1964. Rev: Hornbill   3.00
3. 6 Pence (C-N) 1964. Rev: Morning glory   1.25

4. 5 Shillings (N) 1965. Head of Pres. Kaunda. Rev: Arms. (First anniversary of independence)   7.50
5. 2 Shillings (C-N) 1966. Head. Rev: Oribi buck   5.00
6. 1 Shilling (C-N) 1966. Rev: Hornbill   2.00
7. 6 Pence (C-N) 1966. Rev: Morning glory   1.00

8. 1 Penny (Bro) 1966. (Center hole)   1.00

ZAMBIA (continued)

DECIMAL COINAGE

9. 20 Ngwee (C-N) 1968–78. Head of President K. D. Kaunda. Rev: Oribi buck 2.50

10. 10 Ngwee (C-N) 1968–78. Rev: Hornbill ... 1.25
11. 5 Ngwee (C-N) 1968–78. Rev: Morning glory flower 1.00

12. 2 Ngwee (Bro) 1968–78. Rev: African fish eagle .... .50
13. 1 Ngwee (Bro) 1968–78. Rev: Ant bear ..... .50

14. 50 Ngwee (C-N) 1969. Head of President Kaunda. Rev: Ear of corn. (F.A.O. coin plan, commemorates fifth anniversary of independence) 6.50

15. 50 Ngwee (C-N) 1972. Type of #14, without commemorative inscription. (F.A.O.) 6.50

16. 200 Kwacha (G) 1979. President Kaunda. Rev: African wild dogs. (Conservation Series) ... 500.00
17. 10 Kwacha 1979. Rev: Dove 40.00
18. 5 Kwacha 1979. Rev: Antelope 25.00
19. 10 Kwacha 1980. Rev: Children on gymnastic apparatus. (International Year of Child.) Issued in proof only 50.00

ZANZIBAR

A small island in the Indian Ocean about 20 miles off the coast of East Africa, Zanzibar was a British protectorate until 1963 when it became an independent state within the Commonwealth. A People's Republic was proclaimed in January 1964. In April 1964, Zanzibar merged with Tanganyika to form the United Republic of Tanganyika and Zanzibar, renamed the United Republic of Tanzania (q.v.) in October 1964.

100 Cents = 1 Rupee

1.	1 Rial A.H. 1299 (A.D. 1882). Arabic inscription	300.00

2.	1 Pessa (C) A.H. 1299 (A.D. 1882). Inscription. Rev: Scales	6.50

3.	1 Pessa (C) A.H. 1304 (A.D. 1886). Inscription. Rev: Scales	5.00
4.	20 Cents (N) 1908. Inscription. Rev: Palm tree	450.00

5.	10 Cents (Bro) 1908	300.00
6.	1 Cent (Bro) 1908	200.00

ZIMBABWE

The Republic of Zimbabwe (formerly Rhodesia, and before that Southern Rhodesia) occupies a territory in southeast Africa as large as California. Formerly the British protectorate of Southern Rhodesia, it became the Republic of Rhodesia in 1970 when the Rhodesian Parliament declared complete independence from Britain. After a protracted guerrilla war, in March 1978 Ian Smith, Prime Minister of Rhodesia, and a group of black nationalist leaders came to an agreement calling for black majority rule. The name of the country became Zimbabwe Rhodesia; on April 18, 1980, when a new government was formed, the name became simply Zimbabwe. (See also "Rhodesia and Nyasaland.")

100 Cents = 1 Dollar

1.	1 Dollar (C-N) 1980– . National emblem. Rev: Monument	3.00
2.	50 Cents (C-N) 1980– . Rev: Rayed sun	2.00
3.	20 Cents (C-N) 1980– . Rev: Bridge	1.50
4.	10 Cents (C-N) 1980– . Rev: Tree	1.25
5.	5 Cents (C-N) 1980– . Rev: Rabbit	1.00
6.	1 Cent (C-N) 1980– . Rev: Value	.50

ANCIENT COINS

ANCIENT GREECE AND THE MIDDLE EAST

AEGINA

This was the earliest European state to strike coins. From very early times until its conquest by Athens in 456 B.C. Aegina was one of the greatest commercial states of Greece. For two or three centuries the coins of Aegina had a very wide circulation with little change in style. The sea tortoise which appears on these coins was an appropriate symbol for this state which depended on the sea for its livelihood.

1. Silver Stater 600–450 B.C. Sea tortoise. Rev: Divided incuse square   VG 350.00; VF 1500.00
(A crude archaic-style coin)

AGRIGENTUM (in Sicily)

By far the richest and most magnificent city on the south coast of Sicily.

2. Silver Tetradrachm 400–375 B.C. Standing eagle. Rev: Crab   F 400.00; VF 800.00
(The eagle is a symbol for Zeus; the crab represents the river Akragas)

ARADUS (Ephesus)

The temple of Artemis of the Ephesians was one of the seven wonders of the world.

3. Silver Drachm 174–110 B.C. A large bee. Rev: Stag standing before palm tree   F 125.00; EF 500.00
(Artemis, known to the Romans as Diana, was referred to as goddess of the chase and the fruitfulness of nature)

ASPENDUS (Pamphylia)

A populous and wealthy city of great commercial importance. Its coins are often found with countermarks indicating very wide circulation.

4. Silver Stater 500–450 B.C. Warrior. Rev: Triskeles of human legs and club   VG 250.00
(A crude, archaic, thick coin)

5. Silver Stater 400–300 B.C. Two wrestlers engaged. Rev: Slinger; triskeles in field   F 100.00; VF 350.00

6.

ATHENS

6. Silver Tetradrachm 480–400 B.C. Archaic-style head of Athena. Rev: Owl (the bird of wisdom) in an incuse square; olive sprig in corner   F 65.00; VF 150.00
(The olive spray here probably has no reference to peace, as on modern coins, but very likely refers to the importance of olives and olive oil to the Athenian economy. It has been suggested that the small crescent on the reverse beside the owl was in honor of the Battle of Marathon, which was fought under a waning moon. The archaic style of the coin was preserved for many years due to its wide circulation and fear of possible damage to the commerce of the city if any change were made. The coin circulated throughout the entire known world until at last it was superseded by the still more popular tetradrachm of Alexander the Great. The coins were often cut with a chisel to see if they were good silver throughout.)

7. Silver Tetradrachm 230–200 B.C. Athena. Rev: Owl.   F 150.00; VF 300.00
(New style struck on large planchet)

CAPPADOCIA

A kingdom in Asia Minor.

8. Silver Drachm 300–225 B.C. Head of King Ariarathes. Rev: Athena   VF 150.00

CARTHAGE

Coins of this North African city founded by the Phoenicians were mostly produced during the invasion of Sicily; the type of Persephone is copied from the Sicilian coin.

9. Silver Tetradrachm 400–300 B.C. Head of Persephone in beautiful artistic style. Rev: Horse's head and palm tree   F 600.00; VF 1750.00

569

15.

10. Silver Tetradrachm. Head of Persephone.
Rev: Horse's head and palm tree
F 750.00; VF 1250.00

(Struck by Ptolemy I as Governor of Egypt under Alexander IV, King of Macedon, posthumous son of Alexander the Great)

11. Electrum Stater 350–250 B.C. Head of Persephone. Rev: Standing horse
F 1500.00; VF 2500.00

CORINTH

16. PTOLEMY I: Silver Tetradrachm 323–
305 B.C. His diademed head. Rev: Eagle
F 200.00; VF 400.00
(Struck by Ptolemy I as independent King of Egypt)

17. PTOLEMY II: Very large heavy bronze cast
coin 285–246 B.C. Bearded head of Zeus.
Rev: Eagle   VF 100.00

18. PTOLEMY II: Silver Tetradrachm 285–
246 B.C. His diademed head. Rev: Eagle
F 200.00; VF 400.00
(Similar coins were issued by the Ptolemies through Ptolemy XIII, 55–51 B.C.; value as above)

12. Silver Stater 400–335 B.C. Head of Athena in
typical Corinthian helmet. Rev: Pegasus
(winged horse) in flight   VF 125.00; EF 300.00
(One of the most famous coins in the ancient world, used in all Corinthian colonies)

CROTON (Bruttium)

19. CLEOPATRA VII: Base silver Tetradrachm
51–30 B.C. Ptolemaic head. Rev: Eagle   F 250.00
(This is the famous Cleopatra of history)

GELA (Sicily)

This city was located at the mouth of the river Gela. The swimming man-headed bull on the following coin represents the river.

20. Silver Tetradrachm 500–450 B.C. Forepart of
man-headed bull with horns. Rev: Quadriga, winged Victory above   F 500.00; VF 1500.00

13. Silver Stater 550–480 B.C. Tripod in relief.
Rev: Tripod, incuse   F 400.00; VF 1000.00

14. Silver Stater 420–390 B.C. Standing eagle.
Rev: Tripod   F 350.00; VF 800.00

EGYPT

LARISSA

21. Silver Drachm 400–344 B.C. Facing head of
the nymph Larissa. Rev: Grazing horse
F 150.00; VF 600.00
(After the famous facing-head Tetradrachm of Syracuse by Kimon)

15. PTOLEMY I: Silver Tetradrachm 323–
305 B.C. Head of Alexander the Great in elephant skin. Rev: Athena with javelin and
shield; eagle on thunderbolt   F 200.00; VF 400.00

ANCIENT GREECE AND THE MIDDLE EAST (continued)

LEONTINI (Sicily)

22. Silver Tetradrachm 475–400 B.C. Laureate head of Apollo. Rev: Lion's head with open mouth; border of corn grain   F 300.00; VF 650.00
(The corn is an allusion to the extreme fertility of the region. The lion undoubtedly refers to the name of the town.)

LYDIA (Asia Minor)

Thought to be the first state to issue coins.

23. CROESUS: Gold Stater 561–546 B.C. Forepart of lion facing forepart of bull. Rev: Two incused squares   F 1500.00; VF 3000.00
(A coin of great historical interest)

MACEDON

24. PHILIP II (father of Alexander the Great): Gold Stater 359–336 B.C. Laureate head of Apollo. Rev: Two-horse chariot and driver   F 1500.00; VF 2500.00
(Struck from gold from the mine of Pangaeus, the richest source of ancient times)

25. PHILIP II: Silver Tetradrachm 359–336 B.C. Bearded head of Zeus. Rev: Jockey on horse   F 300.00; VF 450.00
(Rev. refers to Philip's victory in Olympic Games)

26. ALEXANDER THE GREAT: Gold Stater 336–323 B.C. Helmeted head of Athena. Rev: Standing figure of winged Nike   F 800.00; VF 1500.00

27. ALEXANDER THE GREAT: Silver Tetradrachm 336–323 B.C. Head of young Hercules in lion's scalp. Rev: Zeus seated on throne, holding an eagle and leaning on sceptre   F 200.00; VF 400.00
(Probably the most widely circulated coin of ancient times)

28. ALEXANDER THE GREAT: Silver Drachm 336–323 B.C. Type of #27   F 75.00; VF 125.00

29. ALEXANDER THE GREAT: Silver Tetradrachm 336–323 B.C. Type of #27, but struck on a broad, spread planchet in the mints of Asia Minor   F 125.00; VF 250.00
(Sometimes found counterstamped for use in various provinces)

30. UNDER ROMAN RULE: Silver Tetradrachm 158–146 B.C. Head of Artemis in center of Macedonian shield. Rev: War club in oak wreath   F 175.00; VF 300.00
(One of the finest coins struck during this era)

METAPONTUM

This city was in a very fertile region and agriculture was very important. Consequently an ear of corn is invariably pictured on the observe or reverse of each coin.

31. Silver Stater 550–470 B.C. Ear of corn in high relief. Rev: Same type, incuse   F 200.00; VF 500.00

32. Silver Stater 400–350 B.C. Head of goddess Demeter. Rev: Ear of corn   F 1000.00; VF 1750.00

33. Silver Stater 350–330 B.C. Head of the bearded hero Leukippos in Corinthian helmet. Rev: Ear of corn   F 850.00; VF 1500.00
(Some coins show a locust on the reverse, others a mouse; these are thought to be coins issued during a year of poor crops due to havoc wreaked by these pests)

ANCIENT GREECE AND THE MIDDLE EAST (continued)

NEAPOLIS (Naples)

34. Silver Drachm 350–250 B.C. Head of Parthenope. Rev: Man-headed bull   F 250.00; VF 350.00

PARTHIA

Located in Asia, southeast of the Caspian Sea.

35. MITHRIDATES I: Silver Drachm 170–140 B.C. Bearded head. Rev: King seated   F 75.00; VF 150.00

36. PHRAATES IV: Silver Drachm 38–3 B.C. Bust in oriental costume. Rev: Seated and standing figure   VF 150.00

PERGAMUM

37. Silver Cistophorous 200–50 B.C. Cista Mystica with half-open lid from which a serpent appears. Rev: Two serpents coiled around bowcase   F 100.00; VF 175.00
(A popular coin throughout Asia Minor during the first and second centuries B.C.)

PERSIA

38. KING DARIUS: Gold Daric 521–486 B.C. King as an archer kneeling with bow, quiver and spear. Rev: Irregular incusum   F 1750.00; VF 2500.00
(Millions of these coins were struck, and due to the purity of the metal they were the accepted gold currency of the ancient world until the time of Philip II of Macedon)

39. KING DARIUS: Silver Siglos 521–486 B.C. Type of #38   F 150.00; VF 250.00

POPULONIA

40. Silver 20 Litrae 300–265 B.C. Facing Gorgon head with outstretched tongue. Rev: Blank   F 150.00; VF 375.00

SICYON

41. Silver Triobol 400–300 B.C. Dove flying. Rev: Lion walking   F 75.00

SIDE

42. Silver Tetradrachm 190–36 B.C. Head of Athena in Corinthian helmet. Rev: Winged Victory   F 200.00; VF 400.00

SIDON (Phoenicia)

43. STRATO I: Silver Double Shekel 370–358 B.C. Galley with rowers. Rev: King in chariot with driver; Egyptian attendant follows (signifies Egyptian subjection to Persia)   F 250.00; VF 500.00
(This coin is often found with various countermarks)

SYRACUSE

The most important Greek colony in Sicily.

44. Silver Tetradrachm 485–475 B.C. Small archaic head of Arethusa surrounded by dolphins. Rev: Slow-moving quadriga, winged Victory above   F 400.00; VF 650.00

45. Silver Dekadrachm 413–357 B.C. Head of Persephone surrounded by three dolphins. Rev: Victorious quadriga, winged Victory flying above   F 5500.00; VF 7500.00; EF 12,500.00
(Issued after the defeat of the Athenians in the Peloponnesian War, this coin is often considered the finest example of the art of coinage and the most beautiful coin of all time)

46. Silver Tetradrachm. Large head of Persephone. Rev: Fast quadriga   VF 450.00; EF 800.00

SYRIA

47. ANTIOCHUS I: Silver Tetradrachm 293–281 B.C. Very fine head of the King. Rev: Apollo seated with bow and arrow   F 150.00; VF 275.00

TARENTUM

48. Silver Didrachm 400–300 B.C. Horseman galloping. Rev: Taras riding on a dolphin   F 125.00; VF 250.00
(The Tarentines were renowned as expert horsemen. The reverse refers to the legend of Taras being saved from shipwreck by Poseidon, who sent a dolphin to carry him to shore, where he founded the colony that grew into this important city-state.)

49. Silver Drachm 400–300 B.C. Head of Athena in helmet. Rev: Owl   F 70.00; VF 175.00

ANCIENT GREECE AND THE MIDDLE EAST (continued)

TARSUS

Birthplace of the Apostle Paul.

50. AS PERSIAN SATRAPY: Silver Stater 386–333 B.C. Head of Ahura Mazda. Rev: The god Baal standing with sceptre and eagle   F 150.00; VF 300.00

51. KING PHARNABAZUS: Silver Stater 379–374 B.C. Facing head of Arethusa. Rev: Head of Mars in war helmet
    F 150.00; VF 300.00
(The beautiful reverse is copied from Kimon's Arethusa on the coins of Syracuse)

THEBES (Boeotia)

One of the most important Greek cities in ancient times.

52. Silver Stater 400–330 B.C. The shield of Thebes. Rev: Amphora
    F 150.00; VF 300.00; EF 500.00

THRACE

53. LYSIMACHUS: Silver Tetradrachm 323–281 B.C. Head of Alexander the Great wearing horn of Ammon. Rev: Athena seated holding winged Victory   F 250.00; VF 600.00
(One of the most famous coins of antiquity. Lysimachus was an outstanding general under Alexander.)

THURIUM

54. Silver Stater 450–400 B.C. Helmeted head of Athena. Rev: Bull   F 175.00; VF 325.00

TYRE (Phoenicia)

A great trade center of ancient times.

55. Silver Shekel 125 B.C.–100 A.D. Head of Melkarth. Rev: Eagle standing on bow of ship   F 250.00; VF 450.00
(This coin was struck in large numbers and circulated extensively in Judea at the time of Christ. It is generally believed that the "thirty pieces of silver" paid to Judas were made up of these coins.)

VELIA

56. Silver Didrachm 350–275 B.C. Helmeted head of Athena. Rev: Lion prowling, devouring prey or seizing upon a stag
    F 250.00; VF 400.00

ANCIENT ROME

ROMAN REPUBLIC

CAST BRONZE COINAGE, THE *AES GRAVE* ("HEAVY BRONZE") 225–175 B.C.

The reverse of these coins always shows the prow of a galley. The basic unit was the As, equivalent to 12 Uncia, and originally equal in weight to the Latin pound of 12 ounces. Prices quoted for the following coins are for VG–F condition.

1. As (12 Uncia) Head of Janus. Rev: Prow of galley   800.00

2.	Semis (6 Uncia). Head of Jupiter or Saturn	500.00
3.	Triens (4 Uncia). Head of Minerva	375.00

12.	Head of Apollo. Rev: Various types	150.00
13.	Head of Tatius. Rev: "Rape of the Sabines"	125.00

14.	Head of Jupiter. Rev: Various types	75.00

15.	Head of Mars. Rev: Various types	100.00

NOTE: The above are the types most frequently encountered. Many other deities, however, appear on the coinage. The value of these pieces is generally upward of $25.00.

4.	Quadrans (3 Uncia). Head of Hercules	300.00
5.	Sextans (2 Uncia). Head of Mercury	250.00
6.	Uncia. Head of Roma or Bellona	100.00

COINS OF THE CIVIL WARS   59–31 B.C.

NOTE: Prices are quoted for F–VF condition

STRUCK COINS OF THE ROMAN REPUBLIC
269–55 B.C.

The silver Denarius was the chief coin of the Republican period and was equivalent in value to ten bronze Asses, this value being indicated by the "X" frequently seen on the Denarii. Prices quoted for the following silver Denarii (185–55 B.C.) are for F–VF condition.

16.	POMPEY THE GREAT: Denarius. Bare head. Rev: Catanian brothers carrying their parents on their shoulders	475.00

7.	Head of Roma. Rev: Dioscuri galloping	100.00
8.	Head of Roma. Rev: Biga (two-horse chariot)	100.00
9.	Head of Roma. Rev: Quadriga (four-horse chariot)	100.00
10.	Head of Roma. Rev: Romulus and Remus	125.00

17.	JULIUS CAESAR: Denarius. Laureate head of Caesar	650.00
18.	JULIUS CAESAR: Denarius. Head of Venus. Rev: Trophy between two captives	300.00

11.	Head of Janus. Rev: Various types	300.00

19.	JULIUS CAESAR: Denarius. Elephant trampling serpent. Rev: Sacrificial instruments	250.00

20.	BRUTUS: Denarius. Liberty head. Rev: Brutus walking between lictors	275.00
21.	MARK ANTONY: Denarius. Bare head. Rev: Trophy	350.00

22.	MARK ANTONY: Denarius (struck for payment of his legions). Galley. Rev: Eagle and standards of the Tenth Legion	150.00
23.	CASSIUS: Denarius. Liberty head. Rev: Jug	350.00

Commodus	M COMMODVS ANTONINVS AVG PIVS
Clodius Albinus	D CLOD SEPT ALB CAES
Septimius Severus	IMP CAES L SEPT SEV PERT AVG
Caracalla	ANTONINVS PIVS AVG GERM
Geta	P SEPT GETA CAES
Macrinus	IMP C M OPEL SEV MACRINVS AVG
Elagabalus	ANTONINVS PIVS FEL AVG
Severus Alexander	IMP SEV ALEXAND AVG
Maximinus I	MAXIMINVS PIVS AVG GERM
Gordianus III (Pius)	IMP CAES GORDIANVS PIVS AVG
Philip I	IMP M IVL PHILIPPVS AVG
Philip II	M IVL PHILIPPVS CAES
Trajan Decius	IMP C M Q TRIANVS DECIVS AVG
Trebonianus Gallus	IMP CAES C VIB TREBONIANVS GALLVS AVG
Volusian	IMP CAE C VIB VOLVSIANO AVG
Valerian	IMP C P LIC VALERIANVS AVG
Gallienus	IMP C P LIC GALLIENVS PF AVG
Postumus	IMP C POSTVMVS PF AVG
Victorinus	IMP C VICTORINVS PF AVG
Tetricus	IMP C TETRICVS PF AVG
Claudius II	IMP C CLAVDIVS AVG
Aurelian	IMP C L DOM AVRELIANVS PF AVG
Tacitus	IMP C M CL TACITVS AVG
Probus	IMP C PROBVS PF AVG
Diocletian	IMP C C VAL DIOCLETIANVS PF AVG
Maximianus I	IMP CMA MAXIMIANVS PF AVG
Constantius I (Chlorus)	CONSTANTIVS PF AVG
Galerius	IMP C GAL VAL MAXIMIANVS PF AVG
Severus II	IMP C SEVERVS PF AVG
Maxentius	IMP C MAXENTIVS PF AVG
Constantine I (the Great)	CONSTANTINVS PF AVG

ROMAN EMPIRE

LEGENDS ON COINS

These often appear with abbreviations, especially for titles of honor (AVG for Augustus, GERM for Germanicus, etc.). In some cases, of course, these words are completely spelled out; but the abbreviations below are given in order to familiarize the reader with them.

The order of words varies with different coins. The arrangements used here are the most common ones. Thus, IMP may appear as the first word in some cases, as the last in others.

Titles were often added during the course of a reign. Consequently some of the words used here may not be present on all inscriptions. This is particularly true of coins issued during the early phase of a long reign.

The legends used here are the most common ones of any given reign, and the ones most frequently encountered. Commemorative pieces or other material off the beaten track may have altogether different legends.

Augustus	CAESAR AVGVSTVS
Tiberius	TI CAESAR DIVI AVG F AVG
Caligula	C CAESAR AVG GERM
Claudius	TI CLAVD CAESAR AVG
Nero	NERO CLAVDIVS CAES AVG GERM
Galba	IMP SER GALBA CAES
Otho	IMP M OTHO CAES AVG
Vitellius	VITELLIVS GERM IMP AVG
Vespasian	IMP CAES VESP AVG
Titus	T CAES VESPASIAN IMP
Domitian	IMP CAES DOMIT AVG GERM
Nerva	IMP NERVA CAES AVG
Trajan	IMP CAES NERVA TRAIANO AVG GERM
Hadrian	IMP CAES TRAIAN HADRIANVS AVG
Antoninus Pius	ANTONINVS AVG PIVS
Marcus Aurelius	M ANTONINVS AVG ARM
Lucius Verus	IMP CAES L AVREL VERVS AVG

DENOMINATIONS OF COINS

The coinage as reorganized by Augustus included the following denominations and relative values:

Aureus (gold) = 25 silver Denarii: The standard gold coin, gradually reduced in weight until the time of Constantine, when it became known as the Solidus.

Denarius (silver) = 16 Asses: The standard silver coin. During the reign of Caracalla a double Denarius known as an Antoninianus was first coined (A.D. 214). On these coins the ruler's bust has a spiked crown.

Sestertius (bronze) = 4 Asses: These are beautiful, large bronze pieces, much sought after when in choice condition.

Dupondius (yellow bronze) = 2 Asses
As (copper) = 4 Quadrantes
Quadrans (copper) = ¼ As

Many different deities and personifications appear on the reverse of Roman coins. Often the coins of a single emperor carry several different types. In the following listings only obverses are shown. Prices are for VF condition. Coins in extremely choice condition, however, sell for more than the prices listed. This is especially true of copper and bronze coinage. Coins that are poorly struck, much worn or mutilated in any way are worth much less.

Note that bronze coins were issued by authority of the Senate and bear the mark "SC" *(Senatus Consulto)*.

24.	AUGUSTUS (as Octavian, 43 B.C.–27 B.C.; as Emperor Augustus, 27 B.C.–14 A.D.). Aureus (G)	2750.00

25.	Denarius	450.00

43.	Sestertius (Bro)	500.00
44.	Dupondius (Bro)	100.00
45.	As (C)	75.00
46.	Quadrans (C)	30.00
47.	NERO 54–68 A.D. Aureus (G)	1250.00
48.	Denarius	500.00

26.	Sestertius (Bro)	400.00
27.	Dupondius (Bro)	250.00
28.	As (C)	75.00
29.	Quadrans (C)	35.00
30.	TIBERIUS 14–37 A.D. Aureus (G)	2500.00

49.	Sestertius (Bro)	600.00
50.	Dupondius (Bro)	200.00
51.	As (C)	125.00
52.	Quadrans (C)	50.00
53.	GALBA 68–69 A.D. Denarius	350.00

31.	Denarius (Tribute Penny of the Bible)	850.00
32.	Sestertius (Bro)	600.00
33.	Dupondius (Bro)	350.00
34.	As (C)	75.00
35.	Quadrans (C)	35.00
36.	CALIGULA 37–41 A.D. Aureus (G)	3000.00
37.	Denarius	1000.00

54.	Sestertius (Bro)	500.00
55.	Dupondius (Bro)	250.00
56.	As (C)	75.00
57.	OTHO 69 A.D. Denarius	450.00

38.	Sestertius (Bro)	750.00
39.	As (C)	200.00
40.	Quadrans (C)	100.00
41.	CLAUDIUS 41–54 A.D. Aureus (G)	2000.00
42.	Denarius	1000.00

58.	VITELLIUS 69 A.D. Denarius	400.00
59.	Dupondius (Bro)	200.00
60.	As (C)	150.00
61.	VESPASIAN 69–79 A.D. Aureus (G)	2000.00
62.	Denarius	100.00

63.	Sestertius (Bro)	250.00
64.	Dupondius (Bro)	150.00
65.	As (C)	75.00
66.	Quadrans (C)	35.00
67.	TITUS 79–81 A.D. Aureus (G)	1500.00
68.	Denarius	150.00

86.	Sestertius (Bro)	200.00
87.	Dupondius (Bro)	75.00
88.	As (C)	60.00
89.	Quadrans (C)	30.00
90.	HADRIAN 117–38 A.D. Aureus (G)	2000.00
91.	Denarius	100.00

69.	Sestertius (Bro)	275.00
70.	Dupondius (Bro)	100.00
71.	As (C)	125.00
72.	Quadrans (C)	35.00
73.	DOMITIAN 81–96 A.D. Aureus (G)	1750.00
74.	Denarius	100.00

92.	Sestertius (Bro)	250.00
93.	Dupondius (Bro)	100.00
94.	As (C)	50.00
95.	Quadrans (C)	30.00
96.	ANTONINUS PIUS 138–61 A.D. Denarius	100.00

75.	Sestertius (Bro)	275.00
76.	Dupondius (Bro)	125.00
77.	As (C)	75.00
78.	Quadrans (C)	25.00

97.	Sestertius (Bro)	175.00
98.	Dupondius (Bro)	60.00
99.	As (C)	50.00
100.	Quadrans (C)	30.00
101.	MARCUS AURELIUS 161–80 A.D. Aureus (G)	2000.00
102.	Denarius	125.00

79.	NERVA 96–98 A.D. Denarius	300.00
80.	Sestertius (Bro)	500.00
81.	Dupondius (Bro)	100.00
82.	As (C)	50.00
83.	Quadrans (C)	25.00
84.	TRAJAN 98–117 A.D. Aureus (G)	1500.00
85.	Denarius	100.00

103.	Sestertius (Bro)	275.00
104.	Dupondius (Bro)	50.00

105.	As (C)	40.00
106.	Quadrans (C)	50.00
107.	LUCIUS VERUS (Co-emperor with MARCUS AURELIUS) 161–69 A.D. Denarius	150.00
108.	Sestertius (Bro)	300.00
109.	Dupondius (Bro)	75.00

110.	As (C)	100.00
111.	COMMODUS 180–92 A.D. Denarius	85.00

112.	Sestertius (Bro)	275.00
113.	Dupondius (Bro)	85.00
114.	As (C)	65.00
115.	CLODIUS ALBINUS 193–197 A.D. Denarius	500.00
116.	Dupondius (Bro)	400.00
117.	SEPTIMIUS SEVERUS 193–211 A.D. Denarius	75.00

118.	Sestertius (Bro)	300.00
119.	Dupondius (Bro)	250.00
120.	As (C)	200.00
121.	CARACALLA 211–217 A.D. Antoninianus	100.00
122.	Denarius	80.00

123.	Sestertius (Bro)	275.00
124.	Dupondius (Bro)	250.00
125.	As (C)	150.00

126.	GETA (Co-emperor with CARACALLA) 211–12 A.D. Denarius	100.00
127.	MACRINUS 217–18 A.D. Antoninianus	300.00
128.	Denarius	175.00

129.	Sestertius (Bro)	300.00
130.	Dupondius (Bro)	150.00
131.	As (C)	150.00
132.	ELAGABALUS (or HELIOGABALUS) 218–22 A.D.	125.00
133.	Denarius	100.00

134.	Dupondius (Bro)	125.00
135.	As (C)	100.00
136.	ALEXANDER SEVERUS 222–35 A.D. Denarius	85.00

137.	Sestertius (Bro)	100.00
138.	Dupondius (Bro)	125.00
139.	MAXIMINUS I 235–38 A.D. Denarius	150.00

140.	Sestertius (Bro)	100.00
141.	Dupondius (Bro)	100.00
142.	As (C)	85.00
143.	GORDIANUS PIUS 238–44 A.D. Antoninianus	60.00
144.	Denarius	75.00

145.	Dupondius (Bro)	100.00
146.	As (C)	75.00
147.	PHILIP I 244–49 A.D. Antoninianus	85.00

148.	Sestertius (Bro)	100.00
149.	Dupondius (Bro)	100.00
150.	As (C)	80.00
151.	PHILIP II (Co-emperor with PHILIP I) 247–49 A.D. Antoninianus	80.00
152.	Sestertius (Bro)	100.00
153.	Dupondius (Bro)	80.00
154.	As (C)	50.00
155.	TRAJAN DECIUS 249–51 A.D. Antoninianus	60.00

156.	Sestertius (Bro)	100.00
157.	Dupondius (Bro)	75.00
158.	TREBONIANUS GALLUS 251–53 A.D. Antoninianus	75.00

159.	Sestertius (Bro)	125.00
160.	Dupondius (Bro)	85.00
161.	As (C)	85.00
162.	VOLUSIAN (Co-emperor with TREBONIANUS GALLUS) 252–53 A.D. Antoninianus	60.00

163.	Sestertius (Bro)	125.00
164.	As (C)	50.00
165.	VALERIAN 253–60 A.D. Antoninianus	40.00
166.	Dupondius (Bro)	100.00

167.	As (C)	65.00
168.	GALLIENUS (Co-emperor with Valerian) 253–68 A.D. Antoninianus	50.00

(During this reign the Antoninianus, the chief coin at this time, became sadly debased. It was usually bronze with a light silver wash.)

169.	Dupondius (Bro)	75.00

170.	POSTUMUS (Pretender) 259–67 A.D. Antoninianus	50.00

171.	VICTORINUS (Pretender) 265–70 A.D. Antoninianus (Bro)	50.00

172.	TETRICUS (Pretender) 270–73 A.D. Antoninianus (Bro)	50.00

ANCIENT ROME: Empire (continued)

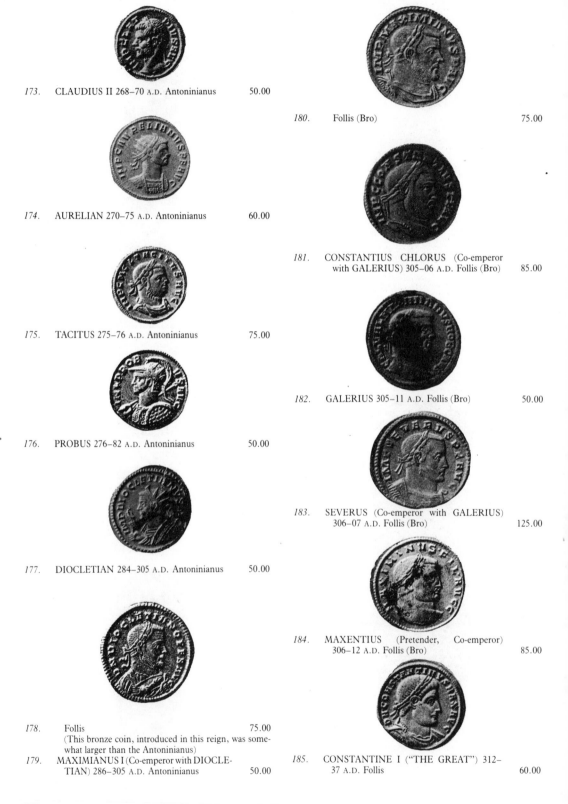

173.   CLAUDIUS II 268–70 A.D. Antoninianus   50.00

174.   AURELIAN 270–75 A.D. Antoninianus   60.00

175.   TACITUS 275–76 A.D. Antoninianus   75.00

176.   PROBUS 276–82 A.D. Antoninianus   50.00

177.   DIOCLETIAN 284–305 A.D. Antoninianus   50.00

178.   Follis   75.00
(This bronze coin, introduced in this reign, was somewhat larger than the Antoninianus)

179.   MAXIMIANUS I (Co-emperor with DIOCLETIAN) 286–305 A.D. Antoninianus   50.00

180.   Follis (Bro)   75.00

181.   CONSTANTIUS CHLORUS (Co-emperor with GALERIUS) 305–06 A.D. Follis (Bro)   85.00

182.   GALERIUS 305–11 A.D. Follis (Bro)   50.00

183.   SEVERUS (Co-emperor with GALERIUS) 306–07 A.D. Follis (Bro)   125.00

184.   MAXENTIUS (Pretender, Co-emperor) 306–12 A.D. Follis (Bro)   85.00

185.   CONSTANTINE I ("THE GREAT") 312–37 A.D. Follis   60.00